Introduction

SHOULD YOU VISIT MYANMAR?

Many people ask us why we publish this book. Our answer is always the same: At Lonely Planet we believe that travel is one of the most powerful forces for tolerance, understanding and democracy the world has.

Independent travellers can bear witness in countries where human rights abuses are perpetrated. Relaying accounts of such abuses to friends, families, colleagues, communities and governments can give a personal and powerful authentication of the news stories filed by international media or the bureaucratic reports of UN and other bodies. The critical attention of the world community can follow.

Travellers who respect their host communities and spend their money with an awareness of who benefits can also make a positive contribution to the lives of the people of the countries they visit (see the Reasons to Go section in the boxed text later in this chapter). By contributing to the economic prosperity and autonomy of individuals, travellers can help to challenge the economic domination of repressive regimes over their people. Economic independence is one of the most important stepping stones towards political independence – and travellers can help individuals to achieve this.

Travellers can also make people in countries governed by repressive regimes aware that the eyes of the international community are focused on the situation in their homeland. Being reminded of this fact, and of the healthy state of democracy in many parts of the world, can give heart to individuals whose political rights have been curtailed for long periods of time. Travellers need to do this sensitively, of course, and without endangering the individuals with whom they communicate, but we know from the many reports we are sent by travellers that this happens every day in every part of the world. It is the type of communication that in the long term can change lives and unseat undemocratic governments.

It would be easy for Lonely Planet to avoid criticism and controversy by choosing

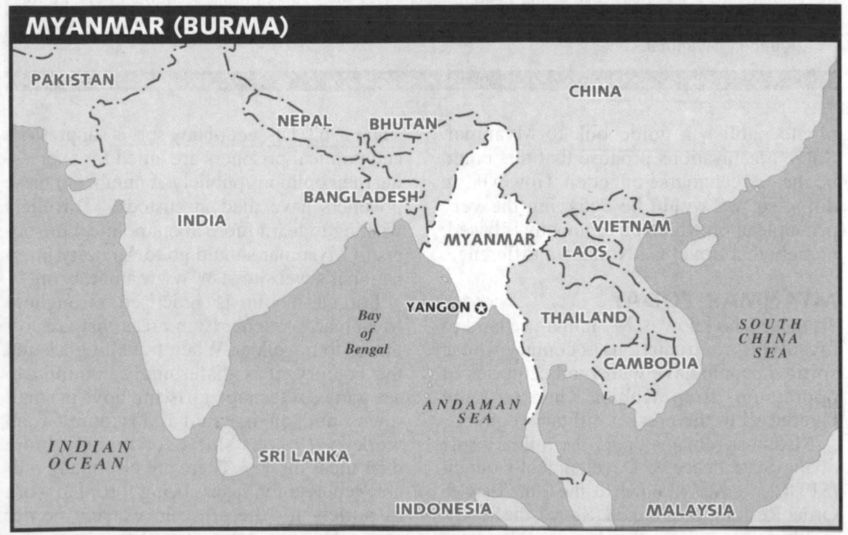

To Go or Not to Go?

Reasons Not to Go:

- International tourism can be seen to give a stamp of approval to the SPDC, and is promoted as such by the government.
- Aung San Suu Kyi and the NLD have called on the international community to boycott travel to Myanmar until the candidates democratically elected in 1990 are allowed to form a government.
- The government still controls which parts of the country travellers can visit, and deliberately keeps travellers away from areas where forced labour or repression of minorities is occurring. (See the Bamar Repression of Minorities text in the 'People of Myanmar' special section on page 53.)
- It is all-but-impossible to avoid some government-owned businesses, tourism sites and transport.
- The mandatory purchase of US$200 worth of FECs by every foreign tourist entering the country provides the government with much-needed foreign exchange.
- Forced labour has been used to construct some of the country's tourism infrastructure.

Reasons to Go:

- Tourism remains one of the few industries to which ordinary Burmese have access. Any reduction in tourism automatically means a reduction in local income-earning opportunities.
- It is becoming increasingly possible to travel around Myanmar without staying in government-owned hotels, using government-owned transport etc.
- The government is sensitive to international criticism and has sometimes modified its behaviour as a result of negative reports by foreign travellers.
- Many pro-democracy activists within Myanmar itself argue that sanctions are counter-productive, and that economic development (as achieved through industries such as tourism) can lead to political liberalisation.
- Keeping the Burmese isolated from international witnesses to internal oppression may only cement the government's ability to rule.
- Human rights–tragedies such as the 1988 massacre (see the 1988 Uprising section on page 22 for more details) are less likely to occur if the members of the international community are on the ground in Myanmar.

not to publish a guidebook to Myanmar. Some organisations propose that this could be the correct course of action. However, in doing so, we would be betraying the very principle upon which our company is based: namely that travel CAN make a difference.

MYANMAR TODAY

To those who know it, Myanmar is a land of mystifying contradictions, a country whose spirited people have withstood centuries of oppression, from Kublai Khan to King George VI to the present military regime.

Myanmar remains under the military rule of the State Peace & Development Council (SPDC), formerly known as the State Law & Order Restoration Council (Slorc), the abominable military junta that has run Myanmar since 1962. Dissent of any sort is suppressed, and political prisoners are jailed for expressing their opinions publicly. A number of these prisoners have died in custody. (Travellers wishing to learn more about political prisoners in Myanmar should go to Amnesty International's website at W www.amnesty.org).

Forced labour is practised throughout Myanmar, particularly in areas that are 'off limits' to travellers. When travelling around the country, it is disturbingly common to see gangs of teenage girls and boys in small towns and on isolated roads doing road work in 10-hour shifts for nothing more than meal money. There are also many reliable reports of villagers being forced to work as porters for the army in warring border areas. Amnesty International's website also

Myanmar (Burma)

Steven Martin
Mic Looby
Michael Clark
Joe Cummings

LONELY PLANET PUBLICATIONS
Melbourne • Oakland • London • Paris

MYANMAR

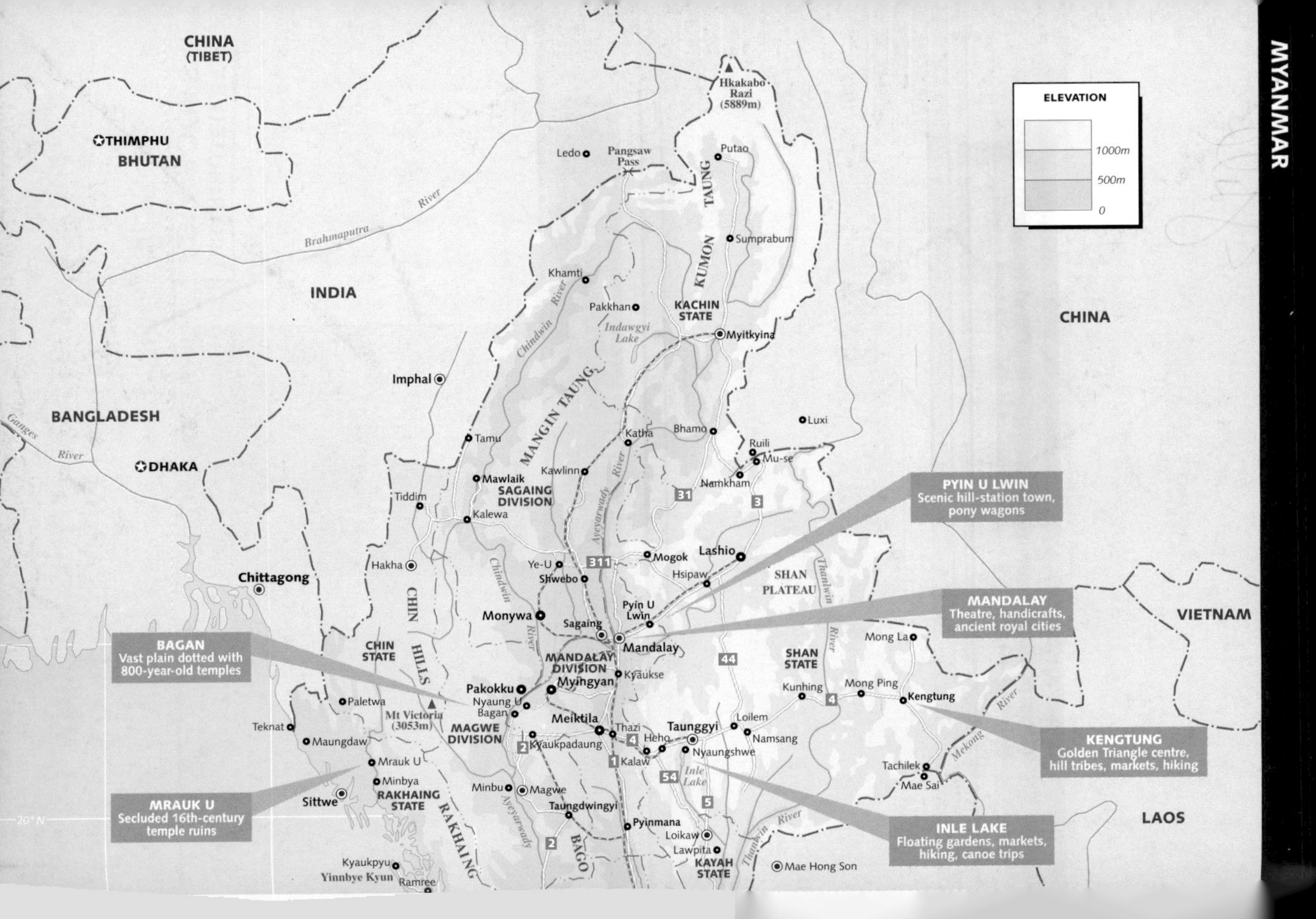

ELEVATION
1000m
500m
0
CHINA (TIBET)
THIMPHU
BHUTAN
Brahmaputra River
INDIA
BANGLADESH
Ganges River
DHAKA
Chittagong
Imphal
CHINA
VIETNAM
LAOS
Hkakabo Razi (5889m)
Ledo
Pangsaw Pass
Putao
TAUNG
KUMON
Sumprabum
Khamti
Chindwin River
Pakkhan
KACHIN STATE
Indawgyi Lake
Myitkyina
MANGIN TAUNG
Tamu
Katha
Bhamo
Luxi
Ruili
Mu-se
Namkham
Kawlinn
Ayeyarwady River
Mawlaik
SAGAING DIVISION
Tiddim
Kalewa
Hakha
Ye-U
Shwebo
Mogok
Lashio
Hsipaw
SHAN PLATEAU
Thanlwin River
Chindwin River
CHIN HILLS
Monywa
Sagaing
Pyin U Lwin
Mandalay
CHIN STATE
MANDALAY DIVISION
Kyaukse
Myingyan
Pakokku
Nyaung U
Bagan
Mt Victoria (3053m)
MAGWE DIVISION
Meiktila
Thazi
Taunggyi
Heho
Kyaukpadaung
Nyaungshwe
Kalaw
Loilem
Namsang
Inle Lake
SHAN STATE
Mong La
Kunhing
Mong Ping
Kengtung
Mekong River
Tachilek
Mae Sai
Paletwa
Teknat
Maungdaw
Mrauk U
Minbya
RAKHAING STATE
Sittwe
Minbu
Magwe
Taungdwingyi
Pyinmana
Loikaw
Lawpita
KAYAH STATE
Mae Hong Son
BAGO
RAKHAING
Kyaukpyu
Yinnbye Kyun
Ramree
20° N
PYIN U LWIN
Scenic hill-station town, pony wagons
MANDALAY
Theatre, handicrafts, ancient royal cities
KENGTUNG
Golden Triangle centre, hill tribes, markets, hiking
INLE LAKE
Floating gardens, markets, hiking, canoe trips
BAGAN
Vast plain dotted with 800-year-old temples
MRAUK U
Secluded 16th-century temple ruins

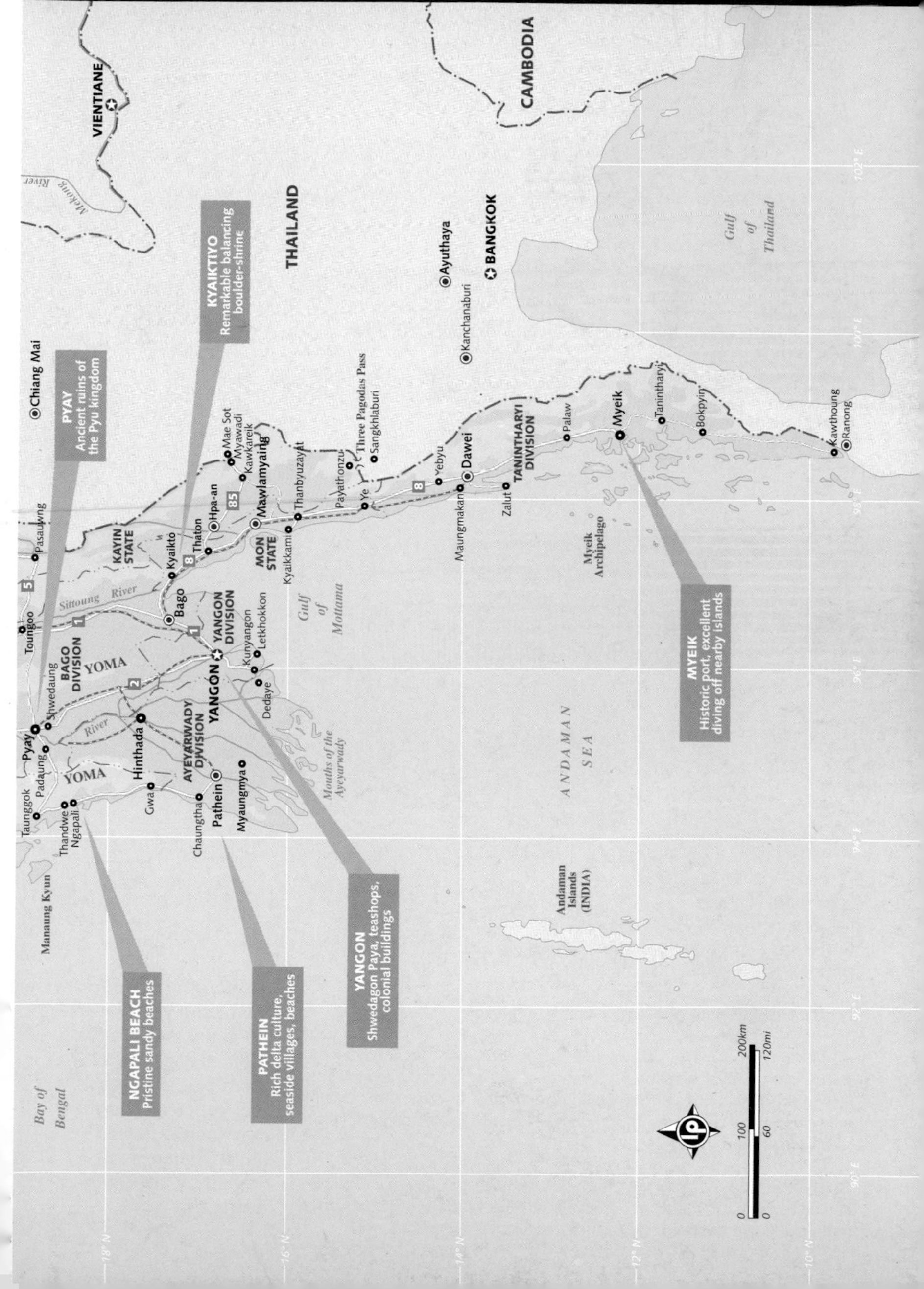

PYAY
Ancient ruins of the Pyu kingdom

NGAPALI BEACH
Pristine sandy beaches

KYAIKTIYO
Remarkable balancing boulder-shrine

PATHEIN
Rich delta culture, seaside villages, beaches

YANGON
Shwedagon Paya, teashops, colonial buildings

MYEIK
Historic port, excellent diving off nearby islands

Bay of Bengal
Manaung Kyun
Taunggok
Pyay
Padaung
Shwedaung
Toungoo
Pasawng
Chiang Mai
Thandwe
Ngapali
YOMA
River
BAGO DIVISION
YOMA
Sittoung River
KAYIN STATE
Mekong River
VIENTIANE
Hinthada
Gwa
Bago
Kyaikto
Thaton
Hpa-an
AYEYARWADY DIVISION
Chaungtha
Pathein
YANGON
YANGON DIVISION
Myaungmya
Kunyangon
Letkhokkon
Dedaye
Mae Sot
Myawadi
Kawkareik
MON STATE
Mawlamyaing
Kyaikkami
Thanbyuzayat
THAILAND
Gulf of Mottama
Mouths of the Ayeyarwady
Payathonzu
Three Pagodas Pass
Ye
Sangkhlaburi
Yebyu
Maungmakan
Dawei
Ayuthaya
Kanchanaburi
BANGKOK
Zalut
TANINTHARYI DIVISION
CAMBODIA
Andaman Islands (INDIA)
ANDAMAN SEA
Palaw
Myeik Archipelago
Myeik
Tanintharyi
Bokpyin
Gulf of Thailand
Kawthoung
Ranong

18° N
16° N
14° N
12° N
10° N
90° E
92° E
94° E
96° E
98° E
100° E
102° E

0 100 200km
0 60 120mi

Myanmar (Burma)
8th edition – October 2002
First published – December 1979

Published by
Lonely Planet Publications Pty Ltd ABN 36 005 607 983
90 Maribyrnong St, Footscray, Victoria 3011, Australia

Lonely Planet offices
Australia Locked Bag 1, Footscray, Victoria 3011
USA 150 Linden St, Oakland, CA 94607
UK 10a Spring Place, London NW5 3BH
France 1 rue du Dahomey, 75011 Paris

Photographs
Many of the images in this guide are available for licensing from Lonely Planet Images.
www.lonelyplanetimages.com

Front cover photograph
Extraordinary gold-leafed Kyaiktiyo boulder-shrine, Mon State (Anders Blomqvist)

ISBN 1 74059 190 9

Printed by Craft Print International Ltd, Singapore

Contents – Text

Contents – Maps

FACTS ABOUT MYANMAR

GETTING AROUND

YANGON

AROUND YANGON

MANDALAY

AROUND MANDALAY

BAGAN REGION

NORTHEASTERN MYANMAR

SOUTHEASTERN MYANMAR

WESTERN MYANMAR

MAP LEGEND

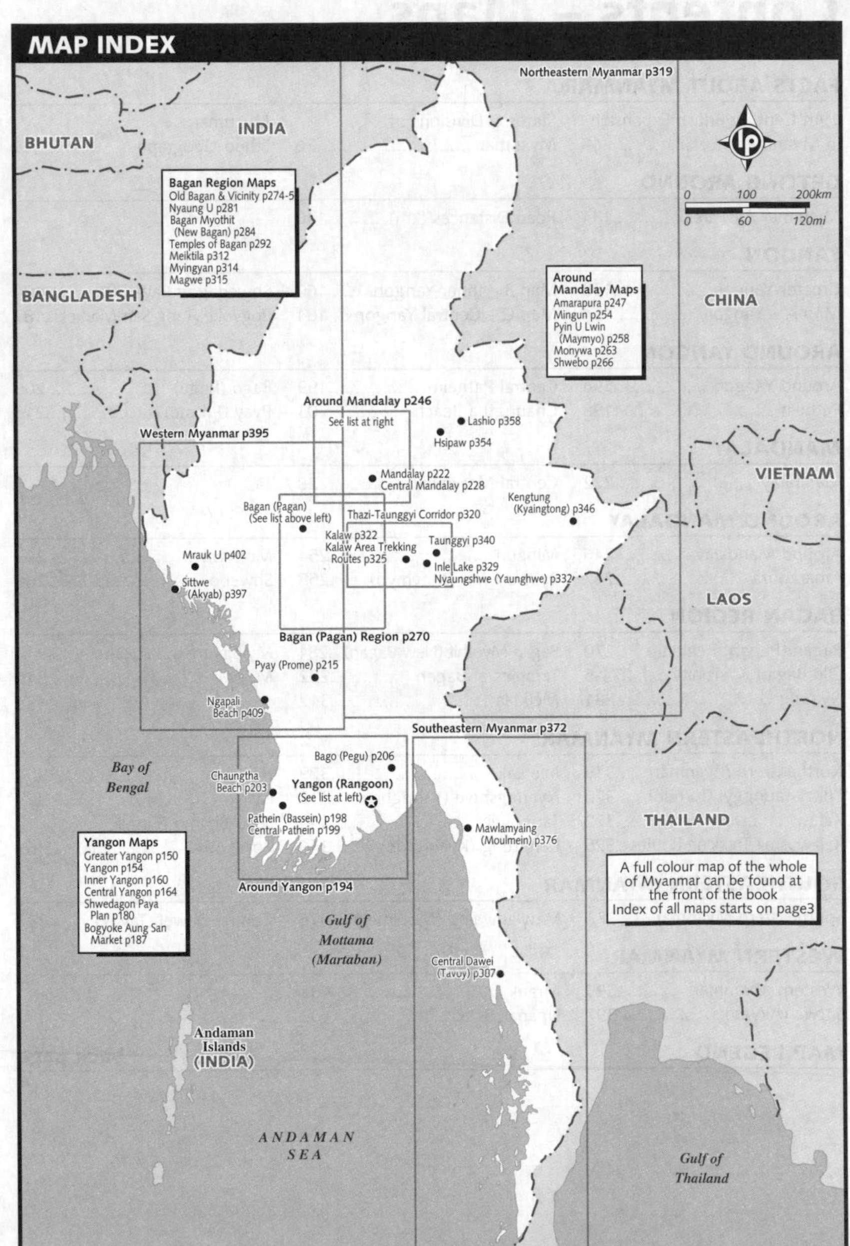
MAP INDEX
Northeastern Myanmar p319
BHUTAN
INDIA
Bagan Region Maps
Old Bagan & Vicinity p274-5
Nyaung U p281
Bagan Myothit
(New Bagan) p284
Temples of Bagan p292
Meiktila p312
Myingyan p314
Magwe p315
0 100 200km
0 60 120mi
BANGLADESH
Around
Mandalay Maps
Amarapura p247
Mingun p254
Pyin U Lwin
(Maymyo) p258
Monywa p263
Shwebo p266
CHINA
Around Mandalay p246
See list at right
Lashio p358
Hsipaw p354
Western Myanmar p395
Mandalay p222
Central Mandalay p228
VIETNAM
Kengtung
(Kyaingtong) p346
Bagan (Pagan)
(See list above left)
Thazi-Taunggyi Corridor p320
Kalaw p322
Kalaw Area Trekking
Routes p325
Taunggyi p340
Inle Lake p329
Nyaungshwe (Yaunghwe) p332
Mrauk U p402
Sittwe
(Akyab) p397
LAOS
Bagan (Pagan) Region p270
Pyay (Prome) p215
Ngapali
Beach p409
Southeastern Myanmar p372
Bay of
Bengal
Bago (Pegu) p206
Chaungtha
Beach p203
Yangon (Rangoon)
(See list at left)
Pathein (Bassein) p198
Central Pathein p199
Mawlamyaing
(Moulmein) p376
THAILAND
Yangon Maps
Greater Yangon p150
Yangon p154
Inner Yangon p160
Central Yangon p164
Shwedagon Paya
Plan p180
Bogyoke Aung San
Market p187
Around Yangon p194
A full colour map of the whole
of Myanmar can be found at
the front of the book
Index of all maps starts on page3
Gulf of
Mottama
(Martaban)
Central Dawei
(Tavoy) p387
Andaman
Islands
(INDIA)
ANDAMAN
SEA
Gulf of
Thailand

The Authors

Steven Martin

Steven Martin has been living and travelling in Southeast Asia since 1981, and has written articles about the region for the Associated Press, Agence France-Presse and *Time*. He is currently based in Bangkok, Thailand.

Mic Looby

After what seemed like an eternity, Mic was born in Australia's Blue Mountains in 1969. Since then, he has been busy growing up, travelling, coming home, travelling again, and becoming a professional writer and freelance illustrator somewhere along the way. He has a degree in journalism, a graduate diploma in animation and interactive media, a 1968 Holden HK station wagon, and – until a recent water filter disaster – a pet crayfish called Eric. Mic has illustrated several Lonely Planet phrasebooks and co-authored Lonely Planet's *Philippines* guidebook.

PREVIOUS EDITION

Michael Clark

Michael first visited Myanmar in 1987, while working in Malaysia as a university lecturer. His overseas travels began with a summer job in the merchant marine, followed by a hitch-hiking trip to Greece, and then a two-year stint in Malawi as a US Peace Corps volunteer. Graduate work in Hawaii and a teaching job in Japan followed. When not on the road, Michael teaches English to international students in Berkeley, California, where he lives with his wife Janet, and kids Melina and Alexander. He has written for the *San Francisco Examiner* and is a co-author of Lonely Planet's *New York, New Jersey, & Pennsylvania* guidebook, and he updated the Myanmar chapter of *South-East Asia on a Shoestring*.

Joe Cummings

Joe has been travelling and working in Southeast Asia since the 1970s, enjoying stints as a translator-interpreter, movie extra, English teacher and freelance writer. He has written over 30 original guidebooks, photographic books, phrasebooks and atlases for countries in Asia and North America, and has recently co-written *Myanmar Style* and edited a book-length biography of Bogyoke

Aung San. For Lonely Planet, he has authored the *Thai* and *Lao* phrasebooks, as well as guides to *Thailand*, *Bangkok*, *Thailand's Islands & Beaches* and *Laos*, parts of *South-East Asia on a Shoestring* and *World Food: Thailand.* Joe has also published articles on culture, politics and travel in many print and online periodicals, including *Ambassador*, *Asia Magazine*, *Asian Wall Street Journal*, *Bangkok Post*, *Expedia*, *Fables*, *Geographical*, *The Nation*, *Outside*, *San Francisco Examiner* and *South China Morning Post*.

FROM THE AUTHORS

From Steven

Many thanks to Ma Thanegi, Matthew Pennington, Daniel Lovering, Thomas Crampton, Joe Cummings, Bo Hill, Rick Heizman, Ross Dunkley, Duncan T MacLean, and to all my friends in Myanmar whose warmth and hospitality make every visit to their fascinating country a thoroughly enjoyable and memorable experience.

From Mic

A thousand golden thank-yous to the following for their information and inspiration: Dr Chan Aye and his family, Ron McIntyre, Win Win, Lotta and Stef, and Mie Mie and her family.

This Book

The first three editions of Myanmar were written by Tony Wheeler. Joe Cummings took over the writing for the 4th, 5th and 6th editions, with Michael Clark helping Joe on the 7th edition. This 8th edition was updated by Steven Martin (who was the coordinating author and updated the Northeastern Myanmar and Southeastern Myanmar chapters) and Mic Looby (who updated the Yangon, Around Yangon, Mandalay, Around Mandalay, Bagan Region and Western Myanmar chapters). Making a brief cameo appearance, Tony Wheeler also added a little to the Inle Lake and Mrauk U sections after a holiday visit.

FROM THE PUBLISHER
This edition of *Myanmar (Burma)* was produced in our Melbourne office under the coordination of Bruce Evans (editing and indexing) and Jack Gavran (mapping and layout). Susie Ashworth (editing) and Pablo Gastar (layout) coordinated the final stages of production. Lending a hand with editing were Melanie Dankel and Victoria Harrison, while Nina Rousseau helped with proofing. Chris Thomas, Meredith Mail, Chris Tsismetzis and Barbara Benson helped with mapping. The climate chart was done by Kusnandar. Illustrations were coordinated by Matt King and the cover was designed by Jenny Jones. Emma Koch compiled the Language chapter and Mark Germanchis gave valuable Quark assistance. Virginia Maxwell did layout checks and revised the Introduction. Lonely Planet Images supplied the colour.

THANKS
Many thanks to the travellers who used the last edition and wrote to us with helpful hints, advice and interesting anecdotes. Your names appear in the back of this book.

Foreword

ABOUT LONELY PLANET GUIDEBOOKS

The story begins with a classic travel adventure: Tony and Maureen Wheeler's 1972 journey across Europe and Asia to Australia. There was no useful information about the overland trail then, so Tony and Maureen published the first Lonely Planet guidebook to meet a growing need.

From a kitchen table, Lonely Planet has grown to become the largest independent travel publisher in the world, with offices in Melbourne (Australia), Oakland (USA), London (UK) and Paris (France).

Today Lonely Planet guidebooks cover the globe. There is an ever-growing list of books and information in a variety of media. Some things haven't changed. The main aim is still to make it possible for adventurous travellers to get out there – to explore and better understand the world.

At Lonely Planet we believe travellers can make a positive contribution to the countries they visit – if they respect their host communities and spend their money wisely. Since 1986 a percentage of the income from each book has been donated to aid projects and human rights campaigns, and, more recently, to wildlife conservation.

Although inclusion in a guidebook usually implies a recommendation we cannot list every good place. Exclusion does not necessarily imply criticism. In fact there are a number of reasons why we might exclude a place – sometimes it is simply inappropriate to encourage an influx of travellers.

UPDATES & READER FEEDBACK

Things change – prices go up, schedules change, good places go bad and bad places go bankrupt. Nothing stays the same. So, if you find things better or worse, recently opened or long-since closed, please tell us and help make the next edition even more accurate and useful.

Lonely Planet thoroughly updates each guidebook as often as possible – usually every two years, although for some destinations the gap can be longer. Between editions, up-to-date information is available in our free, quarterly *Planet Talk* newsletter and monthly email bulletin *Comet*. The *Scoop* section of our web site covers news and current affairs relevant to travellers. Lastly, the *Thorn Tree* bulletin board and *Postcards* section carry unverified, but fascinating, reports from travellers.

Tell us about it! We genuinely value your feedback. A well-travelled team at Lonely Planet reads and acknowledges every email and letter we receive and ensures that every morsel of information finds its way to the relevant authors, editors and cartographers.

Everyone who writes to us will find their name listed in the next edition of the appropriate guidebook, and will receive the latest issue of *Comet* or *Planet Talk*. The very best contributions will be rewarded with a free guidebook.

We may edit, reproduce and incorporate your comments in Lonely Planet products such as guidebooks, websites and digital products, so let us know if you don't want your comments reproduced or your name acknowledged.

How to contact Lonely Planet:

Online: e talk2us@lonelyplanet.com.au, w www.lonelyplanet.com
Australia: Locked Bag 1, Footscray, Victoria 3011
UK: 10a Spring Place, London NW5 3BH
USA: 150 Linden St, Oakland, CA 94607

has detailed information about the prevalence of forced labour in Myanmar.

Nobel Peace Prize Laureate and National League for Democracy (NLD) leader Aung San Suu Kyi advocates boycotting all forms of travel to the country as a means of isolating the government and forcing reform. (See the boxed text 'National League for Democracy & Aung San Suu Kyi' on page 28 for more details.) Inside Myanmar, there are a number of people who support her stance. This pro-boycott group argues that much of the money from tourism goes directly and indirectly into the pockets of the very generals who continue to deny Burmese citizens the most-basic civil rights. They point particularly to the fact that every tourist that enters Myanmar must change a set sum of overseas funds (currently US$200) into Foreign Exchange Certificates (FECs), a transaction from which the military earns a small commission. It is, of course, also one of the most effective ways for the junta to obtain precious foreign currency. (See the Foreign Exchange Certificates section on pages 75-76 for more details.)

However, others involved with Burmese politics, including many current or former members of the NLD, feel that a travel boycott of Myanmar is counterproductive. They maintain that tourism is not only economically helpful, but vital to the pro-democracy movement for the two-way flow of information it provides. (See the boxed text 'The Burmese Fairy Tale' written by pro-democracy activist Ma Thanegi on pages 26-27 for such a viewpoint.) Aung San Suu Kyi, on the other hand, regards tourism for the purpose of exchanging views on democracy as virtually useless. She has dismissed as 'patronising' the argument that tourists can teach something to the Burmese about their own plight.

THIS GUIDEBOOK

We're often asked why we have titled this book 'Myanmar (Burma)' rather than using 'Burma' only. Our decision reflects the official United Nations designation of the country; in using this designation, we are in the

If You Decide to Go

If you do go to Myanmar and would like to maximise the positive effects of a visit among the general populace, while minimising support of the government, follow these simple tactics:

- Stay at private, locally owned hotels and guesthouses, rather than in government-owned hotels.
- Avoid package tours connected with Myanmar Travel & Tours (MTT; the state tourist agency). Many independent tour agencies are available in Yangon.
- Avoid MTT-sponsored modes of transport, such as the Yangon-Mandalay Express trains, the MTT ferry between Mandalay and Bagan, and Myanma Airways (MA) flights.
- Buy handicrafts directly from the artisans, rather than from government shops.
- Avoid patronising companies involved with the military-owned Myanmar Economic Holdings. Companies with solid links to the Tatmadaw (armed forces) are often called Myawadi or Myawaddy.
- Bring a few popular (but not politically sensitive) paperback books or recent magazines to give to Burmese people. Books and magazines are often expensive or hard to find in cash-poor Myanmar, and this simple act will be much appreciated.
- Be conscious that the Burmese are not free to discuss politics with foreigners and may be punished or imprisoned if they are caught doing this by the government. Wait for them to raise political topics and never force or initiate such discussions.
- Write to the Myanmar government and to the Myanmar embassy in your country expressing your views about the human-rights situation there. (See the list of Myanmar embassies and consulates on page 73 for contact details.)

company of organisations such as Amnesty International. (See the boxed text 'Name Changes' on pages 24-25 for more details.)

We are sometimes criticised for making a profit out of publishing books to Myanmar and other countries functioning under repressive regimes. In fact, LP makes very little money out of projects such as this, as they cover destinations that relatively few travellers visit. Of the profit that is made from this and all other LP projects, a proportion is donated to aid projects and human rights campaigns around the world.

At Lonely Planet, we believe that travellers who decide to visit Myanmar should support non-government tourist facilities wherever possible. In this guidebook we have made the decision not to review any restaurants, hotels or shops that we know to be government owned. When we think there's a good chance that travellers will find themselves in these places (by recommendation or because of location) we have noted their existence and highlighted the fact that they are government owned. We have tried to identify government-owned transport services (see the boxed texts 'Government-Owned Services' on pages 128 and 133 for more details) and point travellers towards privately owned alternatives. We have also supplied a list of useful websites (many of which also contain links offering more information about Myanmar) in the Digital Resources section of the Facts for the Visitor chapter (page 82). Useful printed references are listed in the Books & Periodicals section of the same chapter (page 83).

Whether you choose to visit Myanmar or not, we hope that this book has been useful in helping you to arrive at your decision.

Facts about Myanmar

HISTORY

Early Pyu & Mon Kingdoms

Virtually nothing is known of Myanmar's prehistoric inhabitants, though archaeological evidence suggests the area has been inhabited since at least 2500 BC. It may originally have been sparsely populated by Negritos or proto-Malays who are thought to have inhabited the lowland and coastal areas of Myanmar (Burma), Thailand and Malaysia. The remnants of this race appear today in only a few isolated pockets in the interior of the Thai-Malay Peninsula and on a sprinkling of islands in the Andaman Sea. If these Negritos were indeed Myanmar's original inhabitants, one theory holds that they were displaced by peoples who migrated into the area from other parts of Southeast Asia. At any rate, Myanmar's nation-building history really begins with the struggle for supremacy between the various peoples who inhabited different regions of the country around a thousand years ago.

A group known as the Pyu – possibly hailing from the Tibeto-Burman plateau or from India – created city-states in central Myanmar at Beikthano, Hanlin and Thayekhittaya (Sri Ksetra) between the 1st century BC and the 9th century AD. Little is known about these people; the art and architecture they left behind indicate they practised Theravada and Mahayana Buddhism mixed with Hinduism, and that they had their own alphabet. The Pyu were dispersed or enslaved by Yunnanese invaders during the 10th century AD, leaving central Myanmar without any clear political succession.

Around the 6th century the Mon – who may have originated in eastern India or who may have been indigenous to mainland Southeast Asia – settled the fertile lowlands stretching from the Ayeyarwady (Irrawaddy) River delta across present-day Thailand to western Cambodia. Inscriptions left behind by the civilisation they developed referred to this area as Suvannabhumi (Golden Land). According to official

Myanmar's Capitals & Ruling Chronology

It's difficult to create a precise summary of the different historical periods in Myanmar due to the general lack of accurate historical records. The only clearly documented eras are those which have been considered 'Burmese' by Burmese historians: that is, the Rakhaing, Pyu, Mon and Bamar kingdoms. Periods of Shan or Siamese rule – even when power extended well into central Myanmar – aren't counted.

Rakhaing	
Dhanyawady	?–6th C
Wethali	4th–8th or 9th C
Mrauk U	13th–18th C
Pyu	
Beikthano	?–5th C
Hanlin	3rd–9th C
Thayekhittaya	3rd–10th C
Mon	
Thaton (Dvaravati)	?–10th C
Hanthawady	10th–16th C
Bamar	
Bagan	11th–14th C
Sagaing	1315–1364
Inwa	1364–1555
	1629–1752
	1765–1783
	1823–1837
Taungoo	1486–1573
Shwebo	1758–1765
Konbaung	1783–1823
	1837–1857
Mandalay (Yadanapon)	1857–1885
British	
Sittwe & Mawlamyaing	1826–1852
Mandalay	1852–1886
Yangon	1886–1947

Burmese history, the Mon capital occupied the area around Thaton in present-day Myanmar, though outside scholars argue more convincingly that Suvannabhumi was centred in Thailand's Nakhon Pathom.

Enter the Bamar, or Burmans, who came south into Myanmar from somewhere in the eastern Himalayas around the 8th or 9th century. Once the Pyu were vanquished by the Yunnanese, the Bamar supplanted them in central Myanmar, a region that has since been the true cultural heartland of Myanmar. Shortly after they took over the central region, the Bamar came into conflict with the Mon in a long and complicated struggle for control of the whole country. By the time the Bamar had irrevocably ended up on top, the Mon had largely merged with Bamar culture or, bearing in mind how much Mon culture the Bamar had absorbed, it might be more accurate to say that the Bamar had largely merged with Mon culture.

Great Kings of Bagan (Pagan)

It is thought that Bagan (Pagan) was actually founded on the banks of the Ayeyarwady River in AD 849, but it entered its golden period 200 years later when Anawrahta ascended the throne in 1044. He consolidated the kingdom, drawing several regions around it into vassal status and creating the first centralised government. Virtually all written history pertaining to Myanmar begins with this era; legendary Bagan kings from the 2nd century AD are probably invented.

Initially animists, the Bamar had picked up a hybrid form of Buddhism – part Tantric, part Mahayana – in their migration to Myanmar. When the Mon king Manuha of Thaton, to the south, would not cooperate willingly with Anawrahta's request for their *Tripitaka* (the holy canon of Theravada Buddhism), Anawrahta marched south and conquered Thaton in 1057. He took back not just the Buddhist scriptures, but also the king and most of his court. This injection of Mon culture inspired a phenomenal burst of energy from the Bamar. Bagan quickly became a city of glorious temples and the capital of the first Burmese kingdom to encompass virtually all of present-day Myanmar. What we today identify as 'Burmese' is really a fusion of Mon and Bamar cultures that came about at the height of the Bagan era.

Anawrahta was killed by a buffalo in 1077. None of his successors had his vision or energy, and Bagan's power declined slowly but steadily. Kyanzittha (1084–1113) attempted to unify Myanmar's disparate peoples, and later kings like Alaungsithu and Htilominlo built beautiful shrines, but essentially Bagan reached its peak with Anawrahta.

Bagan's decline coincided with the rise to power of Kublai Khan and his Tartars in the north, who invaded Myanmar in 1287. Bagan's rule collapsed before the onslaught. Shan tribes from the hills to the east – closely related to the Siamese – took the opportunity to attack and grab a piece of the low country, while in the south the Mon broke free of Bamar control to establish their own kingdom once again.

Other Kingdoms

For the next 250 years Myanmar remained in chaos. In the south the Mon kingdom remained relatively stable, but in the north there was continuous strife. Between the two, a weaker Bamar kingdom was established at Taungoo, east of Pyay (Prome), and it retained its independence by playing off one major power against the other.

At first the Mon established their new capital close to the present Thai border at Mottama (Martaban) near Mawlamyaing (Moulmein), but after a series of skirmishes with the Siamese it was shifted to Bago (Pegu), near Yangon (Rangoon) and the Mon country became known as the Kingdom of Hanthawady. Around this time Myanmar received its first-known European visitor, Venetian trader Nicolo di Conti, who travelled along the coast in 1435 and left behind brief accounts of Tanintharyi (Tenasserim) and Rakhaing (Arakan).

In 1472 Dhammazedi, considered the greatest of the Bago kings, came to the throne. A major Buddhist revival took place and the first diplomatic contact with Europeans was made. During this time the great Shwedagon Paya in Yangon began to assume its present form.

Meanwhile the Shan took over northern Myanmar once again and founded the Kingdom of Inwa (mistakenly called Ava by the British) near present-day Mandalay in 1364. Along the western coast the Rakhaing (a people living near the Indian border) established Mrauk U (Myohaung), a Buddhist kingdom with fields of temples to rival Bagan. Surprisingly, it was not the establishment of Bago, Inwa or Mrauk U that was to prove the catalyst for the reunification of Myanmar, but tiny Taungoo, which had been founded by Bamar refugees from the new Shan kingdoms.

In the 16th century a series of Taungoo kings extended their power north, nearly to Inwa, then south, taking the Mon kingdom and shifting their own capital to Bago. Their hold was initially fragile, but in 1550 Bayinnaung came to the throne, reunified all of Myanmar and defeated the neighbouring Siamese so convincingly that it was to be many years before the long-running friction between the Burmese and Siamese re-emerged. Burmese historians sometimes refer to this era as the Second Burmese Empire.

With Bayinnaung's death in 1581, this new Burmese kingdom immediately went into decline, and when, in 1636, the capital was shifted north from Bago to Inwa, the idea of a kingdom taking in all of Myanmar was effectively renounced. Inwa was the capital of Myanmar, but it was a long way from the sea, so it was effectively cut off from communication with the outside world. This isolation eventually contributed to the conflict with the British.

Final Kings of Mandalay

In the 18th century the decline became serious as hill tribes once more started to raid central Myanmar, and the Mon again broke away and established their own kingdom in Bago. In 1752 the Mon took Inwa, but in the same year Alaungpaya came to power in Shwebo, 80km north of Inwa, and spent the next eight years rushing back and forth across Myanmar – conquering, defeating and destroying all who opposed him. He was the founder of the last Burmese dynasty and it was his near-invincibility that later deluded the Burmese into thinking they could resist the British.

Alaungpaya's son, Hsinbyushin, charged into Thailand for good measure, and so thoroughly levelled the capital of Ayuthaya that the Siamese were forced to move their capital south to what eventually became Bangkok. Bodawpaya, who came to power in 1782, was also a son of Alaungpaya and managed to bring Rakhaing (Arakan) back under Bamar control. This was to be the direct cause of the first Anglo-Burmese conflict.

Rakhaing, the eastern coastal region of the Bay of Bengal, had long been a border region between Myanmar and India; but its Buddhist populace were ethnically and linguistically akin to the Bamar. By this time the British had colonised much of the Indian subcontinent and were looking for a pretext to expand eastward. Refugees from Rakhaing fled into British-controlled India and from there planned to recapture their country. This so irritated the Burmese that they, in return, mounted raids across the border into British territory.

At this time the British, Dutch and French were all vying for power in the East, and all had established at least some sort of contact with the Burmese. The Portuguese had been the first Europeans to come to Myanmar in numbers, as explorers and later adventurers who hired themselves as mercenaries to the Burmese kings. However, the Burmese showed little interest in dealing commercially with Europeans. The British, increasingly worried about French interest in the region, were keen to gain control of the eastern side of the Bay of Bengal. Border incidents in Rakhaing and Assam soon gave the British the excuse they needed to invade.

In 1819 Bagyidaw came to the throne in Myanmar. A hot pursuit across the Assam border by Burmese troops led to a declaration of the First Anglo-Burmese War by the British. The increasing isolation of the Burmese court at Inwa contributed to this disastrous (for the Burmese) war; but there is little doubt that the British were more motivated by geopolitical considerations than by concern for Assamese refugees.

Under the leadership of General Maha Bandula, the Burmese used guerrilla tactics to score some minor victories, but they were no match for the superior firepower of the British. In May of 1824 a British armada landed at Yangon (Rangoon), taking the Burmese by surprise. The undefended town was abandoned by the Burmese and the British took advantage of the lull in fighting during heavy monsoon rains to turn Shwedagon Paya into a fortress. Maha Bandula attempted to retake the sacred site, but was repelled and finally retreated after his forces sustained heavy casualties. During a subsequent battle in the Ayeyarwady (Irrawaddy) delta region, Maha Bandula was killed by British cannon fire, and the demoralised Burmese troops surrendered.

The British then imposed the Treaty of Yandabo upon the Burmese. The terms of this lopsided treaty were negotiated with the help of an Armenian merchant, Sarkies Manook, who was the official translator for the British. The Burmese court used the translating services of Adoniram Judson, an American Baptist missionary who had been imprisoned by the Burmese at the outbreak of the war (see the Kyaikkami section in the Southeastern Myanmar chapter for details of his life). Judson, for obvious reasons, welcomed the British takeover, and did his best to negotiate terms that were favourable to them. Under the terms of the treaty, Britain gained control of Rakhaing (Arakan) and Tanintharyi (Tenasserim), and Myanmar had to pay a large reparation in silver to the British and accept a British 'resident' (a political officer who oversaw affairs at the royal court) at Inwa. Cowed by the British, Bagyidaw resigned himself to the circumstances in unrealistic hopes that the British would relinquish the occupied territories once the reparation was paid.

Bagyidaw was followed by Tharawaddy Min, and he in turn by his son, Bagan Min, neither of whom were pleased at the prospect of being manipulated by the British. It had long been the custom for a new king to massacre all possible pretenders to the throne, and Bagan Min took this policy to new extremes. In the first two years of his reign 6000 people were executed. The British resident had been forced to withdraw during Tharawaddy's brief reign, and frontier incidents began to flare up again. The British seized upon an extortion incident in Yangon in 1852, during which two British ship captains had allegedly been kidnapped by Burmese government officials, in order to open hostilities in the Second Anglo-Burmese War.

It's possible that this incident never actually took place, and that the British were again motivated by the desire to add territory to their empire. In any case, most historians agree that this war was started on the basis of a grossly exaggerated pretext by the British. It's more likely that they realised what a bad deal they had made in taking over Rakhaing and Tanintharyi, which were of little practical or commercial use. Rather, they sought the use of a suitable port, such as Yangon, and to control the Ayeyarwady River, which would afford access to the interior.

The British quickly took over Yangon, Mottama and Pathein (Bassein), and marched north to Pyay. Unlike the first war, the British conducted this campaign with stern efficiency, and met little opposition from the ill-equipped and disorganised Burmese forces. After a series of skirmishes and one-sided battles, the war was over – this time, the British conquered all of central and southern Myanmar (Lower Burma), which became a province of India.

Bagan Min, now extremely unpopular, was deposed and in 1853 Mindon Min became king of Myanmar, or at least what remained of it. Mindon proved to be a wise realist who eventually came to pragmatic terms with the British, yet cleverly balanced their influence with that of other European (and American) powers. During this period the industrial revolution came to full flower in Europe, and Lower Burma became an important and profitable part of the British Empire due to its enormous teak resources and vast potential for growing rice.

Unhappily for the Burmese, Mindon made one important mistake – he did not adequately provide for a successor. When he died in 1878, the new king, Thibaw Min, was propelled into power by his ruthless wife and scheming mother-in-law. Thibaw was so far down the list of possible successors that the 'massacre of kinsmen' reached unheard-of heights, and in the new age of the telegraph and steamship, the news, described in lurid detail, soon reached the West. In London, public outcry demanded that something be done to quell such 'acts of barbarism' so close to the borders of the Empire, and thus European and British attitudes towards the new king were tarnished from the start.

Thibaw proved to be a totally ineffective ruler. Deprived of the revenue that had traditionally been collected from central Myanmar, northern Myanmar soon became a sorry scene as armed gangs and ruthless officials vied with each other to extort money from the hapless peasants. Enormous numbers of Burmese fled to the stability of British Lower Burma, where there also happened to be a great demand for labour for the new rice trade.

Finally, in 1885, another Anglo-Burmese conflict flared up. The British resident had again withdrawn from Mandalay, and a petty dispute over the exploits of the Bombay Burmah Trading Company was the excuse the British needed to send gunboats north to Mandalay. In two weeks it was all over: the British took Mandalay after only the most token resistance. The royal palace was looted and used to quarter British and Indian troops, and Thibaw and his queen were unceremoniously bundled into oxcarts and then onto a waiting steamer. The former king spent the rest of his life in exile in India, reduced to sending letters to British officials pleading for funds to supplement his meagre pension. Meanwhile, Queen Victoria was presented with the pick of the war booty, including 'Thibaw's best crown, three emeralds from his second crown, an envelope containing eight loose stones which had dropped out of the crown, and a necklace with a diamond peacock and gold comb'.

In order to stamp their authority upon northern Myanmar, the British undertook a brutal two-year military campaign throughout the region. Similar in execution to the Highland Clearances of Scotland approximately a century earlier, British forces ruthlessly crushed any signs of opposition, killing many innocent civilians and destroying numerous villages.

British Period

Once again Myanmar was united, but this time with the British as masters. To the British, Myanmar was just another chunk of Asia that now had the good fortune to be part of the British Empire. To the Burmese, the situation was not nearly so pleasant: Now Myanmar was just a part of British India – and what was worse, Indians, whom the Burmese had traditionally looked down on, came flooding in with the British. As the swampy delta of the south was turned into rice paddies, it was the Indians who supplied the money to improve the land, and those same Indians who came to own it when the less commercially experienced Burmese proved unable to make it pay or to pay for it. By 1930 most of Yangon's population was Indian. Chinese were also encouraged to immigrate and set up businesses to stimulate the economy. As Myanmar's national income grew, the country was flooded with cheap British imports, such as cotton *longyi* (sarongs) produced in the factories of Manchester. Profits from rice cultivation were whisked out of the country to pay for more and more imported goods.

Contrary to the romantic tone of modern English-language accounts of 'Burma under the Raj', much of Myanmar was considered a hardship posting by British colonial officials, who found the Burmese difficult to govern. Myanmar had the highest crime rate in the British Empire. Along with the railroads and schools, the British built numerous prisons, including the massive penitentiary at Insein, the largest prison in the British Empire.

The British applied direct rule only to the areas in which Bamar were the majority – central Myanmar, Rakhaing and Tanintharyi. The 'hill states' belonging to the Chin, Kachin, Shan, Kayin and Kayah were

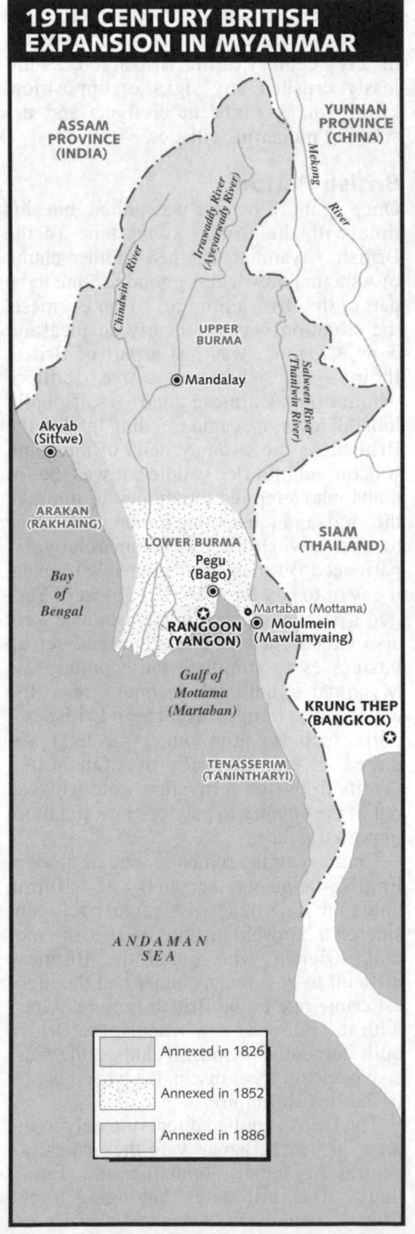

permitted to remain largely autonomous, though officially part of British India. This difference between direct and indirect rule has haunted Myanmar's political history ever since.

Burmese nationalism grew. Inspired by the nationalist movement in India, the resistance took on a unique Burmese flavour: Demonstrations were often lead by Buddhist monks. U Ottama, a Burmese monk who had studied in India and returned to Myanmar in 1921, promoted the concept of religious liberation as a way to bring the independence movement to the attention of the average Burmese Buddhist. After being arrested numerous times for demonstrating against British rule, U Ottama finally died in prison in 1939. U Wizaya, another monk-turned-martyr, died in prison after a 163-day hunger strike that began as a protest against a rule that forbade monks from wearing their Buddhist robes while imprisoned.

By the 1920s and 1930s the British were eventually forced to make a number of concessions towards Myanmar's self-government. In 1937 Myanmar was separated from India, but internally the country was torn by a struggle between opposing Burmese political parties. The era was also marred by sporadic outbursts of anti-Indian and anti-Chinese violence.

WWII

Japanese-Burmese contact had been made well before Japan entered WWII. Indeed Bogyoke Aung San, who had first made his name through university-level political action and was later to become the 'father figure' of independent Burma, had fled to the Japanese in 1940, following his arrest for participation in the Burmese Communist Party (BCP). Aided by the Burmese Independence Army (BIA), the Japanese army marched into Myanmar within weeks of Pearl Harbor and by mid-1942 had driven the retreating British-Indian forces, along with the Chinese Kuomintang (KMT) forces (which had come to their aid), out of most of Myanmar. Japan declared Myanmar an independent country and allowed Aung San and his '30 comrades' to create the

MICK WELDON

Bogyoke Aung San, the famous father of both Myanmar's independence movement and Aung San Suu Kyi, was assassinated in 1947 and is regarded as a martyr.

Burma National Army (BNA). One of the 30 was a Sino-Burmese native of Paungdale (near Pyay) named Shu Maung, who took the nom de guerre Ne Win, meaning Brilliant Like The Sun. Aung San took the position of defence minister; Ne Win became chief of staff of the BNA.

The Japanese were able to maintain Burmese political support for only a short time before their harsh and arrogant conduct managed to alienate the Burmese. Aung San expressed his bitterness during his stay at Japan's 15th Army headquarters in Maymyo (now Pyin U Lwin):

> I went to Japan to save my people who were struggling like bullocks under the British. But, now we are treated like dogs. We are far from our hope of reaching the human stage, and even to get back to the bullock stage we need to struggle more.

The imaginative 'Chindit' anti-Japanese operation, mounted by the Allies with air-supplied troops behind enemy lines, also encouraged further anti-Japanese feeling. Soon an internal resistance movement sprang up, and towards the end of the war the BNA hastily switched sides to the British. The Allies prevailed at a cost of approximately 27,000 casualties; nearly 200,000 Japanese perished in the fierce, protracted battles.

Independence

That Myanmar was heading rapidly towards independence after the war was all too clear, but who should manage this process was a different question. On 27 January 1947 British Prime Minister Clement Attlee and General Aung San signed an agreement on behalf of the UK and Burma respectively. The Aung San–Attlee agreement stipulated that a constituent assembly would be elected in April by, and consisting of, Myanmar nationals only; that certain matters which had previously been formally reserved for the British governor would in future be brought before an executive council that would function as an interim government; that the Burmese army would come under the control of the interim government; and that Burma would receive an interest-free loan of approximately £8 million from the UK.

The executive council, in consultation with non-Bamar representatives, was to nominate a Frontier Areas Committee composed of an equal number of members from 'Ministerial Burma' (British-dominated Myanmar) and the border states which had had some degree of autonomy under the British. This committee would determine ways for frontier peoples to participate in the drafting of a constitution.

In February 1947 Aung San met with leaders from the Shan, Chin and Kachin communities in Panglong, a township in the Shan State. Together, they signed the famous Panglong Agreement, guaranteeing Burma's ethnic minorities the freedom to choose their own political destiny. Although representatives from the Kayin, Kayah, Mon, Rakhaing and many other ethnicities were noticeably absent from the meeting, the agreement was broadly interpreted to mean that it would apply to all ethnic communities in what the British called the Frontier Areas.

When elections for a constituent assembly were held on 9 April 1947, Aung San's

Anti-Fascist People's Freedom League (AFPFL) won an overwhelming 172 seats out of 255. The BCP took seven seats, while the Bamar opposition led by U Saw took three seats. Twenty-four seats were allotted to the Kayin community, four seats to the 'Anglo-Burman' community and 45 seats to the Frontier Areas.

Hoping to retain influence in the region, the British wanted a gradual transition, claiming that time was needed to rebuild the shattered economy and political system before the handover. Bogyoke Aung San wanted independence immediately, because if given time, other political parties could gain ground on his strong position at the close of the war. He also wanted to establish a democratic, civilian government:

> We must make democracy the popular creed. We must try to build up a free Burma in accordance with such a creed. If we should fail to do this, our people are bound to suffer. If democracy should fail the world cannot stand back and just look on, and therefore Burma would one day, like Japan and Germany, be despised. Democracy is the only ideology which is consistent with freedom. It is also an ideology that promotes and strengthens peace. It is therefore the only ideology we should aim for.

However, Aung San's incredibly prophetic views didn't win over his political opponents, and in late 1945 he made another prediction:

> How long do national heroes last? Not long in this country; I do not give myself more than another eighteen months of life.

Eighteen months later, in July 1947, 32-year-old Aung San and six of his assistants were assassinated in a plot ascribed to U Saw, a prewar political leader who had refused to sign the Aung San–Attlee agreement that was to usher in Burmese independence. A few conspiracy theorists speculate that General Ne Win may have ordered the assassination, due to Aung San's plans to demilitarise the government. However, Aung San's main source of political support had been the BNA and Ne Win, and U Saw – who favoured British-style capitalism and Bamar domination rather than the national socialism and ethnic autonomy espoused by Aung San – had more motive than anyone else in the ongoing power conflict between Aung San and his various political opponents. U Saw apparently believed that his position as prime minister in pre-WWII Myanmar would be reinstated if Aung San and the AFPFL could be successfully thwarted.

While Myanmar mourned a hero's death, Prime Minister Attlee and Aung San's protégé U Nu signed an agreement for the transfer of power in October 1947. On 4 January 1948, at an auspicious middle-of-the-night hour, Myanmar became independent and left the British Commonwealth. As Aung San had promised, the national presidency was given to a representative from an ethnic minority group, and Sao Shwe Thaike, a Shan leader, became the first president of the Union of Burma.

Almost immediately, the new government was faced with the complete disintegration of Myanmar. The hill-tribe people, who had supported the British and fought against the Japanese throughout the war, were distrustful of the Bamar majority and went into armed opposition. The communists withdrew from the government and attacked it. Muslims from the Rakhaing area also opposed the new government. The Mon, long thought to be totally integrated with the Burmese, revolted. Assorted factions, private armies, WWII resistance groups and plain mutineers further confused the picture.

In early 1949 almost the entire country was in the hands of one rebel group or another, and even Yangon suffered fighting in its suburbs. At one stage the government was on the point of surrendering to the communist forces, but gradually, and with particularly valuable assistance from loyal hill-tribe contingents, the government fought back, and through 1950 and 1951 regained much of the country.

Although much of Myanmar was now at least tenuously under government control, a new problem sprang up for the battered Burmese. With the collapse of Chiang Kai-Shek's KMT forces before Mao Zedong, the tattered remnants of his army withdrew into Myanmar and mounted raids from northern Myanmar into Yunnan, the bordering Chinese province. Being no match for the Chinese communists, the KMT decided to carve their own little fiefdom out of Burmese territory. The Burmese government now found itself fighting not only a mixed bag of rebels, communists, and gangs of out-and-out brigands and bandits, but also a US-supported, anticommunist Chinese army.

Road to Socialism

In the mid-1950s, although the central government strengthened its hold on the country, the economic situation went from bad to worse. A number of grandiose development projects succeeded only in making foreign 'advisors' rather wealthy, and in 1953 the Burmese bravely announced that aid or assistance from the USA was no longer welcome, as long as US-supplied Chinese nationalist forces were at large within Myanmar. U Nu managed to remain in power until 1958 when, with political turmoil about to become armed chaos yet again and the KMT problem still unresolved, he voluntarily handed the reins over to a military government under General Ne Win.

Freed from the 'democratic' responsibilities inherent in a civilian government, Ne Win was able to make some excellent progress during the 15 months his military government operated. A degree of law and order was restored, rebel activity was reduced and Yangon was given a massive and much-needed cleanup.

In early 1960 elections were held and U Nu came back to power with a much-improved majority, but once again political turmoil developed. His party threatened to break up into opposing groups and in early 1962 Ne Win assumed power again and abolished the parliament. He established his own 17-member Revolutionary Council, announcing that the country would 'march toward socialism in our own Burmese way'. This time U Nu did not hand over power voluntarily, and along with his main ministers was thrown into prison, where he remained until forced into exile in 1966. He later ineffectively opposed the Ne Win government from abroad. In 1980 U Nu returned from exile under an amnesty programme for political offenders and devoted himself to translating Buddhist scriptures, except for a brief period of political involvement in 1988. U Nu died of a heart attack at age 88 in Yangon in February 1995.

Soon after coming to power in 1962, Ne Win announced the new path Myanmar would follow: 'The Burmese Road to Socialism'. It was a steadily downhill path. Nationalisation policies were extended right down to the retail shop level in 1966 when it was announced that a long list of items would only be available from 'Peoples Shops'. The net result was frightening: Many everyday commodities immediately became available only on the black market, and vast numbers of people were thrown out of work by the closure of retail outlets.

A disingenuous 'sock the rich' measure demonetised the largest banknotes (K50 and K100); anybody so unfortunate as to have these notes found them to be worthless. Many of the retail traders who became unemployed following the nationalisation of retail trade were Indians and Chinese – vestiges of the colonial era in Bamar eyes – and they were hustled out of the country with Draconian thoroughness. No compensation was paid for their expropriated businesses, and each adult was allowed to depart with only K75 to his or her name plus K250 in gold – even a woman's jewellery in excess of that amount was to be confiscated. As many as a quarter of a million people of Indian and Chinese descent left Myanmar during the 1960s. Anti-Chinese riots in Yangon in 1967 – spurred by fears that the Chinese were about to 'import' China's Cultural Revolution – resulted in hundreds of Chinese deaths.

In late 1974 there were serious student disturbances over the burial of former United Nations (UN) secretary-general and long-time Ne Win political foe, U Thant, yet overall the government appeared firmly in control and determined to continue its strange progress towards a Burmese Utopia. In late

1981 Ne Win retired as president of the republic (retaining his position as chair of the Burmese Socialist Programme Party, the country's only legal political party at the time), but his successor was more or less hand picked and the government remained guided very much by Ne Win's political will.

1988 Uprising

As Myanmar's economy stagnated, the country's standard of living slid downhill year after year. Finally, in 1987 and 1988, the long-suffering Burmese people decided they had had enough of their incompetent and arrogant government and packed the streets in huge demonstrations, insisting that Ne Win go.

Ne Win voluntarily retired in July 1988, but it was too late to halt the agitation of the people. The massive pro-democracy demonstrations, spurred by the further demonetisation of large notes and a prophecy that Myanmar would become a 'free country' on the auspicious date of 8-8-88, were brutally crushed, with at least 3000 deaths over a six-week period.

Ne Win's National Unity Party (NUP; formerly the Burmese Socialist Programme Party) was far from ready to give up control, and the public protests continued as two wholly unacceptable Ne Win stooges succeeded him. The third Ne Win successor came to power after a military coup in September 1988, which, it is generally believed, was organised by Ne Win.

A newly formed State Law and Order Restoration Council (Slorc) established martial law under the leadership of General Saw Maung, commander in chief of the armed forces, and promised to hold democratic National Assembly elections in May 1989. Slorc also changed the country's official name from the Union of Burma to the Union of Myanmar, claiming that 'Burma' was a vestige of European colonialism.

The opposition quickly formed a coalition party called the National League for Democracy (NLD) and campaigned for all they were worth. U Nu tried to declare a parallel government based on the 1945 constitution, but the long-suppressed Burmese population rallied around charismatic NLD spokesperson Aung San Suu Kyi, daughter of national hero Bogyoke Aung San. Suu Kyi, conversant in Burmese, Japanese, French and English, and married to an Oxford University professor, brought a hitherto unseen sophistication to Burmese politics.

Nervous, Slorc tried to appease the masses with new roads and fresh paint jobs in Yangon, and then attempted to interfere in the electoral process by shifting villages from one part of the country to another and by postponing the election. Perhaps the biggest surprise came with the announcement that the government was abandoning socialism in favour of a capitalist economy in all but a few industries.

In July 1989 Aung San Suu Kyi was placed under house arrest.

1990 Free Election & Aung San Suu Kyi

Once the government was confident it had effectively reduced the opposition, in May 1990 it allowed the country's first free election in 30 years. In spite of all preventive measures, the NUP lost the election to the NLD, which took 392 of the 485 contested seats. Slorc barred the elected members of parliament from assuming power, however, decreeing that a state-approved constitution had to be passed by national referendum first. In October 1990 the military raided NLD offices and arrested key leaders. Since that time over a hundred elected parliamentarians have been disqualified, imprisoned, exiled or killed.

Before her arrest in 1989, Suu Kyi had been appointed secretary general of the party. The main NLD candidates in line for any potential premiership that might have occurred if the 1990 election of MPs had been recognised by the current regime were U Aung Shwe, U Tin Oo and U Kyi Maung, all ex-officers. It was widely acknowledged, even back in 1990, that Slorc would never allow a person of Aung San Suu Kyi's background (ex-resident of Myanmar, and married to a Briton) to run for office; it was equally acknowledged that the candidates who stood the best chance of acceptance by the military dictatorship were those with a military background. It turned out that even this was not enough to make the ruling junta relinquish control.

Had the NLD been installed in government, Suu Kyi may have been given a high position (although the suspended constitution would have to have been rewritten, since it contained a clause forbidding those married to foreigners from holding high public office – a clause supported by Suu Kyi's late father, Aung San), but as long as the NLD remains a besieged opposition, we'll never know.

After the events of 1988–89, the world press at first gave amazingly little coverage to politics in Myanmar. In January 1991 Suu Kyi was awarded the Sakharov Prize for freedom of thought by the European Parliament, and in October of the same year she was honoured with the Nobel Peace Prize; both awards were issued as tributes to her selfless leadership in Myanmar's pro-democracy movement. Another international honour came her way in June 1992 when the United Nations Educational, Scientific and Cultural Organization (Unesco) awarded Suu Kyi the Simon Bolivar Prize. In May 1995, Suu Kyi was honoured with a fourth international award when India presented the leader, in absentia, with the Jawaharlal Nehru Award for International Understanding. Likewise as the world media began to follow events in Myanmar, pro-democracy elements, both within the country and abroad, proved themselves to be much more media savvy than the military junta. The democratisation of 'Burma', as pro-democracy groups still call the country, soon became a cause celebre for sundry activists and Hollywood celebrities.

Much to the joy of the Burmese people and her supporters abroad, the government released Suu Kyi from house arrest in July 1995 after nearly six years. Suu Kyi's detention was the most potent symbol of government repression and the biggest magnet for international attention, but many other high-level dissidents, including the NLD's Tin U and Kyi Maung, were also released – not from house arrest, but from prison. For several months Suu Kyi was allowed to address crowds of supporters from her residence. In May and September of 1996, Suu Kyi held a congress of NLD members in a bold political gambit to demonstrate that the NLD was still an active political force. The junta responded by detaining hundreds who attended the congress and the street leading to Suu Kyi's residence was blockaded, prohibiting her from making speeches at her residence.

Upon the advice of a Washington-based public relations firm, Slorc changed its name to the State Peace and Development Council (SPDC) in November 1997.

In 1998, 18 foreign activists were arrested in Yangon in 1998 for distributing anti-government leaflets. In the same year Suu Kyi attempted to leave Yangon to meet with supporters outside the city but was blocked by the military and forcibly returned to Yangon. In 1999 Suu Kyi's British husband, Oxford professor Michael Aris, died of cancer shortly after Yangon denied him a visa to see Suu Kyi one last time in Myanmar. Although they hadn't seen each other since January 1996, Suu Kyi stayed in Myanmar, fearing that if she left the country to visit her husband's deathbed in England, she would be refused re-entry and forced into exile.

In September 2000, Suu Kyi was arrested again after attempting to leave Yangon to meet with supporters. In October 2000, secret talks began between Suu Kyi and the junta – the most significant step towards reconciliation since the elections. Brokered by a UN special envoy, the talks resulted in the release of hundreds of political prisoners, and a noticeable cessation of open hostility between the government and the NLD. In May 2002 Suu Kyi was released from house arrest and announced that her demands for political reform had not changed as a result of the talks. In the weeks following her release she visited NLD offices in townships in the Rangoon area, and in late June made a triumphant visit to Mandalay.

In May 2003 Suu Kyi was arrested again following a violent clash between her supporters and a pro-government mob while she was visiting northern Myanmar. Around 70 NLD supporters and local villagers were

Name Changes

One of the cursory changes instituted by the government since the 1988 Uprising has been a long list of Roman spelling changes for geographic names, in a further effort to purge the country of its colonial past. In most of the name changes, the new Romanised versions bring the names phonetically closer to the everyday Burmese pronunciation.

Myanmar versus Burma

In 1989 the official English name of the country was changed from the Union of Burma to the Union of Myanmar, to conform with Burmese usage. There has been no change in the Burmese name for the country. Myanmar has, in fact, been the official name since at least the time of Marco Polo's 13th-century writings; the first Burmese-language newspaper, published in 1868, was called *Myanmar Thandawzin*, translated by the British as Burma Herald. In the country's 1947 Constitution, the Burmese version reads Myanmar, the English version Burma.

In Burmese literary contexts, the name Myanmar refers to the whole country, Bamar (from whence the English got Burma) refers to Burman ethnicity, or to the Burman language. In everyday parlance, Bamar-pyi (Land of the Burmans) may also be used to refer to the country. The new government position finds Myanmar more equitable, since it doesn't identify the nation with any one ethnic group. If the current military regime releases control of the government to the National League for Democracy, however, there's always the possibility all the names could revert back to their colonial versions.

Linguistically speaking, the change is quite reasonable, but it has become something of a political football between the opposition and the government. The official United Nations designation is now Myanmar, and Amnesty International uses this name as well; some English-language periodicals recognise the change, while others don't.

The 'r' at the end of Myanmar is merely a British English device used to lengthen the preceding 'a' vowel; it is not pronounced. State enterprises that use Myanmar in their titles typically spell the word without an 'r', eg, Myanma Airways, Myanma Five Star Line, Myanma Timber Enterprise.

allegedly beaten or shot dead in the attack. Suu Kyi was officially 'freed' in November, but at the time of going to press she had elected to stay in custody until 35 NLD colleagues were also released.

New prime minister General Khin Nyunt drafted a new 'road map' to 'disciplined democracy' in September 2003, but this was dismissed as a diversion by the US, which, along with the EU and Japan, tightened sanctions against Myanmar following Suu Kyi's re-arrest.

Change seems unlikely unless, or until, the military leadership decides to relinquish control. Many Burmese say they expect major political changes to occur only after Ne Win (91 years old in 2002) dies.

Post-Election Events

Prompted in part by the stagnant economy, top Slorc officials decided to clean house within their own ranks in November 1997, relieving several corrupt ministers of their positions and replacing the 21-member Slorc with a 19-member group calling itself the State Peace & Development Council (SPDC). The move did very little to improve the government's image either at home or abroad. In November 2001 a similar government overhaul occurred in which regional commanders were recalled to Yangon and replaced. Ten of these commanders, who were reassigned to the Ministry of Defence, now make up part of the scaled-down, 13-member SPDC.

Despite the government's human-rights record, a number of foreign investors – most of them Asian – continue to invest huge amounts of foreign currency into private development projects, especially in the central Yangon to Mandalay corridor. Singaporean and Japanese companies hold

Name Changes

Myanmar versus Burmese

Officially in post-1989 Myanmar, the word now used to mean Burmese – referring to a citizen of Myanmar, the language, or any attribute of the country as a single entity (cuisine, culture etc) – is Myanmar. In other words, it's Myanmar people (or 'the Myanmar'), Myanmar language and Myanmar customs, as in Berber people or Magyar language. Because of the lack of familiarity with the use of Myanmar as an adjective however, Lonely Planet is staying with the word Burmese for references to the people and language. Bamar will be used to refer to the Burman ethnic group and to the cuisine.

colonial name	Burmese name	colonial name	Burmese name
Akyab	Sittwe	Moulmein	Mawlamyaing or Mawlamyine
Amherst	Kyaikkami	Myohaung	Mrauk U
Arakan	Rakhaing or Rakhine	Pagan	Bagan
Ava	Inwa	Pegu	Bago
Bassein	Pathein	Prome	Pyay or Pyi
Burma	Myanmar	Rangoon	Yangon
Chindwin River	(no change)	Salween River	Thanlwin River
Irrawaddy River	Ayeyarwady River	Sandoway	Thandwe
Mandalay	(no change)	Sittang River	Sittoung River
Martaban	Mottama	Syriam	Thanlyin
Maymyo	Pyin U Lwin	Taunggyi	(no change)
Mergui	Myeik (or Beik, in spoken language)	Tavoy	Dawei
		Tenasserim	Tanintharyi

significant investments in the country, while China remains the junta's biggest military supporter.

The land border between Myanmar and China stands wide open for legal and illegal trade, and acts as the main supply line for millions of dollars worth of Chinese weaponry destined for Myanmar's military, along with another estimated billion US dollars in consumer goods annually. Beijing considers Yangon a seaport for western China, conveniently linked to Yunnan Province by the WWII-era Burma Road. A 1994 visit to Yangon by Chinese Premier Li Peng – the man who ordered the Tiananmen Square massacre one year after Myanmar's bloody 1988 putdown – reaffirmed China's firm approval of Slorc rule. The US renewal of 'Most Favoured Nation' trade status for China was received with delight in Yangon. In fact, as long as China remains a major foreign-trade hub in Asia, Myanmar's government believes it need not fear potential trade sanctions from other nations.

Meanwhile the repression of free speech and other human rights continues under SPDC leadership. A report commissioned by the International Commission of Jurists (ICJ) in Geneva describes systematic human rights violations, including arbitrary arrests of anyone opposed to the junta, torture of detainees, severe media restrictions, forced relocation of half a million urban dwellers, and forced conscription of civilians to serve as anything from porters to human mine sweepers for the military. The government also frequently requests 'volunteer beautification' labour (in effect, forced labour) from city, town and village residents, requiring them to paint their houses, dig drainage ditches, build walls and weed the roadside.

The Burmese Fairy Tale

Like many Burmese, I am tired of living in a fairy tale. For years, outsiders portrayed the troubles of my country as a morality play: good against evil, with no shade of grey in between – a simplistic picture, but one the world believes. The response of the West has been equally simplistic: It wages a moral crusade against evil, using such magic wands as sanctions and boycotts.

But for us, Myanmar is no fairy-tale land with a simple solution to its problems. We were isolated for 26 years under socialism and we continue to lack a modern economy. We are tired of wasting time. If we are to move forward, to modernise, then we need everyone to face facts.

That may sound like pro-government propaganda, but I haven't changed since I joined the democracy movement in August 1988. I have lived most of my life under the 1962–88 socialist regime – another fairy tale, this one of isolation. In 1988 we knew it was time to join the world. Thousands of us took to the streets, and I joined the National League for Democracy (NLD) and worked as an aide to Aung San Suu Kyi.

I worked closely with Ma Suu, as we all called her, for nearly a year. I campaigned with her until 20 July 1989, when she was put under house arrest and I was sent to Insein Prison in Rangoon, where I spent nearly three years.

I have no regrets about going to jail and blame no-one for it. It was a price we knew we might have to pay. But my fellow former political prisoners and I are beginning to wonder if our sacrifices have been worthwhile. Almost a decade after it all began, we are concerned that the work we started has been squandered and the momentum wasted.

In my time with Ma Suu, I came to love her deeply. I still do. We had hoped that when she was released from house arrest in 1995 the country would move forward again. So much was needed – proper housing and food and adequate health care, to begin with. That was what the democracy movement was really about – helping people.

Ma Suu could have changed our lives dramatically. With her influence and prestige, she could have asked major aid donors such as the USA and Japan for help. She could have encouraged responsible companies to invest here, creating jobs and helping build a stable economy. She could have struck up a constructive dialogue with the government and laid the groundwork for a sustainable democracy.

Instead, she chose the opposite, putting pressure on the government by telling foreign investors to stay away and asking foreign governments to withhold aid. Many of us cautioned her that this was counterproductive. Why couldn't economic development and political improvement grow side by side? People need jobs to put food on the table, which may not sound grand and noble, but it is a basic truth we face every day.

According to Amnesty International's 2001 report:

> A Shan woman from Laikha township, Shan State, reported that in February she had regularly been forced to cut bamboo, build fences, and maintain military camps and roads.

Western Responses

With the exception of humanitarian assistance, Western countries have maintained an embargo on foreign aid to Myanmar since the military's bloody crackdown on democracy protests in 1988. Moreover, the European Union (EU) also maintains an embargo on arms sales as well as visa restrictions on members of the junta and their families, all in a bid to pressure the Burmese government into instituting democratic reform. Yet European companies remain free to invest in Myanmar. Most notably, Premier Oil of the UK, Total of France and Unocal of the USA have helped to develop the offshore gas fields seen as the Burmese government's most significant hope of boosting state revenues.

The strongest international sanctions were taken in 1997 by the USA, the regime's harshest critic, when it banned new investment by American companies in Myanmar,

The Burmese Fairy Tale

Ma Suu's approach has been highly moral and uncompromising, catching the imagination of the outside world. Unfortunately, it has come at a real price for the rest of us. Sanctions have increased tensions with the government and cost jobs. But they haven't accomplished anything positive.

I know that human-rights groups think they are helping us, but they are thinking with their hearts and not their heads. They say foreign investment merely props up the government and doesn't help ordinary people. That's not true. The country survived for almost 30 years without any investment. Moreover, the USA, Japan and others cut off aid in 1988, and the USA imposed sanctions in May 1997. Yet all that has done nothing except send a hollow 'moral message'.

Two Westerners – one a prominent academic and the other a diplomat – once suggested to me that if sanctions and boycotts undermined the economy, people would have less to lose and would be willing to start a revolution. They seemed very pleased with this idea – a revolution to watch from the safety of their own country.

This naive romanticism angers many of us here in Myanmar. You would deliberately make us poor to force us to fight a revolution? American college students play at being freedom fighters and politicians stand up and proclaim that they are striking a blow for democracy with sanctions. But it is we Burmese who pay the price for these empty heroics. Many of us now wonder: Is it for this that we went to jail?

Unfortunately, the Burmese fairy tale is so widely accepted it now seems almost impossible to call for pragmatism. Political correctness has grown so fanatical that any public criticism of the NLD or its leadership is instantly met with accusations of treachery: To simply call for realism is to be labelled pro-military or worse.

But when realism becomes a dirty word, progress becomes impossible. So put away the magic wand and think about us as a real, poor country. Myanmar has many problems, largely the result of almost 30 years of isolationism. More isolation won't fix the problems and sanctions push us backward, not forward. We need jobs. We need to modernise. We need to be a part of the world. Don't close the door on us in the name of democracy. Surely fairy tales in the West don't end so badly.

Ma Thanegi, a pro-democracy activist and former political prisoner, lives in Yangon.

This article was first published in the *Far Eastern Economic Review* on 19 February 1998. Reprinted with permission.

dealing a blow to the country's struggling market economy. (Unocal invested in Myanmar before the ban was put in place.)

However, no country has enacted an outright ban on trade with Myanmar (as happened with South Africa under apartheid), which some believe would be the most effective tool the international community could use to exert pressure on the regime. Despite this, strong lobbying by activists and threats of consumer boycotts have forced major companies including PepsiCo, Heineken, Carlsberg and Levi Strauss to pull out of the country or decide not to invest there. Critics of these boycott campaigns argue that this hurts the local workforce in an already impoverished country. Garment factories in Myanmar, virtually all of which are privately owned, still employ about 300,000 workers.

In November 1999, the UN International Labour Organization took the unprecedented step of recommending sanctions against Myanmar for its use of civilians for forced labour and military portering. Its 174 member nations were advised to review their links with Myanmar and ensure they did not support forced labour there.

National League for Democracy & Aung San Suu Kyi

Since the National League for Democracy (NLD) was denied its election victory in 1990, it has campaigned through nonviolent protest to apply pressure on Myanmar's military regime and to seek international support. The party has made constant demands that the military respect the people's wishes and step aside so that the NLD can take its place as the democratically elected government of the country, but the military regime has refused. NLD Secretary General and leader, Aung San Suu Kyi, has been put under house arrest twice (the first time for six years and the second for two), and thousands of members of the party have been imprisoned. Despite such obstacles, the party continues to agitate and campaign on a platform of justice and human rights, and its stance on such issues as economic sanctions and tourism boycotts has not wavered. Long-term goals include the liberalisation of the economy, an end to forced labour, and political and personal freedoms for the population.

Through the international media and human rights groups, the NLD has spread its message and has tried to use external pressures to sway the military regime. It has lobbied for economic sanctions, stating that international corporations and governments should not do business with an undemocratic regime. The NLD believes that sanctions will send a clear message to the Myanmar government that its reluctance to give up power and its treatment of the local people are unacceptable. Suu Kyi has called for companies to wait until there is a more responsible government running the country before they invest in Myanmar.

The NLD also disapproves of tourism in the current climate, pointing out that the government's recent drive for the tourist dollar and an influx of tourists will only serve to give legitimacy (and valuable hard currency) to the regime. Suu Kyi has requested that potential tourists be patient and wait until there is justice and a rule of law before making plans to travel through the country. She believes that tourism helps to sustain the regime and is of little benefit to the average Burmese.

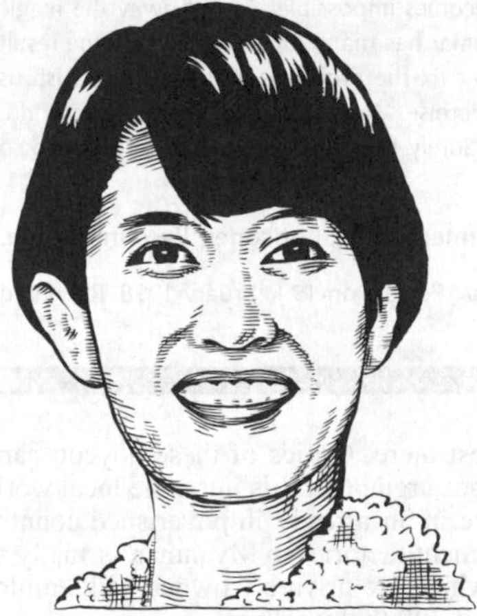

MICK WELDON

Nobel laureate Aung San Suu Kyi: "I could not, as my father's daughter, remain indifferent to all that was going on ... This national crisis could in fact be called the second struggle for national independence."

Though not totally opposed to humanitarian aid projects in Myanmar, the NLD is wary of aid that does not reach the right people in the right way. The party is concerned that aid resources will reach the pockets of the government and its friends, rather than the poor people who need it most. The NLD questions the Myanmar government's claims that its infrastructure programs have improved the lives of the Burmese people. Suu Kyi has expressed concern about the use of forced labour to build roads, bridges, railways and tourism infrastructure, and has called for an end to the practice.

It appears that external pressures have worked to a certain degree. Talks between the NLD and the military junta preceded the unconditional release of Aung San Suu Kyi in May 2002, and the release of other senior NLD members. Although Suu Kyi is cautious about the future, describing the new situation as a 'difficult balancing act', it is also hoped that a new period of meaningful dialogue has begun. Time will tell whether the icy relations between the NLD and the military junta have undergone a permanent thaw.

Not surprisingly, UN agencies based in Myanmar get a clear view of the effects that boycotts and sanctions, combined with Myanmar's unsound economic policies, are having on the impoverished nation. In June 2001, these UN agencies warned in a joint letter to their headquarters that Myanmar was facing a humanitarian crisis and that it was a 'moral and ethical necessity' for the international community to extend more aid. The letter stated that one quarter of Burmese babies were born underweight and, as of the end of 1999, an estimated 530,000 people were HIV-positive. The letter also stated that Myanmar only receives annual foreign aid equivalent to about US$1 per capita, compared with US$35 for Cambodia and US$68 dollars for Laos.

In a controversial move in 2001, Japan broke ranks in the embargo on non-humanitarian aid to Myanmar when it offered US$28 million in technical assistance to repair the Baluchaung hydroelectric power plant in the Kayah State as an incentive for the regime to press ahead with reconciliation talks with Suu Kyi. Other countries maintained that it is too soon to reward the regime for the talks, which have yet to yield any concrete progress towards political change.

Despite highly publicised criticisms and boycotts from several human rights organisations, it remains the editorial policy of Lonely Planet Publications to continue to publish the *Myanmar* guidebook (see the Introduction at the front of this book for more details).

GEOGRAPHY

Size & Shape

Myanmar covers an area of 671,000 sq km, sandwiched between Thailand and Laos to the east and Bangladesh to the west with India and China bordering the north. The country extends from approximately 28°N to 10°N latitude; the Tropic of Cancer crosses just above Mogok in the Mandalay Division and also intersects the Chin, Kachin and Shan States.

The shape has been likened to a parrot facing west, with the beak touching Sittwe (Akyab), the claws gripping Yangon, the tail extending down the Tanintharyi peninsula, and outstretched wings forming the three northernmost states. Its greatest length from north to south is approximately 2000km, while the widest east-to-west distance is around 1000km.

The Bay of Bengal and the Andaman Sea form Myanmar's southern boundaries. The centre is marked by expansive plains and wide rivers emptying into the Bay of Bengal and the Gulf of Martaban (the upper Andaman Sea). Mountains rise to the east along the Thai border and to the north, where you find the easternmost end of the Himalayas (highest elevations around 6000m).

Rivers

Most of the country's agriculture is centred along the floodplains of the 2000km Ayeyarwady River, which flows south from its source (actually the confluence of two rivers), 27km north of Myitkyina, to a vast delta region along the Gulf of Martaban southwest of Yangon. Navigable year-round for at least 1500km, the Ayeyarwady has played a major role in domestic transport and communications for centuries. At the height of British rule, as many as nine million passengers a year were carried along this huge river by the colonial Irrawaddy Flotilla Company.

Other major rivers are the Chindwin (navigable for 792km), which joins the Ayeyarwady between Mandalay and Bagan; the Kaladan (navigable for 177km), which flows from Paletwa in the southern Chin State to the Bay of Bengal at Sittwe; the Sittoung (formerly Sittang; non-navigable due to strong currents), which flows through Taungoo and meets the sea between Bago and Mawlamyaing; and the Thanlwin (formerly Salween; navigable for just 89km), which has its headwaters in China, and for some distance forms the border between Myanmar and Thailand before eventually reaching the sea at Mawlamyaing. The Mekong River forms the border between Myanmar and Laos.

Mountains

The Himalayas rise in the north of Myanmar, and Hkakabo Razi, right on the border between Myanmar and Tibet, is the highest mountain in Southeast Asia at 5889m. Gamlang Razi is only slightly lower at 5835m. West of Bagan towards Rakhaing, Mt Victoria rises to 3053m. A wide expanse of comparatively dry plain stretches north of Yangon, but hill ranges running north-south separate the central plain from Myanmar's neighbours.

Coastline

Myanmar's coastline extends 2832km from the mouth of the Naaf River near Bangladesh to the southern tip of Tanintharyi Division near Ranong, Thailand. Coastal barrier and delta islands are common in the estuarial areas stretching from the Rakhaing State to Mawlamyaing. Off peninsular Myanmar, farther south, over a thousand continental islands dot the littoral sea, forming a mostly uninhabited island group sometimes called the Mergui Archipelago.

Resources

Myanmar is fortunate in possessing huge stands of teak and other hardwoods. According to the most recent UN World Development Report, Myanmar has an estimated natural forest area of 43%, down 12% from 10 years ago, and is ranked 33rd among the world's top 100 countries (ahead of the USA, Australia and most European countries). The Bago Yoma (Bago Mountain Range), extending between the Ayeyarwady and Sittoung river valleys, is the most heavily forested area and the source of most of the country's teak.

The most valued woods are teak and *padauk* (cherry wood). Timber concessions (and smuggling) to India, China, Japan, Thailand and other Asian countries slowed considerably during the Asian economic crisis of 1997–98. The government-owned Myanma Timber Enterprise (MTE) accounts for most of the logging undertaken throughout the country. Reportedly the company follows a sustainable 'selective tender' system devised by the British in 1856 to maintain forest cover. Timber extraction has in fact decreased rather than increased yearly since 1994. Government plans call for the complete elimination of all log exports, figuring that the greatest potential revenue comes from processed wood products rather than raw timber. If this plan is carried out, cutting should slow even further.

The country's lengthy coastline provides a wealth of saltwater fisheries. Until recently, all fisheries were government-owned, but since 1991 several private domestic and foreign companies have begun large-scale processing of marine products along the coast.

The country is also rich in gems, oil, natural gas and mineral deposits, which, like timber, serve as direct sources of foreign currency for the government.

CLIMATE

Myanmar undergoes an annual three-season cycle that follows the classic 'dry and wet monsoon climate' pattern common to other parts of mainland Southeast Asia. The southwest monsoon starts between mid-May and mid-June, bringing frequent rains that continue into late October. The rain tends to fall mainly in the afternoons and evenings. Although it takes the edge off the intense heat, it does tend to make things unpleasantly humid. Generally speaking, travelling in the rainy season is not particularly

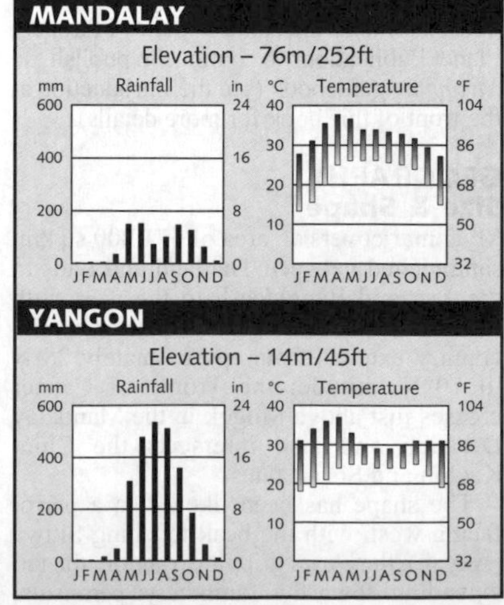

difficult, though unpaved roads may occasionally be impassable. In central Myanmar it rains most during August and September, when occasional floods may occur.

The November to May dry period begins with lower relative temperatures because of the influences of Asia's northeast monsoon. This second monsoon bypasses all but the southeastern-most reaches of Myanmar below Myeik (Mergui) but results in cool breezes throughout the country. As a result, during December and January the temperature can drop to near freezing at night in the highlands of the Kalaw-Taunggyi area.

In February the temperatures start to rise, and during March, April and May it can be unpleasantly hot. In Yangon the temperature often tops 40°C and in Mandalay and Bagan – part of the 'dry zone' lying in the rain shadow of the Rakhaing Yoma (Arakan Range) – it gets even hotter. The annual water festival, when people douse each other with cold water, takes place in April at the height of the hot season.

Dry season rains known as 'mango showers' occasionally bring welcome but temporary relief until the rains begin again in May.

The geography of Myanmar considerably affects the monsoon rains. The delta region around Yangon gets about 250cm a year, but the rainfall rapidly diminishes as the monsoon continues north; the central area of Myanmar (which includes Bagan) is a large, comparatively dry zone with 60cm to 110cm of rain a year. Then, north of Mandalay, the hill ranges force the winds higher and the rain again gets heavier, reaching a drenching annual total of around 350cm. The Rakhaing coastal area near Bangladesh and the Tanintharyi coastal strip beside southern Thailand are exposed to the full force of the southwest monsoon rains, which are often held over the region by the mountain ranges inland. Thus these coastal areas get very heavy rainfall: Sittwe receives over 500cm a year and Mawlamyaing around 440cm, most of which falls during the southwest monsoon.

To get up-to-the-minute information about current temperatures and weather in Myanmar, log onto **W** www.myanmarpyi.com. Here you'll find a nifty link to CNN.com that allows you to check the current weather in over 30 cities and towns in Myanmar.

ECOLOGY & ENVIRONMENT

From the snow-capped Himalayas in the north to the coral-fringed Myeik Archipelago in the south, Myanmar's 2000km length crosses three distinct ecological regions within the vast Indo-Malay biogeographical realm: the Indian subregion along the Bangladesh and India borders; the Indo-Chinese subregion in the north bordering Laos and China; and the Sundaic subregion bordering peninsular Thailand. Together these regions produce what is quite likely the richest biodiversity in Southeast Asia.

Very little natural-history research has been carried out in Myanmar due to the country's self-imposed isolation from the rest of the world since independence. Most of the studies available date to the British colonial era and are not reliable by today's standards. Tertiary education in the country, which has never approached the levels of other countries, has further declined in quality since the 1970s, hence local research is even more scant. Myanmar's new openness to tourism and foreign investment has only recently extended to the reception of trained wildlife researchers. In 1998, the Smithsonian Institute was invited to conduct limited flora and fauna surveys in the country. Additionally, a recent memorandum of agreement cosigned by the Wildlife Conservation Society (WCS) and Myanmar's Ministry of Forestry may further open the country to contemporary natural historians.

FLORA

As in the rest of tropical Asia, most indigenous vegetation in Myanmar is associated with two basic types of tropical forest: monsoon forest (with a distinctive dry season of three months or more) and rainforest (where rain falls more than nine months per year).

Monsoon forests are marked by deciduous tree varieties, which shed their leaves during the dry season to conserve water; rainforests are typically evergreen. The area stretching from Yangon to Myitkyina contains mainly

Environmental Consciousness

At the moment, Myanmar lacks the legal structure for a viable national park system and there are virtually no organised environmental movements. Most Burmese recycle nonbiodegradable materials as a matter of course; unlike in wealthier countries, disposability is still considered a luxury reserved for the rich. However, as the country develops economically its natural resources and environmental purity will come under increasing pressure.

What can the average visitor to Myanmar do to minimise the impact of tourism on the environment? By expressing your desire to use environmentally friendly materials – and by taking direct action to avoid the use and indiscriminate disposal of nonbiodegradables – you can provide an example of environmental consciousness not only for the Burmese but for other international visitors.

Visitors might also avoid all restaurants serving 'exotic' wildlife species (eg, barking deer, pangolin, bear). The main patrons of this type of cuisine are wealthy Burmese, along with visiting Chinese from Singapore, Hong Kong and Taiwan.

When using hired boats in the vicinity of coral reefs, insist that boat operators avoid lowering their anchors onto coral formations. Likewise, volunteer to collect (and later dispose of) rubbish if it's obvious that the usual mode is to throw everything overboard.

Naturally, you should refrain from purchasing coral while in Myanmar. In Chaungtha many souvenir stalls offer coral clusters; although talking to the vendors won't get you anywhere, try expressing your concern to village officials who may take action if they receive enough complaints. Burmese sensitive to Western paternalism are quick to point out that on a global scale the so-called 'developed' countries contribute far more environmental damage than do the poorer countries of Southeast Asia; for example, per capita greenhouse emissions for Australia, Canada or the USA average over five tonnes each, while the Southeast Asian countries contribute less than 0.5 tonnes per capita.

Hence, in making complaints to locals employed in the tourist industry, it's important to emphasise that you want to work with them, rather than against them, in improving environmental standards.

Joe Cummings

monsoon forests, while peninsular Myanmar south of Mawlamyaing is predominantly a rainforest zone. There is much overlapping of the two – some forest zones support a mix of monsoon forest and rainforest vegetation.

In the mountainous Himalayan region above the Tropic of Cancer, Myanmar's flora is characterised by subtropical broadleaf evergreen forest up to 2000m; temperate semi-deciduous broadleaf rainforest from 2000m to 3000m; and evergreen coniferous and subalpine snow forest passing into alpine scrub above 3000m.

Along the Rakhaing and Tanintharyi coasts, tidal forests occur in river estuaries, lagoons, tidal creeks and along low islands. Such woodlands are characterised by mangrove and other coastal trees that grow in mud and are resistant to sea water. Beach and dune forests, which grow along these same coasts above the high-tide line, consist of palms, hibiscus, casuarinas and other tree varieties that can withstand high winds and occasional storm-sent waves.

The country's most famous flora includes an incredible array of fruit trees (see the Food section in the Facts for the Visitor chapter), over 25,000 flowering species, a variety of tropical hardwoods, and bamboo. Of the last, considered one of Asia's more renewable plant resources, Myanmar may possibly contain more species than any country outside China. One pure stand of bamboo in Rakhaing State extends over 7770 sq km. Cane and rattan are also plentiful.

Myanmar holds 75% of the world's reserves of *Tectona grandis*; better known as teak (*kyun* in Burmese). This dense, long-wearing, highly prized hardwood is one of Myanmar's most important exports, for which the biggest consumers are China, Singapore and India.

FAUNA

When Marco Polo wrote about Myanmar in the 13th century, he described 'vast jungles teeming with elephants, unicorns and other wild beasts'. Though Myanmar's natural biodiversity has no doubt altered considerably since that time, it's difficult to say just how much.

The most comprehensive wildlife survey available at the time of writing was undertaken by the Bombay Natural History Society between 1912 and 1921 and published as the *Mammal Survey of India, Burma and Ceylon*. In Myanmar *The Wild Animals of Burma*, published in 1967, is the most recent work available and even this volume simply contains extracts from various surveys carried out by the British between 1912 and 1941, with a few observations dating to 1961.

As with flora, the variation in Myanmar's wildlife is closely associated with the country's geographic and climatic differences. Hence the indigenous fauna of the country's northern half is mostly of Indo-Chinese origin while that of the south is generally Sundaic (ie, typical of Malaysia, Sumatra, Borneo and Java). In the Himalayan region north of the Tropic of Cancer, fauna shares the Indian biogeographical realm with areas of northeastern India. The large overlap area between zoogeographical and vegetative zones – extending from around Myitkyina in the north to Bago Yoma in the central region – means that much of Myanmar is a potential habitat for plants and animals from all three zones.

Myanmar is rich in bird life, with an estimated 1000 resident and migrating species. Coastal and inland waterways of the delta and southern peninsula are especially important habitats for Southeast Asian waterfowl.

Distinctive mammals – found in dwindling numbers within the more heavily forested areas of Myanmar – include leopards, fishing cats, civets, Indian mongooses, crab-eating mongooses, Himalayan bears, Asiatic black bears, Malayan sun bears, gaur (Indian bison), banteng (wild cattle), serow (an Asiatic mountain goat), wild boars, sambar, barking deer, mouse deer, tapirs, pangolin, gibbons and macaques. Sea mammals include dolphins and dugongs.

As recently as the mid-1990s, an estimated 2000 tigers were thought to inhabit the primary forests, but some sources claim that numbers have dropped dramatically due to poaching and the illicit trade in tiger parts. Some 10,000 Asiatic elephants – roughly a third of all those on the planet – are widely distributed in Myanmar. Among these are 6000 making up the world's largest herd of working elephants, most of which are used in logging and agriculture. It's encouraging that this number exceeds by a thousand that tallied by English scholar FT Morehead in his 1944 treatise *The Forests of Burma*.

Both the one-horned (Javan) rhinoceros and the Asiatic two-horned (Sumatran) rhinoceros are believed to survive in very small numbers near the Thai border in the Kayin State. The rare red panda (or cat bear) was last sighted in northern Myanmar in the early 1960s but is still thought to live in Kachin State forests above 2000m.

Burmese Tuskers

The *Elephas maximus* plays such an important role in montane Myanmar that the Burmese use different names for male elephants according to tusk characteristics:

with two tusks	*sweh-zoun*
with one tusk	*hte*
without tusks	*hain*
widely spread, curving tusks	*sweh-ga*
straight, downward-curving tusks	*sweh-zaiq*
short, stumpy tusks	*sweh-touq*
stumpy tusks shaped like banana buds	*ngapyaw-bu*

According to a 1955 edition of the *Journal of the Bombay Natural History Society*, the old rule of thumb that an Asian elephant's shoulder height is about twice the circumference of one of its forefeet is accurate more than 95% of the time.

Joe Cummings

Herpetofauna include four sea turtle species along with numerous snake varieties, of which an astounding 52 are venomous. These include the common cobra, king cobra (hamadryad), banded krait, Malayan pit viper, green viper and Russell's viper.

Endangered Species

Myanmar is not a signatory to the UN Convention on International Trade in Endangered Species of Wild Flora & Fauna (CITES), and neither the International Union for Conservation of Nature & Natural Resources (IUCN) nor the WCS have reliable figures of the status of any species that might be threatened or endangered.

At the moment, deforestation by the timber industry poses the greatest threat to wildlife habitats. In areas where habitat loss isn't a problem, hunting threatens to wipe out the rarer animal species. Even in the nation's nominally protected lands, wildlife laws are seldom enforced due to corruption and a general lack of manpower. As in neighbouring countries, there are restaurants in Myanmar that specialise in serving endangered species. In addition to this, tigers and rhinos are killed for the lucrative overseas Chinese pharmaceutical market.

Marine resources are threatened by a lack of long-range conservation goals. Myanmar's growing industrialisation means that the release of pollutants into rivers and the sea is steadily increasing, and overfishing, especially in the delta regions, is also a growing problem. The country must also deal with illegal encroachment on national fisheries by Bangladeshi, Thai and Malaysian fishing boats.

National Parks

Myanmar claims to have three national parks and 17 wildlife sanctuaries (including two marine and three wetland environments), which together protect about 1% of the nation's total land surface. Compared to international averages, this is very low coverage (Thailand, by comparison, has 12% coverage). The government reported that it had plans to raise protection to 5% by 2000, but at the time of writing the implementation of these plans could not be confirmed. None of these protected areas features any facilities for researchers or visitors of any kind, and most are in fact off-limits to foreigners. Exceptions are the Lampi Island Wildlife Preserve, off the coast of Tanintharyi Division, which can be visited with permission from the regional authorities (best obtained via a travel agency in Yangon), and the more accessible Mt Popa National Park near Bagan.

MARTIN HARRIS

The Irrawaddy dolphin is more likely to be found in coastal regions than in any river.

GOVERNMENT & POLITICS

The System

The Tatmadaw (the Burmese military) and their political junta, the SPDC, continue to rule Myanmar with an iron fist. The Pyithu Hluttaw (People's Assembly) last convened in May 1990, while the Council of People's Justices was dissolved following the events of 1988. In effect Myanmar is centrally ruled by one executive branch, which is controlled by the military.

The military's NUP, founded by General Ne Win, is the only party with real political power, though it is clearly symbolic rather than substantive since there is no pretence that the country functions via party politics.

The true centre of control, the SPDC, is headed by three generals: SPDC chairman and Ne Win's appointed successor, General Than Shwe; vice-chairman General Maung Aye; and first secretary (and head of military intelligence) Lt General Khin Nyunt.

Until quite recently many speculated that Ne Win (commonly spoken of as 'the Old Man') was still running Myanmar through these three generals. Then in March 2002, four of Ne Win's relatives – three grandsons and a son-in-law – were arrested for plotting a coup against the SPDC. While few believed the official reason for the arrests (at least two of the grandsons were thuggish types, given to abusing their connections), the fact that Ne Win was unable to keep them from being arrested is interesting.

Political Freedom

Burmese citizens' political freedom is strictly curtailed. Peaceful political assembly is banned and citizens are forbidden to talk to foreigners about politics. All government workers in Myanmar, from mail carriers to university professors, must sign a pledge not to discuss the government among themselves, at risk of losing their jobs. In everyday practice, plenty of Burmese talk to foreigners about political issues as long as they can be sure no Burmese are listening.

Among the most visible signs of the government's stance are the prominent red-and-white signboards posted in public areas of all Myanmar's major cities. They carry slogans, in Burmese (and occasionally in English), such as:

Only when there is discipline will there be progress.
Anyone who is riotous, destructive and unruly is our enemy.
The Tatmadaw shall never betray the national cause.

In addition, virtually all government publications carry the following list headed 'People's Desire':

Oppose those relying on external elements, acting as stooges, holding negative views.
Oppose those trying to jeopardise stability of the State and progress of the nation.
Oppose foreign nations interfering in internal affairs of the State.
Crush all internal and external destructive elements as the common enemy.

Of course the Tatmadaw never explains how it is they have discerned what the 'national cause' or the 'People's Desire' really might be, since without elected representatives in the government they couldn't possibly know!

Some observers say that the opposition never stood a chance and that the 1990 election was either a small tactical error on the part of the military or simply a way of identifying the opposition (reportedly, anybody who ran for election against the NUP was immediately put on the arrest list). Many younger Burmese still harbour hopes that some day they will be able to wrest control of the country from the military government.

Political Imprisonment Detention of suspected dissidents is common, with many being held for days or weeks of questioning. The government also makes a big show of releasing prisoners at regular intervals each year – an age-old Southeast Asian practice that is supposed to confer merit upon the rulership and, rather ironically, demonstrate Buddhist compassion.

It is estimated by the UN that between 1500 and 1600 political prisoners (including at least 100 women) are being held in Myanmar – about half of whom are connected with the NLD, the remainder made up of members of Myanmar's minority ethnic groups and student activists, including Min Ko Naing, student leader of the revolt in 1988.

According to some UN sources, conditions for political prisoners have improved since the Red Cross was given access to them in May 1999.

Administrative Divisions

For administrative purposes, Myanmar is divided into seven *tain* (divisions) where Bamar are in the majority (Yangon, Ayeyarwady, Bago, Magwe, Mandalay, Sagaing, Tanintharyi); and into seven *pyi* (states) where non-Bamar are in the majority (Shan, Kachin, Chin, Rakhaing, Kayah, Kayin, Mon).

Each state and division is subdivided into *kyay* (villages), *kyay ywa oksu* (village tracts), *myonei* (townships) and *khayain* (districts).

ECONOMY

Pre-Independence Economics

Myanmar's value to the British during the colonial era can be summed up in one word – rice. The 19th century was a time of major upheaval in world economies. With industrialisation, a world market for agricultural products suddenly emerged as

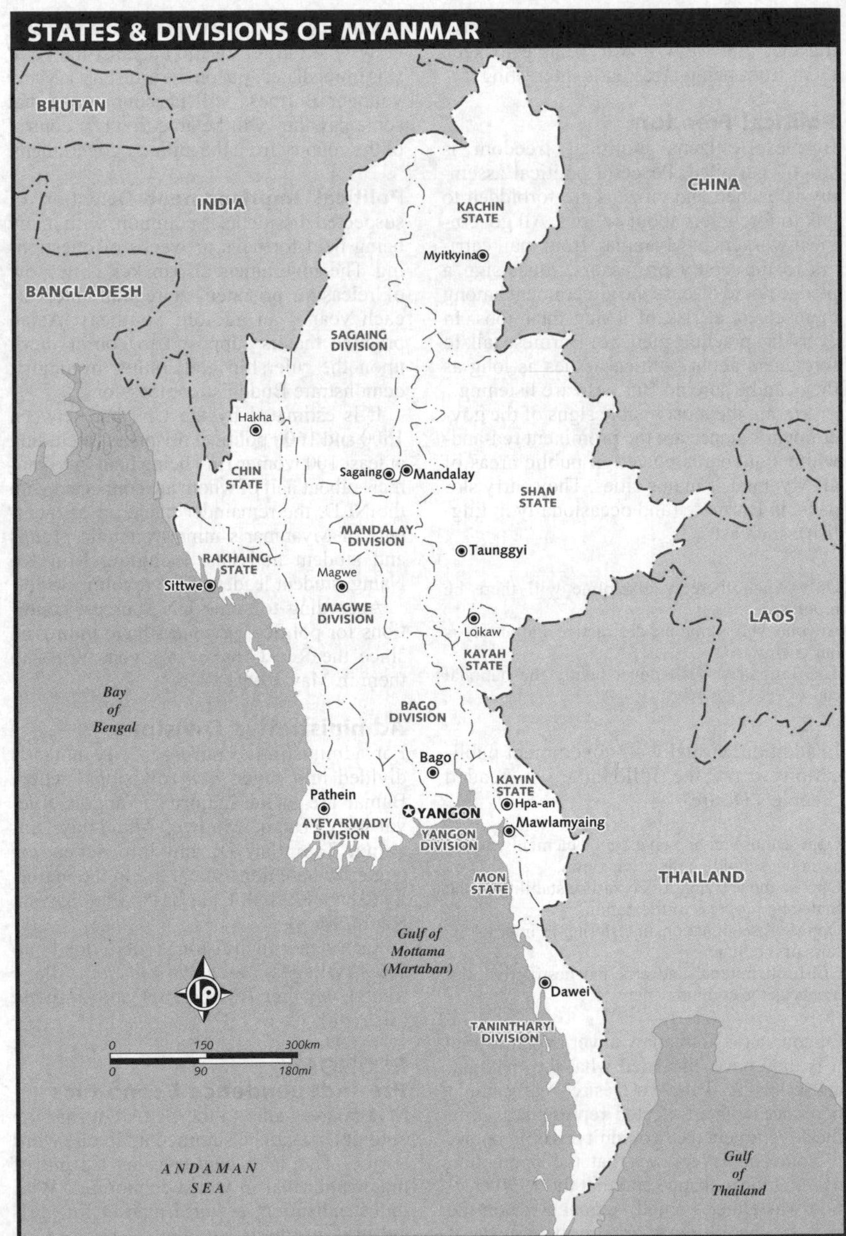
STATES & DIVISIONS OF MYANMAR
BHUTAN
CHINA
INDIA
KACHIN STATE
Myitkyina
BANGLADESH
SAGAING DIVISION
Hakha
CHIN STATE
Sagaing
Mandalay
SHAN STATE
MANDALAY DIVISION
Taunggyi
RAKHAING STATE
Sittwe
Magwe
MAGWE DIVISION
Loikaw
LAOS
KAYAH STATE
Bay of Bengal
BAGO DIVISION
Bago
KAYIN STATE
Pathein
Hpa-an
YANGON
AYEYARWADY DIVISION
Mawlamyaing
YANGON DIVISION
MON STATE
THAILAND
Gulf of Mottama (Martaban)
Dawei
TANINTHARYI DIVISION
0
150
300km
0
90
180mi
ANDAMAN SEA
Gulf of Thailand

some countries found it more profitable to produce industrial goods and import food with the proceeds rather than grow their own food. Myanmar proved ideal for supplying a large proportion of the world's rice.

Prior to WWII, Myanmar exported as much as 3.5 million tonnes of rice a year, but much of the profit went to British or other foreign parties. As in a number of other colonial countries, it was a frequent complaint that foreign rule had turned Myanmar into a one-product country, with all the dangers this entailed. Myanmar's rice-growing potential was devastated along with many other of the country's assets during WWII, and the path of development since the war has not been a happy one.

Myanmar suffered major damage from WWII, far more than most of its neighbours: Malaysia and Indonesia were quickly overrun and thus suffered little damage; Thailand collaborated and thus also escaped damage; and war was never waged on most Indian territory. Yet in Myanmar, air and ground battles raged right to the end and caused enormous destruction. Furthermore, Myanmar quickly threw off the colonial yoke after the war and never enjoyed the benefits of overseas aid for reconstruction and replacement of ruined assets. Internal conflicts following independence and a shift towards a command economy in the 1960s and 1970s further complicated the situation and prevented efficient restoration.

Under Military Rule

For a time, Myanmar remained dependent upon rice as a major source of foreign earnings even though its efficiency as a rice producer was steadily declining. Despite the worldwide advances in agriculture – miracle rice, fertilisers etc – Burmese were managing to produce less per hectare even two decades after independence than before. By the mid-1960s, the area used for rice production was slightly above prewar levels but the actual output was somewhat lower. Yet the population had increased by over 50% compared to prewar levels and by now is probably double what it was. The upshot is that after WWII there was little rice to export and barely enough to feed the country. By 1987, Myanmar was considered one of the poorest countries in the world.

After the government's abandonment of socialism in 1989, the economy changed rapidly. By 1995 it was growing at a rate of 6.4% per year, the highest since before Ne Win took power in the early 1960s. As of 2000 this had slowed to just over 4%. The cause of this downward trend can be attributed to a number of factors, such as the Asian economic crisis of 1997. However, the same opaqueness and corruption that have plagued the economies of many Southeast Asian nations are even more acute in Myanmar. For the first time in its history the government of Myanmar failed to produce a national budget for the fiscal year 2001–02. According to the US government's Country Commercial Guide 2002 report on Myanmar:

> Economic reforms have stagnated since the mid-1990s. The SPDC has continued to exert a heavy hand in the economy with a policy turning increasingly inward. In the past six years, significant backtracking on earlier progress is evident. The concepts of laissez faire, open markets, transparency, accountability and freedom of information are alien to the ruling generals. Thus, under the current regime, there are unlikely to be any reforms that substantially loosen the government's command and control over the economy. Meanwhile corruption is rising and the benefits of the market economy have not been widely shared. As legitimate local and foreign businesses experience growing difficulty in this environment, there has been a noticeable shift to business conducted in the unrecorded sector, as smuggling and the laundering of narcotics proceeds become more prominent.

Inflation runs at an estimated 30% per annum when adjusted for dollar usage and purchasing power parity – more like 70% if judged by a *kyat* (Burmese currency) index alone. Hyperinflation has meant that between this guidebook edition and the previous one, many consumer prices tripled. Burmese citizens must typically spend more than half of their monthly income on food. This leaves little to spend on consumer goods, so most Burmese rely on the inexpensive but shoddy goods that pour into the country from China.

International Trade

The nation's main export revenues come from forest products, rice, gems and pearls, followed by much smaller incomes from maize, rubber, cotton, jute, minerals and marine products.

By far the largest importers of Burmese commodities are Singapore and India, followed by Thailand, China, and the USA. In the reverse direction, most imports to Myanmar originate from Singapore, Thailand, China, Japan and South Korea.

When it comes to direct foreign investment in Myanmar, the single largest players are Singapore, the UK and Thailand, each investing over US$1 billion in 1999, the last year for which figures are available. Some distance behind Thailand march Malaysia (US$587 million), the USA (US$582 million), France (US$470 million) and the Netherlands (US$238 million).

The government continues to control all legal foreign trade in timber, minerals, gems, oil and gas – although foreign companies have been contracted for the exploration and extraction of some minerals and petroleum. These and other large, private ventures must be underwritten or sponsored by someone in the government. Ministers typically take a piece of every project that requires their approval, often as much as 5% of the project's estimated value. Tatmadaw officers, thus enriched, live in colonial-style villas in Yangon's best suburbs and are chauffeured about in the latest-model Japanese cars. Most conduct multiple business affairs that assure a comfortable retirement.

Many Chinese who fled Myanmar following nationalisation in the 1960s are now returning to participate in the liberalised economy. Those who can speak Burmese are able to get national ID cards even though they aren't Burmese citizens; this permits overseas Chinese to use kyat to purchase goods and services that usually require US dollars, enabling them to enjoy lifestyles that are obscenely extravagant by ordinary Burmese standards. Not surprisingly, many Burmese resent this official 'favouritism', and anti-Chinese sentiment among the average Burmese is high.

Underground Economy

In much of rural Myanmar, cash economies revolve around the opium, heroin and methamphetamine trades, which form a large component of Myanmar's underground economy. In 2001, an estimated 865 tonnes of raw opium were produced, a substantial drop from the 1085 tonnes produced in 2000. Still, since the Taliban began enforcing an eradication programme in Afghanistan Myanmar has become the world's largest producer of opium.

Although the government has an explicit anti-narcotics policy and there appears to be no direct political connection with opium/heroin/meth producers, a certain military complicity at local levels is undeniable. On top of this, drug trafficking profits are allowed to circulate freely in Myanmar's laissez faire economy. Practically all large, privately managed businesses have been invaded, from banks to airlines to hotels. As the US government's Country Commercial Guide summed up in its 2002 report:

> While there is no evidence that the government is involved on an institutional level in the drug trade, there are continuing reports that corrupt army personnel may be aiding traffickers and profiting from the trade. The government's ability to pursue drug trafficking is seriously constrained by the cease-fire agreements it has concluded with the major narco-trafficking organisations, which have conducted insurgencies against the government in the past. In several cases, these agreements have ceded a great deal of autonomy over territory and security to the local ethnic organisations, and the government does not have the means to police them.
>
> This situation is further complicated by the fact that the government actively encourages the investment of narcotics profits in the Burmese economy, as part of its strategy to wean the ethnic organisations from heroin production and to offset the shortage of foreign investment. Narcotics proceeds dominate the local economies of the Kokang, Wa, Shan, Kachin, and Mon ethnic areas and figure prominently in the Burmese economy as a whole. Narcotics proceeds are widely and openly invested in business, real estate, and infrastructure projects and, in some cases, investments of narcotics proceeds in public works projects supplement government expenditures.

In the final analysis, the quiet takeover of Myanmar's private-sector economy by narcotics barons and their associates allows for one charitable interpretation: the junta is prepared to turn a blind eye to the process in the overriding interest of securing peace, integrating insurgent-held areas into the national mainstream and promoting economic development – if necessary with dirty money.

Some analysts, prepared to credit the junta with a long-term narcotics strategy, argue that the government may even hope that over time today's drug lords, attracted by the prospect of making real money legally, may mellow into legitimate business tycoons.

Tourism

Tourism, an obvious source of hard currency, came to a temporary halt following the 1988 uprising, but quickly recovered after 1992, as a result of liberalised visa regulations and an expanding tourist infrastructure.

Pre-1988 tourism peaked in 1986–87 at 41,000 arrivals per year. During the restrictive 1990–92 period the incoming stream slowed to around 4000 per annum. By 1992–93 it was back up to 22,000 and in 1994–95 around 60,000 people reportedly visited Myanmar.

In 1996–97 the government mounted a feeble 'Visit Myanmar Year' campaign – and despite their efforts to encourage tourism, visitor numbers peaked at 180,000, far short of the hoped-for half a million.

By far the largest number of visitors to Myanmar are from China (an estimated 250,000 per annum), but since many of these are day-trippers who don't venture beyond border towns, the Myanmar government doesn't include their numbers in tourism statistics. Besides the mainland Chinese, the number of arrivals to Myanmar is said to be approaching the 200,000 mark. Visitors from Taiwan top the list, making up about 15% of total arrivals. Next are the Japanese and Thais at about 10% each; Malaysians (8%); Singaporeans, French and North Americans (about 7% each); Germans (6%); Italians (5%); and Britons (4.5%). Of these arrivals approximately 60% are tourists and 30% are travellers on business.

The Myanmar Tourism Promotion Board estimates revenue generated through tourism at around US$50 million.

POPULATION & PEOPLE

Population

As of 1999 the population is estimated to be between 47 and 49 million, with an annual growth rate of around 1.9%. Approximately 70% live in rural areas.

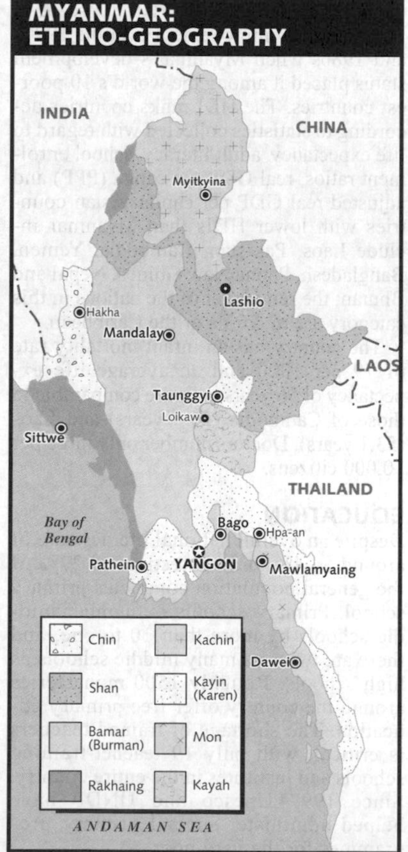

The largest cities, in declining order, are Yangon, Mandalay, Pathein, Mawlamyaing, Taunggyi and Sittwe. Population statistics for each of these cities have not been made public since 1973, and local estimates vary wildly depending on whom you ask; Yangon appears to have four or five million people, Mandalay around one million, the remainder 500,000 or fewer.

Development

The 1999 UN Human Development Report (UNHDR) ranks Myanmar 118 out of 162 countries with regard to overall human development, with a human development index (HDI) rating of 0.551 (on a scale of 10) – quite an improvement over the 1970s and 1980s when Myanmar's development status placed it among the world's 10 poorest countries. The HDI ranks countries according to statistics collected with regard to life expectancy, adult literacy, school enrolment ratios, real GDP per capita (PPP) and adjusted real GDP per capita. Asian countries with lower HDIs than Myanmar include Laos, Pakistan, Cambodia, Yemen, Bangladesh, Papua New Guinea, Nepal and Bhutan; the remainder of the nations in this category are in Africa or the Caribbean.

The country has an infant mortality rate of 79 per 1000 and an average life expectancy of 56 years, a figure comparable to those of Cambodia (56.4 years) and Laos (53.1 years). Doctors number only three per 10,000 citizens.

EDUCATION

Despite an overall national literacy rate of around 84.4%, only an estimated 27% of the general population completes primary school. Primary schools outnumber middle schools by more than 10 to one, and there are twice as many middle schools as high schools. Roughly 1500 monasteries around the country offer free primary education. The shortage of trained teachers is critical, with only 19 teacher-training schools and institutes in the entire country. Since 1997 Unesco and UNDP have helped administer special primary programmes for the very poor.

There are nine public universities and 21 colleges, most of them in Yangon. These were all closed between 1996 and 2000 due to the government's fear that students would organise antigovernment protests or start riots. During that time some schools were relocated to sites outside the city so that protests could be more easily quashed.

ARTS

Burmese court culture has not had an easy time since the forced exile of the last king Thibaw Min; architecture and art were both royal activities which, without royal support, floundered and faded during colonial times. In recent years classical Burmese music and dance have undergone a revival – as the abundance of these performances to be seen on Burmese television will attest. At the street level, Burmese culture is vibrant and thriving, as you'll see at the first *pwe* (show) you visit.

Dance & Drama

Myanmar's truly indigenous dance forms are those that pay homage to the *nat* (spirits). In special nat pwe, one or more nat is invited to possess the body and mind of a medium; sometimes members of the audience are possessed instead, an event greatly feared by most Burmese. Nat dancing styles are very fluid and adaptable, and are handed down from older pwe dancers to their offspring or apprentices.

In contrast, few of Myanmar's classical dance-drama styles are entirely indigenous. Most arrived from Thailand during periods of Burmese conquest of Thai kingdoms. Today the dances most obviously taken from Thailand are known as *yodaya zat* (Ayuthaya theatre), as taught to the Burmese by Thai theatrical artists taken captive from Ayuthaya by King Hsinbyushin in the late 18th century. So thorough is the public perception that Thailand was the primary source for all court arts that the term *yodaya* can be applied loosely to describe any 'elite' art form even today. Around this same period *Zinme pannatha* (Chiang Mai plays) were translated into Burmese, providing the text for another entire dance-drama genre.

The most Burmese of dances feature solo performances by female dancers who wear strikingly colourful dresses with long white trains, which they kick into the air with their heels – quite a feat, given the restrictive length of the train. One wonders how a dancer could walk while wearing such a costume, much less dance in it. A *zat pwe* involves a re-creation of an ancient legend or Buddhist *jataka* (life story of the Buddha) while the *yamazat* picks a tale from the Indian epic *Ramayana*. The arm and head movements often seek to mimic those of Burmese marionette theatre. Burmese dance scholars have catalogued around 2000 dance movements, including 13 head movements, 28 eye movements, nine neck movements, 24 ways of moving only one hand plus 23 using both hands, 38 leg movements, eight body postures and 10 walking movements.

Classical dance-drama is occasionally performed at the National Theatre in Yangon, where around a dozen amateur theatre groups regularly practise and perform yamazat. Traditional yamazat can also be seen in Mandalay, Amarapura and Sagaing. In Mandalay, yamazat performers even have their own shrine, where masks of the principal *Ramayana* characters receive offerings of fruit and flowers. Shorter, excerpted performances may be seen at large banquet-style restaurants in Yangon and Mandalay. Since Burmese classical dancing emphasises pose rather than movement, and solo rather than ensemble performances, it can soon become a little boring for TV-hyped Western tastes. By contrast the less common, but more lively, *yein pwe* features singing and dancing performed by a chorus or ensemble.

Most popular of all is the *a-nyeint pwe*, a traditional-variety pwe somewhat akin to early American vaudeville or Thai *li-keh*; see the boxed text 'A-Nyeint Pwe – From Slapstick to Satire' in the Mandalay chapter for details. One of the easiest ways to tell a-nyeint pwe from zat pwe or yamazat is that in both of the latter the musical instruments sit on the floor (or on the ground in an outdoor performance), while in a-nyeint pwe the instruments are placed on a stage with the dancers and actors.

Marionette Theatre

Youq-the pwe (Burmese marionette theatre) presents colourful puppets up to a metre high in a spectacle that many aesthetes consider the most expressive of all the Burmese arts. Developed during the reign of King Bagyidaw in the Konbaung period, it was so influential that it became the forerunner to zat pwe as later performed by actors rather than marionettes. As with dance-drama, the genre's 'golden age' began with the Mandalay kingdoms of the late 18th century and ran through to the advent of cinema in the 1930s.

The Burmese have great respect for an expert puppeteer; indeed a youq-the pwe is thought to demand a more skilled and artistic performance than a zat pwe. Some marionettes may be manipulated by a dozen or more strings; certain nat may sport up to 60 strings, including one for each eyebrow. The marionette master's standard repertoire requires a troupe of 28 puppets including Thagyamin (king of the gods); a Burmese king, queen, prince and princess; a regent; two court pages; an old man and an old woman; a villain; a hermit; four ministers; two clowns; one good and one evil nat; a Brahmin astrologer; two ogres; a *zawgyi* (alchemist); a horse; a monkey; a *makara* (mythical sea serpent); and an elephant. These figures bring together the talents of singers, puppeteers, musicians, woodcarvers, embroiderers and set designers.

Marionette theatre declined following WWII and is now mostly confined to tourist venues in Yangon, Mandalay and Bagan. Rather less frequently it appears at pwe sponsored by wealthy patrons.

Music

Burmese music, which features strongly in any pwe, can be rather hard for unaccustomed Western ears to enjoy. As with other Asian music, it is very short on the harmony so important in Western music and tends to sound 'harsh, tinkly and repetitive', as one early observer described it. The perceived harshness is probably due to the fact that Burmese scales are not 'tempered' as Western scales have been since Bach. As in Western music, the Burmese diatonic scale has seven tones, but they are arranged equidistantly within the octave, and there is no tempering or retuning of the 4th and 7th intervals as with Western scales.

Traditional Burmese music is primarily two dimensional in the sense that rhythm and melody provide much of the musical structure, while repetition is a key element in developing this structure. Subtle shifts in rhythm and tonality provide the modulation usually supplied by the harmonic dimension in Western music. These techniques have been 'rediscovered' in Western musical trends, as in the minimalism of Steve Reich, Philip Glass, Terry Riley and Brian Eno. There is also a significant amount of improvisation in live performance, an element traditional Burmese music shares with jazz.

Classical Music The original inspiration for much of Myanmar's current musical tradition came from Thailand (then Siam) during the reign of King Hsinbyushin, particularly after the second conquest of Thailand in 1767. During this period, Thai court musicians, dancers and entertainers from Ayuthaya were brought to Myanmar by the hundreds in order to effect 'cultural augmentation'. Interestingly, much of this 'Thai' culture actually originated in Cambodia – the Thais had augmented their own culture with captured Cambodian court musicians, dancers and entertainers after conquering Angkor centuries earlier. Burmese classical music as played today was codified by Po Sein, a colonial-era musician, composer and drummer who also designed the *hsaing waing* (the circle of tuned drums, also known as *paq waing*) and formalised classical dancing styles. Such music is meant to be played as an accompaniment to classical dance-dramas that enact scenes from the jataka or from the Indian epic *Ramayana*.

Musical instruments are predominantly percussive, but even the hsaing waing may carry the melody. These drums are tuned by placing a wad of *paq-sa* (drum food) – made from a kneaded paste of rice and wood-ash – onto the centre of the drum head, then adding or subtracting a pinch at a time till the desired drum tone is attained. By the use of multiple hand-and-stick strokes, Burmese percussionists can create melodic and chordal patterns on the large banks of drums employed in a typical performance.

In addition to the hsaing waing, the traditional *hsaing* (Burmese ensemble) of seven to 10 musicians will usually play: the *kyewaing* (a circle of tuned brass gongs); the *saung gauq* (a boat-shaped harp with 13 strings); the *pattala* (a sort of xylophone); the *hneh* (an oboe-type instrument related to the Indian *shanai*); the *pa-lwe* (a bamboo flute); the *mi-gyaung* (crocodile lute); the *paq-ma* (a bass drum); and the *yagwin* (small cymbals) and *wa-leq-hkouq* (bamboo clappers), which are purely rhythmic and are often played by Burmese vocalists. It is also common to see a violin or two in a hsaing, and even the Dobro (an American acoustic slide guitar played on the lap) is occasionally used. Solo piano music has also become part of the traditional Burmese musical repertoire. At the National Museum in Yangon you can view an exhibit of Burmese musical instruments, including old Mon violins, the use of which may predate that of violins in Europe.

An older performance mode features duets of two female musicians playing Burmese harp and crocodile lute. This style of playing originated during the reign of King Badomintara in the late 18th century, when court maidens were trained on these instruments.

A 1997 CD entitled *White Elephants & Golden Ducks*, recorded in Myanmar using top digital equipment and issued on the Shanachie label, offers a good sampler of traditional Burmese instrumental and vocal music. A 1998 follow-up CD, *Pat Waing: The Magic Drum Circle of Burma*, does a beautiful job of rendering the hard-to-reproduce paq waing (hsaing waing) drum sounds. To hear how the Burmese have been translating their traditional music into piano performance for the last hundred years or so, listen to the equally high-quality *Sandaya: The Spellbinding Piano of Burma* (Shanachie, 1998).

A 2000 CD release entitled *Green Tea Leaf Salad: Flavors of Burmese Music* on the Dutch label PAN brings together many of the unique, surprising and scintillating facets of Burmese music. Some of the instruments presented on this CD – such as the Mon crocodile zither and tuned clay pots – are the first recordings of these instruments available to the outside world.

In the near future Smithsonian will be releasing a double CD entitled *Mahagita: Songs From Burma's Royal Courts*, which will feature the epitome of Burmese classical music – the *saung gauq* (harp) with an accompanying vocalist, performed by singer Daw Yi Yi Thant and Burma's greatest harp player, the late U Myint Maung.

Folk & Pop Older still is an enchanting vocal folk-music tradition still heard in rural areas where the Burmese may sing without instrumental accompaniment while working. Such folk songs set the work cadence and provide a distraction from the physical strain and monotony of pounding rice, clearing fields, weaving and so on. You'll hear this most readily in the Ayeyarwady Delta between Twante and Pathein.

Myanmar's urban ears are fed via radio and cassette tapes by a huge pop music industry based in Yangon. The older generation prefer a pop sound created in the 1950s and 1960s by combining traditional Burmese melodies and rhythms with Western instrumental settings. Younger Burmese listen to heavily Western-influenced sounds – sit in a tea shop and you're likely to hear Burmese-language covers of your favourite oldies. A few Burmese rock musicians, such as Zaw Win Htut, produce quite good compositions of their own. In fact, Myanmar produces some of the best local rock in Southeast Asia – as good as or better than Filipino, Indonesian and Thai bands. Of late Burmese musicians doing home-grown versions of country and even rap music have also become popular.

At one time the government discouraged Western music, but things have loosened up substantially over the last few years. Officially, music performed live still must be sung in Burmese, but pirated copies of albums by American and British musicians are openly sold and nobody seems to mind if they're played in public.

Architecture

Traditional temple architecture brings together all the *pan seh myo* (ten types of flower), the traditional Burmese arts schemata:

gold and silversmithing *(ba-dein)*
blacksmithing *(ba-beh)*
bronze, copper and brass casting *(ba-daing)*
woodcarving *(ba-bu)*
lathe-work *(pan-buq)*
painting *(ba-ji)*
lacquerware *(pan-yun)*
stucco work *(pan-daw)*
stone carving *(pan-ta-maw)*
masonry *(pa-yan)* and stone-cutting *(pan-yweh)*

It is in architecture that one sees the strongest evidence of Burmese artistic skill and accomplishment. Myanmar is a country of stupas (Buddhist reliquaries), often called 'pagodas' in English. The Burmese seem unable to see a hill top without wanting to put a religious monument on top of it. Wherever you are – boating down the river, driving through the hills, even flying above the plains – there always seems to be a stupa in view. It is in Bagan that you see the most dramatic results of this national enthusiasm for religious monuments; for over two centuries a massive construction programme resulted in thousands of shrines, stupas, monasteries and other sacred buildings.

The Paya The *paya* (pa-YAH), the most common Burmese equivalent to the often misleading English term pagoda, literally means holy one and can refer to people, deities and places associated with religion. For the most part it's a generic term for a stupa. There are basically two kinds of paya: the solid, bell-shaped *zedi* and the hollow square or rectangular *pahto*. A zedi or stupa is usually thought to contain 'relics' – either objects taken from the Buddha himself (especially pieces of bone, teeth or hair) or certain holy materials such as Buddha images and other religious

Burmese Iconography

Buddhist architecture in Myanmar – whether old or new – tends to employ a set of common decorative motifs taken from Hindu-Buddhist mythology. These may appear as free-standing sculptures, often placed near gates and doorways; as bas relief on the exterior walls of *thein* (ordination halls) or *pahto* (temples or shrines); or as gold-leaf paintings or woodcarvings on doors. Each motif symbolises a particular positive quality associated with the religion and is meant to confer that quality upon the place as well as the people who enter the place.

motif	Burmese	Pali/Sanskrit	meaning
half-lion/half-dragon	chinthe	singha	courage, royalty
swan	hintha	hamsa	unity
human from the waist up, ostrich-like bird waist down	keinnayi (male) keinnaya (female)	kinnari kinnara	love
sphinx-like, half-lion, half-human	manouq-thiha	manussingha	security
eagle-like bird	galoun	garuda	strength
legless dragon	naga	naga	peace, prosperity
ogre	bilu	yaksha	protection
sea serpent	magan	makara	blessing
earth goddess	wathoundaye	vasundhara	maternal protection
peacock	daun	-	sun or patriotism
rabbit	youn	-	moon or peace
crowned Buddha-like figure holding a lotus flower	lokanat	lokanatha or avalokitesvara	world peace, future brotherhood

objects blessed by a famous *sayadaw* (Burmese Buddhist master, usually abbot). Both zedi and pahto are often associated with *kyaung* (Buddhist monasteries).

The term pahto is sometimes translated as temple, though shrine would perhaps be more accurate since priests or monks are not necessarily in attendance. The so-called Mon-style pahto is a large cube with small windows and ground-level passageways; this type is also known as a *gu* or *ku* (from the Pali-Sanskrit *guha*, cave). In later Bagan structures, indoor passages led to outside terraces on several levels, a style usually ascribed to the Bamar rather than the Mon. The overall Bamar concept is similar to that of the Mayan and Aztec pyramids of Mesoamerica; both architectural styles are designed so that worshippers climb a symbolic mountain while viewing religious reliefs and frescoes along the way.

If all this seems too confusing, just remember that the generic Burmese term for all these structures is paya. The famous Mon zedi in Yangon is called Shwedagon Paya, and Bagan's greatest pahto is known as Ananda Paya.

Paya function basically as a focus for meditation or contemplation. In the case of solid paya (zedi), if there is a need for some sheltered gathering place or a place to house images or other paraphernalia, then this will usually be an ancillary building. There may be small shrines, pavilions, covered walkways or other such places all around a major paya. These are often more heavily ornamented than the zedi themselves. *Hman-si-shwe-cha*, which describes the combination of gilt-work with coloured-glass mosaic, is one of the most popular types of ornamentation in Mon and Bamar temples.

Zedi Styles Zedi go under different names in other Buddhist countries; they may be called *dagoba* in Sri Lanka, *chedi* or *jedi* in Thailand, stupas or *chaitya* in India, but basically they all refer to the same idea. Although at first glance all zedi may look alike, you'll soon realise there have been many, often subtle, design changes over the years. Early zedi were usually hemispherical (the Kaunghmudaw at Sagaing near Mandalay) or bulbous (the Bupaya in Bagan), while the more modern style is much more graceful – a curvaceous lower bell merging into a soaring spire, such as the Shwedagon Paya in Yangon. Style is not always a good indicator of a zedi's original age since Myanmar is earthquake-prone and many have been rebuilt over and again, gradually changing their design through the centuries.

One thing many zedi seem to have in quantity is an air of tranquillity. Even when it's noisy around a zedi, when some sort of festival or ceremony is going on, the atmosphere is still charged with that tranquil magic that seems to pervade everything around it. High above you can hear the wind bells tinkling from the *hti*, the decorative metal 'umbrella' that tops the structure. Around the base, people are meditating, strolling around, or simply chatting. Zedi have a warmth, an easy-going feeling of friendliness that is quite unmatched by any other religious building.

Other Buildings Traditionally, only the zedi, gu and pahto have been made of permanent materials; until quite recently all secular buildings – and most monasteries – were constructed of wood, so there are few old ones to be seen. Even the great palaces were made of wood, and with the destruction of Mandalay Palace during WWII there is no remaining wooden Burmese palace. There are only a few reminders of these beautifully carved buildings, and even these are deteriorating due to lack of protection.

Although so little remains of the old wooden architectural skills, there are still many excellent wooden buildings to be seen. The Burmese continue to use teak with great skill, and a fine country home can be a very pleasing structure indeed. While Myanmar boasts no great buildings of meticulous artistry like Cambodia's Angkor Wat (the emphasis has always been more on quantity than quality), when it comes to location – balancing a delicate stupa on a towering hill top or perching one on the side of a sheer precipice – the Burmese have no match.

Buildings erected during the British colonial period feature a variety of styles and materials, from the rustic wood-and-plaster Tudor villas of Pyin U Lwin to the thick-walled, brick-and-plaster, colonnaded mansions and shop houses of Yangon, Mawlamyaing and Myeik. Much of the ornamentation found on these old colonial dames was inspired by local architecture, replacing, for example, the 'gingerbread' typical of British Victorian rooflines with the Burmese equivalent found on Buddhist monastery buildings. An interesting example of a fusion of Burmese and European styles is the City Hall building in Yangon. Until recently scant attention was paid to preserving colonial architecture – for political as well as economic reasons. Nowadays some are being restored, and many of the grand old government buildings in Yangon, such as the High Court building with its impressive clock tower, are protected from the wrecking ball by government decree. Sadly, this has not been the case with privately owned shop houses and other commercial buildings, many of which have been demolished and replaced by new structures in recent years. Sadder still is the practice of 'modernising' old colonial buildings by covering their facades with ceramic tiles and tinted glass. In recent years Mandalay and Pyin U Lwin have lost countless colonial classics in this manner.

Buddhist Sculpture

Remarkably little research has been carried out on Burmese religious sculpture other than that from the Bagan and Mandalay eras. A rich Buddhist sculptural tradition in wood,

Shapes of the Buddha

Despite stylistic variations, Buddha images in Myanmar are remarkably similar in overall shape and form. This is because sculptors are traditionally bound by certain iconographical parameters that specify the hand and body positions the Buddha may assume, as well as the physical characteristics that the sculptor is required to depict. The way the monastic robes drape over the body, the direction in which the hair curls, the proportions for each body part – all are to some degree canonised. The tradition does leave room for innovation, however, allowing the various 'schools' of Buddhist art to distinguish themselves over the centuries.

One aspect of the tradition that almost never varies is the posture of the Buddha image. Four basic postures (Pali: *iriyapada*) are portrayed: standing, sitting, walking and reclining. The first three postures are associated with the daily activities of the Buddha, namely: teaching, meditating and offering refuge to his disciples, which can be accomplished in any of these three asanas. The reclining position represents the Buddha's dying moments when he attained *parinibbana* (ultimate nirvana). Another key iconographical element is the figure's *mudra* (hand position).

Bhumisparsa (touching the earth) In this classic sitting posture the right hand touches the ground while the left rests in the lap. This hand position symbolises the point in the Buddha's life when he sat in meditation beneath the banyan tree in Bodh Gaya, India, and vowed not to budge from the spot until he gained enlightenment. Mara, the Buddhist equivalent of Satan, tried to interrupt the Buddha's meditation by invoking a series of distractions (including tempests, floods, feasts and nubile maidens) – the Buddha's response was to touch the earth, thus calling on nature to witness his resolve. The bhumisparsa mudra is one of the most common mudras seen in Buddhist sculpture; it's also known as the *maravijaya* (victory over Mara) mudra.

Dhyana (meditation) Both hands rest palms-up on the Buddha's lap, with the right hand on top, signifying meditation. This mudra is always accompanied by a sitting posture.

Vitarka or Dhammachakka (exposition, or turning of the wheel of dharma) When the thumb and forefinger of one hand *(vitarka)* or both hands *(dhammachakka)* form a circle with the other fingers curving outward (similar to the Western OK gesture), the mudra evokes the first public discourse on Buddhist doctrine. A sitting posture is most common with these mudras, though it's occasionally seen in standing images.

Abhaya (no fear) In this posture, one or both hands extend forward, with palms out and fingers pointing upward, to symbolise the Buddha's offer of protection or freedom from fear to his followers. This mudra is most commonly seen in conjunction with standing or walking Buddhas, and occasionally with sitting images.

Bhumisparsa

Shapes of the Buddha

Dhyana

Vitarka

Dana (giving, or offering) Either one or both hands extend forward in this posture, with palms up and parallel to the ground, to signify the offering of *dhamma* (Buddhist teachings) to the world. Rarely seen in seated images, this is almost always accompanied by a standing posture.

Physical Characteristics
According to the Mahapadana Sutta of the Pali canon, there are 32 bodily marks whereby one can recognise a Buddha. Most of these can easily be seen on any Burmese Buddha image:

1 Well-planted feet
2 Wheel marks on the base of the feet
3 Projecting heels
4 Long fingers
5 Soft, delicate hands and feet
6 Hands and feet covered with a network of lines
7 Arched feet
8 Antelope limbs
9 Hands that can reach to the knees without bending
10 Private member in a sheath
11 Golden complexion
12 Delicate skin
13 One hair for every pore
14 Body hairs standing straight up
15 Upright limbs
16 Protuberances on the hands, feet and shoulders
17 Lion chest
18 Full shoulders
19 Rotundity of a banyan tree
20 Well-rounded branching of the trunk
21 Superior delicacy of taste
22 Lion jaw
23 Forty teeth
24 Even teeth
25 Teeth without gaps
26 Very white teeth
27 Large and thin tongue
28 Brahman voice
29 Dark eyes
30 Ox-like lashes
31 White tuft between the eyebrows
32 Protuberance on the crown of the head

bronze, stone and marble existed among the Shan, Mon and Rakhaing peoples but these have received short shrift from both Bamar and foreign scholars. Even Bamar sculpture is hard to come by in the country.

Compared with the inhabitants of neighbouring countries, the Burmese have had a difficult time preserving historical, non- architectural art. Seldom does one come across any Buddha images older than 100 years in Burmese paya or kyaung – one gets the definite impression that most such sculptures have been sold or stolen. This may be partially due to the Burmese belief that images from old kyaung or paya may be unlucky, so why collect them? Mandalay's Mahamuni Buddha image, a Rakhaing sculpture, is just about the only famous image of any age – probably because it's too heavy to steal! Unfortunately the years of war and poverty have taken their toll on the arts and you'll easily find more Burmese religious sculpture for sale or on display in Bangkok, San Francisco and London than in Myanmar.

Painting

Early Burmese art was always a part of religious architecture – paintings were for the walls of temples, sculpture to be placed inside them. Since the decline of temple-building, the old painting skills have deteriorated considerably. Modern Burmese paintings in the Western style reflect only a pale shadow of the former skill, and the one painter of any renown, U Ba Kyi, paints murals and canvases commissioned for the larger hotels and government offices. Many contemporary artists in Yangon and Mandalay work in modern international styles, even when painting traditional subjects.

Woodcarving

Burmese woodcarving was reserved mainly for royal palaces, which were always made of timber and became showpieces for the skilful woodcarver. When royal palaces ceased to be built, woodcarving skills rapidly declined, although the new construction boom has brought about a small but growing woodcarving renaissance – again mostly seen in hotels.

Literature

Religious texts inscribed onto Myanmar's famous *kammawa* (lacquered scriptures) and *parabaik* (folding manuscripts) were the first literature as such, and began appearing in the 12th century. Until the 1800s, the only other works of 'literature' available were royal genealogies, classical poetry and law texts. A Burmese version of the Indian epic *Ramayana* – called *Yama Thagyin* or *Yama Yagan* in Burmese – was first written in 1775 by poet U Aung Pyo. The first printed books in the country were produced by missionaries; the American Baptist Mission was responsible for virtually all publishing until the late 19th century, when the first Burmese-owned press began printing a Burmese-language newspaper.

Today the Burmese are great readers, as you'll realise from the piles of books in the street at every night market. Not all publications are government owned. Magazines and newspapers about everything from soccer news to trends in popular music are published privately in Myanmar, but because of the heavy restrictions placed on verbal expression, everything must pass government censors.

SOCIETY & CONDUCT

Traditional Culture

The social ideal for most Burmese citizens – no matter what their ethnic background – is a standard of behaviour commonly termed *bama hsan-jin* (Burmese-ness).

The hallmarks of bama hsan-jin include: an acquaintance with Buddhist scriptures (and the ability to recite at least a few classic verses); the ability to speak idiomatic Burmese; showing respect for elders; dressing modestly; showing discretion in behaviour towards members of the opposite sex; and most importantly, exhibiting modes of expression and comportment that value the quiet, subtle and indirect rather than the loud, obvious and direct. One also hears the term *myanma hsan-jin* although clearly the cultural norms themselves originally derive from Bamar *(bama)* and/or Mon culture.

[Continued on page 54]

The People of Myanmar

The People of Myanmar

BERNARD NAPTHINE

BERNARD NAPTHINE

BERNARD NAPTHINE

COREY WISE

Title Page: A Karen woman with traditional earring, Shan State (Photograph by Nicholas Reuss)

Top: Man with cheroot, Mingun, Mandalay Division

Middle Left: Novice nun, Mingun, Shan State

Middle Right: Novice monks line up for alms, Bagan, Mandalay Division

Bottom: Chin woman, Kerit Chaung village, Chin State

THE PEOPLE OF MYANMAR

ne of the more exciting aspects of travel in Myanmar is the opportunity to experience a corner of Asia that in many ways has changed little since British colonial times. Due to its isolation – self-imposed and otherwise – Myanmar has yet to be completely overwhelmed by outside fashion influences. Many Burmese still sport some vestiges of their traditional dress: nowhere else in Southeast Asia will you see so many sarongs, turbans and other exotic apparel. Of course, these differences in dress are just a hint of the distinctions between Myanmar's diverse ethnic populations. Less obvious to the casual eye are differences in cultures, customs, languages and religions.

Officially Myanmar is divided up into eight 'national races' – the Bamar, Shan, Mon, Kayin, Kayah, Chin, Kachin and Rakhaing – but the Burmese government further subdivides these eight groups into 67 subgroups. Ethnologists have suggested that there are actually over 100 distinct groups living in Myanmar. While it would take a hefty tome to give a detailed account of all Myanmar's ethnicities, we've made a list of the groups the average visitor to Myanmar is most likely to encounter or read about.

Keep in mind that intermarriage between some ethnicities is quite common in Myanmar. Individual Burmese are usually quite knowledgeable about their own ethnic background and you'll often encounter Burmese with parents from two different ethnicities. Besides the peoples that are indigenous to Myanmar, you'll also encounter the descendents of peoples who migrated to Myanmar in the not-so-distant past – mostly these are people of Indian, Chinese and Nepalese descent who relocated to Myanmar during the British colonial period.

Myanmar is also quite diverse religiously. In towns and cities it's not uncommon to see places of worship for Buddhists, Hindus, Muslims and Christians all within sight of one another.

As in other Southeast Asian countries with ethnically diverse populations, feelings of pride and prejudice have and continue to cause friction between Myanmar's ethnicities. The Burmese outspoken nature can be a boon to travellers who are interested in current ethnic relations. Ask a Bamar (or a Shan or a Kayin) their opinion about their countrymen of different ethnic or religious backgrounds to get an idea of what kinds of challenges governments in Myanmar – both past and present – have faced in their efforts to keep the peace and preserve the borders.

Bamar

The Bamar – also known as Burman – make up the majority of the population (65%) and, not surprisingly, it is they who rule the country. Thought to have originally migrated from the Himalayas, the Bamar ruled much of what is now Myanmar from Bagan by the 11th century. When the British conquered Myanmar in the 19th century, it was the

Bamar who relinquished the most. Many ancient court customs and arts were lost as the Bamar monarchy was abolished.

Devout Theravada Buddhists, the Bamar – from the top generals who run the country on down to the lowliest trishaw drivers – believe that being Buddhist is a key aspect of being Bamar, and the Burmese media reports daily on the merit-making of top government officials at the country's principal Buddhist places of worship. In government efforts at nation-building, the Bamar language (Burmese) has also been established as the language of instruction in schools throughout Myanmar. Thus most non-Bamar speak Burmese as a second language.

Mon

The Mon were one of the earliest inhabitants of Myanmar and their rule stretched into what is now Thailand. As happened with the Cham in Vietnam and the Phuan in Laos, the Mon were gradually conquered by neighbouring kingdoms and their influence waned until they were practically unknown outside the region. As in Thailand, which also has a Mon minority, the Mon have almost completely assimilated with the majority and in most ways seem indistinguishable from the Bamar. In the ancient past, Mon Buddhist sites – including Yangon's Shwedagon Paya – were appropriated by the Bamar, and Mon tastes in art and architecture were borrowed as well. Today the Mon make up just over 2% of the population of Myanmar, but Mon art and culture have influenced that of the Bamar quite thoroughly, as a trip to the Mon Cultural Museum in Mawlamyaing (the capital of the Mon State) will attest.

Shan

The Shan call themselves Tai ('Shan' is actually a Bamar word derived from the word 'Siam'). This is significant, as the Shan are related ethnically, culturally and linguistically to Tai peoples in neighbouring Thailand, Laos and China's Yunnan Province. In fact, if you've spent some time in northern Thailand or Laos and learned some of the respective languages, you'll find you can have basic conversation with the Shan – especially in the eastern Shan State which borders northern Thailand. The Shan are also Theravada Buddhists and at one time they fought the Bamar for the control of Myanmar. Today they make up about 10% of the population.

Traditionally the Shan wore baggy trousers and floppy, wide-brimmed sun hats, and the men were known for their faith in talismanic tattoos. Nowadays Shan town-dwellers commonly dress in the Bamar *lọngyi* (sarong) and are mostly indistinguishable from the Bamar, except on festival occasions when they proudly sport their ethnic costumes.

In former times the Shan were ruled by local lords or chieftains called *sao pha* (sky lords), a word that was corrupted by the Bamar to *sawbwa*.

The Shan are said to be very fond of gambling and festivals, and Shan women are admired throughout Myanmar for their beauty and light complexions.

Kayin

The Kayin (also known as Karen) are a large and diverse group, divided into numerous subgroups. They were originally animists, but some Kayin villages were heavily targeted by Christian missionaries in the 19th and early 20th centuries, while other villages converted to Buddhism.

The Kayin are an independent-minded people but the sheer diversity of the many Kayin subgroups has made it impossible for them to achieve any real political power. To this day Buddhist Kayin often side with the Buddhist Bamar against their Christian Kayin kin. The recruitment of child soldiers is not uncommon in this neck of the woods. This came to the world's attention most recently when a Christian Kayin group calling itself 'God's Army' made headlines with their brief armed struggle against the Myanmar government. The group was led by young twin brothers who reputedly had magical powers and took up arms when they were only nine years old.

The typical dress of both the Kayin men and women is a longyi with horizontal stripes (a pattern that is reserved exclusively for women in other ethnic groups). The Kayin are thought to make up less than 10% of the total population of Myanmar.

Kayah

Also known as the Karenni or Red Karen, the Kayah are settled in the mountainous isolation of the Kayah State.

As with many of Myanmar's ethnicities that traditionally practised animism, the Kayah were targeted for conversion to Christianity by Baptist and Catholic missionaries during the colonial period. The name 'Red Karen' refers to the favoured colour of the Kayah traditional dress, and the fact that their apparel resembles that of some Kayin (Karen) tribes – a resemblance that caused the Kayah to be classified by colonisers and missionaries as 'Karen'. Today the Kayah make up a very small percentage of the overall population of Myanmar – perhaps less than 1% – and the vast majority lead agrarian lives within the Kayah State much as their ancestors have for centuries. A significant number of Kayah also live in Thailand's Mae Hong Son Province.

Kachin

The Kachin (who call themselves Jingpaw) are another ethnicity that was heavily missionised by Christian groups during British colonial times. The Baptists seemed to have been the most successful, with the Catholics following close behind. As much of the Kachin State lies above the tropic of Cancer, the climate is more extreme – stifling hot in the summer months and downright cold in the winter – and the Kachin seem to have abandoned their traditional dress for Western clothes that can be easily changed to suit the seasons.

About the only vestige of Kachin dress that foreign visitors are likely to note are men's longyi of indigo, green and deep-purple plaid. However, during festive occasions Kachin dress is quite impressive. Women sport finely woven wool skirts decorated with zigzag or diamond patterns and dark blouses festooned with hammered silver medallions and tassels. These exotic blouses are admired by the Bamar and until fairly recently it was not uncommon for photo studios in Bamar-majority towns as far south as Pyay to keep a few Kachin blouses on hand so that Bamar women could wear them while posing for photographs.

Chin

The Chin inhabit the mountainous region which borders on India to the west. In the past the Chin, as with most highland dwellers, lead labour-intensive lives and their relatively simple traditional dress reflected this. Men wore loincloths in the warmer months and draped blankets over themselves when the weather turned cool. The women wore a poncho-like garment woven with intricate geometric patterns. These garments and Chin blankets are highly sought-after by textile collectors today.

The most extraordinary Chin fashion of old was the custom of tattooing the women's faces. Chin facial tattoos cover the whole face – starting at just above the bridge of the nose and radiating out in a pattern of dark lines that resemble a spider's web. Even the eyelids were tattooed. The tattooing was traditionally done to girls once they reached the age of 12 or 13. The practice died out after WWII, but in many Chin villages one can see a few tattooed grannies going about their daily chores. Legend has it that this practice was initiated to keep young Chin maidens from being coveted by Rakhaing princes whose kingdom bordered the southern Chin hills.

Rakhaing

The Rakhaing (formerly called Arakanese), who make up about 4% of the population of Myanmar, are principally adherents of Buddhism. Their ancient capital was centred at Mrauk U in what is now the northern Rakhaing State, which borders Bangladesh to the west. Their language is akin to Bamar but, due to their geographical location, they have absorbed a fair amount of culture from the Indian subcontinent. In the eyes of most Bamar, the Rakhaing are a creole race – a mixture of Bamar and Indian – a perception that Buddhist Rakhaing strongly resent.

The Rakhaing State also has a minority population of Muslim Rakhaing, who refer to themselves as Rohingya.

The Rakhaing are skilled weavers and are known in Myanmar for their eye-catching and intricately patterned longyi.

Besides the ruins at Mrauk U, the most visible vestige of the Rakhaing's illustrious past is the Mahamuni Buddha image in Mandalay, plundered by the Bamar from its shrine near Mrauk U in 1784.

Wa

During British-colonial times the Wa were hated and feared. The British distinguished two groups of Wa according to how receptive they were to the coloniser's attempts to control them. The 'Wild Wa' were headhunters, and decorated their villages with the severed heads of vanquished enemies to propitiate the spirits that guarded over their opium fields. The so-called Tame Wa allowed the colonisers to pass through their territory unimpeded, yet the area inhabited by the Wa – east of the upper Thanlwin (Salween) River in the northern Shan State – was never completely pacified by the British. Nowadays the Wa are mostly known for their alleged involvement in the production and smuggling of opium and methamphetamine, and often make headlines in neighbouring Thailand due to frequent border skirmishes with Thai military and police forces.

Naga

The Naga are mainly settled in a mountainous region of eastern India known as Nagaland, but significant numbers live in the western Sagaing Division between the Indian border and the Chindwin River.

When the British arrived in the mid-19th century, the Naga were a fragmented but fearsome collection of tribes. Headhunting was a tradition among them and for many decades they resisted British rule, though a lack of cooperation between the tribes hindered their efforts to remain independent. A turnaround came about during WWI when the British recruited nearly 17,000 Naga to fight in Europe. The unexpected result of this experiment was a feeling of unity among the many Naga tribes, which lead to an organised Naga independence movement that plagued the British until the end of the colonial era.

Among tribal peoples of the world, the Naga must sport one of the most exotic traditional costumes. Naga men at festival time wear a striking ceremonial headdress made up of feathers, tufts of hair and cowrie shells, and carry wicked spears, giving them a look that somehow seems vaguely African, Polynesian and Amazonian – like some fantasy ensemble cooked up by Hollywood.

Bamar Repression of Minorities

With the complete takeover of Myanmar by the British in 1886, new borders were drawn. As with so many of the boundaries superimposed on maps during the European colonisation of the world, these borders had little to do with ethnic groupings, and there were many old rivals and enemies within the British Burma borders. The colonisers managed to keep their hatred of each other under wraps by utilising the carrot of semi-autonomy or the stick of arrest and imprisonment. Over a century later, little has changed. The insurgency between Bamar-majority government troops and minority ethnicities that smoldered for four decades after independence has been largely quelled. Groups that signed ceasefire agreements with the government (the Kachin, Kayah, etc) have been granted limited economic autonomy. Those who continue to fight the government (some Shan and Kayin groups) are dealt with severely. In rebel-controlled areas, Burmese troops have been accused of using rape as a weapon and adopting a scorched-earth policy that regularly sends groups of refugees fleeing across the borders into Thailand and Bangladesh. Some observers of Burmese politics predict that, given democracy and a choice, many of Myanmar's ethnicities would opt for independence and break away from Bamar-controlled Myanmar.

[Continued from page 48]

The degree to which a Burmese can conform to these ideals matches the degree of respect he or she will receive from associates. Although high rank – civil, military or clerical – will exempt certain individuals from chastisement by social inferiors, it doesn't exempt them from the way they are perceived by other Burmese. This goes for foreigners as well, even though most first-time visitors can hardly be expected to speak idiomatic Burmese or recite Buddhist scripture. Still, if you do your best to follow the cultural guidelines on behaviour and dress outlined below, you'll garner much respect from the Burmese.

Dos & Don'ts

The usual Asian rules of conduct apply in Myanmar, and there are also a few specific Burmese ones. As with elsewhere in Asia it is unseemly to show too much emotion – losing your temper over problems and delays gets you nowhere, it just amazes people. Stay calm and collected at all times. The Burmese frown on such displays of anger just as much as they frown on too open a display of affection.

Don't compromise local people by raising political questions and issues in inappropriate situations – be discreet and mindful of possible repercussions for them.

As in other Buddhist countries the head is the highest part of the body – spiritually as well as literally. You should never deliberately touch somebody else on the head or pat a child on the head. Equally, the feet are the lowest part of the body – don't point your feet at anybody or anything. If you accidentally brush somebody with your foot, apologise immediately. Needless to say, using your toes to pick something up off the ground is poor form.

Buddha images are sacred objects, so don't pose in front of them for pictures, or give them a thump to ascertain what they're made of – and definitely do not sit or climb upon them.

A couple of rules apply specifically to women: Women should never ride on the roofs of vehicles or small boats (large passenger ferries with multiple decks are exempted), which would be a cultural insult to any male passengers below.

Monks are not supposed to touch or be touched by women. If a woman wants to hand something to a monk, the object should be placed within reach of the monk, not handed directly to him.

When handing something to anybody, it's polite to give and receive with the right hand. Note how the Burmese will often touch their right elbow with their left hand when giving or receiving something, or especially when shaking hands in greeting. This is considered extra polite, and if a Burmese hands something to you in this way, reciprocate by mimicking the gesture.

As in neighbouring Thailand and Laos, it's very rude to step over anybody who is sitting or lying on the floor (or the deck of a boat), even if it's just their outstretched arms or legs. Do your best to step around instead of over somebody, even if they're asleep. Usually Burmese will make room for you to pass if they notice that they're blocking your way, but if they don't notice you (or are asleep), it's best to touch them gently on the arm to get their attention instead of climbing over them.

Dress One should dress neatly (no shorts or skimpy tops) when visiting religious sites. Most important of all in Myanmar, remember to take off your shoes and socks before entering the grounds of any Theravada Buddhist shrine, zedi, temple, paya or monastery. Even at the most dilapidated, run-down, ruined paya in Bagan the 'no footwearing' rule still applies. You must go barefoot in every part of a Buddhist compound, not just in the shrine buildings as in neighbouring Buddhist countries. In the middle of the day going barefoot can be a little painful as the paved area around a paya often becomes very hot. At major paya there will often be a mat walkway around the platform.

At one time this restriction caused quite a stir between the Burmese and the British. As part of the growing surge of nationalism between the wars, and as a neat way to put the British in their place, the Burmese decided to rigidly enforce the no-footwear rules, from which the Europeans had previously exempted themselves.

Shoes – but not necessarily socks – are also taken off before entering private homes. Actually the Burmese very rarely wear socks. You'll find it easier to deal with temples and private homes if you follow their example and go sockless. Or take it a step further and wear slip-on sandals – the most convenient footwear for travelling in Myanmar – like the locals do.

Beach attire or sloppy lounge clothes are not considered appropriate for walking around town. Men should try to keep their shoulders covered except at the beach or when bathing. Likewise long trousers, *longyi* (sarong-style garment) or skirts are considered more appropriate than shorts in all situations except at the beach. Women can wear sleeveless blouses, but should try to avoid tight or breast-baring tank tops.

If you decide to 'go native' and wear a longyi in public (as a surprising number of travellers do), make sure it has been sewn into a tube before wearing it. Walking around town with an unsewn longyi is the Burmese equivalent of being caught with your trousers unzipped!

Treatment of Animals

Most animal life is considered potential protein in Myanmar. Some Chinese restaurants keep caged live animals – from fish to small bears – both as advertising and as potential dishes from the menu (though this practice is nowhere near as common as in China, Taiwan or Singapore).

RELIGION

Around 87% of Burmese are Buddhist. During the U Nu period Buddhism functioned as a state religion of sorts – as embodied in such catch-phrases as 'the Socialist Way to Nibbana'. Nowadays there is complete freedom of religion, though within the government Buddhists tend to attain higher rank more easily than non-Buddhists, simply because Buddhism is considered a key element in bama hsan-jin.

An appreciation of Buddhism and its history in Myanmar is a prerequisite for outsiders wishing to better understand the Burmese mind.

Burmese Buddhism

Early Buddhism & Theravada Reform

The Mon were the first people in Myanmar to practise Theravada Buddhism, called the Southern School since it took the southern route from India, its place of origin. King Asoka, the great Indian emperor and devout Buddhist convert, is known to have sent missions during the 3rd century BC to Suvannabhumi, the Golden Land – an area taken to be the fertile river deltas of what are today Myanmar, Thailand and Cambodia. A second wave is thought to have arrived in Southeast Asia via Sinhalese missionaries from present-day Sri Lanka, sometime between the 6th and 10th centuries.

By the 9th century the Pyu of northern Myanmar were combining Theravada with elements of Mahayana and Tantric Buddhism brought with them from their homelands on or near the Tibetan Plateau. When the Bamar of Bagan supplanted the Pyu they inherited this amalgamated form.

During the early Bagan era (11th century), Bamar king Anawrahta decided that the Buddhism practised in his realm should be 'purified' of all non-Theravada elements, a task he set for Mon monks captured by his armies in Thaton, southern Myanmar. Although Burmese Buddhism was never totally rid of Mahayana, Tantric, Hindu and animist elements, his efforts were remarkably successful in bringing the Burmese around to a predominantly Theravada world-view.

History & Tenets Theravada Buddhism differs from Hinduism, Judaism, Islam or Christianity in that it is not centred around a god or gods, but rather a psychophilosophical system. Today it covers a wide range of interpretations of the basic beliefs, which all start from the enlightenment of Siddhartha Gautama, a prince-turned-ascetic, in northern India around 2500 years ago.

Neither the Buddha (The Enlightened) nor his immediate pupils ever wrote the *dharma* (Buddhist teachings) down, so after Gautama's death a schism developed and today there are two major schools of Buddhism. The Theravada (Doctrine of the Elders) school holds that to achieve *nibbana* (nirvana), the eventual aim of every Buddhist, you must 'work out your own salvation with diligence'. In other words it is up to each individual to work out his or her own fate.

The Mahayana (Large Vehicle) school holds that individuals should forego the experience of nibbana until all humankind is ready for salvation. The goal is to become a Bodhisattva (Buddha-to-be), rather than a fully enlightened Buddha. From this perspective, no-one can enter nibbana without the intervention of a Bodhisattva.

The Mahayana school does not reject the other school, but claims it has extended it. Hence Mahayanists often refer to Theravada as Hinayana (Small Vehicle) Buddhism. The Theravadins, on the other hand, see Mahayana as a misinterpretation of the Buddha's original teachings. To those who would choose, Mahayana offers the 'soft option' (have faith and all will be well), while the Theravada is more austere and ascetic, and, some might say, harder to practise.

Theravada Buddhism is followed in Cambodia, Laos, Myanmar, Sri Lanka and Thailand. Mahayana Buddhism is practised in China, Japan, Korea, Taiwan, Singapore and Vietnam. There is also a variety of more esoteric divisions of Buddhism such as the Hindu-influenced Tantric Buddhism of Tibet and Nepal, and the Zen Buddhism of Japan, all of which are forms of Mahayana in general principle, since they adhere to the Bodhisattva ideal.

Today the majority of Buddhists in Myanmar belong to the Theravada sect; those who profess Mahayana Buddhism comprise fewer than 1%, virtually all of whom are of Chinese descent.

Buddha taught that the world is primarily characterised by *dukkha* (unsatisfactoriness), *anicca* (impermanence) and *anatta* (insubstantiality), and that even our happiest moments are only temporary, empty and unsatisfactory.

The ultra-pragmatic Buddhist perception of cause and effect – *kamma* in Pali, *karma* in Sanskrit, *kan* in Burmese – holds that birth inevitably leads to sickness, old age and death, hence every life is insecure and subject to dukkha. Through rebirth, the cycle of *thanthaya* (Pali: *samsara*) repeats itself endlessly as long as ignorance and craving – the remote and proximate causes of birth – remain.

Only by reaching a state of complete wisdom and nondesire can one attain true happiness. To achieve wisdom and eliminate craving one must turn inward and master one's own mind through meditation, most commonly known to the Burmese as *bhavana* or *kammahtan*.

The Buddha taught four noble truths:

1. Life is dukkha.
2. Dukkha comes from *tanha* (selfish desire).
3. When one forsakes selfish desire, suffering will be extinguished.
4. The 'eightfold path' is the way to eliminate selfish desire.

The eightfold path is divided into three stages: *sila* (morality), *samadhi* (concentration), and *pañña* (wisdom and insight). It consists of:

1. Right thought
2. Right understanding
3. Right speech
4. Right action
5. Right livelihood
6. Right exertion
7. Right attentiveness
8. Right concentration

Devout Burmese Buddhists adhere to five lay precepts, or moral rules (*thila* in Burmese, *sila* in Pali), which require abstinence from killing, stealing, unchastity (usually interpreted among laypeople as adultery), lying and intoxicating substances.

Buddhism emphasises love, compassion, nonviolence and tolerance of other belief systems. This tolerance has often resulted in its assimilation into other religions, as eventually happened in India with Hinduism, or in its absorption of already extant beliefs, as happened with the Burmese nat. The personal experience one has of Buddhism remains similar from country to country despite local adaptations, changes, amalgamations and inclusions – an overriding impression of warmth and gentleness, and of a religion practised by sympathetic people who are always eager to explain their beliefs.

In spite of Buddhism's obviously profound truths, the most common Burmese approach is to try for a better future life by feeding monks, giving donations to temples and performing regular worship at the local paya. For the average Burmese, everything revolves around the *kutho* (merit), from the Pali *kusala* (wholesome), one is able to accumulate through such deeds. One of the more typical rituals performed by individuals visiting a stupa is to pour water over the Buddha image at their astrological post (determined by the day of the week they were born) – one glassful for every year of their current age plus one extra to ensure a long life. Asked what they want in their next life, most Burmese will put forth such seemingly mundane and materialistic values as beauty and wealth; others choose rebirth somewhere beyond the reach of the military regime.

Monks & Nuns Socially, every Burmese male is expected to take up temporary monastic residence twice in his life: once as a *samanera* (novice monk between the ages of 10 and 20) and again as a *hpongyi* (fully ordained monk, sometime after age 20). Almost all men or boys under 20 years of age participate in the *shinpyu* (novitiation ceremony) – quite a common event since a family earns great merit when one of its sons 'takes robe and bowl'. A samanera adheres to 10 precepts or vows, which include the usual prohibitions against stealing, lying, killing, intoxication and sexual involvement, along with ones forbidding eating after noon, listening to music or dancing, wearing jewellery, garlands or perfume, sleeping on high beds, and accepting money for personal use.

Later in life a male should spend three months as a hpongyi at a monastery during Waso (often referred to by Westerners as 'Buddhist Lent'), which begins in July and coincides with the rainy season. For many men the post–rice harvest, hot-season hiatus between January and April is a more convenient time. Some men spend as little as three to nine days to accrue merit as monks. Others may enter the monkhood a third time, since three is considered an especially lucky number.

As of June 2001, there were 466,524 monks residing at 53,017 monasteries in Myanmar; this number includes the many monks who have ordained for life as well as those undergoing temporary ordination. Of these a significant percentage become scholars and teachers, while some specialise in healing, folk magic or nat exorcism.

All things possessed by a monk must be offered by the lay community. Upon ordination a new monk is typically offered a set of three robes (lower, inner and outer). Bright red robes are usually reserved for novices under 15, darker colours for older, fully ordained monks. Other possessions a monk is permitted include a razor, a cup, a filter (for keeping insects out of drinking water), an umbrella and an alms bowl. The latter are usually plain black lacquer bowls made in Inwa or Sagaing; monks carry them to gather their daily food from householders in their monastery precincts.

At one time the Theravada Buddhist world had a separate monastic lineage for females. The female monks were called *bhikkhuni* and observed more precepts than monks did – 311 as opposed to the 227 followed by monks. The bhikkhuni tradition was begun in the Buddha's time but eventually died out and has never been restored.

In Myanmar, the modern equivalent are women who live the monastic life as *dasasila* ('ten-precept' nuns), often called *thilashin* (possessor of morality) in Burmese. Burmese nuns shave their heads, wear pink robes, and take vows in an ordination procedure similar to that undergone by monks. They don't go out on daily alms-food rounds but they do collect dry food provisions every 15 days in most locales, or as often as once a week in some places.

Generally speaking, nunhood isn't considered as 'prestigious' as monkhood. The average Burmese Buddhist makes a great show of offering new robes and household items to the monks at the local kyaung but pays much less attention to the nuns. This is mainly because nuns generally don't perform ceremonies on behalf of laypeople, so there is often less incentive for self-interested laypeople to make offerings to them. Furthermore, many Burmese equate the number of precepts observed with the total Buddhist merit achieved, hence nunhood is seen as less 'meritorious' than monkhood since nuns keep only ten precepts – the same number observed by male novices.

This difference in prestige represents social Buddhism, however, and is not how those with a serious interest in Buddhist practice regard the nuns. Nuns engage in the same fundamental eremitic activities – meditation and dhamma study – as monks do, activities that are the core of monastic life. When more than a few nuns reside at one temple, it's usually a sign that the teachings there are particularly strong. In Sagaing alone there are 145 nunneries housing over 2000 thilashin.

Monasteries Monastic communities are called *kyaungtaik*, *hpongyi-kyaung*, or simply *kyaung* for short. The most important structure on the monastery grounds is the *thein* (Pali: *sema*, a consecrated hall where monastic ordinations are held). Kyaung may also be associated with one or more zedi or pahto. An open-sided resthouse or *zayat* may be available for gatherings of laypeople during festivals or pilgrimages.

Non-Theravada Elements in Burmese Buddhism The Theravada Buddhism practised by the Burmese is no more a 'pure' form of the belief system than Philippine Catholicism is 'pure' Roman Catholicism. In everyday life it is blended with bits of spirit worship, Hinduism and Mahayana Buddhism. The nat cult (see Nat Worship later in this chapter) in particular plays an important role in the religious life of most Burmese, who, it is said, 'love the Buddha, but fear the nat'.

Mahayana elements survive in the worship of at least two *arahat* (enlightened disciples) of the Buddha, whose images are often encountered at Burmese paya. In Mahayana Buddhism these would be considered Bodhisattvas. The monk Sivali (Shin Thiwali in Burmese) is shown holding a walking staff and fan; he is believed to bring prosperity and good fortune to those who make offerings or pay homage to him, especially in preparation for travel. Upagupta (Shin Upagot) sits cross-legged on a lotus raft in the middle of the ocean with a begging bowl and appears to anyone who faces physical danger. Offerings to Shin Upagot ensure protection in instances of mortal danger; some people pray to Upagot for good weather. Burmese Buddhists also worship Lokanatha, otherwise known as Avalokitesvara, a Mahayana deity who is thought to be protecting the world between the passing of the last Buddha and the coming of the next. The crowned Lokanatha sits on a lotus pedestal, with his left thigh parallel to the pedestal and his right knee upright, holding a lotus flower in his right hand. Almost all major paya in central Myanmar feature separate shrines to these three figures somewhere in the grounds.

Hinduism survives mainly in the form of Burmese astrology, which is based on the Indian system of naming the zodiacal planets for Hindu deities and is very important for deciding the proper dates for weddings, funerals, ordinations and other life-cycle ceremonies. A cabalistic ritual called Paya-kozu (Nine Gods), held on behalf of those who have fallen ill or have experienced serious misfortune, similarly invokes Hindu deities. A *ponna* (or Brahman priest) – usually but not always of Indian descent – often officiates at rituals such as these and may also divine the most auspicious moment for significant occasions.

Ne Win's infamous fascination with numerology was taken to extremes in 1987, when he replaced common currency with brand new bills that were divisible by his favourite number, nine. Many Burmese, who stashed their money at home rather than the bank, were ruined. Their savings had became worthless overnight. Ne Win's obsession is shared by many Burmese Buddhists. Nearly everyone in Myanmar reveres the number nine, which is thought to have an inherent mystic significance. In Burmese the word *ko* (nine) also means 'to seek protection from the gods'; *nat-ko* signifies propitiation of the nat, and offerings are often made in nines, eg, nine candles, nine kinds of food, nine cups of tea and so on.

Recommended Reading If you're interested in learning more about Buddhism, the following books are recommended (publisher supplied when difficult to find):

Buddhism, Imperialism and War, by Trevor Ling
Buddhist Dictionary, by Mahathera Nyanatiloka
The Buddhist World of Southeast Asia, by Donald K Swearer
Essential Themes of Buddhist Lectures Given by Ashin Thittila, Department of Religious Affairs (DRA), Yangon
The Initiation of Novicehood and the Ordination of Monkhood in the Burmese Buddhist Culture, by Sao Htun Hmat Win, DRA, Yangon
In This Very Life: The Liberation Teachings of the Buddha, by Sayadaw U Pandita
Living Dharma: Teachings of Twelve Buddhist Masters, ed Jack Kornfield
The Long View: An Excursion into Buddhist Perspectives, by Suratano Bhikkhu (T Magness)
The Mind and the Way, by Ajaan Sumedho
Religion and Legitimation of Power in Thailand, Laos, Burma, ed Bardwell L Smith
Theravada Buddhism in Southeast Asia, by Robert C Lester
Things as They Are, by Maha Boowa Nyanasampanno
What the Buddha Taught, by Walpola Rahula

Two good sources of publications on Theravada Buddhism are the **Buddhist Publication Society** *(w www.lanka.com/dhamma/bps/bps.htm; PO Box 61, 54 Sangharaja Mawatha, Kandy, Sri Lanka)* and the **Barre Center for Buddhist Studies** *(w www.dharma.org/bcbs.htm; 149 Lockwood Rd, Barre, MA 01005, USA).*

On the Internet, an excellent source is **Access to Insight** *(w www.accesstoinsight.org/index.html)*, from which you can freely download many publications (including many English translations from the Pali canon), all cross-indexed by subject, title, author, proper names and even Buddhist similes. Two other recommended Internet sites with lots of material on Theravada Buddhism include **Buddha Net** *(w www.buddhanet.org)* and **DharmaNet International** *(w www.dharmanet.org).*

To get an interesting and informative look at the unique Burmese spin on Buddhism, check out w www.myaing.com/weizzar.

See Meditation Study in the Facts for the Visitor chapter for a discussion of monasteries and meditation centres in Myanmar where foreigners may study *satipatthana vipassana*, a highly systematic style of Buddhist meditation.

Nat Worship

The widespread adoption of Buddhism in Myanmar suppressed, but never replaced, the pre-Buddhist practice of *nat* (spirit) worship. Originally animistic – associated with hills, trees, lakes and other natural features – the Burmese nat has evolved into a spirit that may hold dominion over a place (natural or human-made), person, or field of experience. Orthographically, the written Burmese word nat is derived from the Pali-Sanskrit *natha* (lord or guardian), though this spelling may have overlaid an existing indigenous term. Despite the continued efforts of some Buddhist leaders to downgrade the nat cult, it remains an important dimension of everyday Burmese life.

Before King Anawrahta came to power in Bagan in the 11th century, it was common for the Burmese to build small shrines or spirit houses dedicated to land nat who were displaced by the construction of houses, monasteries or other buildings, or by the planting of rice and other crops. The owners or tenants of the buildings made daily offerings of food, incense and flowers at the shrines to placate these 'guardian' nat. Unpropitiated, such nat might cause misfortune to befall the land's human tenants.

Separate, larger shrines were built for a higher class of nat, descended from actual historic personages (including previous Thai and Bamar kings) who had died violent, unjust deaths. These suprahuman nat, when correctly propitiated, could aid worshippers in accomplishing important tasks, vanquishing enemies and so on. A few Hindu *devas* (spirit-beings) and Mahayana Buddhist *bodhisattvas* – each with its own magico-religious function – also participated in the nat pantheon.

In his push to make Theravada Buddhism the national faith, King Anawrahta tried to ban nat worship in Bagan, which was (and still is) the strongest bastion of spirit worship in Myanmar. As part of his anti-nat campaign, he ordered the destruction of all nat shrines in the kingdom, and banished all Hindu images to a desecrated Vishnu temple renamed Nathlaung Kyaung (Monastery of the Prisoner Nat). He also forbade the practice of animal sacrifice at nearby Mt Popa, a volcanic outcropping considered the abode of the 36 most powerful human nat. Instead of abandoning their belief in nat, however, the Bamar merely took their practices underground, rebuilding the guardian nat shrines in their homes.

Realising he was turning the people away from Buddhism, rather than destroying their faith in the nat, the king rescinded his total ban and allowed nat images and shrines on paya grounds. He himself led the way by placing images of the 36 nat from Mt Popa at the base of the sacred zedi of Shwezigon. To these universally recognised 36, Anawrahta added a 37th, Thagyamin, a Hindu deity based on Indra, who he crowned 'king of the nat'. Thagyamin thus outranked the previous nat king, Mahagirinat (Lord of the Great Hill, a reference to Mt Popa). Since, in traditional Buddhist mythology, Indra paid homage to Buddha on behalf of the Hindu pantheon, this theistic insertion effectively made all nat subordinate to Buddhism.

Anawrahta's scheme worked, and today the commonly believed cosmology places Buddha and his teachings at the top, with the Hindu and Bamar nat in second and third place. In spite of the nat' lower position in the hierarchy, the Burmese nat cult is nearly as strong as ever. The Burmese merely divide their devotions and offerings according to the sphere of influence: Buddha for future lives, and the nat – both Hindu and Bamar – for problems in this life. A misdeed, for example, might be redressed by offerings made to Thagyamin, who once a year records the names of those who perform good deeds in a book made of gold leaves, and of those who do evil deeds in a book made of dog skin. Offerings to Thurathati (Sanskrit: *Saraswati*), a nat in charge of education, may help a student pass a tough exam.

Since the Bagan era, the house guardian nat has stayed indoors and merged with Mahagiri to form Eindwin-Min Mahagiri (Lord of the Great Mountain [who is] in the House). In most homes, this dual nat is represented by a large, unhusked coconut, which is dressed with a red *gaung baung* (turban), perfumed, and hung from a pillar or post somewhere in the house. This nat must receive daily offerings from the house's inhabitants; for many Burmese, this is the only nat worshipped on a regular basis. Other nat, particularly in Bamar-dominated central Myanmar, have shrines in paya or monastery grounds which receive occasional offerings only during pilgrimages, or bimonthly full-/new-moon visits.

Some of the more animistic guardian nat remain outside home and paya. A tree-spirit shrine, for example, may be erected beneath a particularly venerated old tree, thought to wield power over the immediate vicinity. These are especially common beneath larger banyan trees *(Ficus religiosa)*, as this tree is revered as a symbol of Buddha's enlightenment; an offering made to a banyan nat conveniently doubles as a Buddhist offering. A village may well have a nat shrine in a wooded corner for the propitiation of the village guardian spirit. Such tree and village shrines are simple dollhouse-like structures of wood or bamboo; their proper placement is divined by a local *saya* (teacher or shaman), trained in spirit lore.

Knowledge of the complex nat world is fading fast among the younger Burmese generation, many of whom pay respect only to the coconut-head house guardian. Red and white are widely known to be nat colours; drivers young and old tie red and white strips of cloth onto the side-view mirrors and hood ornaments of their vehicles for protection from the nat. Those with a general fear of nat will avoid eating pork, which is thought to be offensive to the spirit world. The main fear is not simply that spirits will wreak havoc on your daily affairs, but rather that one may enter your mind and body, then force you to perform unconscionable acts in public – acts that would cause other Burmese to shun you. Spirit possession – whether psychologically induced or metaphysical – is a real phenomenon in Myanmar.

Staunch Burmese Buddhists claim to pay no attention to the nat, as if the nat didn't exist. On close questioning, however, they will usually admit this is only because they 'outrank' nat due to their adherence to Buddhism, and thus they have no reason to fear them. It is commonly believed that Buddhists can stay out of the nat's reach as long as they keep the five lay precepts against lying, stealing, killing, harmful sexual behaviour and intoxication. In particular, drunkenness is considered an invitation to spirit possession.

Nat Festivals On certain occasions, the nat cult goes behind simple propitiation of the spirits (via offerings) and steps into the realm of spirit invocation. Most commonly, this is accomplished through *nat pwe* (spirit festivals), special musical performances designed to attract nat to the performance venue. Nearly all indigenous Burmese music is designed for this purpose; the 'classical' forms seen in tourist restaurants came relatively late in the country's music history. When enough money is available, a nat pwe may be hosted the night before a *shinpyu* (Buddhist novice ordination ceremony) as a way of receiving the nat' blessings – perhaps, on some level, even asking the nat' permission for the novice ordination. Often the nat pwe is part of a variety of musical, dramatic and comedic performances that last from dusk till dawn; those spectators who object to nat pwe (or are fearful of the nat world) can then leave during the nat pwe and return later for the rest of the show.

The nat like loud and colourful music, so nat pwe musicians bang away at full volume on their gongs, drums and xylophones, producing what sounds like some ancient form of rock and roll. Such music lures the nat to the vicinity of the pwe, but it still takes a spirit medium, or *nat-gadaw* (literally, nat wife), to make one materialise. Most nat-gadaw are either women or male transvestites who sing and perform special dances that invite specific nat to possess them. Once possessed they continue to sing and dance while in trance, often performing various feats that 'prove' a spirit has taken them over – such as dancing with a large bowl of water balanced on their heads or bending over backwards to snatch an offered K100 bill with their mouths. The highly entertaining androgyny displayed by some nat-gadaw brings the spectacle even closer to rock and roll, à la Mick Jagger or David Bowie at their most outrageous.

Every nat pwe is accompanied by a risk that the invited spirit may choose to enter, not the body of the medium, but one of the spectators. One of the most commonly summoned spirits at nat pwe is Ko Gyi Kyaw (Big Brother Kyaw), a drunkard nat who responds to offerings of liquor imbibed by the nat-gadaw. When he enters someone's body, he's given to lascivious dancing, so a chance possession by Ko Gyi Kyaw is especially embarrassing. We attended a nat pwe near Lawkananda Paya in Bagan, in which Ko Gyi Kyaw possessed a 14-year-old girl in the audience. Her family was mortified when she began dancing drunkenly around the tent, her longyi flapping away immodestly to show her legs.

Once possessed by a nat, the only way one can be sure the spirit won't return again and again is to employ the services of an older Buddhist monk skilled at exorcism – a process that can take days, if not weeks. Without undergoing such a procedure, anyone who has been spirit-possessed may carry the nat stigma the rest of their lives. Girls who have been so entered are considered unmarriageable unless satisfactorily exorcised. Nat-gadaw who choose to devote their minds and bodies to nat possession, and thus live on the fringe of normal Burmese society, usually have a history of involuntary nat trance. By the time they become spirit mediums, they're considered strong enough to handle such trance states.

Though nat pwe are commonly held with festivals throughout Bamar Myanmar, the grandest of all occur during the annual nat festival in Taungbyone, about 20km north of Mandalay. Held each August (more specifically for six days up to and including the full moon of Wagaung, the fifth lunar month) since Anawrahta's reign, the Taungbyone festival honours the so-called Muslim Brothers, Byat-wi and Byat-ta, two of the most famous nat from the Bagan era. Nat-gadaw and nat devotees from all over Myanmar convene in a Woodstock-like collection of tents for a week of drinking, wild music and nat possession. Another nat festival, rather smaller than the one at Taungbyone, follows immediately afterwards at Yadana-gu, a paya south of Amarapura. This one revolves around the ritual bathing of nat images on the banks of the Ayeyarwady River; many festival-goers arrive by sampan from Amarapura.

Other Religions

Among non-Buddhist Burmese citizens, 5% are animist, 4.5% Christian, 4% Muslim and 1.5% Hindu. Most Muslims and Hindus, as well as many Christians, are of Indian descent and live in the larger towns and cities.

Most other Christians in Myanmar are found among the tribal minorities, though the majority of the tribal people remain animist. Christian missionaries have been active in Myanmar for over 150 years. The American Baptists were first on the scene, but they had little success in converting Buddhists. Ethnicities who traditionally practised animism were more receptive to conversion, however, especially the Kayin, Kachin and Chin. Catholic and Anglican missionaries were also active in Myanmar.

With such religious diversity, it's not surprising that there is sometimes friction between religious groups. In October 2001, riots between Buddhists and Muslims caused the government to impose temporary curfews in Taungoo and Pyay.

LANGUAGE

Myanmar's official language is Burmese, the language of the Bamar majority. Speakers of Burmese and related dialects comprise nearly 80% of the population. Making up another 10% of the population are speakers of Tai languages, which include the Shan, Khün, Tai Lü and even a little-known group of Lao living near Payathonzu – descendents of refugees from Lao-Siamese wars in the 19th century. Linguists estimate that there are 107 languages spoken within the borders of Myanmar.

Travellers will find basic English widely spoken in urban areas and around popular tourist sites such as Bagan. Learning a few words of Burmese will make your travel in Bamar-majority areas much more enjoyable. Travellers who have spent some time in northern Thailand or Laos and learned some of the respective languages will be pleasantly surprised to find that many of these words are understood in the Shan State as well. See the Language chapter later in this book for an in-depth look at the Burmese language.

Facts for the Visitor

SUGGESTED ITINERARIES

With the exception of the Myeik Peninsula from Mawlamyaing (Moulmein) to Kawthoung, Myanmar's asymmetric shape doesn't lend itself to simple, linear north-south or east-west routes. Depending on your interests and available time you might pick from the following circuits or combine parts of several to create your own travel route.

The standard tourist visa is valid for 28 days, though only a relatively small percentage of visitors stay that long. This is usually enough for most people but you can get two extensions of 14 days each, for an additional 28 days. Still want to see more of Myanmar? Fly back to Bangkok and get a new visa – there is no mandatory waiting period between visas.

Note that some of the suggested itineraries may involve the use of government-owned transport (see the boxed text 'Government-Owned Services' in the Getting Around chapter for more information).

The following itineraries assume you want to see as much of the country as possible within a given interval. Another approach would be to spend more time in a few places rather than less time in many. Depending on your inclinations, you might decide to spend a full two weeks or even more just exploring the Mandalay-Bagan (Pagan) area. If you're into mountains and minority cultures, several weeks in the Shan State could be very rewarding. Unlike in neighbouring Thailand, where people may reside on one beach for weeks at a time, few visitors in Myanmar choose to hole up in one place for their entire stay.

The majority of visitors begin their journeys in Yangon (Rangoon), but some decide to save the capital until after they've seen other parts of the country. On the other hand, upcountry Myanmar will probably seem less overwhelming if you spend some time acculturating in Yangon first.

We hope there's enough information and evaluation in this guide for you to make up your own mind about where to go during your sojourn in Myanmar. However, if you're unsure of how and where to allot your time, the suggestions below may help. Keep in mind one major caveat for all Myanmar travel: transport delays are entirely normal throughout the country, so always be prepared to alter your itinerary in the face of unforeseen events such as railway repairs, road washouts, cancelled flights and bad weather.

One Week

Yangon, Mandalay & Bagan For a short Myanmar sampler, start with a two-day taste of Yangon's heavily gilded *paya* (pagodas) and urban intensity, then travel to the former royal capital of Mandalay by bus or plane (skip the train, as it's not time efficient) to take in the city's historic Mahamuni temple. The several smaller royal cities surrounding Mandalay are must-sees as well. Two days in Mandalay will suffice for people in a hurry. From Mandalay you can then shift to Bagan by plane, bus, boat or chartered car to revel in Myanmar's greatest archaeological site, a wide plain studded with *pahto* (temples or shrines) and *zedi* (Buddhist stupa) dating from the 10th to 14th centuries. After one or two nights in Bagan, it's back to Yangon to catch your return or onward flight. If you intend to spend two nights in Bagan, you'll have to fly to Yangon to complete this circuit in a week.

Yangon, Bago & Kyaiktiyo A less touristy and less hurried alternative to the Yangon-Mandalay-Bagan circuit would be to head east from Yangon to Bago (Pegu) – home to a huge reclining Buddha and one of the more important zedi in the country – and onward to the famous 'golden rock' mountain-top shrine at Kyaiktiyo. One night each is enough for Bago and Kyaiktiyo, thus leaving more time for Yangon at the beginning and end of the trip. All travel along this circuit can be done by road, using public or private transport, or by train.

A more ambitious eastern route would continue on from Kyaiktiyo to Mawlamyaing, once colonial Burma's most important teak port and an engaging southern Myanmar city of Mon-style paya and historic mosques.

Two Weeks

With two weeks at your disposal you could accomplish both of the previously described one-week circuits back-to-back or spend more time in either Bagan or Mandalay (perhaps adding the hill station of Pyin U Lwin, formerly Maymyo, northeast of Mandalay). Or choose one of the week-long suggestions and add one of the following:

Delta & Western Beaches After completing one of the week-long circuits, start again in Yangon and head west into the huge Ayeyarwady (Irrawaddy) Delta. The scenic overnight boat trip to Pathein (Bassein) is highly recommended, and after a night there you can reach Chaungtha by road in a couple of hours. Staying there one or two nights will leave enough time to continue north along the coast to Ngapali for another couple of days' beach time before catching a flight back to Yangon. Or do the trip in reverse, starting in Ngapali and working your way down the coast and through the delta. During the rainy season parts of this road may be washed out.

Another way to visit these areas is to plan a road circuit from Yangon to Pyay (Prome), then Pyay to Ngapali, down to Chaungtha and Pathein, and back to Yangon. This saves the cost of a flight between Ngapali and Yangon, and allows you to fit in Pyay since it's considerably faster to travel between Pathein and Yangon by road than by boat. You could also proceed instead in the other direction, from Yangon to Pathein and around to Pyay.

Meiktila or Thazi to Inle After doing Mandalay or Bagan, double back to Meiktila or Thazi by road, and then take a week to cover the eastern road out to Inle. Stop at the former British hill station of Kalaw and the Pindaya caves along the way. From Inle you can either fly back to Yangon (via the nearby market town of Heho) or schedule an extra day for the long bus ride(s).

Pyin U Lwin, Hsipaw & Lashio If you want to get a little more off the beaten track in the Shan State, skip Inle and spend a few days in and around Hsipaw, a charming centre for Shan culture, with a side trip to the Shan/Chinese market town of Lashio. Road travel is the most efficient way to reach Hsipaw and Lashio, but railroad bridge buffs may want to sacrifice travel time to ride the rails across the historic Gokteik Viaduct. On the way out of Mandalay, a stopover in the quirky former 'hill station' of Pyin U Lwin is worthwhile.

If the road from Lashio south to Loilem, then west to Taunggyi, ever opens up to foreign visitors, one could make a very interesting and efficient loop from Mandalay to Lashio, then to Inle and back to the centre via Kalaw and Pindaya.

Mrauk U or Pyay The archaeologically minded could skip the beaches, lakes and hill stations and spend their second week at Myanmar's second greatest Buddhist ruins site, Mrauk U (Myohaung). This area is accessible to tourists via flights to Sittwe (Akyab) from Yangon, or you can go overland via Pyay to Taunggok where a ferry runs to Sittwe. Flights between Bagan and Mrauk U are also a future possibility, and this would save having to backtrack to Yangon before hopping on the flight to Sittwe.

If you don't want to spend an entire week in Mrauk U and Sittwe, add more time to your first week in Bagan, perhaps including the smaller ruins site at Salay. Or take a one-night trip from Yangon to Pyay and visit the archaeological site at Thayekhittaya.

One Month

Ruins, Hill Stations & Beaches In a month you can sample many of Myanmar's major highlights. After a few days in Yangon, take a bus or car north with a stopover in Taungoo or Pyinmana, then on to Mandalay, Pyin U Lwin and Bagan. Then head east into the Shan State to experience either the Inle circuit or the Pyin U Lwin–Lashio route. Of course you could do this route in reverse.

[Continued on page 68]

Highlights

Highlights

RYAN FOX

JOHN ELK III

JOE CUMMINGS

RYAN FOX

BERNARD NAPTHINE

RICHARD I'ANSON

HIGHLIGHTS

Current visa regulations permit visitors to stay 28 days (up to 56 days with extensions), allowing time to see close to the full range of Myanmar's plentiful attractions. Still, because of the hassles with road travel and flight delays, it usually pays to be under-ambitious with one's travel plans: don't try to see too much in too short an interval, or your travels will quickly become a chore.

Virtually everyone begins their journey in Yangon (Rangoon). Yangon is a good place to become accustomed to the climate, food and everyday customs before heading upcountry.

Your recreational and aesthetic inclinations will largely determine which direction you take upon leaving Yangon. The basic threads most visitors follow include historic temple architecture, handicrafts, hiking, beaches and culture. These interests are not necessarily mutually exclusive, though it's hard to find one place that has them all!

Historic Temple Architecture

Myanmar's most magnificent temple ruins are of course those at Bagan (Pagan), the country's No 1 tourist attraction and for decades the most popular photo subject for tour brochures and posters. Nearby Salay boasts a little-known set of ruins from the same period, easily visited as a day trip from Bagan.

Nearly as impressive in form and style, if not in number of ruins, are the massive Mrauk U (Myohaung) temples near Sittwe (Akyab) in the Rakhaing (Arakan) State, which sees relatively few tourists. In local colour some people may in fact find Mrauk U superior to Bagan, though recent restoration work on a couple of the major temples has diminished much of the romance of the ruins.

Mandalay is surrounded by the ancient cities of Inwa (Ava), Amarapura, Sagaing and Mingun, all easily visited on day trips. Though not as old or impressive in scale as Bagan and Mrauk U, the atmosphere at the old Mandalay temples is energised by the continued worship of the local population.

Early stupas (Buddhist religious monuments) at the former Pyu capital of Thayekhittaya (Sri Ksetra) near Pyay (Prome) rank fourth in architectural interest and are the most accessible of all the ancient capitals from Yangon. Additional Pyu ruins can be seen at the more obscure – and more off-the-beaten-track – sites of Beikthano and Hanlin. See the Architecture section in the Facts about Myanmar chapter for more information on art and archaeological styles.

Title page: 18th-century frescoes at Hpo Win Daung caves, Sagaing Division (Photograph by Corey Wise)

Clockwise from top left: Ancient pagoda in Bagan region; market at Mawlamyaing; parasol making, Pathein; Intha fisherman, one of the famed 'leg-rowers' of Inle Lake; Maungmagan Beach, Tanintharyi Division; Kuthodaw Paya (World's Largest Book), Mandalay

Handicrafts

Myanmar's incredible ethnic diversity means a wide range of handicrafts are available for study or purchase throughout the country. As the culture and business capital of northern Myanmar, Mandalay has been the main handicrafts centre for over a hundred years. You'll find virtually every type of craft produced in the immediate region, as well as materials from throughout the north. Mandalay specialities include silverwork, woodcarving, stone sculpture, *kalaga* (embroidered tapestries), Burmese marionettes and jade work.

The Shan State is the country's centre for hand-rolled cheroots (Burmese cigars) and for the ubiquitous embroidered shoulder bags carried by practically every Burmese. Bagan is renowned for its lacquerware and antiques.

Multicoloured cotton *longyi* (a loom-woven length of cloth draped around the lower body and legs and tied at the waist) can be found in municipal markets throughout the country, but the most interesting Burman patterns seem to be those produced in small central Myanmar towns such as Inma, Yezin, Pakokku and Lindwin. The various frontier states, ie, the Kachin, Kayah, Mon, Kayin and Rakhaing States, produce patterns unique to their regions.

Beaches

Although Myanmar's coastline is the longest in mainland Southeast Asia, only the Ayeyarwady Division and Rakhaing State sections stretching from the Ayeyarwady River Delta northwest to Sittwe are so far commonly visited by foreigners. Because of the lengthy travel times involved, stays of at least one night are necessary at most seaside areas. Most suitable for overnight visits are Ngapali, Chaungtha, Kanthaya and Letkhokkon. Between these points you'll find plenty of other beaches, but few facilities and no 'licensed-for-foreigners' accommodation.

During the rainy season from June to November, many of the roads in these areas may be washed out and impassable. Only Ngapali is accessible by air. Ngapali is the most attractive beach of the four; the closer you get to the delta, the muddier the beaches become – Letkhokkon being the muddiest.

The beaches and islands south of Mawlamyaing (Moulmein), off peninsular Myanmar, have incredible recreational potential and are just beginning to open up. The drawback so far is that there is virtually no accommodation available at any of the beaches along the Myeik Peninsula or Myeik Archipelago. One of the easiest ways to see these areas is on a liveaboard cruise, all of which are based in Phuket, Thailand. See Diving & Snorkelling in the Activities section of the Facts for the Visitor chapter for more detail on cruising the Myeik area.

Culture

One of the main joys of travelling through Myanmar comes from soaking up the general cultural ambience, which is plentiful throughout the country. You'll obtain less in terms of Burmese culture if you spend most of your time sitting around in foreigner-frequented guest-houses and restaurants in Yangon and Mandalay, both of which are rapidly modernising. Try going to a small to medium-size town well off the main tourist circuit, staying at a local hotel, and eating in Burmese curry shops and tea-shops. It's not as easy as going with the crowd but you'll learn a lot more about the country.

Other Highlights

The Mon State's Kyaiktiyo Paya – the famous, stupa-topped gilded boulder perched on a mountain cliff – is fairly accessible these days and is a favourite among visitors interested in Myanmar's syncretic, animistic Buddhism. Mt Popa, the 'home of the *nat*' (spirits) near Bagan, holds a similar lure although the overall atmosphere runs far behind that at Kyaiktiyo.

The old Mon capital of Bago (Pegu) – with the second-largest reclining Buddha in the country and a highly revered stupa – makes an easy day trip from Yangon or a stopover on the way to Kyaiktiyo.

Inle, in Shan State, offers a nice variety of old Shan temples, boat tripping and relaxed evenings with nothing much to do except walking to the edge of town for a little stargazing before bed.

[Continued from page 64]

With roughly a week left in your itinerary, fly to Ngapali, enjoy a few days at the beach, and then work your way down the western coast through Chaungtha and Pathein back to Yangon.

Want more ruins? Skip Chaungtha and Pathein, and spend your fourth week on the Mrauk U/Pyay circuit described previously. Of course, this would require more internal flights.

East by Southeast If beach resorts don't matter much to you, go for a major intake of culture by starting with the Bago and Kyaiktiyo circuit, then continue eastward to Mawlamyaing's captivating blend of colonial, Indian, Kayin and Mon influences. From Mawlamyaing, continue by road or rail to the old tin port of Dawei (Tavoy), assuming the road is open (it was not at the time of writing). While in Dawei, don't miss Myanmar's largest reclining Buddha, and Maungmagan, perhaps Myanmar's longest undeveloped beach. From Dawei you can catch a flight farther south to Myeik (Mergui), one of Southeast Asia's most historic ports. After seeing Myeik you can either fly back to Yangon to finish your trip, or continue on another plane to Kawthoung at Myanmar's southeasternmost tip. Although Kawthoung has little of interest to offer the traveller, you can exit Myanmar and enter Thailand by boat here, thus avoiding any backtracking to Yangon.

Two Months

In two months you can combine several of these itineraries to link different regions in Myanmar. If Kachin culture interests you, add Bhamo and Myitkyina in northern Myanmar's Kachin State. Neither of these towns is of huge intrinsic interest, unless you manage to arrive during a *manao* (Kachin festival). However, the train trip from Mandalay to Myitkyina or the boat trip from Mandalay to Bhamo are unparalleled in Myanmar in terms of stimulating experiences. A side trip to Katha would be of interest to fans of George Orwell. Both trips are possibly time-consuming; flights are available from Mandalay, but if you fly you'll miss what could be the best parts of these trips.

PLANNING

When to Go

Climate-wise, the best season for visiting most of Myanmar falls between November and February – during these months it rains least and is not so hot.

The cool hill stations of the Shan State or the wind-swept Rakhaing (Arakan) State or Tanintharyi (Tenasserim) Division coasts are best visited when the rest of Myanmar is miserably hot, from March to May. Bagan, Mandalay and the rest of the 'dry zone' in central northern Myanmar can be nearly intolerable during these months. During the height of the monsoon season, from July to September, the dry zone gets less rain and humidity than the rest of the country, while roads along the delta region southwest of Yangon, as well as anywhere along the coast, can become impassable.

The peak months for tourist arrivals are December, February, July and August. The least-crowded months – though as yet Myanmar never actually seems to be overcrowded – are May, June and September.

Where You Can Go

Travel anywhere in the standard tourist circuit – Yangon, Mandalay, Bagan, Inle, Taunggyi – and to any points between or near these destinations is freely allowed for anyone holding a valid passport and tourist visa. This includes places just off the main linking routes, such as Bago, Pyay, Shwebo, Magwe, Monywa, Taungoo and Pyinmana – basically any place in central Myanmar between the Shan Yoma (Shan Range) to the east and the Ayeyarwady (Irrawaddy) River to the west, plus most places in the Ayeyarwady Delta region – Pathein, Twante, Thanlyin (Syriam) and Letkhokkon.

Several other places farther off the beaten path that used to require travel permits no longer require them. These include Bhamo, Myitkyina, Kyaiktiyo, Mawlamyaing, Dawei and Myeik, all of which required permits as recently as five years ago.

Travel to certain other places in Myanmar requires a permit – actually a typed letter stamped with various government seals – issued by the Ministry of Hotels and Tourism (MHT) and approved by the Ministry of Defence. Such permits are available directly from Myanmar Travels & Tours (MTT) in Yangon or through many Yangon travel agencies. There's no charge for the travel permit itself but the catch is that a permit won't be issued unless you arrange for the services of a paid government guide. Travel agencies work similarly; you must contract the services of a government guide or driver before they'll arrange for a permit.

In March 1997 the government finally published an official list of places that are open only to 'package' travel and places open to 'foreign independent travellers'. This list remains unchanged at the time of writing, but there's no way to know how or when it might change in the near future. Most places in the country are now open to individual, nonpackage travellers. Places open only to people who purchase package tours include Muse and Namkham in the northern Shan State. These areas are Myanmar-China border crossings and are for the most part used by Chinese tourists, although in theory any nationality may arrange to travel in them.

Only two states – Kayah and Chin – are entirely off-limits for all tourists, with or without a permit or whether on tours or alone. Certain parts of the Shan State, Kayin State, Mon Division and Tanintharyi Division are also off-limits – usually those areas with active ethnic insurgency or banditry, or where travel conditions are so bad that the government fears for Myanmar's international reputation as a potential tourist destination. Parts of the Shan State, Mon State and Tanintharyi Division fit all three of these criteria. Some areas are off-limits simply because the government doesn't want travellers to visit.

It's obvious that the most touchy destinations are in frontier areas where the headquarters of the few remaining ethnic insurgencies are based. In some of these areas – for example, between Taunggyi and Kengtung in the Shan State – military checkpoints placed at close intervals along every government-controlled road leading into these areas catch anyone who tries to enter from either end.

For specific information see Dangers & Annoyances later in this chapter as well as the relevant destination chapters later in this book.

Even *with* a permit, there's no guarantee the local authorities won't give you the boot – as happened to several visitors to Myitkyina in 1995. That year MTT was issuing permits to Myitkyina with the caveat that upon your arrival, the Myitkyina authorities could arbitrarily refuse entry. For other places, like Mawlamyaing, permits would be easy to get one week and impossible the next, depending on the level of rebel activity in the area. Although visiting either of these places no longer requires a permit, the same principle may still apply in places that do require them.

Once you arrive, permit in hand, at your destination, there are other papers to be filled in. Since these places also require the services of a guide, your guide should take care of these procedures.

Any or all of this could change overnight, especially as Myanmar's frontier areas become more 'secure' following cease-fire agreements with insurgent groups or military victories over other groups. By the time you read this, travel restrictions may have loosened considerably – or things could have gone the other way. Most likely the constant passport checking will persist as long as the ruling junta maintains its warlord mentality.

Maps

Country Maps Good, up-to-date maps of Myanmar are difficult to find outside Myanmar. In Yangon you can pick up the full-colour, folded *Tourist Map of Myanmar*, published on coated stock by Design Printing Services (DPS), from many hotels and bookshops. Sometimes it's free, sometimes it costs up to K1000. All major towns, cities and roadways are clearly marked on this map, and it's relatively up-to-date. The Myanmar government's Survey Department publishes a very good paper sheet map of the country, simply entitled *Myanmar*, with a scale of 1:2,000,000. Although this map is a little large to carry around in a day-pack and the noncoated paper decays rapidly, it's good for general reference. You'll occasionally find it for sale from the footpath book vendors on Pansodan Rd in Yangon.

Periplus Editions' *Myanmar Travel Map*, is a similar folded map that looks better in terms of detail, accuracy and consistency, and is available worldwide.

The inferior and more costly Nelles' *Myanmar*, a folded map on coated stock, contains many errors but is also easily available outside Myanmar so that you can play with it before you arrive.

Myanmar's Survey Department also publishes a multipage 1997 *Myanmar Atlas*, complete with colour relief but labelled in Bamar language only. This atlas provides the most up-to-date and detailed set of maps available. You may find it for sale among the Pansodan Rd book vendors.

City Maps DPS publishes very useful and fairly detailed city maps of Yangon, Mandalay and Bagan. As with its *Tourist Map of Myanmar*, these city maps are printed on durable coated stock and are available from various hotels and bookshops in Yangon, and to a lesser degree in Mandalay and Bagan. If you anticipate spending a lot of time in the capital, look for a new DPS bilingual atlas, *The Map of Yangon*, a detailed street and place directory.

MTT also prints city maps oriented towards tourists, but they tend to be out-of-date and less detailed. These maps are available from the MTT office in Yangon on Sule Paya Rd, or from individual MTT offices in these respective cities.

What to Bring

Even at the height of the cool season you'll rarely need anything more than a sweater while on the plains – and probably only for the nights in Bagan, where it can get a little chilly. It can get rather cold up in the hill country, so if you're going to Pyin U Lwin or Inle bring a warm sweater or light jacket. In Myitkyina and Bhamo in the Kachin State, which lie above the tropic of Cancer, it can get downright cold in the winter months; consider buying a heavy jacket in Mandalay before heading up there during this season. A light sleeping bag might also be useful in other parts of the Shan State, especially in Kalaw and Taunggyi where the one or two blankets per person supplied by guesthouses is not always enough during the cool season.

Otherwise it's normal tropical gear – lightweight, but 'decent', clothes. Myanmar is a prim, conservative country; shorts (particularly when worn by women) or short skirts are inappropriate.

When travelling in Myanmar, we strongly advise that you wear sturdy sandals or thongs (flip-flops) rather than shoes – simply because you take them off and put them on so often when visiting temples and paya. Remember that the sunlight is intense in Myanmar – protect your head in open places like Bagan, or when out on Inle Lake. Mosquitoes can be a major irritant, so bring insect repellent, mosquito coils or even a mosquito net.

Bring any items you feel may not be available in Myanmar – mosquito repellent, film, batteries and medicines are the most likely examples. Simple toiletries like soap, toothpaste and toilet paper are readily available; in fact toilet paper is much easier to find and cheaper than in India.

An unsewn *longyi* (sarong) can be a very handy item; it can be used to sleep on or as a light bedspread (many guesthouses don't supply top sheets or bedspreads), as a makeshift 'shopping bag', as a turban/scarf to keep off the sun and absorb perspiration, as a towel and as a small hammock – to name just a few of its many functions. However, unsewn *longyi* are not appropriate street attire. Be sure to have them sewn into a tube before wearing them in public.

If you plan to wash your own clothes, bring along a universal sink plug, a few plastic clothes pins, and plastic hangers or 3m of plastic cord for hanging your washing.

A small but strong padlock is useful for locking your room in small upcountry guesthouses where locks aren't provided.

Tampons etc Burmese women don't use tampons, and they are almost impossible to find outside Yangon. If you use them, bring them with you. If you're coming through Bangkok, the more upmarket pharmacies there may carry Tampax-brand tampons. Sanitary napkins are widely available from minimarts and supermarkets in Thailand, but not in Myanmar.

TOURIST OFFICES

Local Tourist Offices

Myanmar Tours and Travel (MTT), formerly known as Tourist Burma, is part of the Ministry of Hotels and Tourism (MHT) – the official government tourism organisation in Myanmar. Its **main office** (☎ *01-275328, 278386, fax 282535; 77/91 Sule Paya Rd)* is beside the Sule Paya in Yangon. You should be aware that the government profits from your use of MTT services.

MTT has improved its service to travellers over the years and now has an assortment of brochures and leaflets, as well as train and plane timetables and costs for government-run hotels.

Apart from the main Yangon office there are also MTT desks in Mandalay, Bagan, Nyaungshwe (Yaunghwe) and Taunggyi. Until the early 1990s it was the only travel agency in the country; it now competes with over 100 private travel agencies.

With the privatisation of the tourist industry, it's no longer difficult to avoid MTT while travelling round Myanmar. Two of its remaining monopolies are express train tickets between Yangon and Mandalay and express boat tickets between Mandalay and Bagan, neither of which can be purchased by a foreigner except through MTT (or its representatives at the station/pier). But in both cases there are alternatives to using MTT transport, so even here you can bypass the bureaucrats.

In areas where, until 1995, your only choice for a place to stay was a hotel owned by the MHT (eg, Mawlamyaing), there are now plenty of private hotels or guesthouses. This time around we didn't find any place in the country where you had to stay in an MHT-owned hotel. Even in little-visited Dawei and Myeik, none of the foreigner-approved accommodations were government-run or government-owned. See the Accommodation section later in this chapter for more information on where to stay.

Just as the MHT has sold off almost all its hotel properties, there are rumours it may dissolve MTT in the face of competition from better-run travel agencies.

Tourist Offices Abroad

Myanmar maintains no branches of the MTT abroad, although most Myanmar embassies and consulates around the world disseminate limited tourist information.

VISAS & DOCUMENTS

Passport

Entry into Myanmar requires a passport valid for at least six months from the time of entry. If you anticipate your passport expiring while you're in the country, you should obtain a new one before arrival or inquire from your government whether your embassy in Myanmar (if one exists – see the list of foreign embassies later in this chapter) can issue a new one after arrival.

Visas

The Myanmar government issues 12 types of visitor visas and border permits, including such quaint-sounding ones as 'caravan trader permit', 'seasonal mahjis permit' and 'frontier visa'. Leisure travellers are issued the tourist visa, which is now valid for four weeks (28 days) and is readily available through most Myanmar embassies or consulates abroad. At the embassy in Bangkok you can usually obtain a visa the day after you apply for it. The simple application process requires two passport-size photos and around US$10 to US$18 for the visa fee.

Be mindful that you have to exchange a nonrefundable minimum of US$200 upon arrival into Foreign Exchange Certificates (FECs; this requirement is waived for package-tour visa holders). Most visitors spend their FECs on hotels, train and plane tickets; the average individual easily spends this much when staying three weeks or

Visa Applications

Myanmar's embassies and consulates abroad are scrupulous in checking out the backgrounds of anyone applying for a tourist visa. In particular, writers and journalists may have a difficult time obtaining visas. Therefore it is probably not a good idea to list your occupation as any of the following: journalist; photographer; editor; publisher; motion-picture director or producer; cameraperson; videographer; or writer. Of course plenty of journalists and photographers do get into the country – by declaring a different profession on the visa application.

Myanmar foreign missions may also be suspicious of anyone whose passport shows two or more previous visits to Myanmar in the same five-year period. Obviously the government can't believe anyone would want to visit Myanmar more than once or twice! In cases like these you'll need more of a reason than simply 'tourism' for receiving another visa. We won't suggest any alternatives here, but we encourage you to be creative.

Joe Cummings

more. FECs may also be exchanged for *kyat*, the national currency, at the free-market rate – see the Money section later in this chapter for details.

Beware of travel agents in Bangkok (especially on Khao San Rd) who will try to sell you a 'special visa' (often said to be a business visa) or other type of visa that would exempt you from the US$200/200FEC exchange requirement. Only holders of tourist visas bearing the stamp 'package tour EVT' are exempt from the FEC requirement. Yes, some agencies are able to obtain this type of visa – but don't pay any extra charges till you see the visa first.

Visa Extensions Although some Myanmar embassies abroad will say tourist visa extensions aren't permitted, once in Myanmar you can usually extend your visa up to 14 days beyond the original 28-day validity, and then extend again for an additional 14 days once the first extension has expired. The type of permit issued for such extensions is called a 'stay permit'. To be granted an extension, your passport must be valid for six months after the end of your planned stay in Myanmar. Of course, this is at the discretion of the Department of Immigration and Manpower in Yangon. Note that Yangon is the only place where you can extend your visa. The usual procedure requires five photos plus payment of a US$36 fee for each 14-day extension. Allow two or three days for the extension to go through. Keep in mind that policies concerning visa extensions seem to change frequently.

If you overstay your visa by a day or two due to unavoidable transport difficulties, there's usually little hassle at Yangon or Mandalay international airports, but be prepared to part with some cash for the time you overstayed. The usual fine (or fee) is US$3 per day. Be sure to allow yourself plenty of time at the airport to complete the paperwork involved or you might miss your flight.

Onward Tickets

Myanmar immigration does not seem very concerned with whether or not you arrive with proof of onward travel. Legally speaking all holders of tourist visas are *supposed* to carry such proof. In over 20 years of frequent travel in and out of Myanmar, our onward travel documents haven't been checked once.

Travel Insurance

A travel insurance policy to cover theft, loss and medical problems is a wise idea. There is a wide variety of policies and your travel agent will have recommendations. The international travel policies handled by STA Travel and other student travel organisations are usually good value. Some policies offer lower and higher medical expenses options but the higher ones are chiefly for countries, like the USA, which have extremely high medical costs.

Driving Licence & Permits

Myanmar does not allow tourists to drive motorised vehicles, so you won't need a driving licence.

Paper Games

Wherever you go in Myanmar, your passport is likely to be checked frequently. In fact every airport arrival, anywhere in the country, requires a passport-and-visa check and the filling in of some papers with your name, passport number and visa number. Hotel staff also check passports and visas. At the airport in Sittwe we once had our passports checked by no less than five different people, each of whom wrote our names, passport numbers and visa numbers in ledgers or on little scraps of paper! The scraps of paper were just the corners torn from a plain sheet of paper.

At some point in your Myanmar travels, you come to realise that the country is still run like a loose-knit collection of warlord states. Even when you're just moving from one Bamar-majority division to another, your papers are checked. On top of this, every time you enter a small town or village by car, someone appears to exact a tribute from the driver in the form of a 'road tax'. The same happens for Burmese road travellers.

Joe Cummings

Student Cards

Several readers have reported receiving discounted entry fees for monuments in Myanmar upon presentation of the International Student Identity Card (ISIC). We've never heard of anyone receiving a discount for any other type of student or youth card. We predict that as more foreign visitors try to receive discounted entry fees with ISIC cards, the government will be forced to formulate policy regarding student discounts. In which direction they will go – either allowing such discounts or declaring the cards invalid for Myanmar – remains to be seen.

Hostel & Seniors' Cards

Myanmar recognises neither of these cards for discounts.

International Health Card

These are no longer recognised by many countries and, in fact, medical authorities in some Western countries no longer issue them. In Myanmar the authorities no longer ask to see them at the airport, although visitors from African countries may be asked to show a certificate of yellow fever vaccination. These need not appear on the World Health Organization's (WHO) yellow card; any hospital or clinic stationery will do.

Photocopies

It's a good idea to keep photocopies of all vital documents – passport data and Myanmar visa page, credit card numbers, airline tickets, travellers cheque serial numbers and so on – in a separate place from the originals. In case you lose the originals, replacement will be much easier to arrange if you can provide issuing agencies with copies. You might consider leaving extra copies of these documents with someone at home or in a safe place in Yangon or another point of entry.

EMBASSIES & CONSULATES

Myanmar Embassies & Consulates

Addresses of Myanmar's embassies and consulates include:

Australia (☎ 02-6273 3811) 22 Arkana St, Yarralumla, ACT 2600
Bangladesh (☎ 02-60 1915) 89B Rd No 4, Banani, Dhaka
Canada (☎ 613-232 6434/46) Apt 902–903, 85 Range Rd, The Sandringham, Ottawa, Ontario K1N 8J6
China (☎ 010-6532 1584/6) 6 Dong Zhi Men Wai St, Chaoyang District, Beijing 100600
France (☎ 01-42 25 56 95) 60 rue de Courcelles, 75008 Paris
Germany (☎ 30-206 1570) Zimmerstrasse 56, 10117 Berlin
India (☎ 11-688 9007/8) No 3/50F Nyaya Marg, Chanakyapuri, New Delhi 110021
Indonesia (☎ 021-327 684, 314 040) 109 Jalan Haji Agus Salim, Jakarta Pusat
Israel (☎ 03-517 0760) 26 Hayarkon St, Tel Aviv 68011
Italy (☎ 06-854 9374) Viale Gioacchino Rossini, 18, Int 2, 00198 Rome
Japan (☎ 03-3441 9291) 8-26, 4-chome, Kita-Shinagawa, Shinagawa-ku, Tokyo 140-0001
Laos (☎ 021-314910) Thanon Sok Pa Luang, PO Box 11, Vientiane

Malaysia (☎ 03-456 0380) 10 Jalan Mengkuang, 55000 Kuala Lumpur
Nepal (☎ 01-521 788) Chakupat, Patan Gate, Lalitpur, Kathmandu
Philippines (☎ 02-817 2373) 4th floor, Xanland Center, 152 Amorsolo St, Legaspi Village, Makati, Manila
Singapore (☎ 6735 0209) 15 St Martin's Dr Singapore 257996
Switzerland (☎ 022-731 7540) 47 Ave Blanc, 1202 Geneva
Thailand (☎ 022 337 250) 132 Thanon Sathon Neua, Bangkok 10500
UK (☎ 020-7629 6966, 7499 8841) 19A Charles St, London W1X 8ER
USA (☎ 202-332 9044/5/6) 2300 S St NW, Washington, DC 20008
Vietnam (☎ 04-823 2056) Bldg No A-3, Ground floor, Van Phuc Diplomatic Qrtrs, Hanoi

Embassies & Consulates in Myanmar

Yangon can be a good place to get visas for other countries: because it isn't a big tourist stopover, visas are usually issued quickly. However, embassies for neighbouring countries accept only US dollars for payment of visa fees.

Australia (☎ 01-251810, 251809, fax 246159) 88 Strand Rd
Bangladesh (☎ 01-526145, 515272) 11B Thanlwin Rd, Kamayut Township
Canada Affairs handled by Australian embassy
China (☎ 01-221281) 1 Pyidaungsu Yeiktha Rd
France (☎ 01-212523, 212532) 102 Pyidaungsu Yeiktha Rd
Germany (☎ 01-548951, fax 548899) 32 Natmauk Rd
India (☎ 01-282933) 545–547 Merchant St
Indonesia (☎ 01-254465, 254469) 100 Pyidaungsu Yeiktha Rd
Israel (☎ 01-515155, fax 515116) 15 Kabaung Rd, Hlaing Township
Italy (☎ 01-527100) 3 Inya Myaing Rd, Golden Valley
Japan (☎ 01-549644, 549645) 100 Natmauk Rd
Laos (☎ 01-222482) A1 Diplomatic Quarters, Taw Win Rd
Malaysia (☎ 01-220249) 82 Pyidaungsu Yeiktha Rd
Nepal (☎ 01-545880, fax 549803) 16 Natmauk Rd
Netherlands Affairs handled by German embassy
New Zealand Affairs handled by UK embassy
Pakistan (☎ 01-222881) 4A Pyay Rd

Your Own Embassy

It's important to realise what your own embassy – the embassy of the country of which you are a citizen – can and can't do to help you if you get into trouble. Generally speaking, it won't be much help in emergencies if the trouble you're in is remotely your own fault. Remember that you are bound by the laws of the country you are in. Your embassy will not be sympathetic if you end up in jail after committing a crime locally, even if such actions are legal in your own country. In genuine emergencies you might get some assistance, but only if other channels have been exhausted. For example, if you need to get home urgently, a free ticket home is exceedingly unlikely – the embassy would expect you to have insurance. If you have all your money and documents stolen, it might assist with getting a new passport, but a loan for onward travel is out of the question. Some embassies used to keep letters for travellers or have a small reading room with home newspapers, but these days the mail holding service has usually been stopped and even newspapers tend to be out of date.

Philippines (☎ 01-664010) 50 Pyay Lan
Singapore (☎ 01-525688, 525700) 326 Pyay Rd
Sri Lanka (☎ 01-222812) 34 Taw Win Rd
Sweden Affairs handled by UK embassy
Switzerland Affairs handled by German embassy
Thailand (☎ 01-533082, 512017) 45 Pyay Rd
UK (☎ 01-281700, 281702, fax 289566) 80 Strand Rd
USA (☎ 01-282055, 256020, fax 280409) 581 Merchant St
Vietnam (☎ 01-548905) 36 Wingaba Rd

CUSTOMS

Besides personal effects, visitors are permitted to bring in the following items duty free: 200 cigarettes (or 50 cigars, or 250g of unrolled tobacco), a quart (0.94L) of liquor and 500mL of cologne or perfume. Cameras (including video cameras), radios and cassette players can be brought into the country, but they're supposed to be declared on arrival and taken out upon departure. In reality no-one ever seems to check and if you try to declare your cameras on arrival you're usually waved on through.

Any foreign currency in excess of US$2000 must be declared upon entry. Mobile phones may be confiscated and held by customs personnel on arrival at Yangon international airport and returned upon your departure. If you're holding a tourist visa, bringing a laptop computer into Myanmar may make customs officials suspicious that you are a journalist, and the laptop may be confiscated. Visitors arriving on a business visa don't seem to have this problem.

See Export Restrictions in the Shopping section at the end of this chapter for a list of items that cannot be taken out of the country.

MONEY

Currency

Myanmar uses three currencies, two of which are legal tender for everyone, one of which Burmese citizens need a licence to use. All three currencies are strongly linked to the US dollar and the Japanese yen.

Kyat The first is the everyday national currency, called kyat (pronounced chat) and divided into 100 *pyas* with a confusing collection of coins that is no longer in circulation because the kyat has decreased in value so much over the last decade. In 2000 it was announced that K50 and K100 coins would be issued, but we've yet to see any in circulation. At present the following kyat banknotes were in use: K1, K5, K10, K15, K20, K45, K50, K90, K100, K200, K500 and K1000.

A sum of 100,000 is called *thein* in Burmese, so K100,000 is thein kyat; the Indian term *lakh* (100,000) is also common.

Foreign Exchange Certificates (FECs) Until recently it has been mandatory to exchange US$200 for 200 FECs (Myanmar's second legal currency) on exiting the airport immigration checkpoint at Yangon and Mandalay, but recently travellers have reported that this is no longer required.

Printed in China, the Monopoly-like FEC notes are issued by the Central Bank of Myanmar 'for the convenience of tourists visiting Myanmar'. FECs come in denominations equivalent to US$1, US$5, US$10 and US$20. Note that the government benefits from your purchase of FECs; this is its main way of obtaining hard currency.

Payment for FECs is accepted in US dollars, pounds sterling, Australian dollars, Canadian dollars, Swiss francs and Japanese yen – all in cash – or in US dollars or British pounds only travellers cheques. Credit cards may also be used to purchase FECs at the Yangon international airport; a tiny branch of the Foreign Trade Bank in the arrivals area can perform the transaction. When you buy FECs with travellers cheques a 2% fee is levied on the transaction. Only travellers cheques issued by these banks are accepted in Myanmar: MasterCard, American Express (AmEx), Bank of Tokyo, Citicorp, Visa, Bank of America, National Westminster Bank, Swiss Bankers and Commonwealth Bank of Australia.

One US dollar always equals one FEC; the rate for other currencies fluctuates according to dollar variance. Along with the FECs you'll also receive a Foreign Exchange Certificate Voucher, which you'll only need to save if you plan to convert more than US$200 at the official rate. Reconversion of FEC to US dollars or British pounds sterling is legal only for conversions in excess of US$200 and only when accompanied by the FEC voucher. It used to be possible sometimes to exchange surplus FEC back into US dollars at hotels in Mandalay and Yangon, but since US dollars began getting a higher exchange rate than FEC for free-market kyat, it's become a highly doubtful prospect. Other currencies? Forget it.

FECs can be spent anywhere in Myanmar. Unlike with US dollars, no special licence or permit is necessary for a citizen of Myanmar to accept FECs. Officially approved hotel rooms, airlines, Myanma Railways (most stations) and larger souvenir shops require payment either in US dollars or FECs. So the required US$200 purchase of FECs is not necessarily something to avoid, since they can be used to pay hotel and transportation costs.

FECs can also be exchanged for kyat – at the free-market rate – at hotels, shops or from moneychangers that accept FEC. If you run out of FECs while on the road, MTT is, or course, quite happy to sell you more. FECs may also be purchased at the Central Bank of Myanmar and the Foreign Trade Bank in Yangon, and at government-owned hotels.

On the other hand, FECs aren't absolutely necessary for Myanmar travel, and if you can avoid purchasing them, do so. The staff at the FEC exchange booth at Yangon airport will sometimes permit couples to exchange US$200 for both persons rather than US$200 each. Some individuals have also got away with buying less than the US$200 minimum – this usually involves the offering of a 'present' to the staff behind the exchange counter – figure on at least US$10.

This entire complicated system revolves around the desire of virtually every Burmese person – and of course the government – to get their hands on hard currency, commonly referred to as FE (foreign exchange, pronounced like one word, effee).

Note that just a few years ago, the amount of US dollars that one had to exchange into FEC on arrival was US$300. If, as we've heard may happen soon, the government banishes FECs and goes to a straight exchange rate, none of this will matter anymore.

Note also that the old scheme of buying whisky and cigarettes at Bangkok airport's duty-free shop to sell for free-market kyat is no longer necessary. In fact you'll lose money if you do it! These items are usually less expensive in Yangon than in Bangkok.

US Dollars The FE most desired is the US dollar, Myanmar's third currency – and the most basic to the country's overall economy. Other currencies are accepted for purchase of FECs (see earlier) but for anything else, US dollars are best. In fact, most other currencies get a poor rate of exchange on the free market. Legally speaking, cash dollars can only be accepted by establishments possessing a licence to accept US dollars. In reality all merchants are quite happy to take them. They can also be used to exchange for kyat from licensed moneychangers, at hotels, or on the black market.

Exchange Rates

Depending on where you exchange your US dollars or FEC, there are different rates of exchange. At the time of writing, the rate offered at banks throughout the country was K490 for US$1 or one FEC. On the free market, ie, in hotels and shops, the exchange rate was K700 for one US dollar or K640 for one FEC – note that US dollars get a better exchange rate than FECs when converting to kyat on the free market. Black-market moneychangers, ie, the guys on street corners, were offering slightly better rates; K720 for one US dollar and K670 for one FEC. Not surprisingly, the government was doing its best to shore up the value of the kyat by clamping down on the black-market moneychangers; they were much more furtive in their approach than in the past. Since black-market moneychangers are known for their trickery (short changing is common), it makes sense to do your currency exchanges with hotels or shops.

Exchange rates vary from day to day, sometimes by as much as K50 per dollar, so you need to keep tabs on the rate if you have enough cash on hand to wait for an optimum rate. The rate is usually best in Yangon and Mandalay – typically 5% to 10% higher than the rest of the country. If you want to check the current free-market rate of exchange for US dollars or FECs to kyat before you leave for Myanmar, check out W www.myanmarpyi.com.

Note that the following rates are only rough estimates based on the rate of the US dollar for kyat at time of publication; note also that it is illegal to bring kyat into the country.

country	unit		kyat
Australia	A$1	=	521
Canada	C$1	=	612
China	Y1	=	113
euro zone	€1	=	871
Hong Kong	HK$1	=	120
Japan	¥100	=	751
New Zealand	NZ$1	=	438

Singapore	S$1	=	526
Thailand	B100	=	2215
UK	UK£1	=	1381
USA	US$1	=	950

Exchanging Money

Since the information below was compiled, travellers have reported being unable to exchange travellers' cheques, access funds through ATMs or use credit cards in Myanmar. However, the situation may change.

FEC vs Cash US Dollars Since US dollars get a better free-market rate than FECs, you can maximise your return by reserving FECs for hotel, train and air payments, and using US dollars to buy kyat. Obviously with the difference in exchange rates, hotels and shops would much rather you pay in US dollars. We've heard of smaller hotels politely refusing to accept FECs in hopes that tourists will pay with cash dollars. If this happens, politely insist on paying in FECs. Hotels usually won't push the matter since they are breaking the law by refusing FECs for payment.

When buying kyat on the free market, you'll get better rates for crisp US$100 bills than for any other denomination or currency. The next most wanted are US$50 notes, after which the rate may drop again – so in effect there are three different free-market rates, one for bills less than US$50, one for US$50 and another for US$100.

When to Change If you're newly arrived, ask around for the going rate before changing large amounts. It's best to ignore moneychanging touts at the airport – just use cash US dollars for the taxi into Yangon. Some people bring a few kyat purchased in Bangkok to pay for a bus into town if they're pinching pennies. There's a slight risk here, since it's illegal to bring kyat into Myanmar, but it's rare that anyone is searched on entry. Once in town you can check into a hotel or guesthouse using FECs or US dollars, then ask other travellers what the current rate is.

Where to Change When you're ready to change US dollars or FECs, it's safest to change in hotels or shops rather than on the street. Unscrupulous moneychangers, who usually hang around Sule Paya and outside Mahabandoola Garden in Yangon, are very good at short-changing new arrivals for several thousand kyat. Unless you want to get fleeced, give them a wide berth. Always count the kyat before releasing your US dollars/FECs. And take your time counting: short changing is all the easier with K15, K45 and K90 notes in the mix, as these are hard for first-time visitors to add up quickly.

ATMs So far only one bank in Myanmar, Mayflower, has automated teller machines (ATMs), but these work only for cards issued on Mayflower savings or cheque accounts, and are found only in central Yangon. It's unlikely international ATMs will be established soon, as this would make it somewhat easier for foreign residents and visitors to circumvent Myanmar's banking system and exchange controls.

Credit Cards AmEx, Diners Club, Visa and JCB are the only international credit cards accepted in Myanmar. Of these, Visa seems to be the most hassle-free. MasterCard withdrew in 1998. It is now possible to use credit cards to pay for stays in some mid-range hotels and for purchases in upmarket shops in Yangon and Mandalay. There is usually a fee of 6% for credit-card transactions. The Foreign Trade Bank (and some hotels) will allow you to use a credit card to purchase FECs. The Foreign Trade Bank branch at the airport in Yangon accepts credit cards for the exchange of US dollars for FECs on arrival, which was previously mandatory.

All transactions paid for with foreign credit cards in Myanmar are charged in US dollars, then converted to your home currency by the card's bank of origin.

In 1995 Myanmar Oriental Bank and Yoma Bank became the first private, Burmese-owned banks to issue credit cards. These cards charge in kyat only. Customers must deposit K100,000 to open a credit-card account at either bank.

Travellers Cheques Travellers cheques issued by the following banks are accepted in Myanmar: MasterCard, American Express (AmEx), Bank of Tokyo, Citicorp, Visa, Bank of America, National Westminster Bank, Swiss Bankers and Commonwealth Bank of Australia. As with credit cards, travellers cheques are increasingly easier to use in Myanmar. All of the upmarket hotels accept them. A modest 2% fee is levied on transactions involving travellers cheques.

Banking Myanmar now has around 20 private, locally owned banks, plus 38 foreign banks with representative offices. So far, none of the latter are permitted to handle foreign currencies.

Of the private Burmese-owned banks, only the Cooperative Bank, Mayflower Bank, Myanmar Industrial Development Bank, Myanmar Citizen Bank, Myanmar Livestock and Fisheries Development Bank, Myawaddy Bank, Yangon City Bank, Yoma Bank and Yadanabon Bank are currently permitted to manage US dollar accounts. Mayflower appears to be the best managed and most service-oriented. There is a 10% 'tax' on such accounts.

Security

Give some thought in advance as to how you're going to organise your finances – whether travellers cheques, cash, credit and debit cards, or some combination of these. Many travellers favour hidden pouches that can be worn beneath clothing. Hip-pocket wallets are easy marks for thieves. Pickpockets work markets and crowded buses throughout the country, so it pays to keep your money concealed. See Dangers & Annoyances later in this chapter for more on petty crime.

It's a good idea not to keep all your money in one place; keep an emergency stash well concealed in a piece of luggage separate from other money.

Costs

Travel in Myanmar continues to get cheaper as more private businesses compete to attract tourist dollars. Costs depend largely on where you decide to go, how you decide to get there, and in which hotels you choose to stay.

Goods and services may be priced either in kyat or in US dollars/FECs. Hotel rooms, some train tickets, air tickets, car rental and guide services are generally priced in US dollars/FECs – for some of these services, US dollars/FECs may be the only currencies accepted. Duty-free items at the airport are also priced in US dollars/FECs. Food, taxis, buses and just about everything else in Myanmar are priced in kyat. In keeping with this two-currency system, prices in this guidebook are quoted in either US dollars or kyat; any time US dollars are quoted, FECs are equally acceptable.

Daily Expenses Over the last few years inflation in Myanmar has been high, but this hardly affects visitors using US dollars. Meals are cheap if you avoid restaurants attached to upmarket hotels. Figure on paying US$4 or US$5 worth of free-market kyat per day for food.

Now that the hotel industry has been privatised, it's possible to get rooms in well-touristed areas of Myanmar for as little as US$3 per person per night, comparable with the rest of Southeast Asia. Virtually all hotels licensed to accept foreigners accept only US dollars or FECs for room payments. A few hotels in very out-of-the-way places will allow you to pay entirely in kyat, but the price of a room in such places will be pegged to a US dollar rate, so don't expect to be paying pennies for a bed.

Upmarket hotels and larger tourist restaurants add a 10% hotel and restaurant tax plus a 10% service charge to the bill. Public ground transport is generally inexpensive and so slow that you're unlikely to be able to spend more than US$5 a day on long-distance movement. Using domestic air transportation speeds things up considerably but prices average US$50 to US$160 per flight.

Although it's difficult to pin down a one-figure travel budget due to all the variables in the equation – particularly whether or not your desired itinerary requires a guide – you can expect to spend a rock-bottom minimum of about US$10 a day. This assumes always taking the cheapest room available, using public ground transport (avoiding express services), never using the services of a guide, staying clear of places that require buying package tours, and eating in local restaurants and teashops rather than hotel restaurants or places geared to foreign tourists.

A comfortable budget for those seeking the extra convenience of a private, rather than shared, bathroom, the occasional use of a freelance guide (but not a package) and a broader range of restaurant choices, would be around US$20 a day. Taking express ground transport and flying a couple of domestic air routes might add another US$5 or US$7 per person per day for anyone staying the full 28-day period permitted under the current tourist visa regulations.

Moving farther upmarket you could easily spend US$25 to US$50 per day on the more well-appointed hotels and guesthouses – and in Yangon there are an increasing number of US$75 to US$125 a night places.

Locally purchased travel packages that include guide services, accommodation and meals cost a minimum of US$25 per person a day, or as much as US$100 a day for more deluxe tours.

Inflation It's important to remember that Myanmar has an annual inflation rate of about 30% to 50%, so any prices quoted in kyat in this book will need to be adjusted accordingly. One of the easiest and most accurate ways to calculate overall price increases is to check the price of a cup of tea in a typical Burmese teashop – such prices are more or less standard throughout urban Myanmar. In 2001, for example, you could sip a cup of tea for K40; a year later the same cup of tea had increased to K50. If this formula holds, a cup of tea in 2004 will cost about K70 and a trishaw ride cited in this guidebook as costing K500 would have increased to around K800 – and so on.

Tipping & Bribes

Tipping as known in the West is not customary in Myanmar. However, minor bribes – called 'presents' in Burmese-English (as in 'Do you have a present for me?') – are part of everyday life and can be seen as the moral equivalent of tipping, except that the range of services covered differs completely. Much as tips are expected for a taxi ride or a restaurant meal in the West, extra compensation is expected for the efficient completion of many standard bureaucratic services. A visa extension or customs inspection will move a little more quickly if a present – a little cash – is added.

If a flight is 'sold out', US$10 (or the kyat equivalent) – might buy a seat. Want to ride in the front seat of a passenger pick-up truck instead of crammed in the back? Add 30% to 50% of the regular passenger fare.

In some cases a present may be requested for no special service at all – just to get a government worker to do his or her job. Some visitors refuse to pay in such cases, though from the Burmese perspective you're liable for the unwritten 'leisure class tax' because of your relative wealth. You may have earned your meagre travel budget washing dishes at the dingiest dive in London, but to the Burmese your presence in Myanmar automatically means you're well-off. The same happens to Burmese of obvious means, so it's not always a case of 'foreigners pay more'. The major exception is when it comes to hotels and plane or train transport, where foreigners really get soaked relative to what locals pay.

No matter how this system might bruise your sensibilities, you probably won't get through a Myanmar trip without paying at least a couple of minor bribes – even if you're not aware you've paid.

Touts

As in Thailand and other countries in Southeast Asia, Myanmar has its share of touts who take a commission for each customer they manage to steer toward shops and other businesses, such as car-hire services. The practice is most prevalent in Mandalay where most trishaw drivers act as touts for shops selling handicrafts and antiques. This means that the trishaw driver who brings you to the shop will expect the shopkeeper to give him a commission for bringing in some business. Of course, the cost of this commission (sometimes as high as 50% of the price of a purchase) is passed onto the buyer. It's kind of a hassle, but the best way to avoid this is to go on a 'window shopping' expedition, taking care to get business cards from the shops in which you want to make purchases. Visit the same shops later using a different trishaw driver (and the business cards to help you relocate the shops) and the shopkeepers will no longer be under pressure to pay a commission, since you've already visited their shops and found your own way back. Trishaw drivers in Mandalay also act as touts for drivers with vehicles for hire. If you need a driver, try asking at your hotel instead of taking up a trishaw driver's offer to help you find one. In Yangon, virtually all the black market moneychangers also act as touts for cars for hire.

Taxes & Refunds

Other than the 10% hotel tax, there are no consumer taxes in Myanmar. Companies based in Myanmar are taxed at a flat 30% of adjusted gross income while branches of companies based outside Myanmar are exposed to a sliding scale of 5% to 40% depending on income. Capital gains are taxed at 10% for resident firms, 40% for non-resident firms. Import taxes vary from 0% to 25%. None of these taxes are refundable.

POST & COMMUNICATIONS

Post

Most mail out of Myanmar seems to get to its destination quite efficiently. Or at least we think so: a number of letter writers either agreed that everything they sent arrived OK (even from upcountry) or totally disagreed, saying that nothing at all arrived.

International postage rates are a bargain K35 per postcard to anywhere in the world. The cost of mailing letters is slightly higher, depending on the weight. There is a free poste-restante service on the 2nd floor of the main post office in Yangon.

Officially post offices all over Myanmar are supposed to be open Monday to Friday from 9.30am to 4pm, but in reality, the staff open and close when they feel like it. As a general rule of thumb, the smaller the town, the more the post office deviates from the official schedule. Yangon's main post office keeps fairly rigorous hours; elsewhere it's often difficult to get any kind of service after 3.30pm. In some places it's worse than that; the post office in Kawthoung appears to stay open only an hour or so in the morning, regardless of advertised hours. Most likely the staff are out trying to earn some real money!

Embassies in Yangon recommend that if you are sending any important correspondence in or out of Myanmar you should send it by air freight rather than trust the mail. Some reliable agents are **DHL Worldwide Express** *(☎ 01-664423; 7A Kaba Aye Pagoda Rd, Yangon • ☎ 02-39274; Mandalay)* and **ASAP Express Services** *(☎ 01-228468; 82 8th St, Yangon)*. For larger air or sea freight shipments, **Express Air & Sea Transportation Co** *(EAST; ☎ 01-296098; 100 123rd St, Yangon)* is recommended.

Telephone

Domestic Calling other places in Myanmar is relatively simple and very inexpensive from the **Central Telephone & Telegraph office** *(CTT; cnr Pansodan & Mahabandoola Sts, Yangon)*. Only larger cities with area codes can be direct-dialled. Smaller towns still use manual switchboards, so you must ask the national operator to connect you to a specific town operator, then request the local number. These numbers are usually listed with the name of the town. The telephone number for the Inle Inn in Nyaungshwe, for example, is 'Nyaungshwe 16' – which means you must first be connected with the operator in Nyaungshwe, then ask for the number 16.

A government-regulated mobile cellular phone service is available, but costs – billed in US dollars only – are high compared to elsewhere in the world. All cell phone (hand phone) numbers begin with the code 09.

International There are two ways to make an international call. The fast and expensive

Area Codes

The country code for Myanmar is ☎ 95; the area code for Yangon is ☎ 01, for Mandalay ☎ 02. You need to dial the zero when calling from within Myanmar. Other cities with area codes include:

Aungban	☎ 081
Bagan	☎ 062
Bago	☎ 052
Chauk	☎ 061
Dawei	☎ 036
Heho	☎ 081
Hinthada	☎ 044
Hpa-an	☎ 035
Kalaw	☎ 081
Kyaukse	☎ 066
Lashio	☎ 082
Loikaw	☎ 083
Magwe	☎ 063
Mawlamyaing	☎ 032
Meiktila	☎ 064
Minbu	☎ 065
Monywa	☎ 071
Myeik	☎ 021
Myingyan	☎ 066
Myitkyina	☎ 074
Nyaungshwe	☎ 081
Pakokku	☎ 062
Pathein	☎ 042
Pyay	☎ 053
Pyinmana	☎ 067
Pyin U Lwin	☎ 085
Sagaing	☎ 072
Sittwe	☎ 043
Taunggyi	☎ 081
Taungoo	☎ 054
Thanlyin	☎ 065

way is to use an International Direct Dial (IDD) phone, available in certain hotels in Yangon, Mandalay and Bagan. Calls are charged by the minute, usually at about US$6 to US$7 to anywhere outside of Asia.

The cheaper way is to call from the CTT office in Yangon or Mandalay, or from privately owned long-distance services found mostly in Yangon. Calls to North America are US$5 per minute, while a call to Europe or Australia is US$4 per minute, and Japan and Thailand are US$3 and US$2 per minute respectively.

The CTT phone offices are open from 7am to 6pm weekdays and 8am to 4pm weekends and holidays.

The number of hotels that furnish IDD phones is increasing rather quickly, especially in Yangon and Mandalay. Most mid-range hotels and even some budget guesthouses have IDD service available near reception. The larger Yangon hotels – eg, The Strand, Traders and Equatorial – feature in-room IDD phones, as well as small business centres where guests may make international calls. All add steep service charges onto the regular phone company rates. The Strand permits nonguests to use its business centre, which is open 24 hours, but calls are highly surcharged. Waiting is the norm even at the hotels, since not more than one IDD line is usually available.

Fax

You can also make surcharged phone and fax calls at the **International Business Centre** (*☎ 01-524811, fax 667157; 88 Pyay Rd, Yangon*). Sponsored by the Ministry of Forestry, the International Business Centre has a range of secretarial and business services in addition to basic telecommunications. Fax machines are also available at the CTT office, and many hotels.

Note that if you bring your own fax machine to Myanmar, or purchase one in Yangon or Mandalay to use there, you're supposed to register the machine with the government – though in everyday practice few people do. The International Business Centre can help with registration, or contact the CTT office in Yangon. Note that if you arrive from overseas with a fax machine and a tourist visa, you will certainly be questioned about your intentions.

eKno Communication Service

Lonely Planet's eKno global communication service provides low-cost international calls – for local calls you're usually better off with a local phonecard. eKno also offers free messaging services, email, travel information and an online travel vault, where you can securely store all your important documents. You can join online at **W** www.ekno.lonelyplanet.com, where you will find the local-access numbers for the 24-hour customer-service centre. Once you have joined, always check the eKno website for the latest access numbers for each country and updates on new features.

Email & Internet Access

At the moment, the World Wide Web is not available to the general public. The government does provide an email service, which costs a very steep US$290 to set up, plus US$60 annual dues, plus US$1 per hour of online use. No other service provider is permitted to set up email services, so it's unlikely prices will be dropping any time soon. The government currently offers limited Internet access, similar to the heavily screened access officially available in China.

Despite the cost of getting set up, the number of hotels that offer email service via their private account is growing. Prices vary – the more expensive the hotel, the more they charge for sending and receiving email. Top-end hotels charge by the kilobyte – typically between US$1.50 to US$2.50 per kilobyte (you can squeeze about three or four short sentences into each kilobyte). Mid-range hotels may charge as little as US$2 per message, no matter how many kilobytes it is.

DIGITAL RESOURCES

The World Wide Web is a rich resource for travellers. You can research your trip, hunt down bargain air fares, book hotels, check on weather conditions or chat with locals and other travellers about the best places to visit (or avoid!).

You'll find that the **Lonely Planet website** has an up-to-date Myanmar page at **W** *www.lonelyplanet.com/destinations/south_east_asia/myanmar*. It also offers travel advice, commentary and the Thorn Tree bulletin board, where you can ask questions before you go or dispense advice when you get back. You can also find travel news and updates to many of our most popular guidebooks, and the subWWWay section links you to the most useful travel resources elsewhere on the Web.

One of the best websites we've seen – simply because it carries so many links to other Myanmar-related sites – is called **Ayezay** (**W** *www.ayezay.com/)*. The copious data on geography, travel, business, history, politics, computers and current Myanmar news found on this site is also unique in that it presents several different perspectives on the country, from gung-ho investment news to human-rights reports. Similar websites include **KaByar** (**W** *www.kabyar.com)* and **Nagani** (**W** *www.nagani.com)*.

Naturally the Myanmar government has its own site, called **Myanmar Home Page** (**W** *www.myanmar.com)*, which, despite all the expected government propaganda, contains some hard info on travel and country statistics.

The **Myanmar Times website** (**W** *www.myanmar.com/myanmartimes)* is an abbreviated rundown of the weekly newspaper, including a helpful listings section with current information on hotels, shopping, entertainment and activities in Yangon. There is also an up-to-date schedule for domestic flights.

Also worth a look for its US-dollar-to-kyat exchange-rate information is **Myanmarpi.com** (**W** *www.myanmarpyi.com)*. This site also has a link to CNN.com that enables you to check the weather and temperature in over 30 places in Myanmar.

Other good sources of information include the **Bangkok Post** (**W** *www.bangkokpost.co.th)*, the **Democratic Voice of Burma** (**W** *www.communique.no/dvb)*, **Anti Slavery International** (**W** *www.antislavery.org)*, the **International Labour Organisation** (**W** *www.ilo.org)*, the **Burma Peace Campaign** (**W** *www.burmapeacecampaign.org)*, **Worldview Rights** (**W** *www.worldviewrights.com)* and the **Irrawaddy** (**W** *www.irrawaddy.org)*.

Human Rights–Based Websites

Of the many non-government organisations (NGOs) featuring Myanmar in their web pages, the most interesting are **Free Burma** (w *www.sunsite.unc.edu/freeburma/index.html*) and **The Burma Project** (w *www.soros.org/bur ma.html*). The latter is sponsored by George Soros' Open Society Institute. These sites will give you an idea of the mountain of information available out there regarding human rights in Myanmar. Both sites are openly dedicated to bringing down the current regime in Myanmar and stopping all foreign investment and tourism, at any cost. Addresses for many known rebel groups are included.

Few reports carried on these sites contain independently verified information. Many features, facts and interpretations – particularly on the Free Burma site – are in fact sourced from Burmese refugees living abroad. This does not mean that the reports are false or even exaggerated, it just means that for now most of it must be classified as anecdotal. Both sites mix in occasional mainstream news items from Reuters, Associated Press and so on.

Other sites with human-rights information include the **Burma Action Group** (w *www.burmacampaign.org.uk*), the **Free Burma Coalition** (w *www.freeburmacoalition.org*), **Human Rights Watch** (w *www.hrw.org*), **Partners** (w *www.partnersworld.org*), the **Karen Human Rights Group** (*KHRG;* w *www.khrg.org*) and **Tourism Concern** (w *www.tourismconcern.org.uk*). There are also pages managed by the **US State Department** (w *www.state.gov*) and **Amnesty International** (*AI;* w *www.amnesty.org*).

BOOKS & PERIODICALS

The following titles are recommended reading (publishing details are not always included as they can vary globally).

Lonely Planet

In addition to this guidebook, Lonely Planet publishes the *Burmese phrasebook* by David Bradley, a pocket-sized primer to the majority language in Myanmar.

Description & Travel

Old Burma: As Described by Early Foreign Travellers, published by the University of Rangoon in 1947, collects the writings of the first Europeans to visit Myanmar, beginning with Marco Polo. Polo may have relied upon second-hand accounts rather than personal experience to describe the country he knew as 'Mien', a Chinese shortening of 'Myan-ma', in the 14th century. *Old Burma* ends with Captain Symes' stay in the court of Ava in 1795. Packed with historical trivia not found in any other single volume, this little book is out of print and difficult to find. Similar is Gerry Abbott's newer *The Traveller's History of Burma* (Orchid Press, Bangkok), which also compiles and condenses the chronicles of early European travellers in Myanmar. In this case Abbot uses the quotations of traders, priests and explorers to build a history of Myanmar from 1364 Bago to independence in 1948.

Originally published in 1954 by the Burma Oil Co, and revised for the fifth and final time in 1962, the hard-to-find *Motor Roads of Burma* contains information on motor routes all over the country, from roads still used today, such as Kyaukpadaung-Meiktila, to roads that are now seldom used (eg, the Stilwell Road to India). Although conditions have obviously changed since the book's publication, certain details, such as road distances, have not. Many of the so-called 'circuit houses' described in the book still exist as government or private guesthouses.

Tim Slessor's *First Overland* recounts the journey from London to Singapore made by two Oxford and Cambridge University –crewed Land Rovers in 1956, in which they travelled the Stilwell Road.

Historical guidebook collectors might also keep an eye out for *A Pocket Guide to Burma*, a tiny 56-page booklet distributed to British soldiers at the close of WWII, or the Burmese-produced *A Handbook on Burma* from 1968. The latter is an interesting read if for no other reason than to compare the country then with the country today. A fold-out colour map in the back of the book shows the political divisions of the time; the Kayin State is called Kawthoolei, the name the Kayin (Karen) themselves tend to call their territory. All of the current divisions (Mandalay Division, Bago Division etc) are lumped into one 'Union of

Caring for Your Elephant

One of my favourite Burmese books is *Burmese Timber Elephant* by U Toke Gale. It could be subtitled 'selection, care and use of your pet elephant', for it tells you everything you need to know and many things you don't need to know about timber elephants – even what to do with your elephant when he's in *musth*. There's a chart showing the 90 nerve centres to which an *u-zi* (elephant handler) applies pressure to control his elephant or to get it to do things. But don't press 13, 25, 60, 61 or 63, for 'the animal will be infuriated'!

Tony Wheeler

Burma' – proving the point made by the frontier ethnicities that their autonomy has eroded since independence. Another rarity is *Travellers' Guide to Burma* by Kanbawza Win, published by the YMCA in Yangon in 1977 and banned by the government shortly thereafter.

Golden Earth by Norman Lewis, originally written in 1952, is a delightful tale of a ramble around Myanmar at a time when it was both more, and less, open than it is today. At that time the varied rebellions were in full swing, but Myanmar had not yet entered its reclusive period. Much of the book sounds remarkably like Myanmar today, and the author's descriptions of Myanmar's often antiquated trucks have the real ring of truth – no photograph could do a better job of summing up these miracles of mechanical endurance.

Paul Theroux's amusing and cynical bestseller, *The Great Railway Bazaar*, includes chapters on the train trip from Yangon to Mandalay, and from Mandalay to Pyin U Lwin – with a perfect description of Candacraig (now called the Thiri Myaing Hotel), and his amusing visit to 'forbidden' Gokteik. Another witty account of pre-1988, seven-day-visa Myanmar is found in the essay 'The Raj is Dead! Long Live the Raj!' in Pico Iyer's book *Video Night in Kathmandu*.

Rory Maclean's *Under the Dragon* is a semifictional account of his travels in the Shan State in search of a Palaung basket, set against descriptions of life in 1990s Myanmar.

Early History & Politics

GE Harvey's *History of Burma* (1925) remains the classic work, although parts are naturally out of date from today's historiographical perspective. Maurice Collis, a former British civil servant stationed in Burma in the early 20th century, wrote several books chronicling particular episodes in Burma's colonial and pre-colonial history. Perhaps Collis' best books were *Siamese White*, an account of Samuel White's pernicious sojourn as harbourmaster of 17th century Mergui (now Myeik), and the harder-to-find *The Land of the Great Image*, which follows the remarkable adventures of Friar Manrique, a Portuguese Franciscan monk in 17th century Arakan (Rakhaing). *Into Hidden Burma* is a whimsical first-hand account of Collis' postings in colonial Myanmar that gives an interesting insight into the racism that plagued British rule in Myanmar.

Burma by FSV Donnison gives a concise and very readable history of Myanmar from its earliest development through the British period and into the troubled 1960s. There are also chapters on the country's economy and culture. *The Union of Burma* by Hugh Tinker is a scholarly study of the path to independence in Myanmar and the difficult U Nu period. Frank N Trager's *Burma: From Kingdom to Independence* is an equally scholarly account of this same period and its particular ramifications for Asia.

There are other more recent accounts of earlier Burmese history, such as *The Pagoda Wars* by ATQ Stewart, which covers the British takeover of Myanmar.

Amitav Ghosh's *The Glass Palace* is a bestselling introduction to Burmese history from the final British conquest right through to the present.

English-language accounts of the Burmese perspective on history, including the colonial era, are few in number but worth seeking out. *A History of Burma* by Maung Htin Aung is easily found at used bookseller's shops and stalls in Yangon. Also quite interesting is *Deposed King Thibaw of Burma in India, 1885–1916* by WS Desai. It's long out of print but copies can be purchased at the Bagan Bookshop in Yangon.

A number of books concern the dramatic events in Myanmar during WWII, particularly the behind-enemy-lines actions of Wingate's 'Chindit' forces. Find a complete description of their activities in *The Chindits* by Michael Calvert, or read Bernard Fergusson's more personal accounts in *The Wild Green Earth* or *Beyond the Chindwin*. Fergusson's more recent *Return to Burma* provides an account of the author's post-war travels in Myanmar.

The Longest War 1941–45, by Louis Allen, is an excellent and comprehensive book on the WWII campaign in Burma, probably one of the most interesting but least understood military campaigns of the war.

Essays on the History and Buddhism of Burma by Than Tun (Kiscadale Publications) covers a range of social, religious, political and economic topics within the Burmese context.

Anyone interested in colonial Myanmar's steamer era should read *Irrawaddy Flotilla* by Alister McCrae and Alan Prentice (James Paton), a history of the river fleet established by the British and still running today under the auspices of government-owned Inland Water Transport (IWT). Although the title is out-of-print outside Myanmar, reprints are available in Yangon.

Reader Recommendations

Living in Silence: Burma under Military Rule, by Christina Fink, is an intelligent study on the realities of living under an oppressive military regime. It describes how the regime maintains its power and the forms of resistance the Burmese people take.

Journalist John Pilger's *Hidden Agendas* includes two disturbing but illuminating essays on Myanmar, exposing the truth behind much of the rhetoric that surrounds the political issues, including Western economic involvement with the current regime. It's an invaluable read if you want to travel with your eyes open.

Less widely available, *Welcome to Burma: and enjoy the totalitarian experience*, by Timothy Syrota, describes his 1996 trip, which he took with a self-confessed ignorance of the military dictatorship. The honest style of writing is sometimes clumsy, but often touches on the feelings of many a first-time traveller. It's worth the hunt down.

Howard Ralley

Modern History & Politics

Two books by Myanmar expert David I Steinberg provide what is probably the most complete sociopolitical look at Myanmar between 1962 and 1988. *Burma: A Socialist Nation of Southeast Asia* (Westview Press, Boulder, Colorado) contains an overview of Burmese history, geography, ethnicity, politics and economics, while *Burma's Road Toward Development: Growth & Ideology Under Military Rule* (Westview Press) is a history of the country since 1962, when Ne Win took power.

Myanmar-watcher Martin Smith is without peer when it comes to understanding the country's political situation, and his *Burma – Insurgency & the Politics of Ethnicity* (Zed Press, London) contains an extremely well-researched history and analysis of insurgent politics in Myanmar from the 1940s through to 1988. *Burma's Golden Triangle: On the Trail of the Opium Warlords* by André & Louis Boucaud (Asia Books; or in the French, *Birmanie-Sur la Piste des Seigneurs de la Guerre*, L'Harmattan) presents a collection of accounts detailing the Boucaud brothers' travels in insurgent Myanmar in the 1970s and 1980s, along with some more recently updated material. Although it's sometimes difficult to tell which era is being covered, the book is an entertaining read.

Outrage: Burma's Struggle for Democracy by Bangkok journalist Bertil Lintner (White Lotus, London and Bangkok) chronicles the violent suppression of Myanmar's pro-democracy movement from 1987 to 1990, with particular focus on the events of 1988. It's a somewhat polemic, one-sided look at the student uprisings, but basically it's very informative. Lintner's *Land of Jade* by the same publisher describes a fascinating overland journey he and his Shan wife made through insurgent territories in northern Myanmar in 1985. The reporter's third book-length outing, *Burma In Revolt: Opium and Insurgency Since 1948* (Westview Press), discusses the relationship between opium production and insurgency among the Shan, Kayah, Pa-O, Mon, Lahu and Wa.

Edith Mirante's *Burmese Looking Glass* follows similar political terrain in yet another mid-1980s first-person account.

True Love and Bartholomew: Rebels on the Burmese Border was written by Jonathan Falla, a nurse who worked in the KNU-controlled part of Kayin State during the 1980s. His accounts of Kayin society and the culture of insurgency form an important contribution to the literature on these topics.

Freedom from Fear & Other Writings presents a sometimes brilliant collection of essays by and about Nobel Peace Prize–winner Aung San Suu Kyi. She has also published an account of her father titled *Aung San of Burma* and the hard-to-find *Let's Visit Burma* (Burke Publishing), a thin children's guide to the country. A chapter in the latter, 'My Country and People', is an excellent encapsulation of Burmese culture.

In *Dancing in Cambodia, At Large in Burma* (Ravi Dayal, New Delhi), postcolonial scholar Amitav Ghosh impresses with the length and breadth of his travels in contemporary Myanmar and his knowledge of opposition politics.

People, Culture & Society

Anyone interested in quickly obtaining a broad understanding of Burmese customs and etiquette should pick up a copy of *Culture Shock! Burma* by Saw Myat Yin (Times Editions, Singapore). One of the few titles in the *Culture Shock* series to have been written by a local, this book simply and accurately explains male and female roles, business protocol, common Burmese ceremonies and festivals, the naming system, how to extend and accept invitations, and even how Burmese perceive Westerners.

Mi Mi Khaing's *Burmese Family*, though first published in 1946 by Longman, remains one of the best references on traditional Burmese customs and values. A blend of amateur sociology and personal memoirs, this book is available in reprinted form in Yangon and Bangkok.

The Thirty-Seven Nats by Sir RC Temple, originally published in 1906 by Griggs in London, has been redone in a beautiful colour edition by Kiscadale Publications. Though it costs an astounding US$180, it's still the most venerable description of the Burmese *nat* (spirit) cult available and the colour plates provide artists' renderings of each of the 37 nat. *Nat-Pwe: Burma's Supernatural Sub-Culture* by Yves Rodrigue sheds further light on this fascinating topic and includes reproductions of the same colour plates that appear in *The Thirty-Seven Nats*.

Other notable books from Kiscadale include a new edition of *The Burman: His Life and Notions*, a fascinating collection of essays by Shway Yoe, the pseudonym of Sir JG Scott, a colonial official and specialist in Burmese botany, linguistics and archaeology. In his many years in Myanmar, Scott acquired an extraordinary knowledge about every aspect of the country. Kiscadale has also republished *The Silken East: A Record of Life and Travel in Burma*, a chronicle of travels along the Chindwin, Ayeyarwady and Thanlwin (Salween) rivers early in the 20th century by VC Scott O'Connor. Kiscadale, incidentally, devotes itself to Myanmar-related topics; for a catalogue write to Kiscadale Publications, Murray House, Gartmore, Stirling FK8 3RJ, UK.

The Soul of a People by H Fielding was an 1898 attempt to understand the Burmese. *Thibaw's Queen*, by the same author in 1899, is a romanticised story of the collapse of the final Burmese kingdom before British imperial might. It has been republished in Myanmar by the Buddha Sasana Council and is easily found.

For those interested in the Shan State or the Shan people, a mandatory read is Inge Sargent's *Twilight Over Burma: My Life as a Shan Princess*. It's about an Austrian woman who marries Sao Kya Seng, the last *sao pha* (hereditary Shan chieftain) of Hsipaw, who was arrested in 1962 and never heard from again. Like this guidebook, it's banned in Myanmar.

Somewhere in Myanmar, you may come across a mouldy 1922 booklet on elephant lore entitled *A Short Treatise on the Management of Elephants* by AJW Milroy, deputy conservator of forests for the Raj. Towards the end of WWII Longman published a series of booklets about Myanmar known as *Burma Pamphlets*. You may see some of these long-since out-of-print books on culture and customs in Myanmar; they make interesting reading.

Bamar culture as it relates to religion is well covered in *Folk Elements in Burmese Buddhism* by Maung Htin Aung (Department of Religious Affairs, 1959), reprints of which are easy to find in Yangon since it's a standard exam text for Burmese students. The book most accurately describes what occurs in villages along the Yangon-Mandalay axis and as far north as Monywa and Shwebo only; customs in outer Myanmar – even in the predominantly Buddhist Shan, Rakhaing and Mon States – differ greatly. *Burmese Supernaturalism* by Melford Spiro contains decent explanations of nat worship as well as certain Burmese Buddhist themes.

The Vanishing Tribes of Burma, by Richard K Diran, is a remarkable photographic documentation of 28 different ethnic minorities in Myanmar, including several never before recorded on film. Although this represents only around a quarter of the ethnicities found in Myanmar today, it's nonetheless an important contribution to the visual literature on the nation's multicultural milieu.

On the Road to Mandalay, edited and translated by Mya Than Tint (White Orchid, Bangkok), is a Studs Terkel–inspired collection of recent interviews with ordinary Burmese – an elephant handler, a miner, a fortune-teller, a waitress etc – in which they describe their lives, loves, hopes and dreams.

For gourmets and cooking enthusiasts, *Cook and Entertain the Burmese Way* (Myawaddy Press) by Mi Mi Khaing makes interesting reading. This volume contains a wealth of information on preparing, serving and eating Burmese food in the correct style, and includes instructions on how to mix Burmese salads by hand, recipes for 'salivators and tongue titillators', and a very useful appendix that lists fruits, vegetables, spices and fish with their Burmese and English names. It's available at bookshops in Yangon and at tourist hotels throughout the country. A slicker tome, *Under the Golden Pagoda: The Best of Burmese Cooking* by Aung Aung Taik (Chronicle Books, San Francisco) covers much the same territory.

Art, Archaeology & Design

Myanmar Style: Art, Architecture & Design of Burma by John Falconer et al pulls together many elements of Burmese art and design never seen in one volume before. Luscious photos by Luca Tettoni archive, for the first time in print, both contemporary and historical architecture, along with ritual objects, traditional crafts and everyday items such as patent medicine containers and children's toys.

The slim *Kalagas: The Wall Hangings of Southeast Asia* (Ainslie's, Menlo Park, California) by Mary Anne Stanislaw contains photographs and descriptions of the Burmese *kalaga* (tapestry) craft. Sylvia Fraser-Lu's *Burmese Crafts, Past and Present* is currently the most comprehensive volume covering handicrafts in Myanmar. Those with an interest in tribal textiles will find *Textiles of the Hill Tribes of Burma* (White Lotus, Bangkok), by Michael C Howard, an excellent source of information. Its photographs of textiles from private collections, including many rare pieces collected by American Baptist missionaries, are a valuable visual resource for collectors.

Burmese Art, written by John Lowry and published by the Victoria & Albert Museum, presents a detailed discussion of nonarchitectural art in central and northern

Myanmar from the early Bagan period through to the Mandalay period. It's illustrated with 50 black-and-white photos of works in the museum's Burmese collection.

If you'd like to know a lot more about Shwedagon Paya then get a copy of *Shwedagon* by Win Pe (Printing & Publishing Corporation, Yangon). You might find it in street bookstalls or at the Bagan Bookshop in Yangon.

Several books offer histories and descriptions of the temple architecture at Bagan. The older *Pictorial Guide to Pagan* (Ministry of Culture, Yangon) contains illustrated descriptions of many of the important Bagan buildings plus a map inside the back cover. It's a useful book that you'll find fairly easily in Myanmar. The 1986 release, *Glimpses of Glorious Pagan,* by the University of Yangon's history department, is basically an update of the earlier book. *Pagodas of Pagan* (Buddha Sasana Council Press) is also quite readily available, but not so detailed or interesting. Another good general guide is *Pagan: Art and Architecture of Old Burma* by Paul Strachan (Kiscadale). This modern art history of Bagan monuments is available at larger hotels in Yangon, and costs around US$50 hardcover or US$25 softcover.

If you're really serious about studying the monuments of Bagan, don't need any accompanying art history and can afford US$130 per volume, look for the six-volume *Inventory of Monuments at Pagan* (Weatherhill) by French archaeologist Pierre Pichard. Basically what you get for your investment is a set of monocolour diagrams. Pichard spent several years living in Bagan during the 1980s compiling this series. A softcover version collecting 302 diagrams in the series is available as *Inventory of Monuments at Pagan: Monuments 1137– 1439* for a mere US$160. If you're too cheap to afford that trifle, look for the Department of Archaeology's own two-volume *Inventory of Ancient Monuments in Bagan* (Ministry of Culture, Yangon), which uses Pichard's diagrams but adds a colour photo to accompany each and every diagram – at a cost of US$30 per volume. The latter two-volume set is generally available only in Myanmar.

It is very difficult to find any material on historical places other than the straightforward Yangon-Mandalay-Bagan triangle. *Historical Sites in Burma* by Aung Thaw (Ministry of Union Culture) is an excellent illustrated description of the major buildings at Bagan, Bago, Yangon, Amarapura, Ava, Sagaing, Mingun, Mandalay and a number of other historical spots. It can be found at Yangon's Bagan Bookshop or in Bagan.

Historic Sites and Monuments of Mandalay and Environs by U Lu Pe Win (Buddha Sasana Council Press) is fairly easy to come across and describes the ancient cities around Mandalay: Ava, Sagaing, Amarapura and Mingun.

One of the few books available with any information at all about archaeological sites other than Bagan or Mandalay is *A Guide to Mrauk U* by Tun Shwe Khine (Sittway Degree College). Available only in Yangon and Sittwe, it contains detailed descriptions and floor plans of the impressive Mrauk U monuments.

Theatre & Dance-Drama

Aung San Suu Kyi's former secretary Ma Thanegi has published an informative volume on marionette theatre called *Burmese Puppets* (White Orchid, Bangkok). Around Yangon you may come across reprints of the dryly written *Burmese Drama* by Maung Htin Aung, originally published by Oxford University Press, India, in 1937.

Burmese Dance and Theatre (Oxford University Press, Kuala Lumpur) by Noel F Singer is a small but well-illustrated volume covering the history of Burmese theatre right up into the early 1990s. About the only other printed resource to cover this territory is the out-of-print *Burmese Drama: A Study, with Translation, of Burmese Plays* (Oxford University Press, Calcutta, 1937) by Maung Htin Aung.

Novels, Short Stories & Poetry

Quite a few writers set novels in Myanmar, the most famous, of course, being George Orwell's *Burmese Days* (1934). It makes an engrossing read on upcountry Myanmar in the British days. Orwell served with the British colonial police in Myanmar and his novel exhibits a strong grasp of both local and expat life.

Michio Takeyama's *Harp of Burma*, first published in Japanese in 1949, then in English in 1966, novelises the desertion of a Japanese soldier in Myanmar during WWII.

In 1983 Burmese author Wendy Law-Yone published *The Coffin Tree*, a well written, sensuous novel that follows the young female narrator on a cultural journey back and forth between the USA and Myanmar some time after the 1962 military coup. Law-Yone updated Burmese political themes and turned up the heat for her novel *Irrawaddy Tango*, in which the fictional country Daya stands in for Myanmar and a dictator's mistress turns rebel assassin. Set in colonial times, *John Dollar* by Marianne Wiggins is a riveting, haunting tale about another journey that a young woman makes to Myanmar. It recounts the English schoolteacher's experiences in the tight-knit British community in Yangon as well as an exciting near-death adventure on the high seas.

For a taste of Burmese verse, try *Modern Burmese Poetry* (Thawda Press, Yangon), translated by Richard Win Pe and readily available in Yangon bookshops.

One chapter in *A Traveller's Literary Companion to South-East Asia* contains excerpted material from a number of works by foreign and Burmese writers on Myanmar, and includes an account of Orwell's sojourn in the country. The chapter editor, Anna Allott, also translated and edited *Inked Over, Ripped Out* (Silkworm Press, Chiang Mai), which highlights the restrictions faced by Burmese writers in the 1990s, and contains a number of censored and uncensored Burmese short stories from the Slorc period.

Magazine Articles

National Geographic has done a number of features about Myanmar. The November 1940 issue featured an article called 'Burma Road, Back Door to China', which chronicled a trip through Hsipaw, Lashio and other places in northern Shan State to China. The February 1963 issue covered Myanmar as a whole; March 1971 was about Bagan; June 1974 had an article on the Inle leg rowers; while in the June 1979 issue there was an article about the long-necked Padaung women – revealing that they're actually not long-necked at all – the heavy coils they wear around their necks actually push their shoulder blades and collar bones down, rather than extend their necks. Myanmar featured once again in July 1984, in a general article where it emerges that even *National Geographic* writers couldn't wangle more than a seven-day visa. Myanmar's latest *National Geographic* appearance occurred in the July 1995 issue, wherein the author excoriated the military regime in one of the most political articles the magazine has ever published.

An interesting perspective was given in a piece by Amitav Ghosh in the 12 August 1996 issue of the *New Yorker*. The long article not only encapsulates Myanmar exceedingly well, it was the first article published in the West in the 1990s to question opposition politics.

Archaeology magazine ran an inspiring article on the archaeological significance of Bagan, 'The Power of Pagan', in its September/October 1992 issue.

Hong Kong weekly *Far Eastern Economic Review* features pieces on Myanmar two or three times per month.

Political Publications

Various groups outside the country produce newsletters and reports focusing on current political affairs, especially human rights in Myanmar. Readers should exercise their own judgement about their content. Most groups will gladly send samples of their publications.

All Burma Students Democratic Front (e absdfhq@chmai2.loxinfo.co.th) PO Box 31 Mae Sariang, Mae Hong Son 58110 Thailand

Amnesty International (☎ 212-807 8400, fax 463 9193, w www.aiusa.org) 332 8th Ave, New York, NY, 10001 USA

Burma Action Group (☎ 020-7281 7377, fax 7372 3559) Bickerton House, 25–27 Bickerton Rd, London N19 5JT, UK

Burma Affairs Monitor (☎/fax 020-7924 3147) 3A Chatto Rd, London SW11 6LJ, UK

Burma Alert (☎ 819-647 5405, fax 647 5403) RR 4, Shawville, Quebec J0X 2Y0, Canada
Burma Bureau Germany (☎ 2173-907334, fax 907335) Fahlerweg 08 D-40764 Langenfeld, Germany
The Burma Project (Open Society Institute; ☎ 212-548 0632, fax 548 4655, **W** www.burmaproject.org) 400 W 59th St, New York, NY 10019, USA
Burma Relief Centre (☎ 053 216 894) PO Box 48, Chiang Mai University, Chiang Mai 50002, Thailand; BRC-Japan (☎ 7442-28236, fax 46254) Ozuku-cho, Kashihara-shi, Nara-ken 634, Japan
Human Rights Watch – Asia (☎ 212-290 4700, fax 736 1300, **W** www.hrw.org) 350 5th Ave, New York, NY 10018-3299, USA
National Coalition Government of the Union of Burma (☎ 202-393 7342, fax 393 7343, **W** www.ncgub.net) Suite 910, 815 15th St SW, Washington, DC 20005, USA

FILMS

Michio Takeyama's 1949 antiwar novel *Harp of Burma* was made into a beautiful black-and-white Japanese film directed by Kon Ichikawa in 1956. It's now available on video with English subtitles under the title *The Burmese Harp*.

In 1995, American director John Boorman's graphic *Beyond Rangoon*, a film dramatising the brutal suppression of the 1988 pro-democracy uprising, briefly focused international cinematic attention on Myanmar's plight. As might be expected of a Hollywood production, the film is somewhat melodramatic and oversimplified.

NEWSPAPERS & MAGAZINES

Before the 1962 Burmese military takeover, over 30 daily newspapers – including three in English, six in Chinese, five in Indian languages and 18 in Burmese – were published in the country. Today the only English-language daily newspaper readily available in the country is the *New Light of Myanmar*, a thin, government-owned mouthpiece published by the Ministry of Information. It contains plenty of propaganda – though the rabid attacks against Aung San Suu Kyi have stopped since talks between her and the SPDC began in October 2000.

The weekly *Myanmar Times* is a surprisingly sophisticated effort to bring the local English-language press up to regional standards. The extensive listings section is handy for up-to-date information on domestic and international flights as well as entertainment and shopping venues in Yangon. However, its close ties with the government are worth noting.

There are now only four Burmese-language dailies, *Myanma Alin*, *Kyemon*, *Myodaw* and *Yadanabon* (Mandalay only). Only *Myanma Alin* – the Burmese version of the *New Light of Myanmar* – is circulated in greater numbers than the *New Light* itself.

Recent issues of international magazines like *Time*, *Newsweek* and the *Economist* are often available at newsstands and bookshops in luxury hotels like The Strand, Traders Hotel, Summit Parkview and Sedona Hotel in Yangon. Older issues are sold on the street by pavement vendors. Western newspapers are available at the British and American libraries. You can also get the *International Herald Tribune* at Trader's.

The *Far Eastern Economic Review*, a Hong Kong–based weekly magazine, regularly reports on major events within Myanmar. Thailand's *Bangkok Post* and *The Nation* also carry news on Myanmar.

A tourist-oriented publication called *Today* – published by MTT and available at the MTT office and at many hotels – contains short articles on Myanmar's culture and the tourism industry, along with useful lists of embassies, current festivals, airlines and long-distance express bus services.

See the Bookshops and Libraries entries in the Information section of the Yangon chapter for information on where to find English- and French-language publications.

RADIO & TV

All legal radio and television broadcasts are state-controlled. Radio Myanmar (formerly Voice of Myanmar) broadcasts news in Burmese, English and eight other national languages three times a day at 8.30am, 1.30pm and 9.30pm.

In January 2001, Yangon launched its first FM radio station, 'City FM', which is broadcast at 89 on the dial from 8am to noon and 1pm to 6pm. Programming consists of top-20 Burmese and international hits.

Educated Burmese generally listen to shortwave BBC and VOA broadcasts for an earful of the outside world. Although these programmes appear nightly, the most popular time to listen is each Wednesday evening from 8.15pm to 9pm, when the BBC broadcasts Burmese-language special reports that contain translated Myanmar news stories extracted from the foreign press. Just as popular – perhaps more so – is the Burmese service of Radio Free Asia (RFA).

TV Myanmar (MRTV) operates mornings and evenings via the NTSC system. Regular features include classical song and dance performances, and locally produced news and weather reports.

National news in English is telecast on TV Myanmar nightly at around 9.15pm. A second military-owned station, Myawaddy TV, broadcasts from 7am to 8.30am and 4pm to 11.30pm. Programming is a bit livelier than MRTV and includes sporting events and old Burmese movies, as well as Chinese historical dramas dubbed into Burmese.

One of the most dramatic changes to occur in Myanmar's media since the advent of TV is the relatively recent arrival of satellite TV services. Tens of thousands of satellite dishes have appeared all over the country over the last six years. The main signal received is the 'southern footprint' of AsiaSat 1 and 2, same as for Thailand and Indochina, which beam in channels such as CNN, BBC World Service, Home Box Office, Chinese Channels and MTV Asia. Myanmar also receives Doordarshan India (India Television), India's Hindi/Urdu Zee TV and Yunnan TV via satellite. Many of the newer hotels now provide satellite TV, although they're never able to provide a choice of more than two or three satellite channels at a time.

VIDEO SYSTEMS

Although the standard TV system in Myanmar is NTSC, many people also own PAL sets, a format compatible with that used in Thailand and most of Europe (France's SECAM format is a notable exception) as well as in Australia. Some video shops rent NTSC as well as PAL and SECAM tapes; virtually all videos offered for sale or rent in Myanmar are pirated or unlicensed tapes. A 'multisystem' VCR has the capacity to play both NTSC and PAL, but not SECAM (except as black-and-white images).

PHOTOGRAPHY & VIDEO

Film & Equipment

Myanmar is a very photogenic place, so bring lots of film with you. Colour print films – mostly Kodak, Fuji and Konica brands – are readily and inexpensively available in shops in Yangon and Mandalay. Prices are around K1050 for a 36-exposure roll of Fujicolor 100; Kodak costs a bit more.

Slide film is harder to find but some shops stock it. Generally the only types available are Kodak Elite Chrome and Fujichrome Sensia 100, both of which sell for around K3300 per roll. Pro-grade film like Velvia and Provia are occasionally available in Yangon for K4000 to K4500. Of course if the kyat devalues further these prices will increase exponentially according to the value of the US dollar – you can figure that whatever film costs in Bangkok it will cost about the same or just a bit more here. Black-and-white print (or slide) film is very hard to come by. If you're shooting in this medium, be sure to bring your own supply. Bangkok is a good place to stock up on film of all types. Outside Yangon and Mandalay, film is scarce.

Photographic processing services are available in Yangon and Mandalay and quality has improved in recent years. In these cities processing is probably safe, but if you think you've captured some gems on film, it might be best to wait until you get home to have your film developed.

Technical Tips

The usual tropical rules apply to taking photographs here. Allow for the intensity of the sun after the early morning and before the late evening. Try to keep your film as cool as possible, particularly after it has been exposed. Beware of dust, particularly at the height of the dry season when central Myanmar becomes very dusty indeed. During the Water Festival (Thingyan) in April, be sure to seal your camera and film in a plastic bag or in some sort of waterproof container.

Restrictions

It is forbidden by law to photograph any military facility or any uniformed person. Any structure considered strategic – this includes bridges and train stations – are also supposedly against the law to shoot. If true, it's hardly enforced – nobody's going to hassle you for photographing the Gokteik viaduct or Yangon's colonial-era train station.

Aung San Suu Kyi's home is absolutely off-limits to photographers, whether amateur or professional. We received a letter from an Italian photographer who claimed that when he tried to shoot photos of the house, soldiers promptly confiscated all his film, drove him to the airport and had him deported. Although you might not receive this treatment, we do know of people who have been questioned and turned away from the block on which Suu Kyi lives.

For more on the issue of restrictions, see Dangers & Annoyances later in this section.

Photographing People

The Burmese are not over-exposed to camera-clicking visitors and are not at all unhappy about being photographed. Even monks like to be photographed, although, of course, it's rude to ask them to pose for you and it's always polite to ask anybody's permission before taking photographs.

Airport Security

The X-ray baggage inspection machines at Yangon and Mandalay international airports are all deemed film-safe. Nevertheless if you're travelling with high-speed film (ISO 400 or above), you may want to have your film hand inspected rather than X-rayed. Security inspectors are usually happy to comply. Packing your film in see-through plastic bags generally speeds up the hand-inspection process. Some photographers pack their film in lead-lined bags to ward off potentially harmful rays.

At other airports around the country the X-ray machines are considerably more dubious and we suggest you have all film hand-inspected. On occasion the upcountry machines aren't working at all, in which case there will be no anxiety over the film.

TIME & DATES

Hours

Myanmar Standard Time (MST) is 6½ hours ahead of Greenwich Mean Time (GMT/UTC). Coming from Thailand you turn your watch back half an hour, from India you turn it forward an hour. When it is noon in Yangon, it's 9.30pm the previous day in San Francisco, 12.30am in New York, 5.30am in London and 3.30pm in Sydney and Melbourne. When these cities are on daylight-saving time, these times are one hour behind.

Days

Most Burmese Buddhists recognise an eight-day week in which Thursday to Tuesday conform with the Western calendar but Wednesday is divided into two 12-hour days. Midnight to noon is 'Bohdahu' (the day Buddha was born), while noon to midnight is 'Yahu' (Rahu, a Hindu god/planet). It's rare that the week's unique structure causes any communication problems, however, given that the Wednesday division mainly applies to religious rather than secular matters (for example, which planetary post a worshipper attends at a paya).

Months

The traditional Burmese calendar features 12, 28-day lunar months that run out of sync with the months of the solar Gregorian calendar. To stay in sync with the solar year, the Burmese calendar inserts a second Waso month every few years – somewhat like the leap year day added to the Gregorian February. The Burmese months are:

Tagu	March/April
Kason	April/May
Nayon	May/June
Waso	June/July
Wagaung	July/August

Tawthalin	August/September
Thadingyut	September/October
Tazaungmon	October/November
Nadaw	November/December
Pyatho	December/January
Tabodwe	January/February
Tabaung	February/March

Most traditional festivals take place according to this scheme, making it difficult to calculate festival dates using a Gregorian calendar.

Each lunar month is divided into two 14- or 15-day sections; the two weeks during which the moon waxes are called *la-zan*, while the two weeks of the waning moon are *la-gweh*. These lunar phases determine the Burmese religious calendar. Four monthly 'holy days' – when it's most propitious to visit a paya or *kyaung* (Buddhist monastery) – occur on the 8th and 15th days of the waxing and waning moons.

Burmese months are cited more commonly than the Gregorian months in everyday speech. Ask most Buddhist villagers what the date is and they'll respond with something like: 'It's Pyatho, 8th day of the waning moon'. Urban-dwelling and Christian Burmese are familiar with the Gregorian calendar, which is used in most official capacities and in business situations.

Years

Over the centuries Burmese monarchs have established and counter-established several different year counts. The main one in current use, called *thekkayit*, is 638 years behind the Christian era. Since each new year begins in April (at the end of the Thingyan festival), this means the Christian year 2000 is equivalent to thekkayit 1362 until the month of April, after which it's 1363. Burmese archaeology is particularly challenging since historic chronicles and stone inscriptions use different year counts depending on who was king at the time.

Another calendar in use follows the Buddhist era as reckoned in Thailand counting from 543 BC; hence 2000 was 2543 BE. Private businesses typically cite years following the AD Christian calendar. Some official Burmese documents and many Burmese calendars state the year according to all three systems, ie thekkayit, BE and AD.

ELECTRICITY

Myanmar's national grid system covers only certain parts of central and eastern Myanmar. Most of the power comes from a single hydroelectric plant at Lawpita in the Kayah State. Off the national grid, towns and cities may have their own diesel plants or small hydroelectric facilities.

The supply of electricity to Yangon has improved much over the last few years, but brownouts still occasionally occur. When this happens the voltage drops to levels that are barely enough for anything more than basic lighting. Brownouts and blackouts are common outside the capital, even in Mandalay. In many towns and villages electric power is supplied only during the evening hours from around 6pm to 11pm. Most hotels catering to foreign visitors have their own gas or diesel-powered generators that kick on during scheduled and non-scheduled blackouts.

In many villages lighting, heating and cooking sources are restricted to candles, paraffin and firewood.

Voltages & Cycles

When it's working the current is supposed to run at 230V, 50 Hz AC.

Plugs & Sockets

Most electrical wall outlets have sockets that accept two flat and/or two round prongs. Some older outlets accept British-style plugs with three flat prongs in a triangle.

WEIGHTS & MEASURES

For a country with such a professed anti-colonial stance, Myanmar is amazingly Anglo in the standard units of measures employed in everyday life.

Weight

The most common units of weight used in Myanmar are *viss (peiqtha)*, pounds *(paun)* and *ticals (kyat tha)*. One viss is equal to 3.6lb (1.6kg) or 100 ticals. One tical is equal to 16g.

Volume

At the retail level, rice and small fruits or nuts are sold in units of volume rather than weight; the most common measure is the standard condensed-milk can or *bu*. Eight *bu* equals one small rice basket or *pyi*, and 16 pyi make a jute sack or *tin*.

Petrol and most other liquids are sold by the imperial gallon (4.55L). One exception is milk, which is sold by the viss.

Length & Distance

Cloth and other items of moderate length are measured by the yard (91.5cm), called *gaiq* in Burmese. A half-yard is a *taung* (45.7cm), which is divided into two *htwa* (22.8cm). Half a htwa is a *maiq* (11.4cm).

LAUNDRY

Nearly every hotel and guesthouse in Myanmar offers a laundry service. Rates are generally geared to room rates; the cheaper the accommodation, the cheaper you'll find the washing and ironing. Cheapest of all are public laundries, where you pay by the pound (in weight), but our experience has been that these are available only in Yangon and Mandalay. There are no laundrettes or self-service laundries anywhere in the country.

Some hotels and guesthouses also provide laundry areas where you can wash your clothes at no charge; sometimes there's even a hanging area for drying. In accommodation where there is no laundry, do-it-yourselfers can wash their clothes in the sink and hang them out to dry in their rooms – see the What to Bring section earlier in this chapter for useful laundry tools. Laundry detergent is readily available in general mercantile shops.

TOILETS

In Myanmar, as in many other Asian countries, the 'squat toilet' is the norm, except in hotels and guesthouses geared towards tourists and international business travellers. Instead of trying to approximate a chair or stool like a modern sit-down toilet, a traditional Asian toilet sits more or less flush with the surface of the floor, with two footpads on either side of the porcelain abyss. It takes a bit of getting used to.

Next to the typical squat toilet is a bucket or cement reservoir filled with water. A plastic bowl usually floats on the water's surface or sits nearby. This water supply has a two-fold function; toilet-goers scoop water from the reservoir with the plastic bowl and use it to clean their nether regions while still squatting over the toilet. Since there is usually no mechanical flushing device attached to a squat toilet, a few extra scoops must be poured into the toilet basin to flush waste into the septic system. In larger towns, mechanical flushing systems are common. More rustic toilets in rural areas may simply consist of a few planks over a hole in the ground.

Even in places where sit-down toilets are installed, the plumbing may not be designed to take toilet paper. In such cases the usual washing bucket will be standing nearby so you can wash yourself, or there will be a waste basket where you're supposed to place used toilet paper.

Public toilets are rather uncommon in Myanmar, except in train stations, larger hotel lobbies and airports. While on the road between towns and villages, it is perfectly acceptable to go behind a tree or bush or even to use the road side when nature calls.

BATHING

Smaller hotels and most guesthouses in the country may not have hot water, though places in the larger cities will usually offer small electric shower heaters in their more expensive rooms (though depending on the generator situation these devices may only function for a few hours per day). Boiler-style water heaters are available at all larger international-style hotels and are becoming more common at mid-range places, especially where the weather gets cold in the winter months (eg, Pyin U Lwin, Kalaw and Taunggyi).

Many rural Burmese bathe in rivers or streams or at public wells. Those living in towns or cities may have washrooms where a large jar or cement trough is filled with water for bathing purposes. A plastic or metal bowl is used to sluice water from the jar or trough over the body. Even in homes where showers are installed, heated water is

Burmese Beauty Secrets

Diet

The typical Burmese dietary intake includes plenty of fibre via pulses, vegetables, fruit and grains (rice and noodles). Fish and chicken are preferred to red meat, and vegetable oils (sesame, sunflower and peanut) are used instead of animal fat. Few dairy products are eaten. Very weak green tea is drunk in large quantities and clear soups are often taken with main meals.

Even in the cities, women rarely touch alcohol or cigarettes, and the huge cheroots puffed by country women are very mild.

Climate

Except for the central 'dry zone', the country's normally high humidity is kind to the skin. There are no frosts or drying winds and little pollution. Constant sweat keeps the pores active and flushed.

Personal Hygiene

All-over washing with cold water two or three times a day – using unrefined, unscented soap – is a routine for all. It is believed that warm water is bad for the skin. Herbal shampoo is made by boiling the bark of a small shrub called *tayaw* (grewia) with the pods of soap acacia *(Acacia concinna)*. The resultant brown liquid, which is widely sold in the markets, lathers quite well and leaves the hair soft and glossy. Hair is oiled with coconut oil and adorned with combs of woods, ivory and tortoiseshell.

Cosmetics

The soft outer bark of the *thanakha* tree *(Linoria acidissima)*, which grows in central Myanmar, is ground on a whetstone with a little water and used as a paste on the face. Alternately, it can be bought prepared as a liquid cosmetic or in powder form. The paste is smeared on the face and body; some women cover their whole bodies with it at night. Thanakha is mildly astringent, and used as a combination skin conditioner, sunscreen, perfume and cosmetic. Older women tend to put cold cream and light oil preparations on their faces before applying thanakha.

Traditionally, eyebrows and lashes were blackened with a mixture of oil and soot, but now 'Western' cosmetics – some made domestically, some imported – are readily available. Burmese women are generally very brand-conscious, and genuine Revlon lipsticks are a treasured gift.

Physique

Most Burmese have small bones, high cheekbones in an oval face and slim bodies, although plumpness is frequently considered a sign of health and beauty. The expression *'Wa-laiq-ta!'* ('How fat you're looking!') is considered a compliment. Although they are not tall, the *longyi* (sarong-style garment) makes them appear so.

From early childhood, boys and girls carry water pots or trays of food on their heads, which seems to result in fewer back problems and beautiful carriage. The longyi restricts the stride so the people move slowly and gracefully. Burmese women believe that squatting, rather than standing, helps prevent varicose veins.

Vicki Bowman

uncommon. Most Burmese bathe at least twice a day, and never use hot water.

If ever you find yourself having to bathe in a public place you should wear a longyi; nude bathing is shockingly offensive.

HEALTH

Travel health depends on your predeparture preparations, your daily health care while travelling and how you handle any medical problem that does develop. While

Medical Kit Check List

Following is a list of items you should consider including in your medical kit – consult your pharmacist for brands available in your country.

- ☐ **Aspirin or paracetamol (acetaminophen in the USA)** – for pain or fever
- ☐ **Antihistamine** – for allergies, eg, hay fever; to ease the itch from insect bites or stings; and to prevent motion sickness
- ☐ **Cold and flu tablets, throat lozenges and nasal decongestant**
- ☐ **Multivitamins** – consider for long trips, when dietary vitamin intake may be inadequate
- ☐ **Antibiotics** – consider including these if you're travelling well off the beaten track; see your doctor, as they must be prescribed, and carry the prescription with you
- ☐ **Loperamide or diphenoxylate** –'blockers' for diarrhoea
- ☐ **Prochlorperazine or metaclopramide** – for nausea and vomiting
- ☐ **Rehydration mixture** – to prevent dehydration, which may occur, for example, during bouts of diarrhoea; particularly important when travelling with children
- ☐ **Insect repellent, sunscreen, lip balm and eye drops**
- ☐ **Calamine lotion, sting relief spray or aloe vera** – to ease irritation from sunburn and insect bites or stings
- ☐ **Antifungal cream or powder** – for fungal skin infections and thrush
- ☐ **Antiseptic (such as povidone-iodine)** – for cuts and grazes
- ☐ **Bandages, Band-Aids (plasters) and other wound dressings**
- ☐ **Water purification tablets or iodine**
- ☐ **Scissors, tweezers and a thermometer** – note that mercury thermometers are prohibited by airlines
- ☐ **Sterile kit** – in case you need injections in a country with medical hygiene problems; discuss with your doctor

the potential dangers can seem quite frightening, in reality few travellers experience anything more than an upset stomach.

Predeparture Planning

Immunisations Plan ahead for getting your vaccinations: some of them require more than one injection, while some vaccinations should not be given together. Note that some vaccinations should not be given during pregnancy or in people with allergies – discuss this with your doctor.

It is recommended you seek medical advice at least six weeks before travel. Be aware that there is often a greater risk of disease with children and during pregnancy.

Discuss your requirements with your doctor, but vaccinations you should consider for this trip include the following (for more details about the diseases themselves, see the individual disease entries later in this section). Carry proof of your vaccinations, especially yellow fever, as this is sometimes needed to enter some countries.

Diphtheria & Tetanus Vaccinations for these two diseases are usually combined and are recommended for everyone. After an initial course of three injections (usually given in childhood), boosters are necessary every 10 years.

Polio Everyone should keep up to date with this vaccination, which is normally given in childhood. A booster every 10 years maintains immunity.

Hepatitis A Hepatitis A vaccine (eg, Avaxim, Havrix 1440 or VAQTA) provides long-term immunity (possibly more than 10 years) after an initial injection and a booster at six to 12 months.

Alternatively, an injection of gamma globulin can provide short-term protection against hepatitis A – two to six months, depending on the dose given. It is not vaccine, but ready-made antibody collected from blood donations. It is reasonably effective and, unlike the vaccine, it is protective immediately, but because it is a blood product, there are current concerns about its long-term safety.

Hepatitis A vaccine is also available in a combined form, Twinrix, with hepatitis B vaccine. Three injections over a six-month period are required, the first two providing substantial protection against hepatitis A.

Typhoid Vaccination against typhoid may be required if you are travelling for more than a couple of weeks in most parts of Asia. It is now available either as an injection or as capsules to be taken orally.

Hepatitis B Travellers who should consider vaccination against hepatitis B include those on a long trip, as well as those visiting countries where there are high levels of hepatitis B infection, where blood transfusions may not be adequately screened or where sexual contact or needle sharing is a possibility. Vaccination involves three injections, with a booster at 12 months. More rapid courses are available if necessary.

Yellow Fever A yellow fever vaccination is now the only vaccination that is a legal requirement for entry into certain countries, usually only enforced when coming from an infected area. Vaccination is recommended for travel in areas where the disease is endemic (parts of Africa and South America). You may have to go to a special yellow fever vaccination centre.

Rabies Vaccination should be considered if you will be spending a month or longer in Myanmar, where rabies is common, especially if you are cycling, handling animals, caving or travelling to remote areas; it should also be considered for children (who may not report a bite). Pretravel rabies vaccination involves having three injections over 21 to 28 days. If after vaccination you are bitten or scratched by an animal, you will require two booster injections of vaccine; those not vaccinated require more.

Japanese B Encephalitis Consider vaccination against this disease if spending a month or longer in Myanmar, making repeated trips, or visiting during an epidemic. It involves three injections over 30 days.

Tuberculosis The risk of TB to travellers is usually very low, unless you will be living with or closely associated with local people. Vaccination against TB (BCG) is recommended for children and young adults living in these areas for three months or more.

Malaria Medication Antimalarial drugs do not prevent you from being infected but kill the malaria parasites during a stage in their development and significantly reduce the risk of becoming very ill or dying. Expert advice on medication should be sought, as there are many factors to consider, including the area to be visited, the risk of exposure to malaria-carrying mosquitoes, the side effects of medication, your medical history, your age and whether you are pregnant. Travellers to isolated areas in Myanmar may like to carry a treatment dose of medication for use if symptoms occur. Antimalarial drugs are readily available in Yangon.

Health Insurance Make sure that you have adequate health insurance. See Travel Insurance under Visas & Documents earlier in this chapter for details.

Travel Health Guides Lonely Planet's *Healthy Travel Asia & India* is a handy pocket size and is packed with useful information including pretrip planning, emergency first aid, immunisation and disease information and what to do if you get sick on the road. *Travel with Children* from Lonely Planet also includes advice on travel health for younger children.

There are also a number of excellent travel health sites on the Internet. From the Lonely Planet home page there are links (W www.lonelyplanet.com/weblinks/wlheal.htm) to the World Health Organization and the US Centers for Disease Control & Prevention.

Other Preparations Make sure you're healthy before you start travelling. If you are going on a long trip make sure your teeth are OK. If you wear glasses take a spare pair and your prescription. If you require a particular medication take an adequate supply, as it may not be available locally. Take part of the packaging showing the generic name rather than the brand, which will make getting replacements easier. It's a good idea to have a legible prescription or letter from your doctor to show that you legally use the medication to avoid any problems.

Basic Rules

Food There is an old colonial adage which says: 'If you can cook it, boil it or peel it you can eat it – otherwise forget it'. Vegetables and fruit should be washed with purified water or peeled where possible. Beware of ice cream which is sold in the street or anywhere it might have been melted and refrozen; if there's any doubt (eg, a power cut in the last day or two), steer well clear. Shellfish such as mussels, oysters and clams should be avoided as well as undercooked meat, particularly in the form of mince. Steaming does not make shellfish safe for eating. If a place looks clean and well run and the vendor also looks clean and healthy, then the food is probably safe. In general, places that are packed with travellers or locals will be fine, while empty restaurants are questionable. The food in busy restaurants is cooked and eaten quite quickly with little standing around and is probably not reheated.

Water The number one rule is *be careful of the water* and especially ice. If you don't know for certain that the water is safe, assume the worst. Reputable brands of bottled water or soft drinks are generally fine, although in some places bottles may be refilled with tap water. Only use water from containers with a serrated seal – not tops or corks. Take care with fruit juice, particularly if water may have been added. Milk should be treated with suspicion as it is often unpasteurised, though boiled milk is fine if it is kept hygienically. Tea or coffee should also be OK, since the water should have been boiled.

Water Purification The simplest way to purify water is to boil it thoroughly. Vigorous boiling should be satisfactory; however, at high altitude water boils at a lower temperature, so germs are less likely to be killed. Boil it for longer in these environments.

Consider purchasing a water filter for a long trip. There are two main kinds of filter. Total filters take out all parasites, bacteria and viruses and make water safe to drink. They are often expensive, but they can be more cost effective than buying bottled water. Simple filters (which can even be a nylon mesh bag) take out dirt and larger foreign bodies from the water so that chemical solutions work much more effectively; if water is dirty, chemical solutions may not work at all. It's very important when buying a filter to read the specifications, so that you know exactly what it removes from the water and what it doesn't. Simple filtering will not remove all dangerous organisms, so if you cannot boil water it should be treated chemically.

Chlorine tablets will kill many pathogens, but not some parasites like giardia and amoebic cysts. Iodine is more effective in purifying water and is available in tablet form. Follow the directions carefully and remember that too much iodine can be harmful.

Medical Problems & Treatment

Self-diagnosis and treatment can be risky, so you should always seek medical help. An embassy, consulate or five-star hotel can usually recommend a local doctor or clinic. Although we do give drug dosages in this section, they are for emergency use only. Correct diagnosis is vital. In this section we have used the generic names for medications – check with a pharmacist for brands available locally.

Note that antibiotics should ideally be administered only under medical supervision. Take only the recommended dose at the prescribed intervals and use the whole course, even if the illness seems to be cured earlier. Stop immediately if there are any serious reactions and don't use the antibiotic at all if you are unsure that you have the correct one. Some people are allergic to commonly prescribed antibiotics such as penicillin; carry this information (eg, on a bracelet) when travelling.

Environmental Hazards

Heat Exhaustion Dehydration and salt deficiency can cause heat exhaustion. Take time to acclimatise to high temperatures, drink sufficient liquids and do not do anything too physically demanding. Salt deficiency is characterised by fatigue, lethargy, headaches, giddiness and muscle cramps; salt tablets may help, but adding extra salt to your food is better.

Anhidrotic heat exhaustion is a rare form of heat exhaustion that is caused by an inability to sweat. It tends to affect people who have been in a hot climate for some time, rather than newcomers. It can progress to heatstroke. Treatment involves removal to a cooler climate.

Heatstroke This serious, occasionally fatal, condition can occur if the body's heat-regulating mechanism breaks down and the

Everyday Health

Normal body temperature is up to 37°C (98.6°F); more than 2°C (4°F) higher indicates a high fever. The normal adult pulse rate is 60 to 100 per minute (children 80 to 100, babies 100 to 140). As a general rule the pulse increases about 20 beats per minute for each 1°C (2°F) rise in fever.

Respiration (breathing) rate is also an indicator of illness. Count the number of breaths per minute: Between 12 and 20 is normal for adults and older children (up to 30 for younger children, 40 for babies). People with a high fever or serious respiratory illness breathe more quickly than normal. More than 40 shallow breaths a minute may indicate pneumonia.

body temperature rises to dangerous levels. Long, continuous periods of exposure to high temperatures and insufficient fluids can leave you vulnerable to heatstroke.

The symptoms are feeling unwell, not sweating very much (or at all) and a high body temperature (39° to 41°C or 102° to 106°F). Where sweating has ceased, the skin becomes flushed and red. Severe, throbbing headaches and lack of coordination will also occur, and the sufferer may be confused or aggressive. Eventually the victim will become delirious or convulse. Hospitalisation is essential, but in the interim get victims out of the sun, remove their clothing, cover them with a wet sheet or towel and then fan continually. Give fluids if they are conscious.

Jet Lag Jet lag is experienced when a person travels by air across more than three time zones (each time zone usually represents a one-hour time difference). It occurs because many of the functions of the human body (such as temperature, pulse rate and emptying of the bladder and bowels) are regulated by internal 24-hour cycles. When we travel long distances rapidly, our bodies take time to adjust to the 'new time' of our destination, and we may experience fatigue, disorientation, insomnia, anxiety, impaired concentration and loss of appetite. These effects will usually be gone within three days of arrival, but to minimise the impact of jet lag:

- Rest for a couple of days prior to departure.
- Try to select flight schedules that minimise sleep deprivation; arriving late in the day means you can go to sleep soon after you arrive. For very long flights, try to organise a stopover.
- Avoid excessive eating (which bloats the stomach) and alcohol (which causes dehydration) during the flight. Instead, drink plenty of non-carbonated, nonalcoholic drinks such as fruit juice or water.
- Avoid smoking.
- Make yourself comfortable by wearing loose-fitting clothes and perhaps bringing an eye mask and ear plugs to help you sleep.
- Try to sleep at the appropriate time for the time zone you are travelling to.

Motion Sickness Eating lightly before and during a trip will reduce the chances of motion sickness. If you are prone to motion sickness try to find a place that minimises movement – near the wing on aircraft, close to midships on boats, near the centre on buses. Fresh air usually helps; reading and cigarette smoke don't. Commercial motion-sickness preparations, which can cause drowsiness, have to be taken before the trip commences. Ginger (available in capsule form) and peppermint (including mint-flavoured sweets) are natural preventatives.

Prickly Heat Prickly heat is an itchy rash caused by excessive perspiration trapped under the skin. It usually strikes people who have just arrived in a hot climate. Keeping cool, bathing often, drying the skin and using a mild talcum or prickly heat powder or resorting to air-conditioning may help.

Sunburn In the tropics, the desert or at high altitude you can get sunburnt surprisingly quickly, even through cloud. Use a sunscreen, a hat, and a barrier cream for your nose and lips. Calamine lotion or a commercial after-sun preparation are good for mild sunburn. Protect your eyes with good-quality sunglasses, particularly if you will be near water, sand or snow.

Infectious Diseases

Diarrhoea Simple things like a change of water, food or climate can all cause a mild bout of diarrhoea, but a few rushed toilet trips with no other symptoms is not indicative of a major problem.

Dehydration is the main danger with any diarrhoea, particularly in children or the elderly as dehydration can occur quite quickly. Under all circumstances *fluid replacement* (at least equal to the volume being lost) is the most important thing to remember. Weak black tea with a little sugar, soda water, or soft drinks allowed to go flat and diluted 50% with clean water are all good.

With severe diarrhoea a rehydrating solution is preferable to replace minerals and salts lost. Commercially available oral rehydration salts (ORS) are very useful; add them to boiled or bottled water. In an emergency you can make up a solution of six teaspoons of sugar and a half teaspoon of salt to a litre of boiled or bottled water.

You need to drink at least the same volume of fluid that you are losing in bowel movements and vomiting. Urine is the best guide to the adequacy of replacement – if you have small amounts of concentrated urine, you need to drink more. Keep drinking small amounts often. Stick to a bland diet as you recover.

Gut-paralysing drugs such as loperamide or diphenoxylate can be used to bring relief from the symptoms, although they do not actually cure the problem. Only use these drugs if you do not have access to toilets, eg, if you *must* travel. Note that these drugs are not recommended for children under 12 years.

In certain situations – diarrhoea with blood or mucus (dysentery), any diarrhoea with fever, profuse watery diarrhoea, persistent diarrhoea not improving after 48 hours and severe diarrhoea – antibiotics may be required. These suggest a more serious cause of diarrhoea and in these situations gut-paralysing drugs should be avoided.

In these situations, a stool test may be necessary to diagnose what bug is causing your diarrhoea, so you should seek medical help urgently. Where this is not possible the recommended drugs for bacterial diarrhoea (the most likely cause of severe diarrhoea in travellers) are norfloxacin 400mg twice daily for three days or ciprofloxacin 500mg twice daily for five days. These are not recommended for children or pregnant women. The drug of choice for children would be co-trimoxazole with dosage dependent on weight. A five-day course is given. Ampicillin or amoxycillin may be given in pregnancy, but medical care is necessary.

Two other causes of persistent diarrhoea in travellers are giardiasis and amoebic dysentery.

Giardiasis is caused by a common parasite, *Giardia lamblia*. Symptoms include stomach cramps, nausea, a bloated stomach, watery, foul-smelling diarrhoea and frequent gas. Giardiasis can appear several weeks after you have been exposed to the parasite. The symptoms may disappear for a few days and then return; this can go on for several weeks.

Amoebic dysentery, caused by the protozoan *Entamoeba histolytica*, is characterised by a gradual onset of low-grade diarrhoea, often with blood and mucus. Cramping abdominal pain and vomiting are less likely than in other types of diarrhoea, and fever may not be present. It will persist until treated and can recur and cause other health problems.

You should seek medical advice if you think you have giardiasis or amoebic dysentery, but where this is not possible, tinidazole or metronidazole are the recommended drugs. Treatment is a 2g single dose of tinidazole or 250mg of metronidazole three times daily for five to 10 days.

Fungal Infections Fungal infections occur more commonly in hot weather and are usually found on the scalp, between the toes (athlete's foot) or fingers, in the groin and on the body (ringworm). You get ringworm (which is a fungal infection, not a worm) from infected animals or other people. Moisture encourages these infections.

To prevent fungal infections wear loose, comfortable clothes, avoid artificial fibres, wash frequently and dry yourself carefully. If you do get an infection, wash the infected area at least daily with a disinfectant or medicated soap and water, and rinse and dry well. Apply an antifungal cream or powder like tolnaftate. Try to expose the infected area to air or sunlight as much as possible and wash all towels and underwear in hot water, change them often and let them dry in the sun.

Hepatitis Hepatitis is a general term for inflammation of the liver. It is a common disease worldwide. There are several different viruses that cause hepatitis, and they differ in the way that they are transmitted. The symptoms are similar in all forms of the illness, and include fever, chills, headache, fatigue, feelings of weakness and aches and pains, followed by loss of appetite, nausea, vomiting, abdominal pain, dark urine, light-coloured faeces, jaundiced (yellow) skin and yellowing of the whites of the eyes. People who have had hepatitis should avoid alcohol for some time after the illness, as the liver needs time to recover.

Hepatitis A is transmitted by contaminated food and drinking water. You should seek medical advice, but there is not much you can do apart from resting, drinking lots of fluids, eating lightly and avoiding fatty foods. Hepatitis E is transmitted in the same way as hepatitis A; it can be particularly serious in pregnant women.

There are almost 300 million chronic carriers of **hepatitis B** in the world. It is spread through contact with infected blood, blood products or body fluids, for example through sexual contact, unsterilised needles and blood transfusions, or contact with blood via small breaks in the skin. Other risk situations include having a shave, tattoo or body piercing with contaminated equipment. The symptoms of hepatitis B may be more severe than type A and the disease can lead to long term problems such as chronic liver damage, liver cancer or a long-term carrier state. Hepatitis C and D are spread in the same way as hepatitis B and can also lead to long-term complications.

There are vaccines against hepatitis A and B, but there are currently no vaccines against the other types of hepatitis. Following the basic rules about food and water (hepatitis A and E) and avoiding risk situations (hepatitis B, C and D) are important preventative measures.

HIV & AIDS Infection with the human immunodeficiency virus (HIV) may lead to acquired immune deficiency syndrome (AIDS), which is a fatal disease. Any exposure to blood, blood products or body fluids may put the individual at risk. The disease is often transmitted through sexual contact or dirty needles – vaccinations, acupuncture, tattooing and body piercing can be potentially as dangerous as intravenous drug use. HIV/AIDS can also be spread through infected blood transfusions; some developing countries cannot afford to screen blood used for transfusions. In Myanmar it is uncertain whether proper screening procedures are being followed. If you do need an injection, ask to see the syringe unwrapped in front of you, or take a needle and syringe pack with you.

Fear of HIV infection should never preclude treatment for serious medical conditions.

Intestinal Worms These parasites are most common in rural, tropical areas. The different worms have different ways of infecting people. Some may be ingested on food such as undercooked meat (eg, tapeworms) and some enter through your skin (eg, hookworms). Infestations may not show up for some time, and although they are generally not serious, if left untreated some can cause severe health problems later. Consider having a stool test when you return home to check for these and determine the appropriate treatment.

Sexually Transmitted Infections HIV/AIDS and hepatitis B can be transmitted through sexual contact – see the relevant sections earlier for more details. Other STIs include gonorrhoea, herpes and syphilis; sores, blisters or rashes around the genitals and discharges or pain when urinating are common symptoms. In some STIs, such as wart virus or chlamydia, symptoms may be less marked or not observed at all, especially in women. Chlamydia infection can cause infertility before any symptoms have been noticed. Syphilis symptoms eventually disappear completely but the disease continues and can cause severe problems in later years. While abstinence from sexual contact is the only 100% effective prevention, using condoms is also effective. The treatment of gonorrhoea and syphilis is with antibiotics. The different sexually transmitted diseases each require specific antibiotics.

Typhoid Typhoid fever is a dangerous gut infection caused by contaminated water and food. Medical help must be sought.

In its early stages sufferers may feel they have a bad cold or flu on the way, as early symptoms are a headache, body aches and a fever which rises a little each day until it is around 40°C (104°F) or more. The victim's pulse is often slow relative to the degree of fever present – unlike a normal fever where the pulse increases. There may also be vomiting, abdominal pain, diarrhoea or constipation.

In the second week the high fever and slow pulse continue and a few pink spots may appear on the body; trembling, delirium, weakness, weight loss and dehydration may occur. Complications such as pneumonia, perforated bowel or meningitis may occur.

Insect-Borne Diseases

Malaria This serious and potentially fatal disease is spread by mosquito bites. If you are travelling in endemic areas it is extremely important to avoid mosquito bites and to take tablets to prevent this disease. Symptoms range from fever, chills and sweating, headache, diarrhoea and abdominal pains to a vague feeling of ill-health. One of the telltale signs of malaria is the cyclic nature of the symptoms, coming on, for example, every couple of days or every afternoon. Seek medical help immediately if malaria is suspected. Without treatment malaria can rapidly become more serious and can be fatal.

There is a variety of medications such as mefloquine, Fansidar and Malarone. You should seek medical advice, before you travel, on the right medication and dosage for you. If medical care is not available, malaria tablets can be used for treatment. You need to use a malaria tablet that is different from the one you were taking when you contracted malaria.

You needn't worry about malaria in the cities, but in rural areas, particularly in the eastern Shan, Kayah and Kayin States and along the Thai border, malaria is a real risk.

Travellers are advised to prevent mosquito bites at all times. The main messages are:

- Wear light-coloured clothing.
- Wear long trousers and long-sleeved shirts.
- Use mosquito repellents containing the compound DEET on exposed areas (prolonged overuse of DEET may be harmful, especially to children, but its use is considered preferable to being bitten by disease-transmitting mosquitoes).
- Avoid perfumes or aftershave.
- Use a mosquito net impregnated with mosquito repellent (permethrin) – it may be worth taking your own.
- Impregnate clothes with permethrin, which effectively deters mosquitoes and other insects.

Dengue Fever This viral disease is transmitted by mosquitoes and is fast becoming one of the top public health problems in the tropical world. Unlike the malaria mosquito, the *Aedes aegypti* mosquito, which transmits the dengue virus, is most active during the day, and is found mainly in urban areas, in and around human dwellings.

Signs and symptoms of dengue fever include a sudden onset of high fever, headache, joint and muscle pains (hence its old name, 'breakbone fever') and nausea and vomiting. A rash of small red spots sometimes appears three to four days after the onset of fever. In the early phase of illness, dengue may be mistaken for other infectious diseases, including malaria and influenza.

Minor bleeding such as nose bleeds may occur in the course of the illness, but this does not necessarily mean that you have progressed to the potentially fatal dengue haemorrhagic fever (DHF). This is a severe illness, characterised by heavy bleeding, which is thought to be a result of second infection due to a different strain (there are four major strains) and usually affects residents of the country rather than travellers. Recovery even from simple dengue fever may be prolonged, with tiredness lasting for several weeks.

You should seek medical attention as soon as possible if you think you may be infected. A blood test can exclude malaria and indicate the possibility of dengue fever. There is no specific treatment for dengue. Aspirin should be avoided, as it increases the risk of haemorrhaging. There is no vaccine against dengue fever. The best prevention is to avoid mosquito bites at all times by covering up, using insect repellents containing the compound DEET and mosquito nets – see the Malaria section earlier for more advice on avoiding mosquito bites.

Japanese B Encephalitis This viral infection of the brain is transmitted by mosquitoes. Most cases occur in rural areas as the virus exists in pigs and wading birds. Symptoms include fever, headache and alteration in consciousness. Hospitalisation is needed for correct diagnosis and treatment. There is a high mortality rate among those who have symptoms; of those who survive many are intellectually disabled.

Cuts, Bites & Stings

See Less Common Diseases for details of rabies, which is passed through animal bites.

Cuts & Scratches Wash well and treat any cut with an antiseptic such as povidone-iodine. Where possible avoid bandages and Band-Aids, which can keep wounds wet. Coral cuts are notoriously slow to heal and if they are not adequately cleaned, small pieces of coral can become embedded in the wound.

Bedbugs & Lice Bedbugs live in various places, but particularly in dirty mattresses and bedding, evidenced by spots of blood on bedclothes or on the wall. Bedbugs leave itchy bites in neat rows. Calamine lotion or a sting relief spray may help.

All lice cause itching and discomfort. They make themselves at home in your hair (head lice), your clothing (body lice) or in your pubic hair (crabs). You catch lice through direct contact with infected people or by sharing combs, clothing and the like. Powder or shampoo treatment will kill the lice, and infected clothing should then be washed in very hot, soapy water and left in the sun to dry.

Bites & Stings Bee and wasp stings are usually painful rather than dangerous. However, in people who are allergic to them severe breathing difficulties may occur and require urgent medical care. Calamine lotion or a sting-relief spray will give relief and ice packs will reduce the pain and swelling. Scorpion stings in Myanmar are notoriously painful but not dangerous.

Leeches & Ticks Leeches may be present in damp rainforest conditions; they attach themselves to your skin to suck your blood. Trekkers often get them on their legs or in their boots. Salt or a lighted cigarette end will make them fall off. Do not pull them off, as the bite is then more likely to become infected. Clean and apply pressure if the point of attachment is bleeding. An insect repellent may keep them away.

You should always check all over your body if you have been walking through a potentially tick-infested area as ticks can cause skin infections and other more serious diseases. If a tick is found attached, press down around the tick's head with tweezers, grab the head and gently pull upwards. Avoid pulling the rear of the body as this may squeeze the tick's gut contents through the attached mouth parts into the skin, increasing the risk of infection and disease. Smearing chemicals on the tick will not make it let go and is not recommended.

Snakes To minimise your chances of being bitten always wear boots, socks and long trousers when walking through undergrowth where snakes may be present. Don't put your hands into holes and crevices, and be careful when collecting firewood. Pay particular attention and dress appropriately when exploring ruins such as Bagan and Mrauk U.

Snake bites do not cause instantaneous death and antivenins are usually available. Immediately wrap the bitten limb tightly, as you would for a sprained ankle, and then attach a splint to immobilise it. Keep the victim still and seek medical help, if possible with the dead snake for identification. Don't attempt to catch the snake if there is a possibility of being bitten again. Tourniquets and sucking out the poison are now comprehensively discredited.

Women's Health

Gynaecological Problems Antibiotic use, synthetic underwear, sweating and contraceptive pills can lead to fungal vaginal infections, especially when travelling in hot climates. Thrush or vaginal candidiasis is characterised by a rash, itch and discharge. Nystatin, miconazole or clotrimazole pessaries are the usual treatment, but some people use a more traditional remedy involving vinegar or lemon-juice douches, or yogurt. Maintaining good personal hygiene and wearing loose-fitting clothes and cotton underwear may help prevent these infections.

Sexually transmitted infections are a major cause of vaginal problems. Symptoms include a smelly discharge, painful intercourse and sometimes a burning sensation when urinating. Medical attention should be sought and male sexual partners must also be treated. For more details see the section on Sexually Transmitted Infections earlier. Besides abstinence, the best thing is to practise safer sex using condoms.

Pregnancy It is not advisable to travel to some places while pregnant as some vaccinations normally used to prevent serious diseases are not advisable during pregnancy (eg, yellow fever). In addition, some diseases are much more serious for the mother (and may increase the risk of a stillborn child) in pregnancy (eg, malaria).

Most miscarriages occur during the first three months of pregnancy. Miscarriage is not uncommon and can occasionally lead to severe bleeding. The last three months should also be spent within reasonable distance of good medical care. A baby born as early as 24 weeks stands a chance of survival, but only in a good modern hospital. Pregnant women should avoid all unnecessary medication, although vaccinations and malarial prophylactics should still be taken where needed. Additional care should be taken to prevent illness and particular attention should be paid to diet and nutrition. Alcohol and nicotine, for example, should be avoided.

Less Common Diseases

The following diseases pose a small risk to travellers, and so are only mentioned in passing. Seek medical advice if you think you may have any of these diseases.

Cholera This is the worst of the watery diarrhoeas and medical help should be sought. Outbreaks of cholera are generally widely reported, so you can avoid such problem areas. *Fluid replacement is the most vital treatment* – the risk of dehydration is severe as you may lose up to 20L a day. If there is a delay in getting to hospital, then begin taking tetracycline. The adult dose is 250mg four times daily. It is not recommended for children under nine years nor for pregnant women. Tetracycline may help shorten the illness, but adequate fluids are required to save lives.

Rabies This fatal viral infection is very common in Myanmar. Many animals can be infected (such as dogs, cats, bats and monkeys) and it is their saliva which is infectious. Any bite, scratch or even lick from an animal should be cleaned immediately and thoroughly. Scrub with soap and running water, and then apply alcohol or iodine solution. Medical help should be sought promptly to receive a course of injections to prevent the onset of symptoms and death.

Tetanus This disease is caused by a germ which lives in soil and in the faeces of horses and other animals. It enters the body via breaks in the skin. The first symptom may be discomfort in swallowing, or stiffening of the jaw and neck; this is followed by painful convulsions of the jaw and whole body. The disease can be fatal. It can be prevented by vaccination.

Tuberculosis (TB) TB is a bacterial infection usually transmitted from person to person by coughing but which may be transmitted through consumption of unpasteurised milk. Milk that has been boiled is safe to drink, and the souring of milk to make yogurt or cheese also kills the bacilli. Travellers are usually not at great risk as close household contact with the infected person is usually required before the disease is passed on. You may need to have a TB test before you travel as this can help diagnose the disease later if you become ill.

Typhus This disease is spread by ticks, mites or lice. It begins with fever, chills, headache and muscle pains followed a few days later by a body rash. There is often a large painful sore at the site of the bite and nearby lymph nodes are swollen and painful. Typhus can be treated under medical supervision. Seek local advice on areas where ticks pose a danger and always check your skin carefully for ticks after walking in a danger area such as a tropical forest. An insect repellent can help, and walkers in tick-infested areas should consider having their boots and trousers impregnated with benzyl benzoate and dibutylphthalate.

WOMEN TRAVELLERS

Attitudes Towards Women

The 1999 UN Gender-related Development Index (GDI) ranks Myanmar 107th on a list of 162 nations with regard to a matrix of factors, which include education, health care, employment rate and share of earned income relative to male citizens of Myanmar. By contrast, neighbouring countries Thailand and India are ranked 58th and 105th respectively. The adult literacy rate for Myanmar women is 80.1% versus 88.8% for Myanmar men. In 1998 the average share of earned income, however, totalled 46.4%, which beat the USA (40%), France (39.1%), Canada (37.9%) and Switzerland (32.4%).

In most respects Burmese women enjoy legal rights equal to those of Burmese men; for example, they own property and aren't barred from any profession. Unlike in the West, females do not traditionally change any portion of their names upon marriage; in the event of divorce, they are legally due half of all property accumulated during the marriage. Inheritance rights are also equally shared. Female children are educated alongside male children and, by university age, women tend to outnumber men in university and college enrolment. Most professions grant women a paid maternity leave of six weeks before birth and one or two months afterwards.

Religion is one arena in which women perpetually take a back seat. A small number of Buddhist shrines, for example Mandalay's Mahamuni Paya, have small areas around the main holy image that are off-limits to women. Many Burmese – women as well as men – believe a female birth indicates less religious merit than a male birth, and that it is easier for males to attain *nibbana* (nirvana). A small but devoted minority of men and women refute this view, pointing out that the actual *suttas*, or sayings of the Buddha, do not support this assumption.

Just as boys between the ages of five and 15 usually undergo a pre-puberty initiation as temporary novice monks, girls around the same age participate in an initiatory ear-piercing ceremony (often called 'ear-boring' in Burmese English). Some also become temporary nuns at this age. For details on clerical differences between Buddhist monks and nuns, see the Monks & Nuns entry under Burmese Buddhism in the Religion section of the Facts about Myanmar chapter.

Saw Myat Yin, insightful author of *Culture Shock! Burma*, expresses a viewpoint common among the majority of Burmese women, who see their role as equal but 'supportive and complementary…rather than in competition' and that 'if they accept a role a step behind their menfolk they do so freely and willingly'. Though some Westerners may find this difficult to believe, this represents the most commonly expressed perception in Myanmar. Even Aung San Suu Kyi, Myanmar's torchbearer of democracy, has written:

Although theoretically men are considered nobler because only a man can become a Buddha, Burmese women have never really had an inferior status. They have always had equal rights of inheritance and led active, independent lives. Secure in the knowledge of her own worth, the Burmese woman does not mind giving men the kind of respectful treatment that makes them so happy!

Safety Precautions

In Myanmar no Burmese woman would even consider travelling without at least one female companion, so women travelling alone are regarded as slightly peculiar by the locals. Women travelling alone and being seen off on boats and trains by Burmese friends may find the latter trying to find a suitably responsible older woman to keep them company on the trip.

As in most Buddhist countries, foreign women travelling in Myanmar are rarely hassled on the road as they might be in, for example, India, Malaysia or Indonesia. However, we have received a few reports of foreign women being harassed while travelling in Myanmar. Dressing modestly should help to reduce the risk of sexual harassment. Women travelling in Myanmar during the April Water Festival (Thingyan) should take extra precautions.

As in neighbouring Thailand, drunkenness and an 'anything goes' atmosphere, combined with Western women in tight, wet, T-shirts, is apparently too much for some Burmese men to bear – we've heard of women being groped during the festival. Again, dressing modestly should help to prevent such incidents.

GAY & LESBIAN TRAVELLERS

Most of the cultures of Myanmar are very tolerant of homosexuality, both male and female. Muslim and Christian Burmese communities are exceptions, but as they form relatively small minorities they rarely foist their world perspectives on people of other faiths.

Although it's difficult to tell given the opaqueness of the current military-directed government – which contains no true judiciary branch – there appear to be no laws that discriminate against homosexuals. Certainly we have never heard of anyone facing prosecution or arrest for homosexual behaviour.

The gay/lesbian scene around the country is relatively low-key – certainly nowhere near as prominent as in neighbouring Thailand. Whether speaking of dress or mannerism, lesbians and gays are generally accepted without comment.

Since homosexuals are free to meet wherever they wish without encountering social prejudice, furtive secrecy is much less common than in Western countries and other less liberated parts of the world. Public displays of affection – whether heterosexual or homosexual – are frowned upon.

DISABLED TRAVELLERS

With its lack of paved roads or footpaths – even when present the latter are often uneven – Myanmar presents many physical obstacles for the mobility-impaired. Rarely do public buildings feature ramps or other access points for wheelchairs, nor do any hotels consistently make efforts to provide handicapped access (the single exception is Traders Hotel in Yangon, which has some ramping). Hence you're pretty much left to your own resources. Public transport is particularly crowded and difficult, even for the fully ambulatory.

For wheelchair travellers, any trip to Myanmar will require a good deal of advance planning. Fortunately a growing network of information sources can put you in touch with those who may have wheeled through Myanmar before. There is no better source of information than someone who's done it.

Organisations

There are three international organisations that act as clearing houses for information on world travel for the mobility-impaired. They are: **Mobility International USA** *(☎ 514-343 1284, fax 541-343 6812; Ⓦ www.miusa.org; PO Box 10767, Eugene, OR 97440, USA)*;

Access Foundation *(☎ 516-887 5798; PO Box 356, Malverne, NY 11565, USA)*; and the **Society for the Advancement of Travel for the Handicapped** *(SATH; ☎ 212-447 7284, fax 725 8253; w www.sath.org; Suite 610, 347 Fifth Avenue, New York, NY 10016, USA)*. SATH publishes a very good magazine called *Open World*.

Abilities magazine *(☎ 416-923 9980, fax 923 9829; e info@enablelink.org; w www.enablelink.org; 501-489 College St, Toronto, ON M6G 1A5)* has an article on travel in nearly every issue. The book *Exotic Destinations for Wheelchair Travelers* by Ed Hansen & Bruce Gordon (Full Data Ltd, San Francisco) contains useful information on Southeast Asia (including Thailand), though nothing specific to Myanmar.

SENIOR TRAVELLERS

Senior discounts aren't available in Myanmar, but the Burmese more than make up for this with the respect they typically show for the elderly. In all the cultures of Myanmar, status comes with age; there isn't nearly as heavy an emphasis on youth as in the Western world. Deference for age manifests itself in the way the Burmese will go out of their way to help older persons in and out of vehicles or with luggage, and – usually but not always – in waiting on them first in shops and post offices.

Cross-generational entertainment is more common than in China, Vietnam or Thailand. Although there is some age stratification in karaoke clubs or discos, all ages are welcome. At more traditional events such as rural paya fairs and other temple-centred events, young and old dance and eat together.

TRAVEL WITH CHILDREN

Like many places in Southeast Asia, travelling with children in Myanmar can be very rewarding as long as you come well prepared with the right attitudes, physical requirements and the usual parental patience. Lonely Planet's *Travel with Children* by Cathy Lanigan contains useful advice on how to cope with kids on the road and what to bring along to make things go more smoothly, with special attention paid to travel in developing countries.

The Burmese love children and in many instances will shower attention on your offspring, who will find ready playmates among their local counterparts and an impromptu nanny service at practically every stop.

Due to Myanmar's overall low level of public sanitation, parents ought to lay down a few ground rules with regard to health maintenance – such as regular hand-washing – to head off potential medical problems. All the usual health precautions apply (see the Health section earlier in this chapter for details); children should especially be warned not to play with animals encountered along the way as a precaution against rabies.

DANGERS & ANNOYANCES

Tales of insurgents, terrorists, forbidden areas and so on make Myanmar sound as if it is a rather unsafe country to visit; the truth is actually quite different. In the late 1990s, the government and most insurgent groups signed treaties giving limited economic autonomy to many areas, which has resulted in the pacification of all but a handful of areas.

Sporadic fighting continues along the border with Thailand, but unless you're a Kayin refugee this is unlikely to affect you. An Australian and a Thai national were abducted by Kayin rebels at the border in early 1998, but were released unharmed after a few days.

So long as you do not venture into areas that are not under government control (a possibility that the government is firmly determined not to allow), you're very unlikely to run into any difficulty. For the most part, the few remaining insurgents seem to stick to their own territory and leave the government's territory to the government.

Of course, in the government-controlled areas (the places where you are permitted to go), the possibility of being mugged, robbed, held up or enjoying any of those other unpleasant, everyday Western events is similarly remote. However, we do recommend that you keep a close eye on your valuables, particularly during overnight train trips.

In a few unpacified areas there are bandits who hold up vehicles at night; this seems to be most common in the Tanintharyi division – an area foreign travellers are still prohibited from traversing overland. In some cases the bandits claim to be politically motivated, but their methods and targets leave this seriously in doubt. A group of eight bandits operating in southern Tanintharyi Division, between Myeik and Kawthoung, claim to belong to the All Burma Students Democratic Front (ABSDF), but their activities appear to be confined solely to ripping off passengers in civilian vehicles that ply this road – hardly a revolutionary stance. So far no foreigner has been affected in robberies in any of these areas.

You must also be cautious about talking Burmese politics with the locals, not for your safety but for theirs. The people who have the best chance of filling you in on the latest events are those Burmese who deal with foreign tourists on a regular basis – trishaw drivers, vendors and tour guides. Because of their occupations, these people can talk at length with foreigners without arousing suspicion; when not in the presence of other Burmese they can be surprisingly forthcoming with their views. The average Burmese on the street, however, would be very circumspect about conversing openly with a foreigner about politics.

Be aware that if you make bold gestures of political protest you may get your Burmese contacts in trouble and yourself deported or jailed immediately. One traveller wrote to tell us that during her trip in Myanmar, two foreign bus travellers refused to show their passports at a military checkpoint as a form of protest. As a result, the bus driver was ordered by the army to stand in the sun for three hours while the travellers waited on the bus, completely unaware of the situation they had caused. The government is unlikely to harass tourists, but may well take it out on the locals behind closed doors.

Note also that Myanmar has one of the highest incidences of death from snake bite in the world – watch your step in forest areas! See Cuts, Bites & Stings in the Health section earlier in this chapter.

See also the earlier Health section for cautions on personal health.

Air Travel

Government-operated Myanma Airways (MA) has one of the worst safety records in the world. The year 1998 alone saw two MA crashes that involved fatalities. We recommend that you avoid travel on this airline if at all possible (see the Getting Around chapter for details and recommendations).

EMERGENCIES

For medical emergencies, the **Diplomatic Hospital** (*☎ 550149; Kyaikkasan Rd*) is your best bet in Yangon. The police emergency number is ☎ 199; in Yangon, police headquarters can be contacted on ☎ 282541 or 284764.

LEGAL MATTERS

The Myanmar government contains no judiciary branch as separate from the executive powers vested – by force of totalitarian rule – in the Tatmadaw. Thus you have absolutely zero legal recourse in case of arrest or detainment by the authorities, regardless of the charge. Foreign visitors engaging in political activism risk deportation or imprisonment. However, if you were arrested, you would most likely be permitted to contact your consular agent in Myanmar for possible assistance.

If you purchase gems or jewellery from persons or shops that are not licensed by the government, you run the risk of having them all confiscated if customs officials find them in your baggage when you're exiting the country.

Drugs are another area where you must be very careful. We know of a French traveller arrested for possession of opium or heroin in Kengtung and held for several weeks before he was able to bribe his way out.

Many foreigners have foolishly entered Myanmar illegally from northern Thailand, but not all have succeeded in avoiding arrest. We know a Chinese-Malaysian reporter, stationed in Bangkok, who was arrested near Kengtung for travelling in Myanmar without a valid visa. He spent an uncomfortable year in prison in Kengtung before being released. In late 1998 three Western motorcyclists crossed from Thailand's Mae Hong Son Province into the Shan State illegally; they were held for three months before being released and deported.

See the 'Visa Applications' boxed text earlier in this chapter on the hazards peculiar to journalistic professions.

BUSINESS HOURS

Most government offices are open Monday to Friday from 9.30am to 4.30pm (usually posted as 16.30, according to the 24-hour system). Don't arrive at a government office at 4pm expecting to get anything done; most government workers start drifting away to the local teashops after 3.30pm.

Banks are open from 10am to 2pm on weekdays only. Private shops are generally open from around 9.30am or 10am till 6pm.

PUBLIC HOLIDAYS & SPECIAL EVENTS

Traditionally Myanmar follows a 12-month lunar calendar, so the old holidays and festivals will vary in date, by the Gregorian calendar, from year to year (see Months under Time & Dates earlier in this chapter for a list of these months). Myanmar also has a number of more recently originated holidays whose dates are fixed by the Gregorian calendar.

Festivals are drawn-out, enjoyable affairs in Myanmar. They generally take place or culminate on full-moon days, but the build-up can last for days. There's often a country-fair atmosphere about these festivals – at some convenient grounds there will be innumerable stalls and activities that go on all night. Pwe, music and Burmese boxing bouts will all be part of the colourful scene. The normally calm Burmese can get really worked up during these festivals – at a full-moon festival on one of our visits to Yangon the supporters of the defeated favourite in a boxing bout were so enraged they wrecked the arena, and subsequent bouts had to be cancelled.

January/February

Independence Day This day, 4 January, is a major public holiday marked by a seven-day fair at Kandawgyi (Royal) Lake in Yangon. There are fairs all over the country at this time.

Union Day Celebrated on 12 February, this day marks Bogyoke Aung San's short-lived achievement of unifying Myanmar's disparate racial groups. For two weeks preceding Union Day, the national flag is paraded from town to town, and wherever the flag rests there must be a festival. The month of Tabodwe culminates in a rice-harvesting festival on the new-moon day. *Htamin* (literally, rice), a special food-offering made and eaten at this time, consists of glutinous rice mixed with sesame, peanuts, shredded ginger and coconut. In villages large batches of htamin are cooked over open fires and stirred with big wooden paddles until they become a thick mass, after which the rice is wrapped in small banana-leaf parcels and distributed among all the members of the community.

February/March

Shwedagon Festival The lunar month of Tabaung brings the annual Shwedagon Festival, the largest *paya pwe* (pagoda festival) in Myanmar. The full-moon day in Tabaung is also an auspicious occasion for the construction of new paya, and local paya festivals are held.

Peasants' Day/Armed Forces Day Two holidays fall during March: 2 March is Peasants' Day, while 27 March is Resistance or Armed Forces Day, celebrated with parades and fireworks. Since 1989, the Tatmadaw has made it a tradition to pardon a number of prisoners on Armed Forces Day.

April/May

The Buddha's Birthday The full-moon day of Kason is celebrated as the Buddha's birthday, the day of his enlightenment and the day he entered nibbana. Thus it is known as the 'thrice blessed day'. The holiday is celebrated by the ceremonial watering of *bo* trees, the sacred banyan tree under which the Buddha attained enlightenment. One of the best places to observe this ceremony is at Yangon's Shwedagon Paya, where a procession of girls carry earthen jars to water the three banyan trees on the western side of the compound.

The Water Festival (Thingyan) This is the celebration of the Burmese New Year. See 'The Water Festival' boxed text later for detailed information about this holiday.

Workers' Day Although the government renounced socialism in 1989, the country still celebrates May Day – 1 May – as Workers' Day.

June/July

Start of the Buddhist Rains Retreat The full moon of Waso is the beginning of the three-month Buddhist Rains Retreat (sometimes referred to as 'Buddhist Lent'). Laypeople present monasteries with stacks of new robes for resident monks, since during the rainy season monks are restricted to their monasteries for a prolonged period of spiritual retreat. Ordinary people are also expected to be rather more religious during this time – marriages do not take place and it is inauspicious to move house. The most devout Burmese Buddhist will observe eight precepts – rather than the usual five – for the duration of the season. This is also the traditional time for young men to temporarily enter the monasteries.

Martyrs' Day 19 July is Martyrs' Day, commemorating the assassination of Bogyoke Aung San and his comrades on that day in 1947. Wreaths are laid at his mausoleum north of the Shwedagon Paya in Yangon.

July/August

Wagaung Festival At the festival in Wagaung, lots are drawn to see who will have to provide monks with their alms. If you're in Mandalay, try to get to Taungbyone, about 30km north, where there is a noisy, seven-day festival to keep the nat happy.

September/October

Boat Races This is the height of the wet season, so what better time to hold boat races? They're held in rivers, lakes and even ponds all over Myanmar, but the best place to be is Inle where the Buddha images at the Phaung Daw U Kyaung are ceremonially toured around the lake in the huge royal barge, the Karaweik. The Phaung Daw U festival comes just before the festival of Thadingyut and usually overlaps late September and early October.

Thadingyut In Thadingyut, the Buddhist Rains Retreat comes to an end and all those couples who had been putting off marriage now rush into each other's arms. Monks are free to travel from kyaung to kyaung or to go on pilgrimage to holy spots such as Kyaiktiyo or Mt Popa. The Festival of Lights takes place during Thadingyut to celebrate the Buddha's return from a period of preaching *abhidhamma* (higher Buddhist teachings) in Tavatimsa (the highest *deva* realm), his way lit by devas who lined the route of his descent. For the three days of the festival all of Myanmar is lit by oil lamps, fire balloons, candles and even mundane electric lamps. Every house has a paper lantern hanging outside and it's a happy time – particularly after the solemnity of the previous three months. Pwe may be performed on *pandal* (stage platforms) erected along city streets, particularly in Mandalay.

October/November

Tazaungmon The full-moon night of Tazaungmon is an occasion for another 'festival of lights', known properly as Tazaungdaing. It's particularly celebrated in the Shan State – in Taunggyi there are fire-balloon competitions. In some areas there are also speed-weaving competitions during the night – young Burmese women show their prowess at weaving by attempting to produce robes for Buddha images between dusk and dawn. The results, finished or not, are donated to the monks. The biggest weaving competitions take place at Shwedagon Paya in Yangon.

Kahtein Tazaungmon also brings *kahtein* (Pali: *kathina*), a one-month period at the end of the Buddhist Rains Retreat during which new monastic robes and requisites are offered to the monastic community. Many people simply donate cash; kyat notes are folded and stapled into floral patterns on wooden 'trees' called *padetha* and offered to the monasteries.

National Day Myanmar's national day falls in late November or early December.

November/December

Nadaw During Nadaw, many nat pwe are held; Nadaw is actually spelt with the characters for nat and *taw* (respectful honorific).

Christmas Despite Myanmar's predominantly Buddhist background, Christmas Day is a public holiday in deference to the many Christian Kayin, Kachin and Chin.

December/January

Kayin New Year Held on the first waxing moon of Pyatho, the Kayin new year is considered a national holiday. Kayin communities throughout Myanmar celebrate by wearing their traditional dress of woven tunics over red longyi and by hosting folk dancing and singing performances. The largest celebrations are held in the Kayin suburb of Insein, just north of Yangon, and in Hpa-an, the capital of the Kayin State.

Ananda Festival The Ananda Festival, held at the Ananda Paya in Bagan, also takes place during Pyatho.

The Water Festival

Around the middle of April, the three-day Thingyan (Water Festival) starts the Burmese New Year. Thingyan, from the Sanskrit *samkranta* (fully passed over), celebrates the passage of the sun from the sign of Pisces into the sign of Aries in the zodiac. This is the height of the dry and hot season and, as in Thailand's Songkran, it is celebrated in a most raucous manner – by throwing buckets of cold water at anyone who dares to venture into the streets. Foreigners are not exempt!

In cities, temporary stages called *pandal* (from the Tamil *pendel*) are erected along main thoroughfares. Each pandal is sponsored by civic groups, neighbourhood associations, student societies or government departments, the members of whom stand next to rows of water barrels and douse every person or vehicle that passes by.

On a spiritual level, the Burmese believe that during this three-day period the king of the *nat* (spirits), Thagyamin, visits the human world to tally his annual record of the good deeds and misdeeds humans have performed. Villagers place flowers and sacred leaves in front of their homes to welcome the nat. Thagyamin's departure on the morning of the third day marks the beginning of the new year, when properly brought-up young people wash the hair of their elder kin, Buddha images are ceremonially washed and *hpongyi* (monks) are offered particularly appetising alms food.

Although the true meaning of the festival is still kept alive by ceremonies such as these, nowadays it's mainly a festival of fun. In between getting soaked, there will be dancing, singing and theatre. In the latter, the emphasis is on satire – particularly making fun of the government, the latest female fashions and any other items of everyday interest. Cultural taboos against women acting in a boisterous manner are temporarily lifted, so women can 'kidnap' young men, blacken their faces with soot or oil, bind their hands and dunk their heads in buckets of water until the boys surrender and perform a hilarious monkey dance for the girls.

Joe Cummings

Paya Pwe

In addition to these main pan-Myanmar festivals, nearly every active paya or kyaung community hosts occasional celebrations of its own, often called 'pagoda festivals' in Burmese English. The typical paya pwe features the same kinds of activities as a major festival – craft and food vendors, music and dance – on a smaller scale. The biggest proliferation of paya fairs occur on full-moon days and nights during the January to March period, following the main rice harvest, providing local paddy farmers and their families with a good excuse to party. The festivals also offer added market venues for local basket weavers, potters, woodcarvers, blacksmiths, longyi-weavers and other artisans.

To the professional *hse-hna pwe thi* (twelve-festival traders) who travel from festival to festival following the lunar calendar, the smaller paya fairs serve as convenient fillers between major gigs. Other assorted camp followers include fortune-tellers, movable teashops, tent barbers, homespun beauty consultants, pickpockets and professional beggars.

Particular paya festivals are described in the appropriate destination sections throughout this guidebook.

ACTIVITIES

Cycling

Although one highly publicised package-tour group cycling south from Bagan had problems with permits a couple of years ago, many individuals have brought their bikes into Myanmar and cycled around the unrestricted areas of the country with no problems. Cycling is the ideal form of local transport because bikes are cheap, nonpolluting and keep you moving slowly enough to see everything. The terrain – varying from rutted, unsealed dirt or gravel roads to potholed, semi-paved ones – is definitely not for the average touring bike. Instead you'll need a sturdy mountain bike equipped with thick tyres. Shoulders may be nonexistent, but for the most part drivers are courteous and move over for bicycles. Plain black Indian or Chinese bicycles can be hired in Mandalay, Bagan, Hsipaw, Nyaungshwe and a few other places. Carefully note the condition of the bike before hiring; if it breaks down you are responsible and parts can be expensive.

There is plenty of opportunity for dirt-road and off-road pedalling in all areas of the country, but be sure to stay well within the boundaries of what's allowed for foreign tourists. Don't even think about going north of Lashio, east of Taungoo, east of Taunggyi or south of Kalaw, as these areas are particularly sensitive. Good touring routes include the two-lane roads along the Ayeyarwady between Mandalay and Yangon via Bagan, Pyay and many other less well-known towns. The terrain along the Ayeyarwady is mostly flat and the river scenery is inspiring.

One note of caution: before you leave home, go over your bike with a fine-toothed comb and fill your repair kit with every imaginable spare part. You're highly unlikely to be able to buy that crucial gismo for your machine when it breaks down somewhere in the back of beyond as the sun sets.

No special permits are needed for bringing a bicycle into the country, although bikes may be registered by customs – which means if you don't leave the country with your bike you'll have to pay a customs duty. Most larger cities have bike shops but they usually stock only a few Indian, Chinese, Thai or locally made parts. Japanese bike parts can also sometimes be found. All the usual bike trip precautions apply – bring a repair kit with plenty of spare parts, a helmet, reflective clothing and plenty of insurance.

You can take bicycles on the trains for a relatively small cargo fee. Buses often don't charge (if they do it will be something nominal); on the ordinary buses they'll place your bike on the roof, and on express air-con buses it will go in the cargo hold.

Hiking

Northern Myanmar's potential as a serious hiking venue remains virtually untapped due to the sensitive political nature of the mountainous frontier states. Out-of-town hikes are now permitted in the 'secure' area of the Shan State stretching from Kalaw east to Inle. So far about the only place you'll find hiking guides are in the small towns of Kalaw, Nyaungshwe and Kengtung.

The area around Kalaw and Pindaya offers a variety of possible mountain hikes to minority villages. At present overnight hikes don't seem to be officially permitted, though that hasn't stopped some visitors from spending the night in the occasional village. Guides in Nyaungshwe can lead hikes into the hills east of Inle – but not too far east, as Shan and Red Pa-O insurgent territory crops up quickly in this direction.

The areas around Hsipaw and Lashio are an interesting possibility. Hsipaw is the better or the two as it's possible to get locally drawn maps of trails to the surrounding villages.

Kengtung, in the far eastern section of the Shan State, makes an excellent base for treks to nearby Wa, Shan, Kheun and Akha villages.

Mt Kyaikto, site of Kyaiktiyo Paya in southeastern Myanmar, offers an easily navigated but physically challenging uphill climb if you start from the bottom – about a four-hour hike. Branch trails around the mountain provide at least a couple of days' worth of side hikes that few foreign visitors have so far experienced.

Mountaineers everywhere are awaiting the day when the highest mountain in Southeast Asia, snow-clad Hkakabo Razi (5889m), on the border of Myanmar and Tibet, and nearby Gamlang Razi (5835m) are open to climbers. A team of Japanese and Burmese climbers was allowed to climb Hkakabo Razi in 1997, but there was reportedly much paperwork involved in getting permission. Those few foreigners who have made it as far as Putao – a valley town in the same general region – have been disappointed; until the area north of Putao opens there's little point in going to the trouble of obtaining a permit to fly to Putao.

Diving & Snorkelling

Coastal, insular and marine Myanmar are nearly untouched in terms of their potential for underwater exploration. The only area that has been dived so far – and only since January 1997 – is a small portion of the Myeik Archipelago, a string of some 804 islands running more or less parallel to the coast of the 480km-long Myeik Peninsula.

Myeik Archipelago diving has so far been organised only as live-aboard dive cruises out of Phuket or Kawthoung. Reports say diving conditions are excellent. Many islands feature lofty limestone sea cliffs pockmarked with caves, some of which form extensive submarine networks or lead to enclosed tidal lagoons. The larger islands also contain mountainous, forested interiors with a considerable hiking potential to supplement diving activities. Around a dozen big-league dive sites have so far been identified, from the so-called Burma Banks in the south (claimed by Myanmar but actually in international waters according to international maritime law) all the way to Tanintharyi Kyun (known to the British as Tenasserim Island) west of the port town of Myeik itself.

For the time being the only way to dive in the Myeik Archipelago is to join one of the liveaboard cruises operated by companies based in Thailand. Dive trips last between five to 10 days and cost between US$165 and US$180 per person per day, plus US$140 per person for a Myanmar customs entry permit. Among the more experienced outfitters offering Myeik diving are:

Asian Adventures (☎ 076 341 799, fax 076 342 798, W www.asian-adventures.com) 237 Thanon Rat Uthit, Hat Patong, Phuket, Thailand

Fantasea Divers (☎ 076 281 388, fax 076 281 389, W www.fantasea.net) 43/20 Thanon Viset, Hat Rawai, Phuket, Thailand

Faraway Sail & Dive (☎ /fax 076 280 701, W www.far-away.net) 5/6 Muu 10, Soi Bangrae, Phuket, Thailand

South East Asia Liveaboards Co (SEAL; ☎ 076 340 406, fax 076 340 586, W www.seal-asia.com) 225 Thanon Rat Uthit, Hat Patong, Phuket, Thailand

Paddling

Myanmar's many great rivers, most of which are relatively clean by international standards, bear incredible potential as venues for long-distance canoeing and kayaking. We don't know anyone who has tried it yet, but one might assume that most rivers in the country would be off-limits to foreign paddlers. One exception might be the Ayeyarwady River between Mandalay and Yangon, which is heavily travelled by IWT boats, as well as the occasional tourist boat. River traffic towards Yangon tends to be heavy, so if you were to attempt this stretch, you might best put in no farther north than Mandalay and no farther south than Pyay.

As with bicycles, we know of no customs regulations forbidding the temporary import of a canoe or kayak. Of course the reality of showing up at Mingaladon airport in Yangon with a 4m kayak might be different.

Sea kayaking is another extraordinary possibility. One outfitter based in Thailand, South East Asia Liveaboards Co (see Diving & Snorkelling earlier for contact details), offers a six night 'sea kayaking safari' in the Myeik Archipelago, which features a kayaking component along with sailing, hiking, snorkelling and diving.

MEDITATION STUDY

Several monasteries and meditation centres in Yangon provide opportunities for the study and practice of *satipatthana vipassana,* or insight-awareness meditation, based on instructions in the Maha Satipatthana Sutta of the Theravada Buddhist canon. This type of meditation is also commonly practised in Sri Lanka and Thailand, though the tradition of lay practice is probably stronger in Myanmar. Many Westerners have come to Myanmar to practise at the various centres for periods ranging from 10 days to more than a year. Visitors typically attach themselves to a respected *sayadaw* (abbot) in the Buddhist tradition for the duration.

The most famous centre in Yangon is the Mahasi Meditation Centre (Mahasi Thathana Yeiktha in Burmese), founded in 1947 by the late Mahasi Sayadaw, perhaps Myanmar's greatest meditation teacher. The Mahasi Sayadaw technique strives for intensive, moment-to-moment awareness of every physical movement, every mental and physical sensation, and ultimately, every thought. This technique has spread well beyond Myanmar's borders and is now commonly taught in Buddhist centres all over the world. The Mahasi Meditation Centre is on Thathana Yeiktha Rd (formerly Hermitage Rd) off Kaba Aye Paya Rd, north of Kandawgyi, about 10 minutes from the city centre or 20 minutes from the airport.

Two of the Mahasi centre's chief meditation teachers, Sayadaw U Pandita and Sayadaw U Janaka, have established their own centres – Panditarama and Chanmyay Yeiktha – which are also highly regarded. Although each presents its own slight twist on the Mahasi Sayadaw technique, the basic meditation instructions are similar.

Another famous centre is the International Meditation Centre, founded by the late U Ba Khin, a well-known lay teacher. The U Ba Khin technique focuses on a deep appreciation of impermanence and on consciously moving or 'sweeping' one's mental awareness throughout the body. In India this practice has been perpetuated by SN Goenka. Instruction at all of the above centres is given to foreigners in English.

For practice sessions of less than a month, a tourist visa will suffice. To obtain the necessary 'special-entry visa' for a long-term stay of more than a month, applicants must receive a letter of invitation from the centre where they would like to study, which may in turn require a letter of introduction from an affiliated meditation centre abroad. This invitation is then presented to a Myanmar consulate or embassy that will issue a visa for an initial stay of six to 12 weeks, as recommended by the centre. This may be extended in Yangon at the discretion of the centre and Burmese immigration.

Important points to remember: the special-entry visa takes eight to 10 weeks to be issued and cannot be applied for while a person is in Myanmar on a tourist visa. Food and lodging are provided at no charge at the centres but meditators must follow eight precepts, which include abstaining from food after noon and foregoing music, dancing, jewellery, perfume and high or luxurious beds. Daily schedules are rigorous and may involve nearly continuous practice from 3am till 11pm. Students may be given permission to travel in Myanmar at the end of a long period of study but this is not automatic. Finally, Westerners who have undergone the training say it is not recommended for people with no previous meditation experience.

For further information, contact:

Chanmyay Yeiktha Meditation Centre (☎ 01-661479, fax 667050) 55-A Kaba Aye Paya Rd, Yangon; a second branch (☎ 01-620321) is set among 4 hectares of gardens in Hmawbi, a 50-minute drive north of Yangon.

Dhamma Joti Vipassana Centre (☎ 01-549290) Nga Htat Gyi Paya Rd, Bahan Township, Yangon

International Meditation Centre (☎ 01-531549) 31-A Inya Myaing Rd, Yangon

Mahasi Meditation Centre (☎ 01-541971, fax 289960) 16 Thathana Yeiktha Rd, Yangon

Panditarama Meditation Centre (Shwe Taung Gon Sasana Yeiktha; ☎ 01-531448, fax 527171, e panditarama@mptmail.net.mm) 80/A Shwetaunggyaw Rd (Thanlwin Rd), Yangon; Panditarama Forest Meditation Centre, 3km northeast off the highway to Bago, is a second branch.

Saddhamma Ransi Meditation Centre (☎ 01-661597) 7 Zeyar Khemar Rd, Mayangone Township, Yangon

For further information on the teachings of Mahasi Sayadaw and U Ba Khin, read *Living Dharma: Teachings of Twelve Buddhist Masters* edited by Jack Kornfield (see the Recommended Reading section under Religion in the Facts about Myanmar chapter for more titles).

Other meditation centres can be found outside Yangon, particularly in Sagaing, which is Myanmar's principal monastic centre in terms of numbers of monks, nuns, monasteries and nunneries. In Sagaing, Kyaswa Kyaung hosts occasional Mahasi Sayadaw–style retreats oriented towards foreigners, under the direction of Sayadaw U Lakkhana and a couple of foreign lay teachers. For further information contact e mettadana@aol.com or e nyanodaya@hotmail.com.

In Mawlamyaing, Venerable Pak Auk Sayadaw teaches satipatthana vipassana using a penetrative and highly technical approach at **Pak Auk Forest Monastery** *(☎ 032-22132; c/o Major U Khan Sain, 653 Lower Main Rd)*.

WORK

Although Myanmar is one of the poorest countries in the world, there are, surprisingly, a few employment opportunities for foreigners. As one might guess, the development game flourishes in Yangon, with plenty of NGOs and UN operations in place. Getting information on these can be rather difficult; your best bet is simply to turn up in Yangon and ask around at places where expats hang out, such as the 50th Street Bar & Grill. Or contact known NGO/UN offices overseas and ask whether they have any programmes in Myanmar. To be considered for an NGO or UN position you'll need an educational and experiential background to match, and will most likely have to arrange your visa and work permit outside Myanmar.

English teaching is another possibility. Despite the high demand for English language instruction, the opportunities are much slimmer than in most other Asian countries, simply due to the lack of disposable income. Still there are a few private language schools in Yangon and Mandalay – check the yellow pages of the Yangon phone directory. As might be expected, rates of pay are quite low – basically no more than a subsistence allowance by most standards. Work permits aren't necessarily needed if you're just looking for temporary work.

Foreigners have also obtained temporary work as extras in Yangon's burgeoning film industry. As in India, pay rates are very low – this really isn't a moneymaking proposition as much as it is a sometimes fun experience.

ACCOMMODATION

The accommodation situation in Myanmar has improved dramatically in the past decade, both in the number of places to stay and in the levels of comfort on offer. In the past all places of accommodation open to foreigners were government-run, relatively expensive and sorely lacking in the service department. Over the years nearly all places of accommodation have been privatised. A handful are run as joint ventures with the government. We have not reviewed or recommended such places, and have identified them at the end of each Place to Stay section so that those travellers who wish to avoid staying in government-owned or joint venture accommodation can do so.

Technically any hotel or guesthouse that accepts foreign guests must have a special lodging licence – this is usually displayed somewhere on the wall behind the reception desk. Such a licence requires these hotels and guesthouses to charge US dollars or FECs, and to have a minimum of five rooms and certain room standards that are substantially beyond the usual local inn.

Rates, Services & Taxes

In the past Myanmar accommodation was a bit more expensive than other countries in Southeast Asia, but many of Myanmar's hotels have dropped their rates over the past few years and those that haven't have added amenities to justify their old rates.

Bargaining is acceptable, especially during the low season (March through October) when the drop in visitors makes for plenty of empty rooms. At the top end you're not likely to get much of a discount – but it doesn't hurt to try.

Except for international-class hotels like The Strand, Traders Hotel and the Summit Parkview – where a uniform dollar pricing structure is used – and a few hotels way off the beaten track where everyone pays in kyat, nearly all hotels use a two-tiered pricing system. If you're travelling with a hired vehicle and driver, your driver can get a free room at most hotels – or at least he should get the much lower kyat rate reserved for Burmese.

Fortunately for travellers on a tight budget, there are now quite a number of places in the US$3 to US$5 per person range. Typically this gets you a bare cubicle with two beds and a cold-water bathroom down the hall. Rooms with a private cold-water bathroom cost a few dollars more. A toast-and-egg breakfast is usually included.

Moving up from this category, room rates are a few dollars more as hot water, air-con and TV become part of the picture. For this type of room the minimum rate ranges around US$8 to US$12 for a single and US$10 to US$15 for a double. Toast-and-egg breakfasts, of course, are included. In highly touristed places such as Mandalay and Bagan you can get rooms with these amenities for as little as US$5 to US$6.

The next level of hotels offers larger rooms, usually a bit more atmosphere, and perhaps a sitting garden, for US$20 to US$30. Many of the places in this price range are older hotels that once belonged to the MHT but are now privately owned. The service in these hotels can be terrible at one place, great at another. Some hotels in this range are modern but characterless Chinese-owned buildings with tidy rooms and all the amenities. In this category are a few rare exceptions where the hotel breakfasts include a variety of fresh fruits, eggs cooked in your choice of styles, or where Burmese breakfasts can be taken as an alternative.

Once you're in the US$60 and up range many of the hotels are owned by Singaporean, Taiwanese or Hong Kong companies and usually don't include free breakfasts.

Depending on your luck, you can usually find a few kyat-priced hotels to stay at in out-of-the-way areas, and even in fairly accessible but relatively untouristed towns such as Shwebo, Magwe, Myingyan and Pakkoku. We found other towns where guesthouses cost no more than K1000 a night, sometimes as little as K600. The rooms in such places are very basic – perhaps two hard beds in a room surrounded by wood partitions that stop 30cm short of the ceiling.

Larger, more expensive hotels also add a 10% service charge on top of the room rates.

FOOD

You can eat very well and very inexpensively in Myanmar. Before 1995 it was often difficult to find decent Burmese food in local restaurants, but the economic development in urban areas has brought substantial improvements in the availability and quality of Burmese cuisine. Chinese and Indian foods are also quite popular in the larger towns and cities. Street and market stalls tend to provide the regional dishes, but with these you must be a little wary of cleanliness. Like most Southeast Asians, the Burmese are great snackers, and in the evening many street stalls sell tasty little snacks.

Myanmar has a wide variety of tropical fruits, and in season you can get delicious strawberries in Pyin U Lwin, Mandalay and even Yangon. Don't miss the huge avocados

Table Etiquette

At home, most families take their meals sitting on reed mats around a low, round table about 30cm in height. In restaurants, chairs and tables are more common. The entire meal is served at once, rather than in courses. In ordinary Bamar restaurants, each individual diner in a group typically orders a small plate of curry for himself or herself, while side dishes are shared among the whole party. This contrasts with China and Thailand, for example, where every dish is usually shared.

Traditionally, Bamar food is eaten with the fingers, much like Indian food, but nowadays, it's also common for urban Burmese to eat with a *hkayin* (fork) and *zun* (tablespoon), in the Thai fashion. These are always available at Bamar restaurants and almost always given automatically to foreign diners. The fork is held in the left hand and used as a probe to push food onto the spoon; you eat from the spoon.

Except for *mohinga* (rice noodles and fish soup), which is eaten with a spoon, noodle soups are eaten with a spoon and *tu* (chopsticks).

Joe Cummings

MARTIN HARRIS

In season, delicious mangoes are common throughout Myanmar.

if you're in the Inle area. Bago is known for its tasty pineapples, and Hsipaw has the most delicious papayas we've ever sampled. In Yangon and Mandalay snack bars have excellent, and seemingly healthy, ice cream but you should avoid the ice-cream street vendors unless you have a very strong stomach.

Food can be quite cheap in Myanmar if you stick to the restaurants that cater mainly to locals. On the other hand, the restaurants of big hotels are predictably expensive and only accept US dollars.

Bamar & Regional Cuisines

Mainstream Burmese cuisine represents an intriguing blend of Bamar, Mon, Indian and Chinese influences. *Htamin* (rice) is the core of any Burmese meal, to be eaten with a choice of *hin* (curry dishes), most commonly fish, chicken, prawns or mutton. Very little beef or pork is eaten by the Burmese – beef because it's considered offensive to most Hindus and Burmese Buddhists, pork because the nat disapprove. Many Burmese Buddhists in fact abstain from eating the flesh of any four-legged animal, and, during the Buddhist Waso or rains retreat, may take up a 'fire-free' diet that includes only uncooked vegetables and fruit. Nearly all butchers in Myanmar are either Muslim or Chinese.

Bamar curries are the mildest in Asia in terms of chilli power – in fact most cooks don't use chillies at all in their recipes, just a simple *masala* of turmeric, ginger, garlic, salt and onions, plus plenty of peanut oil and shrimp paste. Heat can be added in the form of *balachaung*, a table condiment made from chillies, tamarind and dried shrimp pounded together, or from the very pungent, very hot *ngapi jaw* (shrimp paste fried in peanut oil with chilli, garlic and onions). Curries are generally cooked until the oil separates from all other ingredients and floats on top. Some restaurants will add oil to maintain the correct top layer, as the oil preserves the underlying food from contamination by insects and airborne bacteria while the curries sit in open, unheated pots for hours at a time. When you're served a bowl of hin, you're not expected to consume all the oil; just spoon the ingredients from underneath.

Almost everything is flavoured with *ngapi*, which is a salty paste concocted from dried and fermented shrimp or fish, and can be very much an acquired taste. A thin sauce of pressed fish or shrimp called *ngan-pya-ye* may also be used to salt Bamar dishes. Mi Mi Khaing, author of one of the seminal works on Burmese cuisine, *Cook and Entertain the Burmese Way*, explains:

> It is sometimes observed that cheeses, and the esoteric pleasures therefrom, are strangely absent in East Asian cuisines. Cheese needs milk, and so too herds lovingly bred; whereas our rivers, spreading into immense deltas and other waters, already abound with fish of kind upon kind there for the netting. Adjoining great fisheries are saltbeds of the long Burmese coastline. Deliciously odoriferous foods result from this conjoining.

One of the culinary highlights of Bamar cuisine is undoubtedly *thouq* (also *lethouq*) – light, spicy salads made with raw vegetables or fruit tossed with lime juice, onions, peanuts, chillies and other spices. Among the most exquisite are *maji-yweq thouq*, made with tender young tamarind leaves, and *shauk-thi thouq*, mixed with pomelo, a large citrus similar in appearance to grapefruit, but sweeter. *Htamin let-thouq* are savoury salads made with cooked rice.

Another common side dish is Indian-influenced *peh-hin-ye* (lentil soup, or dahl); the better restaurants may serve dahl fortified with chunks of boiled turnips, potatoes and okra. A *hin-jo* (mild soup) of green squash may also be available. At an authentic *htamin zain* (rice shop), once you've ordered one or more curries, then rice, dahl, soup, side dishes and Chinese tea come automatically at no charge. Soft drinks, beer or Indian tea cost extra. Hotel restaurants usually have a few Bamar dishes on their menus but these will be toned-down versions of the real thing, with less chilli and seasonings, and they'll usually come with fewer accompanying dishes.

Noodle dishes are most often eaten for breakfast or as light meals between the main meals of the day. By far the most popular is mohinga. Another popular noodle dish, especially at festivals, is *oun-no hkauq-sweh*, rice noodles with pieces of chicken in a spicy sauce made with coconut milk.

Shan hkauq-sweh (Shan-style noodle soup) – thin wheat noodles in a light broth with chunks of chilli-marinated chicken – is a favourite all over Myanmar but is most common in Mandalay and the Shan State. A variation popular in Mandalay is made with rice noodles and called *myi shay*. Another Shan dish worth seeking out is *htamin chin* ('sour rice', a turmeric-coloured rice salad).

A popular finish to Bamar meals is *la-hpeq thouq* (a salad-like concoction of pressed, moistened green tea leaves mixed with a combination of sesame seeds, fried peas, dried shrimp, fried garlic, peanuts, toasted coconut and ginger, and other crunchy flavourings). The 'slimy-looking' mass of leaves puts some foreigners off, but it's actually quite tasty once you get beyond the dish's exotic appearance.

In Mandalay and around Inle (Kalaw, Pindaya, Nyaungshwe and Taunggyi) it is also fairly easy to find Shan food, which is very similar to northern Thai cuisine. Popular dishes are *hkauq sen* (Shan-style wide rice noodles with curry) and various fish and meat salads. Large *maung jeut* (rice crackers), are common throughout the Shan State.

Mon food, most readily available in towns stretching from Bago to Mawlamyaing, is very similar to Bamar with a greater emphasis on curry selections. Where a Bamar restaurant might offer a choice of four or five curries, a Mon restaurant will have as many as a dozen, all lined up in curry pots to see. Mon curries are also more likely to contain chillies.

Rakhaing cuisine most resembles those of Bangladesh and India's Bengal, featuring lots of bean and pulse dishes, very spicy curries and flatbreads. Because of the Rakhaing State's long coastline, seafood is commonly eaten in the larger towns. Seafood is also available and popular in the Tanintharyi Division, which has a similarly lengthy sea coast.

Chinese & Indian Cuisines

Throughout Myanmar in towns large and small you'll find plenty of Chinese restaurants, including quite a few of the regional specialities that are a world (well, half of China anyway) away from Chinese food found in Western countries. In a run-of-the-mill Chinese restaurant a meal will cost around K600. In true Chinese fashion you

Betel

Kunya (betel chews) are often passed round at the end of a meal as a 'digestive'. These take a variety of forms, the most basic being small chunks of dried areca (betel) nut wrapped in a betel leaf with lime paste. More elaborate kunya may contain flavoured tobacco (usually Indian snuff), peppermint and other spices. In areas where areca palms are cultivated, people chew fresh areca nut as well as dried. Experienced chewers can hold a betel quid in their mouths for hours without spitting.

The nut and leaf come from two separate plants, the areca or betel palm *(Areca catechu)* and the betel vine *(Piper betel)*. An alkaloid in the nut produces mild stimulation and a sense of well being. It also kills certain worms that may take up residence in the digestive tract; modern veterinarians use an areca extract to de-worm pets. The chewed nut stains the teeth dark red and is thought to be carcinogenic.

Vicki Bowman

almost invariably get soup with your meal and free Chinese tea.

Indian restaurants are also common, although much more so in Yangon than in other towns. Most are run by Muslim Indians, a few by Hindus. Excellent chicken *dan bauk* (biryani) as well as all-you-can-eat, *thali* (banana-leaf) vegetarian food is easy to find in the capital. The Burmese call Indian restaurants that serve all-you-can-eat thalis 'Chitty' or 'Chetty' restaurants. There are also Muslim-Chinese restaurants serving Yunnanese specialities. You can recognise Muslim (halal) restaurants by the numeral 786 over the door, sometimes flanked by the star and crescent symbol. This number represents the Arabic phrase 'In the name of Allah the most beneficent and merciful'.

DRINKS

Nonalcoholic Drinks

Only drink water when you know it has been purified – which in most restaurants it should be. One should be suspicious of ice although we've had lots of ice drinks in Myanmar without suffering any ill-effects. Many brands of drinking water are sold in bottles and are quite safe.

Burmese tea, brewed in the Indian style with lots of milk and sugar, is cheap. Many restaurants, the Chinese ones in particular, will provide as much weak Chinese tea as you can handle – for free. It's a good, safe thirst quencher and some people prefer it to regular Burmese tea. You can always buy some little snack if you'd like a drink but not a meal. Teashops are a good place to drink safely boiled tea and munch on inexpensive snacks like *nam-bya*, *palata* (kinds of flat breads) or Chinese pastries. See the boxed text 'Burmese Teashops' in the Yangon chapter.

Soft drinks are more costly but reasonable by Asian standards. Since the privatisation of industry there has been a boom in new made-in-Myanmar soft drink brands, including Max, Star, Fruito, Crusher and Fantasy. All are more or less equivalent to international brands like Pepsi, Coca-Cola, Fanta, Bireley's and so on.

Alcoholic Drinks

In the past the Burmese were not big drinkers. This was partially due to the general lack of disposable income but also because alcohol-drinking is looked down upon by the many Burmese Buddhists who interpret the fifth lay precept against intoxication very strictly. However, with the advent of 'beer stations' – places that serve cheap draught beer – the number of urban Burmese who can afford a few glasses of beer after work is on the rise. In fact, beer stations seem to be giving the traditional Burmese teashops some stiff competition.

Beer Apart from international brands such as Tiger, ABC Stout, Singha, San Miguel, Beck and other beers brewed in Thailand, Singapore and Indonesia (typically costing K300 to K500 per 375mL can or bottle), there are a couple of Myanmar brews. These include long-running Mandalay Beer, which is very similar to Indian or Sri Lankan beer – rather watery but not bad on those hot and dusty occasions when only a beer will do. Most bottles contain a layer of sediment on the bottom resulting from inadequate filtration. Unfortunately, considering its low quality, Mandalay Beer also happens to be the most expensive beer in Myanmar at K400 per bottle. Hence few Burmese or foreigners drink the national brew. Founded in 1886, **Mandalay Brewery** *(129 Warden Rd, Yangon)* also produces the New Mandalay Export label, which is better-tasting and doesn't contain sediment. Newer, better brands brewed in Myanmar include 'Myanmar', Dagon, and Skol, all of which cost about the same as Mandalay Beer but taste a lot better. Also worth a try is the new Mandalay Strong Ale, which packs a punch with a 7.5% alcohol content.

Among the locals, Myanmar draught is the favourite, a glass of which will only set you back K100.

Toddy Throughout central Myanmar and the delta, *htan ye* (palm juice) is the farmer's choice of alcoholic beverage. Htan ye is tapped from the top of a toddy palm, the same tree – and the same sap –

that produces jaggery, or palm sugar. The juice is sweet and nonalcoholic in the morning, but by mid-afternoon naturally ferments to a weak beer-like strength. By the next day it will have turned. The milky, viscous liquid has a nutty aroma and a slightly sour flavour that fades quickly.

Villages in some areas have their own thatched-roof toddy bars where the locals meet and drink pots of fermented toddy. The toddy is sold in the same roughly engraved terracotta pots the juice is collected in and drunk from coconut half-shells set on small bamboo pedestals. Favourite toddy accompaniments include prawn crackers and fried peas. Some toddy bars also sell *htan-ayeq* (toddy liquor, also called jaggery liquor), a much stronger, distilled form of toddy sap.

Other Liquors & Wines Very popular in the Shan State is an orange brandy called *shwe leinmaw*, which varies in price from K250 to K400 per bottle, depending on how close to the source you buy it – much of it is distilled in the mountains between Kalaw and Taunggyi. It's a pleasant-tasting liqueur, sort of a poor man's Grand Marnier, and packs quite a punch.

There is also a variety of stronger liquors, including *ayeq hpyu* (white liquor), which varies in strength from brandy-like to almost pure ethyl; and *taw ayeq* (jungle liquor), a cruder form of ayeq hpyu.

Foreign wines – especially those from Australia – are occasionally found in shops and restaurants frequented by foreigners.

ENTERTAINMENT

For most of nonurban Myanmar, local entertainment involves sitting around with friends at home or in a local teashop, telling jokes and recounting the events of the day. Religious and seasonal festivals are an important venue for Burmese folk drama and pop music performances – see Public Holidays & Special Events earlier in this chapter, and Music under Arts in the Facts about Myanmar chapter for details.

Most larger towns or cities have a couple of clubs or restaurants where live music can be heard. Despite its cultural isolation, Myanmar has not been spared the karaoke boom. Even in the tiniest towns there is at least one rustic karaoke bar, usually open to the street, where young men sit, drink and bawl their favourite ballads at ear-splitting volume.

Yangon and Mandalay have a handful of discos or dance clubs, often with live music. Most are associated with hotels but a few operate independently. Burmese-language covers of Western pop songs are usually mixed in with Burmese songs. Sometimes discos and karaoke bars are closed down because of police crackdowns on prostitution. Prostitution has a long history in Myanmar but it is only recently that it has become associated with places that foreign visitors might enter.

More highbrow entertainment, such as classical musical and dance performances, can be seen at top-end restaurants and hotels.

SPECTATOR SPORTS

Burmese Martial Arts

Myanmar has a tradition of kickboxing that's said to date back to the Bagan era, although the oldest written references are found in chronicles of warfare between Burma and Thailand during the 15th and 16th centuries. *Myanma let-hwei* (Burmese kickboxing) is very similar in style to *muay thai* (Thai kickboxing), although not nearly as well developed as a national sport. In fact Burmese boxing matches are never seen or heard on TV or radio, and only occasionally reported in the newspaper.

The most common and traditional kickboxing venues are temporary rings set up at paya pwe rather than sports arenas. Within the last eight years, the martial art's status has raised perceptibly and nowadays occasional championship matches are also held at Aung San Stadium in Yangon. Finding out in advance about such public events can be difficult. If you're interested it's best to drop in on one of the kickboxing classes at Yangon's YMCA and ask whether there are any upcoming matches in the area.

As with Thai boxing, almost anything goes in the ring. All surfaces of the body are considered fair targets and any part of the body except the head may be used to strike an opponent. Common blows include high kicks to the neck, elbow thrusts to the face and head, knee hooks to the ribs and low crescent kicks to the calf. A contestant may even grasp an opponent's head between his hands and pull it down to meet an upward knee thrust. Punching is considered the weakest of all blows and kicking merely a way to 'soften up' one's opponent; knee and elbow strikes are decisive in most matches.

Competition isn't nearly as formalised in Myanmar as in Thailand; in fact you probably won't find two people anywhere in the country who agree on the rules! What's obvious is that the structure and limitations of each match varies with its context and with the calibre of the participants. Unlike Thai boxing, which has borrowed a great deal from the Queensbury rules in international or Western boxing, Burmese boxing represents a more traditional form once shared by the two countries. Rules tend to follow situational norms; fighters, managers and judges get together before each match and work out time limits and scoring criteria.

In the simplest rural matches, fought in a dirt circle, there's no time limit and a fighter loses once he has wiped blood from his face or body three times. In more organised amateur matches, boxers fight in square rings (5.8m by 5.5m), for three to five rounds of three minutes each, usually with two minutes' rest between. Professional matches in larger towns and cities begin with five rounds but may increase round by round to 12 rounds when the scoring is tight – even longer if no clear winner emerges earlier in the match. When such extensions occur, boxers can request a five-minute rest period for every seven rounds fought. Such marathons – gruelling in the extreme by most international standards – are somewhat rare. At both amateur and pro matches, two referees officiate in the ring – this contrasts with Thailand, where there's only one. At ringside are three judges who score the match by pooling their impressions of stamina, skill and bravery.

Fighters bandage their hands but don't wear gloves; they fight barefoot except for nylon anklets for absorbing perspiration. Simple, dark-coloured shorts rather than boxing trunks are usually worn; if the shorts worn by the contestants appear too similar in colour, the fighters may sew coloured bandanas over the front to make it easier for spectators to differentiate the opponents. In championship matches Burmese fighters are beginning to imitate the Thai boxers they see on TV by wearing big, gaudy trunks.

Before the match begins, each boxer performs a dance-like ritual in the ring to pay homage to Buddha and to Khun Cho and Khun Tha, the nat whose domain includes Burmese kickboxing. The winner repeats the ritual at the end of the match. A small musical ensemble consisting of drums, *hneh* (double-reed wind instrument), cymbals and bamboo clappers performs during the rituals and throughout the match; the volume and tempo of the music rises and falls along with events in the ring.

There are no weight divisions in Burmese boxing – perhaps because the pool of professional fighters is relatively small. Instead boxers are ranked by skill into 1st, 2nd and 3rd class. The best boxers are said to hail from the Ayeyarwady Division, Mandalay Division, Kayin State and Mon State, and these regions are where you'll see the best matches. A professional boxer earns around K500,000 for winning in a big match. Many of the more accomplished Burmese professionals end up migrating to the better-paying boxing stadiums of provincial Thailand; some go back and forth.

Myanmar's most famous myanma let-hwei teacher is Saya Pan Thu, founder of the Institute of Myanmar Traditional Advanced Boxing and one of three trainers at Yangon University. Pan Thu comes from a teaching lineage that emphasises Myanmar's most traditional style of kickboxing, but also incorporates a few grappling and wrestling techniques from the judo-like Burmese art of *bando*. Due largely to Pan Thu's steady promotion of Burmese martial arts, the country may soon establish the Myanma Traditional Boxing Federation, an organisation that will regulate boxing rules, introduce new safety measures to the ring and develop overall professionalism.

Another thread follows the YMCA school developed by Nilar Win, who now teaches in Paris. The YMCA/Nilar Win tradition appeals to both the amateur and the aspiring professional with its relative emphasis on physical fitness and on precision of movement. It also borrows more from modern martial techniques outside Myanmar, particularly from Thailand.

Chinlon

Often called 'cane ball' in Burmese English, *chinlon* refers to games in which a woven rattan ball about 12cm in diameter is kicked around. It also refers to the ball itself, which resembles the *takraw* of Thailand and Malaysia. Informally any number of players can form a circle and keep the chinlon airborne by kicking it soccer-style from player to player; a lack of scoring makes it a favourite pastime with Burmese of all ages.

In formal play six players stand in a circle of 22-foot circumference. Each player must keep the ball aloft using a succession of 30 techniques and six surfaces on the foot and leg, allotting five minutes for each part. Each successful kick scores a point, while points are subtracted for using the wrong body part or dropping the ball.

A popular variation – and the one used in intramural or international competitions – is played with a volleyball net, using all the same rules as in volleyball except that only the feet and head are permitted to touch the ball. It's amazing to see the players perform aerial pirouettes, spiking the ball over the net with their feet.

Football (Soccer)

Attending local football matches between different *yaq-kweq* (residential quarters) is good entertainment and a great way to meet locals.

SHOPPING

There are some good bargains to be had in Myanmar, particularly for textiles and handicrafts. It's a good idea to seek out local artisans and buy handicrafts directly from them, rather than directing profits towards government-owned shops.

In larger towns and cities bargains are usually found in the public markets, called *zei*, or *zay*, in Burmese. The main central market is often called *zeigyo* (also spelt *zei-gyo* or *zay-cho*); other markets will be named for the district or township where they're found.

The Bogyoke Aung San Market in Yangon and the zeigyo in Mandalay are good places to look for handicrafts; just about everything that can be bought around the country can be purchased just as cheaply right in these two markets. The big hotel shops, large air-con handicrafts emporiums and the shops in the departure lounge at Yangon airport are very expensive.

Note the following warning on precious-stone rip-offs, but beware of other more mundane rip-offs. See the information about touts and how to avoid their various schemes in the Money section earlier in this chapter.

Precious Stones & Jewellery

Myanmar generates a considerable income from the mining of precious stones, mostly in the north. Be very wary of people who come to you with stories of large profits from taking Burmese gemstones to sell in Western countries. There are a lot of red glass rubies waiting for the unwary.

Precious stones are supposed to be a government monopoly and the government is very unhappy about visitors buying stones from anywhere but licensed retail shops. If *any* stones are found when your baggage is checked on departure, they may be confiscated unless you can present a receipt showing they were purchased from a government-licensed dealer.

The finer imperial jade or pigeon-blood rubies can only be purchased at special dealer sessions during the government-sponsored Myanmar Gems, Jade & Pearl Emporium held each year in October, December and February at a special building next to Kaba Aye Paya in Yangon. Each is typically attended by only around 400 'key' international buyers.

Still, many visitors manage to buy stones from unlicensed dealers, who far outnumber the licensed kind. The government turns a blind eye to most domestic trade; entire districts of southern Mandalay, for example, are engaged in the unlicensed buying, selling, cutting and polishing of jade.

Black-market prices are considerably lower than prices found in licensed retail shops, but of course the risk is far greater as well. The best place to buy unlicensed stones is at the source, where fakes are much less common – the reason being that anyone discovered selling fakes in a well-known gem town would be severely punished by dealers of legitimate minerals.

Dug from pit, strip and tunnel mines, Myanmar's finest rubies and sapphires hail from Mogok (Sagaing Division), Pyinlon (Shan State) and Maingshu (or Mong Shu, Shan State). The Kachin State is the sole domain of jadeite, or Burmese jade, which forms inside football-sized boulders in mountain streams. Emeralds are mined at Myadaung in the Kayah State. At the moment only Mogok is open to the average foreign visitor, but all of these precious minerals are traded heavily in Mandalay and Yangon.

Lacquerware

Probably the most popular purchase in Myanmar is lacquerware – you'll find it on sale in the main markets of Yangon and Mandalay, in the Mahamuni Paya entrance walks in Mandalay, and most particularly in Bagan, where most of the lacquerware is made. Burmese lacquerware is fairly similar to that made in the north of Thailand, and although connoisseurs of Japanese lacquerware say that in comparison the Burmese items are inferior, many people find it highly collectable.

Although the earliest lacquerware found in Myanmar today can be dated to the 11th century and was created in the Chinese style, the incised polychrome techniques, known as *yun,* in use today were imported from northern Thailand. Yun is an old Bamar word for the inhabitants of Chiang Mai; in 1558 King Bayinnaung captured a number of Chiang Mai lacquer artisans and brought them to Bago to establish the Burmese incised lacquerware tradition.

At one time Mandalay artisans made relief lacquerware, a tradition that appears to have all but died out. The oldest bichromatic style applies gold or silver to a black background, a technique dating perhaps to the Pyay era and kept alive by artisans in Kyaukka near Monywa, Mandalay Division. Lacquerware is also made in Kengtung.

Lacquer as used in Myanmar comes from the *Melanorrhea usitata* or *kusum* tree (not to be confused with 'lac', which comes from an insect), and in its most basic form is mixed with paddy-husk ash to form a light, flexible, waterproof coating over bamboo frames.

To make a lacquerware object, the craftsperson first weaves a frame. If the item is top quality, only the frame is bamboo; horse or donkey hairs will be wound round the frame. In lower-quality lacquerware the whole object is made from bamboo. The lacquer is then coated over the framework and allowed to dry. After several days it is sanded down with ash from rice husks, and another coating of lacquer is applied. A high-quality item may have seven layers of lacquer altogether.

The lacquerware is engraved and painted, then polished to remove the paint from everywhere except in the engravings. Multicoloured lacquerware is produced by repeated engraving, painting and polishing. From start to finish it can take five or six months to produce a high-quality piece of lacquerware, which may have as many as five colours. Flexibility is one characteristic of good lacquerware. A top-quality bowl can have its rim squeezed together until the sides meet without suffering damage. The quality and precision of the engraving is another thing to look for.

Lacquerware is made into bowls, trays, plates, boxes, containers, cups, vases and many other everyday items. Octagonal folding tables and folding screens are also popular lacquerware items. If you purchase large lacquerware items, most shops will wrap and crate them for you for easier shipping.

Tapestries

Along with lacquerware, tapestries (kalaga) are one of the better bargains in Myanmar. They consist of pieces of coloured cloth of various sizes heavily embroidered with silver- or gold-coloured thread, metal sequins and glass beads, and feature mythological Burmese figures in padded relief. The greatest variety is found in Mandalay, where most tapestries are produced, but mark-up can be high there because of a tout system. However, if you locate the shops on your own and bargain well, you can get very good prices. You can also purchase tapestries in Yangon at craft shops in the Bogyoke Aung San Market – prices are similar to those in northern Myanmar but the selection is not as great.

Good quality kalaga are tightly woven and don't skimp on sequins, which may be sewn in overlapping lines, rather than spaced side by side, as a sign of embroidery skill. Metals used should shine, even in older pieces; tarnishing means lower-quality materials. Age is not necessarily a factor in value except when related to better-quality

Do Real Men Wear Longyi?

Men throughout South and Southeast Asia commonly wore skirt-like waistcloths until the beginning of this century. European trouser-wearing gradually won over the rest of Southeast Asia, and even in India the wearing of the *lungi* (the Indian equivalent to Myanmar's longyi, a sarong-style garment) no longer predominates.

Myanmar's isolation since independence and general lack of income have thus far preserved the longyi-wearing tradition. Nowadays only around 10% of males in urban areas wear trousers; in many rural parts of the country virtually no male (except for uniformed soldiers) is seen wearing anything other than a longyi. Jokes about what's found beneath a man's longyi parallel similar jokes about Scottish kilts.

The longyi is a very practical clothing choice for Myanmar. In the tropical heat, the billowing cotton keeps one's legs substantially cooler than even the thinnest trousers. The lower length can be pulled between the legs and tucked in at the back of the waist to create 'shorts' for swimming or running. In a country where people often bathe outdoors at riverbanks and streams, the longyi preserves the bather's modesty while he scoops water over his body, and dries quickly afterwards.

And one size fits all. They can easily be loosened at the end of a large meal, and as one's weight moves up or down, there's no need to buy a new set of longyi. More than just an article of clothing, a spare longyi can be used: as a shoulder sling to carry items while travelling; as a bed sheet, picnic blanket or towel; as a baby cradle; tied ankle-to-ankle for safely climbing coconut or toddy palms; and as an impromptu curtain when the hot sun pierces a train or bus window.

Different patterns hail from different parts of the country. In most of central Myanmar, small checks and plaids in relatively bright colours predominate. Solid reds bordered with horizontal stripes at the middle or bottom indicate a Karen-style longyi. Highly favoured – and somewhat expensive – Rakhaing patterns feature a thick, high-relief weave in light, reflective greys and blues. Around Inle Lake, weavers produce red, green and yellow *Zin-me* (Chiang Mai) and blue, brown and green *Ban-gauk* (Bangkok) longyi, modelled after Thai weaving styles introduced to the region in the early 20th century. You can also find *ikat* (tie-dyed) longyi, reminiscent of patterns used in northeastern Thailand and Laos. Deep indigo, green and purple plaids are the hallmark of the Kachin style, which, during the 1988–90 uprisings, became a symbol of the pro-democracy movement – especially when worn with a white Mandarin-collar shirt and reddish-coloured, long-sleeved overcoat (the homespun uniform of Burmese nationalists during the British colonial era). For a Burmese to wear the latter outfit today is to risk being branded as an undesirable dissenter by the authorities.

Joe Cummings

work. Prices vary according to size and quality, from smaller squares (say 30cm by 30cm) for US$5 to US$10, to the larger (say 1.5m by 1.2m) for US$65. You can usually get better deals by paying in cash US dollars rather than the kyat equivalent.

Clothes & Textiles

Myanmar is the only country in Southeast Asia where the majority of the population wear non-Western clothes as part of their everyday dress. Native fabrics are for the most part limited to the longyi.

Men wear ankle-length patterns of checks, plaids or stripes. To tie them they gather the front of the longyi to create two short lengths of material, then twist them into a half-knot, tucking one end in at the waist while allowing the other to protrude from the knot; this protrusion of cloth can be allowed to hang freely or can be formed into a decorative bunch. It can even be used as a small pouch to hold money or keys. Any kind of shirt, from a T-shirt to the formal mandarin-collar *eingyi*, may be worn with a man's longyi. On very formal occasions such as weddings, the *gaung-baung* (Bamar turban) is added to the outfit.

Burmese women favour calf-length longyi in solid colours, stripes or flower prints, topped off by a form-fitting, waist-length blouse. A black waistband is stitched along the waist end, which is folded in front to form a wide pleat, then tucked behind the waistband to one side. The most expensive designs tend to feature wavy or zigzag *acheiq* patterns, the most rare of which are woven using a hundred or more spools of thread and called *luntaya* (hundred spool) *acheiq*. These are so thick and long-wearing they may be handed down from generation to generation like Persian rugs.

Simple flip-flops with leather soles and velvet thongs are the most common footwear for both men and women. If you have large feet and can't find a pair in your size, some shops can have them tailor-made for you in about three days.

Tailoring in Myanmar is very inexpensive compared with just about anywhere else in the world. Many of the textiles seen in tailor shops are imported synthetics. If you want, say, a shirt made from pure cotton, consider buying a longyi in a market or longyi shop and having the tailor cut and sew from that.

Shan-style trousers, of the same cut as those sold in Thailand as 'fisherman's pants', can be found in the Shan State, particularly around Inle Lake, but also in Hsipaw. Unlike the Thai variety, those sold in Myanmar are made of thicker, hand-woven cotton and use natural dyes.

Antiques

They're not all as ancient as made out, but many people like to collect *a-le* (opium weights); the little animal shapes in descending sizes that are traditionally used for weighing opium, gems and other precious goods (see Export Restrictions later in this section, however).

The older scale system used a series of nine weights; the newer system uses six weights. Production of the traditional zoomorphic weights came to a halt once the British colonial administration standardised the system of weights and measures in 1885. The pre-1885 weights were made of bronze; reproductions made for the tourist trade are usually brass. The most common animal figures are *to-aung* (a creature that looks like a cross between a bull and a lion), *hintha* (a swan-like bird) and *karaweik* (the Burmese crane). Folding scales in carved wooden boxes go with the weights. If you can, check prices in shops in Bangkok before blithely looking for bargains in Myanmar.

Kammawa & Parabaik *Kammawa* (from the Pali *kammavacha*) are narrow, rectangular slats painted with extracts from the Pali Vinaya – the *pitaka*, concerned with monastic discipline, specifically extracts having to do with clerical affairs. The core of a kammawa page may be a thin slat of wood, lacquered cloth, thatched cane or thin brass, which is then layered with red, black and gold lacquer to form the script and decorations. The resulting 'pages' aren't bound but are tied in stacks with similarly decorated wooden covers.

Traditionally, a new monk may receive a kammawa from his sponsors (usually his family) upon ordination. They have become less common since the advent of the press-printed page in Myanmar and are now mostly seen in museums and antique stores.

The *parabaik* is a similarly horizontal 'book', this time folded accordion-style, like a road map. The pages are made of heavy paper covered with black ink on which the letters are engraved; some parabaik may feature gouache illustrations, and some can be erased and written over again. Typical parabaik contain *jataka* (stories of the Buddha's past lives) or royal chronicles and, less frequently, Buddhist scriptures.

Both kammawa and parabaik are among the items prohibited for export – though it's difficult to say how well this is enforced. If you pass through Thailand on your way to Myanmar, you'll see plenty of them for sale in the high-end antique shops of Bangkok and Chiang Mai.

Woodcarving

You can still find some pleasantly carved new Buddha images and other items from workshops in Mandalay or in the corridors leading to Shwedagon Paya in Yangon, but in general you will not see too much woodcarving on sale.

Older items from the Amarapura, Yadanapon and Mandalay periods are plentiful but you can't be sure Burmese customs will allow them out of the country. Again, the high-end antique shops of Bangkok and Chiang Mai seem to have an endless supply of Burmese Buddha images and carved wooden ornamentation that once graced Burmese kyaung.

Umbrellas

The graceful and beautifully painted little parasols you see around Myanmar are a product of the port of Pathein – in fact they're known in Myanmar as *Pathein hti* (Pathein umbrellas). Everyday umbrellas have wooden handles, the more ceremonial ones have handles of silver. You can pick up a nice small umbrella for about US$1. The Bogyoke Aung San Market in Yangon is a good place to look. See the Pathein section of the Around Yangon chapter for details on where to observe them being made.

Shan Shoulder Bags

Brightly coloured, embroidered shoulder bags from the Shan State can be found all over Myanmar, but most particularly at Inle. Fancy models have a zip pocket in the front. They are also now made by Chinese and Kachin weavers; the latter produce eye-catching bags decorated with silver-coloured medallions.

Bookshops

Finding books in Myanmar is not that easy, although there are a number of used-book vendors in Yangon. The best selection of English-language books, including many out-of-print editions, can be found at the **Bagan Bookshop** *(Pagan Bookshop; 100 37th St, Yangon)*. Owner U Ba Kyi is a veritable national treasure for rebinding and reprinting rare, out-of-print literature on Myanmar. He has quite a large selection of books about Myanmar topics, though most of the originals are not for sale – if he sells these, he'll no longer be able to make reprints. There are also shelves full of books on many other topics – including a seemingly large number of books about cultural anthropology.

Along 37th St, near Merchant St and not far from Bagan Bookshop, are a number of outdoor book vendors who stock used English-language books and magazines. Here you'll find slightly battered but readable books on Buddhism, Burmese history and archaeology, as well as British-era government publications – including such oddities as the *Civil List* (read *Burmese Days* to understand its all-consuming importance in the colonial era). Be sure to bargain – the street vendors' first price is usually double what they're actually willing to sell a book for.

Along Bogyoke Aung San Rd, across from the Bogyoke Aung San Market, are a number of other bookstalls, and there are some in the streets that run back from the main road. Several of these have a selection of Burmese books if you ask for them. You can also buy old issues of *Time*, *Newsweek* and other foreign magazines here (and elsewhere in the street markets) for about K100 per copy.

Outside Yangon you may well come across similar book vendors displaying their wares along the streets.

Export Restrictions

The following items cannot legally be taken out of the country: prehistoric implements and artefacts; fossils; old coins; bronze or brass weights (including opium weights); bronze or clay pipes; kammawa or parabaik; inscribed stones; inscribed gold or silver; historical documents; religious images; sculptures or carvings in bronze, stone, stucco or wood; frescoes or fragments thereof; pottery; and national regalia and paraphernalia.

Getting There & Away

AIR

The vast majority of visitors to Myanmar arrive by air, but depending on the current political situation, it may be possible to go overland from Thailand and even China (see the Land section later in this chapter).

Airports & Airlines

Yangon international airport (in the township of Mingaladon) is unable to take anything bigger than an Airbus 300 or a Boeing 767, so aircraft such as 747s and DC-10s can't fly there. A new, larger airport (50km northeast of the capital, on the highway to Bago) has been in the planning-and-rumour stage for several years, but so far it's a no-show. Recently a new international airport was opened in Mandalay, adding sorely needed runways capable of accommodating larger aircraft and expanded passenger facilities.

There are several major air-route options. The first and most common is to travel out and back from Bangkok or Chiang Mai in Thailand. A second possibility is to slot Myanmar in between Thailand and Bangladesh or India – many people travelling from Southeast Asia to the subcontinent manage a few weeks in Myanmar in between. Other alternatives include travelling out and back from Calcutta, Karachi, Dhaka, Hong Kong, Taipei, Kuala Lumpur and Singapore.

Airline Offices Ten airlines have offices or agents in Yangon, though only Biman Bangladesh Airlines, Air China, Myanmar Airways International (MAI), Thai Airways International (THAI) and SilkAir actually have flights to/from Yangon international airport.

Government-Owned Services

Be aware that the government profits from your use of the government-owned airline, Myanma Airways (MA).

Air China (☎ 01-666223) 206 Bagwa Lane, Pyay Rd (9 Mile)
Air France (☎ 01-252708, fax 274199) 73–75 Sule Paya Rd
Air Mandalay (☎ 01-525488, fax 525937) 146 Dhammazedi Rd
All Nippon Airways (☎ 01-248901, fax 248904) 339 Bogyoke Aung San Rd, Sakura Tower
Asiana Airlines (☎ 01-549826, fax 531317) Wizaya Plaza, 301 Dhammazedi Rd
Biman Bangladesh Airlines (☎ 01-275882) 106–108 Pansodan St
China Airlines (☎ 01-245484, fax 246330) 353 Bo Aung Gyaw St
EVA Air (☎ 01-298001, fax 296272) 94 Bogalay Zay St
Indian Airlines (☎ 01-254758, fax 248175) 127 Sule Paya Rd
Japan Airlines (JAL; ☎ 01-240400, fax 246859) 380 Bogyoke Aung San Rd, FMI Building
KLM-Royal Dutch Airlines (☎ 01-274466) c/o Myanma Airways, 104 Strand Rd
Korean Air (☎ 01-661524) 341 Mahabandoola Rd
Malaysia Airlines (☎ 01-241007, fax 241124) 335 Bogyoke Aung San Rd
Myanma Airways (MA; ☎ 01-277013) 104 Strand Rd
Myanmar Airways International (MAI; ☎ 01-255260, fax 289609) 123 Sule Paya Rd
Pakistan International Airlines (PIA; ☎ 01-245068) 184 Bo Aung Gyaw St
Silk Air (☎ 01-255287, fax 255290) 339 Bogyoke Aung San Rd
Thai Airways International (THAI; ☎ 01-255499, fax 255490) 339 Bogyoke Aung San Rd
Yangon Airways (☎ 01-251934, fax 251932) 22–24 Pansodan St

Arrival in Yangon

After going through immigration, you must pass the Foreign Exchange Certificate (FEC) counter where you will be asked to change US dollars or British pounds into FECs. (See the Money section in Facts for the Visitor for details.)

At the customs counter, if you are checked, airport officials may ask questions about three items: video cameras, computers with modems, and mobile phones. Video cameras or video tapes are not prohibited, but apparently they remind them of reporters; with computers they are even more suspicious. If you bring any of these items, you might have to do some explaining. Don't be overly paranoid though: on our most recent trips, our bags weren't even checked.

See the Getting Around chapter for information on getting to/from the airport.

Flight Reconfirmation

If you are counting on flying out of Yangon on your scheduled date of departure, you must reconfirm your outbound flight either at the appropriate airport ticket counter or at the relevant airline office in town. This applies regardless of whether or not your flight is officially confirmed (OK status) on the ticket.

For most flights, we have found the airline offices in town to be more reliable than the airport ticket counters – mainly because you can't always find someone at the airport to fill out the proper forms. More airline offices in Yangon are now online with computer reservation systems, but a confirmation may still require calling back the next day to see if you have OK status. If you are trying to connect with an airline that does not fly into Yangon, you may need to call its Bangkok office. However, check first with the airline that flew you into Myanmar; it may be able to help reconfirm your connecting flight (eg, THAI will reconfirm all United Airlines reservations).

If you do not reconfirm, the airlines (this goes for any airlines flying in and out of Yangon) can't guarantee your outbound seat, especially during the height of the tourist season (November to February), when most flights out of Yangon seem to be intentionally overbooked.

If you get bumped, make sure you visit immigration to extend your visa sometime before your rescheduled departure (this usually amounts to paying the routine US$3 per extra day fee). Otherwise the airlines may refuse to give you a seat when you arrive for check-in and you will have to deal with the airport immigration office. This process has been known to delay check-in until the very last minute, in which case you may find yourself bumped a second time.

Departure Tax

A US$10 departure tax payable in dollars or FECs is collected at the airport from all ticket holders after check-in.

In the departure lounge, you can buy any books you missed on your way around the country, or purchase whisky and cigarettes at the duty-free counter – only US dollars are accepted.

The USA

Discount travel agents in the USA are known as consolidators (although you won't see a sign on the door saying 'Consolidator'). San Francisco is the ticket consolidator capital of America, although some good deals can be found in Los Angeles, New York and other big cities.

Council Travel (*☎ 1800-226-8624;* **W** *www.counciltravel.com*), America's largest student travel organisation, has around 60 offices in the USA, and **STA Travel** (*☎ 1800-781 4040;* **W** *www.statravel.com*) also has offices throughout the country.

From the US west coast, fares to Bangkok cost around US$480/820 one way/return. Flights from the east coast are more expensive (from US$540/880). If you're flying out of New York, it might prove just as cheap to fly via London at certain times of year.

Canada

Canadian discount air ticket sellers are also known as consolidators and their air fares tend to be about 10% higher than those sold in the USA.

Travel CUTS (*☎ 800-667 2887;* **W** *www.travelcuts.com*) is Canada's national student travel agency and has offices in all major cities. **STA Travel** (*☎ 1888-427 5639;* **W** *www.statravel.ca*) has offices in Vancouver and Toronto.

Flights from Vancouver to Bangkok start at CA$575/1200 one way/return. Travellers from the eastern side of Canada may want to consider flying to London and then arranging a cheap flight from there to Bangkok.

Australia

STA Travel (*☎ 1300 360 960;* **W** *www.sta travel.com.au*) has offices in all major cities and on many university campuses. **Flight Centre** *(☎ 13 1600; w www.flightcentre.com.au)* also has dozens of offices throughout Australia.

There are usually peak and off-peak rates for flights from Australia to Southeast Asia. The peak season is the December to January school holiday period – flights can often be heavily booked at this time as well as more expensive.

Fares from Sydney and Melbourne to Bangkok cost from A$520/780 one way/return. Fares from Darwin or Perth to Bangkok start at A$580/800.

New Zealand

Flight Centre *(☎ 0800 243 544; w www.flightcentre.co.nz)*, with branches throughout the country, and **STA Travel** *(☎ 0508 782 872; w www.statravel.co.nz)* are the well-known travel agencies.

Tickets between Auckland and Bangkok start from NZ$1225 return.

The UK

The UK is one of the world's best places for picking up cheap tickets. **STA Travel** *(☎ 0870 160 0599; w www.statravel.co.uk)* has branches across the country. The Sunday editions of most of the major daily newspapers have travel sections with advertisements for tickets to Southeast Asia, as do the free magazines widely available in London.

Many budget fares are with airlines that fly via Eastern Europe or the Middle East. Flights from London start as low as UK£200/350 one way/return. A number of cheap airlines offer a free stopover in their home city – Czech Airlines is a good option, as you get the opportunity to visit Prague. One-way flights to Bangkok start at about UK£250. It's worth keeping an eye out for promotional fares during the slow periods of business in February, June and October.

Continental Europe

The best centres for picking up discount tickets in Europe are Amsterdam, Antwerp and Frankfurt. Check out the local press for travel ads. Bear in mind that with the advent of budget airlines such as Buzz, Go and Ryanair, it may be cheaper to fly to London to buy your onward ticket.

Asia

Thailand Bangkok is a good place to look for tickets to Myanmar. Some travel agents will not only sell you tickets at knock-down prices, but will organise your visa too. It's usually cheaper to arrange your visa and ticket separately, however.

One discount ticket agency within walking distance of the Myanmar embassy in Bangkok is **Sun Far Travel** *(☎ 022 333 311; 48/5 Thanon Pan, Bang Rak)*. Typical costs for Bangkok-Yangon-Bangkok tickets are around US$180 on Thai Airways International (THAI), US$160 on Myanmar Airways International (MAI) and as low as US$140 on Biman Bangladesh Airlines. The latter flies Bangkok-Yangon-Calcutta for about US$220. Return flights to/from Kuala Lumpur or Singapore cost US$200 to US$240. Remember that published fares outside Southeast Asia are often higher than you'll find in Bangkok, or other regional capitals.

THAI currently flies Bangkok-Yangon-Bangkok twice daily. The flight takes about 50 minutes. Although slightly more expensive than the equivalent MAI flight, THAI's departure times are more convenient and the service is more reliable.

MAI flies from Bangkok to Yangon and vice versa daily. From 1993 to 1998, MAI was a joint venture between Myanma Airways (MA, the government-owned domestic carrier) and a Singaporean company. In 1998 it was purchased by EVA Airways of Taiwan.

Air Mandalay (AM), one of Myanmar's new, privately owned domestic carriers, has recently started up a regular service between Chiang Mai in Thailand and Yangon twice weekly during the high season (November to February) and once a week for the rest of the year.

Other Countries in Asia MAI flies from Hong Kong twice weekly, from Singapore four times a week and from Kuala Lumpur twice weekly.

Biman Bangladesh Airlines flies Bangkok-Yangon-Dhaka (via Chittagong) once a week. It is usually the cheapest operator, although flights are often delayed and occasionally cancelled.

If you're flying through to Calcutta with Biman, you (sometimes) get a free night's stopover in Dhaka. Note that if you plan to stop in Bangladesh, it's still worth getting a ticket to Calcutta, as the price is the same and you may, therefore, start your Bangladesh travels with free airport transport and a free night's accommodation.

If you plan on an overnight stay in Dhaka, be sure to get a hotel voucher from Biman before leaving Yangon; in fact it might be best to get it in Bangkok (or wherever you buy the ticket) first, just to be safe.

SilkAir, a subsidiary of Singapore Airlines, flies daily between Yangon and Singapore while Malaysia Airlines flies twice-weekly from Kuala Lumpur. Mandarin Airlines flies four times a week to/from Taipei. Indian Airlines flies between Calcutta and Yangon twice weekly. There is also a flight from Beijing to Yangon via Air China.

LAND

Getting into Myanmar overland is gradually becoming an option, though relatively few people do it because of the added expense. Not counting border crossings for day-trippers along the Thai-Myanmar border, there are only two crossings where travellers can enter or exit Myanmar overland from Thailand with relative ease. Unfortunately, both of these crossings require travellers to fly over sections of Myanmar that are currently off limits. One crossing on the China-Myanmar border is now open to travellers (see the following entry).

China

The border crossing between China and Myanmar is open to travellers carrying permits for the region north of Lashio, although you can only legally cross the border in one direction – from the Chinese side (Ruili) into Myanmar via Mu-se in the northern Shan State. This appears to be possible only if you book a visa-and-transport package from Chinese travel agencies in Kunming. Once across the border at Mu-se, you can continue on to Lashio on a good road, and farther south to Mandalay, Yangon and so on.

India

So far the Chin State, which borders India, is still closed to foreign travellers, though rumours that it is about to open to group tours have been circulating for years. If this ever happens, travel for individuals may follow, in which case it will be possible to traverse the state via the Chindwin River, all the way to the Indian border at Tamu. Whether foreigners will be permitted to cross into India (or vice versa) is a matter yet to be decided between the Indian and Burmese governments.

Thailand

A handful of border crossings between Thailand and Myanmar are open to day-trippers, or for short excursions in the vicinity. As yet, only one of these (Ranong-Kawthoung) is an entry/exit point that links up with routes to Yangon or any other cities deep in the interior. Another crossing (Mae Sai–Tachileik) can only be used as an exit point if you've been travelling in the interior of Myanmar.

Note: some travellers report that they have been refused entry into Myanmar at Ranong-Kawthoung.

Ranong-Kawthoung This route is as yet little used by travellers. This is partly because it's relatively newly opened to third-country nationals, and partly because you cannot go overland all the way to Yangon – you must fly from Myeik or Dawei. Before heading down to Ranong make sure to get a Burmese visa in Bangkok. Day trips can be made to Kawthoung from Ranong, but unless you have a valid Burmese visa, you won't be allowed to go any farther. Travellers who intend on entering Myanmar here for anything other than day trips are required to exchange US$200 for FECs. From Kawthoung it's possible to fly to Yangon on Myanma Airways, or take a speedboat to Myeik or Dawei and then fly north to Yangon from those cities.

Mae Sai–Tachileik Travel permits (for up to 14 days) can be obtained from Burmese immigration officials at the border for excursions to Tachileik and beyond (as far north as Kengtung and Mong La), at a cost of US$18 and the exchange of US$100 to US$120 into FECs (depending on whether you're going to Kengtung or Mong La). However, if you only want to cross the border to Tachileik, the cost is US$5 and there is no FEC requirement.

On occasion, the border shuts down because of security reasons – usually involving skirmishes between the Yangon military and the Shan State's splintered Mong Tai Army (MTA) over methamphetamine smuggling.

For similar reasons, travel west from Kengtung to Taunggyi is still off-limits to non-Burmese, as the road is in bad condition and the surrounding area is considered unsafe. It is 163km farther from Tachileik to Kengtung, and the trip by bus or car takes at least six hours.

Rumour has it that an overland route all the way to China via Kengtung will eventually open here, but so far Kengtung is the end of the line, and you must leave the way you came, via Tachileik. In fact, the Burmese immigration officials at Tachileik keep your passport and give you a photocopy of it, along with the paperwork necessary to get past the five military checkpoints between Tachileik and Kengtung – to ensure that you won't attempt to travel deeper into Myanmar from Kengtung.

Three Pagodas Pass This crossing is only open for day trips from Sangkhlaburi, Thailand, to Payathonzu on the Myanmar side.

Warning

The information in this chapter is particularly vulnerable to change: prices for international travel are volatile, routes are introduced and cancelled, schedules change, special deals come and go, and rules and visa requirements are amended. Airlines and governments seem to take a perverse pleasure in making price structures and regulations as complicated as possible. You should check directly with the airline or a travel agent to make sure you understand how a fare (and ticket you may buy) works. In addition, the travel industry is highly competitive and there are many lurks and perks.

The upshot of this is that you should get opinions, quotes and advice from as many airlines and travel agents as possible before you part with your hard-earned cash. The details given in this chapter should be regarded as pointers and are not a substitute for your own careful, up-to-date research.

Mae Sot–Myawadi This crossing is sometimes open to day-trippers from Mae Sot on the Thai side to Myawadi just over the border in Myanmar.

Chiang Dao A dirt track turns left 10km north of Chiang Dao and leads through the small town of Muang Ngai to Na Ok at the border. This was the most popular opium route from Myanmar in the mid-1970s, but now the main illicit trade item is methamphetamine. Gunfights between Thai police and smugglers are very common here and it is recommended that you avoid this area.

Getting Around

AIR

Myanmar has 66 airstrips around the country, 20 of which are served by regularly scheduled domestic flights. Most are short, one-strip fields that can land only one plane at a time. Only the new international airport at Mandalay has instrument landing capability. During the monsoon season (May to November) landings can be especially tricky at airports without this capability.

Planned construction seems to have stalled indefinitely on a new international airport between Yangon (Rangoon) and Bago (Pegu), on a site used by B-29 bombers during WWII. A huge, new international airport has opened at Mandalay, enabling passengers coming from Thailand to bypass Yangon – good news if you plan on spending most of your time travelling upcountry.

An insurance fee of US$3 is tacked onto the price of every domestic flight in Myanmar.

To/From the Airport

A transportation desk with helpful staff just outside the arrival area can arrange taxis into Yangon for US$5 to US$8 per person depending on whether or not the taxi has air-conditioning. If you head for the exit a taxi driver will instantly find you and offer to do the trip for as little as US$3, but be prepared to bargain and give directions to small hotels or guesthouses. Some hotels will provide free transport if you book a room at their airport hotel desk.

Most taxis, official or otherwise, will offer to stop about halfway to town to change money, but you can get a slightly better rate in town rather than anywhere near the airport.

Coming to the airport from Yangon it's a bit cheaper and you can pay in kyat, about the equivalent of US$2.

If you happen to be flying out of Yangon on Union Day, 12 February, you need to get out to the airport before noon because the road to the airport is closed to nonparade traffic after that time.

Air Mandalay & Yangon Airways

AM, the first private carrier in the country, appears to have been created so that foreigners won't compete with Burmese citizens for perpetually tight seating space on MA aircraft. In other words, the government would just as soon see you fly with upmarket AM (or YA) rather than with government-owned MA.

Flying with either AM or YA saves visitors a whole list of headaches. In the first place, they fly to places for which permits aren't necessary, so that's one layer of bureaucracy eliminated in their ticket lines. Secondly, both AM and YA are usually punctual. Finally, both AM and YA planes – recent French-built ATR-72s – are substantially more comfortable, and the attentive, professional service contrasts strongly with the cattle-car ambience at MA. The ATR-72s are comfortably configured to seat 66 passengers, allowing for ample legroom.

AM's Toulouse-trained pilots hail from Australia, France, Singapore and Myanmar; all flight attendants are trained in Singapore. The company has updated safety procedures for flying to each of the airports it serves in Myanmar – the first airline in Myanmar to undertake this task since the 1950s. YA seems to have closely followed

Government-Owned Services

Be aware that the government profits from your use of government-owned or -run transport services. The following is a list of government-owned companies you may choose to avoid:

Inland Water Transport (IWT)
Myanma Airlines
Myanma Five Star Line (MFSL)
Myanma Railways
Road Transport Enterprise

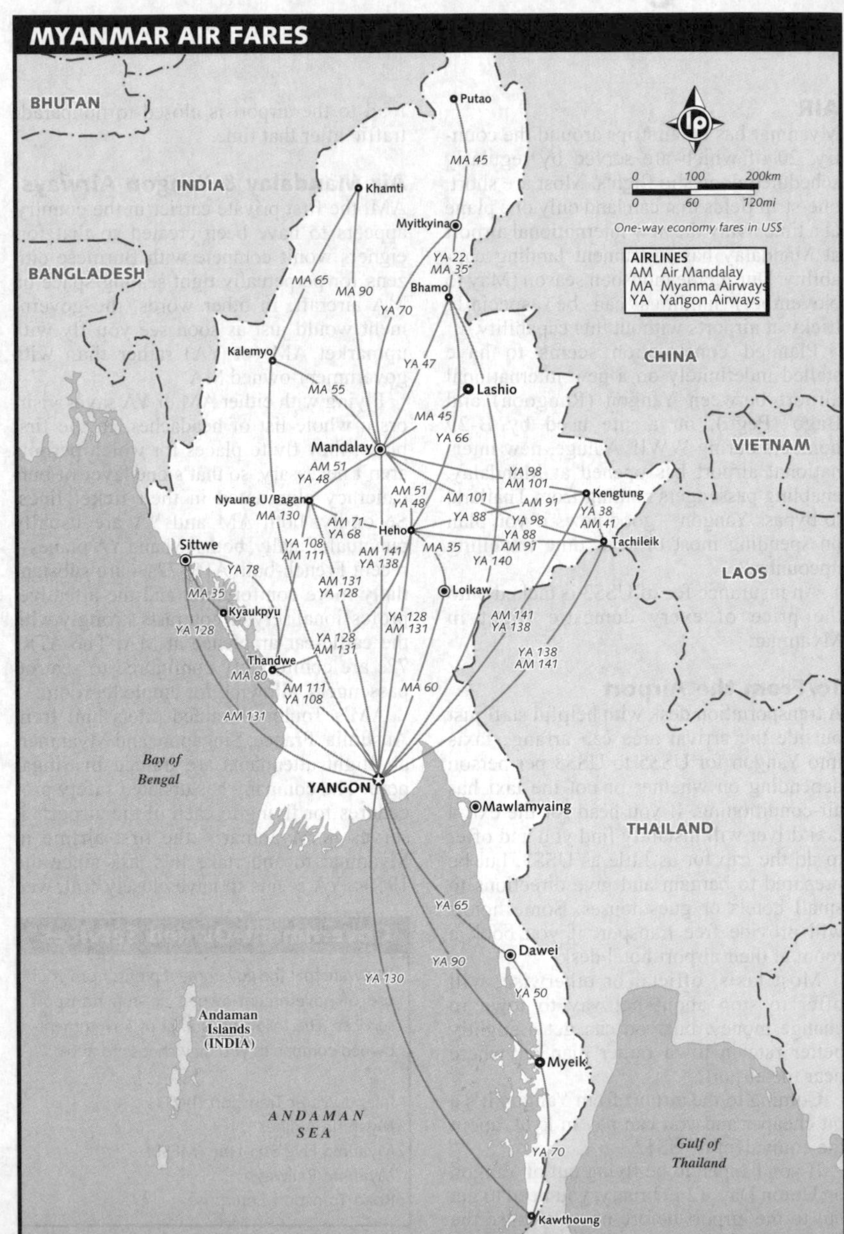
MYANMAR AIR FARES
BHUTAN
INDIA
BANGLADESH
CHINA
VIETNAM
LAOS
THAILAND
Bay of Bengal
ANDAMAN SEA
Andaman Islands (INDIA)
Gulf of Thailand
0 100 200km
0 60 120mi
One-way economy fares in US$
AIRLINES
AM Air Mandalay
MA Myanma Airways
YA Yangon Airways
Putao
Khamti
Myitkyina
Bhamo
Kalemyo
Lashio
Mandalay
Nyaung U/Bagan
Heho
Kengtung
Tachileik
Sittwe
Kyaukpyu
Loikaw
Thandwe
YANGON
Mawlamyaing
Dawei
Myeik
Kawthoung
MA 45
MA 65
MA 90
YA 70
YA 22
MA 35*
YA 47
MA 55
MA 45
YA 66
AM 51
YA 48
AM 51
YA 48
MA 130
AM 71
YA 68
AM 101
YA 88
YA 98
AM 101
AM 91
YA 98
YA 88
AM 91
YA 38
AM 41
YA 108
AM 111
AM 141
YA 138
MA 35
YA 140
YA 78
MA 35
AM 131
YA 128
YA 128
YA 128
AM 131
YA 128
AM 131
AM 141
YA 138
YA 138
AM 141
MA 80
AM 111
YA 108
AM 131
MA 60
YA 65
YA 90
YA 130
YA 50
YA 70

AM in terms of safety procedures and customer service.

AM flies to Yangon, Mandalay, Bagan/Nyaung U, Heho, Thandwe, Sittwe, Tachileik, Kengtung and Kyaukpyu. AM also operates the only arriving international flight into Mandalay, from Chiang Mai in Thailand.

YA flies to Yangon, Mandalay, Bagan/Nyaung U, Heho, Thandwe, Sittwe, Myitkyina, Bhamo, Kengtung, Tachileik, Dawei, Myeik and Kawthoung.

Note that flights to some of these destinations are only available during the high season (December and January).

Ticketing & Reservations Unlike MA, AM has ticketing services overseas – Bangkok and Chiang Mai in Thailand, and Singapore: **Mekong Land** *(☎ 027 125 842, 023 810 881, fax 023 917 212; 399/6 Soi Thonglor 21, Bangkok, Thailand)*; **AM** *(☎ 053 279 992; Chiang Mai, Thailand)*; and **MAS Travel Centre** *(☎ 6235 4411, 6737 8877, fax 6235 3033; 19 Tanglin Rd, Tanglin shopping centre, Singapore)*.

Fares Both AM and YA flights cost a bit more than MA flights to the same destinations, and their fares are slightly higher during the busier November-March period. Keep in mind also that some routes are discontinued during the low season. Ticket prices are cheaper from travel agents than from the airlines. (See the Travel Agencies entry under Information in the Yangon chapter for a list of travel agents.) Note also that AM offers discounts for tickets bought via its website (W www.air-mandalay.com).

The airport codes for domestic airports in Myanmar aren't always easy to figure out, as some of them are based on abbreviations of colonial-era names. A list of Myanmar domestic airport codes follows:

AKY – Sittwe
BMO – Bhamo
HEH – Heho (Inle Lake)
KAW – Kawthoung
KET – Kengtung
MDL – Mandalay
MGZ – Myeik
MYT – Myitkyina
NYU – Nyaung U (Bagan)
RGN – Yangon
THL – Tachileik
TVY – Dawei
SNY – Thandwe (Ngapali)

Myanma Airways

Until 1989, Myanma Airways (MA) was known as Burma Airways Corporation and, before that, Union of Burma Airways. MA's airline code remains UB.

MA's small fleet consists of Fokker F-28 jets and F-27 turboprops. Legroom and carry-on luggage space is minimal, as the airlines have opted for the maximum number of seats the aircraft is designed to carry. All craft are in decidedly tatty condition and the whole operation seems to be a little haphazard, which does not do wonders for one's nerves. The airline employs safety procedures that haven't been updated since the 1950s, and since 1989 MA has logged eight fatal crashes, including two in 1998 – one at Ngapali and another near Tachileik.

Of course, even though there are now two very reliable private domestic carriers, Air Mandalay (AM) and Yangon Airways (YA), there are some routes that are still flown exclusively by MA. Both AM and YA have much smaller route nets, flying only to the more popular tourist destinations. MA flies to virtually every airport in the country.

Air Safety in Myanmar

Until there's a turnaround in its safety record, we see no reason to risk flying government-owned Myanma Air (MA) – not to be confused with Myanmar Airways International (MAI), owned by EVA Air of Taiwan. Travellers on MA have reported broken seats, poor toilets, cancelled flights etc. To make matters worse, recent crashes have been met by government denials and misinformation, with confusion and fear the final results.

Michael Clark

Schedules On MA, even with ticket in hand, things may not go strictly to plan. Schedules don't mean much – if the passengers turn up early the flight may go early. If insufficient passengers show up the flight may not go at all.

Even having a confirmed reservation and being first in line may not get you there, because Burmese VIPs can jump the line with ease and package-tour people also get preference over independent travellers. Dates and departure times are rarely written on MA tickets, so they don't have to honour the days and hours for which reservations were originally made.

Fares & Payment Foreigners must purchase all MA tickets using Foreign Exchange Certificates (FECs) or US dollars. Burmese citizens pay much lower fares in kyat. If you cancel your booking within 24 hours of departure, MA collects a 25% cancellation charge; within six hours it jumps to 50%. Also note that you're not able to purchase tickets for MA outside the country – you can, however, with AM.

Though MA uses both turboprops and jets, in everyday practice the more expensive jets are used only for long hauls – Yangon-Sittwe (Akyab), or Yangon-Myeik – so you'll usually end up paying the lower fare. By the way, all the MA crashes in the last 12 years have been on the F-27 turboprops.

BUS & TRUCK

Private, air-con express buses run from Yangon to Meiktila, Pyay (Prome), Mandalay, Taunggyi, Mawlamyaing and Pathein (Bassein). This private service essentially eliminates the need to consider buses operated by the government-owned Road Transport Enterprise, which tend to be very crowded, ancient and unreliable.

The express buses also beat Myanma Railway's express trains in both speed and ticket price, and they stop for meals along the way. Another major difference between bus and train is that all bus tickets may be purchased using kyat; if there's a dollar/FEC fare posted it's usually close to the kyat fare, figured at the free-market rate. One drawback is that buses don't always have a toilet, so you're at the mercy of the driver, though they'll generally stop whenever asked.

There are also many modern Japanese pick-up trucks installed with bench seats known as *lain-ka* (for 'line car', rather like an Indonesian *bemo* or Thai *songthaew*) coming into use in the country. In fact, most intercity travel off the main routes is accomplished by Toyota pick-ups carrying 20 or more passengers plus cargo.

Foreigners are permitted to buy bus tickets of any class, using kyat, to any destination within or near the main Yangon-Mandalay-Bagan-Taunggyi quadrangle. We also found that buses were easily boarded in most other places in the country too, except for areas of unrestricted travel towards the Thai border.

Trip durations for public road transport are very elastic. Burmese superstition says when you're on a journey, you shouldn't ask 'How much longer?', or 'When will it arrive?', as this is only tempting fate. Some buses even have signs (posted in Burmese) requesting that passengers refrain from inquiring about the arrival time! Upcountry roads in central Myanmar are generally in reasonable condition on the main routes, but they're always narrow. When oncoming vehicles meet, or when one has to overtake another, both vehicles have to pull partly off the road. Breakdowns and tyre punctures are common.

Hitching

Hitching is never entirely safe in any country in the world, and we don't recommend it. Travellers who decide to hitch should understand that they are taking a small but potentially serious risk. People who do choose to hitch will be safer if they travel in pairs and let someone know where they are planning to go.

One extra reason to avoid hitching in Myanmar is that local drivers may not know which areas are off-limits to foreigners, and may unwittingly transport them into such areas. In such cases the driver would probably be punished.

Train Schedules & Fares

train	departure	arrival	fare
Yangon to Mandalay			
11 Up	6.00am	9.10pm	US$30
17 Up	3.15pm	5.20am	US$18-50 (special express)
5 Up	5.00pm	7.00am	US$30
15 Up	6.30pm	8.20am	US$38 (special express)
3 Up	7.30pm	10.35am	US$30
7 Up	9.00pm	11.30am	US$30
Yangon to Thazi			
11 Up	6.00am	5.52pm	US$27
5 Up	5.00pm	4.14am	US$27
17 Up	3.15pm	2.35am	US$33 (special express)
15 Up	6.30pm	5.36am	US$33 (special express)
3 Up	7.30pm	7.17am	US$27
Mandalay to Yangon			
6 Down	3.15pm	5.20am	US$30
18 Down	4.15pm	6.20am	US$38 (special express)
16 Down	5.30pm	7.30am	US$38 (special express)
4 Down	6.30pm	10.00am	US$30
8 Down	8.30pm	12.30pm	US$30
Thazi to Yangon			
18 Down	4.15pm	6.20am	US$33 (special express)
6 Down	6.00pm	5.20am	US$27
16 Down	8.16pm	7.30am	US$33 (special express)

TRAIN

Private Railways

Although most trains are operated by government-owned Myanma Railways, a few private enterprises have come into existence as well. Between Yangon and Mandalay, the private Dagon Mann (DM) line runs express trains that are more pleasant than the state-run express trains. However, the steep US dollar fares are clearly designed to dissuade foreigners from taking the train, which caters to upper crust Burmese rather than tourists. In fact, the only reason the DM accepts foreigners is that the government requires the company to set aside a few seats to help fill the demand for space during the tourist season. For more details, see Train in the Getting There & Away section of the Yangon chapter.

Two private companies, Malihka Mandalar and Mekha Mandalar, operate trains along the Mandalay-Myitkyina line. In this case the only alternative is the very slow and uncomfortable government train. Ticket prices for foreigners are, as usual, in US dollars – and of course, are much higher than those for locals.

Myanma Railways

Myanmar maintains 4684km of metre-gauge railway line – much of which is now open to foreign tourists – and 550 train stations.

The 647km-long trip from Yangon to Mandalay is the only train trip most visitors take – though there are plenty of other routes that could be taken for the more adventurous. On the Yangon to Mandalay route there are daily and nightly reserved cars on express trains, where you can be sure of getting a seat. One way to tell whether an approaching train is express or local is to check the engine colour: express engines are painted yellow, local ones blue. Other train journeys worth considering are the Mandalay (or Pyin U Lwin) train to Lashio (or Hsipaw), which is a scenic and relatively comfortable ride, and the Yangon to Mawlamyaing route.

As an alternative to using the government-owned Myanma Railways train services, you can use the new private bus services, which are cheaper, faster and more punctual. The express trains are far superior to the general run of Burmese trains. In fact we'd recommend avoiding most other trains for any long trip – one 12-hour train trip that ends up running 15 hours late is enough for most people. The Mandalay to Myitkyina route, though scheduled to take around 24 hours, often takes 40 hours; in 1995 this train derailed, killing 120 people, and in 2001 a bridge collapsed killing an equal number. Even on the more travelled Yangon-Mandalay route, delays are common.

Apart from the straightforward Yangon-Bago-Thazi-Mandalay line, you can also take the branch line from Pyinmana to Kyaukpadaung (about 50km south of Bagan) or the branch from Thazi to Shwenyaung (about 11km from Inle Lake). Another express line now runs between Bagan/Nyaung U and Mandalay. At Mandalay there are three branches: one running slightly northwest across the Ava Bridge (Inwa) and up to Yeu, one directly north to Myitkyina in the Kachin State and one northeast through Pyin U Lwin (Maymyo) to Lashio in the northern part of the Shan State. From Yangon, lines also run northwest to Pyay, with a branch-off to Pathein, while from Bago there is a branch off southeast to Kyaikto (jumping-off point for the Kyaiktiyo boulder-stupa) and Mawlamyaing (Mottama train station).

Note also that Burmese trains are classified by a number and either the suffix Up for northbound trains, or Down for southbound trains.

Classes

Express trains offer two classes of passage: upper class and ordinary class. The main differences between ordinary and upper are that the seats recline and can be reserved in advance in the latter, while ordinary class features hard upright seats that can't be reserved. Some trains also offer a third class of service called 1st class, which is a step down from upper in comfort.

The No 15 Up/No 16 Down train between Yangon and Mandalay is a 'special express' that uses relatively new Chinese equipment. The upper-class Chinese cars contain 30 wide seats in rows of three; other express trains may use older, South Korean cars that also seat three across but contain a total of 40 seats (so there's less room).

The No 15 Up/No 16 Down and the No 17 Up/No 18 Down trains have sleeping cars. These are sometimes occupied by Burmese VIPs or foreign tour groups. Some sleeping cars contain five cabins, each with four berths, a fan, a light and a small table with a washbasin underneath. Older sleeping cars are divided into two sections with four berths each, as well as a toilet and shower room in both sections.

Reservations

For booking details for the private Yangon-Mandalay train service, see the Getting There & Away section of the Yangon chapter. For tickets for government services along the Yangon-Mandalay line, all foreigners are supposed to purchase train tickets from MTT or from the **Advance Booking Office** *(Bogyoke Aung San Rd; open 6am-10am & 1pm-4pm daily)*, directly opposite the Sakura Tower.

There are two advantages to booking your express train tickets through MTT in Yangon: this office accepts Visa and American Express (AmEx) – MasterCard withdrew in 1998 – and a seat quota set aside for foreigners means you might be able to get a seat even when the station window says the train is full. Contrary to rumour, we found the fares to be exactly the same at both places, though fares differ according to which express train you take, even along the same line. A day's notice is usually enough for booking a seat. (Also, whenever you try to use a credit card in Myanmar, be prepared to pay a surcharge of 6%).

If you want to try your luck at getting a coveted sleeper, you'll need at least a couple of days notice, longer during the high season. During the November-March tourist season berths are booked weeks in advance; assuming you hold a seat on a train pulling a sleeper car (No 15 Up/No 16 Down or No 3 Up/No 4 Down), your best bet is to try to upgrade to a berth after boarding. If any are available due to last-minute cancellations, you should be able to move from seat to berth by paying the additional fare directly to the conductor.

To buy tickets at other train stations you can use the same ticket windows as the Burmese. For common tourist destinations – Bago, Pyin U Lwin, Kyaiktiyo – a US dollar/FEC fare is usually collected. To other points via nonexpress trains, you may be able to pay in kyat, though this has become increasingly rare over the years – consider yourself lucky if you can pull it off. Foreigners aren't permitted to ride ordinary class on the Yangon to Mandalay line; on most other branch lines where foreigners are allowed to pay in kyat rather than US dollars/FECs, there's usually no problem buying an ordinary ticket if that's what you want.

If you're having trouble buying a ticket or making yourself understood at a train station, try seeking out the stationmaster – the person at the station most likely to speak English, and most inclined to help you get a seat.

Car Rental Precautions

As a rule, it's a good idea to see your car and meet your driver before you agree to anything, or put down a deposit for car rental. You may want to look for a couple of essentials: a spare tyre and working seat belts. I was once offered a seat belt that looked fine at first glance, but had no buckle, or receiving end, to snap into. When the driver noticed the dilemma, he helpfully motioned for me to loop the belt around my neck!

Michael Clark

CAR

Hiring a car and driver is an increasingly popular way to get around the country. Prohibitions on car hire in Myanmar have lifted over the last few years and it's now very easy to hire a reasonably new, air-conditioned car with a driver for around US$35 to US$40 a day, less for older, non-air-con cars. The usual per-day asking price will be around US$50, including the driver and all fuel. If you hire for five days or more and pay for fuel yourself, the cost can drop to as low as US$30 a day. The cost will usually go up a few US dollars per extra person in the car or van. And the price should go down slightly if you plan on having a car for more than a week; the longer you intend to hire the car, the better your bargaining position.

There are no car-rental agencies per se, but most travel agencies in Yangon, Mandalay or Bagan – as well as guesthouses and hotels elsewhere – can arrange cars and drivers. In most cases, you will be asked to sign a simple contract and pay a good-faith deposit. Note that you'll pay more for your hired car if you arrange the deal through touts, such as trishaw drivers and moneychangers.

Foreigners with business or residence visas are permitted to drive themselves, although most still hire drivers. Driving conditions are poor and a driver adds little to the hire cost. Of the 24,000km of roads in Myanmar, about half are bituminous or paved; the remainder are graded gravel, unimproved dirt or simple vehicle tracks. To compound the difficulty, Myanmar traffic law requires vehicles be driven on the right-hand side of the road, even though the vast majority of cars and trucks – because they are low-cost, basic Japanese models – have right-hand drive. This contradictory arrangement is brilliant for keeping an eye on pedestrians and oxcarts alongside the road, but terrible for observing oncoming traffic.

Among the most popular and reliable rental cars in the country are second-hand, reconditioned Toyota hatchbacks imported

Road Distances (km)

	Bago	Kalaw	Lashio	Mandalay	Mawlamyaing	Meiktila	Monywa	Myitkyina	Nyaung U	Pyay	Sagaing	Taunggyi	Yangon
Bago	---												
Kalaw	360	---											
Lashio	557	341	---										
Mandalay	611	166	491	---									
Mawlamyiang	137	469	672	497	---								
Meiktila	461	72	341	150	403	---							
Monywa	747	251	627	136	582	286	---						
Myitkyina	1390	653	1270	779	984	927	915	---					
Nyaung U	377	161	312	183	492	89	268	670	---				
Pyay	307	350	786	595	329	445	731	1470	247	---			
Sagaing	632	179	512	21	510	171	115	800	196	456	---		
Taunggyi	646	44	155	336	519	186	472	1115	205	630	357	---	
Yangon	80	410	882	643	187	541	827	1470	426	286	712	726	---

from Japan and called Super-roofs. Also known as 'vans' in Myanmar, one fresh off the boat costs US$5000. Myanmar assembles its own Mazda jeeps – MJs – using 85% local parts. Though mostly a monopoly of the government, these jeeps make decent off-road vehicles. The old US-made, WWII-era Willys Jeeps that once characterised outback Myanmar travel are becoming few and far between. You'll see a few of them in Mrauk U, usually without windows. As in the Philippines, however, the popularity of the workhorse design has inspired Burmese companies to manufacture reproduction Willys jeeps that are nearly indistinguishable from the WWII originals. You'll see plenty of these in Mandalay.

Myanmar is no longer quite self-sufficient in oil, and petrol can usually only be purchased in the area where the vehicle is registered. Officially, petrol from a government-owned Myanma Electric Power Enterprise (MPPE) station costs just K180 a gallon, but is rationed at four gallons a week. At makeshift black-market pumps – often just around the corner from an MPPE station – petrol costs up to K950 a gallon, over K1000 in remote areas and small towns. When Burmese vehicle owners make an upcountry 'road trip' (the Burmese English term for any ex-Yangon driving), they either have to buy fuel on the black market, or carry along numerous jerry cans of petrol.

Another small cost to consider when travelling by car is the customary K25 to K65 'toll' collected upon entering many towns and villages throughout Myanmar – a legacy of the tributes paid to warlord states in centuries past. More a curiosity than a true financial burden, the road toll means that you or the driver should carry lots of small kyat bills – Burmese drivers are adept at handing these to the toll collectors while barely slowing down.

MOTORCYCLE

Apparently there's no longer any restriction on hiring motorcycles in Myanmar – you may even drive them yourself if you possess a valid International Driving Permit. The problem is finding a place that will rent out motorcycles. This time around we found no-one willing to rent out motorcycles to foreigners.

BICYCLE

Bikes can easily be hired in Mandalay, Bagan, Pyin U Lwin and around Inle Lake. Guesthouses often have a few for rent at only K500 per day. Just about anywhere outside Yangon, bikes are the ideal form of local transport since they're cheap, nonpolluting and keep you moving slowly enough to see everything. Outside Yangon and Mandalay vehicular traffic is generally very light. Carefully note the condition of the bike before hiring; it's not unusual to get one that needs a brake job or new pedal. And if it breaks down you are generally responsible and parts can be expensive.

If renting doesn't appeal, you can buy a sturdy new made-in-India Hero for US$40, a slightly better Five Rams from China for US$50 or a top-of-the-line Crocodile from Thailand for US$150. All are plain, utilitarian, all-black city bikes with moderately heavy frames.

A few visitors bring their own touring bikes into Myanmar; there doesn't seem to be any problem with customs as long as you make the proper declarations upon entering the country. Grades in most parts of Myanmar open to tourism are moderate. Frontier regions, on the other hand – particularly the Shan, Kayin, Kayah and Chin States – tend to be mountainous. You'll find plenty of opportunity everywhere for dirt-road and off-road pedalling – in fact you must come prepared for it! Especially in the north, where main roads can resemble off-roads elsewhere, a sturdy mountain bike would make a good alternative to a touring rig.

One of the most scenic routes starts in Thazi (accessible by train) and runs east through hilly Kalaw and Pindaya to Inle Lake. Another starts in Mandalay and down the flat Ayeyarwady (Irrawaddy) River plains to Bagan. Shorter trips out of Mandalay to Monywa, Pyin U Lwin, Sagaing, Inwa (Ava) and Amarapura also make satisfying rides.

Anyone with previous Third World cycling experience will find Myanmar a fairly straightforward pedal, though an extra measure of resourcefulness and cycling savvy is called for, due to the overall lack of accommodation and transport infrastructure. November to February are the best cycling months in terms of weather. Larger towns have bike shops – there are several in Mandalay and Yangon – but they often stock only a few Indian, Chinese or locally made parts. All the usual bike trip precautions apply – bring a small repair kit with plenty of spare parts, a helmet, reflective clothing and plenty of insurance.

BOAT

River Ferries

A huge fleet of riverboats, heir to the old Irrawaddy Flotilla Company (IFC), still ply Myanmar's major rivers. In the last few years, several newer boats have been put into service. A few of the boats date back 80 or 100 years to the British era. In Burmese-English they're still called steamers, even though the original stern-wheelers have all been converted to diesel. River ferry is, without doubt, one of the most enjoyable ways to cover long distances in Myanmar. The main drawback is speed; where both modes of transport are available, a boat typically takes three to four times as long as road travel along the same route.

Inland Water Transport (IWT) is the government-owned water-transport corporation, and has over 500 boats totalling nearly 1.5 million tonnes and carrying at least 14 million passengers annually. Another thousand or so private cargo and passenger boats travel the waterways. That is just a pale shadow of the former glory of the original Glasgow-owned IFC, which ceased operations in 1948.

There are 8000km of navigable river in Myanmar, with the most important river being the Ayeyarwady. Even in the dry season, boats can travel from the delta all the way north to Bhamo, and in the wet they can reach Myitkyina. Other important rivers include the Twante Chaung, which links the Ayeyarwady to Yangon, and the Chindwin River, which joins the Ayeyarwady a little above Bagan. The Thanlwin (Salween) River in the east is only navigable for about 200km from its mouth at Mawlamyaing.

Today most of the red-and-black boats of the IWT are rather rundown and ramshackle, but it still takes great expertise to navigate Myanmar's waterways. Rapidly changing sandbanks and shallow water during the dry season mean the captains and pilots have to keep in constant touch with the changing pattern of the river flows. For example, seven pilots are used on the stretch from Mandalay to Pyay. Each is an expert on his own particular segment of the river.

Many of the passengers on the long-distance ferries are traders who make stops along the way to pick up or deliver goods. Along the heavily travelled 423km-long Yangon-Pyay-Mandalay route, there are 28 ferry landings, where merchants can ply their trade.

Only a few riverboat routes are regularly used by visitors. These new 'tourist boats' carry foreigners on the upper deck, and locals on the lower. Best known is the Mandalay-Bagan service. Other routes include Mandalay-Katha-Bhamo, Sittwe-Mrauk U, Mawlamyaing–Hpa-an and Yangon-Pathein. On the Ayeyarwady, there is a quite amazing amount of transport shuttling up and down this riverine 'road to Mandalay' and it's a trip that most people seem to enjoy. Other boats can extend the trip south to Pyay, or all the way to Yangon; it's two days travel downriver from Bagan to Pyay, where you change boats and have another couple of days travel before reaching Yangon.

Mandalay-Bagan Express Ferry The new private Mandalay-Bagan Express ferry, operated by the Shwe Kinari Company, departs every Monday, Tuesday, Thursday, Friday and Saturday at 6am, and the trip takes about eight hours. (See the Boats entry in the Getting There & Away section of the Bagan Region chapter later in this book for more information.)

A slower, MTT (government) ferry does the same Mandalay-Bagan route every Sunday and Wednesday at 5.30am, taking roughly 14 hours and costing just US$10 for deck class with a chair. The slower boat stops overnight at Pakokku.

Ayeyarwady River Luxury Cruises There are several luxury ferries now travelling the upper and lower reaches of the Ayeyarwady River. The most conspicuous, and by far the most expensive, is the *Road to Mandalay*, an E&O luxury liner (Orient-Express Cruises, London) that offers package tours between destinations on the Ayeyarwady. For information about routes and rates check out **W** www.orient-expresstrains.com/tplanner/rtm/index.html.

Since 1996 the revived IFC has been operating old-fashioned 'expedition cruises' along several sections of the upper and lower Ayeyarwady River (see 'The RV *Pandaw* & the Irrawaddy Flotilla Company' boxed text later in this chapter.) If you've got the money, these boats are by far the most interesting vessels in Myanmar, relying on shallow-draft technology pioneered in Scotland over 100 years ago by naval architects; the RV *Pandaw* has a draft of just three feet – helpful on a river that bulges with sand bars during the dry season. Although the original stern-paddle design has been replaced by modern engines, the boats have the feel of a classic river steamer, with breezy promenades and teak and brass fittings throughout. Prices for one/two-night cruises between Bagan and Mandalay range from US$150/250; up to US$3000 for a 12-day cruise that reaches Bhamo on the upper Ayeyarwady.

Thanlwin River Ferry Double-decker ferries from the Hpa-an jetty, on the river's eastern bank in Mawlamyaing, depart twice daily to Hpa-an. This four-hour cruise (three hours downriver) is one of the most scenic river trips in the country. The fare for foreigners is US$2 for upper deck class, and US$12 for a cabin. See Getting There & Away in the Hpa-an section of the South-eastern Myanmar chapter for more details.

There are other, lesser known, river trips that the adventurous traveller can also consider. For example, Twante is only a few hours from Yangon via the Twante Chaung, and you can continue all the way to Pathein. The overnight river journey between Bhamo and Mandalay on the upper Ayeyarwady also has some spectacular scenery.

Another shorter trip you can make quite easily is the trip upriver from Mandalay to Mingun. You can also make short day-excursions by rented boat from Yangon, Mandalay and Bagan.

Reservations The government's IWT fares, calculated by mileage, used to be quite inexpensive when you could pay in kyat. As with train travel, the collection of US dollars/FECs versus kyat seems to be somewhat arbitrary. However, we've noticed more and more that foreigners are asked to pay the US dollar amounts. That goes for the privately owned ferries as well. Of course, with small boats that you might charter for part of a day, you can pay in kyat.

The main IWT ticket office in Yangon is one street back from Lan Thit jetty, in Bldg No 63. Foreigners are always referred to the **deputy division manager's office** *(☎ 01-284055)* in a corner of Bldg No 63. To be safe, try to book a week in advance of travel, although a day's advance purchase may sometimes be sufficient.

The **IWT office** *(☎ 02-36035; 35th Street)* in Mandalay is near the jetty. For information on ferries to Bagan or Pyay, see the appropriate Getting There & Away sections in the Bagan Region chapter, the Pyay section in the Around Yangon chapter, and the Bhamo section in the Northeastern Myanmar chapter.

Boats & Classes The standard long-distance ferry features two large decks, a lower deck consisting of the bare steel hull and an upper deck finished in wood. These ferries typically hold 286 passengers, 123 on the more costly upper deck and the remainder below. Only upper-deck passage can be reserved in advance; assigned numbers painted on the deck indicate the reserved spots. Some boats feature a dozen or so sling chairs toward the bow of the upper deck; these cost a bit more than regular upper-deck class. Boats running day routes usually feature a saloon compartment in the upper deck of the bow, with a few wooden chairs and an attached toilet. Monks usually ride in a separate, wired-off section of the upper foredeck.

Those craft running overnight routes may contain a few beds in the saloon compartment. A few boats even have cabins with sleeping berths in the bow, usually no more than six cabins sleeping two people each. On most routes, saloon and cabin-class space is very difficult to come by, though foreigners have a better chance than the Burmese. Military officers, of course, always have first choice.

The Mandalay-Bagan express boats have forward-facing row seating, though you're free to roam the decks for the price of a ticket. All the express boats have a snack bar serving noodles, beer, soft drinks etc.

Three new Chinese-built ferries featuring a triple-deck design have recently gone into service along the Yangon-Pathein route and along the Ayeyarwady River from Mandalay to Pyay via Bagan/Nyaung U. These vessels feature 18 double cabins in 1st class, 10 double cabins in 2nd class, three 16-berth cabins in 3rd class and deck space for 270 passengers. First-class cabins on the triple-deckers have attached toilets and showers.

Ships

Myanma Five Star Line Although the obstacles standing in your way are daunting, it may be possible to travel along Myanmar's coastline via Myanma Five Star Line (MFSL), the country's government-owned ocean transport enterprise. MFSL maintains just 21 craft, which sail north and south from Yangon about twice a month. Only eight vessels offer passenger service: MV *Taunggyi*, MV *Hakha*, MV *Myitkyina*, MV *Loikaw*, MV *Lashio*, MV *Bagan*, MV *Hpa-an* and MV *Htonywa*. Shipping dates vary from month to month and are announced via a public chalkboard at the main MFSL **office** *(☎ 01-295279, fax 295174; 132–136 Theinbyu St)* in Yangon. There's another office and chalkboard in Sittwe.

Southbound MFSL ships sail regularly to Kawthoung, a two-day and two-night voyage from Yangon, to pick up goods

The RV *Pandaw* & the Irrawaddy Flotilla Company

The RV *Pandaw* is a teak-and-brass Raj-era fantasy, forging down the Ayeyarwady at a stately eight knots. In 1920 the original Irrawaddy Flotilla Company (IFC), the Scottish-owned 'fabulous flotilla,' was the largest privately owned ship fleet in the world. In 1942, with Japanese troops flooding into Burma, all 650 ships were scuttled. In 1996 another Scot, Paul Strachan, whose Kiscadale Publications produce a range of interesting books about the country, revived the IFC name and in 1997 took over the RV *Pandaw*.

The 46m-long *Pandaw* was built in Glasgow in 1947 to the same steam-powered, stern paddlewheel design as the prewar flotilla ships. She was actually sailed out to Burma from Scotland. Although her sides were boarded up for the voyage to make her more seaworthy, it would have be an amazing feat to sail a vessel with just a metre draft across the open seas. For nearly half a century the *Pandaw* plied the rivers of Burma carrying passengers and cargo.

The IFC's old Siam Class steamers carried 4200 deck-class passengers and 40 more passengers in staterooms; they were 100m long and until recently travelled upriver faster than present-day government boats could manage downriver! The captains of these mighty riverboats were so important that a Mandalay shop once had a sign announcing they were 'Silk Mercers to the Kings and Queens of Burma and the Captains of the Steamers.' IFC was struck a disastrous blow by WWII, and many wrecks of their boats are still at Mandalay, scuttled in the river to deny them to the Japanese.

The new operators stripped the old *Pandaw* down and rebuilt it with modern luxuries – all 16 cabins have attached bathrooms and air-conditioners – but with a decidedly old-fashioned feel. The ancient steam engine and paddlewheel had already been replaced with modern diesels driving outboard propellers. Lounging outside your room in a cane armchair or sipping a gin and tonic in the bar it's hard to avoid humming that old Kipling ditty:

Come ye back to Mandalay
where the old Flotilla lay
Can't you 'ear their paddles
chunkin' from Rangoon to Mandalay

The *Pandaw* operates one- and two-day Mandalay-Bagan and Bagan-Mandalay trips. A typical two-night cruise from Mandalay departs soon after noon. Passengers enjoy lunch as the stately ship passes the old capital of Sagaing and sails under the Ava Bridge, just south of Mandalay. That

shipped through Thailand's Ranong Province, with calls at Dawei and Myeik. During the rainy season the journey can take a week.

Northbound ships call at Thandwe (a full day from Yangon), Taunggup and Kyaukpyu (one night ashore) before docking in Sittwe (five more hours) for cargo from India and Bangladesh.

Schedules can be irregular and you may have to wait several days for a ship going your way. If you're bent on trying for a ticket, it would be best to have a Burmese citizen make inquiries on your behalf, as the bureaucracy can be staggering. Tickets can only be purchased two days ahead; at times they are in such demand that locals are only able to buy them via a lottery system.

Foreigners who have persevered will usually be issued one of the 20 coveted berths in saloon (upper) class. All Yangon ships leave from the MFSL jetty (also known as the Chanmaye Seikkan jetty), just west of Pansodan Lan jetty. Saloon fares are: Kawthoung K4423; Dawei K2474; Myeik K2696; Thandwe K1538; Kyaukpyu K2179; and Sittwe K2592.

The RV *Pandaw* & the Irrawaddy Flotilla Company

evening the passengers enjoy sundowners on the upper deck as the sun sinks below the horizon. Dinner is served after the ship moors for the night by the riverbank near the town of Myinmu.

The next morning the Pandaw is on its way before dawn and by breakfast it moors beside the village of Yandabo. It was under a tree on the riverbank at Yandabo that the treaty was signed ending the first Anglo-Burmese War (1824–26), when the Burmese ceded Arakan, Assam, Manipur and Tenasserim to the British and allowed a British resident to set up at Ava. The village is not connected to the road network so its contact with the outside world is principally by river. Almost everyone in the village is engaged in making pottery and during the dry season there will be thousands of pots lined up at various stages of manufacture. The pots are traded up and down the river and even exported to the West. The IFC has sponsored the rebuilding and operation of the village school.

There's a steady flow of traffic up, down and across the river. Sometimes approaching ships carry a couple of bowmen, sounding the river depth with long red-and-white striped poles. There are always pilots on board the *Pandaw*, each of whom knows his own stretch of river with its constantly shifting shallows and sandbanks. Periodically the riverboat pulls in at some small settlement to drop off one pilot and pick up another.

Late that afternoon the *Pandaw* moors at Pakokku, a busy little provincial town only 25km north of Bagan. A fleet of chartered trishaws takes the passengers to the town's colourful little market, to a blanket-weaving workshop and to a cheroot manufacturer, all the while pursued by a cheerful posse of bicycling women, all intent on selling blankets and other crafts. That night the *Pandaw* moors only a few kilometres south of the town and by the time breakfast is over the next morning she's in Bagan.

From time to time the *Pandaw* travels further afield on five- and 10-day 'expedition' cruises up the Ayeyarwady to Bhamo or up the Chindwin River. It's even possible to charter the whole ship and plan your own expedition. The ship's shallow draft allows it to reach as far as 600km north of Mandalay or 500km up the Chindwin. Bhamo, the furthest navigable point up the Ayeyarwady, is about 1500km from the Indian Ocean, the wide plains of central Myanmar giving way to jungle and spectacular narrow gorges. The Chindwin rises in the heavy rainfall area of Assam in India and cuts through a series of mountain ranges to merge with the Ayeyarwady just north of Bagan. Although the Lower Chindwin can be kilometres wide in the dry season its average depth is only a metre. Navigating around the constantly changing sandbanks is a considerable feat. The IFC has recently added the slightly larger *Pandaw II*, a brand-new riverboat built in Yangon to the same style as its historic predecessors.

Tony Wheeler

Cargo Ships If you don't mind sleeping on potato and onion sacks, cargo ships are a cheap alternative to the government-MFSL ships that sail up and down the Bay of Bengal. See the Getting There & Away section for Mrauk U in the Western Myanmar chapter for more information.

LOCAL TRANSPORT

Larger towns in Myanmar offer a variety of city buses *(ka)*, bicycle rickshaws or trishaws (*saiq-ka*, for side-car), horse carts *(myint hlei)*, vintage taxis *(taxi)*, more modern little three-wheelers somewhat akin to Thai tuk-tuks (*thoun bein*, three wheels), tiny four-wheeled Mazdas (*lei bein*, four wheels) and modern Japanese pick-up trucks (also lain ka).

Small towns rely heavily on horse carts and trishaws as the main mode of local transport. In the five largest cities (Yangon, Mandalay, Pathein, Mawlamyaing and Taunggyi), public buses take regular routes along the main avenues for a fixed per-person rate, usually no more than K15. Standard rates for taxis, trishaws and horse carts are sometimes 'boosted' for foreigners. A little bargaining may be in order; ask around locally to find out what the going fares are. The supply of drivers and vehicles often exceeds demand, so it's usually not hard to move the fare down towards normal levels.

ORGANISED TOURS

Itineraries for Myanmar tours booked anywhere in the world look much the same. The cheapest (around US$400) is a four-day-three-night Yangon package that includes a visa, airport transfers in Yangon, guide service and accommodation only, booked through travel agencies in Bangkok. With a package of this sort, you must book your own return flight to Yangon, arrange your own local transport outside Yangon and buy your own meals.

More-expensive trips costing US$2000 or more run for 14 or 15 days in Yangon, Mandalay, Pyin U Lwin, Bagan, Kalaw, Pindaya, Inle Lake, Taunggyi and Bago, including visa, return air fare from Bangkok, local transport, accommodation, all meals and guide service. Such tours can be booked easily in the USA, Europe, Japan, New Zealand and Australia, or from agencies in Bangkok.

Deluxe river cruises on the upper and lower reaches of the Ayeyarwady River are available for periods of two to 14 days. Discerning travellers will be able to choose between government-run and privately operated cruises. See the River Ferry section in this chapter for more information.

It's also possible to arrange tours locally, out of Yangon and Mandalay. There are well over 100 travel agencies in Yangon, so it pays to shop around (see the Travel Agencies entry under Information in the Yangon chapter). Many will custom-design a tour according to your requests, for about the same price as a package tour booked abroad. Many travel agents can competently arrange tours for groups of just two or three people, and also get big discounts at top-end hotels.

Yangon

☎ 01

Yangon (formerly Rangoon) lies in the fertile delta country of central Myanmar, on the wide Yangon River, about 30km from the Andaman Sea. Although the population hovers around four million, the city gives a very different impression from other Asian capitals of similar size. It seems full of trees and shade – even old growth teak here and there – and some outlying neighbourhoods are refreshingly overgrown. The city centre's eclectic combination of British colonial architecture, Buddhist stupas, Hindu temples, Christian churches and Muslim mosques make it one of the most exotic and striking cities in Southeast Asia.

The city has changed dramatically following the 1989 banishment of socialism. Since 1992, when the relatively moderate, pro-capitalist General Than Shwe took power, many new cars and trucks have taken to city roads, mobile phones are commonly seen in the city centre and satellite dishes dot the horizon. The capital is still easygoing and there's little of the frenetic, neon-lit clamour of Bangkok. Nevertheless, the term rush hour can now be applied in relation to the city centre. Of course, the Yangon rush hour is a combination of weaving cars, buses, trucks, trishaws, taxis, bicycles and pedestrians. Somehow, people and vehicles coexist in the middle of large intersections. The sound of horns seems constant at times, and there are even posted signs here and there on city centre alleyways forbidding their use. Of course, no-one seems to pay attention to either the signs or the honking.

History

As Myanmar's capital city, Yangon is comparatively young – it only became capital in 1885 when the British completed the conquest of northern Myanmar and Mandalay's brief period as the centre of the last Burmese kingdom ended.

Despite its short history as the seat of national government, Yangon has been in existence for a long time – although very much as a small town, in comparison to places like Bago (Pegu), Pyay or Thaton. In 1755 King Alaungpaya conquered central Myanmar and built a new city on the site of Yangon, which at that time was known as Dagon. Yangon means 'end of strife': the king rather vainly hoped that with the conquest of central Myanmar, his struggles would be over.

In 1756 with the destruction of Thanlyin (Syriam) across the river, Yangon also became an important seaport. In 1841 the city

Highlights

- Glittering Shwedagon Paya with its dazzling mix of pavilions, stupas, images and bells
- Colonial architecture of old 'Rangoon', including the legendary Strand Hotel
- Serene Sule Paya in the heart of the busy city centre
- Pro-democracy landmarks such as Bogyoke Aung San's house-museum and the Martyrs' Mausoleum
- Sprawling Bogyoke Aung San Market and Theingyi Zei
- Peaceful Kandawgyi and Inya Lakes

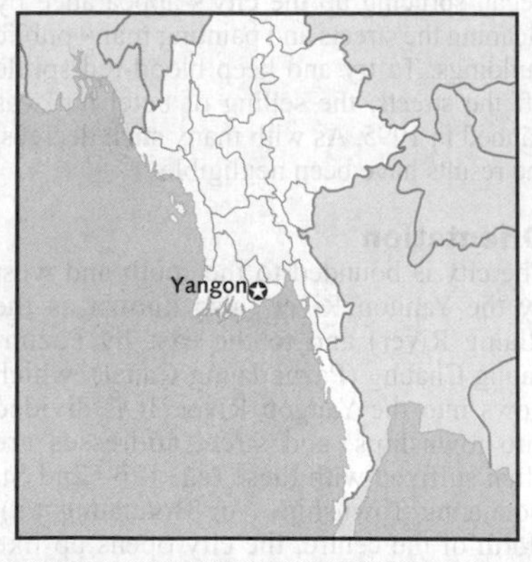

was virtually destroyed by fire; the rebuilt town again suffered extensive damage during the Second Anglo-Burmese War in 1852. The British, the new masters, rebuilt the capital to its present plan and corrupted the city's name to Rangoon.

Yangon's early history as Dagon is tied very closely to its grand Buddhist stupa, the Shwedagon Paya. It doesn't stand in the city centre, rather about 3km to the north – yet it totally dominates the Yangon skyline.

In 1988 around 15% of Yangon's city centre population – all squatters – were moved to seven *myo thit* (new towns) north-east of the city centre. Many of the old colonial buildings once occupied by the squatters have now been refurbished for use as offices, businesses and apartments.

Starting in the early 1990s, the government began sprucing up the city's appearance by cleaning the streets and painting many public buildings. To try and keep blood-red spittle off the streets, the selling of betel nut was banned in 1995. As with many such decrees, the results have been negligible.

Orientation

The city is bounded to the south and west by the Yangon River (also known as the Hlaing River) and to the east by Pazundaung Chaung (Pazundaung Canal), which flows into the Yangon River. It is divided into townships, and street addresses are often suffixed with these (eg, 126 52nd St, Botataung Township – or Botataung t/s). North of the centre, the city opens up like the top of a funnel and spreads along a network of long, curving avenues.

At the northern end, most businesses and hotels are along Pyay Rd, Kaba Aye Paya Rd or Insein Rd – long thoroughfares running south from the airport area to the city centre. Addresses in this northern area often quote the number of miles from Sule Paya – the landmark *paya* (pagoda) in the city's centre. For example, 'Pyay Rd, Mile 8' means the place is 8 miles (13km) north of Sule Paya on Pyay Rd.

Two of the most important townships outside the central area are Dagon – where you'll find Shwedagon Paya, People's Park and several embassies – and Bahan, site of many of the city's mid-range and top-end hotels and inns.

Central Yangon is a relatively simple area to find your way around, and pleasant enough to explore on foot. The main central streets are laid out in a grid system, with the minor north-south streets numbered in the North American fashion. Many of the major roads were renamed after independence.

Most of the other old names are fading from memory, however, and are of interest perhaps only to those in search of a bygone era. Mention of China St (Shwedagon Paya Rd), Godwin Rd (Madaw Rd) or Montgomery St (Bogyoke Aung San Rd) will probably elicit little more than a shrug. One exception: locals may indicate their political opinions by their choice of pre-junta terms such as Burma and Rangoon.

The English terms street and road are often used interchangeably in Yangon for the single Burmese word *lan*. Hence, some maps may read Shwegondaing St, while others will say Shwegondaing Rd; in Burmese, it's simply Shwegondaing Lan.

Maps The *Yangon Tourist Map,* printed by Design Printing Services (DPS) and distributed by Myanmar Travels & Tours (MTT), is usually free and useful enough for most people. If you anticipate spending a lot of time in the capital, look for a new bilingual atlas, *The Map of Yangon*, a detailed street directory with both a street and place index, first published in 1998, and easily found in most bookshops or large hotels for about US$3 or the *kyat* equivalent.

Harder to find, but still useful, is the older *Yangon City Map* (Printing & Publishing Enterprise), or the more detailed *Yangon Guide Map* (Ministry of Forestry, Survey Department). Both of these maps were first published in 1993. You might find used versions of these and other maps at the rambling sidewalk bookstalls on Pansodan St, just north of Merchant St.

Information

Tourist Offices The **MTT office** *(Map C; ☎ 275328, tourist information ☎ 282075;*

77-91 Sule Paya Rd; open 8.30am-5pm daily), on the corner of Mahabandoola Rd and across the street from Sule Paya, is the main centre for tourist inquiries. Basically nothing more than a government-run travel agency, its main purpose seems to be to discourage visitors from venturing away from the main tourist quadrangle, while encouraging the use of government-sponsored transportation like Myanma Airways (MA) and the Yangon-Mandalay train. Decent city maps of Bagan (Pagan), Mandalay and Yangon are sold for K50 each; postcards are also cheap here. Though seemingly helpful, information here is inconsistent at best, and should be double-checked; this means destinations, prices – everything.

Money With the Foreign Exchange Certificate (FEC) system in place, no-one bothers to change money at the so-called official rate any more. If you're foolish enough to want to, you'll have to convince someone you're serious. Even the MTT cashier will take foreign currency at close to the going rate.

Yangon is usually the best place in the country for changing money at the free-market rate. On the other hand, we've found that news of a drop in rates sometimes takes longer to reach the provinces. Ask around to establish what the current rate is. If you've bought FECs at the airport, the best place to change them is at a hotel or shop licensed to accept FECs. In general, Bogyoke Aung San Market is a good place to shop for moneychangers; several here are licensed to exchange kyat for FECs. If you don't have FECs, US dollars are the only alternative; free-market moneychangers usually aren't interested in other foreign currencies.

Cash Advance on Credit Cards Obtaining a cash advance from your credit card (Visa and American Express only) in Yangon is possible. And all up, it's quite an adventure in government-sanctioned bureaucracy. Grab your passport and credit card and head for the shabby-looking **Myanmar Foreign Trade Bank** *(MFTB; Map C; Mahabandoola Garden St)*. Make your way through the often crowded main foyer, then go straight ahead, down the back steps, over a laneway, into a separate building of tellers – it's here that you can buy and sell travellers cheques – then take a right up the stairs where you'll find a small office. Fill out a form here and you'll be handed a slip stating the amount you get (minus a 4% bank commission), then you head back down to the main foyer again, where a teller will hand over your cash – FECs only – you can't get US dollars.

Post The **main post office** *(Map C; Strand Rd; open 9.30am-4.30pm Mon-Fri)* is a short stroll east of The Strand Hotel. It's best to arrive by 4.15pm.

Telephone & Fax The **Central Telephone & Telegraph office** *(CTT; Map C; cnr Pansodan St & Mahabandoola Rd; open 8am-4pm Mon-Fri, 9am-2pm Sat, Sun & holidays)* was recently the only public place in the country where international telephone calls could be conveniently arranged. There are now two more methods: International Direct Dial (IDD) and trunk calls. IDD calls are very expensive, and can be made from many hotels; trunk calls are quite cheap, and can be made from many shops in the city centre area. The CTT office also has fax machines. Some hotels also have fax machines.

Internet Access Yangon isn't overrun with Internet outlets, and Internet cafés as you might know them are yet to appear. Several hotels offer Internet access, as do a steadily growing number of small businesses. One of the best organised of these is **Uniqcom Business Services** *(Map C; ☎ 251765, fax 251765; ⓔ uniqcom@mptmail.net.mm; 535 Merchant St; open 9am-5pm daily)* in the city centre. Rates are cheap at K600 per hour, but you aren't allowed to access your own email (eg, Hotmail) – you must send and receive email via a Uniqcom address.

Travel Agencies Most visitors to Myanmar only use domestic travel agencies to book a tour, hire a car or book a domestic flight (air ticket prices are usually cheaper

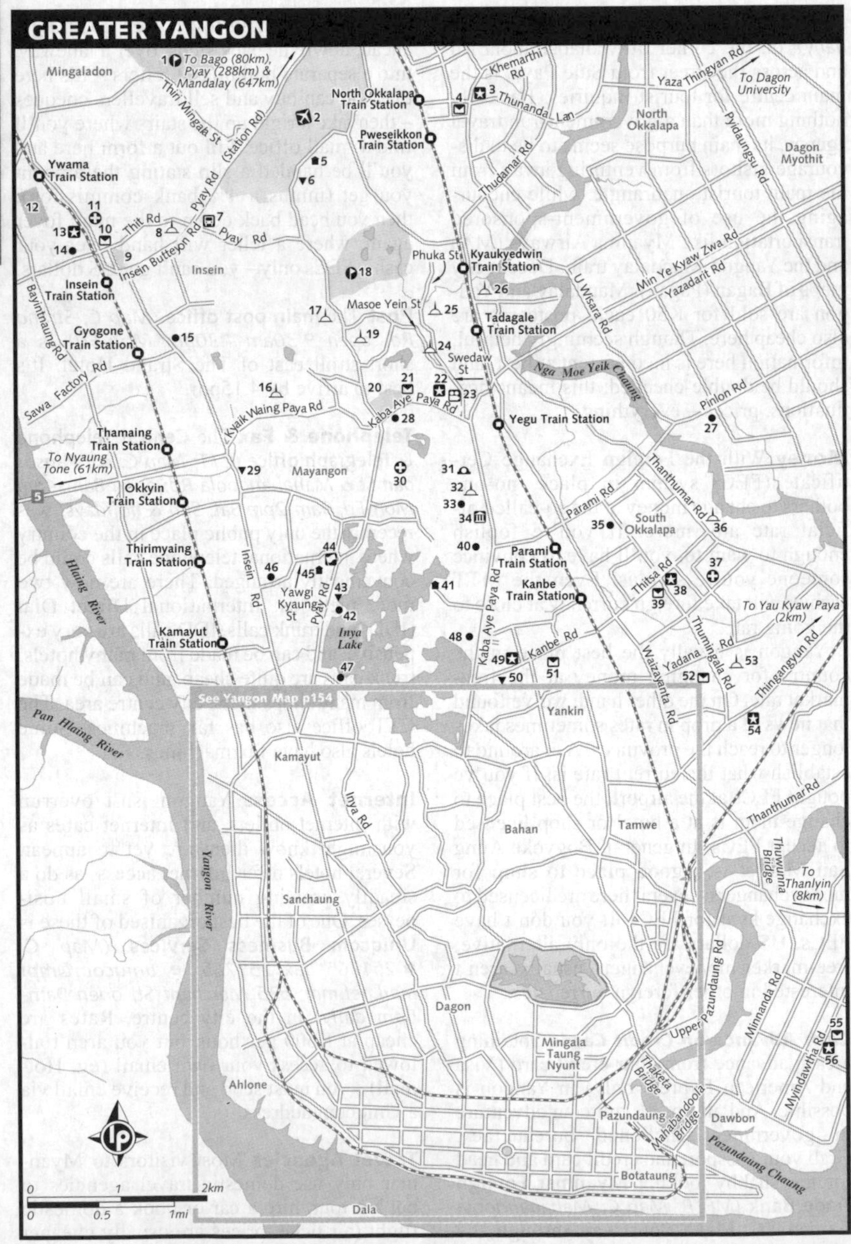
GREATER YANGON
Mingaladon
To Bago (80km), Pyay (288km) & Mandalay (647km)
Thiri Mingala St
(Station Rd)
North Okkalapa Train Station
Pweseikkon Train Station
Khemarthi Rd
Thunanda Lan
Yaza Thingyan Rd
To Dagon University
North Okkalapa
Pyidaungsu Rd
Dagon Myothit
Thudamar Rd
Ywama Train Station
Thit Rd
Pyay Rd
Insein Butteyon Rd
Insein
Bayintnaung Rd
Insein Train Station
Gyogone Train Station
Sawa Factory Rd
Phuka St
Kyaukyedwin Train Station
Min Ye Kyaw Zwa Rd
Yazadarit Rd
U Wisara Rd
Masoe Yein St
Tadagale Train Station
Swedaw St
Nga Moe Yeik Chaung
Kaba Aye Paya Rd
Kyaik Waing Paya Rd
Yegu Train Station
Pinlon Rd
Thamaing Train Station
To Nyaung Tone (61km)
Mayangon
Okkyin Train Station
Thanthumar Rd
Parami Rd
South Okkalapa
Thirimyaing Train Station
Hlaing River
Yawgi Kyaung St
Pyay Rd
Insein Rd
Inya Lake
Parami Train Station
Kanbe Train Station
Thitsa Rd
To Yau Kyaw Paya (2km)
Kamayut Train Station
Kanbe Rd
Waizayanta Rd
Yadana Rd
Thuminggala Rd
Thingangyun Rd
See Yangon Map p154
Pan Hlaing River
Yankin
Kamayut
Inya Rd
Bahan
Tamwe
Thanthumar Rd
Thuwunna Bridge
To Thanlyin (8km)
Yangon River
Sanchaung
Dagon
Upper Pazundaung Rd
Minnanda Rd
Myindawtha Rd
Mingala Taung Nyunt
Thaketa Bridge
Mahabandoola Bridge
Ahlone
Pazundaung
Dawbon
Pazundaung Chaung
Botataung
Dala
0 1 2km
0 0.5 1mi
1 2 3 4 5 6 7 8 9 10 11 12 13 14 15 16 17 18 19 20 21 22 23 24 25 26 27 28 29 30 31 32 33 34 35 36 37 38 39 40 41 42 43 44 45 46 47 48 49 50 51 52 53 54 55 56

GREATER YANGON

PLACES TO STAY
5 Ramada Airport Hotel
41 Renaissance Inya Lake Hotel; International FOF Medical Centre
45 Shwe Hinthar Inn

PLACES TO EAT
6 Airport Oasis Garden Restaurant
29 Nawarat Hotel Restaurant
43 Silom Village Restaurant
50 L'Opera Restaurant

OTHER
1 City Golf Resort Club
2 Yangon International Airport
3 Police Station
4 Post Office
7 Highway Bus Station
8 Ah Lain Nga Sint Paya
9 Insein Park
10 Post Office
11 Insein General Hospital
12 Insein Prison
13 Police Station
14 Insein Market
15 Yangon Institute of Technology
16 Kyaikwaing Paya
17 Shan Kyaung Paya
18 Myanmar Golf Club
19 Nagayon Paya
20 Myaing Haywun Park
21 Post Office
22 Police Station
23 Nawaday Cinema
24 Swedawmyat Paya (Buddha Tooth Relic Pagoda)
25 Naga Cave Paya
26 Me La Mu Paya
27 Pinlon Market
28 DHL Express Mail
30 Sangha Hospital
31 Maha Pasan Guha
32 Kaba Aye Paya
33 State Pariyatti Sasana University
34 Myanma Gems Museum & Gems Market
35 Nandawun Market
36 South Okkalapa Paya
37 Women and Children Hospital
38 Police Station
39 Post Office
40 Chanmyay Yeiktha Meditation Centre
42 International Business Centre
44 Philippines Embassy
46 Na-Gar Glass Factory
47 Yangon Boat Club; Sailing Club
48 Yone Yang Antique Shop
49 Police Station
51 Post Office
52 Post Office
53 Kyaikkasan Paya
54 Police Station
55 Post Office
56 Police Station

through a private travel agency). However, of the more than 100 enterprises in Yangon calling themselves travel agencies, only a handful can be considered full-service, experienced tour agencies.

Among the more reliable agencies are:

Columbus Travels & Tours (Map B; ☎ 221881, fax 229246, ⓔ columbus@mpt-mail.net.mm) 586 Strand Rd (corner of Strand Rd and 7th St)
Diethelm Travel (☎ 527110, fax 527136, ⓔ leisure@diethelm.com.mm) 1 Inya Rd
Free Bird Tours (Map C; ☎ 245489, fax 275638, ⓔ freebird@myanmars.net) 357 Bo Aung Gyaw St
Golden Express Limited (Map B; ☎ 225569) 97-B Wadan St
Gulliver Tours & Travel (☎ 526100, fax 513160, ⓔ gulliver@mptmail.net.mm) 51B Inya Maing Rd
Insight Myanmar Tourism (Map B; ☎ 297798, fax 295599, ⓔ insight@mptmail.net.mm) 85–87 Theinbyu Rd, Botataung Township
Santa Maria Travel & Tours (Map A; ☎ 201996, 709488, fax 297946, ⓔ santa-maria@mptmail .net.mm) 123 (Ground Floor) 43rd St, Bottataung Township
Tour Mandalay (Map B; ☎ 294729, fax 297917, ⓔ kzn.tmc@mptmail.net.mm) 2nd floor, 194/196 Mahabandoola Rd
Woodland Travels (☎ 246636, fax 240377, ⓔ woodlandtravels@mptmail.net.mm) 24 Yawmingyi St

Bookshops The **Bagan Bookshop** *(Map C; ☎ 277227; 100 37th St)* has the country's most complete selection of English-language books on Myanmar and Southeast Asia. The owner often has the front gate pulled across the entrance, but this doesn't necessarily mean the place is closed unless the door inside the gate is closed too. The Bagan even has a photocopier so you can copy rare, out-of-print books. Also it's worth checking out the many bookstalls around Bogyoke Aung San Market (formerly known as Scott Market) or along 37th St.

Libraries The **British Council Library** *(Map C; ☎ 295300; Strand Rd; open to the public 8.30am-3.30pm Mon-Sat)*, in the UK embassy, has a small library of English-language magazines and books. The **American Center** *(Map B; ☎ 223140; 14 Taw Win St; open 9am-4pm Mon-Fri)*, behind the Ministry of Foreign Affairs, also has a collection of books and magazines, which can be perused.

For French-language material, check the **Alliance Française** *(Map B; ☎ 282122; Pyidaungsu Yeiktha Rd; open Tues & Fri)*, attached to the French embassy.

If visiting Shwedagon Paya, you can visit the Library & Archives of Buddhism, located in the western arch.

Religious Services For travellers seeking houses of worship:

Anglican/Episcopal/Protestant

English Methodist Church (Map B; ☎ 284165) 65 Alaungpaya St

Holy Trinity Cathedral (Map B; ☎ 272326) 446 Bogyoke Aung San Rd

Immanuel Baptist Church (Map C; ☎ 250079) Mahabandoola Garden St

Catholic

St Augustine's Church (Map A; ☎ 530620) 64 Inya Rd

St Mary's Cathedral (Map B; ☎ 294896) 372 Bo Aung Gyaw St

Jewish

Moseah Yeshua Synagogue (Map C; ☎ 275 062) 85 26th St (services on special occasions only)

Muslim

Cholia Jama Mosque (Map C) Bo Sun Pet St

Narsapuri (Moja) Mosque (Map C) 227 Shwebontha St

Sikh

Sikh Temple (Map B) 256 Theinbyu Rd

Meditation Centres The following meditation centres are recommended:

Chanmyay Yeiktha Meditation Centre (Greater Yangon map; ☎ 661479) 55A Kaba Aye Paya Rd

Mahasi Meditation Centre (Map A; ☎ 541971, 552501, fax 289960/1) 16 Sasana Yeiktha St

Panditarama Golden Hill Meditation Centre (☎ 531448) 80A Shwetaunggyaw St

The International Meditation Centre (☎ 531549) 31A Inya Myaing Rd

Laundry Professional laundry services usually do a better job of washing and ironing than Yangon's guesthouses and small hotels. **Ava Laundry** *(Map B; ☎ 245575)* and **Anglo Myanmar Laundry Service** *(Map B; ☎ 284602)*, two places on the southern side of Mahabandoola Rd, between 41st and 42nd Sts, are fast, reliable and cheap. Both shops are open 7.30am to 9.30pm daily.

Medical Services If you want medical attention in Yangon, your best bet is the **International FOF Medical Center** *(Greater Yangon map; ☎ 667871, 24-hr alarm centre ☎ 667877; 37 Kaba Aye Paya Rd)*, on the ground floor of the Renaissance Inya Lake Hotel; you can also call the **hotel** *(☎ 662866)*, and ask for FOF International.

There are several private and public hospitals in Yangon, but the fees, service and quality may vary. One that has been recommended to us is the **Pacific Medical Centre & Dental Surgery** *(Map A; ☎ 548022; 81 Kaba Aye Paya Rd)*.

Pharmacies There are two pharmacies just north of Sule Paya and opposite one another – the **AA Pharmacy** *(Map C; 142/146 Sule Paya Rd)* and **Global Network Co** *(Map C; 155/161 Sule Paya Rd)*. **May Pharmacy** *(Map C; 542 Merchant St)* is nearby, on the northwest corner of Pansodan St. All three shops have 24-hour counters. The well-stocked **City Mart Supermarket** *(Map B; cnr Anawrahta Rd & 47th St)* includes a pharmacy. Tampons are available at the City Mart Supermarket.

Emergency An ambulance can be summoned by dialling ☎ 192 or calling the **Red Cross** *(☎ 295133)*. For police, call ☎ 199. In the case of fire, call ☎ 191. There isn't always an English-speaking operator on these numbers; you may have to enlist the aid of a Burmese speaker to make these calls.

Your embassy (see the list of foreign embassies in the Embassies & Consulates section in the Facts for the Visitor chapter) may also be able to assist with emergencies or serious problems. Many embassies and consulates maintain after-hours phone numbers, which they'll disclose to passport holders from the appropriate country. It's a good idea to register with your embassy upon arrival, so that the embassy staff will know where to reach you in case of an emergency at home.

Shwedagon Paya (Map A)

ရွှေတိဂုံဘုရား

The highlight of any visit to Yangon, and indeed Myanmar itself, Shwedagon Paya *(admission US$5)* is located to the north of central Yangon, between People's Park and Kandawgyi. See the special section for full details about Shwedagon, its design and historical significance.

In the compound's northwestern corner is a huge bell that the British dropped into the Yangon River while trying to take it. Unable to recover it, they gave the bell back to the Burmese, who refloated it by tying logs and bamboo beneath it.

The official admission fee includes an elevator ride to the raised platform of the stupa. Of course, like most Burmese, you may walk up one of the long graceful entrances. If you're taking photos rather than praying, a roving foreigner-ticket-checker may ask you to pay the US$5 on the spot. There's also a K5 camera fee, not always enforced.

Maha Wizaya (Vijaya) Paya (Map A)

မဟာဝိဇယ

Almost opposite Shwedagon Paya's southern gate, a pedestrian bridge links the Shwedagon complex with a well-proportioned *zedi* (Buddhist stupa) built in 1980 to commemorate the unification of Theravada Buddhism in Myanmar. The king of Nepal contributed sacred relics for the zedi's relic chamber and Burmese strongman Ne Win had it topped with an 11-level *hti* (decorated top) – two more levels than the hti at Shwedagon.

Foreign media and some locals often refer to the monument as 'Ne Win's paya', due to Ne Win's involvement in the project (a common practice among top military figures). However, many Burmese citizens resent this phrase, pointing out that since the zedi was built by donations from the people, it should rightfully be called the 'people's paya'. They emphasise that any *kutho* (Buddhist merit) created by its construction should accrue not to Ne Win, but to the Burmese people, who have enriched the man and his regime since 1962. Politics and religion aside, the Maha Wizaya *(admission free)* is one of the most attractive to have been built in Myanmar in decades.

Sule Paya (Map C)

ဆူးလေဘုရား

Situated in the centre of Yangon, across from the MTT office, the tall zedi at Sule Paya *(admission free)* makes an excellent landmark; in fact it's used as a milestone from which all addresses to the north are measured. Legend says it's over 2000 years old but, as with many other ancient Burmese shrines, it has been rebuilt and repaired many times over the centuries, so no-one really knows when it was built. The central stupa is said to enshrine a hair of the Buddha; its Mon name, Kyaik Athok, translates as 'the stupa where a Sacred Hair Relic is enshrined'. Most likely, as with the zedi at Shwedagon, it was originally built by the Mon in the middle of this century.

The golden zedi is unusual in that its octagonal shape continues right up to the bell and inverted bowl. It stands 46m high and is surrounded by small shops and all the familiar non-religious activities that seem to be a part of every Burmese zedi. In fact, unlike the more pristine Shwedagon Paya, Sule's busy location seems to enhance its soulful place in daily Yangon life, and it's a popular meeting place for many Burmese.

Botataung Paya (Map B)

ဗိုလ်တထောင်ဘုရား

Bo means leader (usually in a military sense) and *tataung* means 1000 – the Botataung Paya *(Strand Rd)* was named after the 1000 military leaders who escorted relics of the Buddha, brought from India over 2000 years ago. This ancient monument stood close to the Yangon wharves, and during an Allied air raid on 8 November

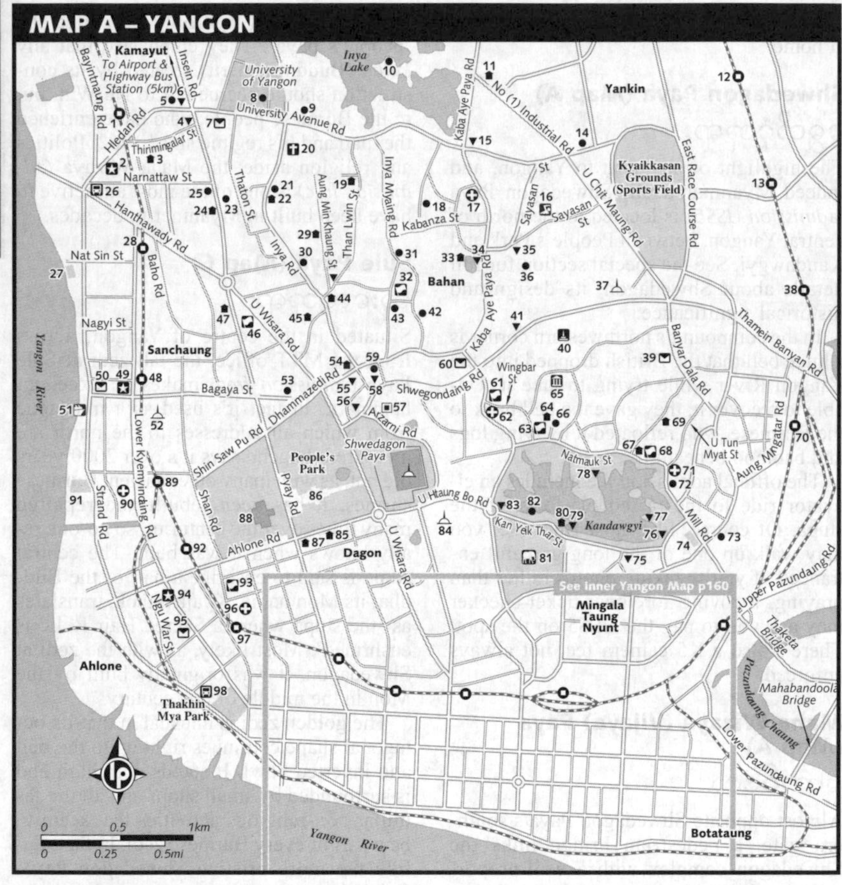

1943, a bomb scored a direct hit on the unfortunate paya.

After the war, the Botataung was rebuilt in a very similar style to its predecessor, but with one important and unusual difference: unlike most zedi, which are solid, the Botataung is hollow, and you can walk through it. There's a sort of mirrored maze inside the stupa, with glass showcases containing many of the ancient relics and artefacts, including small silver-and-gold Buddha images, which were sealed inside the earlier stupa. Above this interesting interior, the golden stupa spire rises to 40m.

To the western side of the stupa is a hall containing a large gilded bronze Buddha, cast during the reign of King Mindon Min. At the time of the British annexation, it was kept in King Thibaw Min's glass palace, but after King Thibaw was exiled to India, the British shipped the image to London. In 1951 the image was returned to Myanmar and placed in the Botataung Paya. Also on the grounds is a *nat* (spirit) pavilion containing images of Thurathadi (the Hindu deity Saraswati, goddess of learning and music) and Thagyamin (Indra, king of the nat) flanking the thoroughly Burmese nat Bobogyi.

MAP A – YANGON

PLACES TO STAY
3 Aurora Inn
11 Sedona Hotel
19 Motherland Inn
22 Yoma Hotel 2
24 Summer Palace Hotel
29 Windermere Inn
33 Mya Yeik Nyo Royal Hotel
44 Winner Inn
45 Comfort Inn
47 Liberty Hotel
54 Savoy Hotel
64 Beauty Land Hotel
67 Hotel Nikko Royal Lake Yangon
69 Bagan Inn; Silver Palace Restaurant
80 Kandawgyi Palace Hotel
85 Summit Parkview
87 Yangon International Hotel; Ashoka Restaurant

PLACES TO EAT
4 Green Elephant Restaurant
6 MacBurger
15 Royal Taj Restaurant
34 Yadana Garden Restaurant
35 Mr Guitar Café
41 Vietnam House Restaurant
55 Sabai Sabai Thai Restaurant
56 Hla Myanma Htamin Zai
58 Aung Thuka Restaurant
75 Sei Taing Kya Teashop
76 Royal Garden Restaurant
77 Karaweik Palace Restaurant
78 Lone Ma Lay Restaurant
79 Seafood Market & Lakeview Restaurant
83 Dolphin Seafood Restaurant

OTHER
1 Hledan Train Station
2 Police Station
5 Hledan Zei (Market)
7 Post Office
8 Institute of Myanmar Traditional Advanced Boxing
9 Unicef
10 Tatmadaw Boat Club
12 Bauktaw Train Station
13 Tamwe Train Station
14 Sanpya Zei (Market)
16 Kokine Swimming Pool
17 Pacific Medical Centre & Dental Surgery
18 Golden Valley Art Centre
20 St Augustine's Church
21 Inya Gallery of Art
23 Institute of Medicine 1
25 Myanmar Book Centre
26 Hsimmalaik Bus Station
27 San Pya Fish Market
28 Hanthawady Train Station
30 Diethelm Travel
31 Gullivers Tours & Travel
32 Italy Embassy
36 Mahasi Meditation Centre
37 Chaukhtatgyi Paya
38 Myittar Nyunt Train Station
39 Post Office
40 Ngahtatgyi Paya
42 Yangon International School
43 Traditions Gallery
46 Singapore Embassy
48 Kyemyindaing Train Station
49 Police Station
50 Post Office
51 Htee Dan Jetty (Passenger Ferry to Dalah)
52 Kohtatgyi Paya
53 Yuzana Supermarket
57 Martyrs' Mausoleum
59 Air Mandalay; A&T Bakery
60 Post Office
61 Vietnam Embassy
62 Jivitdana Hospital
63 Japan Embassy
65 Bogyoke Aung San Museum
66 Mogok Meditation Centre
68 Germany; Nepal Embassy
70 Manlwagon Train Station
71 Kandawgyi Hospital
72 UNDP & FAO
73 Yuzana Plaza
74 Mingala Zei (Market)
81 Yangon Zoological Gardens
82 National Aquarium
84 Maha Wizaya Paya
86 People's Square
88 Pyithu Hluttaw (National Assembly)
89 Panhlaing Train Station
90 People's Hospital
91 Thirimingala Zei (Market)
92 Ahlone Lan Train Station
93 Chinese Embassy
94 Police Station
95 Post Office
96 Children's Hospital
97 Shan Rd Train Station
98 Buses to Thanlyin

A short walk from Botataung Paya at Botataung jetty, you can watch ferryboats and oared water taxis cross the Yangon River.

Kaba Aye Paya (Greater Yangon Map)

ကမ္ဘာအေးဘုရား

The 'world peace' zedi was built in 1952 for the 1954–56 Sixth Buddhist Synod. The 34m-high stupa also measures 34m around its base. It stands about 11km north of the city centre, a little beyond the Renaissance Inya Lake Hotel. This attempt to construct a modern paya was not terribly successful – it does not have the same visual appeal of Myanmar's older, more graceful stupas. The interior of the monument, however, is hollow and inside are some nice Buddhist sculptures, including a *lei-myet-hna* (four-sided Buddha sculpture).

Maha Pasana Guha (Greater Yangon Map)

မဟာပါသနလိုဏ်ဂူ

The 'great cave' is a totally artificial one, built close to the Kaba Aye Paya. It was here that the Sixth Buddhist Synod was held to coincide with the 2500th anniversary of the Buddha's enlightenment. The participants at the Synod were attempting to define a definitive text for the *Tripitaka* (Buddhist canon). The cavern measures 139m by 113m.

Chaukhtatgyi Paya (Map A)

ခြောက်ထပ်ကြီးဘုရား

The reclining Buddha at Chaukhtatgyi *(Shwegondaing Rd; admission free)* is almost as large as the enormous figure in Bago. It's housed in a large metal-roofed shed, only a short distance northeast beyond the Shwedagon Paya. Surprisingly, this huge figure is little known and hardly publicised at all – if you can't get to Bago to see the Shwethalyaung, then don't miss this colossal image. Fortune-tellers on the surrounding platform offer astrological and palm readings.

Other Paya, Temples & Shrines

South of the Chaukhtatgyi Paya, there's a huge seated Buddha image at the **Ngahtatgyi Paya** *(Map A)*. It's appropriately known as the five-storey Buddha and is located in the Ashay Tawya monastery. In Kyemyindaing (also called Kyimyindine and Kemmedine), in the west of the city, there's another huge seated Buddha in the **Kohtatgyi Paya** *(Map A; Bagaya St)*; it stands (or sits) 20m high. There are many monasteries in the vicinity. Kyemyindaing also has a busy night market.

Near the airport, the **Me La Mu Paya** *(Greater Yangon map)* has a series of images of the Buddha in his previous incarnations, and a reclining Buddha image. The paya is named after the mother of King Ukkalapa, the founder of the city of Dagon. In Insein, west of the airport, the **Ah Lain Nga Sint Paya** *(Greater Yangon map)* has a five-storey tower and a particular connection with the nats and other spirit entities of Burmese Buddhism.

Near the International Buddhist University is **Swedawmyat Paya** *(Buddha Tooth Relic Pagoda; Greater Yangon map; Swedaw St)*, between Kaba Aye Paya Rd and Thudhamar St, architecturally one of the best new paya in Yangon. However, it contains not just another tooth relic from the Buddha, but a replica of a relic brought from China in 1997 by pilgrims.

The **Yau Kyaw Paya** is a 30-minute drive from the city, past the Kyaikkasan Paya. It's an interesting complex of buildings with tableaux depicting Buddhist legends, pet monkeys, deer and peacocks and an interesting museum crammed full of Burmese antiques. The paya is beside the Pazundaung Chaung in a rural setting.

Kheng Hock Keong *(Map B; Strand Rd)* is the largest Chinese temple in Yangon. Supported by a Hokkien association, the 100-year-old temple is most lively from around 6am to 9am when it's thronged with worshippers offering candles, flowers and incense to the Buddhist and Taoist altars within. Old men play Chinese checkers in the temple compound throughout the day.

The **Moseah Yeshua Synagogue** *(Map C; 85 26th St)*, near Mahabandoola Rd, was founded over a hundred years ago by Sephardic Jews. In the classic Sephardic style, it contains a *bimah* (platform holding the reading table) in the centre of the main sanctuary and a women's balcony upstairs. The wooden ceiling features the original blue-and-white Star of David motif. Myanmar had around 2500 Jews – a combination of B'nai Israel, Cochin (Indian) and Iraqi heritages – until nationalisation in the 1960s and 1970s, when many began leaving the country. Today there are no more than 50 or so Burmese Jews left in Myanmar, but surviving trustees maintain the synagogue for the occasional special service given by visiting rabbis from India. Caretaker Moses Samuels is happy to talk with visitors and show them the nearby Jewish cemetery, with over 700 graves dating back to 1856.

Several Hindu temples can be found in the centre of the city, including **Sri Sri Siva Krishna** *(141 Pansodan St)*, **Sri Kali** *(Anawrahta Rd)*, between 26th and 27th Sts, and **Sri Devi** *(Map B; cnr Anawrahta Rd & 51st St)*. These are the centres for the city's annual Murugu Festival, famous for colourful street processions featuring acts of ritual self-mutilation.

National Museum (Map B)

အမျိုးသားပြတိုက်

In 1996 the National Museum (*☎ 282563; Pyay Rd; adult/child & student US$5/10 kyat; open 10am-4pm daily)* was moved to a larger site, about 1km north of Bogyoke Aung San Rd, and just south of the Indonesian embassy. The collection remains unspectacular, cavernous and sparsely labelled.

Nevertheless, you can find several interesting exhibits, especially the 8m-high Sihasana (Lion Throne), which belonged to King Thibaw Min, the last Burmese king. There is also a fair range of royal regalia, much of which was plundered by the British but later returned (in fact you'll find a more impressive Burmese collection in London's Victoria and Albert Museum). Also worth a look are some extraordinarily intricate examples of 19th-century Burmese woodcarving.

The main floor contains jewellery, old black-and-white photos of Mandalay Palace and Yangon, royal relics, Hintha opium weights and inscribed tablets.

Note that the museum has three other floors that are very easy to miss. Upstairs you'll find Burmese archaeological finds as well as traditional musical instruments. The fourth floor features about 40 mannequins dressed in the traditional dress of various ethnic groups in the country. Other exhibits include dazzlingly ornate (and no doubt quite heavy) examples of Burmese court costumes, as well as royal furniture, including the royal couch that belonged to King Mindon's queen. There are also some excellent old maps and modern Burmese paintings by the talented U Ba Nyan and others.

Camera use is discouraged by a sign near the entrance announcing a US$100 fee for using still cameras, and US$200 for video.

Bogyoke Aung San Museum (Map A)

ဗိုလ်ချုပ်အောင်ဆန်းပြတိုက်

Located in the Bahan Township, this quiet and secluded house-museum (*☎ 550600; Bogyoke Aung San Museum St; admission US$2; open 10am-3.30pm Tues-Sun)* is the former home of General Aung San and his wife Daw Kin Kyi, and contains remnants of another era. The house itself dates from the 1920s and the rooms, stairway, railings and furniture are fairly intact. There are several old family photos, which of course include daughter Suu Kyi as a little girl. A glass-encased English-language library reveals the general's broad interests; titles range from *Cavalry Training*, *Armoured Cars*, *Children's Play Centre*, *The Mahatma Letters to Schemes of Constitutional Reform in Burma – if Separated*, *Left-wing Democracy in the English Civil War* and Adam Smith's *The Wealth of Nations*.

Martyrs' Mausoleum (Map A)

အာဇာနည်ဗိမာန်

Close to Shwedagon, on a hill offering a good view over the city, stands this memorial *(admission US$3; open 9am)* to Bogyoke Aung San and his fellow cabinet officers who were assassinated with him. It was also here that a bomb set off by North Koreans killed a number of South Korea's top government officials in late 1983. The mausoleum itself is only open one day a year – 19 July.

Mahabandoola Garden (Map C)

မဟာဗန္ဓုလပန်းခြံ

Just southeast of Sule Paya, this square urban park *(admission K5)* offers pleasant strolling in the city centre's heart, especially in the early morning when the Chinese come to practise tai chi, and the air hasn't yet filled with traffic fumes. Occupying the centre of the park's northern half, an **Independence Monument** is surrounded by two concentric circles of *chinthe* (half-lion, half-dragon sculptures). A large fountain in the northwest corner sometimes functions; geese live in the somewhat stagnant pond at the park's southern end, where there is also a children's playground with a couple of mechanical rides.

For a year or two following the 1988–90 uprisings, the park was occupied by Burmese soldiers; many of the more violent events of the time took place nearby.

Yangon Zoological Gardens (Map A)

ရန်ကုန်တိရစ္ဆာန်ဥယျာဉ်

These 0.7-hectare gardens *(☎ 274244; Kan Yeik Thar St)* are a nice place for a stroll and encompass a zoo *(foreign tourist/resident US$5/2; open 6am-4pm daily)*. The entrance is opposite the Dolphin Seafood Restaurant. Originally developed in 1906 by the British, the nicely landscaped grounds include a couple of artificial lakes, a playground and a miniature train circuit for kids, English and Latin labels (even on many of the trees) and maps of distribution. On weekends it's a favourite family picnic spot.

Tigers and lions pace about in the stately **King Edward VII Carnivora House**, built in 1915. Other open-air exhibits display an elephant house (unfortunately the elephants are chained) and a fair selection of both common and scarce Asian animals (including sambar, leopard, serow, Eld's deer, Malayan sun bear, goral, Indian muntjac, great hornbill, python, cobra and the huge marsh crocodile).

A two-storey, school-like building on the grounds contains a **Natural History Museum** *(☎ 272923; free with zoo admission)*, with labelled static exhibits on rocks and minerals, mammals, birds, fish, reptiles and amphibians – most of the specimens are stuffed or bottled.

A restaurant on one of the lakes offers cafeteria-style service.

Kandawgyi Lake (Map A)

ကန်တော်ကြီး

Also known by its literal translation, Royal (Dawgyi) Lake (Kan), this natural body of water close to the city centre is another good place for strolling or picnicking. The lake seems its most attractive at sunset, when the glittering Shwedagon is reflected in calm waters; you'll find the best sunset view from the lake's southwestern edge.

Several of the city's embassies, clinics and smaller hotels are in the lake's vicinity. Just east of the Kandawgyi Palace Hotel (formerly the Baiyoke Kandawgyi Hotel, and before that, the British Boating Club), on the southern side of the lake, floats a **Shin Upagot shrine**. Upagot is a bodhisattva or Buddhist saint who is said to protect human beings in moments of mortal danger.

The renovated **Karaweik**, a reinforced concrete reproduction of a royal barge, sits (it certainly doesn't float) at the eastern edge of the lake. Apart from being something of a local attraction in its own right, the Karaweik (Sanskrit: *garuda*), the legendary bird-mount of the Hindu god Vishnu, is also a restaurant – see the Places to Eat section later in this chapter. Traditional dance performances are held here in the evenings.

Inya Lake (Greater Yangon Map)

အင်းလျားကန်

Further north of the city, stretching between Pyay Rd to the west and Kaba Aye Paya Rd to the east, Inya Lake is roughly five times larger than Kandawgyi. Like the latter, it's a popular weekend relaxation spot for locals, although certain areas along the lake-shore – occupied by state guesthouses and ministerial mansions – are off-limits to the general public.

Two important figures in contemporary Burmese history reside on opposite sides of the lake, like powerful nat locked in a battle of wills. At the southern end, at 54 University Ave, is Aung San Suu Kyi, who was under house arrest until 1995, and again from 2000 to 2002; at the other end is willing recluse Ne Win, housed with his wizards and astrologers.

Myanma Gems Museum & Gems Market (Greater Yangon Map)

မြန်မာ့ကျောက်မျက်ပြတိုက်နှင့် အရောင်းပြခန်း

Just north of Parami Rd, this museum *(☎ 531071; Kaba Aye Paya Rd; admission US$3; open 9am-5pm Tues-Sun)* is meant to impress – starting with the world's largest sapphire that comes from Mogok, measures 17cm in height, and is nearly 12kg in weight; this somehow translates to 63,000 carats. Other exhibits display gemstones from the raw to the polished. In a poor country famous for valuable resources, the museum offers an unintended lesson in beauty, politics and money.

Na-Gar Glass Factory (Greater Yangon Map)

နဂါးဖန်မြေမှုန်မြေစက်ရုံ

The Factory (☎ *526053; 152 Yawgi Kyaung St, Hlaing Township; admission free; open 9.30am-11am & 12.30pm-3.30pm daily)* is an interesting place to explore, with lots of hand-blown glass on display, in a surprisingly pleasant indoor-outdoor setting. It was this place that provided the huge, mesmerising eyes of the reclining Buddha at Chaukhtatgyi Paya (see earlier in this section). Unusual wine glasses, small vases and the like are also for sale at very reasonable prices. It's worth a visit. The friendly, giggly owner is usually on hand to give you a tour of the workshop.

The factory isn't signposted, and is well hidden down a jungly driveway. Most taxi drivers in the downtown area aren't familiar with the factory, and it definitely helps if you tell them it's located in Hlaing (pronounced *lie-eng*) Township. A taxi from the downtown area should take about 15 minutes one way and cost around K3000 to K4000 for a return trip.

Defence Services Museum (Map B)

စစ်သမိုင်းပြတိုက်

This large, typically grim complex (☎ *25 4852; cnr Shwedagon Pyay Rd & Pantra St; admission $3; open 9am-4pm daily)* incorporates the Air Force Museum and may be of interest to the military minded.

Other Attractions

Opposite Shwedagon Paya to the west, **People's Park** *(Map A; admission US$4)* is a huge expanse of grass and trees bisected by **People's Square**, a wide, socialist-style pedestrian promenade. Near a set of fountains south of People's Square is a children's playground area, and in the southeastern corner of the park a couple of armoured tanks are on display. The park entrance faces the eastern side, opposite Shwedagon's western gate. Photo permits cost US$2 for still cameras, US$4 for video.

The Strand Hotel (Map C) 'When in Singapore stay at the Raffles', the saying used to go. (Actually it was 'feed at the Raffles' and stay somewhere else, but never mind.) Similarly, when you are in Yangon, the place to stay, if you can afford it, is The Strand (☎ *243377, fax 289880;* ⓔ *strand.ygn@mptmail.net.mm; 92 Strand Rd)*. Located between 38th St and Seikkantha St, The Strand was originally constructed by the Sarkies brothers, of Raffles fame, in 1896, and was one of those glorious outposts of the British empire early in the 20th century. During WWII it was forced to close, only to reopen in 1948, under the auspices of London's Steel Brothers Co.

Ne Win nationalised the property in 1963 and in its latter-day socialist role The Strand became a run-down shadow of its former self – certainly no competition for the well-kept likes of Raffles or The Oriental in Bangkok. Yet somehow, the old colonial era lived on at The Strand.

All of this changed again in 1991, when Dutch-Indonesian resort impresario Adrian Zecha and his company began spending US$36 million to renovate the grande dame. By the beginning of 1995, 32 rooms had been totally redone and opened to the public. A planned renovation of the once-popular annexe was abandoned in 1998.

Our verdict: of the three major Sarkies hotel renovations in Southeast Asia, this one seems the most faithful to the original spirit. Though perhaps well beyond the budget of many visitors to Myanmar as a place to spend the night, The Strand is well worth a visit for a drink in the bar, high tea in the lobby lounge or a splurge lunch at the café. Unlike the Oriental or Raffles, the

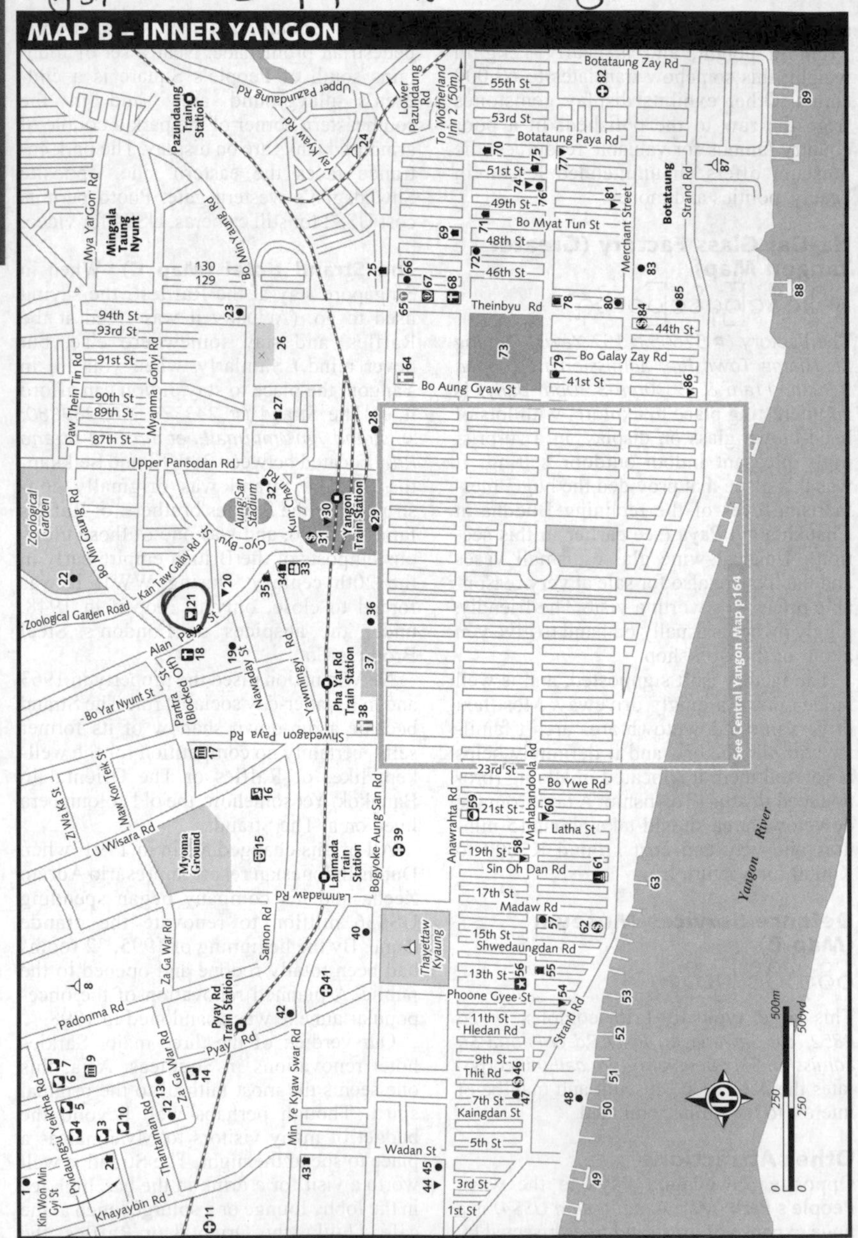
MAP B – INNER YANGON
Botataung Zay Rd
55th St
53rd St
Botataung Paya Rd
51st St
49th St
Bo Myat Tun St
48th St
46th St
Theinbyu Rd
44th St
Bo Galay Zay Rd
41st St
Bo Aung Gyaw St
Merchant Street
Botataung
Strand Rd
Upper Pazundaung Rd
Pazundaung Train Station
Lower Pazundaung Rd
To Motherland Inn 2 (50m)
Yay Kyaw Rd
Bo Min Yaung Rd
Mingala Taung Nyunt
Mya YarGon Rd
94th St
93rd St
91st St
90th St
89th St
87th St
Daw Thein Tin Rd
Myanma Gonyi Rd
Upper Pansodan Rd
Zoological Garden
Bo MinGaung Rd
Aung San Stadium
Gyo Pyu St
Kun Chan Rd
Yangon Train Station
Kan Taw Galay Rd
Zoological Garden Road
Alan Paya St
Pantra (Blocked Off)
Bo Yar Nyunt St
Nawaday St
Yawmingyi Rd
Pha Yar Rd Train Station
Shwedagon Paya Rd
Zi Wa Ka St
Maw Kon Teik St
U Wisara Rd
Myoma Ground
Lanmadaw Rd
Lanmadaw Train Station
Bogyoke Aung San Rd
Samon Rd
Za Ga War Rd
Padonma Rd
Pyay Train Station
Pyay Rd
Min Ye Kyaw Swar Rd
Thantaman Rd
Pyidaungsu Yeiktha Rd
Kin Won Min Gyi St
Khayaybin Rd
Thayettaw Kyaung
Anawrahta Rd
Mahabandoola Rd
23rd St
Bo Ywe Rd
21st St
Latha St
19th St
Sin Oh Dan Rd
17th St
Madaw Rd
15th St
Shwedaungdan Rd
13th St
Phoone Gyee St
11th St
Hledan Rd
9th St
Thit Rd
7th St
Kaingdan St
5th St
Wadan St
3rd St
1st St
Yangon River
See Central Yangon Map p164
0 250 500m
0 250 500yd

MAP B – INNER YANGON

PLACES TO STAY
2 Pansea Yangon; Pansea Restaurant
25 Yoma Hotel
27 Sunflower Inn
34 Thamada Hotel
35 Hotel Equatorial
43 Panda Hotel
55 Lai Lai Hotel
69 Queen's Park Hotel
70 Cozy Guest House
71 Three Seasons Hotel
75 Haven Inn
78 YMCA

PLACES TO EAT
20 Yuzana Garden Hotel Snack Bar
44 Maw Shwe Li Restaurant
54 Singapore's Kitchen
58 Chinese Street Stalls
60 Indian Street Stalls
74 Lashio Lay Shan Restaurant
77 Home Sweet Home
81 50th Street Bar & Grill
86 Palei Kywe Restaurant

OTHER
1 J's Irrawaddy Dream
3 Sri Lanka Embassy
4 Malaysia Embassy; Philippines Embassy
5 Pakistan Embassy
6 Indonesia Embassy
7 French Embassy
8 Ein Daw Yar Paya
9 National Museum
10 Laos Embassy
11 Central Women's Hospital
12 American Center & USIS
13 Ministry of Foreign Affairs
14 Israel Embassy
15 National Theatre
16 Yangon Swimming Club; He & Me Food Centre
17 Defence Services Museum
18 English Methodist Church
19 Yuzana Pickle Tea
21 British Club
22 Amusement Park
23 Theinbyu Zei (Market)
24 Shwe Pon Pwint Paya
26 Muslim Cemetery
28 Morning Market
29 Dagon Mann Private Train Ticket Office
30 Sakhantha Hotel Restaurant
31 Yoma Bank
32 City Bus Ticket Offices (Long Distance Buses)
33 Thamada Cinema
36 FMI Centre
37 Bogyoke Aung San Market
38 Holy Trinity Cathedral
39 Yangon General Hospital
40 Institute of Medicine No 1
41 New Yangon General Hospital
42 Than Zei (Market)
45 Golden Express Limited
46 AWB Bank
47 Columbus Travels & Tours
48 Inland Water Transport Office
49 Wadan St Jetty
50 Kaingdan St Jetty
51 Lan Thit St Jetty
52 Hledan St Jetty
53 Pongyi St Jetty
56 Police Station
57 Iron Bazaar
59 Pick-ups to Bago
61 Kheng Hock Keong
62 Myanma Agricultural Bank
63 Sin Oh Dan St Jetty (Vehicle Ferry to Dalah)
64 St Mary's Cathedral
65 Public Toilets
66 Ivy Gallery
67 Sikh Temple
68 Salvation Army Church
72 City Mart Supermarket
73 Ministers' Offices
76 Tour Mandalay Travel
79 Ava Laundry; Anglo Myanmar Laundry
80 Myanma Five Star Line
82 East Yangon General Hospital
83 Myanma Railways Office
84 FEC Money Exchange
85 Insight Myanmar Tourism
87 Botataung Paya
88 Myanma Five Star Line (MFSL) Cargo Jetty
89 Botataung Jetty

hotel isn't appended to touristy shopping malls and souvenir shops. The decor doesn't bowl you over with a surplus of ornamentation either, and the staff seem to be a bit more laid-back and less snobbish to non-guest visitors – as long as you dress decently for your visit.

Swimming & Golf

Three public pools in Yangon charge small fees (usually $3) for daily use and are generally open from 6am to 8pm: **Yangon University Swimming Pool** *(Map A; ☎ 531889; Inya Rd)*; **Kokine Swimming Club** *(☎ 550034; 34 Sayasan St)*; and **Yangon Swimming Club Pool** *(Map B; ☎ 278550; U Wisara Rd)*. The Yangon Swimming Club Pool is attached to the He & Me Food Centre & Music Pub, which offers snacks and drinks in an open-air setting overlooking the pool.

Yangon has two main public golf courses, both near the airport: **City Golf Resort Club** *(also known as YCDC; Greater Yangon map; ☎ 641342; Thirimingalar St)* and **Myanmar Golf Club** *(Greater Yangon map; ☎ 661702; Pyay Rd)*. Note that most clubs in Myanmar have ties to the Burmese military. Players tend to be a cross-section of Tatmadaw (armed forces) officers and Singaporean and Japanese business executives. Greens fees, on average, range from US$20 to US$30 for foreigners; a caddy is about US$3 for 18 holes. Clubs can be rented for about K2000.

Martial Arts & Weight Training

Burmese kickboxing instruction for beginners is offered on the ground floor of th

YMCA *(the Y; Map B; ☎ 294128, 296435; Mahabandoola Rd near Theinbyu Rd; open beginners 7am-9am Tues, Thur & Sat, experienced 3pm-5pm Mon, Wed & Fri)*. The instructor is Ko Chit, an accomplished student of the renowned Nilar Win, who founded the Y programme and is now teaching Burmese kickboxing in Paris. There's usually someone around who can translate the essentials, though you should mostly expect to learn by example. The techniques taught at the Y incorporate some moves borrowed from Thai and international boxing.

A bodybuilding/weight room, next to the kickboxing room at the Y, features a full range of cast-iron free weights. Visitors are welcome to participate in boxing or weight training upon becoming members; if you're staying at the Y, you're welcome to use the facilities for a small donation. Inquire at the main office on the upper floor for more information.

Saya Pan Thu, founder of the **Institute of Myanmar Traditional Advanced Boxing** *(Map A; 15 Aung Chan Tha St, Hledan Rd, Kamayut Township)* teaches a more traditional Burmese kickboxing style on most Saturdays at 4pm at the Yangon University campus. Pan Thu doesn't speak much English, nor apparently do any of his students. If you're interested in learning Burmese kickboxing, watch a few training sessions at both the Y and Pan Thu's to see which style seems more suitable.

The art of **Tai Chi** is practised daily at dawn at Mahabandoola Garden, near Sule Paya.

Running & Walking

The **Yangon Hash Harriers** meet at the Sailing Club *(Greater Yangon map; ☎ 531298; 132 Inya Rd)*. A walk/run through central Yangon leaves at 4.30pm on Saturday (meet at 4pm), and takes about 30 to 45 minutes at an easy pace that allows even children to keep up. Another informal group does a 3km and 6km run between the Traders Hotel and the Zoological Garden/Kandawgyi area every Sunday. Inquire at the **Traders Hotel** (see Places to Stay – Top End later in this chapter).

Train Ride

More in the category of sightseeing rather than transportation, the **Yangon Circle Line** *(contact Yangon train station: ☎ 274027)* is a three-hour trip around Yangon and the neighbouring countryside. At K15, it's a great way to get a quick overview of the sprawling capital. The train is least crowded on weekends.

Places to Stay

Since the privatisation of the hotel industry in 1993, there has been an explosion of hotel and guesthouse development in Yangon. The number of places licensed to accept foreigners leapt from eight in 1992 – when you still had to book a package deal to receive a tourist visa – to 160 by the beginning of 1999, when occupancy at many of the top-end hotels (many of them joint ventures) was running at about 20% on average. The hotel boom has slowed considerably since the time of the failed Visit Myanmar Year 1996, when central planning and overbuilding reigned. Yangon's budget and mid-range hotels and guesthouses, however, have continued to enjoy considerable success.

Places to Stay – Budget

When Yangon's smaller hotels and guesthouses began receiving licences allowing them to accept foreigners as guests in 1993, many proprietors reckoned they'd strike it rich by charging US$15 to US$20 per person per day for very basic rooms with shared bathroom. By 1996 most budget places had dropped their rates quite a bit – several to as low as US$5 to US$10 per person. There still seems to be a general surplus of rooms, and rates may continue to decline. Price quotes at the following places almost always include tax and service, as well as a rudimentary eggs-and-toast breakfast. Payment is accepted in US dollars, FECs, and sometimes kyats. Note that some categories overlap; the same guesthouse or hotel may have budget rooms for US$5 per person, but air-con doubles for US$25. Most of the budget spots are in the city centre area.

Zar Chi Win Guest House *(Map C; ☎ 275407; 59 37th St; singles/doubles with shared bathroom & toilet US$5/10, with private bathroom US$8/15)*, conveniently located on the western side of 37th St, just south of Merchant St and near the book vendors and Bagan (also called Pagan) Bookshop, comes with a funky red-and-yellow colour scheme. Rooms are the usual windowless cubicles. Rates include breakfast and a left-luggage service is available. Like many places in this price range, you may be able to bargain for a dollar's reduction, if you can do without the bleak breakfast.

Pyin Oo Lwin II Guest House *(Map C; ☎ 243284; 3rd floor 184 Mahabandoola Garden St; singles/doubles US$10/18)*, a few blocks northwest of Zar Chi Win Guest House, just south of Anawrahta Rd, is much better than it looks from the outside. Rooms are windowless but clean, and have hot water. It's in a good location and has helpful staff.

White House Hotel *(Map C; ☎ 240780, fax 240782; ⓔ whitehouse@mptmail.net.mm; 69/71 Konzaydan St; singles/doubles with air-con & shared bathroom US$8/14)*, back in the city centre, is a friendly and popular place west of Sule Paya, between Merchant St and Mahabandoola Rd. It has windowless, low-ceilinged, crazy-paved rooms, and offers a big breakfast in an open-air rooftop environment.

Daddy's Home *(Map C; ☎ 252169, fax 252061; 170 Konzaydan St; rooms per person US$3-8)*, a few doors up from the White House, has similar prices, facilities and service.

Golden Smile Inn *(Map C; ☎ 273589; 644 Merchant St; singles/doubles US$3/6)*, about four blocks from Daddy's Home and the White House, is a similar standard, well-run guesthouse with helpful staff. The rooms are tidy and simple with private bathroom – water pressure from the cold-water showers here can be very low. Rooms include breakfast.

Mayshan Guest House *(Map C; ☎ 283599, 252986; 115/117 Sule Paya Rd; ⓔ mayshan@mptmail.net.mm; low season singles/doubles US$13/18, high season singles US$15, doubles US$18-23)*, half a block north of Sule Paya, is clean and friendly, well managed and centrally located. Tiled rooms come with air-con, bathroom, TV and phone. It has a very comfortable lobby with email for guests, and breakfast is included. A handful of three-bed rooms fronting the building have spectacular views of the heart of Yangon.

Mahabandoola Guest House *(Map C; ☎ 248104; 93 32nd St; singles/doubles with shared bathroom US$3/5)*, on the southeast corner of Mahabandoola Rd, has 18 rooms – all small, mostly windowless and relatively clean. This is one of the cheapest deals in Yangon. Rates don't include breakfast, but they do include quite a climb up an antique staircase to reach the guesthouse.

Near the train station, on the corner of U Pho Kya St and Bo Min Yaung Rd, are the best of the budget places:

Sunflower Inn *(Map B; ☎ 252197, fax 254095; 59 U Pho Kya St; singles/doubles with air-con, shared bathroom & breakfast US$10/15, superior singles/doubles US$15/25, economy singles with fan US$8)* doesn't look like much from the street, but upstairs it offers clean, if small, air-con rooms with communal bathroom. There are also four superior rooms with private hot-water bathroom, fridge and TV, and two single economy rooms with fan. The Indian proprietors are friendly and helpful.

Sunflower Hotel *(Map C; ☎ 240014, fax 254095; 259/263 Anawrahta Rd; economy singles with fan US$6; singles/doubles with air-con, bathroom, TV & fridge US$15/20)*, owned by the same family that runs the Sunflower Inn, is on the corner of Shwebontha St and Anawrahta Rd in the Indian quarter. It is slightly more expensive and offers a variety of neat, if a little airless, rooms. Rooms over the street are noisy. All rates include breakfast.

YMCA *(Map B; ☎ 294128, 296435; 26 Mahabandoola Rd, entrance off Mahaba doola Rd; singles/doubles with shared ba room & fan US$7/14)* has been frequer by budget travellers for many years. spartan but reliable place, near The

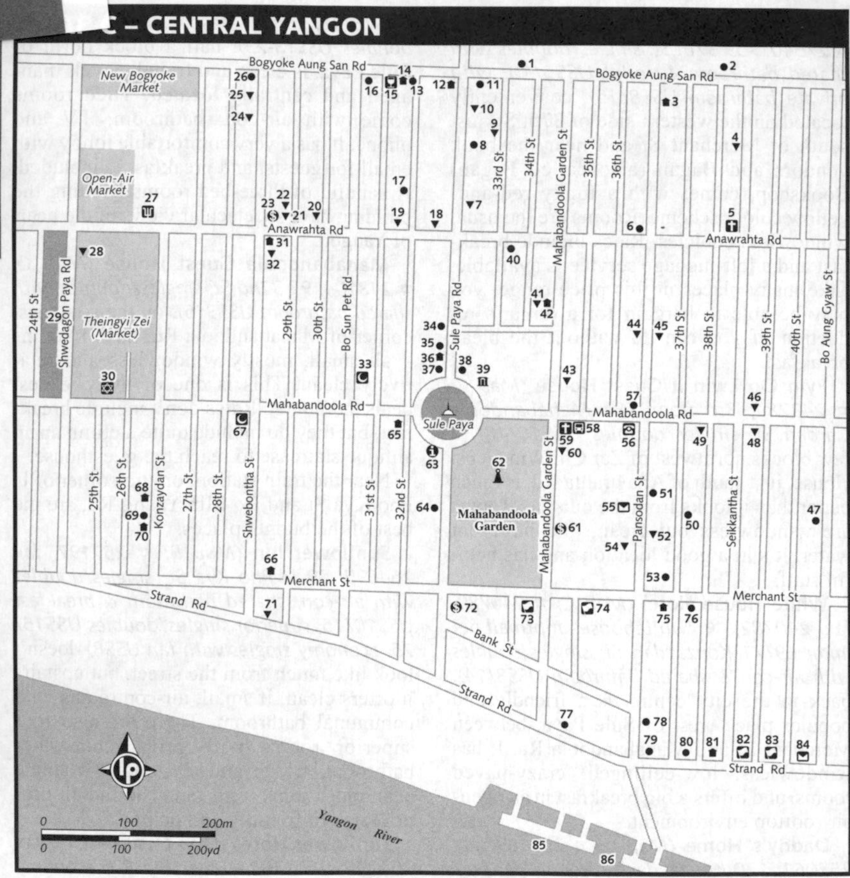

Rd, has 18 large rooms in reasonable, if somewhat tatty, condition, and all have windows – a plus in the budget category. The Y offers clean economy rooms, and there are two air-con rooms. Free transport to/from the airport is available and guests can store luggage while travelling upcoun- y. Both men and women are welcome at is Y, although double rooms are ostensi- for married couples. Room rates in- le breakfast.

ozy Guest House *(Map B;* ☎ *291623, 292239;* e *cozyhouse@mptmail.net 126 52nd St; singles/doubles US$10/ 15)*, down the street from the Three Seasons (see City Centre later in this section), is a family-run place with five small air-con rooms (three with windows), all with a shared hot-water bathroom down the hall. Rates include breakfast.

Motherland Inn 2 *(☎/fax 291343; 433 Lower Pazundaung Rd; dorm beds per person US$3, economy rooms with fan & shared bathroom US$7, standard rooms with fan & bathroom per person US$9)*, though a bit far from the central area, is popular, exceptionally clean and friendly, and good value. In addition to rooms, it also has a huge air-con

MAP C – CENTRAL YANGON

PLACES TO STAY
3 Panorama Hotel
12 Traders Hotel
14 Central Hotel
31 Sunflower Hotel
36 Mayshan Guest House
42 Pyin Oo Lwin II Guest House; City Star Hotel
65 Mahabandoola Guest House
66 Golden Smile Inn
68 Daddy's Home
70 White House Hotel
75 Zar Chi Win Guest House; Uniqcom Business Services
81 The Strand Hotel

PLACES TO EAT
4 Theingi Shwe Yee Tea House
7 Golden City Chetty Restaurant
9 Lay Tan Kon Teashop
10 Café Aroma
18 Shami Food Centre
19 Nila Biryane Shop
20 Shwe Htoo Restaurant
21 New Delhi Restaurant
22 Danubyu Daw Sawyi Restaurant
24 J'Donuts
25 Pizza Corner
28 Theingyizei Plaza Rooftop Restaurants
32 The Var Lunch Home
41 999 Shan Noodle Shop
43 Tokyo Fried Chicken
44 J'Donuts
45 MacBurger; Myanmar Oriental Bank
46 Bharat Restaurant
48 Yatha Teashop
49 Nilar Win's Cold Drink Shop
52 Donburiya Japanese Restaurant
54 Nan Yu
60 Mandarin Restaurant
71 Golden Duck Restaurant

OTHER
1 Dagon Mann Private Train Ticket Office
2 Morning Market
5 Methodist Telugu Church
6 Ava Tailoring
8 Inwa Book Store
11 Silk Air; Thai Air
13 Malaysia Air
15 Diamond White Bar
16 Globe Tailoring
17 Santa Maria Travel & Tours
23 Myanmar Oriental Bank
26 Super One Department Store
27 Sri Kali Temple
29 Theingyizi Plaza
30 Moseah Yeshua Synagogue
33 Cholia Jama Mosque
34 Yangon Duty Free Store
35 Indian Airlines
37 Global Network
38 AA Pharmacy
39 City Hall
40 Camera/Film Shops
47 Free Bird Tours
50 Bagan Books
51 Biman Bangladesh
53 Bookstalls
55 Post Office
56 Central Telephone & Telegraph Office
57 May Pharmacy
58 Buses to Thanlyin
59 Immanuel Baptist Church
61 Myanma Foreign Trade Bank (MFTB)
62 Independence Monument
63 Myanmar Travels & Tours (MTT)
64 Air France
67 Narsapuri (Moja) Mosque
69 Diamond Luck Ticketing
72 Central Bank of Myanmar
73 US Embassy
74 India Embassy
76 Sarpay Beikman Book Centre
77 Customs
78 Yangon Airways Office
79 Myanma Port Authority
80 Myanma Airways
82 Australia Embassy
83 UK Embassy
84 Main Post Office
85 Myanma Five Star Line (MFSL) Passenger Jetty
86 Pansodan St Jetty (Passenger Ferry to Dalah)

dorm. Even if you're not staying here, it's a very good place for breakfast.

Motherland Inn *(Map A; ☎ 513182; 99 Than Lwin St; rooms with air-con/fan & shared toilet US$7/5)* is further out of the city centre, in a quiet neighbourhood. There are decent standard air-con rooms and budget rooms with fan and shared toilet. All rates include breakfast.

Places to Stay – Mid-Range

Yangon's accommodation in this category has expanded rapidly. Many of the newer, mid-range places consist of large converted residences in the Bahan, Dagon and Mingala Taung Nyunt townships, just north of the city centre in the vicinity of Kandawgyi and Shwedagon Paya. Unless otherwise noted, rates do not include the 20% tax and service charges. This tax often appears only at more expensive establishments, many of them joint ventures, or government-backed. Some hotels in this price range will accept credit-card payment.

City Centre Not far from the Y, **Three Seasons Hotel** *(Map B; ☎ 293304, fax 297946; 83/85 52nd St; singles/doubles US$12/18, 4-bed rooms US$20-40)* is a two-storey hotel north of Mahabandoola Rd. It offers seven large rooms, plus two large four-bed rooms. All come with hot-water showers, fridge, air-con, high ceilings and wooden floors. This is one of the quieter central neighbourhoods; other pluses include a tastefully decorated lobby, and the very friendly and resourceful staff, led by manager Mie Mie who has plenty of good travel advice. Rates include a part-Western part-Burmese breakfast, served in an airy room overlooking the street.

Lai Lai Hotel *(Map B; ☎ 27878, fax 27342; 783 Mahabandoola Rd; singles/doubles US$15/25)*, on the edge of Chinatown, is a modern, eight-storey, thoroughly Chinese-style hotel, with good city views from the upper floors. All rooms come with hot shower, satellite TV, phone, minibar and air-con. A Chinese restaurant is downstairs.

Panorama Hotel *(Map C; ☎ 253077, fax 251986; ⓔ panorama@mptmail.net.mm; 294-300 Pansodan St; standard singles/doubles US$20/22, superior singles/doubles US$25/30)* is a popular 10-storey hotel, aptly named with most of its rooms offering good views of downtown Yangon. All rooms are large, tidy and well-appointed, with air-con and satellite TVs. Throw in email facilities, buffet breakfast and the very central location, and you have one of the city's best value mid-range hotels.

Thamada Hotel *(Map B; ☎ 662866; 37 Alaung Paya St; singles US$40, doubles US$45-50, triples US$78)* is a six-storey hotel just across the railway line from the town centre, at the northern end of Sule Paya Rd. It has very helpful staff and nicely furnished rooms. The Thamada is a very popular venue for local wedding receptions. Done in the old socialist style, the hotel has 58 large rooms, all with high ceilings, air-con, TV and hot water; some have fridges. Roadside rooms offer bathtubs as well as showers but these get the most street noise. Rooms at the rear don't have tubs, but they're quieter.

Queen's Park Hotel *(Map B; ☎ 296447, fax 293596; 132 Anawrahta Rd; singles US$12, standard doubles US$18, superior singles/doubles US$15/22, suite singles/doubles US$28/32)*, on the corner of Bo Myat Tun St, is a popular city centre choice. The 11-storey hotel has helpful staff, a generator to cover frequent power outages, and the room rates are a steal. Even the standard single rooms have good views, TV, fridge, telephone, private bathroom and air-con. All rates include breakfast.

City Star Hotel *(Map C; ☎ 286377, fax 285877; ⓔ citystar@cityhotel.com.mm; 169-71 Mahabandoola Garden Street; standard singles/doubles US$20/24, superior singles/doubles US$22/26)* is a modern 10-storey hotel right in the heart of Yangon, and offers tidy, well-equipped rooms with good views of the city. All rates include breakfast.

Haven Inn *(Map B; ☎ 295500, fax 297946; 216 Bo Myat Tun St; singles/doubles US$10/15)* is a small, quiet family-run retreat close to the central area. It has only five rooms, so it's often full during the high season. All rooms have air-con, hot-water shower and telephone, and come with a good breakfast. Two of the larger rooms have a desk and fridge. Haven Inn also has a generator, so it can handle the power outages. The place has a very homey feel, even though none of the rooms have windows.

Yoma Hotel *(Map B; ☎ 297725, fax 297957; ⓔ yoma.one@mptmail.net.mm; 146 Bogyoke Aung San Rd; superior singles/doubles US$15/18, junior suite singles/doubles US$18/21)*, like its Yoma 2 counterpart (see the North & Inya Lake Area entry later in this section), is a popular mid-range place with business travellers, offering computer use, including email access. All rates include breakfast. Monthly rates are available on request.

Shwedagon & Kandawgyi Area This area of the city is generally quieter than central Yangon. It's also convenient for walking to Shwedagon Paya, the zoo and Kandawgyi.

Beauty Land Hotel *(Map A; ☎ 549772; 9 Bo Cho St; rooms US$10-50)*, a residential compound-style inn, typical of those found in Bahan Township, offers a wide variety of rooms. Rates vary, depending on whether you get hot water or cold water, shared or private bathroom, air-con or fan. All rooms come with breakfast and the proprietors offer free airport transport.

Bagan Inn *(Map A; ☎ 541539, fax 549660; 26 Natmauk St 2 – Po Sein St; standard singles US$40, doubles US$60-70, superior doubles US$70-80)* is a well-managed place sitting in its own large, landscaped compound on a quiet street, just north of Kandawgyi. Owned by Hong Kong Chinese, the inn's 25 rooms, in three separate two-storey buildings, are large and nicely decorated with Burmese *kalaga* (tapestries). All rooms feature fridge, TV, air-conditioning and phone; IDD phone and fax services are available. There are also more-expensive suites. Rates include full breakfast and laundry service.

Next door and under the same ownership, the **Silver Palace Restaurant** offers a European, Thai, Chinese and Burmese menu.

Summer Palace Hotel *(Map A; ☎ 527211, fax 525424; 437 Pyay Rd; singles/doubles US$20/25)* is a popular six-storey business-oriented hotel, set back from the road, near the Myanma TV and radio broadcast station. It has an efficient business centre and a large pool. There are 56 rooms at very reasonable rates.

Comfort Inn *(Map A; ☎ 533377, fax 524256; 4 Shwe Lin St; standard singles/doubles US$35/45, superior singles/doubles US$55/65)* sits in a large compound between Inya Rd and U Wisara Rd, and north of People's Park. Similar in standard to the Bagan Inn, the Comfort Inn offers two standard rooms with air-con and TV, and 10 superior rooms with air-con, large bathrooms, TV and fridge. There is a putting green on the grounds, and rates include breakfast and free airport transfer.

Winner Inn *(Map A; ☎ 531205, fax 524196; ⓔ winnerinn@mptmail.net.mm; 42 Thanlwin St; 1- & 2-person rooms US$25)*, in a quieter part of Yangon north of the centre between Inya Lake and Shwedagon Paya, is good value, complete with private bathroom, air-con, fridge and satellite TV; there is a dining room overlooking the garden.

Windermere Inn *(Map A; ☎ 524613, fax 533846; 15A Aung Min Khaung St; singles/doubles US$15/25)* is near Winner Inn, near Thanlwin St. Roughly located between the University of Yangon and Hledan Rd Market, this is one of the quieter small hotels off the main roads. Rooms have air-con, bathroom, TV and fridge, and breakfast is included.

Panda Hotel *(Map B; ☎ 212850, fax 229837; ⓔ pandahotel@mptmail.net.mm; 205 Wadan St; standard singles/doubles US$24/30, junior suite singles/doubles US$30/40)*, on the corner of Min Ye Kyaw Swar Rd and Wadan St, is another excellent mid-range hotel in a residential area, west of the city centre. All rooms in the 13-storey Panda are air-con, with fridge, telephone, TV and private bathroom. There are standard rooms and a larger junior suite.

Travellers keen to avoid government-owned hotels should bypass the **Yangon International Hotel** on Ahlone Rd.

North & Inya Lake Area The remainder of the hotels in this category are well north of the centre; the majority are along or just off Insein Rd or Pyay Rd, which are both long avenues running north to south.

Yoma Hotel 2 *(Map A; ☎ 531065, fax 526945; 24A Inya Rd; superior singles/doubles US$21/28, junior suite singles/doubles/triples US$25/32/40)* is a small, 17-room hotel that, like its Yoma 1 counterpart, is very service-oriented and a popular spot with business travellers in this price range (both Yoma hotels have computers with email access). There are superior rooms with either king or twin beds, or a junior suite. Lower long-term rates are available.

Aurora Inn *(Map A; ☎ 525961, fax 525400; 37A Thirimingalar St; singles US$10-16, doubles US$20-30, triples US$30-45)* is a 15-minute bus ride north of Sule Paya, hidden down a narrow street off Pyay Rd. The inn encompasses two older buildings; the one at the back is decorated with antiques and contains a snack bar. Guest rooms are spacious, and rates vary depending on whether they come with fan or air-con. All room rates include breakfast and laundry. IDD phone service is available.

Shwe Hinthar Inn *(Greater Yangon map; ☎ 533295, fax 524170; ⓔ roswin01@mptmail.net.mm; 51 Pyay Rd; singles/doubles US$30/40)* is a converted colonial building offering 18 well-appointed rooms on spacious grounds; rates include continental breakfast. All rooms have air-con, fridge and private bathroom, and there is a large garden and poolside bar on the grounds. It's near the northern end of Inya Lake, next to the Philippines embassy.

Liberty Hotel *(Map A; ☎ 530050, fax 524144; 343 Pyay Rd; standard singles/*

doubles US$20/25, family room US$45), near the Hanthawady roundabout in an elite residential neighbourhood, is a two-storey colonial mansion converted to a hotel. There are large, high-ceilinged, standard rooms, and a much larger family room. Rates include breakfast.

Places to Stay – Top End

With the exception of The Strand, hotels in this category often discount rooms depending on demand.

City Centre Each suite at **The Strand Hotel** *(Map C; ☎ 243377, fax 289880; ⓔ strand.ygn@mptmail.net.mm; 92 Strand Rd; superior suite singles & doubles US$425, deluxe suites US$450, Strand Suite US$900)* is elegantly finished in the colonial style, with plenty of brass and teak, and has air-con as well as ceiling fans, IDD phone, satellite TV and all the other amenities expected at hotels of this calibre. The renovated guest rooms are divided into eight superior suites, 23 deluxe suites and one apartment-like Strand Suite. To all rates, add the mandatory 20% tax and service. Among the public facilities are a dinner-only restaurant, an opulently finished bar decorated with local art, a café and a small business centre. All guests are met at the airport.

Traders Hotel *(Map C; ☎ 242828, fax 242800; ⓔ thyn@shangri-la.com; 223 Sule Paya Rd) Most rooms US$94-108, suites US$170-800)*, on the corner of Bogyoke Aung San Rd, is the best of the newer upmarket city-centre hotels. It's owned by the Shangri-La chain. Despite its imposing 500-room size, the hotel has a reputation for good service. It has a very decent book/gift shop, business centre, pool and fitness centre and excellent restaurant and bar facilities. As usual in Yangon, rooms generally go for less than the advertised tariff. All rates include breakfast, airport transfer, laundry and local phone calls. The Traders also has a free laundry service and a generous check-out time of 6pm.

Hotel Equatorial *(Sofitel Plaza Yangon; Map B; ☎ 250388, fax 252478; ⓔ sofitelplaza ygn@mptmail.net.mm; 33 Alan Pya Paya Rd; singles/doubles US$60/70, deluxe suite US$150)* is a swanky 350-room hotel just north of the city centre, complete with wood and rattan furnishings, Japanese and Chinese restaurants, café, disco/pub, business centre, fitness centre, tennis court and swimming pool.

Central Hotel *(Map C; ☎ 241007; 335-357 Bogyoke Aung San Rd; standard singles/doubles US$50/70, suites US$86-125)*, next to the Traders Hotel and across the road from Bogyoke Aung San Market, offers large and clean, if unremarkable, standard rooms and larger suites. All rooms have air-con with private bathroom, fridge and phone. The hotel has a good Chinese restaurant and a very popular bar/café adjacent to the large lobby.

Shwedagon & Kandawgyi Area Tucked away in the embassy quarter northwest of the central area, **Pansea Yangon** *(Map B; ☎ 229860, fax 228260; ⓔ panseaygn@mptmail.net.mm, ⓦ www.pansea.com; 35 Taw Win St; singles/doubles US$150/170)* is a very elegantly restored colonial teak mansion. The hotel is worth a visit just to see the beautiful grounds. It has 45 spacious rooms, in addition to two junior suites and one family suite. The Pansea's Mandalay Restaurant serves excellent French and Asian cuisine in a pond-side setting.

Mya Yeik Nyo Royal Hotel *(Map A; ☎ 548310, fax 548318; 20 Pa-le St; singles/doubles from US$50/60)*, off Kaba Aye Paya Rd, between Kandawgyi and Inya Lake, is a stately, two-storey edifice built by the British as an office for the legendary Irrawaddy Flotilla Company (IFC). It served later as a bank, kindergarten and state guesthouse. Large, kitsch, high-ceilinged rooms contain IDD phone, adjustable air-con, and minibar. The MYN Royal's 2.4-hectare landscaped perch affords clear views of Shwedagon Paya. A Burmese music ensemble performs nightly in the spacious lobby/dining room, which is decorated with antiques and handicrafts. On the grounds are a pool and tennis court.

Kandawgyi Palace Hotel *(Map A; ☎ 249255, fax 280412; ⓔ kphotel@mptmail.net.mm; Kan Yeik Thar St; singles/doubles*

US$80/90) is a striking 200-room teak building on the lakeside. Before its extensive renovation in the mid-1990s, it was known as the Baiyoke Kandawgyi Hotel, a state-owned enterprise. The original building once housed the British Boating Club. The hotel has several fine restaurants with Myanmar, Asian and European fare, including a nightclub and 24-hour coffee shop. There is also a business centre, gym equipment and a beautiful outdoor swimming pool. There is a 10% tax and 10% service charge.

Summit Parkview *(Map A; ☎ 211888, fax 227991; 350 Ahlone Rd; singles/doubles US$120/130, studio suites US$220/230)* is a top choice among business travellers, and stands within walking distance of Shwedagon Paya. The voluminous marble lobby is designed to impress; the US$30 million hotel is owned by a three-company consortium, which includes Singapore's Tiger Balm Corp (owned by the Ow family, originally from Myanmar). All 252 rooms come with IDD phones, satellite TV, in-house movies and 24-hour room service; suites and junior suites cost more. In addition to a useful hotel clinic and dispensary, the Summit features a swimming pool, fitness centre, newsstand, bakery/café and a restaurant.

Hotel Nikko Royal Lake Yangon *(Map A; ☎ 544500, fax 544400; e nikko@nikkoyangon.com.mm; 40 Natmauk St; superior singles/doubles US$100/120, deluxe US$120/140)*, overlooking Kandawgyi Lake, is an imposing hotel with 303 rooms and suites, a business centre with secretarial service and email access, a fitness centre and large pool (K1500 for non-guests), a grand ballroom, a very good Japanese restaurant and a brasserie serving excellent Bamar, Mediterranean and Thai cuisine.

Savoy Hotel *(Map A; ☎ 526289, fax 524891; 129 Dhammazedi Rd; singles/doubles US$120/135, suite singles/doubles US$160/180)*, close to Shwedagon Paya, seems to be a cosier version of The Strand – without the history. Only open since 1996, the hotel has 30 teak- and antique-adorned rooms in addition to six suites, a small business centre, pool, a fine international restaurant, plus café and bar – all are open till late. Rooms are good value for a top-end hotel. A full breakfast is included in the tariff. This is a popular place in this price range.

North & Inya Lake Area Near Inya Lake, **Sedona Hotel** *(Map A; ☎ 666900, fax 666911; 1 Kaba Aye Paya Rd; superior singles/doubles US$120/140, deluxe singles/doubles US$140/160)* offers well-appointed rooms in this price range. Discounts are usually available for stays of three days or more. The hotel boasts a popular fitness centre, sauna, large swimming pool, tennis courts, business centre and good bookshop.

Renaissance Inya Lake Hotel *(Greater Yangon map; ☎ 662857, fax 655537; 37 Kaba Aye Paya Rd; superior singles/doubles US$82/92)* is a 239-room place, about 6km north of the city centre on Inya Lake. It's one of the nicest renovations in Yangon. Originally built in 1961 with Russian aid and run by Israelis, the hotel was completely renovated in 1995 by the same company that did The Strand. The hotel offers excellent facilities, including outdoor pool, fitness centre, tennis courts, business centre and several restaurants and cafés. Room rates here are quite reasonable for a top-end Yangon hotel.

Ramada Airport Hotel *(Greater Yangon map; ☎ 666699, fax 666979; Yangon airport compound; deluxe singles or doubles US$50, superior rooms US$84)*, near the Department of Aviation, is adjacent to the international airport and is frequented largely by business travellers. The hotel has a swimming pool, fitness centre and business centre.

Places to Eat

Yangon has some interesting culinary possibilities for those willing to do some exploring. At the mid-range and top end of the scale are the ubiquitous Chinese restaurants, while the many Indian and Bamar places are cheap and basic. Eat early in the evening – by 9pm all but a couple of 24-hour places, a few large hotel cafés and The Strand will be ready to close. There are also a few music clubs/cafés that serve food until 11pm.

Bamar Two humble-looking restaurants in the Shwedagon Paya area enjoy reputations for serving the best traditional Bamar cuisine in the capital; figure on spending no more than K600 per person for a full spread, not including beverages:

Aung Thuka *(Map A; 17A 1st St; open 10am-7pm)*, between Shwegondaing and Dhammazedi Rds near Shwedagon Paya, People's Park and the Royal Hotel, features a clean, simple dining room decorated with Burmese calendars and movie posters, and furnished with linoleum-top tables and wooden chairs. A long table along one side of the room displays dozens of pots containing the day's curries and special dishes, so all you need to do is point to what appeals to you. Curries made with prawn or venison are particularly good here, as are such side dishes as *kazun ywet* (stir-fried watercress and mushrooms) and *shauk thouq-thi* (citron salad). If you order one or more curries, you'll automatically receive soup, dhal, rice and side dishes. Prices are very reasonable.

Hla Myanma Htamin Zain *(Beautiful Myanmar Rice Shop; Map A; 27 5th St; open 10am-7pm)*, near the Aung Thuka restaurant, is sometimes called Shwe Ba because a famous Burmese actor of that name once had his house nearby. Like Aung Thuka it's a very simple, plain restaurant, where the food is served from rows of curry pots. There are also some Chinese and Indian dishes. It's a difficult place to find; it's best to go by taxi with a driver who knows the place.

Green Elephant Restaurant *(Map A; ☎ 531231; ⓔ smeh@mptmail.net.mm; 519A Thirimingalar St)*, off Pyay Rd, offers upmarket and slightly Westernised Bamar curries, salads, meat and seafood dishes (around K1500 per dish) in an attractive, tranquil covered garden setting. The food and service are very good. It's tucked down the narrow side street known as Thirimingalar St, near the large intersection of Pyay Rd and University Ave Rd. The restaurant includes an upmarket craft shop.

Foodstalls serving curries and rice – for experienced stomachs only – can be found along the eastern side of Bo Galay Zay St. The **noodle stalls** on 32nd St, near Sule Paya, are very cheap and very good.

Shan Behind City Hall, a short walk from Sule Paya, is **999 Shan Noodle Shop** *(Map C; 130B 34th St; most noodle dishes K100; open 6.30am-around 7pm)*, a small shop serving some of the best Shan-style noodles in Yangon. The menu, printed in English and Burmese, includes delicious and filling *Shan hkauq sweh* (thin rice noodles in a slightly spicy chicken broth), *gyon hkauq sweh* (same with wheat noodles), *Shan htamin chin* ('sour' rice salad), *myi shay* (Mandalay-style noodle soup) and other delights. Noodle dishes are served with fried tofu triangles and jars of pickled cabbage. We'd recommend eating no later than 6pm, since the kitchen may sell out of some items. Also, this can be a particularly noisy street when all its generators are chugging away.

Maw Shwe Li Restaurant *(Map B; ☎ 221103; 316 Anawrahta Rd, Lanmadaw Township)* is another good Shan eatery west of the city centre. The small, friendly, out-of-the-way place is usually crowded with Burmese people, and the curries are excellent and cheap; Shan specialities include *pei pot kyaw* (sour bean condiment) and *hmo chawk kyaw* (fried mushrooms).

Lashio Lay Shan Restaurant *(Map B; ☎ 259015; 71 51st St; mains under K1000)* is a popular, simple little place near the Three Seasons Hotel that dishes up excellent Shan mains. It's near the corner of Mahabandoola and 51st Sts.

Other Southeast Asian Just across from the Savoy Hotel, **Sabai Sabai Thai Restaurant** *(Map A; ☎ 525526; 126 Dhammazedi Rd; dishes K600-800)* serves excellent and authentic Thai food in a cosy Thai-style wooden building. Prices are in US dollars and kyat.

Malai Thai Restaurant *(Map A; ☎ 533147; 116B Inya Rd)*, near the Yangon Yacht Club, is popular with visiting Thais, and the prices are moderate.

Silom Village Restaurant *(Greater Yangon map; ☎ 527448; 647A Pyay Rd)* is just north of Inya Rd, near the International Business Centre. The Thai food is quite good, and the bustling outdoor atmosphere is fun – although the service can be spotty when they're busy.

Vietnam House Restaurant *(Map A; ☎ 550957; 287 Shwegondaing Rd; most dishes K450-700)*, between Kaba Aye Paya Rd and Chaukhtatgyi Paya, has an excellent local reputation, and the prices are moderate.

Indian Along Anawrahta Rd, west of Sule Paya Rd towards the Sri Kali temple, are a number of **shops** serving Indian biryani (*kyettha dan bauk* in Burmese), and at night the **roti and dosa makers** set up along the pavement on the side streets. Indian food is probably the cheapest way of eating in Yangon, particularly at places that serve *thali* (all-you-can-eat meals of rice and various vegetable curries piled on a fresh banana leaf or stainless-steel thali plate), which often cost only K200. Biryani costs a bit more, around K300.

Nila Biryane Shop *(Map C; Anawrahta Rd)*, between 31st and 32nd Sts, is the most popular biryani place in the city centre. It's always crowded but the service is snappy.

Shami Food Centre *(Map C; Anawrahta Rd)*, a block east on the same side of Anawrahta Rd, serves equally tasty fare to the Nila Biryane and is owned by the same family. Both offer vegetarian biryani, as well as the usual chicken. If one place is out of your favourite biryani, it may send an order to the other shop.

New Delhi Restaurant *(Map C; Anawrahta Rd)*, between 29th and Shwebontha Sts, has more variety. This reasonably clean place serves a wide selection of North and South Indian dishes for as little as K100, including *puris* (puffy breads), *idli* (rice ball in broth) and *dosa* (thin crepe filled with potato; spelt *toeshay* on the menu) with curry and coconut chutney in the morning, banana-leaf thalis and a variety of curries for lunch and dinner. Most Indian places serve tea; the New Delhi serves only coffee, South-Indian style.

Shwe Htoo Restaurant *(Map C; cnr Anawrahta Rd & 30th St)* is open later than most and is good for a quick *palata* (fried flatbread) or biryani plate; it's between the New Delhi and Nila Biryane.

Bharat Restaurant *(Map C; ☎ 281519; 356 Mahabandoola Rd; mains from K600)*, on the corner of Seikkantha St, is dependable and cheap; it's similar to the New Delhi with more of a focus on South-Indian flavours. Bharat's a bit smaller than the New Delhi – it's generally easier to get served – and the marble-topped tables make a nice change from the long cafeteria-style tables at the Indian places on Anawrahta Rd.

Golden City Chetty Restaurant *(Map C; 170 Sule Paya Rd)*, just north of Sule Paya, on the eastern side of the street, follows the usual pattern for Yangon's Indian restaurants – white-tiled walls and bright fluorescent lights. The dosas, thalis etc are nothing special, but it's one of the few city-centre Indian places open after 7pm.

The Var Lunch Home *(Map C; Shwebontha St)*, two doors south of Anawrahta Rd and the **Sunflower Hotel**, serves tasty dhal as well as chicken, mutton and vegie curries – all on banana leaves, South Indian style. You're supposed to use your fingers (after washing up), but if you insist on a fork and spoon, be careful not to tear a hole in your banana leaf. Good, cheap and authentic – it's about K800 for two people.

Two more upmarket Indian restaurants away from the central area are worth a try:

Ashoka Indian Restaurant *(Map A; ☎ 514401; 1A Pyay Rd; entrees/mains from US$5/8)* serves excellent and mostly North Indian cuisine. It's in front of the Yangon International Hotel.

Royal Taj Restaurant *(Map A; ☎ 542899; 138C University Ave Rd)* is another very good North Indian eatery just east of Kaba Aye Paya Rd and Inya Lake with excellent tandoori dishes and vegie curries. Prices are moderate.

Chinese You can sample the whole range of Chinese cuisine in Yangon – from the familiar Cantonese through to the less well known Shanghai, Sichuan, Beijing or Hokkien dishes.

Palei Kywe Restaurant *(Map B; ☎ 296094; 44 Bo Aung Gyaw St; open 10am-9pm daily)* is in the city centre near the main post office, between Strand Rd and Merchant St. It serves excellent northern Chinese fare at reasonable prices. Roasted duck is a speciality, and the menu has several vegetarian dishes.

Mandarin Restaurant *(Map C; ☎ 272960; 126 Mahabandoola Garden St; dishes around K800)*, near the corner of Mahabandoola Rd and Sule Paya, just across from the park and next door to the Methodist Church, is owned by the same family that runs the Mayshan Guest House. The Mandarin offers the usual wide assortment of northern Chinese dishes, vegetarian fare and fresh fish in a clean and friendly setting.

Singapore's Kitchen *(Map B; ☎ 226297; 524 Strand Rd; open daily 10am-1am)* is one of the best Chinese restaurants in town. It's between 12th and Phoone Gyee Sts, and offers excellent food and good service with a choice of upstairs or down, fresh fish on display, an open kitchen and tables that spill onto the footpath during fair weather. At night it's a bright and busy place, and even better is the late closing time. Besides seafood, it does a good job of crispy-fried duck, as well as lots of vegie and noodle dishes. For a variety of dishes and a couple of bottles of beer expect to pay about K3000 for two.

Golden Duck Restaurant *(Map C; ☎ 241234; 222-224 Strand Rd; open daily 10am-10pm)* is a busy, popular little place offering seafood and, of course, duck, for around K1800 per dish. It doesn't have the ambience of nearby Singapore's Kitchen, but it serves excellent food and is good value.

Nan Yu *(Map C; ☎ 252702; 81 Pansodan St; open 10am-8.30pm daily)* has been in business since 1968 and has all the usual Cantonese specialities (including crabs' thumbs) – soups are particularly good here and it's air-con.

Lakeview Restaurant *(Map A; ☎ 249255; Kan Yeik Thar St; most dishes US$5-7; open 10.30am daily)* is a covered outdoor restaurant overlooking the lake at the Kandawgyi Palace Hotel with a quiet, serene atmosphere, and decent and plentiful Bamar food. Prices are reasonable, given the lakeside perch. The restaurant is part of the Seafood Market building, next door to the Kandawgyi Palace Hotel.

Yadana Garden Restaurant *(Map A; ☎ 543561; cnr Palae St & Kaba Aye Paya Rd)* has an extensive offering of Chinese, Bamar and international entrees. The food is good, and prices are moderate to expensive.

Royal Garden Restaurant *(Map A; ☎ 297716; off Kan Yeik Thar St)*, overlooking Kandawgyi, serves excellent Singapore-Chinese cuisine. Prices are moderate to expensive.

For noodles, fried rice and other quick Chinese meals, try the **night market** on Madaw Rd in Chinatown, around the corner from the Cantonese temple.

The **Chinese street stalls** *(Map B; 19th St)*, at Mahabandoola Rd, are particularly tasty and clean; try the **Tin Ohn** stall for good pork and squid satay. Another good **Indian stall** (selling good barbecued fish) is nearby on Latha St, just south of Mahabandoola Rd, next to Vilas Beauty Salon.

Good Chinese food is also available at the larger, banquet-style places described as dinner show restaurants in the Entertainment section of this chapter.

Japanese It's not cheap by Yangon standards, but the serves are very generous at **Danburiya Japanese Style Restaurant** *(Map C; ☎ 280528; 112 Pansodan St; mains around K2000; open lunch-1am daily)*, an unpretentious place offering plenty of good Japanese favourites.

French At the ritzy Pansea Yangon, **Mandalay Restaurant** *(Map B; ☎ 221462; 35 Taw Win St; prices from US$10)* is a serene restaurant serving outstanding French- and Burmese-style cuisine; it's a perfect place to splurge. It also has a good assortment of imported wines.

Le Planteur Restaurant & Bar *(Map A; ☎ 549389; ⓔ leplanteur@mptmail.net.mm; 16 Sawmaha St; mains US$15-25)*, near Hotel Nikko Royal Lake, serves fine French-Swiss food in an outdoor setting. It has a smokehouse and produces its own smoked hams and salamis. The bar offers the speciality of the house, 'Les Planteurs' (planters' punch), plus a variety of delicious fruit punches at US$5 per jug. To find it, follow the signboard on Natmauk St, next to Kandawgyi Lake.

Italian East of Inya Lake and just south of Kanbe St, **L'Opera Restaurant** *(Greater Yangon map; ☎ 566662; e lopera@myanmars .net; 20 Thu Ka Waddy St; dinner with wine around US$25 per person)* is worth a try for excellent, though pricey, Italian cuisine.

Western Near the corner of Merchant St, **50th Street Bar & Grill** *(Map B; ☎ 298096; fax 298287 9-13 50th St; dishes around US$7.50)* is well worth a look for the swank colonial-era interior. It's a hangout popular with expats and Burmese. A pool table, plenty of newspapers and magazines and a bulletin board give the place a homely touch that goes with the excellent brick-oven pizzas, sandwiches, pastas and meat and seafood dishes. Like most upmarket eateries in Yangon, prices are in US dollars, though you may pay in kyat as well. The prices are cheekily high (US$2 for a Coke?!), but the happy hours are generous – there are half-price drinks weekdays 5pm-8pm, Friday 4pm-9pm, and all day Sunday. Lunches are also half-price Monday to Friday.

Fast Food Modest Western-style restaurants serving 'short eats', and catering to well-heeled Burmese clientele by offering sandwiches, burgers, pizza, spaghetti, donuts and the like, are multiplying quickly in the city.

Home Sweet Home *(Map B; ☎ 293001; cnr Mahabandoola Rd & 52nd St; set menus around K850; open 9am-10pm daily)* is typical of the Western-style genre. When the voltage is running, the place is air-conditioned. White-shirted waiters serve sandwiches and a variety of burgers made with a choice of chicken, beef, fish or pork, for around K400 each. Other menu items include grilled lobster, pizza, omelettes, spaghetti, macaroni and cheese, ice cream, fried cashews, milk shakes and imported beers.

Tokyo Fried Chicken *(Map C; 156 Mahabandoola Garden St; open 8am-9pm daily)*, just north of Mahabandoola Rd, is another popular spot; there are tables, but you order and pick up your meal at the counter.

In the central area, try **Pizza Corner** *(Map C)* and **J' Donuts** *(Map C)*, both on Shwebontha St, just south of Bogyoke Aung San Rd; **MacBurger** *(Map C)* and another **J' Donuts** *(Map C)* are on Pansodan St, between Mahabandoola and Anawrahta Rds. All are open 8am to 9pm daily.

Nilar Win's Cold Drink Shop *(Map C; ☎ 278364; 377 Mahabandoola Rd; open 8am-11pm daily)*, four blocks east of Sule Paya (between 37th and 38th Sts), is a long-running place founded by a famous Burmese boxer who now lives in Paris. It's a clean little café where you can get yogurt, lassi (a delicious Indian yogurt drink, plain or blended with fruit) as well as fruit salad, avocado salad, toast and egg (just K80), French toast and other traveller delicacies.

Hotel Restaurants For years, The Strand has been among the very best hotel kitchens in town. **The Strand Grill** *(Map C; ☎ 243377; 92 Strand Rd; open 6pm-11pm)* features a changing continental menu; the Grill is also one of Yangon's most expensive restaurants, with dinners starting at about US$25. Less formal (and less expensive) is the hotel's **Strand Café** *(entrees from US$9; open 6.30am-11pm daily)*, off the southern end of the lobby facing Strand Rd. The menu offers well-prepared soups, salads and sandwiches, as well as a number of Burmese and Asian-inspired dishes. There is also a proper and filling high tea, daily from 2pm to 5pm. The cost is US$14 per person.

Traders Hotel Restaurant *(Map C; ☎ 24 2828, fax 242800; 223 Sule Paya Rd)*, in the Traders Hotel, on the corner of Bogyoke Aung San Rd, serves fine international, Cantonese, Japanese and Burmese cuisine. Buffet dinners here are extremely lavish, as they should be for US$18. There is also a good café and bakery. The small **Gallery Bar** on the 2nd floor serves drinks and snacks. For an expensive splurge on a Sunday morning, you'll get your fill at the lavish brunch, which includes well-prepared Bamar curries, Chinese steam pot, roast duck, soufflés, desserts – you name it. The tab is US$12. While you're there, check out the pianist in the lobby.

Restaurants at the **Summit Parkview** *(Map A; 350 Ahlone Rd)* and **Nawarat** *(Greater Yangon map; 257 Insein St)* Hotels offer somewhat predictable, but reliable, menus featuring Chinese, European and pseudo-Bamar dishes. Both places are open daily for breakfast, lunch and dinner. Food at the **Renaissance Inya Lake** *(Greater Yangon map)* and **Kandawgyi Palace** *(Map A)* **Hotels** is excellent, and includes both Bamar and international cuisines. The **Thamada Hotel Restaurant** *(Map B)* also gets good reviews for Chinese cuisine, and prices are moderate.

Sakhantha Hotel Restaurant *(Map B; ☎ 249518; Kun Chan St)*, in front of Yangon railway station, has Chinese, Bamar and Western dishes. The food is nothing special, but it's part of the train station and it's definitely got atmosphere. There are two dining rooms, one for hotel guests and one for nonresident diners and drinkers (usually people waiting for a train). They're both throwbacks to colonial days, with high ceiling fans and people waiting to go somewhere.

Bakeries In Myanmar, bakeries where cakes and sweet pastries are produced are usually called confectioneries. Yangon's teashops are where you'll find the Bamar-style pastries and sweet snacks.

A & T Bakery *(Map A; ☎ 526763; 150 Dhammazedi Rd)*, near the Air Mandalay office, has Western-style breads and cakes.

The restaurant in the **Summit Parkview Hotel** *(Map A)* stocks a small selection of European-style pastries in a bakery cabinet at the front for ordering in the dining room or for takeaway. Both the **Traders Hotel** *(Map C)* and the **Sedona Hotel** *(Map A)* have good bakeries. The Sedona has fresh bread every morning, although if you happen to drop by later in the day, you'll find that whatever's left has been discounted.

Teashops & Cafés Yangon abounds in teashops, where cups of milk tea or coffee, followed by endless tiny pots of Chinese tea and cheap Burmese, Chinese and Indian snacks, are available. For breakfast, in fact, you're often better off spending a few kyat in a teashop, rather than eating the boring toast, egg and instant coffee breakfasts provided by many hotels and guesthouses.

Sei Taing Kya Teashop *(Map A; 53 Za Ga War St; open 7am-5pm)* is the most famous tea-tippling spot in Yangon, perhaps all Myanmar. It has six branches and the most happening branch is near the Israeli embassy. It serves first-quality tea, samosa, palata, *mohinga* (rice noodles, fish and eggs) and *ei-kya-kwe* (deep-fried pastries). A branch east of the city centre is at 103 Anawrahta Rd, on the corner of 51st St, near the taxi stand. There's another just south of the Theinbyu Playground and Kandawgyi, on Theinbyu Rd.

Theingi Shwe Yee Tea House *(Map C; ☎ 289542; 265 Seikkantha St; open 7am-8pm daily)* is another famous teashop, although smaller and more intimate than Sei Taing. It is conveniently located if you're staying in the city centre. Quality tea is served here, along with sliced *bei moq* (poppy-seed cake), a moist, delicious brown cake made with poppy seeds and topped with slivered coconut. Other house specialities include seasoned sticky rice with pigeon peas, flaky coconut puffs, curry puffs and *sanwin makin* (literally, turmeric unavoidable; sweetened sticky rice steamed in banana leaves). The teashop also makes hamburgers, which are popular throughout the day.

Mahabandoola Rd has a couple of more-modest establishments that typify the general division between Chinese-influenced and Indian-influenced teashops.

Yatha Teashop *(Map C; ☎ 349341; 353 Mahabandoola Rd)*, between Seikkantha and 39th Sts, represents the latter, providing fresh samosas and palata.

The train station platform teashop attached to the **Sakhantha Hotel** *(Map B)* features worn wooden booths under a corrugated metal shelter cooled by huge ceiling fans. Since it's rarely crowded, it's a relaxed spot

Burmese Teashops

At all times of day you'll see Burmese sitting in teashops, where the tea flows freely and the assorted pastries are very inexpensive. Teashops are an important social institution in Myanmar, serving as meeting places for friends, family and business associates, as well as a source of inexpensive nutrition and caffeine.

The shops come in all shapes and sizes, indoor and outdoor, morning-oriented and evening-oriented. The morning teashops are typically open from 5am to 5pm, and generally serve the best-quality tea; many will also serve Burmese-style coffee. Evening teashops open from 4pm or 5pm and stay open till 11pm or later – even all night in some places.

The tea quality can vary dramatically from one teashop to the next. The best shops use only fresh, first-quality Indian-style tea for every brewing cycle, while the worst recycle tea leaves until the flavour and colour are gone – to be replaced by ground tamarind and other natural flavour enhancers. The price differences between the good and the bad differ by only K1 or K2 per cup, so it's usually worth seeking out the top-quality places – ask around, everyone knows the superior ones. For example, in a city of 12 teashops, two will stand out clearly as the best. If Burmese tea has received bad international press in the past, it most likely comes from the low-quality brews served in the lower-class teashops. At a good place, the tea is very drinkable.

Most teashop servers know the English word 'tea' if nothing else, but if you want to order in Burmese ask for *lahpeq ye* (tea water). Burmese tea is always served with milk and sugar. The shops will lighten up on the sugar if you say *cho bouk* (less sweet), or add more if you say *kyauk padaung* (the name of a famous sugar palm-growing region near Bagan).

Many tea drinkers pour hot tea from the cup into the saucer and sip from the latter, as it cools faster. Some Burmese add a dash of salt to their tea, perhaps a legacy of their Tibetan origins. A thermos of *ahka ye* (Chinese tea, also known as *lahpeq ye gyan*) sits on every table and is drunk as a chaser after finishing a cup or two of the Burmese-style milk tea. Don't remove the steel wool plug stuffed into the top of the thermos – it's meant to filter the tea leaves while pouring.

Tea Snacks

A good deal more than tea is available in a Burmese teashop. Cigarettes and cigars can be purchased singly, along with an array of snacks. Teashop menus fall into two main types, depending on whether they're mostly Chinese or Indian-influenced. A Chinese-style place typically offers *paug-si* (steamed buns), *kaw pyant sein* (fried egg rolls) and *ei-kya-kwe* (long, deep-fried pastries known as *youtiao* in China).

An Indian-style teashop – slightly more common than the Chinese style – typically serves *samosa* (fried triangular-shaped pastries stuffed with vegetables) and *palata* (Indian *paratha*, or fried flatbread). The latter sounds like bladder in Burmese pronunciation; a tasty variation is palata filled with mashed banana (ask for banana bladder!). Another popular variation, *bei palata,* is stuffed with pigeon peas. Some Indian-style teashops also offer *nam-bya* (baked, unleavened bread similar to Indian *nan*, often served with a spicy split-pea dip).

Other more Burmese snacks that may be available at a teashop include *hsi htamin* (turmeric-coloured sticky rice topped with sesame seeds and shredded coconut); *kauk hnyin bauq* (sticky rice with salted and mildly spiced pigeon peas); *kua pyant leiq* (deep-fried Burmese egg rolls stuffed with potatoes and vegetables); and *sanwin makin* (literally, turmeric unavoidable, a packet of sweetened sticky rice and banana hunks steamed in banana leaves). Some urban teashops also sell hamburgers, which are gaining popularity as a breakfast food in Myanmar.

Joe Cummings

to sip a slow tea or coffee, compared to the average Yangon teashop. Snacks are limited: in addition to the very average tea and coffee there's a small selection of cakes and curry puffs, plus *dan bauk* (chicken biryani).

Lay Tan Kon Teashop *(Map C; 165 33rd St)* is where a certain crowd of Burmese writers often congregate on the upper block near Sarpe Lawka Bookshop.

Café Aroma *(Map C; Sule Paya Rd)* is a new addition to Yangon, and has several outlets around the city. The Sule Paya Rd branch, next to the cinema, is the most central, and offers fine, freshly brewed coffee and fruit smoothies (from about K500) in a swish, stylish air-con setting. Pasta and pizza dishes are also available for K800-1400. Other Café Aroma outlets are at the Yuzana Plaza, near the corner of Mill Rd and Banyardala St, just east of Kandawgyi Lake and at the New Bogyoke Market on Bogyoke Aung San Rd. All branches are open 8am-11pm daily.

Entertainment

Yangon entertainment, never the highlight of any foreigner's Myanmar visit, was dealt a near-deathblow by the 11pm curfew imposed from 1988 to late 1992. The main form of local recreation is hanging out in the teashops or 'cold drink' shops.

On festival days, local bands occasionally organise live outdoor concerts. During the water festival, sizable rock-music shows are set up along Inya Rd and University Ave and feature local underground rockers such as Iron Cross, Emperor and Aurora. Foreign observers who have seen the leather-clad performances said they are amazed the events are allowed by the State Peace & Development Council (SPDC), the gang formerly known as the State Law & Order Restoration Council (Slorc).

National Theatre The Yangon government recently revived the performance of Burmese classical dance-drama at the National Theatre *(Map B; Myoma Kyaung Rd)*, a government-sponsored facility, northwest of Bogyoke Aung San Market.

Scenes from *Ramayana* – called *Yama thagyin* in Burmese – are only occasionally held. Finding out about them is the trick; check at the theatre itself or try asking staff at the larger hotels.

Dinner Shows In the last couple of years, a number of large, semi-outdoor, banquet-style restaurants with floorshows have opened in Yangon. Heavily used by the visiting business community, these dining spots are typically Chinese-owned and feature extensive Chinese menus plus a few Burmese dishes. Entertainment is provided by Burmese bands that perform a mixture of Burmese, Western, Chinese and Japanese pop songs – usually sung by a changing roster of female vocalists. Some places also feature Burmese classical dance and/or marionette theatre. There is no charge for entertainment, and no set charges for dinner – you simply order from a menu. Tax and service charges amounting to 20% of the bill are usually added.

Lone Ma Lay Restaurant *(Map A; ☎ 550357; Natmauk St, Kandawgyi Lake; dishes from around K700; breakfast 6am-10am, lunch & dinner 10am-11pm)* is among the best of the bunch of restaurants at Kandawgyi Lake, which seems almost ringed by banquet-style restaurants, as a lake view is considered a prime asset for an evening out on the expense account. Entertainment focuses on Burmese classical and folk dance early in the evening, and pop later on. The Chinese food here is quite respectable, with huge portions and fresh ingredients at lunch and dinner. The Burmese dishes aren't too shabby, even if they show a little extra Chinese influence. The restaurant is also open in the morning for Burmese teashop snacks and noodles.

Dolphin Seafood Restaurant *(Map A; ☎ 250240; Kan Yeik Thar St)* is also on the lake, near the aquarium. It's a little less formal and is known for employing the best Burmese pop singers in town. A recent addition to the restaurant is karaoke in English, Burmese and Chinese. If it's peace and quiet you're after, drop in for lunch when you tend to get the restaurant and lake views all to yourself.

[Continued on page 186]

The Shwedagon Paya

The Shwedagon Paya

BERNARD NAPTHINE

JULIET COOMBE

BERNARD NAPTHINE

RICHARD I'ANSON

RICHARD I'ANSON

Title Page: The gleaming Shwedagon illuminates the night sky. (Photograph by Corey Wise)

Images on this page: The Shwedagon isn't just one stupa, but a maze of shrines and images creating a vibrant hub of spiritual intensity.

THE SHWEDAGON PAYA

Kipling called it 'a golden mystery ... a beautiful winking wonder'. As the setting sun casts its last rays on the soft orange dome of the great Shwedagon Paya, you can feel the magic in the air. In the heat of the day, the stupa glitters bright gold. It can be quiet and contemplative, or colourful and raucous. The Golden Dagon is the essence of Myanmar, and a place that never fails to enchant.

For Burmese Buddhists, Shwedagon is the most sacred of all Buddhist sites in the country, one which all Burmese hope to visit at least once in their lifetime.

The great golden dome rises 98m above its base. According to legends, this stupa – of the solid *zedi* (bell-shaped monument) type – is 2500 years old, but archaeologists suggest the original stupa was built by the Mon, sometime between the 6th and 10th centuries. In common with many other ancient zedi in earthquake-prone Myanmar, it has been rebuilt many times and its current form dates back only to 1769.

History

The legend of Shwedagon Paya tells of two merchant brothers meeting the Buddha, who gave them eight of his hairs to take back to be enshrined in Myanmar. With the help of a number of *nat* (spirits), the brothers and the king of this region of Myanmar discovered the hill where relics of previous Buddhas had been enshrined. When the chamber that would house the hairs was built and the hairs were taken from their golden casket, some quite amazing events took place:

> ... there was a tumult among men and spirits ... rays emitted by the Hairs penetrated up to the heavens above and down to hell ... the blind beheld objects ... the deaf heard sounds ... the dumb spoke distinctly ... the earth quaked ... the winds of the ocean blew ... Mount Meru shook ... lightning flashed ... gems rained down until they were knee deep ... all trees of the Himalayas, though not in season, bore blossoms and fruit.

Fortunately, hairs of the Buddha are not unveiled every day.

Once the relics were safely enshrined, a golden slab was laid on their chamber and a golden stupa built on it. Over this, a silver stupa was built, then a tin stupa, a copper stupa, a lead stupa, a marble stupa and finally, an iron-brick stupa. Or so the legend goes. Later, the legend continues, the stupa at Dagon fell into disuse and it is said the great Indian Buddhist emperor Asoka came to Myanmar, finding the site only with great difficulty, and subsequently had the encroaching jungle cleared and the stupa repaired.

During the Bagan period, the story of the stupa emerges from the mists of legend and becomes hard fact. Near the top of the eastern stairway you can see an inscription recording the history of the stupa to 1485. King Anawrahta visited Dagon from his capital at Bagan (Pagan) in the 11th century, while King Binnya U, during his reign at Bago (Pegu; 1353–85), had the stupa rebuilt to a height of 18m. Succeeding kings alternately neglected, then improved, the stupa. During the 15th century, it was rebuilt several times, eventually reaching 90m, a little under its present height.

During this period, the tradition of gilding the stupa also began – Queen Shinsawbu, who was responsible for many improvements to the stupa, provided her own weight (40kg) in gold, which was beaten into gold-leaf and used to gild the structure. Her son-in-law, Dhammazedi, went several better, by offering four times his own weight and that of his wife's in gold. He also provided the 1485 historical inscription on the eastern stairway.

In 1586 the English visitor Ralph Fitch made probably the best early European description of the great stupa:

> ... it is called Dogonne, and is of a wonderful bignesse, and all gilded from the foot to the toppe ... it is the fairest place, as I suppose, that is in the world; it standeth very high, and there are foure ways to it, which all along are set with trees of fruits, such wise that a man may goe in the shade above two miles in length ...

The zedi suffered from a series of earthquakes that caused great damage during this time. In 1612 De Brito raided the stupa from his base in Thanlyin and carried away Dhammazedi's great bell, with the intention of melting it down for cannons. As the British were to do later, with another bell, he dropped it into the river. During the 17th century, the monument suffered earthquake damage on eight occasions. Worse was to follow in 1768, when a quake brought down the whole top of the zedi. King Hsinbyushin had it rebuilt to virtually its present height, and its current configuration dates from that renovation.

British troops occupied the compound for two years after the First Anglo-Burmese War in 1824. In 1852 during the Second Anglo-Burmese War, the British again took the *paya*, the soldiers pillaged it once more and it remained under military control for 77 years, until 1929. In 1871 a new *hti* (the decorative top of a paya), provided by King Mindon Min from Mandalay, caused considerable head-scratching for the British, who were not at all keen for such an association to be made with the still-independent part of Myanmar.

During the 20th century, Shwedagon Paya was the scene for much political activity during the Burmese independence movement and also suffered from a serious fire in 1931. It started at the bottom of the western stairway, which had been reopened to the public for less than two years, after the British military occupation had closed that entrance. The fire rushed up the stairway and right around the northern side of the paya, before being halted halfway down the eastern stairway. The huge earthquake of 1930, which totally destroyed the Shwemawdaw in Bago, only caused minor damage to Shwedagon. After another minor earthquake in 1970, the zedi was clad in bamboo scaffolding beyond King Mindon's 100-year-old hti, and was refurbished.

Design

There are four covered walkways up Singuttara Hill to the platform on which Shwedagon stands. The southern entrance, from Shwedagon Paya Rd, is the one which can most properly be called the main entrance. Here, and at the northern entrance, there are lifts available, should you not feel fit enough for the stroll up the stairs. The western entrance features a series of escalators in place of stairs, and is the only entrance without vendors. The eastern stairway has the most traditional ambience, passing adjacent *kyaung* (monasteries) and vendors selling monastic requisites.

Two 9m-high *chinthe* (the legendary half-lion, half-dragon figures) guard the southern entrance. You must remove your shoes and socks as soon as you mount the first step. Like the other entrances, the southern steps are lined with a whole series of shops, where devotees buy flowers – both real and beautifully made paper ones – for offerings. Ceremonial paper umbrellas, Buddha images, golden thrones, ivory combs, books, antiques and incense sticks are also on sale. However hot it may be outside, you'll find the walkway cool, shady and calm. It's this quiet, subdued atmosphere on the entrance steps that makes the impact so great as you arrive at the platform.

You emerge from semigloom into a visual cacophony of technicoloured glitter – for Shwedagon is not just one huge, glowing zedi. Around the mighty stupa cluster an incredible assortment of smaller zedi, statues, temples, shrines, images and *tazaung* (small pavilions). Somehow, the bright gold of the main stupa makes everything else seem brighter and larger than life.

Stupas, indeed all Buddhist structures, should be walked around clockwise, so turn left at the top of the steps and, like the crowds of Burmese, start strolling. During the heat of the day, you'll probably have to confine yourself to the mat pathway laid around the platform – unless your bare feet can take the heat of the uncovered marble paving.

The hill on which the stupa stands is 58m above sea level and the platform covers over 5 hectares. Prior to the British takeover of southern Myanmar, there had been Burmese defensive earthworks around the paya, but these were considerably extended by the British, and the emplacements for their cannons can still be seen outside the outer wall.

The main stupa, which is completely solid, rises from its platform in a fairly standard pattern. First there is the plinth, which stands 6.4m above the clutter of the main platform and immediately sets Shwedagon above the lesser structures. Smaller stupas sit on this raised platform level – four large ones mark the four cardinal directions, four medium-sized ones mark the four corners of the basically square platform and 60 small ones run around the perimeter.

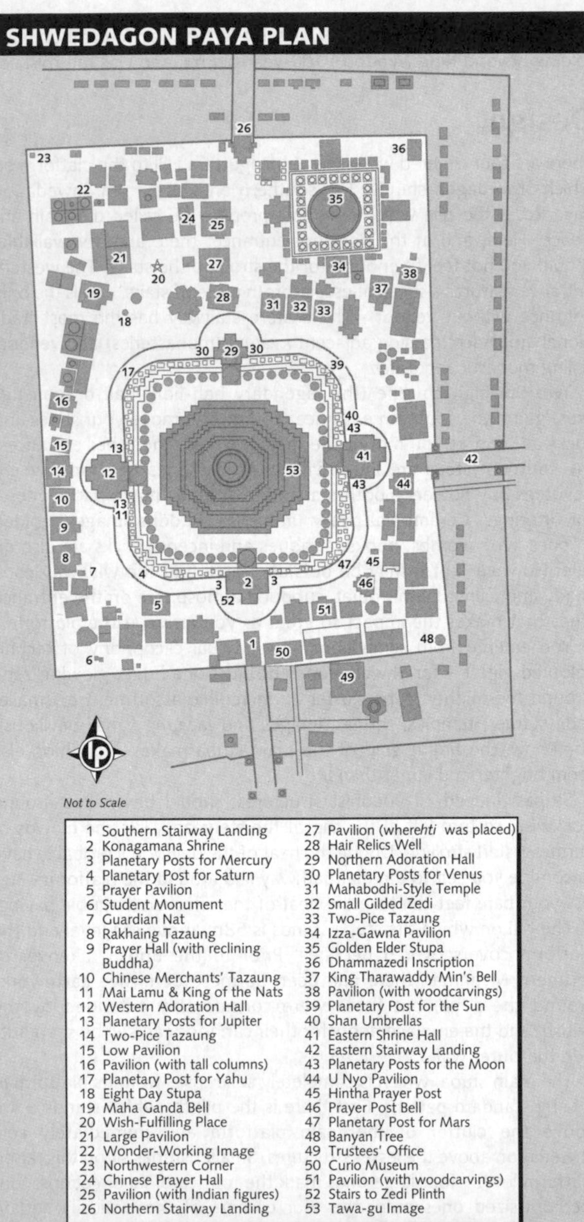
SHWEDAGON PAYA PLAN
Not to Scale
1 Southern Stairway Landing
2 Konagamana Shrine
3 Planetary Posts for Mercury
4 Planetary Post for Saturn
5 Prayer Pavilion
6 Student Monument
7 Guardian Nat
8 Rakhaing Tazaung
9 Prayer Hall (with reclining Buddha)
10 Chinese Merchants' Tazaung
11 Mai Lamu & King of the Nats
12 Western Adoration Hall
13 Planetary Posts for Jupiter
14 Two-Pice Tazaung
15 Low Pavilion
16 Pavilion (with tall columns)
17 Planetary Post for Yahu
18 Eight Day Stupa
19 Maha Ganda Bell
20 Wish-Fulfilling Place
21 Large Pavilion
22 Wonder-Working Image
23 Northwestern Corner
24 Chinese Prayer Hall
25 Pavilion (with Indian figures)
26 Northern Stairway Landing
27 Pavilion (where *hti* was placed)
28 Hair Relics Well
29 Northern Adoration Hall
30 Planetary Posts for Venus
31 Mahabodhi-Style Temple
32 Small Gilded Zedi
33 Two-Pice Tazaung
34 Izza-Gawna Pavilion
35 Golden Elder Stupa
36 Dhammazedi Inscription
37 King Tharawaddy Min's Bell
38 Pavilion (with woodcarvings)
39 Planetary Post for the Sun
40 Shan Umbrellas
41 Eastern Shrine Hall
42 Eastern Stairway Landing
43 Planetary Posts for the Moon
44 U Nyo Pavilion
45 Hintha Prayer Post
46 Prayer Post Bell
47 Planetary Post for Mars
48 Banyan Tree
49 Trustees' Office
50 Curio Museum
51 Pavilion (with woodcarvings)
52 Stairs to Zedi Plinth
53 Tawa-gu Image

From this base, the zedi rises first in three terraces, then in the 'octagonal' terraces and then in five circular bands – together these elements add another 30m to the stupa's height. This is a normal solution to a standard architectural problem associated with stupas – how to change from the square base to the circular upper elements? Here, as in many other Burmese zedi, that transition is achieved with the help of the octagonal sections, which make a transition from the horizontal design of these lower elements to the smooth vertical flow of the bell.

Earlier stupas were commonly hemispherical; a good example in Myanmar is the Kaunghmudaw at Sagaing near Mandalay. The more graceful bell design, as seen here, is a comparatively recent development. The shoulder of the bell is decorated with 16 'flowers'. The bell is topped by the 'inverted bowl', another traditional element of stupa architecture, and above this stand the mouldings and then the 'lotus petals'. These consist of a band of down-turned lotus petals, followed by a band of up-turned petals.

The banana bud is the final element of the zedi before the hti tops it. Like the lotus petals below, the banana bud is actually covered with no less than 13,153 plates of gold, measuring 30 sq cm each – unlike the lower elements, which are merely covered with gold-leaf. The seven-tiered hti is made of iron and again plated with gold. Even without the various hanging bells, it weighs well over a tonne. The hti tiers descend in size from bottom to top, and from the uppermost tier projects the shaft which is hung with gold bells, silver bells and various items of jewellery. The topmost vane, with its flag, turns with the wind. It is gold-and silver-plated and studded with 1100 diamonds totalling 278 carats – not to mention 1383 other stones. Finally, at the very top of the vane rests the diamond orb – a hollow golden sphere studded with no less than 4351 diamonds, weighing 1800 carats in total. The very top of the orb is tipped with a single 76-carat diamond.

This central zedi is regilded every year. By 1995 it had reportedly accumulated 53 metric tonnes of gold leaf.

Around the Stupa

The mighty zedi is only one of many structures on the hilltop platform. Reaching the platform from the southern stairway (1), you encounter the first shrine (2), which is to Konagamana, the second Buddha. Almost beside the shrine stand the planetary posts for Mercury (3). If you were born on a Wednesday morning (as was the Buddha), then this is your post, and the tusked elephant is your animal sign. Continuing around the plinth, you pass a double-bodied lion with a man's face, a laughing necromancer with his hands on his head, and an earth goddess. At the southwestern corner of the plinth, you reach the planetary post for Saturn (4). Come here if you were born on a Saturday; your animal sign is the *naga* (serpent being). The pavilion (5) directly opposite has 28 images to represent the 28 previous Buddhas.

Back towards the corner of the platform is a monument (6) with inscriptions in four languages, recounting a 1920 student revolt against British rule. Continuing around the platform, you come to a glass case with two figures of nat (7) – one is of the guardian nat of Shwedagon Paya. Close to these figures is a prayer hall (8), bare inside, but with fine woodcarving on the terraced roof. It is known as the Rakhaing Tazaung, since it was donated by brokers from the Rakhaing (Arakan) coast bordering Bangladesh. An 8m-long reclining Buddha can be seen in the next prayer hall (9). Next to this is the Chinese Merchants' Tazaung (10), with a variety of Buddha figures in different poses.

On the plinth opposite this prayer hall are figures of Mai Lamu and the king of the nat (11), the parents of King Ukkalapa who, according to the legend, originally enshrined the Buddha hairs here. The figures stand on top of each other. The western adoration hall (12) was built in 1841, but was destroyed in the fire that swept the zedi platform in 1931. The planetary posts for the Thursday-born (13) stand to the right and left of this pavilion: your planet is Jupiter and your animal sign is the rat. A figure of King Ukkalapa can be seen further to the left, on the zedi plinth.

Directly opposite the west adoration hall is the Two Pice Tazaung (14) at the head of the western stairway. It was built with the proceeds of a daily collection of two pice (a discontinued unit of Burmese currency) from the stalls in Yangon market. The western stairway, the steepest of the four entrances, was also built from this collection after the 1931 fire. The low pavilion (15) next to the entrance was built by manufacturers of monastery requirements – in contrast to the rather Chinese-looking roof. Next along is a pavilion (16), with tall columns and the *pyatthat* (wooden, multiroofed pavilion) rising from the upper roof. Almost opposite this tazaung, at the northwestern corner of the main zedi, is the planetary post (17) for those born on Wednesday afternoon, whose animal symbol is the tuskless elephant, and whose planet is Yahu (Rahu, a mythical planet in Hindu astrology that allegedly causes eclipses).

A small stupa with a golden spire (18) has eight niches around its base, each with a Buddha image. Between the niches are figures of animals and birds – they represent the eight directions of the compass and the associated sign, planet and day of the week. To get over the small complication of having an Eight Day Stupa and a seven day week, Wednesday is divided into Wednesday morning and Wednesday afternoon. The eight days, which can also be found with their corresponding planetary posts around the main stupa are (from the southern entrance):

direction	day	planet	sign
south	Wednesday am	Mercury	tusked elephant
southwest	Saturday	Saturn	naga

west	Thursday	Jupiter	rat
northwest	Wednesday pm	Yahu	tuskless elephant
north	Friday	Venus	guinea pig or mole
northeast	Sunday	Sun	garuda
east	Monday	Moon	tiger
southeast	Tuesday	Mars	lion

Close to this small Eight Day Stupa stands the bell pavilion (19) housing the 23-tonne Maha Ganda Bell. Cast between 1775 and 1779, it was carted off by the British after the First Anglo-Burmese War in 1825. The British dropped it into the Yangon River while trying to get it to the port for shipping to England; after repeatedly trying to raise it from the river bottom, they gave up and told the Burmese they could have the bell back if they could get it out of the river. The Burmese placed logs and bamboo beneath the bell until it eventually floated to the surface.

Venturing back into the open area of the platform, you come to the star-shaped 'wish-fulfilling place' (20), where there will often be devotees, kneeling down and looking towards the great stupa, praying that their wishes come true.

The large pavilion (21) across from the bell pavilion houses a 9m-high Buddha image and is often used for public meetings. Behind this pavilion stands a small shrine (22) with a highly revered 'wonder-working' Buddha image covered in gold leaf. From the northwestern corner of the platform (23), you can look out over some of the British fortifications and the country to the north of the hill. There are also two banyan trees growing here, one of them grown from a cutting from the actual tree at Bodhgaya in India, under which the Buddha sat and was enlightened.

Among the cluster of buildings on this side of the platform is the Chinese prayer hall (24), with good woodcarvings and Chinese dragon figures on the sides of the zedi in front of it. The adjacent pavilion (25) has life-size figures of Indians guarding the side and front entrance doors. No-one quite understands their relevance or that of the very British lions that guard the next pavilion.

In 1824 a force of Burmese 'Invulnerables' fought their way up the northern stairs to the entrance (26) of the platform before being repulsed by the better-armed British forces occupying the paya. The crocodile-like stair bannister dates from 1460. The Martyrs' Mausoleum of Bogyoke Aung San and his compatriots stands on the western side of the hill reached from this stairway.

Walking back towards the stupa, you pass the pavilion (27) built on the site where the great zedi's hti, provided by King Mindon Min, was placed before being raised to the zedi summit. The Hair Relics Well (28) was located at the position of the Sandawdwin Tazaung (28) and is said to reach right down to the level of the Ayeyarwady (Irrawaddy) River and to be fed from it; the Buddha hairs were washed in this well before being enshrined in the zedi. In the northern adoration hall (29), the main image is of Gautama, the historical Buddha. On either side of the hall stand planetary posts for Friday (30), domain of the planet Venus, and the guinea pig or mole.

Modelled after the Mahabodhi temple in Bodhgaya, India, the temple (31) a few steps away is distinctly different from the general style of buildings on the platform. A small gilded zedi (32) stands next to this temple, and next again is another 'two-pice' tazaung (33) enshrining a 200-year-old Buddha image. An opening behind this image is, according to legend, the entrance to a passage that leads to the chamber housing the Buddha hair relics. Although seen from the 'two-pice' tazaung, the image is actually in the adjacent stupa.

Izza-Gawna (the name means goat-bullock) was a legendary monk whose powers enabled him to replace his lost eyes with one from a goat and one from a bullock. In his pavilion (34), the figure off to the left of the main Buddha image has eyes of unequal size as a reminder of this unique feat. The golden Elder Stupa (35) is built on the spot where the hair relics were first placed before being enshrined in the great zedi. A straight line drawn from the centre of this stupa to the centre of Shwedagon would pass through the small stupa reputed to be the entrance to the passage that leads to the relic chamber. Women are not allowed to ascend to the platform around the Elder Stupa, which is also known as the Naungdawgyi Stupa.

Back in the corner of the platform is the Dhammazedi inscription (36), which dates from 1485 and was originally installed on the eastern stairway. It tells in three languages – Pali, Mon and Burmese – the story of Shwedagon.

Cast in 1841, King Tharawaddy Min's bell is housed in an elegant pavilion (37). The Maha Titthadaganda (three-toned bell) weighs 42 tonnes. Note the ceiling made of lacquer inlaid with glass. If you look closely, you can also discern red-billed green parrots nearly hidden in the scrolling among the *devas* (celestial beings). The adjacent small pavilion (38) has some good panels of woodcarvings. Back on the main platform the planetary post (39) for those born on Sunday (the sun) stands at the northeastern corner of the stupa platform. The bird-like creature beneath the post is the garuda of Hindu-Buddhist mythology, called *galoun* by the Burmese. Further around you will see golden Shan umbrellas (40) among the plinth shrines; there is also one over the Friday planetary post by the northern pavilion.

Facing the eastern stairway, the eastern shrine hall (41) is said to be the most beautiful on the platform. It was renovated in 1869, but destroyed by the 1931 fire and subsequently rebuilt. The main image is that of Kakusandha, the first Buddha. The eastern stairway (42) is the longest and is lined with shops selling everyday articles as well as religious goods and antiques. On either side, the people born on Monday worship at the planetary posts (43) ruled over by the moon and the tiger.

The graceful U Nyo pavilion (44), beside the eastern entrance, has a series of interesting woodcarved panels illustrating events in the life of Gautama Buddha. The prayer post (45) close to the southeastern corner of the zedi is topped by a mythological *hintha* bird. An interesting bell (46) hangs near this prayer post. Opposite these on the zedi plinth is the planetary post for Tuesday (47), presided over by the lion and the planet Mars.

In the corner of the platform stands another sacred banyan tree (48), also said to be grown from a branch of the original tree under which Gautama Buddha gained enlightenment in India. There is a good view from this corner of the platform over Yangon and across the Yangon River towards Thanlyin. On a clear day, you can see the Kyaikkhauk Paya, just beyond Thanlyin. The paya trustees have their office (49) on this side of the platform, and there's also a small curio museum (50). In front of the museum is a pavilion (51) with very fine woodcarvings. There is also a revolving hti and a telescope, possibly for looking at the real hti on top of the zedi.

Beside the southern shrine (2), the first stop on this circular tour, stairs (52) lead up onto the zedi plinth. With permission from the paya trustees, men only are allowed to climb up to the plinth terrace. Men come up here to meditate; the terrace is about 6m wide – a circular walkway between the great zedi and its 68 surrounding zedi. There's a K5 fee for entering the terrace. Behind the eastern shrine is a Buddha image (53) known as the Tawa-gu, which is reputed to work miracles.

Visiting Shwedagon is far more than just wandering around and looking at the shrines, pavilions, images, bells and stupas. It's a place you feel as much as see. There's a quite amazing atmosphere here – sometimes serene, sometimes exciting, but always enjoyable. Sunrise and sunset are the best times for a visit.

[Continued from page 176]

There are four similar **rooftop restaurants** *(Map C)* in Theingyizei Plaza, on Shwedagon Paya Rd in Chinatown. Access to all four is provided by a single lift open to the street. Directly opposite the lift exit on the roof is **Roof Top** *(☎ 244267)*, with the usual Chinese food and pop singers. Turn right to reach **Ambassador** *(☎ 578911)*, which is similar to Roof Top, followed by the popular **Smile** *(☎ 664504)*, whose dynamic pop music show packs in lots of Burmese who let their *longyi* fly on the dance floor. The food isn't bad at Smile either. Be prepared for the occasional tethered and neurotic bear, peacock or lemur in some of these restaurants; it's apparently part of the show.

Airport Oasis Garden Restaurant *(Greater Yangon map; ☎ 665865; airport compound)* is a good place to repair to if you're waiting for a plane and haven't had enough fun yet. It's a karaoke-style restaurant near the airport, with good Chinese and European food.

Travellers keen to avoid government-owned restaurants should bypass the **Karaweik Palace Restaurant**.

Cinemas A half-dozen or so cinemas along Bogyoke Aung San Rd, east of Sule Paya, show films for K50 or less per seat. The normal fare is pretty awful; a succession of syrupy Burmese dramas, kung-fu smash-ups and 'made for Third-World consumption' European or American action thrillers. On the other hand, it's quite a scene.

Thamada Cinema *(Map B; ☎ 246962; 5 Alaung Paya St; tickets K350)* is easily the best cinema for foreigners. The theatre is newly renovated, quite popular and bookings can be made in advance for the fairly recent American and international films. There are usually five screenings per day, the first at 10am, the last at 9.30pm.

The American Center *(Map B; 14 Taw Win St)*, behind the Ministry of Foreign Affairs, shows free American movies every Monday at noon. Older music programmes such as *Austin City Limits* are also sometimes shown.

Bars & Cafés Inside the swish Strand Hotel, **The Strand Bar** *(Map C; ☎ 243377; open 11am-11pm)* has any foreign liquors you may be craving behind its polished wooden bar. Modern watercolours of Burmese scenes decorate the walls and occasionally there's someone around to play the baby grand. Friday afternoon is a two-for-one happy hour (there's a standard happy hour all other days from 5pm to 7pm), usually graced by a couple of fine musicians playing near the end of the bar.

Two other popular bars with local Burmese and expats are the **50th Street Bar & Grill** *(Map B; ☎ 298069)*, at 9-13 50th St, which has a pool table and brick-oven pizza, and all-day happy hour on Sunday; and **The Bar** *(Map A; ☎ 526289; 129 Dhammazedi Rd; open until midnight)* at the Savoy Hotel.

Diamond White Bar *(Map C; Bogyoke Aung San Rd)* is a popular drinking hole and café on the ground floor of the Central Hotel, just west of Traders Hotel. It's a bit seedy, but there's a steady stream of satellite TV sport, and prices are good and low.

Mr Guitar Café *(Map A; ☎ 550105; 22 Sayasan St; open 6pm-midnight)*, founded by famous Burmese vocalist Nay Myo Say, is a small café/bar decorated with old guitars. Live folk music is featured from about 7pm to midnight nightly. Well-known Burmese musicians drop by frequently, especially on weekends, to sit in with the regular house group (during music breaks Mr Bean videos are shown). The clientele is a mix of Burmese and local expats. Along with music, the café offers espresso and coffee drinks, plus Asian and European food.

A word of warning: prostitutes are a regular feature at many of Yangon's hot night spots. Though the government keeps them on the move, there is little concern for their health or safety, or that of their clients.

Shopping

Markets Shopping at the various *zei* (markets, often spelt *zay*) in central Yangon can be fun and very educational.

Bogyoke Aung San Market *(Map B; Bogyoke Aung San Rd; open until around*

5pm Tues-Sun)* is a sprawling, 70-year-old market (sometimes called by its British name, Scott Market). It has the largest selection of Burmese handicrafts you'll find under one roof (actually several roofs). Along the maze-like aisles you'll find a whole variety of interesting Burmese souvenirs, from lacquerware and Shan shoulder bags to T-shirts and cheroots. Gems and jewellery are also on hand, but be sure to read the Precious Stones & Jewellery entry in the shopping section of the Facts for the Visitor chapter before buying any.

Some of the more interesting shops in Bogyoke Aung San Market include: **Depi Store** *(39 West Block)*, for cheroots and cigars; **Myanmar Lacquerware** *(1/2 East Wing)*, for lacquerware; **Eastern Queen** *(1st floor, 18 Face Wing)*, for rattan furniture; **Maung Maw & Brothers** *(115 Inner West Wing)*, for both modern and traditional musical instruments; **Myat Sanda** *(138 West Wing)* and **Sein Pan** *(69 West C)*, for *lapheq* (pickle tea); and **Mya Malar Longyi** *(Myanmar Traditional Nether Garments; West Wing)*. At least 20 other places in the market also specialise in longyi.

The long southern stairway at Shwedagon Paya is lined with small shops catering to pilgrims and tourists alike. Popular items include sandalwood bracelets, small drums, papier maché animals etc. Bargaining is expected here.

The biggest market in Yangon, **Theingyi Zei** *(Map B)*, is especially good for locals who find Bogyoke Aung San Market a little too pricey. It extends four blocks east to west from Konzaydan St to 24th St, and north to south from Anawrahta Rd to Mahabandoola Rd. Most of the merchandise for sale represents ordinary housewares and textiles, but the market is renowned for its large selection of traditional Burmese herbs and medicines. A snake section features the fresh blood and organs of various snakes – including the deadly banded krait – disembowelled on-the-spot for medicinal consumption. Of more general interest is traditional Burmese herbal shampoo, made by boiling the bark of the *tayaw* shrub with big black *kin pun* (acacia pods) and sold in small plastic bags; this is

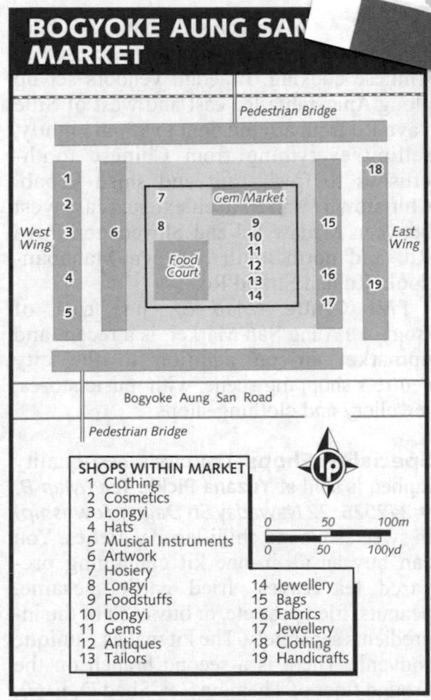

the secret of Burmese women's smooth, glossy hair. A new mall-like section on Shwedagon Paya Rd, Theingyizei Plaza, contains less-interesting modern shops.

Thirimingala Zei *(Map A; Yangon River bank, Ahlone Township)*, off the northern end of Strand Rd (straight west about 1km from People's Park), is a labyrinth of vendors selling fresh foodstuffs, vegetables, fruits and meat – it's worth a stroll for the amazing sights and smells, not all of them especially pleasant. Catch even more of an aroma further north along the riverfront, at the **San Pya Fish Market** *(Map A)*.

Mingala Zei *(Map A)*, a little southeast of Kandawgyi, proffers textiles, clothes, electrical appliances, plastic ware, preserved and tinned foodstuffs, modern medicines, and cosmetics from Thailand, China and Singapore. This is the place to come if you're setting up house in Yangon on the cheap.

There are other markets around, such as the **iron bazaar** *(cnr Mahabandoola Rd &*

Madaw Rd) in Yangon's Chinatown – here you can find all the items that are used in Chinese cooking. Itinerant vendors set up along Anawrahta Rd east and west of Sule Paya Rd from around 6pm to 10pm nightly, selling everything from Chinese toothbrushes to fresh fruit and shish kebab. **Chinatown** *(Map B)* itself extends east-west between Madaw Rd and Shwedagon Paya Rd, and north-south between Mahabandoola Rd and Strand Rd.

FMI Centre *(Map B)*, just east of Bogyoke Aung San Market, is a recent and upmarket air-con addition to the city centre's shopping scene, with music stores, jewellery and clothing shops.

Speciality Shops The city's best-quality lapheq is sold at **Yuzana Pickle Tea** *(Map B; ☎ 242526; 22 Nawaday St, Dagon Township)* in sweet, sour and chilli-laced varieties. You can buy an all-in-one kit containing prepared tea leaves, fried garlic, sesame, peanuts, fried peas etc, or buy each of the ingredients separately. The kit makes a unique souvenir. There is a second branch on the ground floor of Theingyi Zei, Shed D, E-60.

The **morning market** *(cnr 38th St & Bogyoke Aung San Rd)* has fresh flowers at cheap prices. Also try the back entrance to **Bogyoke Market**, or early mornings/evenings at **Hledan**, **Myaynigone** or **Kyimyindaing** markets.

J's Irrawaddy Dream *(☎ 221695; 59 Taw Win St; open 9am-8pm daily)*, a block north of the Pansea Yangon Hotel, is a handsome shop featuring Burmese textiles, clothes, lacquer and other handicrafts.

Arts & Crafts There is a small but thriving local gallery scene in Yangon.

Traditions Gallery *(Map A; Claudia Saw Lwin, director; ☎ 513709; 24 Inya Myaing Rd)* has quality reproductions of traditional Burmese handicrafts.

Ivy Gallery *(Map B; ☎ 297654; 159 45th St)*, between Bogyoke Aung San and Anawrahta Rds, is run by the director Myat Min. It features a fine collection of modern Burmese art. Ivy also has a shop in Bogyoke Aung San Market at 438 West Row.

Yone Yang Antique Shop *(☎ 240167; 1B Kaba Aye Paya Rd, at Inya Ave)* is a good antique shop to browse, even if much of its stock is not for export.

Both **Golden Valley Art Centre** *(Map A; ☎ 533830; 54(D) Golden Valley)*, and **Inya Gallery of Art** *(Map A; ☎ 530327; 50(B) Inya Rd)* feature exhibits by contemporary Burmese painters.

For recommendations on where to buy books, see the Bookshops section at the beginning of this chapter.

Tailors Yangon isn't a place you would usually think of for tailor-made clothes, but prices for tailoring are among the lowest in Southeast Asia. The selection of fabrics at tailor shops, however, is mostly restricted to synthetics. Cotton lengths in prints, plaids, solids and batiks can easily be found in the larger markets, so you may do better to buy cloth at a market and bring it to a tailor shop for cutting and sewing.

If you want a traditional, Mandarin-collar Burmese shirt (for men), try **Ava Tailoring** *(Map C; ☎ 248156; 124 Pansodan St)*, near the train station at the Anawrahta Rd intersection. If you're measured the day you arrive, they can have it ready by the time you return from upcountry.

Globe Tailoring *(☎ 273416; 367 Bogyoke Aung San Rd)* is well regarded by local expats for women's and men's tailoring. Globe is especially good for quick alterations.

Photography Supplies Along Anawrahta Rd, between Sule Paya Rd and Mahabandoola Garden St, are at least a dozen shops that sell film and photography supplies. Several stock slide film – usually Kodak Ektachrome 100 and Fujichrome Sensia 100 – for around K1800 per roll. Colour print film is plentiful and cheap; black-and-white film is very scarce. Slide film isn't common in Myanmar, and it's a good idea to check the date on the packaging. For camera repair, **Pacific Camera Repair**, on the same block, has been recommended.

If you want a handful of cheap visa photos there are lots of photo shops around the Sule Pagoda in central Yangon.

Duty-Free Goods Most merchandise at the **duty-free shop** at Yangon international airport is cheaper than Bangkok, Hong Kong or Singapore. There's also a branch in town just north of Sule Paya. It's called **Yangon Duty Free Store** *(Map C; Sule Paya Rd)*. Both branches carry the usual airport stuff – perfume, cigarettes (US$9 a carton), alcohol (average US$10 per litre) and watches – plus a variety of other imported goods, such as chocolates and breakfast cereal. Both branches are open 10am to 6pm daily.

Getting There & Away

Air See the introductory Getting There & Away chapter for information on air travel to/from Yangon.

Bus Most public and private buses to destinations outside of Yangon leave from the Highway bus station (also known as Sawbwagyigon), at the intersection of Pyay Rd and Station Rd, just southwest of Yangon's international airport in Mingaladon. Each bus line has an office at the station; these offices are mostly lined up according to general routes, eg one section for Nyaung U/Bagan, another for the Mandalay area, another for Taunggyi/Inle Lake and one for Mawlamyaing/Dawei. There are snack shops with rice and noodle dishes if you get hungry while waiting for a departure.

Ordinary government buses are the cheapest and slowest: so slow that the Road Transport Enterprise won't even give arrival times. Private bus companies generally run better vehicles on tighter schedules, for up to twice the government fare. You can buy tickets at the station (a day or two in advance is recommended), or at several central locations, mostly opposite the central train station, alongside Aung San Stadium.

The most impressive buses are the newer air-con express ones, which run to Pyay, Meiktila, Mandalay, Taunggyi and Mawlamyaing. These are typically large Japanese, Chinese or Korean air-con (more or less) vehicles with around 45 reclining seats, and even on-board video. Typical fares are around US$7/FEC for Mandalay, Meiktila or Taunggyi and US$4/FEC to Pyay or Mawlamyaing (Mottama is the actual stop; from there you take a ferry or longtail boat across the river). These lines may also stop in Bago and Taungoo, where small offices are maintained at roadside restaurants.

To the North Buses between Yangon and Mandalay take 12 to 15 hours, to Pyay around four to five hours, and to Thandwe over the mountains 16 to 17 hours, depending on road conditions and the health of your bus. The cheaper, non-air-con buses leave daily, usually throughout the morning, and the air-con buses of companies such as Leo Express and Sun Moon Express head off daily, usually at around 5pm or 6pm.

Bus companies operating up and down Highway 1 (and based at the Highway bus station) include: **AKM Express** *(☎ 636441)*; **Hnin Thu Wai** *(☎ 246283)*; **Rainbow Express** *(☎ 272250)*; **Sin-ma-lite** *(☎ 286588)*; **Saw Bwa Gyi Gon** *(☎ 665545)*; and **Sun Moon Express** *(☎ 642903)*.

The major players on the popular Yangon to Mandalay route are Leo Express, Kyaw Express and Transnational Express, all of whom maintain offices at the Highway bus station as well as in central Yangon, across from the train station near Aung San Stadium. Meals, snacks and water are usually provided. Most companies transfer passengers from several central locations to the Highway bus station in vans or pick-ups for no extra charge.

Express bus offices opposite the central train station include:

Kyaw Express (☎ 242473) 8–11 Aung San Stadium (South Wing)
Leo Express (☎ 252001, fax 240668) 23–25 Upper Pansodan St at Aung San Stadium (Eastern Wing)
Sun Moon Express (☎ 642903) Aung San Stadium (Southern Wing)
Transnational Express (TNE; ☎ 249671) 22–29 Aung San Stadium (Southern Wing) at Kunchan St

Bago, Kyaiktiyo, Pathein/Chaungtha Beach & Thanlyin Buses for Bago and Pathein/Chaungtha Beach leave from the Hsimmalaik bus station near the intersection of Hanthawady and Hledan Rds in the northwestern part of Yangon (a K1000 taxi ride from downtown). Hsimmalaik is a bustling, dusty compound, and mostly caters for bus trips within 320km of Yangon. Most signs are in Burmese, but people are very helpful.

There are two private buses to Pathein and/or Chaungtha Beach, with departures at 4.30am, 6am, 9am, noon and 2pm. The cost – depending on the standard of bus – can range between K1000 and K3000. The cheapest and most crowded buses from Yangon to Chaungtha Beach usually leave at noon or 1pm, and cost K1200 (on the Pathein-Chaungtha Beach leg of the journey, all foreigners are expected to pay a further US$5 for the ferry crossing). The more comfortable buses tend to leave early in the morning, and these should be booked the day before. You can usually buy same-day tickets for the noon or 2pm departure. Most hotels can arrange bookings for you.

One of the better Yangon-Pathein/Chaungtha Beach bus companies is **Ktet Aung Express** *(☎ 5131730; Hsimmalaik; open 7am-6pm daily)*. The bus to Pathein takes approximately five hours; to Chaungtha Beach another two to three hours. From Chaungtha Beach to Yangon, the most comfortable bus heads off at 6.30am, and costs K2000. For some reason, this is K1000 less than the same trip from Yangon to Chaungtha. In Chaungtha Beach, most hotels and guesthouses can arrange bus tickets for you.

Minibuses to Kyaikto (and Kinpun, the base camp to Kyaiktiyo Paya) leave hourly from 6am to 11am (K400, five hours).

Pick-ups to Bago (K100) leave hourly from 6am to 3pm. Small pick-ups to Bago and Kyaikto also leave from the eastern side of Latha St, south of Anawrahta Rd. Buses to Thanlyin leave from the southern side of Mahabandoola Rd, east of Sule Paya.

Train In addition to the many trains operated by government-owned Myanma Railways, one private company runs out of Yangon train station along the Yangon to Mandalay line. **Dagon Mann** *(Map B; ☎ 249024)* reserves four berths and six upper-class seats for foreigners on its express train (No 17 Up on the public schedule), which departs from Yangon at 3.15pm daily, arriving in Mandalay at 7am the next morning. Theoretically foreigners are not allowed to buy tickets for any berths below 1st class. For this privilege, they are rewarded with a meal choice of hamburger, fried noodles or fried rice, plus one soft drink, and – except in 1st class – video programmes. A 1st-class seat costs US$30 (no air-con or video); an ordinary upper seat US$42; a special upper seat (reclining) US$45; an ordinary sleeper US$48; and a superior sleeper (with private bathroom and fridge) US$50.

All Dagon Mann tickets must be purchased in advance; the company recommends four days, but tickets may be reserved up to a month in advance. Reservations and tickets are available at the **Dagon Mann ticket office** *(open 6am-4pm daily)* on the Bogyoke Aung San Rd side of Yangon train station (near the corner of Sule Paya Rd). The ticket booth is on the right as you enter from Bogyoke Aung San Rd.

Government trains from Yangon to Mandalay leave from Yangon daily at 6am, 5pm, 6.30pm, 7.30pm, and 9pm. These trains usually take about 14 hours. A one-way ticket costs US$35 (US$30 for the 5pm train).

For general government-run rail enquiries, call **Yangon train station** *(☎ 274027)*.

See the Getting Around chapter for information on rail travel within Myanmar using Myanma Railways.

Boat Along the Yangon River waterfront, which wraps around southern Yangon, are a number of jetties with boats offering long-distance ferry services. Four main passenger jetties service long-distance ferries headed up the delta towards Pathein or north along the Ayeyarwady (Irrawaddy) River to Pyay, Bagan and Mandalay: Pongyi, Lan Thit, Kaingdan and Hledan. Named for the respective streets that extend north from each jetty, all four are clustered in an area just south of Lanmadaw township and southwest of Chinatown. When you come to purchasing a ticket for a particular ferry from the **Inland Water Transport** *(IWT; ☎ 284055)* deputy division manager's office, at the back of Lan Thit jetty, be sure to ask which jetty your boat will be departing from.

Myanma Five Star Line *(MFSL; Map B; ☎ 295279)* ships leave from the MSFL jetty – also known as Chanmayeiseikan jetty – next to Pansodan St jetty.

Pathein Boats from Yangon to Pathein leave at 5pm daily (arriving 10am the next day). The cost is US$7 (for a spot on the deck, with an easy chair if you're early enough) or $42 per person for a cabin with private bathroom. From Pathein to Yangon, boats also leave at 5pm and arrive at 10am the next day.

Getting Around

To/From the Airport See the Air section in the Getting Around chapter for details on getting to/from the airport.

Bus Over 40 numbered city bus routes connect the townships of Yangon. Many buses date back to the 1940s and carry heavy teak carriages. Often, they're impossibly crowded; a Burmese bus is not full until every available handhold for those hanging off the sides and back has been taken. Other routes use newer air-con Japanese and Korean buses that aren't too bad; some routes also use pick-up trucks with benches in the back. If you can find a space you can go anywhere in central Yangon for K5. Longer routes cost from K10 to K20. Prices often double at night – still cheap and still crowded.

Useful bus routes include:

Bogyoke Aung San Market to Mingala Zei (southeast of Kandawgyi) – Japanese pick-up No 1 (၁)
Sule Paya to Thamaing Junction (Eight-Mile Junction) along Insein Rd – bus No 44 (၄၄), No 45 (၄၅) and No 53 (၅၃)
Sule Paya to Hledan junction, then Pyay Rd University of Yangon, along the western side of Inya Lake to Yangon City Hotel and the airport – blue bus No 51 (၅၁), No 53 (၅၃) and air-con No 51 (၅၁)
To Kaba Aye Paya and on to Mae La Mu Paya – bus No 43 (၄၃)
Starting from Insein, continuing on to Theinbyu Rd in the vicinity of the YMCA, Three Seasons Hotel, Cozy Guest House – green pick-up No 48 (၄၈)
Mahabandoola Garden St to the Highway bus station – yellow No 51 (၅၁)
To Shwedagon Paya – bus No 37 (၃၇), No 43 (၄၃) and No 46 (၄၆)
To the Chaukhtatgyi Paya – bus No 42 (၄၂), No 47 (၄၇)

Train A circular train route loops out north from Yangon to Insein, Mingaladon and North Okkalapa townships and then back into the city. There are actually two trains, one clockwise and one counter-clockwise, and it takes about three hours to complete the loop in either direction. A run around this loop will give you a cheap (US$1 per foreigner), but not necessarily comfortable, look around; trains depart approximately every 30 minutes between 6am and 8pm, but not all do the full circuit. Trains which complete the full circuit are as follows: Clockwise – 6.20am, 8.10am, 11.10am, 1.15pm, 2.12pm, 3.55pm, 4.55pm. Counter-clockwise – 6.05am, 7.10am, 9.10am, 12.12pm, 1.40pm, 2.55pm, 5.18pm.

The Kyaukyedwin station is not far from the airport, and there are also convenient stations for Hledan, Kamayut and Insein northwest of the city centre. Buses to these same areas are quicker, of course, unless you've just come from upcountry by train and are at Yangon train station anyway. Yangon's main station is off Sule Paya Rd, north of Bogyoke Aung San Rd; to buy tickets for the circular train, look for the ticket window next to an oval track map at the eastern end of the station.

Sunday is the least crowded time to use the circular train to get a quick glimpse of the city and surroundings.

Taxi Licensed taxis carry red licence plates, though there is often little else to distinguish a taxi from any other vehicle in Yangon. The most expensive are the car taxis – usually older, mid-sized Japanese cars. Fares are highly negotiable – most trips around the central area shouldn't cost more than K500 one way, K800 to K1000 for longer trips. You can also hire a taxi for about K1000 an hour. For the entire day, you should pay about K5000 or US$12 to US$15. Be sure to work out all details before you agree to a price and itinerary. A taxi from downtown to the airport should cost around K1200, but from the airport to the downtown area drivers often ask more, especially late in the day.

For all types of taxis the asking fares usually leap by 30% or so after sunset and on weekends, when rationed petrol isn't available. Late-night taxis – after 11pm or so – often cost double the day rate, mainly because the supply of taxis on hand is considerably lower than in the day, so the drivers are able to charge more.

Trishaw Every Asian country seems to have its own interpretation of the bicycle trishaw. In some countries the passengers sit beside the rider, side by side in a sort of sidecar; in others they sit in front or in the back. In Myanmar, trishaw passengers ride beside the driver, but back to back – one facing forward, one backward. These contraptions are called *saiq-ka* (as in side-car) and to ride one costs roughly K10 per person for every kilometre.

Nowadays trishaws are not permitted on the main streets between midnight and 10am. They're most useful for side streets and areas of town where traffic is light. So far, trishaws have survived the rumours of their imminent banning from the city centre.

Boat Cross-river ferries to Dalah (US$1), on the southern bank of the Yangon River, leave about every 20 minutes from Pansodan St jetty (for pedestrians), at the foot of Pansodan St. Sin Oh Dan St jetty (for vehicles) is at the foot of Sin Oh Dan St. Dalah is the departure point for excursions to Twante and Letkhokkon; departure times are 9am, 1pm and 5pm (from Dalah, boats leave at 8.30 am, 12.30pm and 4.30pm). See the Getting There & Away in the Twante section of the Around Yangon chapter for further details on cross-river transport.

You can hire privately owned *sampans* (flat-bottomed skiffs) from the Pansodan or Botataung jetties for K500 per hour if you just want to have a look at river life. On a grander scale, for US$1000 you can charter a government-run deluxe double-decker (normally reserved for VIP dinners and the like) from the IWT office near Lan Thit jetty for a four-hour cruise between Thanlyin to the northeast and Bayinnaung Bridge to the northwest.

Around Yangon

Several destinations in the Yangon, Bago and Ayeyarwady Divisions surrounding the capital make good one- to three-day excursions from Yangon (Rangoon). Thanlyin (Syriam) and Twante can be seen in day trips, while relaxing Letkhokkon requires an overnight stay. If your tastes are broad, the varied sights in Bago may well be worth an overnight stay; Pathein and Chaungtha Beach perhaps warrant several nights between them. Pyay, in the northwestern corner of Bago Division on the Ayeyarwady (Irrawaddy) River, is a rewarding two-day detour for the modest ruins of Thayekhittaya (Sri Ksetra), a Pyu kingdom that was in existence around 1500 years ago.

Taungoo, a town in Bago Division off the highway between Yangon and Mandalay, once held little interest for the average visitor except as a good resting place between Yangon and Mandalay. These days it's also the starting point for an excursion to nearby Seine Forest Camp, a working elephant teak forest area.

Highlights

- Day trips to the pottery town of Twante and peaceful Thanlyin
- Rich delta life of the Pathein region, and nearby Chaungtha Beach
- Imposing paya of Shwemawdaw, the enormous reclining Shwethalyaung Buddha and the unusual Kyaik Pun Paya in Bago
- Pyu ruins of Sri Ksetra near Pyay

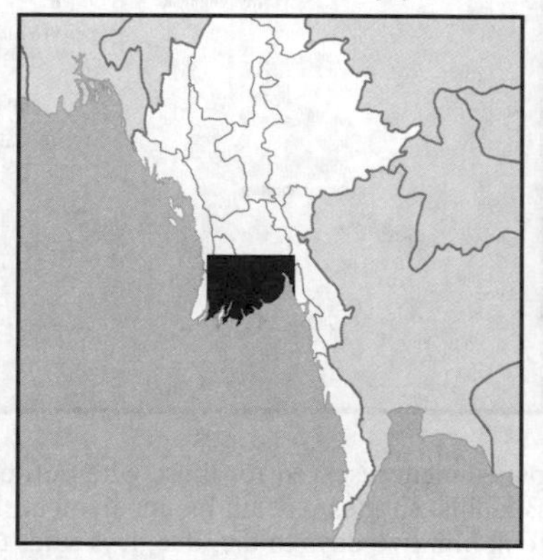

Delta Region

A vast basin stretching from the Bay of Bengal coast across to the Bago Range receives year-round drainage from several major rivers, including the Ayeyarwady (Irrawaddy), Bago, Yangon (Hlaing) and Pathein (Ngawan). Interlaced with canals, streams and tributaries, this riverine network irrigates millions of hectares of farmland, making the delta the central, and essential, 'rice bowl' of Myanmar. In addition, the estuarine environments along the coast provide much of the country's saltwater and freshwater fish harvest. Because of such natural abundance, the delta has attracted Burmese people from all around the country; hence it's one of Myanmar's most populated – and interesting – regions to explore.

THANLYIN & KYAUKTAN

သန်လျင် / ကျောက်တန်း

If you've got a morning or afternoon to spare in Yangon, you can make an excursion across the river to Thanlyin and on to the 'mid-river' *paya* (stupa) at Kyauktan. Thanlyin was the base during the late-16th and early-17th centuries for notorious Portuguese adventurer Philip De Brito. Officially a trade representative for the Rakhaing, he actually ran his own little kingdom from Thanlyin, siding with the Mon (when it suited him) in their struggle against the Bamar. In 1599 his private army sacked Bago, but in 1613 the Bamar besieged Thanlyin and De Brito received the

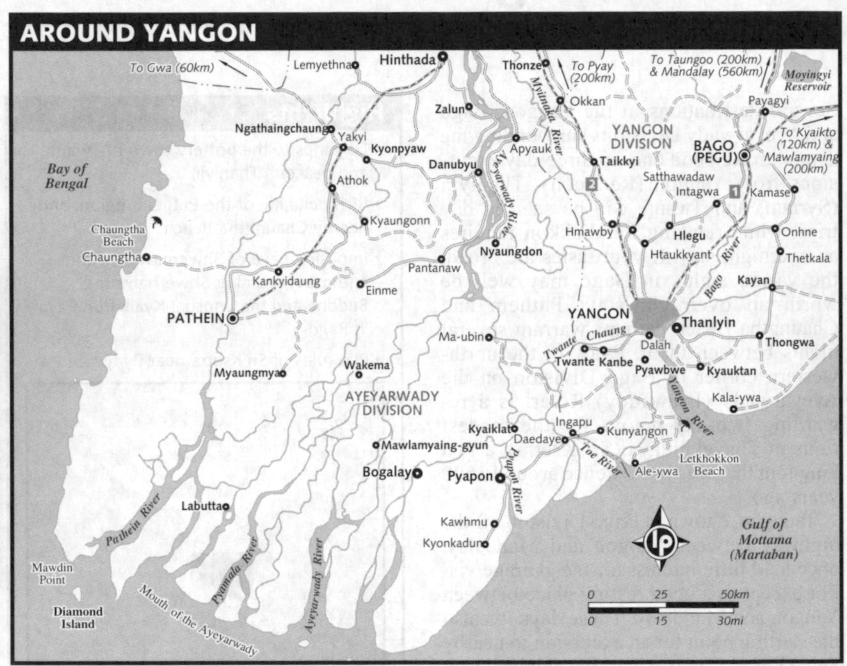

punishment reserved for those who defiled Buddhist shrines – death by impalement. It took him two days to die, due, it is said, to his failure to take the recommended posture where the stake would have penetrated vital organs. Thanlyin continued as a major port and trading centre until it was destroyed by Alaungpaya in 1756, after which Yangon took over this role.

Although there is no longer any of this ancient city to be seen, Thanlyin is a relaxing change of pace, with shaded streets and a busy market to stroll through. A short bus ride out of town will take you to the large, golden **Kyaik-khauk Paya**, rising on a hillock to the north of the road. It's said to contain two Buddha hairs delivered to the site by the great sage himself, although the paya looks to be no more than a couple of hundred years old. Most likely the first stupa on this hillock was erected by the Mon 600 to 800 years ago. Just before this stupa are the tombs of two famous Burmese writers: Natshingaung and Padethayaza. If it's too hot to climb the stairs, you can always take the lift for K5.

If you continue 12km further, until the road terminates at a wide river, you can visit the **Yele Paya** (Mid-River Pagoda) at Kyauktan. It's appropriately named since the complex is perched on a tiny island in the middle of the river. In the temple there are pictures of other famous paya all over Myanmar and further afield. To reach the islet shrine, catch one of the many launch ferries from the riverbank for a few kyat. Near the ferry landing are several food vendors.

Places to Stay & Eat

White House Restaurant & Guest House is about the only alternative as, so far, none of the several guesthouses in Thanlyin is licensed to accept foreigners. Until that changes, check out this friendly place, about 100m off the main road, which serves good Chinese fare in a small air-conditioned café.

Bonsai Restaurant is the place to try for more ambience. It has a courtyard setting on the main road leading to Kyaik-khauk Paya.

Getting There & Away

With the opening of a Chinese-built bridge over the Bago River several years ago, the journey from Yangon to Thanlyin no longer involves a ferry trip. Large pick-ups to Thanlyin leave frequently throughout the day from a spot on Sule Paya Rd opposite City Hall, a little east of Sule Paya. The 25km trip takes about an hour by bus or pick-up; half an hour by car or taxi. The fare is K15 by pick-up. Minibuses also make the short trip out to Thanlyin from a spot next to Thakhin Mya Park, near the corner of Tha Khin Mya Garden St and Strand Rd west of the central Yangon area. The bus fare is K30 to Thanlyin, and K40 if you continue on to Kyauktan and the Yele Paya.

In Thanlyin, horse carts are a good way to get around. You can hire one to go to Kyaik-khauk Paya for about K500 each way.

TWANTE

တွံတေး

It's an interesting day trip from Yangon to Twante, a small town noted for its pottery and cotton-weaving, and for an old Mon paya complex. One can travel there by hiring a jeep from Dalah (on the opposite bank of the Yangon River) for about K1000, or by taking a ferry along the Yangon River and Twante Canal. The latter mode of transport is slower but provides a glimpse of life on and along the famous canal, which was dug during the colonial era as a short cut across the Ayeyarwady Delta.

A large market in the centre of town near the canal banks was destroyed by fire in January 1995 but has since been rebuilt.

Shwesandaw Paya

ရွှေဆံတော်ဘုရား

Standing 76m tall, this Mon-built *zedi* (bell-shaped paya), a kilometre or two south of the canal, is just a few years younger than the one at Yangon's Shwedagon Paya. Though the stupa itself fits the standard central Burmese mould, a walk around the compound will yield a few minor surprises. In a chicken-wire enclosure to one side is a casual display of ancient Twante pottery, plus religious and royal regalia from early Mon and Bamar kingdoms. One corner of the compound, used by worshippers as a 'wish-fulfilling' station, commemorates King Bayinnaung's (also spelt Bayint Nyaung) defeat of a local rebellion.

Along the western side of the stupa stand some old bronze Buddhas. Continuing counterclockwise, near the southern entrance you'll come to a 100-year-old sitting bronze Buddha in Mandalay style with unusual 'capped' shoulders in which the flowing monastic robes curl away from the shoulders. The left hand hovers above the crossed legs rather than resting on them – a difficult casting feat. Instead of focusing on the floor, the Buddha's eyes stare straight ahead. A low blue ledge in front of the image marks off 'footprints' allegedly left by an ogress who made a pilgrimage here.

The ruins of a smaller, older-looking zedi stand adjacent to the main compound, just off the road from the ferry landing.

Oh-Bo Pottery Sheds

အိုးဗိုအိုးလုပ်ငန်း

Pottery is a major cottage industry in Twante, which supplies much of the delta region with well-designed, utilitarian containers of varying shapes and sizes. The pots are made in huge thatched-roof sheds in the Oh-Bo district south of the canal, about 15 minutes' walk from the dock.

Near the entrance to the sheds are the potters' wheels. Twante pots are typically half wheel-thrown, half coil-shaped, then air dried on huge racks in the middle of the shed. After drying, the pots are fired in large wood-fired adobe kilns set towards the back of the sheds. To one side of the sheds stand piles of cut wood – assorted jungle hardwoods, but especially rubberwood, are the fuels of choice. The kilns are divided into two chambers, one for drying wood and one for firing the pots with a brown-black glaze. It takes around 15 days for the firing and cooling of one kiln-full. The typical shed turns out 70,000 pots a year, all of them handmade.

Twante pots can be purchased directly from the sheds or, perhaps more conveniently, at the central market near the Twante ferry landing.

Getting There & Away

The quickest way to get to Twante is via a short cross-river ferry and public jeep or pick-up ride. Pedestrian ferries from Pansodan St jetty (near the foot of Pansodan St and opposite The Strand Hotel) take passengers across the Yangon River to Dalah on the opposite bank (US$1, 20 minutes). In Dalah catch one of the dark green jeeps that leave for Twante every 45 minutes or so throughout the day. The jeeps are gradually being replaced by pick-ups. The ride takes 30 to 45 minutes and the fare is a negotiable K50 or so for a front seat in a jeep; or about K100 for a front seat in a Hi-Lux. Come prepared for a crush – drivers cram as many people as possible into and onto the vehicle. Minibuses (K150) round out the possibilities.

The seemingly slower but more scenic trip along the Yangon River and Twante Canal takes two hours – even though it's only 24km from landing to landing. Although there are several boats that pass by Twante on their way across the western delta, including the Yangon-Pathein ferry (which leaves from Lan Thit jetty), the most frequent departures are aboard Hpayapon-bound craft (US$1). These leave from the Hledan Rd and Kaingdan St jetties in Yangon daily at noon, 1pm, 2pm, 3pm and 4pm, returning hourly till 7pm.

When you add up the waiting times for the cross-river ferry/jeep departure versus the canal ferry, both modes of transport end up taking about the same amount of time from start to finish. A good way to vary the trip would be to do the ferry-jeep combo out to Twante, then catch one of the canal ferries back to Yangon around sunset when the waterways look their best.

Getting Around

Trishaws from the ferry dock to the Oh-Bo pottery sheds cost K30 per person. From the dock to Shwesandaw Paya, the cost is K100. A horse cart from Shwesandaw back to the dock is about K150.

LETKHOKKON BEACH

လက်ခုပ်ကုန်း

Letkhokkon, about three to four hours by road from Dalah, is the closest beach to the capital. Located in Kunyangon township, near the mouth of the Bago River, Letkhokkon is a delta beach facing the Gulf of Mottama (Martaban), with fine powder-beige sand and a very wide tidal bore that tends towards mudflats at its lowest ebb. Copious coconut palms along the beach help make up for the less than crystalline waters. The lack of clarity is part of the estuarial milieu here and doesn't mean the water isn't clean. At low tide the local kids like to stage mud fights.

A day or overnight excursion to Letkhokkon is more than just a beach trip; it offers a glimpse of relaxed delta life. Along the way, the road passes by rice paddies, betel-nut gardens and several Karen villages. At Kunyangon a large stupa called **Payagyi** (Big Paya) is a common stop for Burmese day-trippers. West of the road between Kawhmu and Ingapu is a hilly area studded with the porcelain remains of ceramics left behind by hundreds of years of sea trade.

Adjacent to the main beach area, the village of Letkhokkon itself is a fairly typical seaside town that thrives on coconuts and fishing. Farther southeast in a neighbouring village is a **monastery** with a bizarre collection of mutant fruits, including a pineapple plant that bears a blossom not seen on other pineapples; coconuts whose outer husks bear likenesses to Kyaiktiyo Paya and the late *sayadaw* (abbot); and dead logs that bear fruit. Using a magnifying glass, the abbot likes to show visitors markings in the fingerprint of his left index finger resembling a dancing peacock.

Myaseinthaun, a delta island offshore, is visited by many native and migratory waterfowl. **Daedaye**, on a delta peninsula northwest of Letkhokkon, is a small town that thrives on the production of processed seafood for export. Though the town itself isn't too interesting, there's a long beach nearby called **Anauntphettokan** (Westward-moving Beach, named for its heavy sand drift). The beach can be approached by boat from Ingapu or other spots along the coastline. You can rent a launch for visiting these areas from the Letkhokkon Beach Hotel. The asking price is K3000 per hour, but you should be able to arrange a better deal for multi-hour hires.

Places to Stay & Eat

As you approach Letkhokkon from the north, there's a two-lane, palm-flanked avenue leading off to the right where you'll see a tidy row of brightly painted wooden beach bungalows. **Letkhokkon Beach Hotel** *(booking office ☎ 01-224346; 68 11th St, Lanmadaw Township, Yangon; singles/doubles US$38/45)* has spacious rooms with air-con, mosquito nets and private hot-water showers. However, when we visited the power was not on for more than six hours a day. Rates include a choice of Western or Asian breakfasts. Good seafood is sometimes available at the hotel restaurant.

There are a couple of other simple **eateries** in the village, as well as a thatched-roof **bar** where various palm distillates are available.

Getting There & Away

Vehicle ferries (passengers US$5, 15 minutes) cross the Yangon River to Dalah from Sin Oh Dan St jetty between 18th and 19th Sts in Yangon at 9am, and 1pm and 5pm; from Dalah they leave at 8.30am, 12.30pm and 4.30pm. The fare for autos and small trucks is K160, and there's a K20 tax to be paid on either side of the river.

Pedestrian ferries (K5) cross to Dalah from Pansodan St jetty about every 20 minutes in either direction, starting at 5am and stopping at 8pm.

The road between Dalah and Letkhokkon is in very poor condition in places. Count on close to four hours to complete the journey without stops, more by public transport. It's not easy getting to Letkhokkon by the latter. First you must cross to Dalah via the Pansodan St jetty pedestrian ferry (K5) or charter a sampan (K100). Near the row of restaurants and teashops on the Dalah side you'll see a cluster of pick-up trucks and jeeps; ask around to see if anyone's going to Letkhokkon. This isn't too common – usually only a couple of vehicles a day do this route direct. There are more frequent departures to Kunyangon, but there's no guarantee you'll find a vehicle there to continue to Letkhokkon.

Expect to pay about K3500 each way to hire a car or jeep from Dalah to make the trip. Of course you could always hire a car and driver in Yangon; however, some drivers refuse to do the trip because the road is so hard on their vehicles.

Once in Letkhokkon it's usually not difficult to find a vehicle heading back to Dalah.

PATHEIN

ပုသိမ်

☎ **042**

Situated on the eastern bank of the Pathein River (also known as the Ngawan River) in the Ayeyarwady Delta, about 120km west of Yangon, Pathein is the most important delta port outside the capital, despite its distance from the sea. It is surrounded by a major rice-growing area that produces the best rice available in Myanmar, including a high quality variety called *pawsanmwe htamin* (fragrant rice).

Noted for its colourful hand-painted umbrellas, the town is of some historic interest and was the scene for major clashes during the struggle for supremacy between the Mon and the Bamar. Later it became an important trade relay point for goods moving between India and Southeast Asia. The city's name may derive from the Burmese word for Muslim – *pathi* – due to the heavy presence of Arab and Indian Muslim traders here centuries ago. The colonial Brits – or more likely their imported Indian civil servants – corrupted the name to Bassein.

Today, Pathein's population of 200,000 includes large contingents of Kayin (Karen)

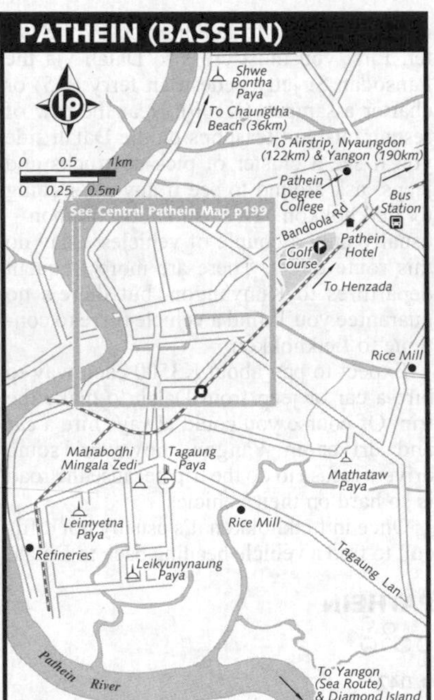

and Rakhaing. Although once part of a Mon kingdom, Pathein is home to only a few Mon today. During the 1970s and 1980s, the Kayin villages surrounding Pathein generated insurgent activity that has calmed to the point where Pathein is now open to foreign tourists. The recent growth of delta trade, particularly rice exports, has contributed to a general air of prosperity in Myanmar's fourth-largest city.

The waterfront area, markets, umbrella workshops and colourful paya make the city worth a stay of at least a night or two. It also serves as a jumping-off point for excursions to the beach resort of Chaungtha and further north to Gwa and Thandwe in the Rakhaing State.

Post & Communications

The main post office is located towards the western end of Mahabandoola Rd near the clock tower. Since there's no air service between Pathein and Yangon, mail is slow, but the Pathein postal service is supposed to be reasonably reliable.

You can make domestic trunk calls and international calls from the telephone office next door. However, the wait can be up to an hour for either.

Shwemokhtaw Paya

ရွှေမုဋ္ဌောဘုရား

In the centre of Pathein, near the river front, looms the golden, bell-shaped stupa at Shwemokhtaw Paya. One legend says it was originally built by India's Buddhist king Asoka in 305 BC as a small stupa called Shwe Arna. Standing 2.3m tall, this original stupa supposedly enshrined Buddha relics and a 6-inch gold bar. Another legend says a Muslim princess named Onmadandi requested each of her three Buddhist lovers to build a stupa in her honour. One of the lovers erected Shwemokhtaw, the others the less distinguished Tazaung and Thayaung-gyaung paya.

Whichever story you believe, Bagan's King Alaungsithu is thought to have erected an 11m stupa called Htupayon over this site in AD 1115. Then, in 1263, King Samodagossa took power, raised the stupa to 40m and changed the name to Shwemokhtaw Paya, which means Stupa of the Half-Foot Gold Bar.

The stupa's main shape has remained the same since then, although the changing of the decorative *hti* (umbrella-like decorated top) has increased the height to its present 46.6m. The current hti consists of a topmost layer made from 6.3kg of solid gold, a middle tier of pure silver and a bottom tier of bronze; all three tiers are gilded and reportedly embedded with a total of 829 diamond fragments, 843 rubies and 1588 semiprecious stones.

The southern shrine of the compound houses the **Thiho-shin Phondaw-pyi** sitting Buddha image, which supposedly floated to the delta coast on a raft from Sri Lanka in ancient times. According to legend, an unknown Sinhalese sculptor fashioned four different Buddha images using pieces from the original bodhi tree mixed with a cement

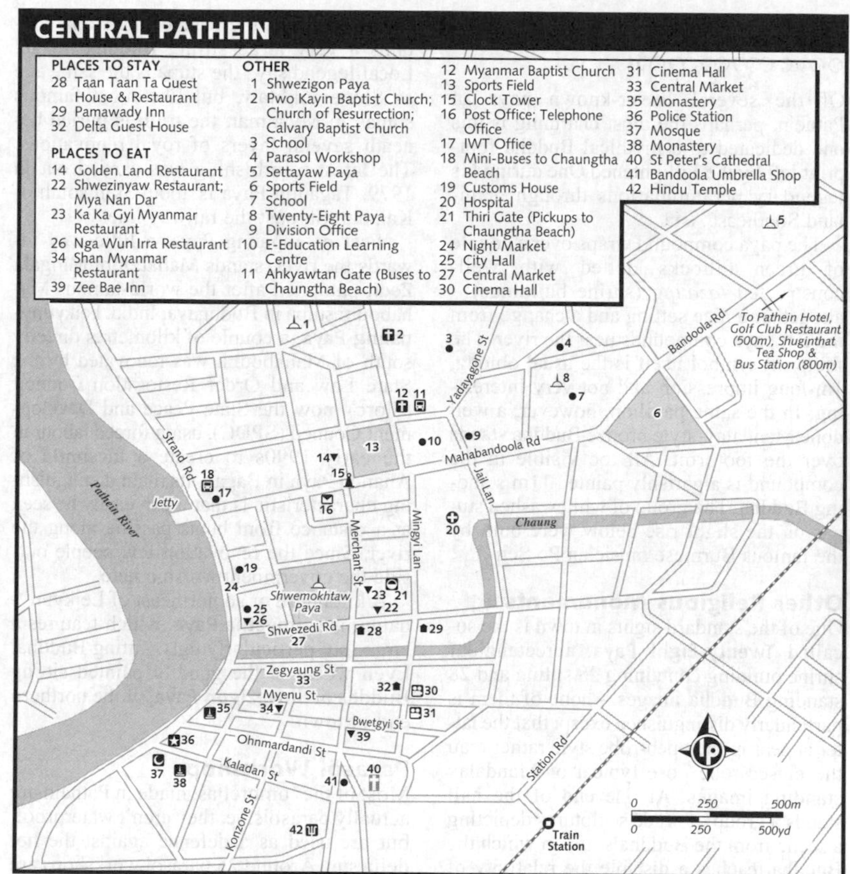

composite. He then placed them on four wooden rafts and set the rafts adrift on the ocean. One landed in Dawei (Tavoy), and is now housed at the Shinmokhti Paya; another landed at Kyaikkami (Amherst), and is now at Yele Paya; the third landed at Kyaikto and is now at Kyaikpawlaw; and the fourth landed near Phondawpyi, a fishing village about 97km south of Pathein. In 1445 the Mon queen Shinsawpu purportedly brought the latter image to Pathein, then known as Kuthima.

A marble standing Buddha positioned in a niche in the fence running along the western side of the stupa marks a spot where Mon warriors once prayed before battle. In the northwestern corner of the compound is a shrine to Shin Upagot, the bodhisattva who floats on the ocean and appears to those in trouble. At this shrine his lotus raft is flanked by blue dragons representing the sea; turtles swim in the water surrounding the small pavilion.

The people of Pathein celebrate Vesakha (celebrating the Buddha's birth, enlightenment and passing away) with a huge *paya pwe* (pagoda festival) during the full moon of Kason (April/May).

Settayaw Paya

စက်တော်ရာဘုရား

Of the several lesser-known paya in Pathein, perhaps the most charming is this one dedicated to a mythical Buddha footprint left by the Enlightened One during his legendary perambulations through mainland Southeast Asia.

The paya compound wraps over a couple of green hillocks dotted with well-constructed *tazaung* (shrine buildings) – altogether a nice setting and a change from the flat paya compounds near the river. The footprint symbol itself is the usual oblong, 1m-long impression and not very interesting. In the same pavilion, however, a well done Mandalay-style bronze Buddha stands over the footprint. All too visible in the compound is a garishly painted 11m standing Buddha. The group of whitewashed stupas on the slight rise below were built by the famous Burmese musician Po Sein.

Other Religious Monuments

One of the standard sights in town is the so-called **Twenty-Eight Paya**, a rectangular shrine building containing 28 sitting and 28 standing Buddha images – none of them is particularly distinguished except that the latter appear in the open-robe style rather than the closed-robe pose typical of Mandalay standing images. At one end of the hall stands a group of crude sculptures depicting a scene from the Buddha's life, in which the Buddha teaches a disciple the relativity of physical beauty by comparing a monkey, the disciple's wife and a *deva* (celestial being). Although it's not that interesting a sight, the shrine is a short walk from Pathein's main umbrella workshops. You may have to ask the caretaker to unlock the building.

More interesting from an artistic perspective is **Tagaung Mingala Zeditaw** (Tagaung Paya), centred around a graceful stupa that sweeps inward from a wide, whitewashed base to a gleaming silver superstructure. Look for the small squirrel sculpture extending from the western side of the upper stupa and representing a previous life of the Buddha as a squirrel. One of the pavilions at the base of the stupa contains a very large sitting Buddha image. Local legend says the stupa is the same age as Shwemokhtaw, but like most famous stupas in Myanmar, the truth is buried beneath several layers of royal renovations. The latest refurbishing was carried out in 1979. Tagaung Paya is about 3km south of Kaladan St, past the railway line.

West of Tagaung Paya, a little way towards the river, stands **Mahabodhi Mingala Zedi**, patterned after the world-famous Mahabodhi stupa in Bodhgaya, India. **Leikyunynaung Paya**, a couple of kilometres directly south of Mahabodhi, was renovated by the State Law and Order Restoration Council (Slorc), now the State Peace and Development Council (SPDC), using forced labour in the early 1990s to create a facsimile of Ananda Paya in Bagan. Its main distinguishing characteristic is that it can easily be seen at a distance from boats passing along the river. Since the renovation few people outside the government worship here.

A kilometre or so northeast of Leikyunynaung is **Leimyetna Paya**, which features a large, but particularly ugly, sitting Buddha. Even worse is the gaudily painted sitting Buddha at **Shwezigon Paya**, at the northern end of town.

Parasol Workshops

Most of the 'umbrellas' made in Pathein are actually parasols; ie, they aren't waterproof, but are used as a defence against the hot delta sun. Around 25 parasol workshops are scattered throughout the northern part of the city, particularly in the vicinity of the Twenty-Eight Paya, off Mahabandoola Rd. The parasols come in a variety of colours; some are brightly painted with flowers, birds and other nature motifs. One type that can be used in the rain is the saffron-coloured monks' umbrella, which is waterproofed by applying various coats of tree resin; a single umbrella may take five days to complete, including the drying process. Parasols and umbrellas can be ordered in any size directly from the workshops. Bargaining usually isn't too fierce as the basic parasols are reasonably priced, even cheap.

Most workshops welcome visitors who want to observe this craft. One of the easiest to find – and one with high-quality work – is the **workshop** *(open 8am-5pm daily)* opposite the entrance to the Twenty-Eight Paya.

Other Attractions

At the **night market** *(Strand Rd)* that is set up each evening in front of Customs House, vendors purvey food, clothing, textiles, tools, housewares and just about every other requisite for daily life at low prices. Just south of Shwemokhtaw Paya is the **central market**, and just south of that is a newer market, with all manner of goods. Both markets are closed on Sunday.

The **golf course** *(green fees K1500)* next to the Pathein Hotel has 18 holes.

Places to Stay

Taan Taan Ta Guest House & Restaurant *(Merchant St; standard singles/doubles US$5/6, larger singles/double US$7/10)* is centrally located and offers simple, clean rooms with private bathroom. The larger rooms come with hot shower. The restaurant serves decent Chinese and Bamar food, with a fairly ordinary breakfast included in the room price.

Pamawady Inn *(☎ 21165; 14-A Mingyi St; singles/doubles US$8/15, with breakfast US$10/20)* is about a 10-minute walk from the harbour. It is a rather run-down hotel offering air-con rooms with private hot-water bathroom.

Delta Guest House *(☎ 22131; 44 Mingyi St; downstairs/upstairs rooms US$3/6)* is a sleepy, central choice with small, simple and well-kept rooms with common bathroom downstairs, or upstairs rooms for one or two people with air-con and private bathroom.

Pathein Hotel *(☎ 22599, fax 24323; Kanthonesint, Pathein-MonyBandoolaa Rd; singles US$25-28, doubles US$35)* is an L-shaped, two-storey building on spacious grounds near the bus station off Bandoola Rd. It is the top-of-the-range in Pathein. Very comfortable rooms on the upper floor come with air-con, fridge, TV and excellent hot-water shower. A rather meagre breakfast is included in all room prices. This place is quite nice overall, but very pricey considering the distance from town, and the minibar charges – US$1 for bottled water!

Places to Eat

Pathein has several simple, decent restaurants, most of them central. Thanks to the Bamar restaurant revival that started in Yangon and Mandalay, there's now a choice in Pathein, to go with the usual assortment of Chinese or Indian dishes.

Shan Myanmar Restaurant *(cnr Konzone & Bwetgyi Sts)* and **Ka Ka Gyi Myanmar Restaurant** *(Merchant St)*, across from Shwemokhtaw Paya, both offer good curries and hot-sour soups for lunch or dinner.

Shwezinyaw Restaurant *(24/25 Shwezedi Rd; open 8am-9pm daily)*, near Merchant St, is a Bamar/Indian-Muslim hybrid with good curries and *biryani*. Nearby is the equally good **Mya Nan Dar** restaurant, serving tasty Bamar dishes.

Zee Bae Inn *(Merchant St; open 9am or 10am-10pm)* is among the more well-known and longest-running Chinese places. It is a saloon-style, popular little place that has been serving large bowls of noodles and other Chinese dishes since the 1950s. The downstairs area opens onto the street, while upstairs there's an air-con dining room.

Nga Wun Irra Restaurant *(Cnr Shwezedi & Strand Rds; mains from K300; open 10am-9pm)* is a pleasant little dinner spot next to the night market down by the water. This simple place offers friendly service but, strangely enough, only chicken, pork and vegetable dishes – no seafood.

Golden Land Restaurant *(Merchant St; mains around K2000; open 9am-10pm)*, just north of the clock tower, has a nice, quiet front-yard, open-air eating area. The menu is a wide-ranging mixture of Chinese and Bamar dishes, mostly chicken and seafood. It's pricey by Pathein standards, but servings are large.

Shuginthat Tea Shop *(Bandoola Rd)*, opposite the golf course, near the Pathein Hotel, is a tea shop (the English sign reads Golf Restaurant). The tranquil indoor/outdoor spot is a good place to enjoy tea and Bamar snacks at a leisurely pace.

Several **noodle shops** occupy 1940s-vintage buildings along Konzone St, near the central market.

Yegyi If you're coming by car from Pyay, the town of Yegyi (pronounced *yeh-she*) makes the best mid-point stop. **U Ba Gyi Rice Shop** (no sign), behind the train station in the central market, is a dirty-looking place with decent Bamar food. A very good hot-sour vegetable soup comes as a side dish with all meals.

Getting There & Away

Air Pathein has an airstrip out at the north-eastern edge of the city, but at the time of writing it didn't field any regularly scheduled flights. If it's ever expanded to handle Myanma Airways' (MA) Fokkers, it will only be a half-hour flight from Yangon.

Bus Buses are available from Yangon's Hsimmalaik bus station. From here, there are two private buses to Pathein and/or Chaungtha Beach, with departures at 4.30am, 6am, 9am, noon and 2pm. The cost – depending on the standard of bus – can range from K1000 to K3000. The cheapest, and most crowded, buses from Yangon to Chaungtha Beach usually leave at noon or 1pm, and cost K1200 (on the Pathein-Chaungtha Beach leg of the journey, all foreigners are expected to pay a further US$5 for the ferry crossing, which goes every two hours, on the hour, throughout the day). The more comfortable buses tend to leave early in the morning, and these should be booked the day before. You can usually buy same-day tickets for the noon or 2pm departure. Most hotels can arrange bookings for you. One of the better Yangon-Pathein/Chaungtha Beach bus companies is **Ktet Aung Express** (*☎ 01-5131730; Hsimmalaik; open 7am-6pm daily)*. Be prepared to ask around; most of the signs are in Burmese, although there are usually enough ticket touts around to help you out and take their small commission.

The bus to Pathein takes approximately five hours; to Chaungtha Beach another two to three hours. From Chaungtha Beach to Yangon (via Pathein), the most comfortable bus heads off at 6.30am, and costs K2000. For some reason, this is K1000 less than the same trip from Yangon to Chaungtha (via Pathein). In Chaungtha Beach, most hotels and guesthouses can arrange bus tickets for you.

Buses from Pathein to Chaungtha Beach (K350) leave from the bus station on Pathein's Yadayagone St daily (as well as some minibuses from Strand Rd), with most heading off during the morning, roughly on the hour. There is a US$5 charge for the ferry crossing en route. The ferry leaves every two hours, on the hour throughout the day, and most bus drivers time their journeys well enough to avoid long waits.

Train Pathein is accessible by train, but since you have to travel some distance north towards Pyay and then turn south, making a ferry crossing along the way, the train trip takes a lengthy 14 hours minimum.

Car Pathein can be reached by car from Yangon in about five hours. The usual route is to drive one to two hours (68km) north-west to Nyaungdon (Yandoon or Yangdon on some maps) on the eastern bank of the Ayeyarwady River. Experienced drivers will know when it's best to leave to meet the vehicle ferry across the Ayeyarwady – it leaves every two hours between 6am and 6pm. From Nyaungdon to Pathein is another 122km; about two to three hours under normal driving conditions. Along the way you must cross several rivers and streams by bridge. There are a few military checkpoints along this route – including one where Aung San Suu Kyi was detained while on her way to a National League for Democracy (NLD) political rally in Pathein, after slipping unnoticed out of Yangon. This 1998 stand-off between the country's most outspoken dissident and the embarrassed military lasted six days. Ma Suu stayed with the car and her companions the entire time, before returning to Yangon.

To reach Pathein from Pyay, you must first drive a little north to meet the ferry across the Ayeyarwady. Once across the river you continue west towards Taunggok, turning south at the first major junction. From here, a road south to Myanaung runs smooth and wide for 60km or so, then deteriorates considerably for the rest of the journey to Pathein. There are many checkpoints along this route. Yegyi is the most well equipped stop-off point for trucks, buses and cars along the Pyay-Pathein road.

Boat Chinese triple-deckers sail between Yangon and Pathein, and foreigners have had to pay in dollars; ordinary class costs US$7, and puts you on the open deck (with an easy chair if you get in early). For US$42 you can get an air-con cabin with private bathroom. These express boats leave Yangon's Lan Thit jetty daily at 5pm, arriving the next morning in Pathein at 10am. Foreigners must buy tickets from the deputy division manager's office next to Building 63 on Lan Thit jetty.

AROUND PATHEIN

Horseshoe-shaped **Inye Lake**, 70km northeast of the city near the village of Kyonpyaw, is a favourite weekend picnic spot. Local fishermen sell fresh fish from the lake.

If you follow the Pathein River till it empties into the Andaman Sea you'll reach **Mawdin Point** (Mawdinsoun), the site of a famous festival during the lunar month of Tabodwe (February/March). On the sea side of the cape, at its point, is a sandy beach and the revered stupa of **Mawdin Paya**. Once a week or so, a boat to Mawdin leaves the main Pathein jetty around 6am and arrives at 2pm, but since there's no lodging licensed for foreigners at Mawdin, this is strictly a trip for risk-takers.

During the Mawdin Point festival there are special boats running daily – this would probably be the best time of year to attempt a trip since more guesthouses open especially for the festival.

Diamond Island lies in the midst of the mouth of the Pathein River and is an important sea-turtle hatchery.

Other interesting delta towns include **Labutta** and **Hpayapon**, both of which can be reached by long-distance ferry from Yangon.

Chaungtha Beach

ချောင်းသာကမ်းခြေ

☎ 042

About 40km west of Pathein, on the Bay of Bengal coast, Chaungtha Beach is a rapidly developing resort area. As western-coast beaches go, this one fits somewhere between Letkhokkon, farther south, and Ngapali, to the north, in terms of quality. At low tide the very wide beach has a touch of the 'muddy delta' look, but overall at medium and high tide it's attractive enough, with fine, beige sand, backed by coconut palms

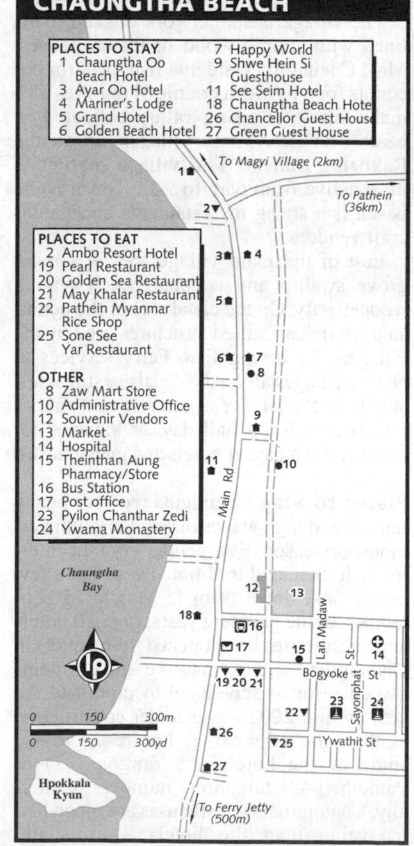

and casuarina trees. The beaches to the north of town, an easy stroll along the sand, are gorgeous and pretty much deserted. Offshore lies a modest coral reef with decent snorkelling except during the rainy season, when water clarity is poor, as well as **Whitesand Island**. Whitesand can be explored in a day trip from Chaungtha Beach. A boat (K1500 return) leaves for the island daily at 8am, returning at 5pm. There's good swimming and snorkelling around the island, as well as a stall selling cold drinks and snacks. For more information, ask at any of the hotels or guesthouses in Chaungtha, or contact **U Tin Ohn** *(☎ 24880)*, the island's Chaungtha-based manager.

The village has a network of sand roads lined with simple wood or thatch houses. Most Chaungtha residents fish, or farm coconuts for a living; a couple of families also make furniture using rattan collected in nearby jungles. Many villagers speak the Rakhaing dialect. The village **market** is most active from 6am to 9am. Towards the beach is a string of restaurants and handicraft vendors.

East of the main village area is a mangrove swamp and a canal beach with a wooden jetty. On the canal side of the peninsula are rickety stilted structures used by the villagers for drying fish. Ferry services to nearby villages along the canal are still available from the jetty. You can also rent canoes for about K700 a half-day, or bicycles for about K500 a day, at hotels and guesthouses.

Places to Stay Chaungtha receives heavy rainfall and high waves during the southwest monsoon season. Few people from the interior visit then, and traditionally all but a few hotels close down from 15 May to 15 September. In the past few years, over 20 hotels and guesthouses have opened for business at Chaungtha, and a massive government-owned resort – scheduled to dominate the area by mid-2002 – was under construction at the time of writing. For reservations, some of the hotels list Yangon (01) or Pathein (042) telephone numbers. Generally, Chaungtha's guesthouses are much better value than the hotels – especially considering only one establishment (Grand Hotel) offers hot showers.

Chaungtha Beach Hotel *(☎ 22587; standard rooms per person US$8, superior singles/doubles US$20/36)* is one of the oldest hotels in Chaungtha, and is now a little frayed around the edges. Standard rooms have fan and private bathroom. Superior rooms come with air-con, fridge and TV.

See Seim Hotel *(☎ 22909; singles/doubles US$15/20, family room per person US$7)* is a sprawling place right on the beach with clean, bungalow-style rooms with fan and private bathroom. The rooms are a little gloomy due to black tinted windows, and only those facing the water are anywhere near good value. The hotel's Pyin Oo Lyin Restaurant is quite good.

Chaungtha Oo Beach Hotel *(☎ 01-254708; singles/doubles US$20/30)* has large, bright blue-and-white chalet-type rooms. It is at the far end of the beach north of the village.

Similarly, **Ayay Oo Hotel** and **Golden Beach Hotel** both offer big, bright bungalows on the beach for US$20/30 per single/double.

Several good budget-level guesthouses are clustered around the village. Among the cleanest and friendliest are **Green Guest House** and **Chancellor Guest House**, both with fan and private bathroom for US$4 to US$5 per person. A good breakfast is included in the price at the Green Guest House.

Shwe Hein Si Guest House *(☎ 153; rooms per person US$4)*, in a quieter spot set back from the road, outside the main village, has very good rooms with private bathroom, and rates include a large breakfast. This place has an attractive communal balcony, and is supremely well run by the tireless Kyaw Kgi (pronounced *chaw-gee*), who is always around to help organise bus tickets and the like. He can also cook up a great seafood feast if you provide the seafood (available at the local market).

Other nearby budget places set back from the beach and worth a look include **Mariner's Lodge** *(singles/doubles US$5/10)*, with no-frills hotel-style rooms; and the strange A-frame **Happy World**, with something similar for around the same price.

Places to Eat The main street of the village is lined with seafood restaurants. Most offer good seafood mains for around K600-800. The better ones include **Pearl Restaurant, Sone See Yar Restaurant, Golden Sea Restaurant, Pathein Myanmar Rice Shop** and **May Khalar Restaurant**, all of which serve fresh lobster, clam, scallop and fish. There are also a few **teashops** along this strip, one of which opens early in the morning and serves decent *hsi htamin* (turmeric-coloured sticky rice topped with sesame seeds and shredded coconut) and other Bamar tea snacks.

Getting There & Away The rough 36km road to Chaungtha from Pathein can be traversed in two hours by private car; public minibuses and pick-ups usually take about three hours. Two buses (K300) leave the Pathein bus station daily at 7am and 11am for Chaungtha. Pick-ups are also available from a road stop near the Shwemokhtaw Paya at 1pm for half the bus fare. Buses and trucks from Chaungtha Beach to Pathein leave at the same times: 7am, 11am and 1pm from the bus station in the village. Several of the Yangon to Pathein buses continue to Chaungtha Beach. Unless you're in a hurry to get to the coast, stop in Pathein for a night before continuing on the rugged delta roads.

If you're happy to skip Pathein and make Chaungtha in one long day's road trip, Yangon's Hsimmalaik bus station has direct buses to Chaungtha (K1200, nine hours) leaving several times daily in the morning and around lunchtime. You often have to swap from bus to crowded pick-up in Pathein, and it's a bad road to Chaungtha, so it makes for a long day's travelling.

Whether by public or private vehicle, from Pathein you first cross the Pathein River by ferry; the ferry runs daily, roughly every hour from 6am to 6pm. In the reverse direction, if you get stuck waiting for a ferry back from Pathein, there are five thatched-roof restaurants where you can hang out.

Parts of the road to Chaungtha are sealed, some are unsealed. The road passes through nearly barren scrubland before crossing the U Do Chaung by bridge, and after that climbs forested hills to an elevation of around 300m. This area is said to be inhabited by elephants, monkeys and leopards; at one point you'll pass through a lush forest reserve with an upper canopy of tall dipterocarps. From there, the road descends into an area of coconut groves and rice paddies. Over half the villages passed along the way are Kayin.

Until the road was cut from Pathein, the only way to reach Chaungtha was by ferry along the U Do Chaung. From the Chaung jetty in Chaungtha, you may be able to book a passage on a boat to Mawdin Point, 12 hours south by schooner.

North of Yangon

HTAUKKYANT

ထောက်ကြံ့

On the road to Bago, beyond Yangon's airport at Mingaladon, you reach Htaukkyant, where the road to Pyay forks off to the northwest, while the Bago and Mandalay road continues on to the northeast. Shortly beyond the junction is the huge Htaukkyant War Cemetery with the graves of 27,000 Allied soldiers who died in the Burma and Assam campaigns of WWII. Maintained by the Commonwealth War Graves Commission, the cemetery is beautifully landscaped.

You can get to Htaukkyant on a No 9 bus from Yangon or aboard any Bago-bound bus from either the Highway bus station or Hsimmalaik bus station.

BAGO (PEGU)

ပဲခူး

☎ 052

Situated only about 80km from Yangon, Bago is easily reached from the capital yet is just far enough off the beaten track to avoid tourists. There are now several hotels and guesthouses where you can spend the night, and if you're on your way to Mt Kyaikto or Mawlamyaing (Moulmein), an overnight stay here will break up the journey nicely.

Bago was reputedly founded in AD 573 by two Mon princes from Thaton, who saw

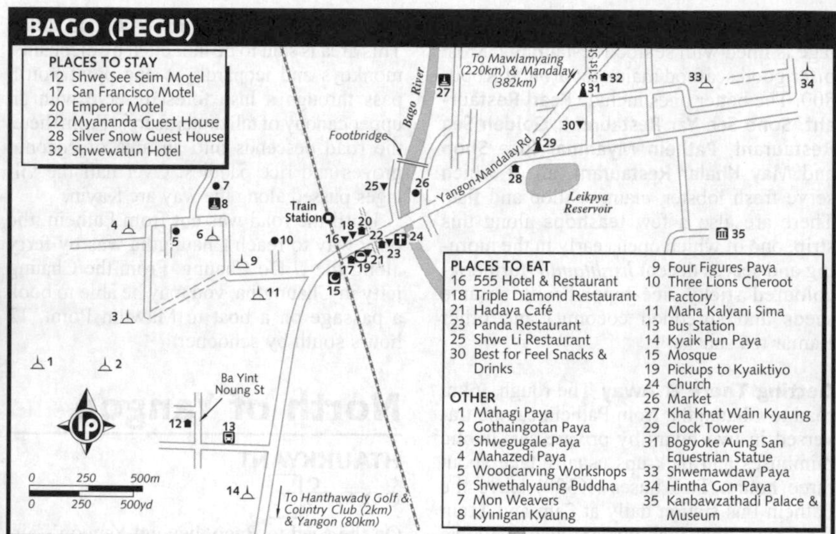

a female swan standing on the back of a male swan on an island in a huge lake. Taking this to be an auspicious omen, they founded a royal capital called Hanthawady (from the Pali-Sanskrit Hamsavati, Kingdom of the Swan) at the edge of the lake. During the later Mon dynastic periods (1287–1539), Hanthawady became the centre of the Mon kingdom of Ramanadesa, which consisted of all southern Myanmar.

The Bamar took over in 1539 when King Tabinshwehti annexed Bago to his Taungoo kingdom. The city was frequently mentioned by early European visitors – who knew it as Pegu – as an important seaport. In 1740 the Mon, after a period of submission to Taungoo, re-established Bago as their capital, but in 1757 King Alaungpaya sacked and utterly destroyed the city. King Bodawpaya, who ruled from 1782 to 1819, rebuilt it to some extent, but when the river changed its course the city was cut off from the sea and lost its importance as a seaport. It never again reached its previous grandeur.

In deference to legend, the symbol for Bago is a female *hamsa* (*hintha* or *hantha* in Burmese; a mythological bird) standing on the back of a male hamsa. At a deeper level, the symbol honours the compassion of the male hamsa in providing a place for the female to stand in the middle of a lake with only one island. Hence, the men of Bago are said to be more chivalrous than men from other Burmese areas. In popular Burmese culture, however, men joke that they dare not marry a woman from Bago for fear of being henpecked!

Kanbawzathadi Palace & Museum

ကမ္ဘောဇသာဒီ / နန်းတော်နှင့်ပြတိုက်

Recently, the original Hanthawady site surrounding a former Mon palace was excavated just south of the huge Shwemawdaw Paya. Walled in the Mon style, the square city measured 1.8km along each side and had 20 gates. The palace compound in the centre, known as Kanbawzathadi, housed King Bayinnaung from 1553 (or 1566 according to some sources) to 1599 and covered 82 hectares. About 26 hectares of this area have been excavated. Bayinnaung, the brother-in-law of a Taungoo king, moved to Bago after conquering an older Mon principality called Oktha-myo, east of the Hanthawady site.

Only the palace's brick foundations are visible today. Everything else is being built anew, as at the Mandalay Palace (see the Mandalay Fort section in the Mandalay chapter), including the king's apartment and audience hall. Among other copied marvels, the original audience hall featured a seven-level roof, two levels higher than Mandalay Palace, and was topped with solid gold tiles. The entire palace compound was originally surrounded by a teak stockade, a few stumps of which can be seen in the new museum. The government is keen to make the site into a showpiece of sorts, since King Bayinnaung ruled during an era when Burmese domains reached their farthest in Southeast Asia. The nearby Mon site of Oktha-myo, meanwhile, is all but ignored.

The small, well stocked, octagonal-shaped museum *(admission US$4; open 9am-4pm daily)* displays Mon, Siamese and Bagan-style Buddhas; clay tobacco pipes; glazed tiles and pots; 'Martaban' jars (huge water jars from the delta area); bronze weights and scales; pieces of the original teak stockade; and weaponry. There's a K50 camera fee.

Shwemawdaw Paya

ရွှေမောဓောဘုရား

Shwemawdaw Paya *(Great Golden God Paya; admission US$2)* stands northeast of the train station. You can't miss it, since its height of 114m dominates the town. The Shwemawdaw is said to be over 1000 years old and was originally built by the Mon to a height of 23m to enshrine two hairs of the Buddha. In AD 825 it was raised to 25m and then to 27m in 840. In 982 a sacred tooth was added to the collection; in 1385 another tooth was added and the stupa was rebuilt to a towering 84m. In 1492, the year Columbus sailed the Atlantic, a wind blew down the hti and a new one was raised.

King Bodawpaya, in the reconstruction of Bago after the ravages of Alaungpaya, rebuilt the stupa to 91m in 1796, but from that point it has had a rather chequered career. A new hti was added in 1882, but a major earthquake in 1912 brought it down. The stupa was repaired, but in 1917 another major quake again brought the hti down and caused serious damage. Again it was repaired, but in 1930 the biggest quake of them all completely levelled the stupa and for the next 20 years only the huge earth mound of the base remained.

Reconstruction of the Shwemawdaw commenced in 1952 and was completed in 1954, when it reached its present height. The glittering golden top of the stupa reaches 14m higher than the Shwedagon in Yangon. Shady trees around the base make it a pleasant place to stroll or simply sit and watch the Burmese. At the northeastern corner of the stupa a huge section of the hti toppled by the 1917 earthquake has been mounted into the structure of the stupa. It is a sobering reminder of the power of such geological disturbances.

Like the Shwedagon, the stupa is reached by a covered walkway lined with stalls – some with interesting collections of antique bits and pieces. Along the sides of the walkway a collection of rather faded and dusty paintings illustrates the terrible effects of the 1930 earthquake and shows the subsequent rebuilding of this mighty stupa.

The mouths of the two *chinthe* (a half-lion/half-dragon guardian beast) at the western entrance contain two Mahayana bodhisattvas, Shin Upagot (Upagupta, on the left) and Shin Thiwali (Sivali, on the right).

On the full moon of the Burmese lunar month of Tagu (March/April) the Shwemawdaw Paya festival attracts huge crowds of worshippers and merrymakers.

There's a K50 camera fee and a K200 video fee.

Hintha Gon Paya

ဟင်္သာကုန်းဘုရား

Located behind the Shwemawdaw, this shrine *(admission free)* has good views over Bago from the roofed platform on the hilltop. According to legend, this was the one point rising from the sea when the mythological bird (the hintha) landed here. A statue of the bird, looking rather like the figures on opium weights, tops the hill. The stupa was built by U Khanti, the hermit monk who was also the architect of Mandalay Hill. You can walk to it by taking the steps down the other side of the Shwemawdaw from the main entranceway.

Shwethalyaung Buddha

ရွှေသာလျောင်းဘုရား

To the west of the Yangon-Bago road, only a little over 1km on the Yangon side of the train station, the Shwethalyaung *(admission US$2)* is a huge reclining Buddha. Measuring 55m long and 16m high, it is a good 9m longer than the reclining Buddha at Wat Pho in Bangkok, but still 19m short of the Buddha in Dawei. A sign on the platform in front of the image gives the measurements of each body part; the little finger alone extends 3.05m.

The Shwethalyaung is reputed to be one of the most lifelike of all reclining Buddhas. The Burmese say the image represents Buddha in a 'relaxing' mode – instead of *parinibbana* (death) – since the eyes are wide open and the feet lie slightly splayed rather than parallel.

The sturdy iron shed that houses the image may look rough and ready, but it's spacious and airy and gives you a far better view than offered by the cramped cells of most reclining Buddhas. The walkway up to the platform is crowded with souvenir and handicraft stalls.

Originally built of brick and stucco in AD 994 by the Mon King Migadepa II, the Shwethalyaung was allowed to deteriorate and was then restored several times during its existence before the destruction of Bago in 1757. The town was so completely ravaged that the huge Buddha was totally lost and overgrown by jungle. It was not found until the 1880s British era, when an Indian contractor, digging in a large earth mound for fill to be used in the construction of the railway line, rediscovered the image. Restoration began in 1881 and the present iron and steel tazaung, a product of a Calcutta engineering company, was completed in 1903. The 1930s saw another flurry of renovative activity, as mosaic was added to the great pillow on which the Buddha's head rests, and Italian marble was laid along the platform.

Near the huge head of the image stands a **statue of Lokanat** (Lokanatha or Avalokitesvara), a Mahayana Buddhist deity borrowed by Burmese Buddhism. Behind the reclining Buddha image is a set of huge painted reliefs depicting the legend of the founding of the image. The admission is worth it.

A Japanese war cemetery, **Kyinigan Kyaung**, can be seen on the grounds of a monastery just north of Shwethalyaung. Northwest of this monastery, a settlement of Mon weavers uses handlooms to produce cotton *longyi* (sarong-style garments) and other textiles.

Maha Kalyani Sima (Maha Kalyani Thein)

မဟာကလျာဏီသိမ်

This 'Sacred Hall of Ordination' was originally constructed in 1476 by Dhammazedi, the famous alchemist king and son of Queen Shinsawpu. It stands beside the road en route from the train station to the Shwethalyaung. It was the first of 397 similar *sima* (ordination halls) he built around the country, copying plans brought back from Ceylon. De Brito, the Portuguese adventurer, burnt it down in 1599 during his period of plunder, and during the sack of Bago it was destroyed once again.

Subsequently it suffered from fires or quakes on a number of occasions before being levelled by the disastrous 1930 quake. As with the Shwemawdaw, reconstruction was completed in 1954. Next to the hall are 10 large tablets with inscriptions in Pali and Mon. The hall itself features rows of tented arches around the outside, with an impressive separate cloister and marble floors inside. Niches along the inside upper walls contain 28 standing Buddha images.

Across the road from the Maha Kalyani Sima, by the corner, is a curious monument with four Buddha figures standing back to back, in somewhat similar fashion to the four seated Buddhas at the Kyaik Pun (see later Kyaik Pun Paya entry later in this

BERNARD NAPTHINE

Ghosts keep out! Demon face in the Shwedagon Paya, Yangon

BERNARD NAPTHINE

Ten-storey Buddha, Pyay

COREY WISE

Traditional house on stilts on the Ayeyarwady (Irrawaddy) delta near Pathein

ANDERS BLOMQVIST

Sule Paya in Yangon

RICHARD I'ANSON

Downtown Yangon: Mahabandoola Rd leading to Sule Paya

RICHARD I'ANSON

Chaukhtatgyi Paya, Yangon

COREY WISE

Showing the years: colonial architecture in Yangon

BERNARD NAPTHINE

A red cow may indeed be faster: public transport in Yangon

COREY WISE

Aspiring soccer pros show their stuff in Bago.

RICHARD I'ANSON

Parasols for sale in Pathein

section) on the outskirts of town. An adjacent open hallway has a small reclining Buddha image, thronged by followers, and some macabre paintings of wrongdoers being tortured in the afterlife.

Mahazedi Paya

မဟာစေတီဘုရား

Continuing beyond the Shwethalyaung brings you to the Mahazedi (Great Stupa) Paya *(admission US$2)*. Originally constructed in AD 1560 by King Bayinnaung, it was destroyed during the 1757 sack of Bago. An attempt to rebuild it in 1860 was unsuccessful and the great earthquake of 1930 comprehensively levelled it, after which it remained a ruin. This current reconstruction was only completed in 1982. Stairways lead up the outside of the stupa, and from the top there are fine views over the surrounding area. Note the model stupa by the entrance.

The Mahazedi originally had a Buddha tooth, at one time thought to be the actual Buddha tooth of Kandy, Sri Lanka. After Bago was conquered in 1539, the tooth was later moved to Taungoo and then to Sagaing near Mandalay. Together with a begging bowl supposed to have been used by the Buddha, it remains in the Kaunghmudaw Paya, near Sagaing, to this day.

Women are not allowed to climb to the top of the stupa.

Shwegugale Paya

ရွှေဂူကလေးဘုရား

A little beyond the Mahazedi, this zedi *(admission free)* has a dark *gu* (tunnel) around the circumference of the cylindrical superstructure. The monument dates to 1494 and the reign of King Byinnya Yan. Inside are 64 seated Buddha figures. From here you can take a short cut back to the corner in the road, just before the Shwethalyaung.

Kyaik Pun Paya

ကျိုက်ပွန်ဘုရား

About 1.5km out of Bago on the Yangon road, and then a couple of hundred metres to the west of the road, stands Kyaik Pun Paya *(admission free)*. Built in 1476 by King Dhammazedi, it consists of four 30m-high sitting Buddhas placed back-to-back around a huge, square pillar. According to legend, four Mon sisters were connected with the construction of the Buddhas; it was said that if any of them should marry, one of the Buddhas would collapse. One of the four disintegrated in the 1930 earthquake, leaving only a brick outline. It has since been fully restored.

En route to the Kyaik Pun Paya, you can detour to the picturesque **Gaung-Say-Kyan Paya**, reached by crossing a wooden bridge over a small lake.

Other Attractions

North of the main town centre, near the eastern bank of the river, is one of the three largest monasteries in the country, **Kha Khat Wain Kyaung**. Watching the long line of monks and novices file out of the monastery in the early morning for their daily alms round is quite a sight.

Many Bago women work in local cheroot factories – there are around 15 large ones, many smaller ones. The **Three Lions factory** lies a little north of the road to Shwethalyaung, from the main avenue through town; the proprietors don't mind receiving visitors. Farther west, towards Mahazedi Paya, you can visit a **woodcarving workshop**.

On the highway to Yangon, south of town, is **Hanthawady Golf & Country Club** *(green fees US$15)*, a military-built 18-hole golf course, now operated by a Japanese company. A caddy is US$2, and you can rent clubs.

Places to Stay

Most budget places are on the busy main road. Rooms towards the back of these hotels will be quieter.

Emperor Hotel *(☎ 21349; singles/doubles US$6/10, with air-con US$8/16, family room US$40)* is a six-storey, modern-looking hotel. On the main avenue through town between the railway and the river, it is where buses to and from Yangon stop. Small, OK rooms have fan and private

Asian-style toilet and bath; there are also rooms with air-con and hot water, and a much larger family room is also available. Standard rooms on the eastern side of the building tend to be a bit dank and humid.

Myananda Guest House (☎ *22275; economy rooms per person US$4, triples US$12)* is a small and friendly guesthouse on the main road a few doors towards the river from the Hadaya Café (see Places to Eat later in this section), and is a good budget choice. Economy rooms have fan, shared bathroom and toilet. One triple room has air-con, fridge, TV and attached cold-water bathroom.

San Francisco Motel (☎ *22265; rooms per person from US$2; singles/doubles with private bathroom US$8/12, doubles in new wing US$10)*, farther southwest near the railway crossing, has single and double rooms both with and without shared toilet. Double rooms in the new wing (west) are cleaner and brighter looking.

Silver Snow Guest House *(economy rooms per person US$5, singles/doubles US$15/20)* is across the Bago River, near the reservoir and opposite the clock tower. It has clean economy rooms, as well as rooms with private bathroom. There is no air-con, but all rooms have fan and a mosquito net upon request.

Shwe See Seim Motel (☎ *22118; 354 Ba Yint Noung St; singles/doubles US$24/30)* is a nine-room place near the bus station which is slightly fancier. Bungalow units and regular rooms cost the same. There is a small and fairly dirty pool.

Travellers keen to avoid government-owned hotels should bypass the **Shwewatun Hotel**, out towards the Shwemawdaw Paya.

Places to Eat

555 Hotel & Restaurant is a friendly but shabby place, a few doors west of the Emperor Hotel. It is a popular eatery and not a hotel. The menu is a combination of Bamar, Chinese, Indian and European; the food is cheap and good, and the menu includes 'goat fighting balls' (goat testicles) prepared in a number of ways.

Triple Diamond Restaurant (*rice or noodle dishes K200)* is next door to 555 Hotel & Restaurant. It's popular with locals and a bit cheaper than 555.

Panda Restaurant, just west of the river, offers a good, medium-priced, standard Chinese menu.

Shwe Le Restaurant *(194 Strand St; curries K200-400)* is a clean and quiet gem half a block north of the main road, just west of the river. The menu features Shan, Indian and Malaysian curries.

Hadaya Café, opposite the Emperor Hotel, is a very popular teashop with a nice selection of pastries, ice cream and good-quality tea.

Best for Feel Snacks & Drinks *(248 31st St)* features both Western-style snacks and good Bamar curries in a quiet and comfortable setting.

In the centre of town on the small street facing the market are a number of **food stalls**, including some good Indian biryani stalls.

Getting There & Away

You can get to Bago by either rail or road; in either case the trip takes about 2½ hours. It's very easy to day trip to Bago from Yangon, but put aside the whole day. An early start is probably the best idea, as Bago can get very hot around noon.

By road, the route to Bago follows the Mandalay road to Taukkyan, about 30km from the capital, where the Pyay road branches off. From here to Bago the country is much more open and the traffic somewhat lighter.

Air A new international airport southwest of town, towards Yangon, has been talked about for several years, but at the time of writing, the plan seemed to be on semi-permanent hold.

Bus Buses (K300) from Yangon operate approximately hourly from 5am or 6am and depart from the Highway bus centre near the airport. GEC Bus Company and Taung Hta Ban Company both make the two-hour trip in relative comfort. Pick-ups (K100, front seat K200) depart from Hsimmalaik bus station, but they can often take as long as four hours as they stop and start so often. Avoid Sunday, however, when Bago is a

AROUND YANGON

very popular excursion from Yangon and the buses get very crowded. It can also be difficult to get back to Yangon because the buses will be booked out until late in the evening; you may want to catch a train back.

Inle Lake Air-con buses from Bago to Inle Lake (K2000) leave at around 1.30pm from near the Emperor Hotel. Tickets are available from the Emperor Hotel. The trip takes about 16 hours – unfortunately, this means arriving in Inle Lake at around 4.30am. It's worth noting that this bus trip can get quite chilly, and some warm clothing or a blanket is recommended.

Mandalay Most of the private bus companies running air-con express buses between Yangon and Mandalay stop in Bago. While they usually won't sell tickets for the short distance between Yangon and Bago, you can book tickets from Bago onward to Mandalay – for the full Yangon-Mandalay fare (around K3000). The Mandalay buses usually arrive in Bago by 7pm; inquire at the Bago bus station, or the travel desk in the lobby of the Emperor Hotel.

Train It is possible to visit Bago by breaking the Yangon-Mandalay train journey here. During the high season (November to February), it is wiser to do this coming down from Mandalay rather than going up from Yangon, because of the difficulties of getting a seat from Bago to Mandalay; from Bago to Yangon you could easily stand, so wait for another train or change to the bus.

From Yangon, there are about six trains a day from around 6am to 8pm (US$2/5 express train ordinary/upper class).

Another train runs between Bago, Kyaikto and Mawlamyaing three times a day. The cost between Bago and Kyaikto is US$3/6; between Bago and Mawlamyaing it's US$6/15. These are not express trains and, as usual, the buses are faster.

Taxi A more expensive but more convenient alternative is to hire a taxi from Yangon. A taxi between Yangon and Bago should cost about US$10 to US$15 each way, with a bit of bargaining – and has the additional advantage of giving you transport from place to place once you get to Bago. Inquire at any Bago hotel. Some drivers may feel that getting you to Bago and back, and to the two big attractions – the Shwemawdaw and the Shwethalyaung – is quite enough for one day. Don't accept excuses that other sites are 'too far off the road', are down tracks 'only fit for bullock carts' or are simply 'closed'. A good place to hire taxis for a Bago trip is near The Strand Hotel. Choose a driver with reasonable English-language skills.

If you hire a taxi in Bago, be sure that your driver agrees to drop you in Yangon at your hotel. Some drivers who lack the proper licence may get close to central Yangon, only to announce they risk a fine by continuing farther.

Kyaiktiyo A guide and driver to Mt Kyaikto (for the Kyaiktiyo boulder-stupa) can be hired through any of the central Bago hotels for around US$50. The same tour booked in Yangon costs US$80. See the Kyaiktiyo section in the Southeastern Myanmar chapter for more information. Pick-ups to Kyaiktiyo depart from in front of Hadaya Café. The five-hour trip costs K500. Buses to Kyaiktiyo leave throughout the day from near the Emperor Hotel, and cost around K400 one way. Buy a ticket on the bus rather than from the ticket booth next to the Emperor Hotel, which charges an inflated K700 or so.

Getting Around

Trishaw is the main form of local transport in Bago. A one-way trip in the central area should cost no more than K50. If you're going further afield – say from Shwethalyaung Paya, at one end of town, to Shwemawdaw Paya, at the other – you might as well hire a trishaw for the day, which should cost about K400.

TAUNGOO

တောင်ငူ

☎ 054

Although Taungoo (often spelt Toungoo) was once the centre of one of the most powerful post-Bagan kingdoms, virtually nothing visibly historic remains to indicate its former 15th to 16th century glory. Today it's simply a typical central Myanmar town supported by the timber trade. It's situated towards the northern end of the Bago Division, within sight of mountain ranges to both the east and west, the source of teak and other hardwoods.

Among Burmese the town is most known for its bounteous areca (betel) palms. In Myanmar, when someone receives unexpected good fortune they are likened to a betel-lover receiving a paid trip to Taungoo.

Kayin State is less than 35km east, and another 65km or so further east is Kayah State. Karen and Kayah insurgents have been known to operate within these distances, and until very recently, Taungoo was considered off-limits for foreigners. A dry-weather road continues east all the way to Loikaw, but any travel beyond the Sittoung (Sittang) River a few kilometres to the east of Taungoo still requires special permission. Such permission is nearly impossible to obtain unless you're a teak buyer or mineral engineer.

Shwesandaw Paya

ရွှေဆံတော်ဘုရား

Situated in the centre of town west of the main road, this is Taungoo's grandest pilgrimage spot. The central stupa, a standard-issue bell shape, is gilded and dates to 1597; local legend says an earlier stupa on the site was built centuries before and contains sacred hair relics. A pavilion on the western side of the stupa contains a large bronze Mandalay-style sitting Buddha, given to the paya in 1912 by a retired civil servant who donated his body weight in bronze and silver for the casting of the image. He died three years after the casting at age 72; his ashes are interred behind the image, which stands 3.6m high.

Another pavilion in the northwestern corner of the compound houses a garish reclining Buddha surrounded by devas and monastic disciples. Glass cabinets along the wall display small religious objects and Buddhas donated by the faithful; only a few are old. Among the other tazaung is one that displays sculptures of the seven Taungoo kings, a small Kuan Yin pavilion to placate the Chinese, a *nat* (spirit) shrine with images of Saraswati and her attendants, and a Shin Upagot shrine.

Myasigon Paya

မြစည်းဂုံဘုရား

Though not as well known as Shwesandaw, this is the most interesting of the three famous zedi in town. A brick *pahto* (hollow shrine or temple) beneath the stupa features glass mosaic arches, paintings of Taungoo kings and a huge, bronze-and-silver-faced sitting Buddha in royal attire. The image is surrounded by planet Buddhas (Buddhas for specific planets, corresponding to the days of the week), an arrangement usually reserved for stupas. Smaller Buddhas, some of them old, are displayed in glass cases in the same building. Opposite the large sitting image, against a couple of pillars, are two Chinese bronze goddess statues, one sitting on an elephant, the other on a Fu dog. An inscription says the figures were donated to the paya in 1901 by a German Buddhist.

A small **museum** *(admission free; open 9am-4pm daily)* on the grounds contains bronze images of Erawan (the three-headed elephant who serves as Indra's mount), a standing Buddha captured from Thailand by King Bayinnaung and two British cannons dated 1897. Other items of lesser artistic or historic import include modern sculptures of famous disciples of the Buddha, such as Moggallana and Sariputta, 100-year-old *hsun ok* (food-offering pedestals), terracotta votive tablets, old coins and stamps.

Other Attractions

In spite of the fact that seven kings reigned over Taungoo for a total of 155 years, all that's left of the secular kingdom known then as Kaytumadi are a few earthen ramparts and a moat on the western side of town. Nearby **Lay Kyaung Kandawgyi**, the town's 'royal lake', features a few small islands topped with pavilions.

Follow the road west of the lake to reach **Kawmudaw Paya**, said to be the oldest religious site in Taungoo. The central pink-and-white, bell-shaped stupa is not that impressive. A mirrored pillar marks the 'earth-conquering' spot from which Taungoo kings set off to conquer other armies. Worshippers walk clockwise around the pillar in the hope of conquering their personal problems.

Elephant Camp Over the past few years, Taungoo has become the starting point for trips to nearby **Seinyay Forest Camp**, a working elephant camp in a mountainous area of Karen villages and teakwood plantations. Visitors who reach the camp can proceed into the forest either on foot or by riding an elephant. How far you get and how much you see depends on whether you're on a day-return trip, or spending the night at a camp 'resort', or even in one of the villages.

There are two ways to do the trip: either by making your own arrangements, or by arranging a one- or two-day tour out of Taungoo. In either case, your best bet is to inquire at the Myanmar Beauty Guest House (see the following Places to Stay entry for contact details), but most guesthouses can arrange a day-return trip for US$40 per person, which includes the necessary permits, transportation there and back, a walk into the forest area and a chance to ride on an elephant. The price includes a Chinese lunch and plenty of bottled water. Tours can also be arranged in Yangon. Contact **Woodland Travel** *(☎ 01-246636)* for 'eco-tour' information; expect to pay about US$100 a day.

The breakdown for your average elephant camp tour goes something like this: taxi hire (on quite bad roads) US$35; camp entry fee US$10 per head; guide US$10; elephant US$5 per head. Yes, elephant handlers charge on average US$5 for each member of the tour group to spend time with their elephant. This fee may vary depending on whether the elephant and handler are private or government operated. It is possible to forego the taxi in place of a public pick-up, with guide. In this case, you'd be paying K500 to K1000 per head for transport, and US$10 to US$15 for a guide.

Another point to remember is that the elephants in this area work daily from 6am to around 10am, so an early start is essential if you want to see the elephants doing anything more than snoozing.

The more adventurous alternative is to hire your own jeep or pick-up with driver for about US$25 to US$30 (or kyat equivalent), obtain the necessary permits (US$20 per person total) and go. If you visit overnight, you can make arrangements to stay in one of two Karen villages (Shwe Daung or Mgwe Taung), or splurge at the **Seinyay Forest Camp** *(doubles US$35)* 'resort', which has basic double rooms; it's not fancy, but it has hot water and everything you'll need for a comfortable night's sleep. Meals are extra, at US$5, and elephant demonstrations – as opposed to genuine working elephants – are US$10 per head.

Places to Stay

Myanmar Beauty Guest House *(☎ 21270, 21527; 7/134 Bo Hmu Pho Kun St; rooms with fan/air-con US$4/6)* has hot showers. To get there from the main road through Taungoo, turn west before the Taungoo Baptist Church onto Bo Hmu Pho Kun St to reach this place (also known as Myanma A-Hla). It's one block north of the main market. This is easily the best value in town, with sparkling clean rooms with bathroom and air-con, or similar rooms with fan and shared bathroom. All rooms have mosquito netting on request, and an excellent Bamar-Western breakfast is included – complete with fresh fruit and local coffee and tea. The guesthouse is owned by two doctors (husband and wife), Dr Tin Thein and Dr Yee Yee Aye, who seem to delight in conversing with international travellers. At the front of the compound is a clinic, now run by the couple's son and daughter-in-law, Dr Chan Aye and Dr Yi Lay Mon. Dr Chan is also an energetic and knowledgeable guide.

Min Kyee Nyo Guest House *(652 Nanda Kyaw Hti St; economy rooms US$3, singles/doubles US$10/15)* is a small place off the main road with clean and comfortable standard rooms plus a couple of economy rooms with fan and shared bathroom facilities.

Travellers keen to avoid government-owned or -leased hotels should bypass the

Myanma Thiri Hotel, well off the eastern side of the main road towards the southern end of town.

Places to Eat

For tasty, Chinese-Bamar fare, try either **Happy Restaurant**, opposite the Myanmar department store, or the similar **Golden Myanmar Restaurant**, across the road. Both of these indoor-outdoor eateries are on the main road through town, near the corner of Bo Hmu Pho Kun St.

Mandalay Htamin Zain *(Mandalay Rice Shop)* has been serving Bamar food since 1914 (at its current location since 1964), and thus claims the honour of being the oldest restaurant in Myanmar. It's on a side street, off the western side of the main road, near the main market – look for two peacock reliefs over the door.

At the **night market** that convenes next to the central market, vendors specialise in chapatis and meat-stuffed *palata* (fried flatbread).

Win Sanda and **Sein Taik,** nearby Nansanda Guest House at the corner of the market, are two popular side-by-side teashops. One focuses on samosas, the other on *paug-si* (Chinese buns); they're open from 5.30am to around 9pm.

Getting There & Away

Bus If you can, avoid buses running all the way from Yangon to Mandalay, as you may have to pay the full K2500 fare even though you're hopping on/off at Taungoo.

Taungoo is considered a midway point for road trips between Yangon, Mandalay and Taunggyi. Kyaw Express and Leo Express stop at the Golden Myanmar Restaurant on the main road just after midnight. Fares to either Yangon or Mandalay should be about K1000, but in reality you may have to pay closer to K1500 to either destination, especially during the high season (November to February). The trip in either direction takes seven to eight hours. One bus, the air-con *Yangyi Aung Express*, collects passengers near the central market in Taungoo, and makes the overnight trip to Yangon for K450.

Yoma and Gandawin bus lines tend to be the best options for getting to Taungoo from Yangon – they have air-con, are comfortable and charge a very reasonable K800.

Cheaper public buses are available to Yangon and Mandalay around 6pm daily for just K250. These can be flagged down anywhere along the main road or at the central market. Count on around 10 hours to either city. See the Getting There & Away section in the Yangon chapter for bus departure times from Yangon.

Train The express train No 18 Down leaves Taungoo for Yangon around midnight, and No 16 Down leaves at about 1.30am. Both trains reach Yangon in about six hours, and the fare (upper class only) is US$18. Two other ordinary class trains leave for Yangon at 6am and 8am and reach Yangon in about seven hours. The fare is US$4 to Bago and US$6 to Yangon.

In the northerly direction, the No 17 Up to Mandalay (US$18 upper class) leaves around 2am and arrives at 10am; the No 15 Up departs at 11pm and arrives at 5am; and the No 7 Up leaves at 3am and gets to Mandalay around 11am. Step lively, as the train only stops in Taungoo for 10 minutes. Two other ordinary class trains (US$7) leave for Mandalay at 3pm and 10pm and reach Mandalay in about seven hours.

See the Getting There & Away section in the Yangon and Mandalay chapters for information on the Mandalay-bound express trains, which stop briefly in Taungoo. If you're coming from Yangon or Mandalay, express bus would be a considerably cheaper option.

Car Taungoo makes an especially good stopover if you've hired a car. If you have your own vehicle and are feeling adventurous, the 100km unpaved logging road from Oktwin (15km south of Taungoo) to Pakkaung provides a unique shortcut to Pyay. From Pakkaung the road is sealed the remaining 39km to Pyay. This is a lengthy and tiring all-day trip; start early and bring at least one spare tyre, plus food and plenty of water.

Forget about travelling east to Loikaw. Not only is the road beyond the Sittoung River in miserable condition, you may have to deal both with military checkpoints (at the river) and bandits (in the mountains).

PYAY (PROME)

ပြည်

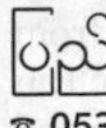

☎ 053

Seven hours north of Yangon by road or an overnight riverboat trip south of Bagan, the small town of Pyay lies on a sharp bend in the Ayeyarwady. Nearby are the ruins of the ancient Pyu capital of Thayekhittaya and, although few visitors get there, it was the centre of the most intensive archaeological work in Myanmar throughout the 20th century.

The current town site was established as a trade centre during the Bagan era, but Pyay didn't really hit its stride until the British developed the Irrawaddy Flotilla Company (IFC) in the late 1890s. Today the town serves as an important trans-shipment point for cargo moving between northern and southern Myanmar along the Ayeyarwady River, and between the Rakhaing coast and the interior along the road from Taungup to Sinte (just across the river from Pyay). Sometimes the name of the city is spelt Pyi, although the everyday pronunciation is always Pyay. The British called it Prome.

Shwesandaw Paya

ရွှေဆံတော်ဘုရား

In the centre of Pyay itself, the Shwesandaw Paya is the main point of interest. Two elevators take visitors from street level to the main stupa platform, which, like the Shwedagon in Yangon, is perched on top of a hill. Don't forget to take your shoes off before you head for the elevators.

As the name Golden Hair Relic suggests, the zedi Shwesandaw purportedly contains a couple of Buddha hairs. Just over 1m

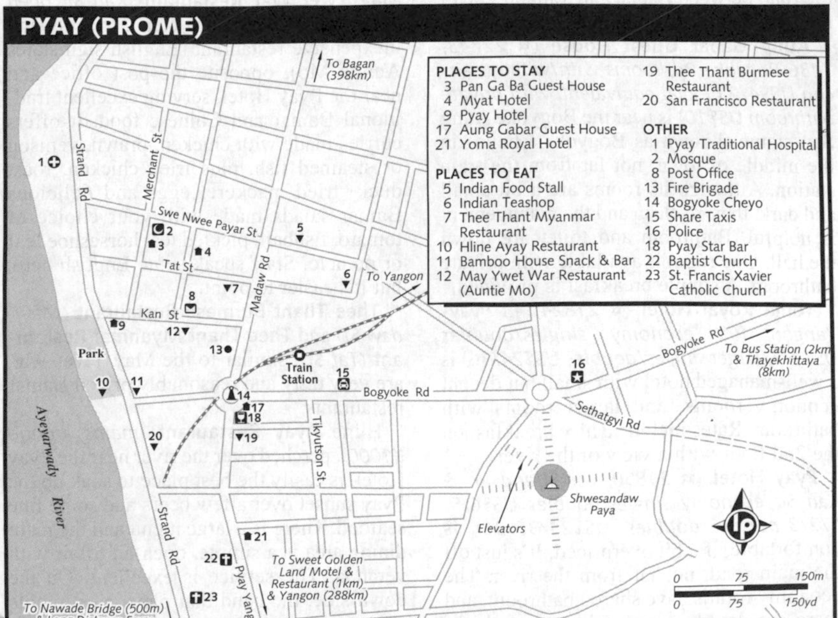

PYAY (PROME)
To Bagan (398km)
PLACES TO STAY
3 Pan Ga Ba Guest House
4 Myat Hotel
9 Pyay Hotel
17 Aung Gabar Guest House
21 Yoma Royal Hotel
PLACES TO EAT
5 Indian Food Stall
6 Indian Teashop
7 Thee Thant Myanmar Restaurant
10 Hline Ayay Restaurant
11 Bamboo House Snack & Bar
12 May Ywet War Restaurant (Auntie Mo)
19 Thee Thant Burmese Restaurant
20 San Francisco Restaurant
OTHER
1 Pyay Traditional Hospital
2 Mosque
8 Post Office
13 Fire Brigade
14 Bogyoke Cheyo
15 Share Taxis
16 Police
18 Pyay Star Bar
22 Baptist Church
23 St. Francis Xavier Catholic Church
Strand Rd
Merchant St
Swe Nwee Payar St
Tat St
Madaw Rd
To Yangon
Kan St
Park
Train Station
Bogyoke Rd
Tikyutson St
Ayeyarwady River
Sethatgyi Rd
To Bus Station (2km) & Thayekhittaya (8km)
Shwesandaw Paya
Elevators
To Sweet Golden Land Motel & Restaurant (1km) & Yangon (288km)
Pyay Yangon Rd
To Nawade Bridge (500m) & Long Distance Ferry Terminal (500m)
0 75 150m
0 75 150yd

taller than the main zedi at Shwedagon, the Shwesandaw stupa follows classic Bamar lines similar to those seen at Bagan's oldest paya, Shwezigon. Along with Kyaiktiyo, Shwemawdaw, Mahamuni (see the Mandalay chapter) and Shwedagon, this is one of the most sacred Buddhist pilgrimage spots in Myanmar.

It's also one of the country's more impressive zedi, especially on its hillside setting. Looking east from the stupa you'll see an enormous seated Buddha figure rising up from the tree line. From the Shwesandaw terrace you look across to the image eye-to-eye; it's known as **Sehtatgyi Paya** (Big Ten-Storey) for its height. Shwesandaw is at its most atmospheric at night, when the zedi is illuminated and the cityscape sparkles below.

Places to Stay

Since Pyay opened to tourists several years ago, it has become a convenient stopover on the road between Bagan and Yangon – with new places to stay continuing to open.

Aung Gabar Guest House *(☎ 22743; 1436 Bogyoke Rd; rooms with/without air-con US$4/2 or kyat equivalent, with private bathroom US$10)* is near the Bogyoke Aung San statue (known as Bogyoke Cheyo) in the middle of town, not far from the train station. Although its rooms are a bit small and dark, they're clean and the management is helpful. Bathroom and toilet are down the hall. One room is available with private bathroom. A simple breakfast is provided.

Yoma Royal Hotel *(☎ 21824; 43 Pyay-Yangon Rd; economy singles/doubles US$4/7, larger singles/doubles US$24/36)* is a well-managed hotel with small but decent economy rooms, and larger rooms with bathroom. Rates include a nice breakfast on the 2nd floor with a view of the river.

Pyay Hotel *(☎ 21890; cnr Strand Rd & Kan St; economy singles/doubles US$6/9, 1/2/3-person doubles US$24/30/36)* is comfortable, if a bit overpriced. It's just off the main road, not far from the river. The economy rooms have shared bathroom, and there are double rooms with private bathroom, fan and air-con (when the electricity is working). All rates include a bleak breakfast of eggs and toast.

Sweet Golden Land Motel & Restaurant *(☎ 22526; 12 Nawaday St; singles/doubles US$20/30)* has a turn-off just south of the town gate and, unless you have a car, it's a good 20-minute walk from the main road. You can also hire a three-wheeled taxi from town for about K50. This collection of clean and spacious bungalows is picturesque and peaceful, if a bit isolated. Rooms have private bathroom and satellite TV. Rates are possibly cheaper in the low season. The owners can also arrange boat tours of nearby weaving villages and Shwe Bone Daw Paya along the river.

Myat Hotel *(☎ 21361; singles/doubles US$6/10, with bathroom US$10/16)* is a converted bungalow with a homey feel, even though the rooms are small. The more expensive rooms have air-con.

Places to Eat

May Ywet War Restaurant *(Kan St; open 11am-around 7pm)* is a clean, friendly and inexpensive restaurant (English sign states Auntie Mo), opposite the post office and near the Pyay Hotel, serving excellent traditional Bamar and Chinese food. It offers curries made with chicken, prawn, venison or steamed fish, plus fried chicken, roast duck, fried mackerel eggs and delicious Bamar salads made with your choice of tomato, fishball, pickled tea, horseshoe leaf or pomelo. Staff speak some English here, but it's easier to point.

Thee Thant Burmese Restaurant *(Mawdaw St)* and **Thee Thant Myanmar Restaurant** *(Tat St)*, similar to the May Ywet War, are very tasty and reasonably priced Bamar restaurants.

Hline Ayay Restaurant *(mains around K1000)*, perched over the river near the Pyay Hotel, is easily the best place to soak up the Pyay sunset over a few beers and some fine seafood. There is a large menu and the main dining area is a simple, open-air affair with veranda. The service is excellent. On the down-side, the band that plays most nights tends to drown out conversation, and the toilets are a tad on the malarial side.

San Francisco Restaurant *(Strand Rd; mains from K400)*, a block south of the Pyay Hotel, on the same side of Strand Rd, offers OK Chinese fare, including one mysterious menu item called 'Chicken and Jerry in Cold'. There are outdoor and indoor tables here.

Further from the town centre, try the restaurant at **Sweet Golden Land Motel & Restaurant** for good Chinese-style food.

Indian Food Stall, about 50m off Madaw St, serves all-you-can-eat *thalis* (set meals) in a tidy, bright little dining area.

The **Indian teashop** (no name), half a block south of the Indian food stall, offers decent potato curry and stuffed palatas for breakfast. There are also a number of **teashops** located along Bogyoke Rd, east of the Bogyoke Cheyo.

If your tastes run to palm toddy, there's a **toddy bar** behind the Ministry of Forestry's 'Static Workshop', just a bit west of Payagyi, on the road to Hmawzaw. Take the narrow dirt road alongside the workshop till it ends next to a field of toddy palms. The rustic, thatched-roof bar is on the left; in addition to toddy sold by the pot or by the bottle, the bar sells prawn crackers and other snacks.

Other watering holes of note in Pyay include the long, narrow **Bamboo House Snack & Bar** *(cnr Bogyoke & Strand Rds)* near the river, and the **Pyay Star Bar** *(Strand Rd)* with its second storey overlooking the bustling junction of Bogyoke Cheyo.

Getting There & Away

Bus Pyay lies 288km northwest of Yangon via a decent, sealed two-lane road (considered the best road in the country). From Yangon there are several choices from the Highway bus station at the northern end of Yangon, starting with Rainbow Express's air-con, 45-seat bus (US$3 or kyat equivalent). Two other companies – Sun Moon Express and Rubyland Express – run good buses (US$3) between Yangon and Pyay. Departures begin at 7am and continue hourly until about 5pm. All three companies have shuttle offices opposite the Yangon train station and you can usually catch a free shuttle from this central location out to the Highway bus centre; from there it's about a six-hour trip to Pyay.

From Yangon, ask to be dropped off at the centrally located Bogyoke Cheyo, rather than the bus centre, which is 2km east of town. In fact, any help you can get in Pyay regarding buses will usually save you a lot of hassle at the bus station where information is hard to come by.

Other companies at Yangon's Highway bus station operate passenger transport to/from Pyay in the K300 to K400 range for ordinary pick-ups (seven to eight hours).

To reach Bagan/Nyaung U from Pyay, try the Ye Thu Aung Express Bus (K1500), departing at 5pm and arriving in the junction town of Kyaukpadaung between 2am and 3am. There should be several connecting buses to Bagan from here, which take about two hours to reach Bagan/Nyaung U.

From the main bus station in Mandalay you can get an overnight express bus (three a day) for K900; these take a grinding 12 to 15 hours to reach Pyay, however. If you're coming from the north it would be better to break your journey in Nyaung U, Kyaukp Padaung or Magwe. The road between Magwe and Pyay is decent, but it's still a five hour stretch.

Other bus routes to/from Pyay include: Kyaukp Padaung (K500, 10 hours, three times daily), Taungup (K650, 13 hours, once daily), Taundwingyi (K200, four hours, three daily), Magwe (K100, five hours, three daily), Meiktila (K500, 12 hours, three daily), Pathein (K400, 10 hours, once daily) and Thandwe (K600, 12 hours).

The Pyay bus station is about 2km east of Shwesandaw Paya off the road to Paukkaung.

Train A branch railway line north of Yangon terminates at Pyay. There is only one express train per day, the No 71 Up, which leaves Yangon train station at 1pm sharp and is scheduled to arrive in Pyay at 8pm, but may arrive up to two hours late. From Pyay, the No 72 Down is scheduled to depart at 10pm for a 5am Yangon arrival. This is an ordinary train with 1st, not upper, class seats available to foreigners for US$9.

Car A car and driver from Yangon to Pyay will cost less per day than hire to most other places outside the capital, since the road is decent and it's no more than a day's drive one way. Figure on paying around US$40 for an older, non air-con car and up to US$50 for a newer model with air-con.

If you're coming to Pyay by private vehicle, you may wish to break your journey in Paungde, a small town with a very trim, old colonial-style market building. It's only about 64km short of Pyay, but is well endowed as far as small Burmese towns go, as it was Ne Win's birthplace (another reason why the Yangon-Pyay road is so good).

The **Nawade Bridge** that crosses the Ayeyarwady between Pyay and Sinte opened in January 1998, and allows for easier road access to Ngapali Beach and Thandwe on the Rakhaing coast, 218km to the west over a good but hilly road. A car can be hired, but you may have to pay the return-trip price, about US$50 or kyat equivalent. This same road crosses the road south to Pathein.

Boat By private ferry, the trip between Pyay, Bagan and Mandalay should cost US$9 for ordinary deck class, or about US$27 for a 1st-class cabin for the overnight journey.

You can continue to Yangon on a government boat (US$2 lower deck, US$7 upper deck cabin), though most people find the cabins very stuffy; this stretch takes 2½ days, with overnight stops in Myaungmya and Wakema. From Yangon, you could take the ferry upriver from Kaingdan Lan jetty, but it's a slow four-day journey.

The ferry pier in Pyay is about 500m south of the San Francisco Restaurant. As the river level lowers during the dry season, the pier usually migrates downriver. You can book tickets at the Inland Water Transport (IWT) office on the opposite side of Strand Rd from the high-water pier or, for deck class only, on the boat itself.

From Pyay, other ferry trip possibilities include Pakokku and Mandalay.

Getting Around

Shared taxis are the main way to get around Pyay. There are still a few three-wheeled taxis and horse carts, either of which should cost no more than K50 per trip anywhere in town, including the bus station. You can hire a horse cart for most of the day for about K500. Most of the taxis gather in a dirt site about 200m west of the Bogyoke Cheyo.

A trishaw from downtown Pyay to the bus station should be about K100.

AROUND PYAY

Hmawza & Thayekhittaya

မှော်ဇာ / သရေခေတ္တရာ

The ancient site of Thayekhittaya – known to Pali-Sanskrit scholars as Sri Ksetra – lies 8km northeast of Pyay in the village of Hmawza, along a good road that leads to Paukkaung. Taking this road, you'll first come to the towering **Payagyi**, an early, almost cylindrical, roadside stupa about 2km from the edge of the city.

Legend says Payagyi was erected by mythical King Duttabaung in 443 BC, but most likely it dates to the early Pyu kingdom that ruled the surrounding area from the 5th to 9th centuries AD – or from the 3rd to 10th centuries according to some sources. Nearby stand a couple of lofty teak trees, safe from the woodcutter's axe since they occupy sacred ground. Payagyi is thought to mark one of four corners that delineated Thayekhittaya. Only two others are visible today: Bawbawgyi and Payama.

Very little is known about this kingdom or about the Pyu themselves. The earliest Pali inscriptions found here date to the 5th or 6th centuries and indicate the coexistence of Mahayana and Theravada Buddhism. A Chinese chronicle based on a Tang dynasty (AD 618–905) survey of the Pyu kingdom reads:

> When the Pyu king goes out in his palanquin, he lies on a couch of golden cord. For long distances he rides on an elephant. He has several hundred women to wait on him ... (The Pyu) are Buddhists and have a hundred monasteries, with bricks of glassware embellished with gold and silver ...

A few kilometres further brings you to the junction where you turn off the Bagan road towards Paukkaung. The road runs alongsid the extensive city walls of Thayekhittaya, and ahead on the left to the north of the road you can see the decaying **Payama**, similar in form to the Payagyi, to the north of the road. Surrounded by rice fields, Payama is at its most picturesque in the rainy season but well worth a look anytime. To reach it you must walk 500m or so from the highway along a trail that winds through these fields. On the grounds stands a stone plinth that once supported a *thein* (monastic ordination hall). A large brick-and-plaster pedestal near the stupa was a gift from the British to hold a large Buddha image (now in the Hmawza museum) excavated at the site. Some stucco relief still adheres to the pedestal. Two venerable banyan trees flank the stupa.

Just before crossing a stream, there's a turn-off south that leads into the village of Hmawza. This road terminates at a small train station on the Yangon-Pyay line, which was built straight through the middle of Thayekhittaya. About 1.5km from the highway turn-off (6km total from Payagyi), by the old palace site, stands a small **museum** *(admission US$4)* and a map of the area. Inside the museum is a collection of artefacts collected from Thayekhittaya excavations, including royal funerary urns; stone reliefs; a couple of bodhisattvas; a *dvarapala* (gate guardian); statues of the Hindu deities Tara Devi, Vishnu and Lakshmi; several 6th-century Buddha images; tile fragments; terracotta votive tablets; and silver coins minted in the kingdom. There are no regular hours but the museum is usually unlocked for visitors. The most-interesting stuff can be seen by just walking around the grounds.

Inquire at the museum for a guide to the outer ruins to the south, as these ruins can be hard to find. There's no charge for the service if someone's available, but a K100 tip is appreciated. At one time this area was considered dangerous due to the presence of 'insurgents' but it now appears secure. Archaeological enthusiasts could easily spend some time here investigating these rarely visited ancient sites. The village itself holds some interest as an example of a typical farming settlement where rice, vegebles and flowers are brought to market, or for shipment by train. Handmade basketry and pots are also for sale in the village.

South of the museum, outside the city walls, are the cylindrical **Bawbawgyi Paya** and cube-shaped **Bebe Paya**. Standing over 45m high, the brick-and-plaster Bawbawgyi is the oldest stupa in the area. Bebe looks like a prototype pahto for some of the temples at Bagan; some sources say it was constructed in the 9th century, but it actually may have evolved during the Bagan era. The *sikhara* (a mound-like superstructure atop the cubic base) has been partially restored. Other cube-shaped pahto in the area include one thought to have been used by a hermit, featuring eight Buddha reliefs along the lower half of the interior wall and a vaulted ceiling of brick. **East Zegu Paya** exhibits a similar vaulted brick ceiling, while **West Zegu Paya** lies in total ruins.

Leimyethna Paya is wider and squatter than the others; its doorways have been blocked off to prevent destruction by looters seeking valuable relics. The vaulted ceiling, no longer accessible for viewing, is reportedly supported by a pillar faced with original Buddha reliefs. The blocking of the doorways may be temporary until these precious reliefs can be restored and moved to a museum.

The best English-language reference available on the Thayekhittaya/Sri Ksetra monuments is an article entitled 'Excavations at Hmawzaw, Prome', which appeared in the 1911–12 annual report of the *Archaeological Survey of India*. The article contains detailed descriptions of objects and inscriptions found at each site, but almost no architectural information on the Pyu stupas.

Getting There & Away The most convenient way to reach Hmawza from Pyay is by pick-up, which should cost around K100 one way and take no more than 15 or 20 minutes.

To hire a taxi for a half-day to visit Payama, Payagyi and Hmawza, plus the ruins, expect to pay about K3000.

There are three local trains per day between Pyay and Hmawza at 7am, 10am and 5pm. The fare is K5 and the journey takes about 15 minutes. Hitching might also be

AROUND YANGON

possible as far as the turn-off to Hmawza, as the road to Paukkaung is fairly well travelled.

Shwedaung

ရွှေတောင်

This small town about 14km south of Pyay, via the road to Yangon, contains two famous paya. The more well known is **Shwemyetman Paya** (Paya of the Golden Spectacles), a reference to a large, white-faced sitting Buddha inside the main shrine. The Buddha wears a gargantuan set of eyeglasses with gold-plated rims. Coming south from Pyay, the turn-off for Shwemyetman is located on the right-hand side of the road, opposite a small whitewashed mosque bearing a 1962 imprimatur. At the roadside, there's also a small green-and-white sign in English that reads 'Shwemyethman Buddha Image – 1 furlong'.

Spectacles were first added to the image during the Konbaung era, when a local nobleman offered them to the temple in an attempt to stimulate local faith through curiosity. Word soon spread that the bespectacled Buddha had the power to cure all kinds of ills, especially afflictions linked to the eyes. The first pair of spectacles was stolen at an early stage, and a second pair was made and enshrined inside the image to protect it from thieves.

An English officer stationed in Pyay during the colonial era had a third pair fitted over the Buddha's eyes after his wife suffered from eye trouble and the abbot suggested such a donation. Naturally, as the story goes, she was cured. It requires nine monks to remove the glasses for their fortnightly cleaning. The attendant who watches over this charming paya seems to have the duty of clapping his hands loudly whenever a few birds try to alight on the huge pair of classic gold wire-rims.

The second major paya in Shwedaung, located south of the first, and several kilometres west of the road, is **Shwenattaung Paya** (Golden Spirit Mountain). As a stupa site, Shwenattaung reportedly dates back to the Thayekhittaya era, though the current 37m stupa features the post-Bagan style. Legend takes it back all the way to 283 BC, from which point it was supposedly reconstructed by a long line of Bamar kings – hardly likely since there were no Bamar in the area before the 9th century AD – with the aid of local nat. Although there is a nat shrine in the paya compound, there is little to suggest that nats play a more important role here than at any other central Burmese paya. A large paya pwe is held here each year on the full moon of Tabaung (February/March), the same time as Yangon's Shwedagon festival.

The town of Shwedaung is also famous for *hkauq sweh* (rice noodles). Several **noodle shops** along the main road through town sell them from early morning till early evening.

Getting There & Away Large and small pick-ups leave for Shwedaung frequently throughout the day, from the bus station east of Pyay, for around K50 per person for the 20-minute ride. The last pick-up back to Pyay passes the turn-off for Shwemyetman Paya around 5pm.

Mandalay

☎ 02

Mandalay was the last capital of Myanmar (Burma) before the British took over and it still has great importance as a cultural centre. Historically, it's the most Burmese of the country's large cities, a place where you'll come close to the 'heart' of Myanmar despite China-style modernisation. Mandalay still has considerable cultural and religious significance and its Buddhist monasteries are among the most important in the country – about 60% of all the monks in Myanmar reside in the Mandalay area. It's also said that Mandalay residents speak better Burmese than anyone in the country.

The city takes its name from Mandalay Hill, the 236m-high bluff that rises just to the northeast of Mandalay Fort and its royal palace. Today the population ranges somewhere between 600,000 and 800,000 people; the largest in the country after that of the capital, Yangon (Rangoon), 695km to the south. It lies in the centre of Myanmar's 'dry zone' and is a surprisingly sprawling place – you may find wandering around the city in the hot season a dry and dusty experience.

New townships are springing up along the edges of the city, many inhabited by former squatters who are being pushed out of the central area in the city's rush to modernise. The Chinese presence has become very large since the easing of foreign trade restrictions. Government truces with northern insurgents and trade with China have brought a boomtown atmosphere to Mandalay, with an assortment of new hotels, office buildings and department stores, not to mention a flourishing vice scene – especially in Kywezun and Ma Yan Chan, two districts on the river in the north-western part of the city, long considered 'black' by the authorities, due to the presence of gambling, prostitution and heroin.

Although it suffered considerable damage in the fierce fighting at the end of WWII – Mandalay Fort was completely burnt out – there is still much to be seen both in Mandalay and in the surrounding deserted cities of the old capitals.

Highlights

- Performances by pwe troupes, including the famous Moustache Brothers
- Mandalay Hill, with its spiralling stairways, temples and sweeping views
- The ancient Rakhaing Buddha image at Mahamuni Paya
- Kuthodaw Paya, the world's 'biggest book'
- Bustling markets with produce and handicrafts from northern Myanmar

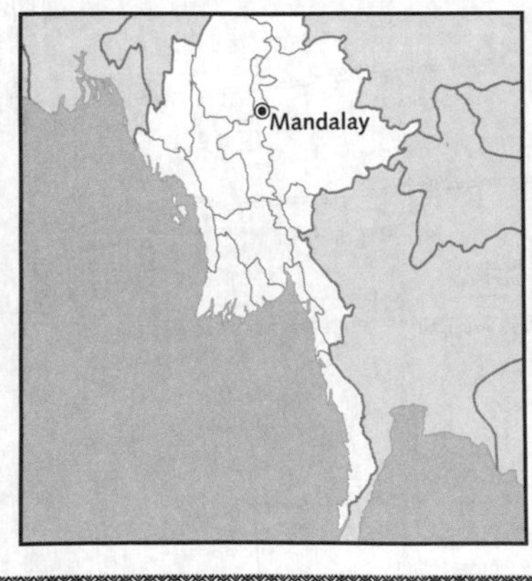

History

Despite erroneous references to the contrary, Mandalay is a comparatively young city, and its period as the capital of the last Burmese kingdom was short. Most of the monuments and buildings are therefore fairly recent, although some temples long predate the city. For centuries this area of Myanmar was the site of the capitals of the Burmese kingdoms; from Mandalay you can easily visit three former royal cities – all now deserted.

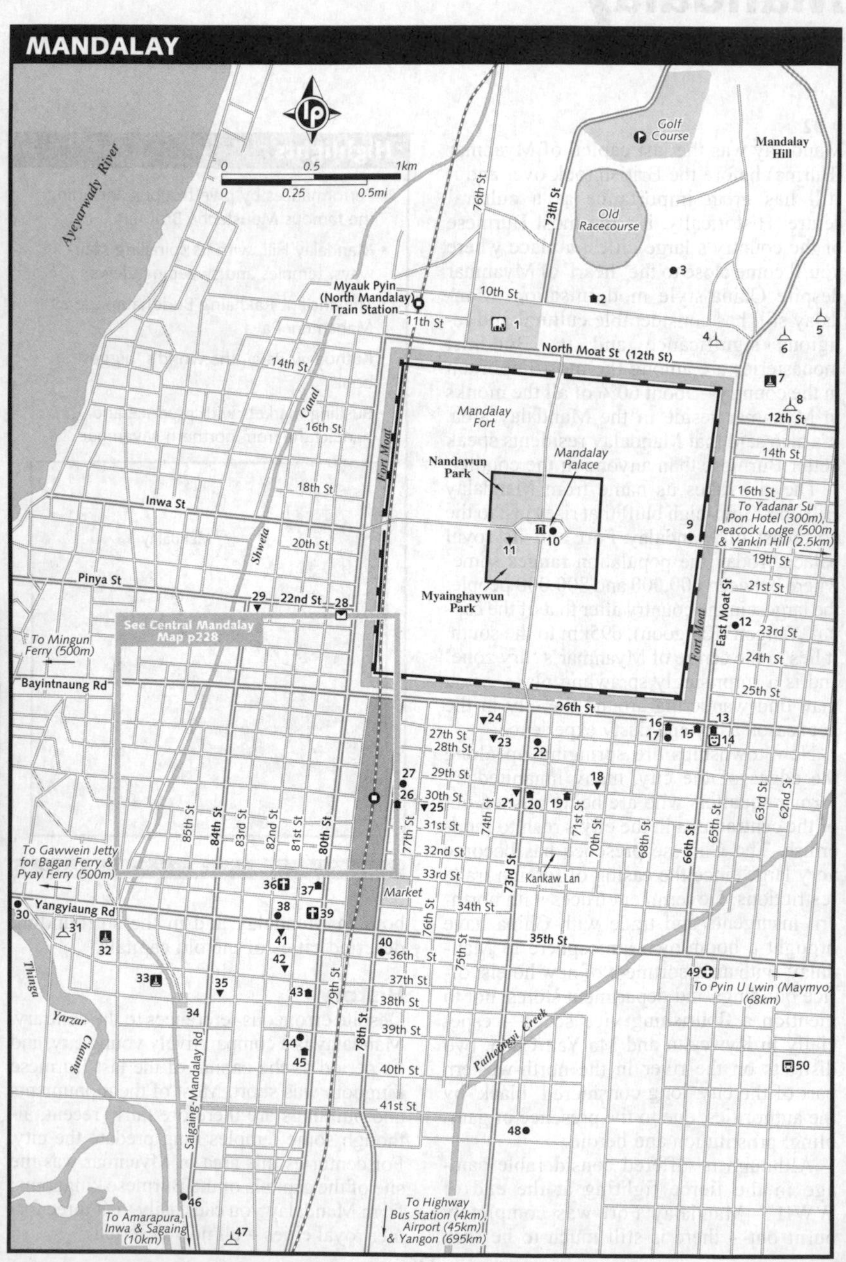
MANDALAY
Ayeyarwady River
Golf Course
Mandalay Hill
Old Racecourse
76th St
73rd St
10th St
Myauk Pyin (North Mandalay) Train Station
11th St
North Moat St (12th St)
14th St
Canal
16th St
Mandalay Fort
12th St
14th St
Nandawun Park
Mandalay Palace
18th St
Fort Moat
Inwa St
16th St
To Yadanar Su Pon Hotel (300m), Peacock Lodge (500m) & Yankin Hill (2.5km)
20th St
Shweta
19th St
Pinya St
Myainghaywun Park
22nd St
21st St
See Central Mandalay Map p228
East Moat St
23rd St
To Mingun Ferry (500m)
24th St
Bayintnaung Rd
25th St
26th St
27th St
28th St
29th St
30th St
31st St
32nd St
33rd St
34th St
35th St
36th St
37th St
38th St
39th St
40th St
41st St
85th St
84th St
83rd St
82nd St
81st St
80th St
79th St
78th St
77th St
76th St
75th St
74th St
73rd St
71st St
70th St
68th St
66th St
65th St
63rd St
62nd St
To Gawwein Jetty for Bagan Ferry & Pyay Ferry (500m)
Market
Kankaw Lan
Yangyiaung Rd
Thinga Yarzar Chaung
Saigaing-Mandalay Rd
Pathedngyi Creek
To Pyin U Lwin (Maymyo) (68km)
To Amarapura, Inwa & Sagaing (10km)
To Highway Bus Station (4km), Airport (45km) & Yangon (695km)
0 0.5 1km
0 0.25 0.5mi

MANDALAY

PLACES TO STAY
2 Novotel Mandalay
13 Mandalay View Inn
15 Sedona Hotel Mandalay
16 Mandalay Swan Hotel
19 Mandalay Royal Hotel
20 Taim Phyu (Silver Cloud) Hotel & Restaurant
26 Pacific Hotel
37 Myit Phyar Ayer Hotel
43 Tiger Hotel
45 Power Hotel

PLACES TO EAT
11 Outdoor Cafe
18 Honey Garden Restaurant
21 Pakokku Daw Lay May Restaurant
23 Too Too Restaurant
24 Marie-Min Vegetarian Restaurant; Sunflower Arts & Crafts
25 Indonesia Biryani Restaurant
29 Thai Yai Restaurant
35 Minn Thi Ha Teashop
41 Shwe Taung Food Centre
42 Aya Myit Tar Myanmar Restaurant

OTHER
1 Yadanapon Zoo
3 Military Cemetery
4 Kyauktawgyi Paya
5 Kuthodaw Paya
6 Sandamani Paya
7 Shwenandaw Kyaung
8 Atumashi Kyaung
9 Main Entrance (Foreign Tourist Entrance)
10 Nan Myint Saung (Watch-tower)
12 School of Fine Arts, Music & Drama
14 Mandalay Marionettes & Culture Show
17 MTT Information
22 Mann Swe Gon Handicrafts
27 Yangon Airways
28 Main Post Office
30 Inland Water Transport Office (IWT)
31 Shwe In Bin Kyaung
32 Thakawun Kyaung
33 Kin Wun Kyaung
34 Jade Markets
36 Judson Baptist Church
38 Myawady Travel & Tours; Honda Motorcycles
39 Father Lafon's Catholic Church
40 Goldleaf Workshops
44 Moustache Brothers Troupe
46 Stone-carrers' Workshops
47 Mahamuni Paya
48 Mandalay Arts & Sciences University
49 Drug Addicts Hospital
50 Highway Bus Station

King Mindon Min, penultimate ruler in the Konbaung dynasty, founded the city in 1857 and began construction of his new capital. The actual shift from nearby Amarapura to the new royal palace took place in 1861. In true Burmese tradition, the new palace was mainly constructed from the dismantled wooden buildings of the previous palace at Amarapura. Mandalay's period of glory was short – Mindon was succeeded by the disastrous Thibaw Min and in 1885, Mandalay was taken by the British. Thibaw and his notorious queen were exiled and 'the centre of the universe' or 'the golden city' (as it was known) became just another outpost of the British empire.

Fifteen years after independence in 1947, Mandalay slumbered, like the rest of the country, through the socialist mismanagement of Ne Win and company. With the reopening of the Burma Road through Lashio to China, however, the city is now undergoing an economic boom. The money fuelling this boom is generated by three trades, known locally as the red, green and white lines – rubies, jade and heroin – and controlled by Kachin, Wa, Shan, Kokang and Chinese syndicates.

Orientation

The hill with the huge grounds of old Mandalay Fort at its base is the natural focus of Mandalay. The city sprawls away to the south and west of the fort, bounded on the west by the busy Ayeyarwady (Irrawaddy) River.

The city streets are laid out on a grid system and numbered from north to south and east to west. Some people may make a distinction between east-west 'roads' and north-south 'streets', but in everyday practice the Burmese use these terms interchangeably, and also the word *lan*. The east-west streets run into the 40s only, while the north-south streets start in the 60s and run through to the 80s. For moving across the city quickly, 35th St serves as the main east-west thoroughfare, while 80th St is the main north-south street. The two major business thoroughfares are 26th and 84th Sts. It's also worth remembering that between 35th and 26th street, the major thoroughfares of 81st and 83rd streets are north-bound one-way streets, and 82nd street is a south-bound one-way street.

If you're thinking of making day trips to the ancient cities outside Mandalay, it's best to do Sagaing one day and save Inwa (Ava) and Amarapura for another day.

Addresses In Mandalay a street address that reads 66th (26/27) means the place is located on 66th St between 26th and 27th Sts. Some of the longer east-west streets take names once they cross the Shweta Chaung (Shweta Canal) heading west. Hence 19th St becomes Inwa St, 22nd St becomes Pinya St, 26th St changes to Bayintnaung Rd and 35th St is Yangyiaung Rd.

Information

Tourist Offices **Myanmar Travels & Tours** *(MTT; ☎ 27193; cnr 68th & 27th Sts; open 8.30am-5.30pm daily)* has an office behind the Mandalay Swan Hotel.

MTT also has a desk at the airport to meet flights, and at the train station to meet tourist trains – in order to steer you towards their favourite overpriced hotels.

The Ministry of Information's *Map of Mandalay* (K50) is useful for getting to the main tourist sites, and has a fairly extensive restaurant and hotel key.

Admission Fees Fees in historical Mandalay can add up quickly – US$3 per person for Mandalay Hill, US$5 for Kuthodaw (Biggest Book) Paya and Sandamani Paya together, US$5 for both Shwenandaw (or Shwe Dangi) and Atumashi Kyaung (Incomparable Monastery), US$2 for Mandalay Museum, US$2 for Kyauktawgyi Paya, US$5 for Mandalay Palace and US$4 for Mahamuni Paya. If you continue to the ancient cities, add US$3 to see Mingun, US$4 to visit Sagaing Hill and US$6 to visit Inwa. On the other hand, the five-minute ferry ride to Inwa is only K10.

If you visit all these sights, the fees will total US$30. The MTT office will also collect fees for the various tourist attractions around the city, but most people pay as they go.

The Ministry of Hotels & Tourism (MHT) receives a steady trickle of complaints about these relatively high entrance fees. They typically respond by either raising the fees, or creating new ones.

Guides Although most places in and around Mandalay can easily be visited on your own, if you want someone to take care of all the travel details and provide a running commentary, there are several good guides in town. The going rate for a licensed guide is around US$20 a day, not including extras like car or driver.

Some trishaw drivers act as guides for about US$5 a day. Generally, their foreign language skills aren't great and neither is their knowledge of Burmese history and architecture, but at least they know where everything is.

Trishaw drivers accustomed to transporting foreigners through town usually park near the popular guesthouses. But you don't have to worry about finding them – they'll find you. Bear in mind that the typical trishaw driver will try to steer you to at least one or two handicraft shops, where he'll earn commissions from anything you buy. Figure on paying K2000 per day for all-day trishaw sightseeing in the central part of the city, or K3000 with jaunts to Mahamuni Paya to the south, or Mandalay Hill to the north. A better idea might be to hire your trishaws one-way only, so you don't feel pressured to hurry to the next spot. A one-way ride from the clock tower to Mahamuni should cost around K300.

Post & Communications The **Central Telephone & Telegraph** *(CTT; 26th St; open 7am-5pm daily)* is near the corner of 80th St. International calls can be made here at outrageously high government rates, eg, around US$5 per minute to the USA. The international calls booth is on the right, towards the back of the building, as you enter from 26th St. Many of the top-end hotels offer an even more expensive International Direct Dial (IDD) phone service.

The **main post office** *(cnr 22nd & 81st Sts; open 9.30am-4pm Mon-Fri)* is next door to a new DHL Worldwide Express office. In typical Burmese government fashion, the staff wander off for tea at around 3pm, and by 3.30pm there's usually no-one at the windows.

Email While all upmarket, and many midrange, hotels have email services, there are precious few public email offices around

Mandalay. A public **email outlet** *(27th St; open 8.30am-8pm daily)*, one of the few, is between 80th and 81st Sts in the downtown area. The place is little more than a booth attached to the Central Hotel, a few doors along from the Dream Hotel. It costs K1500 per outgoing email message.

Mandalay Fort

မန္တလေးနန်းတွင်း

King Mindon Min ordered the construction of his imposing walled **palace compound** *(admission US$5)* in 1857. The immense walls measure 8m high and 3m thick at the bottom, tapering to 1.5m thick at the crenellated top, and are made of fired brick backed by earthen ramparts. Each of the four sides extends 2km; the surrounding moat is 70m wide and over 3m deep. A channel from the Mandalay irrigation canal fills the moat. After the British occupied the city in 1885, the compound was named Fort Dufferin and became the seat of the colony's government house and British Club.

On 20 March 1945, in fierce fighting between advancing British and Indian troops and the Japanese forces, who had held Mandalay since 1942, the royal palace within the fort caught fire and was completely burnt out. All that remains of the original palace are the huge walls and moat, the base on which the wooden palace buildings and apartments stood, and a few masonry buildings or tombs. The Burmese army has reoccupied the fort; soldiers grow their own fruit and vegetables in the middle of the base to supplement meagre wages.

There were originally three gates to the fort on each of the walls. There were also five bridges leading into the fort, four running to the main gates. Each of the gates was topped by a *pyatthat* (wooden pavilion). Smaller pyatthat stood at each corner and between the large ones – making 32 in all. Apart from some damage repaired after the war and changes made when the railway was directed through the palace grounds, the wall and its pavilions are original.

Mandalay Palace was far more than just royal living quarters – it was really a walled city within Mandalay. A massive reconstruction project and a new palace is nearly completed – all for the benefit of tourists. Some visitors like the reconstruction, while others abhor it. Instead of flammable wood, the new version sports concrete construction topped by aluminium roofs. Only the renovated moat surrounding the fort seems to have improved.

A 33m-high watchtower, **Nan Myint Saung**, reached via a spiral staircase, commands a view of the entire compound and cityscape. Nearby is the partly original '**tooth relic tower**' and the **tomb of King Mindon**. The latter was once gilded and decorated with glass mosaics, but an 1898 restoration obliterated all traces of the earlier craftsmanship. The large open sheds here contain over 600 inscribed stone slabs that were collected by King Bodawpaya (1782–1819) and were later moved to the palace from Amarapura just before WWII. Other reminders of the former glory of the old palace are the Royal Mint and the Sabbath Hall, which are also close by.

Much of the restoration of the palace and moat has been carried out using prison labour. The municipal government required all young males in the city to contribute one day's worth of forced labour per month to the project, but this practice was discontinued due to the negative publicity generated in the foreign press.

The main entrance to the palace compound is the gate on the eastern wall – and this is the only entrance that admits foreigners. Admission also entitles you to visit the still-drab palace **Cultural Museum**.

Mandalay Museum

မန္တလေးပြတိုက်

Opposite the southwestern corner of Mandalay Fort's wall, on the corner of 24th and 80th Sts, the museum *(admission US$2; open 10am-4pm Wed-Sun)* contains a collection of Mandalay regalia, royally commissioned art and palm-leaf manuscripts that were formerly housed in the palace. Most of the articles date from the reigns of the last two Mandalay kings – Mindon and Thibaw.

Mandalay Hill

မန္တလေးတောင်

An easy half-hour barefoot climb up the sheltered steps brings you to a wide view over the palace, Mandalay and the *paya* (pagoda)-studded countryside. The main entrance saves you a walk, as it's a three-storey escalator, with an elevator to bring you back down.

A US$3 fee is collected at the top of the hill. Two immense carved lions guard the southwest entrance to the hill and the south-east entrance is watched over by the *Bobokyi Nat* (Boboki spirit). If you're certain to leave the way you came, it's perfectly safe to leave your shoes with one of the attendants. If you keep them with you, it's considered respectful to keep them in a bag and out of view.

Kyauktawgyi Paya

ကျောက်တော်ကြီးဘုရား

Close to the southern entrance to Mandalay Hill stands the Kyauktawgyi Paya *(admission US$2)*, the construction of which commenced in 1853 and was completed in 1878. It was originally intended that this paya, like its namesake located a few kilometres south in Amarapura, would be modelled after the famous Ananda Pahto (temple) of Bagan, but due to a palace rebellion this grand plan was not carried through.

It is chiefly interesting for the huge seated Buddha image carved from a single block of marble. The marble block from the mines of nearby Sagyin was so colossal that it required 10,000 men labouring for 13 days to transport it from a canal to the current site. Ornamented with royal attire, the image was completed and dedicated in 1865. Around the shrine are figures of the Buddha's 80 *arahats* (enlightened disciples), arranged in groups of 20 on each of the four sides.

Mandalay's biggest festival is held here for seven days in early to mid-October to commemorate Thadingyut (see the Facts for the Visitor chapter).

Sandamani Paya

စန္ဒာမုဏိဘုရား

To the southeast of Mandalay Hill, close to the bus stop, is the Sandamani Paya *(admission US$5, includes Kuthodaw Paya)*, a cluster of slender whitewashed *stupas* (Buddhist religious monuments) built on the site of King Mindon's temporary palace – used while the new Mandalay Palace was under construction. King Mindon had come to power after the successful overthrow of King Pagan Min, an operation in which he had been assisted by his younger brother Prince Kanaung.

Mindon tended to concentrate on religious matters and leave the niceties of secular rule to his brother, but in 1866 Prince Kanaung was assassinated in an unsuccessful revolt inspired by Prince Myingun. The Sandamani Paya was built as a memorial to Prince Kanaung on the spot where he was killed.

The Sandamani Paya enshrines an iron image of the Buddha cast in 1802 by Bodawpaya and transported here from Amarapura in 1874. Around the stupa lies a large collection of marble slabs inscribed with commentaries on the Tripitaka (Buddhist canon). They were another project of the venerable U Khanti. Do not confuse them with the 729 inscribed marble slabs of the Kuthodaw Paya, which stands to the east of Sandamani Paya.

The admission fee for this paya is also valid for Kuthodaw Paya.

Kuthodaw Paya

ကုသိုလ်တော်ဘုရား

Also known as the Maha Lawka Marazein Paya *(admission US$5)*, the central stupa here was modelled after Shwezigon Paya at Nyaung U near Bagan. Building commenced in 1857, at the same time as the royal palace. The paya complex has been dubbed 'the world's biggest book', for standing around the central stupa are 729 marble slabs on which are inscribed the entire Tripitaka. Each slab is housed in its own individual small stupa. Admission here is also valid for the Sandamani Paya.

A Stroll Up Mandalay Hill

Since it's such a natural focus for the city, and the only place with a good view over the pancake-flat central plain, Mandalay Hill is where many people start their visit to Mandalay. The famous hermit monk, U Khanti, is credited with inspiring the construction of many of the buildings on and around the hill in the years after the founding of the city.

From the south, two covered stairways wind their way up the hill, meeting about half-way up. Another path ascends more steeply from the west. It's a pleasant stroll, with plenty of places to stop for a rest. Shoes must be removed as you enter the walkways. For those who don't want to make the climb, a minibus to the top can be boarded for K10 per person. For the majority of the year, it makes most sense to climb before 10am or after 4pm, to avoid the midday heat.

Close to the top of the hill, you come to a huge **standing Buddha image**, looking out towards the royal palace with an outstretched hand pointing in that direction. This image, known as the Shweyattaw, represents a rather interesting legend. The Buddha, accompanied by his disciple Ananda, was said to have climbed Mandalay Hill while on one of his visits to Myanmar. In the 2400th year of his faith, he prophesied, a great city would be founded below the hill. By our calendar that 2400th year was 1857 – the year King Mindon Min decreed the move from Amarapura to Mandalay. The statue represents the Buddha pointing to where the city would be built.

The first shrine you come to, half-way up the hill, contains the so-called **Peshawar Relics**, three bones of the Buddha. The relics were originally sent to Peshawar, now in Pakistan, by the great Indian king Asoka. The stupa into which they were built was destroyed in the 11th century, but in 1908, the curator of the Peshawar Museum discovered the actual relic casket during excavations. Although Peshawar had once been a great Buddhist centre, it had by that time been Muslim for many centuries; so the British government presented these important relics to the Burmese Buddhist Society, and this relatively neglected temple was built to house them.

From the summit, 230m above the surrounding plain, there's a fine view back over the battlements of the palace to the city of Mandalay, while to the east you can see the hazy blue outline of the Shan hills. Those interested in military history can also find, in a small building attached to one of the shrines at the top of a wide, steep flight of steps, a monument to the British regiment which retook the hill from the Japanese in fierce fighting in 1945. The Mandalay Hill monasteries were renovated and enlarged in the early 1990s to accommodate Burmese army sentries.

There's a US$3 charge for the use of video cameras. Mandalay Hill can be reached via bus No 4 or 6, or via the red Mann Sit Thi bus.

Joe Cummings

It took an editorial committee of over 200 to produce the original slabs. It has been estimated that, reading for eight hours a day, one person would take 450 days to read the complete 'book'. King Mindon convened the Fifth Buddhist Synod and used a team of 2400 monks to read the whole book in a nonstop relay lasting nearly six months! In 1900 a paper edition of the stone original was printed in 38 volumes, each with about 400 pages. A 730th slab in the corner of the inner enclosure tells of the construction of this amazing book.

Atumashi Kyaung

အတုမရှိကျောင်း

The ruins of Atumashi Kyaung *(Incomparable Monastery; admission US$5, includes Shwenandaw Kyaung)*, built by King Mindon in 1857, stand a little to the south of Kuthodaw Paya. Built at the same time as the Kuthodaw Paya, this *kyaung* (monastery) was of traditional Burmese monastic construction – a masonry base topped by a wooden building – but instead of the usual multiroofed design it consisted of

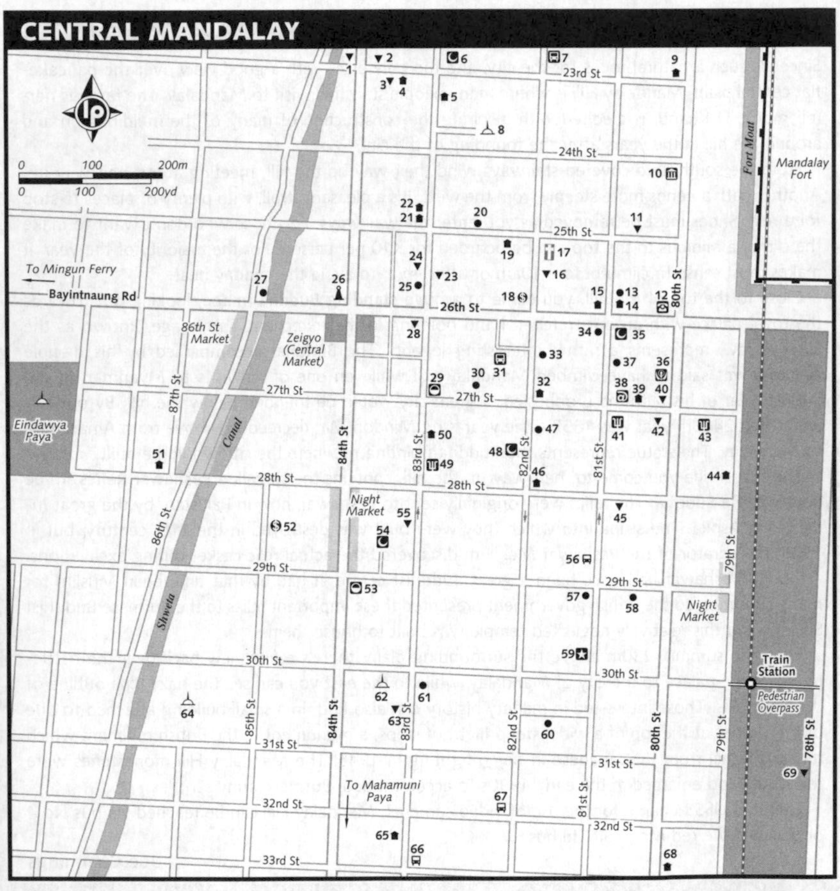

graduated rectangular terraces. By all accounts, it was one of the most magnificent temples in all Southeast Asia. Inside was a famous Buddha image, clothed in the king's silk clothing and with a huge diamond set on the forehead. The image was stolen in 1885, during the British takeover of the city.

In 1890 the monastery caught fire and, together with its contents, which included four complete sets of the Tripitaka in teak boxes, was completely gutted. Today only a huge quadrangle of colonnaded and arched walls, the main stairway and a few fine stucco reliefs survive. Although it's now only a pale shadow of its original form, the ruined building is still impressive. Inside you can see the stumps of the teak pillars that once supported the roof. Using convict labour, the government is currently renovating the site – one hopes the atmosphere won't be lost completely, as at Mandalay Fort. In the nearby Shwenandaw Kyaung you can see an early photograph of the Atumashi Kyaung taken prior to its destruction.

Admission to this paya is also valid for nearby Shwenandaw Kyaung.

CENTRAL MANDALAY

PLACES TO STAY
4 Classic Hotel
5 ET Hotel
9 Natural Inn
14 Sabai Phyu Guest House
15 Taung Za Lat Hotel
19 Royal Guest House
21 Nylon Hotel
22 Garden Hotel
32 Unity Hotel
39 Dream Hotel
44 Mother's World Hotel
46 Bonanza Hotel
50 Universe Hotel
51 AD-1 Hotel
65 Silver Swan Hotel
68 Palace Hotel

PLACES TO EAT
1 Mingalar Confectionery; Lashio Lay Pub
2 Lashio Gyi Restaurant
3 Lashio Lay Restaurant
11 Shwe Pyi Moe Teashop
16 Devi Indian Restaurant
23 Mann Restaurant
24 Nylon Ice Cream Bar
28 Min Min Restaurant
40 Punjab Food House
42 Everest Restaurant
45 Lakshmi Restaurant
55 May Myo Biryani
63 Yumana Dairy Products
69 Banana Food House

OTHER
6 Mosque
7 Buses to Taunggyi
8 Shwekyimyint Paya
10 Mandalay Museum & Library
12 Central Telephone & Telegraph Office
13 Myanma Airways Office
17 Sacred Heart Cathedral
18 Myanmar Economic Bank (MEB)
20 Bicycle Hire
25 Bicycle Hire
26 Clock Tower
27 Mann Thiri Market
29 Pick-ups to Monywa
30 Yamaha
31 Central/Main Bus Centre
33 Air Mandalay Office
34 Hong Kong Store
35 Central Mosque
36 Sikh Temple
37 Shining Star Tours
38 Email Office
41 Hindu Temple
43 Hindu Temple
47 Seven Stars Travel Agency; Penta Money Exchange
48 Am Yauk Tan Mosque
49 Hindu Temple
52 Myanmar Economic Bank (MEB) No 2
53 Pick-ups to Amarapura, Ava & Sagaing
54 Mosque
56 Bus to Hsipaw
57 Fire Lookout Tower
58 Fuji Film Development
59 Police
60 Yi Yi Color Lab
61 Kodak Express
62 Small Paya
64 Setkyathiha Paya
66 Leo Express; Kyaw Express Ticket Office
67 Shwe La Min (Golden Moon) (Bus to Inle Lake)

Shwenandaw Kyaung

ရွှေနန်းတော်ကျောင်း

Close to the Atumashi Kyaung stands the Shwenandaw Kyaung (Golden Palace Monastery). This monastery is of great interest, not only as a fine example of a traditional Burmese wooden monastery, but as a fragile reminder of the old Mandalay Fort. At one time, this building was part of the palace complex and was used as an apartment by King Mindon and his chief queen, and it was in this building that he died. After Mindon's death, King Thibaw Min had the building dismantled and reassembled on its present site in 1880 as a monastery. It is said that Thibaw used the building for meditation, and the couch on which he sat can still be seen.

The building is covered inside and out with carved panels, but unfortunately many of the exterior panels have weathered badly and some have been removed. At one time the building was gilded and decorated with glass mosaics. The carved panels inside are still in excellent condition, particularly the 10 *jataka* (past-life stories of the Buddha).

Mahamuni Paya

မဟာမုနိဘုရား

Southwest of the town, or about 1.5km northwest of Mandalay airport, stands the Mahamuni Paya *(Great Sage Pagoda; blue No 1 bus from zeigyo & Kuthodaw Paya; admission US$4)*. It is also sometimes called Payagyi (Big Paya), or the Rakhaing Paya. It was originally built by King Bodawpaya in 1784, when a road paved with bricks was constructed from his palace to the paya's eastern gate. You can still find traces of this royal highway. In 1884 the shrine was destroyed by fire; the current one is comparatively recent.

The centrepiece of the shrine is the highly venerated **Mahamuni Buddha image**, which was transported to Myanmar from Mrauk U (Myohaung) in Rakhaing (Arakan) in 1784. It was believed to be of great age even at that time – it may have been cast during the 1st century AD – and the surrounding complex was specially built for it. The 4m-high seated image is cast in bronze, but over the years thousands of devout Buddhists have completely covered the figure in a 15cm-thick layer of gold leaf. Only men are permitted to walk up to the Mahamuni image and apply gold leaf. In the rainy season it is cloaked in monastic robes.

During festivals, the image is thronged by so many worshippers that caretakers have installed video monitors in other parts of the complex so that the Burmese can pay their respects to the Mahamuni's video image; you'll actually see people bowing down before the TV screens. Each morning at 4am, a team of monks washes the Mahamuni's face and even brushes its teeth – an event well worth getting up early to see. Photography of the image is forbidden.

In the courtyard a small building houses **six bronze Khmer figures** brought back from Rakhaing along with the Mahamuni Buddha. Three are lions (the heads of which have been replaced with ones in the Burmese style), two are images of the Hindu god Shiva and one is Airavata, the three-headed elephant. Originally, these figures were enshrined at Angkor Wat in Cambodia, then were taken from Angkor by the Thais in 1431. King Bayinnaung subsequently looted them from Ayuthaya in 1564 and brought the figures to Bago (Pegu), where in 1663 they were nabbed by King Razagyi of Rakhaing. According to legend, rubbing a part of the image will cure any affliction on the corresponding part of your own body. Local legend has it that there were once many more Khmer figures here, but they were melted down by order of King Thibaw to cast cannons for the defence of the Mandalay Palace.

The temple courtyard contains more **inscription stones** collected by King Bodawpaya, who appears to have had quite a thing about this pursuit. Another small building, next to the one containing the bronze figures, has two large statues shouldering a pole between them, from which is slung a **traditional Burmese gong** said to weigh five tonnes. There are many interesting **shop stalls** at the entrance to the shrine; this was one of the few places in the country where photographs of Aung San Suu Kyi were openly sold during the long period of her house arrest.

During the Mahamuni Paya *pwe* (festival) in early February, thousands of people from nearby districts make pilgrimages to Mahamuni. The temple is always a centre of activity and during this festival it explodes with energy.

Shwekyimyint Paya

ရွှေကျီးမြင်ဘုရား

Located on 24th St between 82nd and 83rd Sts, a little northeast of *zeigyo* (the central market) or the clock tower, the original construction of this quiet paya *(admission free)* considerably predates Mandalay itself. It was founded in 1167 by Prince Minshinzaw during the Bagan period. He was the exiled son of King Alaungsithu and settled near the present site of Mandalay.

The shrine is notable because it contains the original Buddha image consecrated by the prince. It also contains many other images, made of gold, silver or crystal, that were collected by later Burmese kings and removed from Mandalay Fort after it was occupied by the British. These images are generally kept under lock and key and only shown to the general public on very important religious occasions. Here, and at the Setkyathiha Paya, you can find the ridiculous in close proximity to the sublime – glass cases with figures of the Buddha and his disciples, which parade around to noisy music when you put a coin in the slot.

Shwekyimyint is often a good place to meet Burmese people who wish to serve as unofficial tour guides to other religious sites, for nothing more than a chance to practise their tourist-English skills. Of course, a tip or small gift is always appreciated.

Setkyathiha Paya

စကြာသီဟဘုရား

A short distance southwest of zeigyo on 85th St, this stupa *(admission free)* rises from an elevated masonry platform. It was badly damaged during WWII, but was subsequently repaired. Its main point of interest is the impressive 5m-high seated Buddha image, cast in bronze by King Bagyidaw in Inwa in 1823, just before the First Anglo-Burmese War broke out.

In 1849 King Pagan Min moved the image to Amarapura, just as the second war was about to begin. When the third and final conflict was about to commence, the image was brought to Mandalay in 1884. Reclining Buddha images can be seen in the paya courtyard, along with a sacred bodhi tree planted by U Nu, a former prime minister of Myanmar.

Eindawya Paya

အိမ်တော်ရာဘုရား

The beautifully proportioned stupa at Eindawya Paya *(admission free)* stands west of zeigyo. It is covered in gold leaf and makes a fine, shimmering sight on a sunny day. The stupa was built by King Pagan Min in 1847, on the site of the palace where he lived before he ascended the throne – which at that time was still at Amarapura.

The shrine houses a Buddha image made of chalcedony – a quartz mineral with an admixture of opal – which was said to have come to Myanmar from Bodhgaya, India, in 1839. Eindawya Paya was the site of one of Myanmar's many small battles for independence. In 1919, a group of Europeans who defied the Buddhist ban on shoe-wearing within the monastery were forcibly evicted by outraged monks. Four monks were convicted by a colonial court and their alleged leader, U Kettaya, was given a life sentence.

Shwe In Bin Kyaung

ရွှေအင်ပင်ကျောင်း

This large and elegant wooden monastery *(admission free)* was commissioned in 1895 by a pair of wealthy Chinese jade merchants. The wood-carved ornamentation along the balustrades and roof cornices is of exquisite quality. You'll find it just west of Thakawun Kyaung and south of 35th St. It is seldom crowded and well worth a visit.

Churches

Mandalay has some churches among the many temples. On the western side of 80th St between 34th and 35th Sts, **Father Lafon's Catholic Church** was built by the French in 1894. Rebuilt in 1919, its gothic facade remains intact. **Sacred Heart Cathedral**, on the eastern side of 82nd St between 25th and 26th Sts, was constructed in 1873, bombed in WWII and rebuilt in 1951. Masses are held daily at both churches, twice on Sunday. The congregations are predominantly Indian and Chinese.

The **Judson Baptist Church**, named for the American missionary who has virtually become a saint in Myanmar, stands on 82nd St between 33rd and 34th Sts. A sign posted on the church claims the church fathers oppose 'liberalism, modernism, ecumenism, formalism and worldliness'.

Other Attractions

Something is always happening on the streets of Mandalay, whether bustling street markets or neighbourhood pwe. The town's centre is a short walk west from the southwestern corner of the fort. Here you will find the clock tower, and nearby, the relocated **zeigyo**. This sprawling old market, designed in 1903 by Count Caldari (the Italian first secretary of the Mandalay Municipality) was dismantled – much to the dismay of the local folk – around 1990 and moved to two new three-storey buildings done in the People's Republic of China–style on 84th St between 26th and 27th Sts. In spite of the less atmospheric location, the market still represents a fascinating collection of stalls selling every sort of Burmese ware you could imagine – and a fair assortment of smuggled goods from outside Myanmar. In the usual Asian manner, there are sections for everything from jewellery or textiles to books or hardware. When a lift and escalators were added several years ago, it proved to be quite a marvel. Nowadays however, people in power-erratic Mandalay often ignore the hitech facilities and take the stairs.

In the evening, busy **night markets** spring up around the intersections of 84th and 28th Sts, and 79th and 29th Sts. A picturesque

open-air market west of zeigyo specialises in onions, potatoes, and jaggery (the old English term for sugar produced by the sugar palm).

If you continue west along 26th St beyond the market you will eventually come to the **riverfront**, a scene of constant activity and interest; something is always happening down here. The boat landing at the end of 26th St (called Bayintnaung Rd at this point) is where foreigners must come for the riverboats heading upriver to Mingun. You can see working water buffaloes at the western end of Pinya St (22nd St), the next landing north. A short distance north of the Mingun jetty is an area where people come to do their laundry; it can be a very colourful place. This may change if the government pursues its plan to move everyone out of the riverfront districts.

Yankin Paya, perched on Yankin Hill about 2.5km to 3km east of Mandalay Fort, is a good spot for watching sunsets. If you go by rented bicycle you can park at the bottom and climb the hill on foot. Or you can take a white No 5 bus for K8 to the foot of the hill, then board one of the local pick-ups that climb the hill for K10 per person. Unlike at Mandalay Hill, there's no charge for climbing Yankin Hill.

Yadanapon Zoo *(admission K10)*, opposite the northern side of the fort moat, has a small collection of animals, but is a quiet place to wander around.

Places to Stay – Budget

Room rates at the budget end have dropped considerably, as more hotels and guesthouses obtain licences to accept foreigners. Rates now average US$4 to US$8 per person – high by Burmese standards but the lowest they've been in years. Many budget hotels also have a few larger and slightly more expensive rooms – just as several mid-range places have a few economy rooms. Discounts are often available, especially during off-peak times. These days, virtually all budget hotels offer good information on travelling out of Mandalay.

At most of these places, you can expect electricity and water pressure to be intermittent. The importance of a fan can become apparent during a low-electricity episode. Quite often, there isn't enough power for the air-conditioning units, but there is enough for lights and fans. In Mandalay, it's a good idea to ask upon check-in about the power schedule in general, and your room in particular.

Prostitution is no longer as common at most of the budget places as it was just a few years ago, although a few continue as part-time brothels.

At the moment, several hotels and guesthouses in the central district stand out in terms of quality and variety of accommodation.

Royal Guest House *(☎ 22905; 41 25th St; singles/doubles with shared toilet & cold-water shower US$3/4; with attached toilet & hot-water shower US$5/10; triples US$15)* is a very popular, well-managed, 32-room guesthouse. The rooms with shared toilet and cold-shower facilities are clean, if small; the corridors adjacent to these rooms are air-conditioned, and open transoms allow some of the cool air to reach the room, though on a hot night it's a stretch. There are also two triple rooms with bathroom, air-con and small fridge. All rates include breakfast.

Sabai Phyu Guest House *(☎ 25377; 58 81st St; singles/doubles US$4/5, bungalow singles/doubles US$6/8)* is another popular place in the same vicinity as the Royal Guest House. It's a multistorey building offering economy fan rooms with bathroom and bungalow-style rooms with bathroom and air-con. Breakfasts, which are included in the room price, are served on the rooftop, which affords views of Mandalay Hill.

Taung Za Lat Hotel *(☎ 33967; 60 81st St; singles US$8-10, doubles US$15)* is a well-run, well-placed multistorey hotel opposite the Sabai Phyu Guest House, on the corner of 81st and 26th Sts. It's been newly renovated, and although most of the renovations seem to have been external, the air-con rooms are tidy and comfortable, and come with TV and attached bathroom. Steep stairs take you up to the top floor, where a complimentary breakfast is served.

ET Hotel *(☎ 25491; 129A 83rd St; singles US$6, doubles US$8-12, family rooms US$15-20)* is a convenient hotel between 23rd and 24th Sts, with 22 very tidy, light-filled fan- and air-con rooms and another five with fan only. All rooms come with hot-water shower and a decent breakfast.

AD-1 Hotel *(☎ 34505; singles from US$3, doubles US$4-5)*, just east of Eindawya Paya, near the corner of 87th and 28th Sts, is one of Mandalay's cheapest. There are basic rooms with fan and hot water. Another dollar gets you a room with air-con. Rates include breakfast. One or two travellers have suggested that the hotel attracts tour guides who are less than honest.

Classic Hotel *(☎ 25635; 59 23rd St; singles/doubles US$8/15)*, in the Shan district between 83rd and 84th Sts, is a quiet place offering comfortable air-con rooms with TV, fridge and attached bathroom. Breakfast is included. Some rooms have hot water; others only cold water – though it doesn't seem to affect the price. The standard of rooms is very similar to that of the nearby ET Hotel, although the Classic is a little more expensive. The Lashio Lay Restaurant is next door.

Nylon Hotel *(☎ 33460; ⓔ nylon@mptmail.net.mm; cnr 25th & 83rd Sts; standard rooms per person US$4, larger singles/doubles US$8/12, suites US$20)* is an ever-popular choice a block west of the Royal Guest House. It has clean rooms with fan, air-con, minibar, TV and bathroom attached, and a few larger rooms with the same. As usual, quieter rooms are towards the back, although in this case they're quiet because they have no windows. The solid old showers in this place are particularly good – hot and high-pressured. Breakfast is included in the price, and served on the fourth floor, which has good views.

Garden Hotel *(☎ 25184; 174 83rd St; economy singles/doubles US$8/12, rooms with private bathroom US$10-20)*, next door to the Nylon, is a typical Burmese-style hotel with decent economy rooms with common bathroom, as well as rooms with private bathroom. All rooms come with air-con, TV, fridge and breakfast.

Taim Phyu (Silver Cloud) Hotel *(☎ 27059; cnr 73rd & 29th Sts; singles/doubles US$15/20)* is impressive looking and has comfortable rooms with air-con, bathroom, fridge and TV. All rates include breakfast. Around the corner, on 29th St, is the hotel's own Taim Phyu Restaurant, a good Bamar-style eatery.

Palace Hotel *(☎ 33145; 80th St; singles/doubles US$10/20)*, between 32nd and 33rd Sts, is a tall, narrow, modern hotel with some good, large rooms with views. All rooms include attached bathroom, TV and air-con. Breakfast is not included in the price.

Places to Stay – Mid-Range

Mandalay has added a number of hotels with rooms in the US$25 to US$45 per night range.

Silver Swan Hotel *(☎ 32178, fax 36567; ⓔ silverswanhotel@mptmail.net.mm; 568 83rd St; standard singles/doubles US$15/20, superior singles/doubles US$20/25)* is south of the train station between 32nd and 33rd Sts. It has clean rooms with teak floors, air-con, tub and shower, fridge and TV. A good-value hotel in this price range, it also has an email service for guests. All rates include breakfast. Some travellers have suggested that the staff at this hotel are not as friendly as they could be.

Natural Inn *(☎ 71079; ⓔ natural@mptmail.net.mm; 4 23rd St; singles/doubles US$12/18)*, in a quiet but central location between 80th and 81st Sts, a stone's throw from the palace moat, is a rather kooky-looking place with large, well-furnished air-con rooms with TV, fridge and bathtub. It's family-run, set back from the street, and offers a good breakfast with all room rates.

Myit Phyar Ayer Hotel *(☎ 27242, fax 35648; 568 80th St; singles US$25-35, doubles US$30-40)*, between 33rd and 34th Sts, has an interesting lobby decorated with marionettes and classical musical instruments. The well-managed, newish 42-room place is reasonably good value, if a little gloomy. There is a variety of rooms with teak furnishings; the larger rooms have a tub. All prices include an American breakfast.

Power Hotel *(☎ 52406; 686 80th St; singles US$18-32, doubles US$25-32)*, between 39th and 40th Sts, is fairly typical of the Chinese-style multistorey box hotels. Rooms feature air-con, fridge, TV and attached hot-water bathroom, and rates include breakfast.

Tiger Hotel *(☎ 23134; 628 80th St; singles/doubles US$12/15)*, between 37th and 38th Sts, recently replaced its old building with a stylish new one, set back from the street. The old building still stands, but is now a gem shop. The new-look Tiger is one of the cleanest, quietest and best-value establishments in town. Rooms come with TV, full-size fridge, bathtub and checker-board tiled floors. Rates include breakfast.

Mandalay View Inn *(☎ 22347; e mandalay.viewinn@mptmail.net.mm; 17B 66th St; standard singles/doubles US$25/30, superior singles/doubles US$30/35)*, east of the train station between 26th and 27th Sts, is one of the nicer and quieter places to stay outside the central district. Dwarfed by the Sedona Hotel over the road, it's a two-storey residential compound, just north of the Mandalay Marionettes' theatre. It has well-maintained, nicely decorated standard rooms as well as slightly larger superior rooms with balcony and bathtub. Rates include breakfast. All rooms come with air-conditioning, TV, phone and hot-water showers; IDD phone service is available, as is email.

Mandalay Royal Hotel *(☎ 23702; 5 71st St; singles/doubles US$10/15)*, between 29th and 30th Sts, offers comfortable rooms with air-con, TV and fridge. Most rooms have a balcony. Rates are very reasonable, and include breakfast.

Pacific Hotel *(☎ 32507; cnr 30th & 78th Sts; singles/doubles US$20/25)* is a vast eight-storey Chinese hotel opposite the train station. The clean and airy rooms all have air-con, TV, fridge and bathtub. A Chinese-style buffet breakfast is included.

Universe Hotel *(☎ 33246, fax 33245; 215 83rd St; singles/doubles US$30/36, larger singles/doubles US$36/42)* is part of a cluster of hotels west of the train station between 27th and 28th Sts. It has clean, air-con rooms with private bathroom. Breakfast is included and the hotel will pick up guests from the airport or train station. There are also slightly larger rooms with fridge. The spacious lobby has satellite TV and IDD phone service.

Dream Hotel *(☎ 26054, fax 35656; e dream@mptmail.net.mm; 152 27th St; singles/doubles US$10/20)*, between 80th and 81st Sts, presents a strong contrast between the busy outside world and a quiet interior. Run by an Indian family, the hotel offers well-appointed rooms with attached bathroom, TV, hot water, air-con and fridge. Email access is available and room rates include breakfast.

Unity Hotel *(☎ 28860; cnr 27th & 82nd Sts; standard singles/doubles US$12/15, superior singles/doubles US$25/30)* is another centrally located Chinese-style place with clean, though dark, rooms to suit a good range of budgets. Breakfast is included. The Unity's lobby is a popular hangout for travellers who need to make IDD calls, or who want to catch a bit of satellite TV (it's also, according to rumour, a popular hangout for government agents). Free airport transportation is also provided.

Bonanza Hotel *(☎ 31032; cnr 82nd & 28th Sts; singles US$7-15, doubles US$18-25)* is a Chinese-style place offering good-sized rooms with air-con, TV, fridge and private hot-water showers at reasonable rates. The lobby is up one flight of stairs.

Mother's World Hotel *(☎ 33627, fax 36599; 58 79th St; singles/doubles US$25/30)* is an imposing hotel overlooking the railway line between 27th and 28th Sts. It offers fairly large, carpeted rooms with TV, fridge, air-con, hot water and a small writing desk. The bathroom is particularly nice, although overall the rates are a little high. Breakfast is included in the price.

A few blocks east of the Mandalay Palace, in a quiet residential area, there are two thoroughly worthwhile budget-to-mid-range places to stay. Both are on 61st St, which is also known as Ye Zarni St. **Peacock Lodge** *(☎ 33411; 5 61st St; rooms with bathroom & air-con per person US$8)* is a well-run place operated by the friendly and helpful Alice. It has comfortable rooms. Breakfast is included, and is served in a garden overlooking a lily pond.

A little further north is the **Yadanar Su Pon Hotel** (*☎ 31019; 12A 61st St; singles & doubles US$10*), an exquisitely eccentric cluster of bungalow-style rooms in a dense garden setting complete with lily ponds. Even though this place is a little out of the way – and trishaw drivers don't like it because the hotel doesn't pay them commission – it's often fully booked. There's no English sign at the Yadanar Su Pon.

Places to Stay – Top End

Mandalay's recent hotel boom has produced three new top-end hotels. Like similar establishments in Yangon, occupancy is running well below expectations. The three hotels in this category are also among the only ones in Mandalay where you can reliably use a credit card (Visa or American Express).

Novotel Mandalay (*☎ 35638, 35680, fax 35639; 9 10th St; singles & doubles US$45, suites US$125-200*), at the foot of Mandalay Hill, is an impressive affair complete with a large pool and fitness centre, business centre, several shops, café, Chinese restaurant and yet another Burmese bar called Kipling's. A variety of smart rooms is available, and there are also larger suites. All room rates include full breakfast, air-con, minibar, satellite TV and airport transport.

Sedona Hotel Mandalay (*☎ 36488, fax 36499; ⓔ sales.shm@sedona.com.mm; cnr 26th & 66th Sts; standard singles & doubles US$75, Mandalay Hill–view singles/doubles with balcony US$130/140, suites US$150-300*), opposite Mandalay Palace, easily meets all the large resort hotel expectations, from pool bar and gymnasium to business centre and banquet facilities. All rates include a full Western-style breakfast, satellite TV and free airport transportation.

Travellers keen to avoid government-owned hotels should bypass the **Mandalay Swan Hotel** on 26th St.

Places to Eat

As in Yangon, the variety and quality of restaurants in Mandalay have multiplied with the recent economic development. You'll find that Bamar, Shan and Chinese restaurants are particularly good, but Indian food in Mandalay isn't quite up to Yangon's standards.

Bamar The long-running **Too Too Restaurant** (*27th St; meals K800*), between 74th and 75th Sts, serves traditional Bamar food from pots lined up on a table, in typical Burmese fashion. There's no menu, but the friendly staff will happily explain what dishes are on offer. It's a little more expensive than other restaurants of this type but the place is spotless and the food is very good – especially the soup. Keep in mind Too Too can be an early closer, often shutting up shop before 9pm.

Aya Myit Tar Myanmar Restaurant (*81st St*), between 36th and 37th Sts, serves excellent Bamar curries. The owners are friendly and the food is plentiful and cheap. Similar in quality and price is **Pakokku Daw Lay May Restaurant** (*73rd St*), opposite the Taim Phyu (Silver Cloud) Hotel, between 29th and 30th Sts. This place is well run and very popular with locals. Both places are open from 10am to around 10pm.

The upmarket, two-storey **Shwe Taung Food Centre** (*☎ 23127; 35th St; mains around K1000*) offers fine Bamar food, along with a lively performance of traditional music and dance nightly at 8pm. The show is performed upstairs, so if you'd prefer to eat un-entertained, you can dine on the ground floor. Mains here include a very good crispy duck. It's between 81st and 82nd Sts.

Along the eastern side of 80th St between 28th and 30th Sts, many **food stalls** open up at night, selling everything from *mohinga* (rice noodles and fish soup) and chicken biryani to *ayeq hpyu* (homemade liquor) and tea. Food is generally quite tasty here and you'll meet interesting people – it's less insular than most indoor restaurants in town.

Similarly, along 30th St, east of the downtown area between 68th and 66th Sts, there's a cluster of popular, late-night **restaurants** and **bars**.

Shan The best Shan restaurants are found in the vicinity of 23rd St, west of the moat.

The popular **Lashio Lay Restaurant** *(23rd St; mains around K450)*, next to the Classic Hotel between 83rd and 84th Sts, is one of Mandalay's best cheap eateries. The open-air place offers a large array of spicy and mild Shan dishes which changes on a daily basis and usually includes four or five vegetarian dishes. The food is very good and it's easy enough to point out the dishes that look most appetising.

Lashio Gyi Restaurant *(23rd St; mains K450)*, just across the street from the Lashio Lay Restaurant, is just about as good as its better-known rival. The large menu includes plenty of tasty curries, as well as many good vegetarian dishes.

Thai Yai Restaurant *(22nd St; open 6am-10pm)*, between 83rd and 84th Sts, serves both Shan and Thai dishes. Among the house specialities are Thai-style roast chicken, papaya salad, noodles and chicken rice. It's open later than most of the other Shan places. Lashio Lay and Thai Yai both serve delicious *Shan hkauq sweh* (spicy rice noodles) in the morning; this makes a nice change from teashop fare or the standard toast-and-egg breakfasts served at most guesthouses and hotels.

Indian & Vegetarian Strictly vegetarian – though not strictly Indian – **Marie-Min Vegetarian Restaurant** *(27th St; most dishes under K160; open 8am-10pm daily)*, between 74th and 75th Sts (enter via laneway), has one of the cleanest kitchens we've seen and is a godsend to many travellers. Owned and operated by an Indian Catholic family, Marie-Min serves delicious chapatis, *pappadum* (thin crackers), curries, pumpkin soup and eggplant dip, plus such delights as strawberry lassis (yogurt shakes), muesli, guacamole, hash-brown potatoes, pancakes and various Western-style breakfasts (served all day). The menu, written in 12 languages, is quite reasonably priced. This traveller-friendly oasis has an information bulletin board and also offers a breakfast box for early-morning riverboat or train trips. On Christmas Eve the devout owners arrange special candlelit dinners accompanied by live Burmese music. (Of course, like many Mandalay eateries, you may also have a candlelit dinner anytime the power suddenly goes out.)

Other traditional Indian places can be found near the Hindu and Sikh temples and the Central Mosque around the intersection of 81st and 26th Sts. A good find among these is the cosy **Punjab Food House** *(80th St; open 8.30am-7.30pm daily)*, near 27th St. This friendly, Sikh-run curry shop serves tasty chapatis, rice and vegetarian curries. In the morning they usually have *aloo puri* (fried flatbread with potato curry).

Across the street from Punjab Food House, next to the Nepali temple, is the slightly larger **Everest Restaurant** *(open 7am-7pm daily)*, with a tasty 'morning *nasta*' (sweet or savoury tapas-style dishes) of chapati with vegetables, *dosa* (crepe and vegetables) and aloo puri on occasion. Rice and vegetable curry is served for lunch and dinner.

Chan Myae South Indian Restaurant *(English sign: India Restaurant; 81st St)* is a roomy place near the corner of 28th St. The food is good, and there's lots of it for the price – and it serves beer.

Lakshmi Restaurant *(28th St)*, in the same general vicinity as the Chan Myae South Indian Restaurant between 80th and 81st Sts, isn't bad for curries and rice.

The very basic **Devi Indian Restaurant** *(82nd St)*, opposite the Arya Samaj temple between 25th and 26th Sts, does puri and dosa from 6am to 8am, rice and curries from 10am to 9pm. Though it's basically a hole-in-the-wall place, it's one of the few Indian eateries in town that serves beer (also tea and soft drinks).

Indonesia Biryani *(30th St; open 6am-10pm daily)* is nearly always busy, and serves very tasty biryani. It's between 76th and 77th Sts, two blocks east of the train station.

May Myo Biryani *(no English sign; 83rd St; open 10am-10pm daily)*, opposite the Nadi Myanmar Inn, between 28th and 29th Sts, is another reliable biryani shop.

Chinese There's quite a selection of Chinese eating places on 83rd St, between 26th and 25th Sts, not far from zeigyo.

You'll find the popular **Mann Restaurant** *(☎ 22920; 171 83rd St; mains around K350)* – one of the city's better Chinese eateries – near the Nylon Hotel. Lively and friendly, it dishes up very good, very cheap Chinese food with a Myanmar touch. The soups are tasty and enormous.

Min Min Restaurant *(83rd St)*, near Mann Restaurant between 26th and 27th Sts, has Muslim food (indicated by the number 786 throughout Myanmar) – it's reasonably cheap, the food is quite OK, but don't expect alcohol to be served.

Moving upmarket, the posh **Honey Garden Restaurant** *(☎ 24098; cnr 70th & 29th Sts; open 9am-10pm daily)* offers superb service and a long list of well-prepared Chinese dishes (and a few Bamar ones) in outdoor dining areas.

There are many small **Chinese restaurants** along 80th and 81st Sts in the central district, most open till 9pm or 10pm – late for Mandalay. Another string of basic **Chinese eateries** is along 29th St, between 83rd and 84th Sts, and along 30th St, between 70th and 76th Sts.

Teashops & Cafés Although Mandalay is absolutely jammed with teashops, two stand out from the pack:

Shwe Pyi Moe Teashop *(25th St; open 5am-8pm daily)*, between 80th and 81st Sts (look for the thick phalanx of bicycles parked out front), serves probably the best tea in town. The selection of snacks leans towards Chinese, with *ei-kya-kwe* (long, deep-fried pastries, known as *you tiao* in Chinese) a house speciality.

Minn Thi Ha Teashop *(no English sign; 38th St; open 5am-9pm daily)*, between 83rd and 84th Sts near the entertainment district, is of similar high quality to the Shwe Pyi Moe Teashop, and is also very popular.

Western Food, Snacks, Ice Cream & Beer Across the road from Mann Restaurant is the very popular **Nylon Ice Cream Bar** *(176 83rd St)*. It's a strange name (actually Nai Lon), but the ice cream and lassis are excellent and seem to be safe. You can sit out at the pavement tables and try large servings of strawberry, pineapple or even durian ice cream for about K50.

Yumana Dairy Products *(83rd St)*, between 30th and 31st Sts, also does delicious lassis and ice cream.

The upmarket **Banana Food House** *(☎ 36446; 18 78th St; mains around K700; open 10am-11pm daily)*, despite the name, is a fast-food restaurant serving mostly Italian dishes, with a few Asian specialities thrown in. If you're craving a pasta, you could definitely do worse than this place. You'll find Banana Food House near the train station, between 31st and 32nd St.

At Myainghaywun Park, inside Mandalay Fort, an informal outdoor **café** serves cheap draught beer from Mandalay Brewery.

Towards the end of the dry season Mandalay becomes a very dusty, thirsty place. All over town there are sugar-cane vendors with their big, heavy crushing wheels ready to fix you a glass of iced sugar-cane juice (with a dash of lime). It's very refreshing and appears to be fairly safe. In season there are strawberry vendors around town; take a basket (after rinsing) to one of the ice-cream bars and try strawberries and ice cream!

The large and lively **Lashio Lay Pub** on the corner of 23rd and 84th Sts has a simple, open-air rooftop drinking area and is often open late. There is no English sign, but you can hardly miss it, as it overlooks the Lashio Lay Restaurant. The building includes the little **Mingalar Confectionery** shop (also with no English sign), which has good sweets.

Entertainment

Marionette Theatre Near the Sedona Hotel, between 26th and 27th Sts, is the **Mandalay Marionettes & Culture Show** *(☎ 34446; Garden Villa Theatre, 66th St; admission K1000)*, a small theatre where marionette shows, music and dancing are performed nightly at 8.30pm. The show lasts around an hour and features selections from the *zat pwe* (recreation of Buddhist jataka tales) and *Yamazat* (tales from the Indian

A-Nyeint Pwe – From Slapstick to Satire

TONY WHEELER

Call it folk opera, call it vaudeville or even guerrilla street theatre – the *a-nyeint pwe* is one of the most fluid and adaptable, yet traditional, of contemporary Burmese entertainment forms. In a-nyeint pwe, the emphasis shifts among comedy, dancing, melodrama and instrumental music – in the typically lengthy performance there is plenty of time for all. Accessible and enjoyable even to non-Burmese-speaking visitors, a-nyeint pwe is the everyday, all-purpose Burmese entertainment genre: a religious festival, wedding, funeral, celebration, monastic ordination, fair, sporting event – almost anything – can be a good reason to host one. Once under way a performance traditionally goes on all night in rural areas (or from around 8pm till midnight in the cities), which is no strain – if the audience gets bored at some point during the performance they simply fall asleep and wake up when something more to their taste is on.

These old-time variety shows appeal to all generations, from young children to grannies. During the comedy segments in particular, it is very easy to understand what is happening – slapstick comedy hardly needs to be translated. At one pwe we saw in Yangon, a prolonged skit involved an obviously henpecked and accident-prone husband who, at every opportunity, showed his nervousness by untying, hitching up and then retying his longyi. An equivalent gesture in Western culture might be compulsively straightening a necktie or fiddling with a ballpoint pen. It soon had the audience, and us, falling around with laughter.

Pwe comedians often work subtle political commentary into their routines. U Par Par Lay, a famous comedian with a Mandalay a-nyeint pwe troupe called the Moustache Brothers, was arrested for comparing farmers' hats with his cohort on stage. The cohort said 'My hat is so large it protects my head from sun and rain all day long', to which the comedian replied, 'My hat is so large it protects all Myanmar', a reference to the star-topped hat that served as a symbol for the National League for Democracy (NLD) before Aung San Suu Kyi was arrested in 1989. Par Pay Lay spent six months in jail for that innocuous-sounding reference. He and 13 other performers were arrested again following an Independence Day performance at Aung San Suu Kyi's compound in January 1996 in which more pointed satire poked fun at the generals running the country. This time the pwe comedian was sentenced to seven years hard labour in a Myitkyina prison camp; even his family was not permitted to visit him.

After serving his seven years, Par Par Lay was released in July 2001, and the occasion was celebrated by the Moustache Brothers with a series of gala performances, attended – inevitably – by government agents with video cameras. On July 26th Par Par Lay was summoned by the regional commander and told not to perform any more at home. By the time he returned home, some Westerners had already gathered to see the evening show, so he and his family cleverly decided to perform without costumes and makeup. Thus they performed for the tourists (as well as the MI people in the audience) but explained that they were really just 'demonstrating' a performance since they couldn't do a 'real' performance without costumes and makeup. By the end of the evening even the sheepish-looking MI people put some money into the hat. Since that defiant evening they have generally been left alone by the authorities, except that they are still banned from performing outside their home.

Joe Cummings

MANDALAY

epic *Ramayana*) traditions. This includes colourful marionette dances. The puppet masters are former students of the famous master Shewi-bo U Tin, who passed away some time ago. Preceding the marionette theatre are short performances of traditional music played on the *saung gauq* (Burmese harp) and *pattala* (xylophone). Trishaw drivers often bad-mouth the show or say it's closed because the theatre owners refuse to pay commissions. Handmade marionettes are available for sale.

Folk & Classical Pwe Mandalay is the cultural heart of Myanmar, and there is an active entertainment scene, most notably dozens of **pwe troupes** that combine music, drama and improvisation to the delight of Burmese audiences. Pwe troupes often perform at important Burmese social functions including paya festivals, novitiations, weddings and monastic ceremonies.

If you'd like to delve a little deeper into the art of the Burmese pwe, pay a visit to **Moustache Brothers troupe** *(39th St)*, between 80th and 81st Sts. One of several pwe troupes headquartered in this district, brother Lu Maw and family have opened their house to visitors interested in learning more about Burmese dance, comedy, music and puppetry. The Moustache Brothers' ensemble is somewhat unusual, in that they use nothing but traditional instruments in their performances. Comedian Lu Maw speaks fair English and is very knowledgeable about the history of Burmese dance-drama and comedy (see boxed text '*A-Nyeint Pwe* – From Slapstick to Satire').

All of the pwe troupes in this area practise their craft during the months of June and July from 10am to 4pm daily. Visitors are welcome to wander from house to house and watch for free (however, donations are appreciated). During other times of year the troupes perform locally and travel intermittently to festivals and religious ceremonies.

Abbreviated examples of Burmese classical music and dance are performed at the Shwe Taung Food Centre on 35th St.

Shopping

Markets Worth a visit is **Zeigyo** *(central market; 84th St)*, which encompasses two large buildings on 84th St; one between 26th and 27th Sts, the other between 27th and 28th Sts. You can find just about anything made in Myanmar here, from everyday consumer goods to jewellery and fine fabrics. One of the largest food markets can be found on 86th St.

Several markets have sprung up in the area surrounding zeigyo, including the large open-air **Kaingdan Market** a couple of streets west of zeigyo, which specialises in fresh produce and jaggery.

A **night market** that extends southwards from the intersection of 84th and 28th Sts offers all kinds of food, audio tapes and clothing.

In Mandalay's unofficial and expanding Chinatown, there's a **daily market** that sets up along each street between 29th and 33rd Sts, running east of 80th St and west of the railway. General produce and household goods are cheaper to buy here than anywhere else in Mandalay.

Arts & Crafts Mandalay is a major crafts centre and you can get some really good bargains if you know what you're looking for. There are many little shops in the eastern part of the city near the Mandalay Swan Hotel selling a mixture of gems, carvings, silk, *kalaga* (tapestries) and other crafts. If you enter without a tout (most of the younger trishaw or horse-cart drivers are into this), you'll get better deals, as they are usually paid high commissions.

Among the better shops is **Mann Swe Gon Handicrafts** *(27th St)*, between 72nd and 73rd Sts. The proprietors maintain a particularly good selection of kalaga as well as other handicrafts.

Near Mann Swe Gon Handicrafts, **Sunflower Arts & Crafts**, adjacent to Marie-Min restaurant, has a good number of decent puppets, lacquerware and kalaga at moderate prices.

Sein Myint Artist *(☎ 26553; 42 Sanga University St, Nan Shei)* makes excellent kalaga. You're also free to wander the indoor-outdoor workshop which is adorned with antique looms, as well as a small gallery of very fine antique paintings and carvings, which are not for sale.

Try the eastern entrance of Mahamuni Paya for religious crafts. **Thein Hteik Shin Myanmar Handicrafts** is a reliable shop with reasonable prices.

Handicrafts are also available at a few vendor stalls in zeigyo. Keep in mind that some of the items sold at these shops – older kalaga, *parabaik* (folding manuscripts), *kammawa* (lacquered scriptures), gems, jade and any authentic antiques – aren't legally supposed to be taken out of the country.

If you have a dilapidated stupa in need of refurbishing, then head for the western exit of the Mahamuni – here you will find workshops manufacturing all sorts of **temple paraphernalia**. If the *hti* (umbrella-like decorated top of stupa) has toppled then this is the place to come for a new one.

Mandalay's **gold-leaf makers** are concentrated in the southeast of the city, near the intersection of 36th and 78th Sts. Sheets of gold are beaten into gossamer-thin pieces which are cut into squares and sold in packets to devotees to use for gilding images or even complete stupas. The typical gold-leaf square measures just .000127cm, thinner than ink on the printed page. Gilding a Buddha image or a stupa with gold leaf brings great merit to the gilder, so there is a steady growth of gold leaf on many images in Myanmar. Gold-leaf stickers cost a few kyat. Other crafts you may see around Mandalay include silk weaving and silversmithing.

Precious Stones & Sculpture Kyawzu and Minthazu, two villages attached to the urban sprawl of southern Mandalay, specialise in the cutting, polishing and carving of jade. Just north of the villages, outdoor **jade markets** meet daily in several spots along 86th St. The best-quality jade is generally purveyed during the late morning (from 10am to 1pm) at the intersection of 38th and 86th Sts, where you'll see throngs of Burmese standing and squatting on the roadside or sitting in teashops, poring over red, white and green chunks laid out on empty rice sacks. Both rough and polished pieces, some carved, can be purchased here. None of the trade, of course, is 'government approved'. While most of the jade seen here is genuine, not all is of high quality. Beware of vendors selling jade 'boulders' smuggled in from Kachin State. Some are fakes with thin sheets of jade peering through the brown outer 'skin'; the inside may contain cement or worthless stone.

A street close to Mahamuni Paya has a whole series of **stone-carvers' workshops**. Buddha images of all sizes are hewn from solid stone slabs. The best stone and marble cutters are on the corner of 45th and 84th Sts.

Bronze foundries and **woodcarving workshops** are clustered off Aung San St in the Tampawadi Quarter, south of Mahamuni. Bells and gongs are hand-beaten at **workshops** near the Myohaung train station (take bus No 7).

Photographic Supplies There are several photographic film and development outlets in Mandalay. These include **Kodak Express** *(83rd St)*, near the corner of 30th St; **Fuji Film Development** *(29th St)*; and **Yi Yi Color Lab**, down a side street between 81st and 82nd Sts and 30th and 31st Sts.

Getting There & Away

For information on travel between Mandalay and Bagan or Mandalay and Taunggyi, see the Bagan or Inle Lake sections in the relevant chapters.

From Yangon you can fly, bus or rail upcountry. Mandalay is the starting point for travel to most of northern Myanmar – by riverboat, bus, train or air.

Air As elsewhere in much of the country, there are now two alternatives to flying on the government's risky Myanma Airways (MA). Both Air Mandalay (AM) and Yangon Airways (YA) have daily flights between Mandalay from Yangon; between Mandalay and Bagan (Nyaung U); and between Mandalay and Heho.

The **AM office** *(☎ 27439; 82nd St)* is between 26th and 27th Sts; the **YA office** *(☎ 36012; 78th St)* is between 29th and 30th

Sts; and the **MA office** *(☎ 22590; 81st St)* is between 25th and 26th Sts.

The Yangon-Mandalay fare averages US$140 each way for all three airlines. The only significant difference between AM and YA seems to be that the latter allows Burmese citizens to pay in kyat.

The new Mandalay international airport is a staggering 40km from Mandalay, with a taxi from the airport to the city centre costing around K4000. Allow a good hour each way.

As elsewhere in Myanmar, tickets are cheaper purchased from an agent. Even the airlines will usually send you to a nearby agent to purchase your ticket. In the city centre, try **Seven Stars Travel Agency** *(☎ 28909; 269 82nd St)* between 27th and 28th Sts, or nearby **Shining Star Tours** *(☎ 36335; 279 81st St)* between 26th and 27th Sts. The government's **MTT office** *(☎ 27193)* is in the lobby of the Mandalay Swan Hotel.

Bus Kipling never actually took the 'road to Mandalay', but you can. Private air-con buses from Yangon's Highway bus station cost around K2500. Both **Leo Express** *(☎ 31885)* and **Kyaw Express** *(☎ 27611)* depart for Yangon at 5pm from the corner of 83rd and 33rd Sts. Shuttle vans take you out to the Highway bus station. Another good long-distance bus company, **Aung Kyaw Moe** *(AKM; ☎ 38346)*, operates from the Highway bus station, with similar prices and departure times. The Mandalay-Yangon fare is K2500. For most other destinations outside Mandalay, the usual mode of transport is Japanese pick-up truck or minibus.

For fares, departure times and trip durations, see the Getting There & Away section in the Yangon chapter.

Bagan Minibuses to Bagan (K1200, seven hours) leave thrice daily from the **Highway bus station** *(☎ 21807)*. Buy tickets at least a day in advance from Nyaung U Mann Bus Co, inside the second building under the circular stairway, or from New Bagan Express in the same area.

Inle Lake Shwe La Min (Golden Moon) buses depart from the corner of 82nd and 32nd Sts several times daily for Inle Lake (K2000).

Taunggyi Buses bound for Taunggyi leave from the Highway bus station. Golden minibuses (25 seats; K1000) depart at 5.30am. Slightly larger and more expensive, both **Tiger Head** *(Kya Khaung; ☎ 28814)* and **Lion King** *(Chinthay Min; ☎ 21280)* express buses depart for Taunggyi at 5am (K1500). All three companies also do central district pick-ups near the northeastern corner of 82nd and 23rd Sts.

Pyin U Lwin, Hsipaw, Lashio Pick-ups and buses leave for Pyin U Lwin, Hsipaw and Lashio from the Central bus station (also called Main bus station) in a bustling lot near the corner of 26th and 82nd Sts in the city centre. Pick-ups to Pyin U Lwin cost about K300, or K500 for a minibus. Buses to Hsipaw cost K700; to Lashio K800.

With most pick-ups, if you want to ride at the front of the cab, figure on paying at least 50% more of the regular fare.

For departures to the following towns, inquire at the Highway bus station: Monywa (K500, 3½ hours), Nyaungshwe (Yaunghwe, near Inle Lake; K1500, eight hours), Kyaukpadaung (K800, five hours), Shwebo (K300, three hours), Pyinmana (K700, six hours), Taungoo (K1500, 11 hours) and Bago (K2000, 14 hours).

Pick-ups and minibuses to Meiktila (K400, four hours) leave from both the Highway bus station and the Central/Main bus station, on the corner of 82nd and 26th Sts.

Train The old British-designed Mandalay train station has been replaced with a seven-storey complex, including two floors devoted to a hotel, which was still under construction at the time of writing.

The tourist information office is on the right hand side, ground floor, as you enter from 78th St. It usually closes around 3pm.

Although there are a number of trains each day between Yangon and Mandalay, you should only consider the day or night expresses, as the other trains represent everything that can be wrong with Burmese rail travel – slow, crowded and uncomfortable. It's also possible to reserve a seat on the express services, and on these special 'impress the tourists services' you really do get a seat. Upper class even has reclining seats and is quite comfortable. Sleepers are available but hard to reserve.

Trains leave from both ends at the same time and in theory should arrive at the same time, but are frequently a few hours late. However, your chances of boarding an on-time train are better if you take one of the 'special express' trains between Mandalay and Yangon, which depart at 5.30pm and are scheduled to arrive at 7am the next morning. The cost is US$38 per person, one way. Get an excellent chicken biryani wrapped in a banana leaf at one of the stations on the way or, if you take the night train, on the platform. Meals in the often packed dining car aren't bad; Myanmar Beer is available.

Upon arrival in Mandalay you may be given a ticket for 'free transport' to your hotel, endorsed by Myanma Railways. Although this does entitle you to a free ride to the hotel or guesthouse of your choice, it means Myanma Railways takes a small commission from the place you stay. As with any kind of tout/commission system, this means they may try to steer you away from places that don't pay commissions.

Myanma Railways also operates daily trains from Mandalay to Hsipaw (1st class US$6), Lashio, Monywa, Myitkyina and Pyin U Lwin; see the Getting There & Away sections in the appropriate chapters for details.

The Dagon Mann (private express train) ticket booking office is on the first floor of the train station. There's no English sign, but if you count six ticket windows along from the left (facing the ticket windows), you should be in the right queue.

For schedule and fare information for trains to and from Yangon, see the Getting Around chapter earlier in this book.

Car & Taxi Cars (with licensed driver) can be rented through a number of sources, including most hotels and guesthouses. Expect to pay about US$25 to US$35 a day for trips outside Mandalay. Prices will vary according the number of passengers and the price of petrol. As always, check out the vehicle before you sign an agreement. Your hotel or guesthouse should be of help. Drivers can usually be found at the Nylon Hotel, the Royal Guest House and the Mandalay Royal Hotel, among others. Kyaw Shwe, a driver who can be contacted through the Nylon Hotel, is highly recommended for his safe driving, reliability and flexibility.

The MTT office quotes the following rates for saloon car taxis, but you can usually beat these prices by about 20% with a privately owned taxi:

destination	cost (US$)
Mandalay city tour	$25–30
Mandalay, Amarapura & Sagaing	$30–35
Mandalay–Pyin U Lwin	$35–40
Mandalay-Bagan (one-way)	$75–80
Mandalay-Taunggyi (one-way)	$80–85

Motorcycle Although motorcycle rental hasn't really caught on yet in Mandalay, you may be able to rent a motorcycle at **Honda Motorcycles** (*☎ 22620; Bldg 5, Room 2, 35th St*), between 81st and 82nd Sts, or **Yamaha** (*☎ 24243; 216 27th St*) between 82nd and 83rd Sts.

Boat The **Inland Water Transport office** (*IWT; ☎ 86035; open 10am-2pm daily*) is located near the Gawwein jetty, at the western end of Yangyiaung Rd (35th St). It sells tickets to Bagan, Pyay and Bhamo. The office doesn't sell tickets to Bagan on Tuesday or Saturday. Boat tickets can also be purchased from the MTT office behind the Mandalay Swan Hotel, but you'll have to pay an additional US$2.

Mandalay-Bagan Ferry There is now a private ferry service from Mandalay to Bagan, in addition to the old government ferry. The private ferry *Shwe Kein Nayi* (Mandalay-Bagan Express) is faster, making the trip in about eight or nine hours, for US$16 to US$19 (depending on commissions taken by your hotel, tout etc). Departures are every Monday, Tuesday, Thursday, Friday and Saturday at 6am. Food is available on board but it's pricey. Most hotels and guesthouses can arrange tickets for you, or you can buy tickets (at least one day before is recommended) at the jetty at the end of 35th St.

MTT's government boat departs twice weekly, on Wednesday and Sunday at 5.30am, at a cost of US$11 deck class or US$33 for a stuffy cabin. MTT also sells ferry tickets, but adds an extra US$2 for the service. These boats usually take about 14 hours, although they can take up to 17 hours.

For more information on ferries to Bagan, Bhamo or Pyay, see the appropriate Getting There & Away sections in the relevant chapters.

Getting Around

Bus Mandalay's buses are virtually always crowded, particularly during the 7am to 9am and 4pm to 5pm rush hours. The atmosphere on the buses is also surprisingly friendly – so if that's more important to you than smooth comfort, you'll probably quite enjoy bussing around Mandalay. Some of the useful services include:

From Mahamuni Paya to zeigyo and Kuthodaw Paya – blue bus No 1 (၁)
To Gawwein jetty, train station and airport – blue bus No 2 (၂)
To Mandalay Hill from the clock tower and zeigyo – bus No 4 (၄)
Between Yankin Hill, zeigyo and the boat jetty to Mingun – white bus No 5 (၅)
To the other side of Mandalay Hill, to the Institute of Indigenous Medicine – bus No 7 (၇)
Via Setkyathiha Paya, Mahamuni Paya and Amarapura to Inwa; starts from the corner of 27th and 84th Sts – red or black bus No 8 (၈)
To U Bein's Bridge – yellow bus No 8 (၈)
Mandalay Hill to south of the city and airport – red bus No 12 (၁၂)
Mahamuni Paya to Mandalay Hill through Mandalay Fort – red-and-yellow Mann Sit Thi bus

Pick-up Pick-ups to Amarapura, Inwa and Sagaing leave throughout the day from zeigyo at 26th and 84th Sts for around K50 each. You can also hop on at any point along the way.

Taxi There are now many taxis in Mandalay, and fares average about K300 for trips within the central district. Around zeigyo you'll find a few three-wheelers and more four-wheelers – tiny pick-ups that hold four passengers. They operate within the city for around K200 per trip. The level of English among most drivers is virtually nil; our experience is that it's easier for non-Burmese speakers to take a little time to make sense of the city bus system than it is to try and work out your destination with a taxi driver. It helps if you have the address of your destination written in Burmese.

There is usually a group of taxis waiting at the airport; these should cost around K4000 for the hour-long trip into town.

Car Cars (with licensed driver) can be rented through a number of sources, including most hotels and guesthouses. Expect to pay around US$10 to US$15 for a half day in Mandalay and about US$20 for the whole day. MTT also arranges car hire, but as usual it's more expensive. To visit nearby Amarapura and Sagaing, or Pyin U Lwin (Maymyo) expect to pay US$20 to US$25 for the day.

It's also possible to hire pick-ups by the day for tours around Mandalay. Count on around K5000 for a day trip to Amarapura and Sagaing that includes an English-speaking guide; the trucks take up to eight people, so it needn't be expensive.

Trishaw The familiar back-to-back trishaws are the usual round-the-town transport. Count on K100 for a short ride in a trishaw, K300 for a longer one – say, from Mandalay Hill to zeigyo. Figure on at least K800 per day per trishaw for all-day sightseeing in the central part of the city. You must bargain for your fare, whether by the trip, by the hour or by the day. In the evening, expect to pay a bit more.

Trishaws can easily be flagged down just about anywhere. Many drivers tend to hang out near the popular guesthouses, like the Royal Guest House or the Nylon Hotel. Some of the trishaw drivers in these areas speak English or French. However, unless you know the driver, it is best not to shop in a trishaw, as drivers often have 50% deals with shop owners. Shops that refuse to go along with this may still be hassled by the driver later on, or the driver might tell you that a particular shop is now closed.

Bicycle There are several places in the city centre to rent bicycles, including diagonally opposite the Royal Guest House on 25th St and opposite the Mann Restaurant on 83rd St. Further east, the Mandalay Marionettes & Culture Show theatre, on 66th St, rents out bikes as well. All three places charge K500 per day.

Walking The city of Mandalay is a surprisingly sprawling place. Think three times before setting out on a little stroll around the fort walls or out to Mandalay Hill. The central district area, however, is easily traversed on foot.

Around Mandalay

The area around Mandalay has a number of attractions well worth visiting. The four ancient cities (Amarapura, Inwa/Ava, Sagaing and Mingun) are all within easy day-tripping distance, as is the atmospheric old 'hill station' of Pyin U Lwin (Maymyo). To the northwest, bustling Monywa is not as historic, but it is one of Myanmar's most typically Burmese cities.

Highlights

- Day trips to the 'deserted' royal capitals of Inwa (Ava), Amarapura and Sagaing
- Rickety and picturesque U Bein's Bridge at Amarapura
- Ferry rides along the Ayeyarwady River to the massive Mingun Paya
- The scenic colonial hill station of Pyin U Lwin (Maymyo)
- Bustling Monywa and nearby Thanboddhay Paya

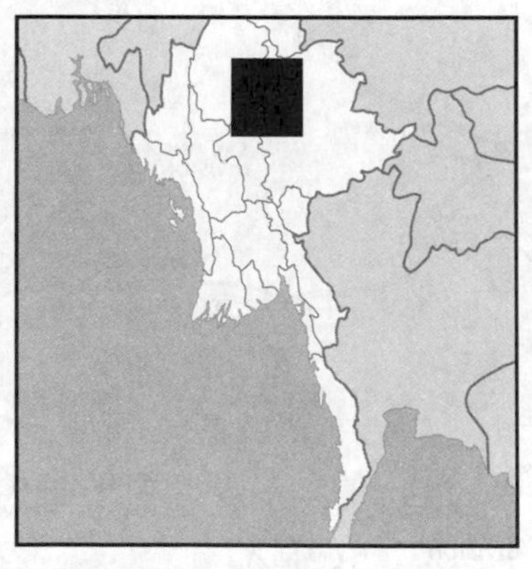

Ancient Cities

After the fall of Bagan (Pagan), right up to when the third and last Anglo-Burmese War reached its final (and for the Burmese, disastrous) conclusion in 1885, the capitals of Myanmar's kingdoms stood in, or close to, Mandalay. Perhaps it's part of the Buddhist belief in the temporary nature of life, but many kings developed an overpowering urge to commence their reign with a new capital and a new palace. Thus, the capital seemed to play musical chairs around the countryside.

In addition, masonry or brick construction was reserved almost solely for religious buildings. The palaces, though magnificent and extensive, were made of wood. When the shift was made to a new capital, the wooden buildings of the old palace were often dismantled and taken along. When the royal entourage departed, the mighty cities soon reverted to farming villages – with neglected stupas picturesquely dotting the fields.

In the chaos after the fall of Bagan, it was Sagaing that first rose to prominence in the early 14th century, but in 1364 Inwa succeeded it. Not until 1760 was the capital shifted back across the river to Sagaing, where it remained for just four years. Inwa (Ava) only regained its pre-eminent position from 1764 to 1783, after which time Amarapura became the capital. In 1823 Inwa was again the capital, but following the terrible earthquake of 1838, which caused great damage to all these cities, the capital was moved back to Amarapura in 1841. Amarapura was capital again for only a short period, and in 1860 the seat of power was transferred to Mandalay, where it remained until the end of the British conquest of Myanmar 25 years later. This seemingly constant moving of capitals around Mandalay gives the area its second nickname: Deserted Cities.

Three of the ancient cities are south of Mandalay. Amarapura and Inwa are on the eastern (Mandalay) side of the Ayeyarwady (Irrawaddy) River, while Sagaing lies to the west of the river, but is easily reached by the long Inwa Tada (more commonly known as

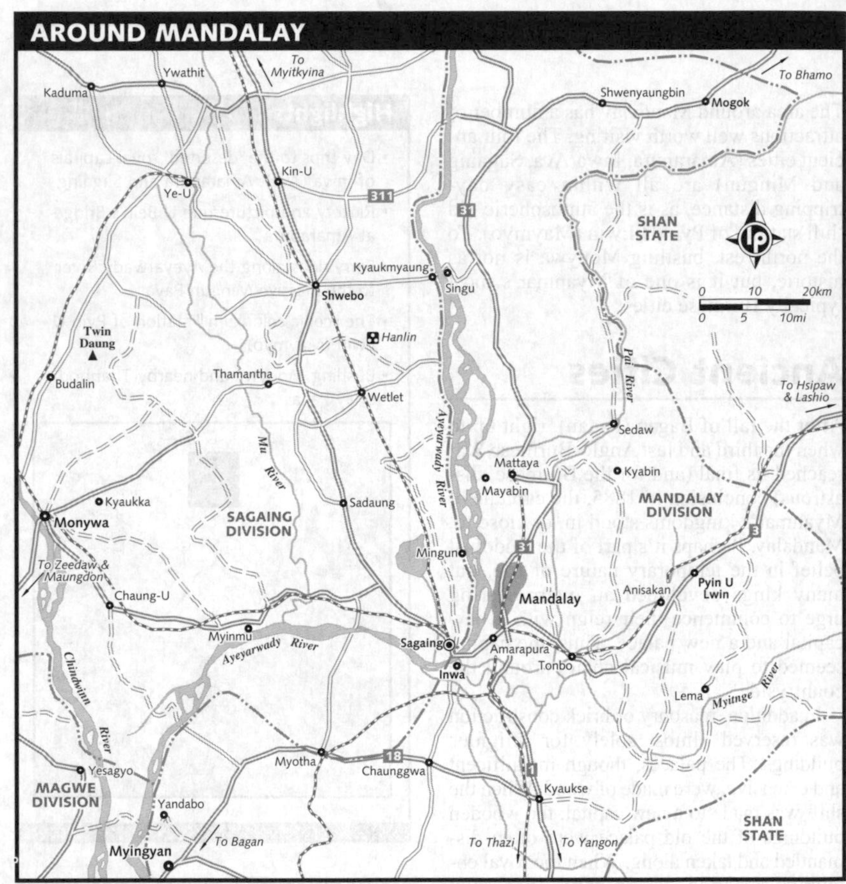

Ava Bridge). Mingun, which was never a capital, is on the western bank of the Ayeyarwady to the north of Mandalay. It's easily reached by frequent riverboats running from Mandalay.

Don't try to do all the cities in one day. It's best to devote a half day each to Sagaing and Mingun; Amarapura and Inwa can be seen together on a separate day.

The Last Kings

Alaungpaya founded the last dynasty (the Konbaung dynasty) of Burmese kings in 1752. It ended 133 years later, when King Thibaw was deposed by the British and exiled to India. Two of the kings, Hsinbyushin and Bodawpaya, were Alaungpaya's sons.

The kings and their reigns were:

Alaungpaya	1752–1760
Naungdawgyi	1760–1763
Hsinbyushin	1763–1776
Singu Min	1776–1782
Bodawpaya	1782–1819
Bagyidaw	1819–1837
Tharawaddy Min	1837–1846
Pagan Min	1846–1853
Mindon Min	1853–1878
Thibaw Min	1878–1885

AMARAPURA

အမရပူရ

The modern town of Amarapura, 11km south of Mandalay, is often referred to as Taungmyo (Southern City) to distinguish it from Mandalay, the northern city. The name Amarapura means City of Immortality, but its period as capital was brief. It was founded by Bodawpaya as his new capital in 1783, not long after he ascended the throne, but in 1823 Bagyidaw moved his court back to Inwa. In 1841 Amarapura again became the capital, but in 1857 Mindon Min decided to make Mandalay the capital, and the changeover was completed in 1860. Amarapura was also the site for the first British embassy in Myanmar in 1795.

Today, little remains of the old Amarapura palace area, although there are several interesting sites. They are widely scattered, so if you don't have transport, allow enough time and energy for walking. The city walls were torn down to make quarry material for railway lines and roads, while most of the wooden palace buildings were dismantled and taken to the palace in Mandalay.

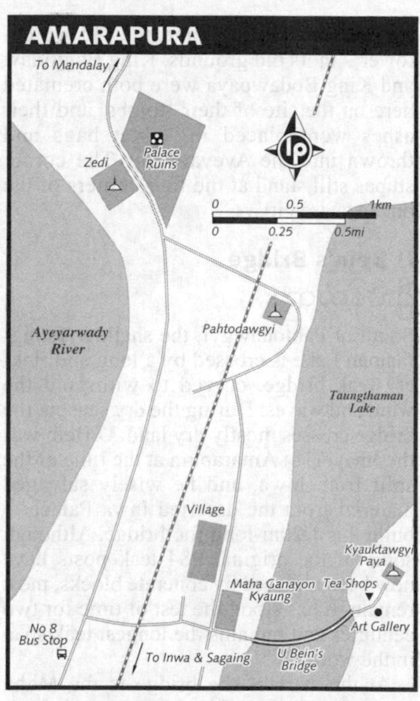

Pahtodawgyi

ပုထိုးတော်ကြီး

Built by King Bagyidaw in 1820, this well-preserved *paya* (pagoda) stood outside the old city walls. The lower terraces have marble slabs illustrating *jataka* (stories of the Buddha's past lives) scenes. There's a fine view over the surrounding countryside from the upper terrace. An inscription stone within the temple precinct details the history of the monument's construction.

Bagaya Kyaung

ဘားကရာကျောင်း

The Bagaya Kyaung in Amarapura was built when Bodawpaya moved the capital to Amarapura, but was destroyed by fire in 1821. Its Inwa predecessor of the same name is still standing. A second Amarapura version, built in 1847, was again burnt down in 1866, leaving only eight brick stairways. These were gradually overgrown until the Myatheindan *sayadaw* (abbot) built a two-storey brick building in 1951, in which he deposited 500 Buddha images and 5000 sets of *pe-sa* (palm leaf manuscripts) from throughout Burma. Between 1993 and 1996, the State Law and Order Restoration Council (Slorc), now known as the State Peace and Development Council (SPDC), reconstructed the monastery, based on drawings and ground plans in frescoes in the Kyauktawgyi Paya, near U Bein's Bridge. It's no longer a monastery, but houses a museum and library, of interest for its collection of palm-leaf manuscripts. The museum is kept locked, but the caretaker will open it on request.

Palace Ruins

နန်းတော်ရာ-အမရပူရ

Little remains of the old Amarapura palace, but you can find two masonry buildings –

the treasury building and the old watchtower – in its old grounds. King Bagyidaw and King Bodawpaya were both cremated here on the site of their 'tombs' and their ashes were placed in velvet bags and thrown into the Ayeyarwady. The corner stupas still stand at the four corners of the once square city.

U Bein's Bridge

ဦးပိန်တံတား

South of Pahtodawgyi, the shallow Taungthaman Lake is crossed by a long and rickety teak bridge, curved to withstand the wind and waves. During the dry season, the bridge crosses mostly dry land. U Bein was the 'mayor' of Amarapura at the time of the shift from Inwa, and he wisely salvaged material from the deserted Inwa Palace to build this 1.2km-long footbridge. Although some of the original 984 teak posts have now been replaced by concrete blocks, most remain. It has stood the test of time for two centuries and remains the longest teak span in the world.

At the start of the bridge is the **Maha Ganayon Kyaung**, home to several thousand young monks. It was founded around 1914 and is renowned as a centre for monastic study and strict religious discipline. If you visit at about 11am, you can watch the whole monastery eating silently. There is also a new and garish-looking temple with a gigantic seated Buddha. Near the bridge is a cluster of shaded tables where you can take tea, beer and snacks under an arcade of *meh-zeh* trees planted in 1875. The best times to visit the bridge are just after sunrise or just before sunset, when hundreds of villagers commute by foot or bicycle back and forth across it. You can also hire a small boat to take you in either direction for about K200 if you only want to cross the bridge once.

During the dry season, look for a cement stairway leading down to a little island with a single teashop (no sign) serving cold drinks and a few snacks. It's about halfway across the bridge and makes a nice break on a hot day.

Kyauktawgyi Paya

ကျောက်တော်ကြီးဘုရား

If you stroll across the bridge (there are fine views from here across the lake to Pahtodawgyi, and rest places where you can shelter from the sun and sample fresh palm toddy), you'll come to Taungthaman village and Kyauktawgyi Paya. Constructed in 1847 by Pagan Min, this paya is said to have been modelled on the larger Ananda Pahto at Bagan, but it has more the look of a Tibetan or Nepali temple, with its five-tiered roof.

While the paya does not have the perfectly vaulted roofs or the finer decorations of the original, it does have an excellent seated Buddha image and interesting and well-preserved frescoes in the four entrance porches. Religious buildings, zodiac charts and scenes from everyday life are all illustrated in the frescoes. You can even find some suspiciously English-looking figures in the crowd scenes – they were beginning to make their presence felt at the time of the temple's construction. The *paya pwe* (pagoda festival), known as the Festival of Lights, takes place during Thadingyut (October).

The atmosphere around Kyauktawgyi is very peaceful and shady, and this is a good place to hang around at sunset, when people, bicycles and bullock carts pass by on their way back from a day's work in the fields that surround the shrine. There are several smaller overgrown stupas to be seen in the vicinity, including a unique honeycomb-shaped stupa covered with Buddha niches. Lay people often come here to practise meditation, getting away from the worldly distractions of Mandalay. There are a couple of traditional outdoor **teashops** where those with time on their hands sit on woven mats or small stools around low tables, drinking small pots of Chinese tea, relaxing and eating snacks such as fried gourd, soy cake and fried lentil balls dipped in a tasty tamarind sauce.

Look for a small and friendly **art gallery** near the teashops.

Other Attractions

On the bank of the Ayeyarwady, north of the bridge, stand two 12th-century paya – the **Shwe-kyet-kya** and the **Shwe-kyet-yet**, or Golden Fowl's Run, a string of *zedi* (stupa) ruins cascading down from a high bluff. If the river level is not too high, you can pay a boatman about K200 to take you out in a local *hgnet* (swallow-tailed boat) for a fabulous view of the two paya, the Sagaing hills, and the sun setting behind the Ava Bridge. Amarapura also has a **Chinese joss house**; when the decision was made to shift to Mandalay, the Chinese traders preferred to remain.

Amarapura is noted for silk- and cotton-weaving, and there are reportedly around 40,000 Siamese-style, four-heddle looms in the area. As you wander through the wooden buildings of the modern town you'll hear the looms' steady clackety-clack. Bronze casting is also done in Amarapura.

In August, a week after the end of the Taungbyone *nat pwe* (spirit festival) and the full moon of Wagaung, Myanmar's nat worshippers move to the Irinaku (Yadanagu) Festival, just south of Amarapura, and to the east of the road. The festival celebrates Popa Medaw, the mother of the Taungbyone brothers. The authorities have clamped down on some of the wilder activities in recent years, but this festival and Taungbyone are still the main nat festivals of the year, and important dates in Myanmar's gay scene.

Getting There & Away

A No 8 bus from 84th St, near the corner of 26th St in Mandalay, will take you to Amarapura for K20 and on to Inwa for another K20. Get off the bus when you come to the palace wall on the left of the road, and a temple guarded by elephants on the right, with the Ayeyarwady visible behind it. From here you can walk to Pahtodawgyi and through the village of Taungthaman to U Bein's Bridge.

Touring by bicycle is another alternative. Bikes can be rented in Mandalay for around K500 a day. Pedalling to Amarapura should take 45 minutes or so.

INWA (AVA)

အင်းဝ

The ancient city of Inwa (Mouth of the Lake), for a long time a capital of northern Myanmar after the fall of Bagan, is on the Mandalay side of the Ayeyarwady River close to the Ava Bridge, a few kilometres south of Amarapura. Just south of the bridge, the Myitnge River flows into the Ayeyarwady, and south of this river stands Inwa. A channel, known as the Myittha Chaung (Myittha Canal), was cut across from the Myitnge to the Ayeyarwady to make Inwa an island.

From 1364 Inwa was the capital of a Burmese kingdom for nearly 400 years (apart from brief interludes), until the shift was made to Amarapura in 1841. No other capital has lasted as long. Although Inwa was known to the outside world as Ava until comparatively recently, the classical Pali name of the city was Ratnapura (City of Gems), pronounced Yadanabon in Burmese.

Before 1364, Sagaing had been the capital of the central Bamar kingdom, but after Sagaing fell to the Shan, the capital was moved across the river to Inwa. The kings of Inwa set about re-establishing Bamar supremacy, which had been in decline since the fall of Bagan. Although the power of Inwa soon extended as far as Pyay (Prome), the Mon rulers of Bago (Pegu) proved to be a strong match for the Bamar.

In 1555 Inwa fell to another Bamar kingdom, that of Taungoo, but in 1636 the capital of Taungoo was returned to Inwa. This period as capital lasted only a century. The Mon again rose up and destroyed Inwa in 1752. A few years later Alaungpaya vanquished the Mon forever, and after a period with Shwebo in the north as capital, Inwa once again became the centre of the kingdom.

When the British occupied southern Myanmar following the Second Anglo-Burmese War, much of northern Myanmar was known as the Kingdom of Ava. An embassy report of a visit to Inwa in 1795 enthused:

The Burmans are certainly rising fast in the scale of Oriental nations. They have an undeniable claim to the character of a civilised and well instructed people. Their laws are wise and pregnant with sound morality; their police is better regulated than in most European countries; their natural disposition is hospitable to strangers.

During his reign, Bodawpaya moved the capital to Amarapura, but his successor Bagyidaw shifted it back to Inwa. When the disastrous earthquake of 1838 caused serious damage, the city was finally abandoned as a capital, in favour of Amarapura, in 1841.

A number of small villages have sprung up inside the city walls, and peasants can be seen tilling the soil where once the palace used to stand – the massive old city walls are still easily traced. To the south, an ancient brick causeway leads from the city gate towards the town of Tada-u, where an Italian-Thai company has recently completed a US$150 million international airport for Mandalay that's capable of receiving jumbo jets.

Nanmyin

နန်းဝင်မျှော်စင်

The 27m-high masonry watchtower, Nanmyin, is all that remains of the palace built by Bagyidaw. The upper portion was shattered by the 1838 earthquake and the rest has taken on a precarious tilt – it's known as the 'leaning tower of Inwa'.

Maha Aungmye Bonzan

မဟာအောင်မြေဘုံစံ

Also known as the Ok Kyaung, this is a brick-and-stucco monastery built by Meh Nu, the chief queen of Bagyidaw, for her royal abbot U Po (Nyaunggan Sayadaw) in 1818. Monasteries were generally built of wood and were prone to deterioration from the elements or destruction by fire. Although this monastery was built in imitation of the traditional wooden style, its masonry construction has ensured its survival. The 1838 earthquake badly damaged it, but it was restored in 1873.

Bagaya Kyaung

ဘားကရာကျောင်း

Fire and earthquake aren't the only threats to Myanmar's architectural heritage, and one of Inwa's finest attractions is the happily unrenovated Bagaya Kyaung, which dates from 1834. The entire monastery is built of teak and supported by 267 teak posts (the largest measures 18m in height and 2.7m in circumference). The cool and dark interior feels old and inviting. On the outside, look for the Keinayi peacock – half-bird and half-female. How long this pristine wooden structure will escape the heavy hand of renovation is not certain, but visit it while you can. A small sign in Burmese at the entrance warns: 'No footwear; if you are afraid of the heat on the floor, stay in your own house.'

Ava Bridge

အင်းဝတံတား

This British-engineered, 16-span bridge dates to 1934 and was the only structure that crossed the Ayeyarwady River, until 1998 when a new Chinese-engineered bridge was completed at Pyay, followed shortly afterwards by one at Myitkyina. The Ava Bridge (also called Inwa Tada) was put out of action by the British in 1942, when they demolished two spans in order to deny passage to the advancing Japanese. Not until 1954 was the bridge repaired and put back into operation. It carries two lanes of traffic, plus a railway line.

Tolls are collected for every moving vehicle that crosses, from bullock carts and trishaws to cargo trucks. Due to the route's strategic importance, photography of – or from – the bridge is strictly forbidden.

Other Attractions

Farms, villages, *kyaung* (monasteries) and ruined zedi are scattered around the area within the old city walls. The walls are in particularly good condition near the northern gate, facing the Ayeyarwady. This was known as the **Gaung Say Daga** (Hair-Washing Gate), since kings had their hair ceremonially washed here. In places the moat outside the walls is also visible.

Located nearby, **Htilaingshin Paya** dates back to the Bagan period; in a shed in the compound an inscription records the construction of the wooden palace during the first Inwa dynasty.

To the southern side of the city stand the remains of the huge four-storey **Le-htat-gyi Paya**. There is also the **Lawkatharaphu Paya**, while to the south of the city stands the **Inwa Fort** and nearby **elephant stockade**.

The Inwa Nat Pwe celebrates the nat Thon Ban Hla from the 10th day of the waxing moon through to the full moon of Tabaung (February/March).

A few miles southeast of Inwa, but best accessed by car from the Mandalay-Meiktila road, is Paleik and the Yadana Labamuni Hsu-taung-pye Paya, said to have been founded in 1093 by Alaungsithu. It is better known as **Hmwe Paya** *(Snake Pagoda; admission 3 Foreign Exchange Certificates – FECs)* after the two pythons that sleep curled around a Buddha image and are lovingly washed and fed every morning at 11am. It receives very few foreign visitors. A festival including *a-nyeint* (similar to vaudeville/slapstick) and *zat* (recreation of an ancient legend or Buddhist jataka) performances takes place in the two weeks following the full moon of Waso (June/July).

Paleik is a well-kept village surrounded by an estimated 325 stupas and paya in varying states of repair, many from the Konbaung period. It is like a mini-Bagan, but with much more greenery, and worth a visit if you are travelling between Mandalay and Meiktila by car. The turn-off to the right for Paleik is about 20km south of Mandalay, after the river and beyond Myitnge, or 30km north of Kyaukse.

Getting There & Away

Bus No 8 to Amarapura, Inwa and Sagaing leaves from the clock tower, near the *zeigyo* (central market) in Mandalay. Bus numbers are in Burmese script. The cost is about K50 for each segment along the way. Pick-ups bound for Sagaing leave from the corner of 83rd and 29th Sts and drop off at Ava Bridge. You can then follow the extremely dusty (in the dry season) track down to the ferry landing on the Myitnge River. You'll be ferried across for K10. During the wet season, you have to take a ferry from Thabyedan Fort near Ava Bridge. Ferries also shuttle across the Ayeyarwady between Inwa and Sagaing for K5.

A saloon taxi can be hired from Mandalay for US$15 to US$25 to take you to Amarapura, Inwa and Sagaing, and back again. A 'blue taxi' (the dinky little Mazda pick-ups) can be hired to do the same job for US$10.

Getting Around

Inwa makes an interesting break in the ancient city circuit because so few travellers seem to make it there – due, in part, to the admission fee of US$5, collected at the ferry crossing. However, to get around you'll either need a bicycle (which may be available at the small ferry landing), or you must hire a horse cart; several await the arrival of each small ferry, and the cost is about K800 for a three-hour tour.

SAGAING

စစ်ကိုင်း

If you're unable to get to Bagan to poke around the ruins, Sagaing may provide an interesting substitute. There are certainly plenty of stupas here, and those scattered over the Sagaing hills – which rise on the western bank of the Ayeyarwady, just north of the modern town – provide a very picturesque spectacle from across the river.

Sagaing became capital of an independent Shan kingdom around 1315, after the fall of Bagan had thrown central Myanmar into chaos. Its period of importance was short, for in 1364 the founder's grandson, Thado Minbya, moved his capital across the river to Inwa. For four brief years, from 1760 to 1764, Sagaing was once again the capital, but its historic importance is comparatively minor.

Today, it's mostly known as a religious centre that supports dozens of Buddhist monasteries and nunneries as well as a major monastic hospital. During the full moon of Tazaungmon (October/November), devotees from Mandalay and beyond flock to Sagaing to offer robes. Kyaswa Kyaung offers an annual 'foreign yogis retreat' (in the Mahasi Sayadaw tradition) each January.

Thabyedan Fort
သပြေတန်းခံတပ်

Just to the left of the Ava Bridge, on the Mandalay and Inwa side, is the fort of Thabyedan, which was built as a last-ditch defence by the Burmese before the Third Anglo-Burmese War. It was taken by the British with little effort.

Kaunghmudaw Paya
ကောင်းမှုတော်ဘုရား

The best known of the Sagaing stupas, this huge whitewashed edifice is actually situated 10km beyond the town of Sagaing. The enormous dome, whose name means work of great merit, rises 46m in the shape of a perfect hemisphere and was modelled after the Mahaceti (Great Stupa) in Sri Lanka – although legend also says that it represents the perfectly shaped breast of a well endowed Burmese queen. Also known by its Pali name, Rajamanicula, the zedi was built in 1636 to commemorate Inwa's establishment as the royal capital of Myanmar.

Around the base of the zedi are 812 stone pillars, each 1m to 1.5m high and with a small hollow for an oil lamp. Images of nat can be seen in the 120 niches that also circle the base. A nearly 3m-high polished marble slab stands in a corner of the paya grounds – the 86 lines of Burmese inscriptions on the slab record details of the monument's construction.

Tupayon Paya
ထူပါရုံဘုရား

Constructed by King Narapati of Inwa in 1444, Tupayon is of an unusual style for Myanmar: it consists of three circular storeys each encircled with arched niches. A temporary wooden bridge was constructed across the Ayeyarwady when the *hti* (the umbrella-like decorated top) was raised, and a huge festival was held. The 1838 earthquake toppled the superstructure, and although it was partially repaired in 1849, the reconstruction was never completed.

Aungmyelawka Paya
အောင်မြေလောကဘုရား

Situated on the riverfront, near Tupayon Paya, this zedi was built in 1783 by Bodawpaya on the site of the residence he owned before he became king. It is built entirely of sandstone, in imitation of the Shwezigon Paya at Nyaung U, Bagan. It is also known as the Eindawya Paya.

Other Paya
The **Datpaungzu Paya** is comparatively recent, but houses many relics from other, older temples that were demolished when the railway was built through Sagaing. **Ngadatkyi** to the west of Sagaing was built in 1657 and houses a fine and very large seated Buddha image.

Hsinmyashin Paya is on the way to the Kaunghmudaw Paya and is known as the Pagoda of Many Elephants, because of the elephant statues stationed at each entranceway – a departure from the usual *chinthe* (half-lion, half-dragon guardian statues). Built in 1429, it was badly damaged in an earthquake in 1485. Although subsequently repaired, it suffered even worse damage in a 1955 earthquake.

Sagaing Hill
စစ်ကိုင်းတောင်

The hill itself has a number of zedi and kyaung, some of which are comparatively recent. **Padamya Zedi** dates from 1300, while **Umin Thounzeh** (30-Caves), contains 45 Buddha images in a crescent-shaped colonnade. The impressive **Soon U Ponya Shin Paya** nearby was constructed in 1312 and reaches 29.3m high with a 7.8m hti above that; in front of the principal altar, large bronze frogs on wheels serve as collection boxes. The view of Sagaing from Soon U Ponya Shin and its approach are outstanding. Mural paintings can be seen in the **Tilawkaguru** cave temple, which was built around 1672. The **Pa Ba Kyaung** is typical of the many monasteries on the hillside. Sagaing also has the remains of a fort by the riverbank. The nearby village of **Ywataung** is renowned for its silversmiths.

The village of Sagaing, at the foot of Sagaing Hill, makes an interesting visit – it's chock-a-block with markets, shops and restaurants. Foreigners are charged an entry fee of US$4 to climb Sagaing Hill.

If you don't want to go up the hill, you can still soak up Sagaing's atmosphere by roaming along the pathways that cover the hillsides and link up the hundreds of *tazaung* (shelters). Covered walkways lead down to Thayetpin jetty where you can hire a row boat down the river and pick up other pathways.

Places to Stay & Eat

Although a day trip to Sagaing seems sufficient to many visitors, an overnight stay allows you to take in the sights at a leisurely pace while absorbing the local ambience.

Happy Hotel (*☎ 072-21420; rooms per person US$3-5*), a quiet place on a side street of the main road near the central market, offers 21 basic but clean rooms. Rates include breakfast. Shower and toilet facilities are down the hall. Downstairs, you'll find a very decent **restaurant** serving Chinese and Bamar food. Coming from Mandalay, turn right, just past the cinema on the right-hand side of the road, then make the first left and you'll see it on your left.

Some travellers have managed to stay at **unlicensed guesthouses** in Sagaing for as little as K2000 a night. There are plenty of **teashops** and **restaurants** in the vicinity of the Happy Hotel and central market, including **Kant Kaw Thu Zar Ywataung**, on the main road.

Getting There & Away

Sagaing is about 20km southwest of Mandalay and is easily reached by road. The Ayeyarwady flows south by Sagaing, then turns west and north, encircling the town in a loop. The road to Sagaing crosses the river on the 16-span Ava Bridge, which is well over 1km long and also carries the railway line.

A Sagaing-bound pick-up (from the intersection of 84th and 26th Sts in Mandalay, and from Amarapura and other stops along the way) will take you right to the middle of town for about K50. To continue to the Kaunghmudaw Paya, it costs another K10.

MINGUN

မင်းကွန်း

If we had to choose just one of the four ancient cities around Mandalay to visit, it would be Mingun. Not only are there some very interesting things to see within a comparatively compact area, it's also a very pleasant boat trip.

Mingun, about 11km upriver from Mandalay, on the opposite bank of the Ayeyarwady, is accessible only by river. It's just long enough a trip to give you a pleasant feel for the river and a glimpse of river life.

The village itself is a very friendly place – although the hawkers are a little too friendly. Several **teashops** and **curry stalls** in the vicinity of the huge Mingun Bell offer snacks, noodles and beverages. A footpath parallel to the river runs the length of the ruins area and beyond and makes an interesting walk, plus it's less dusty than the main road in dry weather.

The Mingun Sanitarium (also called the Buddhist Infirmary), a nursing home for the elderly, is worth checking out. Visitors are welcome. The head nurse here is Than Than Sue. She speaks excellent English and is happy to impart information on the Mingun area. You might be able to stay the night if there's room.

The Mingun Nat Festival takes place between the 5th and 10th days of the waxing moon of Tabaung (February/March). This celebration pays homage to the brother and sister of the Teak Tree, who drowned in the river while clinging to a trunk.

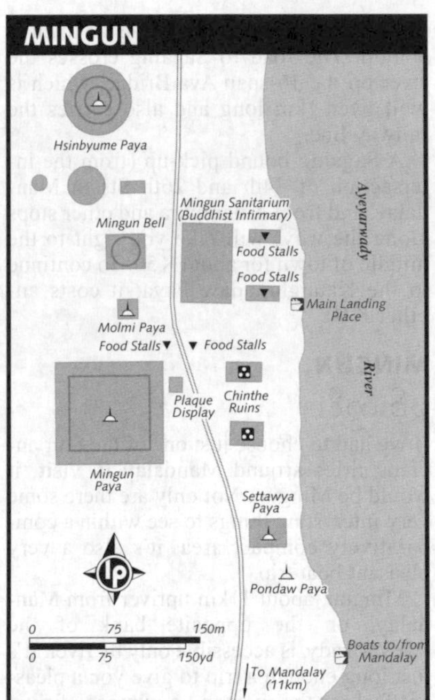

Foreigners are expected to pay a US$3 government-enforced 'restoration' fee to explore Mingun.

Mingun Paya

မင်းကွန်းဘုရား

If King Bodawpaya had succeeded in his grandiose scheme, Mingun might now boast the world's largest zedi. Thousands of slaves and prisoners of war laboured to build the massive stupa, beginning in 1790. Work halted in 1819 when Bodawpaya died, leaving a brick base that stands about a third of the intended height of the stupa.

An earthquake split the monument in 1838 and reduced it to partial rubble – possibly the world's largest pile of bricks. But what a pile of bricks! The base of his projected stupa, badly cracked by the earthquake of 1838, stands 50m high, overlooking the river. Each side of the enormous base measures 72m, and the lowest terrace measures 140m. There are projecting four-layer lintels over the porticoes on each of the four sides. Beautiful glazed tiles in brown, pale brown, cream and green were intended to be set in panels around the terrace; some of these tiles can be seen in the small building in front of the enormous ruin. Had the stupa been completed, it would have stood 150m high.

Despite its dilapidated state, you must still go barefoot if you intend to climb the base. You can climb the zedi on the crumbled corner, and from the top you have a fine view of the Hsinbyume Paya, Mingun village and the river. The view of the delta region alone makes this trip worth it.

A pair of large chinthe have just about crumbled away at their guard posts closer to the river. They, too, were badly damaged by the 1838 quake.

You can enter the paya to view the Buddha, light a candle, and perhaps pay a voluntary donation.

Pondaw Paya

ပုံတော်ဘုရား

Closer to the riverbank, a little downstream from the Mingun Paya, is this 5m-high working model for the gigantic structure. It gives a clear picture of just what Bodawpaya intended to achieve with Mingun Paya. During the 15 years it took to build the base of his stupa, he frequently set up residence on an island in the Ayeyarwady to supervise the construction.

Mingun Bell

မင်းကွန်းခေါင်းလောင်း

In 1808 Bodawpaya had a gigantic bell cast to go with his gigantic zedi. Weighing 55,555 *viss* (90 tonnes), it is claimed to be the largest hung, uncracked bell in the world. There is said to be a larger bell in Moscow, but it is cracked.

The same earthquake that shook the zedi base also destroyed the bell's supports, so it was hung in a new tazaung, close to the riverboat landing. The bell is about 4m high and over 5m in diameter at the lip. You can scramble right inside it and some helpful bystander will give it a good thump so that you can hear the ring from the interior.

Between Mingun Paya and the bell stands a new pavilion sheltering a life-size standing bronze statue of Molmi Sayadaw, a famous Buddhist abbot from the nearby village of Molmi.

Hsinbyume Paya

ဆင်ဖြူမယ်ဘုရား

Also known as Myatheindan, and built by King Bagyidaw in 1816, three years before he succeeded Bodawpaya as king, this stupa was constructed in memory of his senior wife, the Hsinbyume princess. It is built as a representation of the Sulamani Paya, which, according to the Buddhist plan of the cosmos, stands atop Mt Meru (the mountain that stands at the centre of the universe). The seven wavy terraces around the stupa represent the seven mountain ranges around Mt Meru, while the five kinds of mythical monsters can be found in niches on each terrace level. This zedi was also badly damaged in the 1838 quake, but King Mindon had it restored in 1874.

Settawya Paya

စက်တော်ရာဘုရား

Close to the riverbank, upstream from the Pondaw Paya, this hollow, vaulted shrine has a footprint of the Buddha that was brought to Mingun by King Bodawpaya when the relic chamber in the base of his huge *pahto* (temple) was sealed up. The temple was built in 1811.

Getting There & Away

Riverboats to Mingun depart from the foreigners river transport jetty in Mandalay, at the western end of 26th St, daily at 9am. A return ticket costs K500. The upriver journey usually takes about 45 minutes, though sometimes it can take as long as two hours. Depending on the currents, coming back may be rather quicker. It's best to arrange transport to the jetty the night before. The boat back to Mandalay leaves at 1pm from Mingun, so don't miss it! Since there's nowhere to stay in Mingun, you would have to charter a boat back at a cost of around K4000 to K8000. It's best to buy tickets at the nearby Inland Water Transport (IWT) office on 35th St the day before you travel (or have your hotel or guesthouse arrange tickets for you), although you can usually buy a ticket at the jetty.

It's a pleasant, interesting trip with plenty to see along the way – fishing villages, bullock carts, corn fields, market boats, people doing their washing. If you're lucky you may even spot a pod of rare Irrawaddy dolphins along this stretch of the river.

Pyin U Lwin (Maymyo)

ပြင်ဦးလွင်

☎ 085

In 1887, during the British annexation of Myanmar, Pyin U Lwin was renamed Maymyo (May-town) after a British Colonel May, of the 5th Bengal Infantry, which was stationed in the military headquarters there, and among many locals (and tourist touts) the town is still known by its colonial name. From 1896, Pyin U Lwin was a British hill station. The British legacy can be seen in many well-preserved colonial buildings dotted around town, some of which are now hotels. Pyin U Lwin is 67km east of Mandalay and, at 1070m, is considerably higher. The altitude makes all the difference. Even at the height of the hot season, it is pleasantly cool and at certain times of the year it can get quite chilly. Best of all, the air is fresh.

Originally a Shan Danu village, as a legacy of the influx of South Asians during the British colonial era, Pyin U Lwin is home to around 5000 Nepalis and 10,000 Indians. Sweater-knitting is a prominent occupation in town; most of this work is done by women, while the men roam the streets and hang out in teashops. The town has a faint khaki hue, thanks to the much expanded Defence Services Academy, Myanmar's elite military training school. The cadets can often be seen in the teashops.

Getting to Pyin U Lwin is part of its attraction. From Mandalay, you can take a pick-up or bus that chugs its way across the plains, then up the twisting road into the hills. There's no hurry about the trip, which is interspersed with stops to top up the vehicle's radiator. At the halfway mark you pass View Point, which has spectacular views. Along the way, villagers sell wooden blocks that are supposed to keep truck tyres from slipping while parked on the steep grades.

Getting around Pyin U Lwin can be equally enjoyable; the standard transport around town is a miniature, enclosed wagon pulled by a pony. You're never sure if it's a half-scale replica from the Wells Fargo days of the American West or something from the British 'stand and deliver' era. The lodgings can be the most fun of all – see the Places to Stay section, or read Paul Theroux's delightful account of Pyin U Lwin in his book *The Great Railway Bazaar*.

Many of the colonial-era buildings along the town's main streets are being replaced by modern ones built by Chinese developers. You'll find the most intact colonial mansions along the circular road west of the centre. Chinese immigrants from Yunnan Province are buying up many of these old mansions, using profits earned in the border trade.

Pyin U Lwin is a centre for growing many temperate-climate vegetables and flowers: strawberries in season (February/March) are cheap and delicious. A flower market on the main road to Mandalay just south of town sells gladioli, roses, dahlias and other flowers typical of an English country garden. Mulberry trees, used to raise silk worms, are another important township product, and coffee is grown nearby.

The town itself is easygoing and full of interest – a good place for an evening stroll, or an interesting morning at the markets. There are still many English signs around.

At the turn of the century, old Maymyo was considered a 'hornet's nest of dacoits (highwaymen)'. Today, the local tout-mafia still try to keep tabs on all foreigners coming into town from Mandalay. As the number of visitors arriving here by private vehicle increases, their operation seems less secure. But it works like this: upon arrival in Pyin U Lwin you may be approached by a friendly chap asking where you plan to stay. Whatever your answer is – and regardless of whether you take the tout's recommendation or not – he will later make a trip to collect a 'commission' from the hotel or guesthouse owner of the place you stay. There are two main gangs running this operation, both centred at Indian-owned crafts shops in Pyin U Lwin.

Botanical Garden

ရုက္ခဗေဒဥယျာဉ်

Colonel May used Turkish prisoners of war to develop this 96-hectare Botanical Garden *(admission K1000; open 7am-5.30pm daily)* during WWI. The garden features wide expanses of manicured grass, large flower beds, 20 hectares of natural forest with walking trails, a rose garden, an orchid house, a small stupa on an islet in a pond and several other ponds. It's very popular with picnicking families on weekends and holidays.

An open-air **snack shop** sits on a slope overlooking the park.

Other Attractions

Purcell Tower, the clock tower near the town entrance coming from Mandalay, was a present from Queen Victoria, who offered an identical tower to Cape Town in South Africa. Another version of the story has it that the clock was made in 1934 by Gillette & Johnson of England, in commemoration of George V's Silver Jubilee. Part of the cost was paid by Mr Purcell, a resident of Mandalay, descended from Armenian traders who were favourites of Kings Mindon and Thibaw. Naturally, its chime copies Big Ben's.

There's a good view from **Naung Kan Gyi Paya** on a hilltop overlooking town, just north of the train station. You can leave

BERNARD NAPTHINE

The charming main street of Pyin U Lwin, Shan State

BERNARD NAPTHINE

Puppets for sale at Mingun, Mandalay Division

BERNARD NAPTHINE

Horse carts, a cool way to get around Pyin U Lwin

BERNARD NAPTHINE

Guardian lion, Mingun Paya

BERNARD NAPTHINE

Monks crossing the U Bein Bridge, Amarapura, Mandalay Division

JULIET COOMBE

The colossal base of the unfinished Mingun Paya, Mandalay Division, dwarfs its visitors.

BERNARD NAPTHINE

Scenic pathway in the Botanical Garden, Pyin U Lwin

BERNARD NAPTHINE

Anisakan Falls near Pyin U Lwin

your bicycle at the shops at the bottom of the hill.

The 100-year-old **Church of the Immaculate Conception**, south of the central area, features a large brick sanctuary with a bell-tower and cruciform floor plan. The vaulted wooden ceilings and well-appointed interior are more impressive than the outside. According to the Mother Superior here, Pyin U Lwin has around 5000 Catholics; there are two other Catholic churches in town and a Lisu Baptist Theological Seminary.

A few minutes walk from the Candacraig hotel is a colourful **Chinese temple** built by Yunnanese immigrants. There is an orphanage and nursing home within the temple compound.

For five days after the full moon of Tabaung (February/March), Pyin U Lwin holds a nat festival for Ko Myo Shin, the main nat of northern Shan State.

Maymyo Golf Club

မေမြို-ဂေါက်ကွင်း

This fairly well tended 18-hole golf course *(green fees K1000)* 4km from the Botanical Garden is one of the best in Myanmar. Clubs (K500), shoes (K150) and caddies (K500 each) can be hired at the pro shop. With club rental you are provided with 10 balls; you'll be fined K200 for each ball you lose. Men may be refused play if they're not wearing collared shirts (polo or tennis-style shirts are OK).

Places to Stay – Budget

There are several decent places in the vicinity of Purcell Tower that are licensed to accept foreigners.

Golden Dream Hotel *(☎ 22142; 42/43 Lashio-Mandalay Rd; rooms with cold-water shower per person US$3, with hot-water shower per person US$4)* is a rambling four-storey hotel close to the tower and pick-up stop. The rooms with hot water are larger. Room rates include Indian or Western breakfast. Rooms towards the back are quieter than those facing the street.

Grace Hotel *(☎ 21230; 114 Nan Myaing St; singles/doubles US$6/12)* has bicycles for rent for the short ride to town. Although past its prime and not particularly cheap, the Grace is in a quiet location, with a garden sitting area out front.

Dahlia Motel *(☎ 22255; 105 Eindaw St; economy singles/doubles US$5/10, with bathroom US$6/12, standard singles/doubles US$8/15, superior singles/doubles US$10/18)* is a friendly place a bit far from the town centre, but it has plenty of character and is excellent value. It has tidy, simple economy rooms with and without bathroom, and larger standard rooms with bathroom, TV and fan. There are also a few larger superior rooms. Most rooms have hot water, and breakfast is included. There is also free transport to town.

April Inn *(☎ 21001; 51F Eindaw St; bungalow singles/doubles US$7/14)* is further from town than the Dahlia, but easy to get to on a bike. It's in a pleasant garden setting and is very quiet (when the in-house karaoke isn't in full swing), and staff will pick you up from the train station or bus stop. The inn's large, solid, free-standing bungalows have balconies and even chalet-style decorative fireplaces, but also a touch of damp. A good Bamar- or Western-style breakfast is available for K300. Bikes can be rented for K300 for a half-day, and K500 for the whole day.

Places to Stay – Mid-Range & Top End

Royal Parkview Hotel *(☎ 21616, fax 21210; 107 Thaya St; standard singles/doubles US$20/24, superior singles/doubles US$30/36, suite $40)* on Thaya St, near the corner of Eindaw St, is the town's best modern hotel, and is easily the best value in this price range. All rooms are bright and airy, with high ceilings and hot water, fridge, satellite TV and teak furnishings. An in-house restaurant serves Bamar and European dishes. Room prices include breakfast.

Two fairly new hotels offer decent facilities on the outskirts of town:

Thiri Myanmar Hotel *(☎ 22483; 38B Forest Rd; standard singles/doubles US$20/30, superior singles/doubles US$50/60)*, east of town, is a brightly painted Chinese-style two-storey place with a restaurant and small

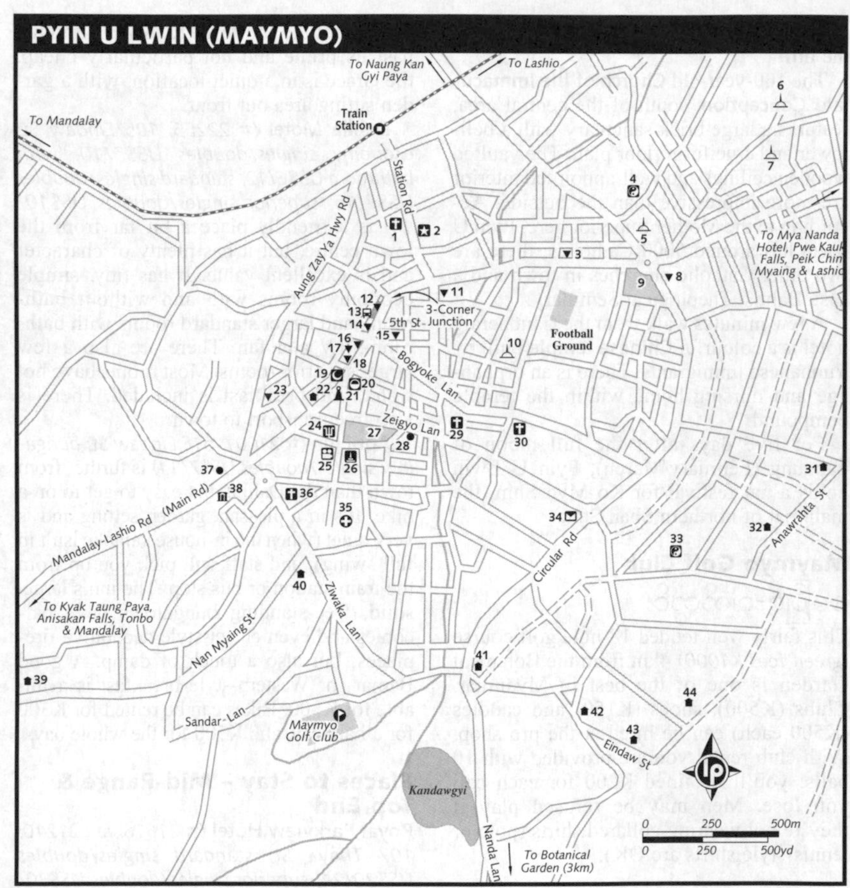

swimming pool. The rooms are decent, with hot water, TV and fridge.

Mya Nanda Hotel *(☎ 21015; singles/doubles US$24/30)*, just out of town on the road to Lashio, has clean and comfortable rooms. Rates include breakfast.

Many travellers will have heard of the **Thiri Myaing Hotel**, but as long as it remains government-owned, we will not review or recommend it.

Places to Eat

Apart from the hotels, there are a number of places to eat in the town centre, including several inexpensive Chinese and Indian restaurants.

Myitta Thit Tea Shop, close to the clock tower on the northern side of the street, is a large tea shop serving good-quality tea, crispy biscuit-like *nam-bya* (flat bread cooked in a clay oven, similar to Indian *nan*) with dhal dip and fresh butter from local Gurkha-run dairies, samosas (stuffed pastries; morning only) and *mohinga* (noodles, fish and egg dish; evening only).

Maymyo Restaurant, next door to the Myitta Thit Tea Shop, serves decent and cheap Chinese food.

PYIN U LWIN (MAYMYO)

PLACES TO STAY
- 22 Golden Dream Hotel
- 31 Thiri Myanmar Hotel
- 32 Thiri Myaing Hotel (Candacraig)
- 39 Nann Myaing Hotel
- 40 Grace Hotel
- 41 Gandamar Myaing Hotel
- 42 Royal Parkview Hotel
- 43 Dahlia Motel
- 44 April Inn

PLACES TO EAT
- 3 Win Yatana Restaurant
- 8 Aung Padamya Restaurant
- 11 Lay Ngoon Restaurant
- 12 Summer Feeling Café; Daw Khin Than Restaurant; Diamond Confectionery
- 14 Shanghai Restaurant
- 15 Rainbow Bar & Restaurant
- 16 Maymyo Restaurant
- 17 Family Restaurant
- 18 Myitta Thit Tea Shop
- 23 Yoe Yar Restaurant

OTHER
- 1 Methodist Church
- 2 Police Station
- 4 Cantonese Temple
- 5 Aung Chantha Paya
- 6 Shwe Myan Tin Paya
- 7 U Chanti Paya
- 9 Shan Market
- 10 Shwezigone Paya
- 13 Buses to Mandalay
- 19 Mosque
- 20 Pick-ups to Mandalay & Lashio
- 21 Purcell Tower
- 24 Hindu Temple
- 25 Cinema
- 26 Monastery
- 27 Zeigyo (Central Market); La Vie Artt Gallery
- 28 Fire Brigade
- 29 St Matthew's Kachin Baptist Church
- 30 Church of the Immaculate Conception
- 33 Chinese Temple
- 34 Post Office
- 35 Hospital
- 36 Church
- 37 Pacific World Curio
- 38 Town Hall

The **Yoe Yar Restaurant** *(Ashe Pyithu Panjan St)*, a couple of blocks southwest of the Hindu Temple, is a roomy place serving very good Bamar, Thai and Chinese dishes.

Family Restaurant *(13 Block 4, 3rd St)*, near Yoe Yar Restaurant on a side street off the main road, is clean and popular. The menu mixes Bamar and Indian dishes; order a chicken, vegetable or mutton curry and you'll also receive three or four side dishes, including vegetables and a delicious dahl, plus rice.

Aung Padamya Restaurant *(Site 44, 28 Thumingala Quarter, Zaythit St; mains around K800; open 11am-6pm daily)*, further east near the Shan Market, is a family-run place serving excellent and reasonably priced home-cooked Indian food. Mains include vegetable side dishes. The restaurant is owned by the golf pro from Maymyo Golf Club and his Indian Catholic family. The same family operates **Win Yatana Restaurant** on the main road, opposite the football ground.

Hlaing Tea Shop near the central market is a Nepali-style place serving good egg fried rice, chapatis, *aloo puri* (potato curry) and samosas for breakfast, plus other snacks during the day.

A cluster of good eateries along the main Mandalay-Lashio road begins with **Shanghai Restaurant**, a few blocks northeast of Purcell Tower, which specialises in Shanghai and Szechuan-style food. Several blocks further east, the Cantonese **Lay Ngoon Restaurant** is equally popular.

Indulge your sweet tooth at nearby **Diamond Confectionery**, founded by an Italian who left Myanmar following nationalisation. Although it may not look like much from the street, the shop produces a nice variety of baked goods and Indian snacks, including shortbread, butter cookies, chocolate-cashew muffins, coconut puffs, vegetable puffs and various cakes.

Next door to Diamond Confectionery is **Daw Khin Than Restaurant**, which serves good Bamar and Chinese food, and the **Summer Feeling Café**, a popular teashop. Opposite these eateries is the **Rainbow Bar & Restaurant** *(16, Block 7, 5th St)*, a small popular Chinese place.

Shopping

The main shed of the **central market** near the clock tower contains vendor stalls selling textiles and household goods from India, China, Thailand and Myanmar. Behind this main shed is a large area where fresh produce and other goods from the countryside are sold. Don't believe any touts in town who say there's nothing local for sale at this market; they're just trying to steer you away from the rival commission mafia and towards their own mafia at the smaller **Shan market** in the eastern part of town. Both markets are visited by tribespeople; the only real difference between the two is size, though it's true there are more Shan people at the Shan market. The Shan market is only open in the morning.

Several handicraft shops on or near the main street vie for your dollars and kyat. The best, or at least the most interestingly cluttered, is **Pacific World Curio** *(401 Mandalay-Lashio Rd)*. Like several smaller stores nearby, it has collections of marionettes, *kalaga* (tapestries), Shan bags, woodcarvings, old British clocks, lacquerware, brass and other materials from northern Myanmar. Beware of shipping things back to your home country from these shops. We've had reports of less than successful results. Also beware of offers of precious stones at these or any other shops; Pyin U Lwin has a very low reputation when it comes to dealing in gems. Many travellers have ended up with handfuls of worthless sapphires that they thought were a big score.

La Vie Art Gallery *(☎ 21266; 7-8 Duwan St, AM Block, central market)* displays paintings and other work by local artists, some of it very good. The owner, Muu Muu, speaks English and is knowledgeable about the artwork.

Getting There & Away

Bus & Pick-up From Mandalay you can take a bus or pick-up to Pyin U Lwin for K300 to K500 per person. These now depart, when full, from one central location in an alley lot near the northeast corner of 82nd St and 26th Sts, from 5am until about 3pm. For comfort and view, you are better off grabbing the front seats (which cost extra) and letting the hardier Burmese people cram themselves into the back. The trip takes about three hours up and about 2½ hours down – barring breakdowns of course, which are always possible.

From Pyin U Lwin, pick-ups depart in the opposite direction from the Shan market, train station, Chinese temple, clock tower and central market.

A private taxi with driver/guide to Pyin U Lwin costs about US$25.

Pick-ups and buses to Hsipaw and Lashio leave from the same area near 82nd and 26th Sts. The buses from Pyin U Lwin to Hsipaw and Lashio are very cold. Comfortable Toyota 'Super-roof' share-taxis take up to four passengers to Hsipaw (K1500, four hours), and Lashio (K2000, six hours).

Train There is a daily train to Pyin U Lwin from Mandalay, but this is more for train enthusiasts than a sensible means of transport. The train (No 131 Up) departs Mandalay at 4.35am and climbs the hills by a switchback system; the schedule says it takes 3½ hours to reach Pyin U Lwin, but this is optimistic – count on four to five hours. The same train continues to Hsipaw and Lashio. This trip across the spectacular Gokteik Viaduct is well worth taking, and the armed guards standing about 2m away from the track seem friendly enough (see the Northeastern Myanmar chapter for a detailed description of this trip). The mandatory-for-foreigners 1st-class fare from Mandalay to Pyin U Lwin is US$6; to Hsipaw another US$7; to Lashio another US$4. Purchase tickets the day before travel.

Getting Around

Most of the town's colourful horse carts are stationed near the mosque on the main road. Fares are steep by Myanmar standards: roughly K100 to travel from the mosque to the Shan market, K500 for the return trip to Thiri Myaing (Candacraig) Hotel or the Botanical Garden, K1000 for half-day sightseeing. You can hire bicycles to explore the town at the Grace Hotel, Dahlia Motel, April Inn and Golden Dream Hotel, or at either of the two crafts shops on the Mandalay-Lashio road. The going rate is about US$1 per day.

AROUND PYIN U LWIN

Waterfalls & Caves

There are several natural attractions around Pyin U Lwin, including a number of caves, waterfalls and tribal villages. Most can be reached by a combination of public transport and hiking, though Pacific World Curio or Zaw Crafts in Pyin U Lwin can arrange a guided trip to any, or all, of them. Rates are negotiable depending on where you want to go.

Pwe Kauk Falls Called Hampshire Falls in British times, Pwe Kauk Falls *(admission K20)* is about 8km from town, off the Lashio road. Although the falls themselves aren't that spectacular, it's a very pleasant picnic spot – popular on weekends and holidays with the locals. During, or just after, the rainy season, you can swim in the upper reaches, but not at the bottom, where the undertow can be quite dangerous. There's a K100 fee if you have a camera.

Three **Shan villages** – Mogyopyit, Yechando and Ye Ngeye – can be visited on the way to Pwe Kauk Falls. Or from Pwe Kauk, you can take a one-hour hike to **U Naung Gu**, a natural cave containing several Buddhas and used by local meditators. You can ask around at Pwe Kauk for a local guide to the cave.

You can charter a pick-up out to the falls from any of the truck stops in Pyin U Lwin for K500 each way. To visit the Shan villages, you can sometimes hire a bullock cart at Pwe Kauk.

Anisakan Falls Although a fairly long and steep walk is required to get to these falls, the hike is worth it. At the village of Anisakan, about 8km from Pyin U Lwin on the road to Mandalay, turn right at the train station, continue about 600m to the railway crossing, then turn left on a dirt road for about 800m to a fork, where you again take a left turn. After about 500m, you reach a parking place from where you continue on foot. It's a 45-minute descent through a river gorge to reach the falls, which consist of five sections; the third is particularly impressive.

Pick-ups go to Anisakan village from Pyin U Lwin for K30 per person – catch them in front of the cinema opposite the central market. You should allow at least a half-day for the whole trip. It's possible to ride a bicycle there, but the ride back is more up than down.

Peik Chin Myaing

ပိတ်ချင်းမြောင်

This large Hindu-Buddhist shrine cave, 27km towards Lashio and another 3.5km off the main road, was developed by local Nepalis and later co-opted by the government as a tourist attraction in 1990. (They also managed to rename it Maha Nan Damu Sacred Cave, though everyone seems happy with the old name.) A 600m path leads through the cave, which is decorated with quite new Buddha images and models of Myanmar's most famous stupas, eg, Shwedagon Paya and Kyaiktiyo. Pick-ups make the one-hour trip direct to Peik Chin Myaing for K400 per person. You can also charter a pick-up and driver for around K3000; ask around at the handicraft shops near the Golden Dream Hotel, or at the Lashio truck stop.

On the way, a few kilometres outside Pyin U Lwin, you will pass a new shrine. On 17 April 1997, four stone Buddhas were being transported by truck to China, when one fell off the truck and could not be hauled back on. The driver of the vehicle (conveniently!) claims that the night before he had dreamt that one of them did not want to leave Myanmar. A shrine and souvenir stall has now grown up around the Buddha. Four months after the event, pilgrims in this desperately poor country had already donated about 19 million kyat to the Buddha.

Shwesayan Paya

ရွှေစာရံဘုရား

This paya was built in 1054 by Shan princess Saw Mon Hla, daughter of the *sawbwa* (hereditary chieftain of the Shan) of Maingmaw. The wife of Anawrahta, she stopped here on her way home to the Shan State from Bagan, having been expelled from court for alleged witchcraft. A festival takes place in the two weeks following the full moon of Tabaung (February/ March). A bamboo platform and teashop is built out over the river, and there is plenty of water splashed around for those who can't wait for Thingyan (Water Festival). Shan traders descend to sell products such as sesame brittle, dried tofu and medicinal herbs and roots. The trademarks of the festival are the colourful locally made *htan-yweq ba-di* (necklaces) and fish, all made out of dyed toddy palm leaves. By car, turn off to the south at Tonbo, the limestone quarry and prison labour camp town 50km southwest of Pyin U Lwin at the foot of the Shan plateau on the Mandalay–Pyin U Lwin road. After a few kilometres, you reach the paya on the Myitnge (Dohtawadi) River. During the festival, you can catch a Mandalay–Pyin U Lwin pick-up as far as Tonbo, and then a pony trap to the paya.

Monywa & Shwebo

မုံရွာ / ရွှေဘို

These two cities in Sagaing Division, to the northwest and north of Mandalay, are known as the most typically 'Burmese' towns in all Myanmar. Although thriving Monywa has been open to foreigners for some time, Shwebo only opened in 1994; neither place has so far received many tourists at all. At the time of writing, visiting nearby Mogok (to the northeast) was forbidden for tourists, by order of the government. A centre for gem mining and trading, it is reportedly rife with dodgy government-run forced-labour operations.

MONYWA

မုံရွာ

☎ 071

Monywa is a worthwhile trip for temple enthusiasts or others who just want to go where there are few travellers. It lies 136km northwest of Mandalay along the Mandalay-Budalin branch railway line, but is best reached by bus or car.

Situated on the eastern bank of the Chindwin River, with a population of 300,000, Monywa is now the second-biggest town in northern Myanmar and serves as a major trade centre for agricultural produce from the surrounding Chindwin Valley, especially beans, pulses and jaggery (palm sugar). In addition to some 600 warehouses, Monywa supports mills for the production of cotton, flour, noodles and edible oils. Rough cotton blankets from Monywa are famous in Myanmar; some even end up being sewn into knapsacks sold to tourists in Bangkok. Other regional crafts include mats and baskets made of bamboo and reed, bullock carts and agricultural implements such as hoes and machetes.

Goods coming from India pass through Monywa on their way to other parts of the country. A forest reserve, west of the Chindwin River, produces teak and various other hardwoods. The Monywa area – particularly the region west of the river – was for many years a centre for the Burmese Communist Party (BCP).

The old market near the river is still active, despite the large new market sheds built by the government near the Monywa Hotel and Great Hotel. This is probably because the government ordered the relocation of a Muslim cemetery to make way for the new market; people fear the nat that may have been left behind.

Monywa is one of the hottest places in Myanmar in April and May, when temperatures approaching, or exceeding, 40°C are not uncommon.

Festivals

Monywa sits at the northwestern edge of what might be termed the nat belt, a region of northern Myanmar where the nat cult is particularly strong. Nat pwe followers will find the Zeedaw Nat Festival at Zeedaw and Maungdon (cross the Chindwin River at Monywa and travel 22km west along the Yinmabin road) in the fortnight around the new moon of Tabaung (February/March).

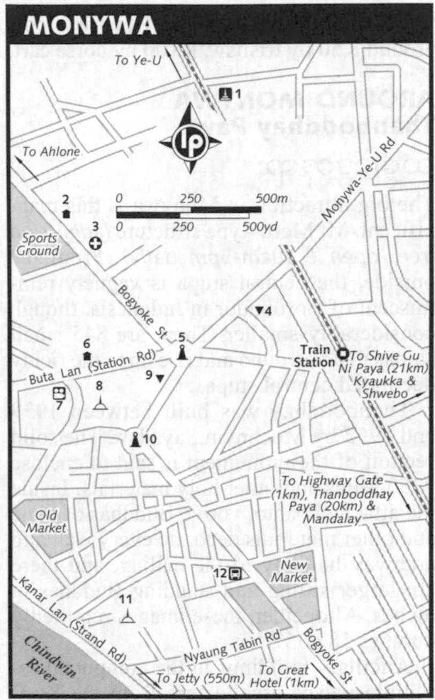

MONYWA

PLACES TO STAY
2 Monywa Hotel
6 Shwe Taung Tan Hotel & Restaurant

PLACES TO EAT
4 Shwe Kyar Restaurant
9 Pann Cherry Restaurant

OTHER
1 Lehdi Kyaung (Stone Inscription Monastery)
3 Hospital
5 Bogyoke Statue
7 Moonlight Cinema
8 Shwezigon Paya
10 Clock Tower
11 Zedi
12 Bus Station

Coinciding with the festival at Zeedaw, the Ma Ngwe Daung Nat Festival is celebrated at Ahlone (12km north of Monywa on the Shwebo road). Ma Ngwe Daung was unlucky in love, and the festival is frequented by those who have suffered similar misfortune.

Places to Stay & Eat

Shwe Taung Tan Hotel & Restaurant (*☎ 21478; rooms per person US$2-5*), near the Moonlight Cinema, is a bit shabby but good value. The smallest, cheapest rooms start at US$2 without bathroom. The US$4 to US$5 rooms have air-con (when the power is working) and cold-water bathroom, and a basic breakfast is included in the rates.

Great Hotel (*☎ 22431; Bogyoke St; singles/doubles US$10/14*), on the main road into town, has quite good air-con rooms with attached shower and toilet.

Monywa Hotel (*☎ 21581; Bogyoke St; singles/doubles US$18/24, with TV US$30/36*) a bit farther past the town centre, is a privatised place with wooden bungalows with corrugated metal roofs divided into four rooms, each with fridge, air-con and attached hot-water bathroom. There are also slightly better furnished rooms with TV. The rooms are clean (if a little overpriced), and rates include breakfast. One of the Monywa Hotel's main advantages is its pleasant outdoor bar and rambling grounds.

Shwe Kyar Restaurant (*Thazi St*), a block northeast of the Bogyoke roundabout, serves quite good Bamar and Chinese dishes.

Pann Cherry Restaurant, in the centre of town near the clock tower, serves good Chinese food in both the open-sided dining room downstairs and the air-con room upstairs.

Getting There & Away

Bus & Pick-up From Mandalay, you can catch a pick-up to Monywa from 27th St, near the corner of 83rd St, or from Central/Main bus station in the lot near the northeast corner of 26th and 82nd Sts. Pick-ups (K150, K300 in front, three hours) leave about every 45 minutes between 4am and 3pm in either direction. Private minibuses (K300) leave hourly between 5am and 3pm in either direction.

There are many buses throughout the day, although the best is Aung Kyaw Moe Express, which runs a large air-con bus between Monywa and Mandalay for K500 (three hours). In Mandalay, it leaves from the Highway bus station; in Monywa from the bus stop near the new market. The same company runs a bus from Monywa to Yangon for K2000, which leaves town at noon, arriving the next morning at 7.30am.

You can also travel from Monywa to Bagan directly (ie, without having to double back to Mandalay) by taking a bus to Pakokku. These head off three times daily and take about three to four hours.

Train Myanma Railways operates twice-daily trains from Mandalay to Monywa at 5.35am (No 123 Up) and 1.45pm (No 125 Up), but the journey is a slow six hours, compared to the 3½ hours by bus. The return journeys are scheduled for 1.20pm (No 124 Down) and 6.50am (No 126 Down). The fare is just K80, but even locals don't bother with the train, preferring the bus option.

Car By car it's only a 2½-hour drive from Mandalay via a decent two lane road. The going rate for car and driver between the two cities – as a long day trip only – is US$35, although it can vary according to the price of petrol. You may be able to find a driver willing to stay overnight in Monywa.

Boat Ferries upriver to Kalewa take around four days and cost K250 per person in funky two-bed cabins, about half that price for deck class. If more foreigners take this ferry, expect the price to be in US dollars soon. Food can be arranged through the crew, or at ferry stops along the way.

If you catch the early morning bus to Pakokku, you should be able to connect with the government-run boat from Pakokku to Nyaung U (Bagan), which departs at 1pm and 2pm daily and takes about 1½ hours. Private boats between Pakokku and Nyaung U can be chartered for around K5000.

Getting Around

Horse cart and trishaw are the main forms of local transport. A trip between the Chindwin River and the Monywa Hotel will cost around K50 by trishaw, K100 by horse cart.

AROUND MONYWA

Thanboddhay Paya

သမ္ဗုဒ္ဓေဘုရား

The big attraction in Monywa is this magnificent, Mt Meru–type structure *(admission free; open 6.30am-5pm daily)*. From the outside, the central stupa is vaguely reminiscent of Borobudur in Indonesia, though considerably smaller. There are 845 small stupas that surround and rise up to the richly decorated central stupa.

Thanboddhay was built between 1939 and 1952 by Moehnyin Sayadaw. The solid section of the monument is said to enclose 7350 relics and other holy materials. Inside the attached pahto, votive Buddhas of bone and other materials decorate every wall and archway halfway to the ceiling, and there are larger sitting and standing Buddhas in niches. Altogether, these images reportedly number 582,357.

Ancillary buildings in the compound resemble palace architecture from the Konbaung era (18th and 19th centuries) and feature three-dimensional jataka reliefs on their exteriors.

The annual festival takes place in the month of Tazaungmon (October/November). Thanboddhay is 19km southeast of Monywa on the northeastern side of the main road from Mandalay, just past a small bridge.

Four kilometres past Thanboddhay Paya is a 90m-long **reclining Buddha**, with a very small (and free) **museum** on the inside containing 9000 Buddha images. Nearby is **Boddhi-tataung** (1000 Buddhas), a grove of banyan trees, each with a Buddha at its foot, and **Aung Setkya Paya**, standing 130m high on the Po Khaung hills, surrounded by 1060 smaller zedi, and including an impressive reclining Buddha.

Twin Daung

တွင်းတောင်

About 3km east of the river in Budalin township, Twin Daung (Well Hill) stands only 200m above the surrounding plain, but features a 50m-deep round lake known as Myitta Kan (The Lake of Love), whose water level reportedly rises and falls with the Chindwin. According to some sources the depression holding the lake was left behind by a volcanic eruption; others say a meteorite bounced off the earth's crust here and went on to land in a similar depression in Kani, further north. Whatever the source, there is now an algae processing plant there. To reach the lake by car, take the road west from Budalin for about 12km.

Ledi Kyaung

လယ်တီကျောင်း

This monastery, at the northeastern edge of the town on the road to Ye-U, was constructed in 1886 by order of renowned Pali scholar Ledi Sayadaw. Similar in concept to Kuthodaw Paya in Mandalay, the kyaung features 806 stone slabs inscribed with Buddhist scriptures.

Shwe Gu Ni Paya

ရွှေဂူနီဘုရား

About 20km east of town, via a scenic two-lane road, is one of the most important pilgrimage spots in northern Myanmar. Dating to the 14th century, the main zedi of Shwe Gu Ni Paya rises to 33m (an auspicious height, made even more so when measured in feet – 108) and is famous for its 'wish-fulfilling' powers. The main antechamber to the shrine hall contains exemplary jataka paintings and is well decorated with mosaics.

Kyaukka

ကျောက်ကာ

This village just beyond Shwe Gu Ni Paya has been a centre for lacquerware since the Konbaung era. The pieces produced are for the most part more basic and utilitarian than those made in Bagan. Consisting of simple bamboo frames finished in black, silver or gold (or some combination thereof), the lacquerware shows more links to the pre–Chiang Mai styles that existed before the Bagan artisans began using a wider palette, finer materials, more layers of lacquer and incising techniques, which allowed different colours to show through the outer layers. Because Kyaukka is less frequented by tourists, prices are particularly low, though you won't find any pieces as striking as in Bagan. In output, however, the village is second only to Bagan and the pieces made here are very strong.

Just east of the village, look for the small **Paw Daw Mu Paya**, which commands a good view of the countryside.

The road to Kyaukka is lined with picturesque tamarind trees and rice paddies. Pick-ups to Kyaukka leave a couple of times in the morning from Monywa's central market; the last one back leaves around 4pm.

Hpo Win Daung Caves

ဖိုးဝင်းတောင်ဂူ

It's a short ferry ride from the main jetty in Monywa across the Chindwin River to Nyaungbingyi, followed by a 25km drive to this system of quite impressive sandstone caves situated in a cleft in the Hpo Win Daung (Hpo Win Hills). The hills have probably been occupied since the dawn of human habitation in Myanmar; to the southwest lies the Pondaung-pon-nya mountain range, where the fossilised remains of 'Pondaung Man' – a primitive primate ancestor who may have lived 30 million years ago – were found.

The caves *(admission US$2)* and surrounding hills are named after U Hpo Win, a famous *zawgyi* (alchemist) who once lived among them. The caves themselves contain Buddhist statues, wood carvings and murals dating to the 17th and 18th centuries. Most exhibit the Inwa style, though some may date as far back as the 14th to 16th centuries. A covered stairway climbs a hill to the main cave shrine, but there are dozens of large and small caves in the area filled with old Buddhas. There are said to be over 400,000 images in these and other nearby caves. The main festival takes place in the week leading up to the full moon of Tazaungmon (October/November). Some travellers have been able to stay overnight at the nearby monastery.

Shwebataung Paya, just beyond Hpo Win Daung, features unique pavilions cut from the surrounding sandstone and filled with plain Buddha images. The hill is reached via a series of steps beginning in the village of Minzu.

The last ferry in either direction across the Chindwin River departs at 6pm.

SHWEBO
ရွှေဘို

The flat plain that lies between the Mu and Ayeyarwady Rivers around Shwebo has been continuously inhabited since at least the 3rd century AD, when the Pyus founded a city-state at nearby Hanlin. With the coming of the Bamar from the north, Hanlin crumbled and the area became an agricultural supply satellite for the rotating Bamar kingdoms of northern Myanmar.

During the early 17th century, when the Portuguese adventurer Philip De Brito was defeated at Thanlyin (Syriam), all the Portuguese and Eurasians living at De Brito's 13-year-old colony were exiled to the villages of Monhla and Chantha near Shwebo. Called *bayingyis*, the rare fair-haired resident may occasionally be seen in these villages, although no linguistic or cultural legacies remain.

Shwebo served as a royal capital from 1760 to 1764 under King Alaungpaya. A Shwebo native, Alaungpaya used the city as a base for the reconquest of Inwa and southern Myanmar, establishing what is known as the Third Burmese Empire. It was previously called Yangyiaung, Yadanatheinga, Konbaung (Embankment) and Moke-so-po (The Hunter Po), but Alaungpaya changed the name to the more royal Shwebo – Golden Banyan Tree. After defeating the Shan and the Mon, Alaungpaya destroyed several British trading posts, one of the first aggravated assaults against the Raj. His successor, Hsinbyushin, moved the capital to Amarapura in the 1780s.

Shwebo today has a Bamar majority with sizable Muslim and Christian communities. The town has little of Monywa's energy or appeal but, as in Monywa, the local economy depends on the trading of

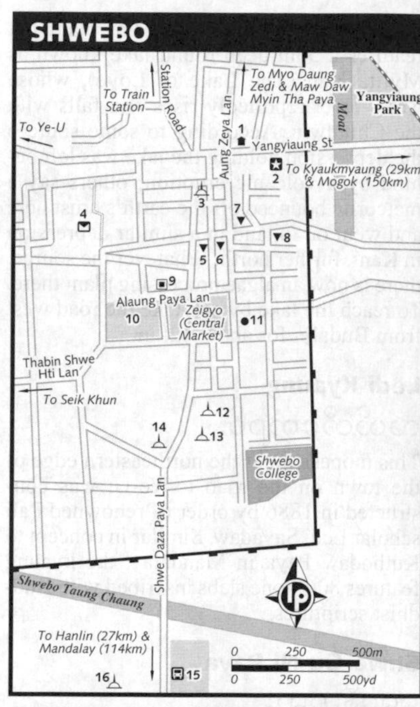

SHWEBO

PLACES TO STAY & EAT
1 Zin Wai Lar Guest House
5 Khine Thazin Restaurant
6 Shwe Taung Chinese Restaurant
7 Eden Culinary Garden
8 Win Myint Gyi Muslim Restaurant

OTHER
2 Police Station
3 Shwekyettho Paya
4 Post Office
9 Alaungpaya's Tomb
10 Alaungpaya Palace Grounds
11 Aung Mitha Pharmacy
12 Chanthaya Paya
13 Chanthaya-gyi Paya
14 Shwe Daza Paya
15 Highway Bus Station
16 Aung Mye Hsu

nuts, pulses, rice and sesame cultivated on the surrounding plains. A signboard in Burmese and English is posted at either end of town proclaiming this a 'Hi-Tech Model Township'. During the months of April and May, Shwebo is extremely hot and dry.

Things to See & Do

You can get a good view of the city from **Maw Daw Myin Tha Paya**, on Eindathaya Hill at the northeastern corner of town. The paya was built in 1755 by Alaungpaya and is said to enshrine an emerald alms bowl belonging to Gautama Buddha. Other famous religious monuments include the typical Burmese-style **Myo Daung Zedi** nearby and **Shwe Daza Paya** in the southern part of town (said to have been built by King Narapatisithu over 500 years ago).

Nay Rapan Paya, which is distinguished by having five entrances instead of the usual four, is located southwest of the town centre. **Aung Mye Hsu Taung** (the town's wishing-ground) is said to be the spot used by King Alaungpaya as a staging point before going into battle. You'll find it just outside the city entrance towards Mandalay, within a larger paya compound.

The water-filled eastern moat, the most visible legacy of Alaungpaya's original city plan, stretches a couple of kilometres and is about 10m deep. The British built a jail on the Alaungpaya palace grounds, next to the central market north of the centre. Burmese residents recently moved the jail to the outskirts of town to excavate the site. **Alaungpaya's remains**, entombed nearby, are marked with a headstone inscribed in English. To enter the gated compound, you must first find the market administrator whose office is about 50m east.

Places to Stay & Eat

Only three guesthouses are licensed to accommodate foreigners in Shwebo. Of those, only one is worth recommending:

Zin Wai Lar Guest House *(☎ 075-21263; Yangyiaung St; doubles with shared/private bathroom K500/1500)* is a relatively new place (sign in Burmese) in the eastern part of town on Yangyiaung St towards Kyaukmyaung. It's a modern, three-storey affair with 14 ordinary doubles with common bathroom and squat toilet, two double rooms with attached bathroom and western toilet, and one triple with attached bathroom, fridge and local TV. Breakfast is included in the price.

Eden Culinary Garden *(Aung Zeya St)* offers a mixed menu of European, Chinese and Bamar dishes (around K200) in a relatively clean setting.

Shwe Taung Chinese Restaurant, north of the market, is Shwebo's most popular Chinese restaurant.

Khine Thazin Restaurant *(Min Nyo San St)* is a quiet, well-decorated place serving Bamar and Chinese food, near the cinema north of the town centre.

There are several small no-name **Bamar restaurants** north of the central market along Aung Zeya St.

For good biryani and other Indian Muslim dishes, head to **Win Myint Gyi Muslim Restaurant**, near the city wall.

Getting There & Away

Bus & Pick-up Several transport companies operate along the 114km route between Shwebo and Mandalay. The busiest line, ie, the one with the most departures, is the Yangyiaung Mahn 35-seat minibus, (K350, three hours). All lines leave hourly from the Central/Main bus station in Mandalay between 6am and 3pm. Shwebo's Highway bus station stands opposite Alaungpaya's wishing-ground paya, just outside the city entrance towards Mandalay. Dyna Transport Co runs several small and medium-sized pick-ups throughout the day between Shwebo and Mandalay for K100 (K150 front seat).

Train Shwebo is linked to Katha and Myitkyina in the north, and to Mandalay in the south by rail. From Mandalay the No 55 Up leaves at 3pm and normally arrives in Shwebo at 6pm, although it attracts very few passengers.

Getting Around

Trishaws and horse carts are the main modes of public transport. Pick-ups can be chartered for K2000 a day for around town excursions, K5000 for half-day out-of-town excursions.

AROUND SHWEBO

Hanlin

ဟန်လင်း

The architectural remains of the Pyu kingdom (3rd to 9th centuries) at Hanlin (also called Halin and Halingyi) consist of a few crumbling city walls, gates, pillars and melting zedi, but little else. Pots and other artefacts excavated at the site are displayed in a small museum in the local monastery.

Hanlin is 26km southeast from Shwebo. There are no buses to Hanlin, but it's possible to hire a jeep for around US$20 return the same day.

Bagan Region

Bagan (Pagan) is the most wondrous sight in Myanmar, if not Southeast Asia. Across 40 sq km of country, stretching back from the Ayeyarwady (Irrawaddy) River, stand thousands of stupas and *pahto* (temples). In every direction you'll see ruins of all sizes – huge and glorious temples like the Ananda Pahto soar towards the sky; small, graceful *zedi* (stupas) stand alone in fields. Some come with all manner of historical tales, while others are identified only by a number. Still others, like 900-year-old Gubyaukgyi in Myinkaba, contain elegant mural paintings, though visitors require a light to see them.

One could easily spend a week or more exploring the Bagan region. In addition to the more well-known monuments in the main archaeological zone of Old Bagan, there are sites worth visiting in several other nearby towns and villages.

What you will be able to see is limited by the amount of time at your disposal and how you intend to use it. If you can afford to hire a car (or horse cart) and a guide, you'll be able to visit more temples, particularly those off the beaten track. Renting bicycles also makes the sites much more accessible than on foot.

If your time is very limited – just an afternoon or a day, for example – we suggest that you restrict yourself to the temples and stupas in the central Bagan Archaeological Zone, which is where most of them are concentrated.

Detailed discussions of the history and archaeological styles of Bagan's ancient temples and stupas have been combined in a special section titled 'Archaeology of Bagan' in this chapter.

Highlights

- Spectacular plain of Bagan dotted with thousands of 800-year-old temple ruins
- Sunset over the Ayeyarwady River, viewed from Mingalazedi or Bupaya
- Mystical Mt Popa, home to Myanmar's nat
- Little-known Bagan-era ruins and monastery museum of Salay

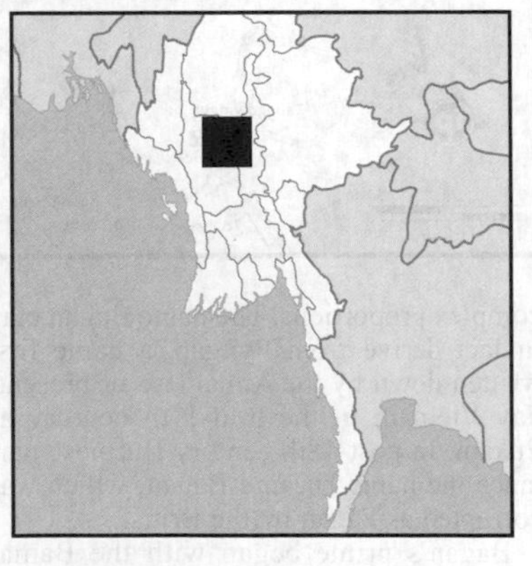

HISTORY

The extraordinary religious fervour that resulted in this unique collection of buildings lasted two and a half centuries. Although human habitation at Bagan dates back almost to the beginning of the Christian era, Bagan only entered its golden period with the conquest of Thaton in AD 1057. Just over 200 years later Bagan declined, and in 1287 was overrun by the Mongols of Kublai Khan. But what fantastic effort went into those two and a half centuries! It's as if all the medieval cathedrals of Europe had been built in one small area, and then deserted, barely touched over the centuries.

Originally, this bend in the Ayeyarwady River was occupied by a stable and thriving Pyu city-state, perhaps allied with Beikthano and Thayekhittaya (Sri Ksetra) to the south as well as Hanlin to the northeast. Excavations along the ruined city walls indicate that by 850 the city had reached

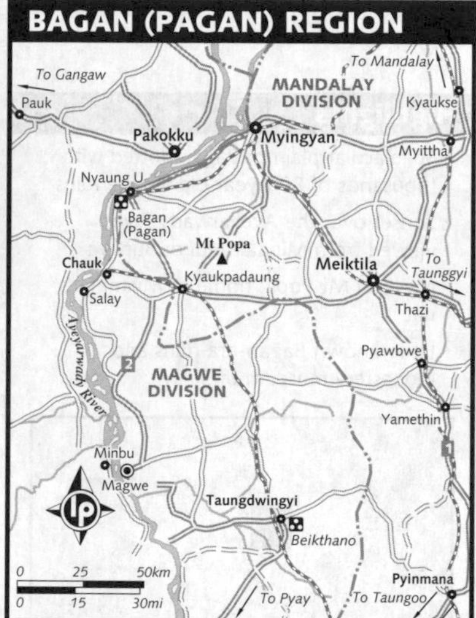

complex proportions. The name Bagan may in fact derive from Pyugan, a name first written down by the Annamese of present-day Vietnam in the mid-11th century as Pukam. In post-18th century Burmese parlance the name became Bagan, which was corrupted as Pagan by the British.

Bagan's prime began with the Bamar King Anawrahta's ascent to the throne in 1044. At this time, Myanmar was in a period of transition from Hindu and Mahayana Buddhist beliefs to the Theravada Buddhist beliefs that have since been characteristic of Myanmar. Manuha, the Mon king of Thaton, sent a monk to convert Anawrahta; the latter met with such success that Anawrahta asked Manuha to give him a number of sacred texts and important relics. Manuha, uncertain of the depths of Anawrahta's beliefs, refused the request. Anawrahta's reply to this snub was straightforward – he marched his army south, conquered Thaton and carted everything worth carrying to Bagan – including 32 sets of the *Tripitaka* (the classic Buddhist scriptures), the city's monks and scholars and, for good measure, King Manuha himself. All in all, some 30,000 Mon prisoners of war were brought to Bagan from Thaton.

Immediately Anawrahta set about a great programme of building, and some of the greatest Bagan edifices date from his reign. Among the better known monuments he constructed are the beautiful Shwezigon Paya, considered a prototype for all later Burmese stupas; the Pitaka Taik (Scripture Library), built to house the *pitaka* (scriptures) carried back from Thaton by 30 elephants; and the elegant and distinctive Shwesandaw Paya, built immediately after the conquest of Thaton. Thus began what the Burmese call the First Burmese Empire, which became a major centre for Theravada Buddhism and a pilgrimage point for Buddhists throughout Southeast Asia.

King Anawrahta's successors, particularly Kyanzittha, Alaungsithu and Narapatisithu, continued this phenomenal building programme, although the construction work must have been nonstop throughout the period of Bagan's glory. Pali inscriptions of the time called the city Arimaddanapura (City of the Enemy Crusher) and Tambadipa (Copper Land). Marco Polo described the city-state in his famous 1298 chronicle:

> The towers are built of fine stone; and then one of them has been covered with gold a good finger in thickness, so that the tower looks as if it were all of solid gold; and the other is covered with silver in like manner so that it seems to be all of solid silver ... The King caused these towers to be erected to commemorate his magnificence and for the good of his soul; and really they do form one of the finest sights in the world, so exquisitely finished are they, so splendid and costly. And when they are lighted up by the sun they shine most brilliantly and are visible from a vast distance.

Historians disagree on what exactly happened to cause Bagan's apparently rapid decline at the end of the 13th century. The popular Burmese view is that millions of Mongols sent by Kublai Khan swept over the city, ransacking and looting. A more thoughtful view holds that the threat of invasion from China threw the last powerful ruler of Bagan into a panic; after a great number of temples were torn down to build fortifications, the city was abandoned, in which case the Mongols merely took over an already deserted city. This view finds support in Marco Polo's observation that the kingdom was taken by Kublai Khan's 'clowns and court jugglers'.

Bagan scholar Paul Strachan argues in *Pagan: Art and Architecture of Old Burma* that the city was never abandoned at all. For him the evidence suggests:

> ... the physical arrival of the Mongols would seem to have affected Pagan little ... Despite the political imbalances that the Mongols brought about Pagan remained a cultural centre, possibly even up to the present.

Evidence suggests Bagan may have continued as an important religious and cultural centre into the 14th century, after which its decay can be blamed on the three-way struggle between the Shan, Mon and Bamar for supremacy over northern Myanmar. Whatever happened, although some minor rebuilding and maintenance continued through the centuries, the state's growth was effectively halted by 1300. Many of the religious monuments were later damaged by looters seeking precious metals and stones hidden in Buddha images and shrine walls.

From the 14th to 18th centuries, Bagan was considered a spooky region, riddled with bandits and *nat* (guardian spirits). The Burmese only began moving back to Nyaung U and Bagan in some numbers after the British established a presence in the area to provide protection from robbers and marauders.

It's hard to imagine Bagan as it once was because, like other Burmese royal cities, only the major religious buildings were made of permanent materials. The kings' palaces were all constructed of wood, and even most *kyaung* (monasteries) were partly or wholly wooden. So what remains is just a frail shadow of Bagan at its peak. Today, a few small farming villages are the only occupants of the great city. Grain fields stand where there were palace grounds.

The kings who reigned over Bagan during its golden period were:

Anawrahta	1044–1077
Sawlu	1077–1084
Kyanzittha	1084–1113
Alaungsithu	1113–1167
Narathu	1167–1170
Naratheinkha	1170–1173
Narapatisithu	1174–1211
Nantaungmya	1211–1234
Kyaswa	1234–1250
Uzana	1250–1255
Narathihapati	1255–1287

1975 Earthquake & Restoration

In 1975 Bagan was shaken by a powerful earthquake, registering 6.5 on the Richter scale. Contrary to initial fears, this 1000-year-old site was not totally ruined. Many of the more important temples were badly damaged, but major reconstruction started almost immediately.

Since renovation of these important religious monuments has been an ongoing project for many centuries, the old skills have not been lost and many monuments were rebuilt using traditional means. Unesco's recent restoration projects now support dozens of local artisans and, although you certainly won't see any modern construction equipment in Bagan, modern techniques are being employed as well. For example, Unesco engineers are reinforcing some of the monuments by inserting iron beams in the masonry to preserve the structural integrity in case of an earthquake.

As for the hundreds of lesser monuments, anything that was likely to fall off in an earthquake would have fallen off centuries ago. While it was quite evident which of the major temples were repaired, Bagan has never looked like a huge building site. Some of the restoration, such as the repairs to the Gawdawpalin Pahto, took until the early 1980s to complete. Others continue.

Recent History

Although the whole area is known to tourists as Bagan, only the Archaeological Zone is properly called Bagan nowadays. The village that grew up in the middle of the zone during the 1970s was moved to the middle of a peanut field several kilometres away just before the May 1990 elections. Old Bagan residents were only given about a week's notice by the government to move and rebuild in the new location, known as Bagan Myothit. Now it's hard to tell that a village ever existed here, so thorough were the authorities in erasing all traces. Despite the forced removal, the resilient residents of Bagan Myothit have put together a respectable existence, and many continue to depend on tourist services – lodging, food, souvenirs and moneychanging – for their livelihood.

Bagan Archaeological Zone

ပုဂံရှေးဟောင်းယဉ်ကျေးမှုနယ်မြေ

☎ 062

Orientation

Old Bagan sits on the eastern bank of a deep bend of the Ayeyarwady River. A paved road follows the river bend from Nyaung U, the largest town in the area, and through the Bagan Archaeological Zone to the village of Myinkaba, and finally to Thiripyitsaya and Bagan Myothit (New Bagan). Branching off this road is a vast network of tracks and trails between the various monuments.

Clearing Old Bagan of guesthouses had the effect of eliminating the tourist ghetto that had developed. Accommodation is now scattered around Nyaung U, Wetkyi-in, Myinkaba, Bagan Myothit, Tetthe and Old Bagan.

The main town in the area, Nyaung U, is about 5km upriver from Bagan. Nyaung U is also the terminus for buses and riverboats from Mandalay or further afield, and the airport is a couple of kilometres southeast near the village of Tetthe. The train station is another 2km beyond the airport.

For K500, you can purchase *The Map of Bagan* at the airport, several hotels, and the MTT tourist information office (see the Information section following).

Photography & Sunset-Viewing For a panoramic view of as many temple ruins and stupas as possible, Mingalazedi is among the best choices, now that the upper terraces of the tallest monuments (Thatbyinnyu, Gawdawpalin, Dhammayangyi, Sulamani) are closed to visitors. The light for the eastward view from Mingalazedi is at its best in the late afternoon. Excellent, lesser-known stupas that can be climbed include Minyeingon, near the Bagan Hotel, and the more remote Pyathada, due east of Mingalazedi.

The westward view from Mingalazedi is, of course, also good at sunset, though some people prefer the sunset view from Shwesandaw Paya, as it encompasses silhouettes of the monuments within Old Bagan to the northwest.

For Ayeyarwady River views at sunset, the best choices are Bupaya in Old Bagan or Lawkananda Paya in Bagan Myothit; both stupas stand on the eastern bank of the river. Upali Thein in Wetkyi-in and Nanpaya in Myinkaba are also good spots for catching a sunset, especially if another favourite is crowded.

An incredibly spectacular way to see the sun rise over Bagan is to treat yourself to a balloon flight. **Balloons Over Bagan** *(☎ 70145, fax 70313; e bob@mptmail.net.mm; w www.balloonsoverbagan.com)* offers flights daily for US$190 per person (or less, depending on the numbers). Champagne is served after the flight. For more information, contact the company's sales desk at the Bagan Hotel.

Information

Old Bagan itself contains only a few hotels and restaurants, the offices of Myanma Airways (MA), Air Mandalay (AM) and Yangon Airways (YA) and Myanmar Travels &

Tours (MTT). The **MTT tourist information office** *(☎ 70217; open 8am-4pm daily)* is inside the government-run MTT Guesthouse, on the road to Nyaung U. The office offers tour guides at a rate of US$10 to US$15 per day, or US$20 for two to three days.

Post & Communications There is a post office in Nyaung U; airmail letters are carried aboard daily flights to Yangon (Rangoon), so it's fairly reliable.

Most of the hotels in the area have International Direct Dial (IDD) phones, but they cost around US$10 a minute, and the service can be erratic. Fax machines are sometimes available, but they are slow and therefore expensive.

You can make much cheaper 'booking' calls, but from only three locations in the vicinity. A telephone office in Nyaung U near the Thante Hotel (Nyaung U) charges K3000 for a three-minute overseas call. As usual, you first book the call, then wait at least half an hour for the switchboard to contact the Yangon operator, who then calls back to Nyaung U. A smaller branch telephone office is on the main road between Old Bagan and Nyaung U. Another telephone office *(open 24 hrs)* is on the main east-west road in Bagan Myothit.

Admission MTT charges a US$10 entry fee for the first two nights spent in the archaeological zone. In theory, an additional US$2 is levied per night thereafter, although no-one bothers to collect it. For those arriving by air, boat or train, the US$10 fee is collected upon arrival on behalf of MTT. Hotels collect the fee from those arriving overland. Hotels are also required to ask to see your entry receipt.

Getting There & Away

Air All three airlines (MA, AM and YA) fly to Nyaung U-Bagan airport from Yangon, Mandalay and Heho.

AM flies daily from Yangon (US$131, 75 minutes) and AM or YA fly from Mandalay (US$51, half an hour). On any flight, if you sit on the right-hand side of the aircraft flying Mandalay-Bagan or the left-hand side flying Bagan-Mandalay, you can keep the Ayeyarwady in sight for most of the way. You also get an excellent view of Bagan on the Bagan-Yangon flights.

From Heho, all the airlines fly daily to Bagan with a stopover in Mandalay. Aboard AM or YA, a ticket for this route costs US$71; on MA it's US$68.

AM flights can be booked or confirmed at the AM office in Bagan Myothit. The YA office is in Nyaung U near the *zeigyo* (central market). Ostensibly, MA flights can also be booked at the MA office on the opposite side of the road in Old Bagan, but repeated visits indicate that the staff are less than helpful. It's very difficult to find out whether you have a confirmed seat on the plane until it's too late to book the bus-train connection. Our recommendation – especially in light of MA's abysmal efficiency and horrible safety record – is to forget about trying to fly in/out of Bagan on MA. Stick to AM or YA – even though it costs a little more – or come via land or river.

Bus, Pick-up & Share Taxi There are a number of options for travelling to the Bagan region by bus:

Mandalay After flying, the fastest way to get to Bagan is on the bus from Mandalay to Nyaung U. Buses operate daily from Mandalay's Highway bus station, also known as the Central/Main bus station, on the corner of 26th and 82nd Sts, for around K650 per person for the seven-hour trip. Pick-ups also go from Mandalay to Bagan for a bit less. Along the way you make a couple of tea stops – breakfast at Kumeh, lunch at Yewei. See the Getting There & Away section in the Mandalay chapter for more information.

From Bagan, Mann Express Co buses depart for Mandalay from the Nyaung U bus station near Shwezigon Pagoda at 4am, 7am and 9am (K650, non air-con).

There are also share taxis – Toyota 'Super-roof' hatchbacks – available to Bagan for around K2000 per person. These same cars can usually be chartered between Mandalay and Bagan for around US$60; new air-con vans for US$100. By share taxi

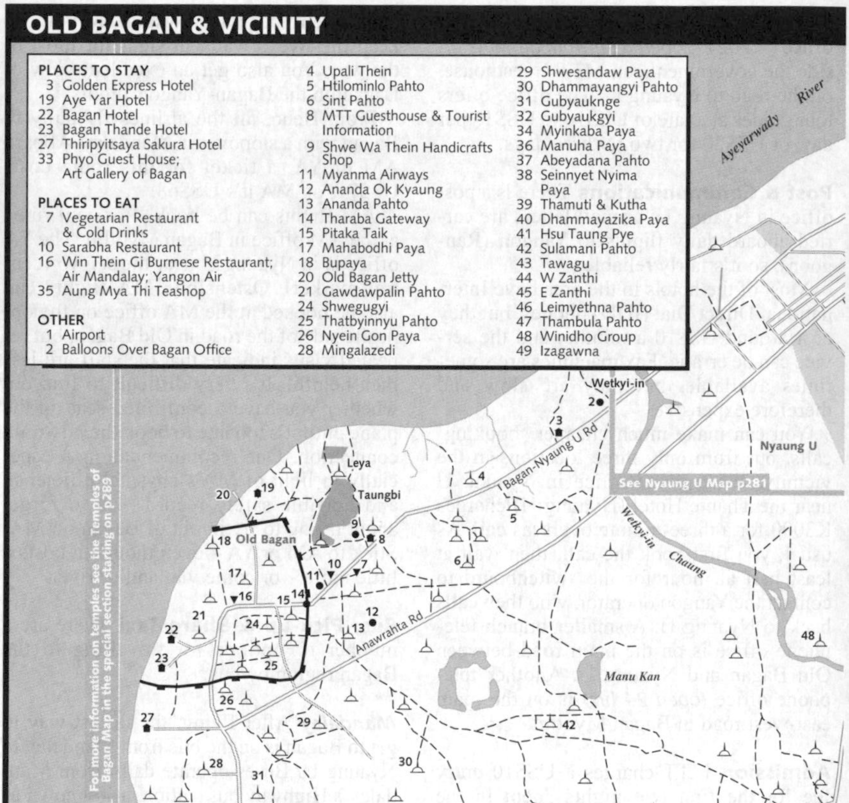

OLD BAGAN & VICINITY
PLACES TO STAY
3 Golden Express Hotel
19 Aye Yar Hotel
22 Bagan Hotel
23 Bagan Thande Hotel
27 Thiripyitsaya Sakura Hotel
33 Phyo Guest House; Art Gallery of Bagan
PLACES TO EAT
7 Vegetarian Restaurant & Cold Drinks
10 Sarabha Restaurant
16 Win Thein Gi Burmese Restaurant; Air Mandalay; Yangon Air
35 Aung Mya Thi Teashop
OTHER
1 Airport
2 Balloons Over Bagan Office
4 Upali Thein
5 Htilominlo Pahto
6 Sint Pahto
8 MTT Guesthouse & Tourist Information
9 Shwe Wa Thein Handicrafts Shop
11 Myanma Airways
12 Ananda Ok Kyaung
13 Ananda Pahto
14 Tharaba Gateway
15 Pitaka Taik
17 Mahabodhi Paya
18 Bupaya
20 Old Bagan Jetty
21 Gawdawpalin Pahto
24 Shwegugyi
25 Thatbyinnyu Pahto
26 Nyein Gon Paya
28 Mingalazedi
29 Shwesandaw Paya
30 Dhammayangyi Pahto
31 Gubyauknge
32 Gubyaukgyi
34 Myinkaba Paya
36 Manuha Paya
37 Abeyadana Pahto
38 Seinnyet Nyima Paya
39 Thamuti & Kutha
40 Dhammayazika Paya
41 Hsu Taung Pye
42 Sulamani Pahto
43 Tawagu
44 W Zanthi
45 E Zanthi
46 Leimyethna Pahto
47 Thambula Pahto
48 Winidho Group
49 Izagawna
Ayeyarwady River
Wetkyi-in
Nyaung U
See Nyaung U Map p281
Bagan-Nyaung U Rd
Wetkyi-in Chaung
Leya
Taungbi
Old Bagan
Anawrahta Rd
Manu Kan
For more information on temples see the Temples of Bagan Map in the special section starting on p289
Minnanthu
Myinkaba
West Pwasaw
East Pwasaw
See Bagan Myothit (New Bagan) Map p284
Bagan Myothit (New Bagan)
Thuhekan
To Chauk & Salay

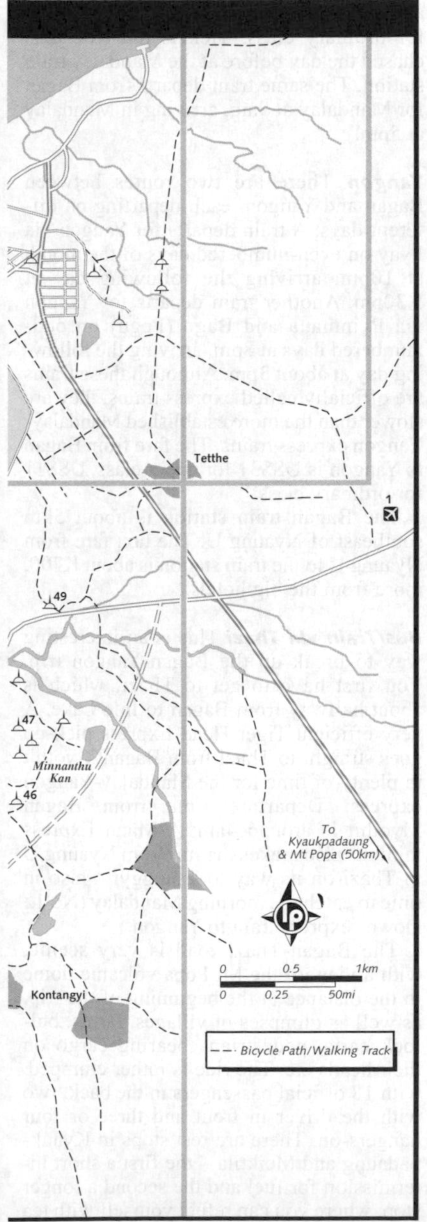

or chartered private vehicle, the drive time for the 305km between Mandalay and Bagan/Nyaung U drops to around six hours.

Taunggyi You can travel by bus, pick-up or private car directly between Nyaung U or Bagan Myothit and Taunggyi, to Inle Lake. From Bagan Myothit, Tiger Head Express operates Japanese pick-ups to Taunggyi for around K1000 per person. The pick-up leaves the main north-south road in Bagan Myothit at 4am and arrives in Thazi around 8.45am, in time to catch the No 12 Down special express train to Yangon, which is scheduled to depart from Thazi at 9.28am. The pick-up continues, arriving in Taunggyi around 2pm, stopping for lunch along the way in Yemabay. Most travellers get off before Taunggyi at the junction town of Shwenyaung and take the short bus or taxi ride to Nyaungshwe (Yaunghwe) at the northern end of Inle Lake.

Mann Express Bus Co operates the only bus (no air-con) from Nyaung U to Taunggyi. Daily departure is at 5am from Nyaung U, arriving in Taunggyi at around 1pm. The fare is K1100.

If you're really counting kyat you can hopscotch to Taunggyi/Inle Lake by taking a public pick-up from Nyaung U to Kyaukpadaung, changing to another pick-up bound for Meiktila, changing again to a Thazi-bound pick-up and finally catching a pick-up in Thazi all the way to Shwenyaung or Taunggyi. It's doubtful you'd make this trip all the way without having to spend the night somewhere. If you decide to stay overnight along the way, Thazi is your least expensive choice.

Those with a less limited budget can charter a car all the way from the Bagan region to Taunggyi or Inle Lake for around US$45, or a new air-con van for up to US$90. Up over the hills east of Thazi, the road is winding – beware if you suffer from motion sickness. Whether by public pick-up or chartered van, this is a long and trying trip. You can usually arrange to stop at Mt Popa on the way for the same price, to make it approximately a 10-hour trip. If you want to break the journey with an overnight stop in Kalaw, expect to pay another K3000.

Meiktila & Thazi If seats are available, Tiger Head Express will drop passengers off in Meiktila or Thazi on the way to Taunggyi for K500. If there's competition for the seats, Tiger Head sometimes charges the full Taunggyi fare, which is K1000.

Yangon Several buses leave daily from Nyaung U for Yangon, via Pyay (Prome). The best is the air-con Ye Thu Aung Express bus, departing at 4pm and arriving early the next morning at Yangon's Highway bus station. The fare is K2000. A slower and less comfortable government bus makes the same trip for K600.

There's also the trip from Nyaung U to Kyaukpadaung, about 50km southeast (K75, two-hours). The Dagon-Popa bus line in Kyaukpadaung departs for Yangon twice daily at 4am and 8am (K800, 12 to 14 hours). Book tickets the day before in Kyaukpadaung.

You could also take a bus to Meiktila and catch one of several Yangon-bound air-con express buses from Mandalay – see the Getting There & Away section in the Mandalay chapter for details.

Pyay Air-con buses depart from Nyaung U at 8.30pm for Yangon and will drop you in Pyay for K1500. Arrival time is around 6am.

From Pyay you can continue to Yangon by public bus (three departures daily) for just K400 and a ride of around seven hours. Air-con Sun-Moon Express or Rainbow Express buses from Pyay to Yangon are also available once a day at around 5pm for K400 – see the Pyay section in the Around Yangon chapter for more details.

By private vehicle you can drive between Bagan and Pyay in as little as six or seven hours, now that the road has been improved.

Train There are a few train options to/from Bagan:

Mandalay There is a daily 10pm departure from Mandalay to Bagan that should arrive at 6am. Upper-class fare is US$9 or US$4 for ordinary class. Tickets must be purchased the day before at the Mandalay train station. The same train departs from Bagan for Mandalay at 9am, arriving in Mandalay at 5pm.

Yangon There are two routes between Bagan and Yangon, each departing on different days. A train departs for Yangon via Pyay on even-numbered days of the month at 10pm, arriving the following day at 5.30pm. Another train departs for Yangon via Pyinmana and Bago (Pegu) on odd-numbered days at 8pm, arriving the following day at about 3pm. Although these trains are officially called express trains, they are slower than the more established Mandalay-Yangon express trains. The fare from Bagan to Yangon is US$31 for upper class, US$11 for ordinary class.

The Bagan train station is about 5km southeast of Nyaung U. The taxi fare from Nyaung U to the train station is about K700, more from the big hotels.

Bus/Train via Thazi This is an interesting way to break up the Bagan-Yangon trip. You first have to get to Thazi, which is about halfway from Bagan to Inle Lake. A very efficient Tiger Head Express pick-up goes straight to Thazi from Bagan Myothit in plenty of time for the Mandalay-Yangon express. Departure time from Bagan Myothit is around 4am. A Mann Express minibus also makes the run from Nyaung U to Thazi on its way to Taunggyi – also in time to catch the morning Mandalay (No 12 Down) express train to Yangon.

The Bagan-Thazi road is very scenic, with a view of the Mt Popa volcanic dome in the distance at the beginning of the trip, as well as glimpses of villages, farms, bullock carts, pedestrians bearing cargo on their heads etc. The ride is rather cramped, with 18 official passengers in the back, two with the driver in front and three or four hangers-on. There are rest stops in Kyaukpadaung and Meiktila – the first a short intermission for fuel and the second a longer stop, where you can refuel yourself with tea and *nam-bya* (Bamar roti). The fare is K500 per passenger.

If you want to spend the day in Thazi, you can wait for the 6.30pm evening express from Mandalay that arrives around 9.30pm and leaves a few minutes later. You can book your Thazi-Yangon tickets in Mandalay or Thazi, but if you wait till Thazi to buy your ticket there's no guarantee of a seat. An MTT official is sometimes at the station to meet foreigners coming from Bagan. See the Thazi section in the Northeastern Myanmar chapter for things to do while you're waiting for the train. See the boxed text 'Train Schedules & Fares' in the Getting Around chapter at the start of this book for the Thazi-Yangon train schedule.

Boat It's possible to travel along the Ayeyarwady in both directions from Bagan, although the trip from Mandalay to Bagan is the one most commonly taken by travellers.

Mandalay There is now a better alternative to the MTT *Mandalay-Bagan* ferry (which departs from Mandalay at 5.30am every Wednesday and Sunday at a cost of US$11 deck class or US$33 for a stuffy cabin). The new *Mandalay-Bagan Express* ferry departs every Monday, Tuesday, Thursday, Friday and Saturday (US$16 nine hours). Food is available on board, but it's pricey.

Travelling upriver from Bagan to Mandalay involves another night stop on the way, so unless you can spare at least two full days, the upriver trip (on either ferry) is not worth considering unless you really have formed an attachment to Burmese river travel. In Mandalay, you must purchase tickets for the ferry at either the Mandalay MTT office or the Irrawaddy Water Transport (IWT) office. Most guesthouses or hotels will also help you get boat tickets. The IWT office in Nyaung U is near the jetty.

A slower, much cheaper ferry does the same route daily, except Thursday and Sunday, taking approximately 26 to 29 hours and costing just K100. The slower boat stops one night on the western bank of the river at the busy river port of Pakokku.

The next morning it's a further 1½ to two hours downriver to Nyaung U, but don't worry if you oversleep in Pakokku and miss the boat, as other boats pass by later in the morning. If you find yourself stranded in Pakokku, you can usually charter a long-tail boat to make the trip for about K5000.

Only the faster express ferries go all the way to Old Bagan; all other boats land at the Nyaung U jetty, about 6km northeast of Old Bagan. Pick-ups, taxis and horse carts from the Nyaung U jetty to Old Bagan are always plentiful.

Although it's quite an experience to travel by boat on the mighty Ayeyarwady, the river is wide and the banks flat, with most of the villages set well back due to the risk of seasonal flooding, so you won't see too much from the river. There are plenty of stops, however, and people are always on hand to sell food and drink.

Towards the end of the dry season (March to early May), inquire about river conditions before leaping on a Mandalay-Bagan ferry. Getting stuck on sand bars can happen at any time of the year, but as the river level falls, you're more likely to get stuck and it's likely to take longer to get unstuck. People have wasted days while at a standstill on the Ayeyarwady.

Pyay & Yangon From Nyaung U, the slow ferries continue daily, except Thursday and Sunday, downriver to Pyay, where you can change boats and continue all the way to Yangon. The first day takes you from Bagan to Magwe, the second day from there to Pyay. From Pyay it's another two and a half-day boat trip to Yangon. You'd use up a quarter of your four-week visa on this trip, but it would be quite a ride. At the time of writing, a new Chinese-built triple-deck ferry was scheduled to begin service along the Ayeyarwady River between Pyay, Bagan/Nyaung U and Mandalay. See the Pyay section in the Around Yangon chapter for more details about the boat.

Getting Around

To/From the Airport The Nyaung U-Bagan airstrip is about 5km southeast of

Nyaung U, which is 5km northeast of Old Bagan. A taxi from the airport to Nyaung U or Wetkyi-in costs around K800; to Old Bagan or Myinkaba it's around K1000; and to Bagan Myothit it's around K1200.

Bus There is a bus service (pick-up trucks once again) between Nyaung U and Bagan for K10; it departs about 200m from the bus station in Nyaung U.

Horse Cart & Trishaw You can hire horse carts from place to place or by the hour; count on around K200 per hour, K800 for a half-day and K1500 for the whole day. A horse cart from the Old Bagan jetty to Bagan Myothit costs around K300 (with bargaining). Some of the horse cart drivers are pretty knowledgeable too, and some visitors prefer carts to bikes. Technically speaking, only drivers holding MTT licences may act as guides, and they will charge a separate guide fee. One of the best licensed guides/drivers is Win-Win, who is the proud owner of the Number 1 horse cart. He can usually be found outside the Bagan Hotel.

Trishaws are mostly confined to Nyaung U and Bagan Myothit, though they're occasionally seen elsewhere and always show up to meet the boats coming from Mandalay. A trishaw ride costs approximately K50 per kilometre.

Bicycle Although you can comfortably walk around the more central Bagan sites, if you want to travel further afield you'll need transport. Bicycles – available for hire at most hotels and guesthouses – are a great way to get around. Traffic around Bagan is so light that bike riding is a joy, although you should steer well clear when the occasional motor vehicle does chance by. The usual cost is K400 to K1000 for the day. Riding can be hard-going down the dustier tracks – beware the soft sand – and punctures are inevitable, but they're fixed, or the bike is swiftly replaced. An early-morning or late-afternoon ride along the sealed road between Wetkyi-in and Myinkaba is particularly pleasant.

When renting a bike, check it thoroughly before accepting it – make sure it steers properly, the brakes work and the tyres hold air. One traveller told of seeing a rider discover his machine's total lack of braking just at the bottom of the long slope. People picked him up and carried him inside to a bar, where a few beers restored his equilibrium. The same traveller was offered a bike with the suggestion that he pedal back every hour or so, 'to refill the tyres'.

Riding out to some of the more remote temples (eg Minnanthu) can be hard going through the deep and dusty sand; for these destinations a horse cart is preferable.

Boat From the jetty near Bupaya in Old Bagan you can charter small boats for scenic trips along the river and to visit riverside shrines such as Lawkananda (near Bagan Myothit) and Kyauk Gu Ohnmin (east of Nyaung U). Hire rates are around K1000 an hour. To Salay and back, expect to pay about K10,000 for a charter.

Any of the riverside hotels in Old Bagan can arrange hourly charters.

OLD BAGAN

ပုဂံမြို့ဟောင်း

Although Old Bagan is no longer inhabited (except by hotel and government employees), it represents the core of the Bagan Archaeological Zone and contains several of the main temple sites, city walls and museum. It's right on a bend of the Ayeyarwady River – some time during your stay, wander down to the waterfront and watch the coming and going of the river trade. Boats will be passing by or pausing to unload goods, and villagers will come down to the river with oxen carts to collect water. You can even take a boat across the river to the village on the other side. Note how Bagan's water supply is pumped up from a point just below the Aye Yar Hotel.

Tharaba Gateway

သာရပါတံခါး

The ruins of Tharaba Gateway (also known as Sarabha Gateway), on the eastern side, are all that remain of the old 9th-century city wall. Traces of old stucco can still be seen on the gateway. The gate is guarded by highly revered brother and sister nat, the male (Lord Handsome) on the right, the female (Lady Golden Face) on the left. In their human histories, the siblings died in a fire, so worshippers offer the images flowers and water, rather than candles or incense.

Anawrahta's original palace is thought to have been located near Tharaba.

Places to Stay

The accommodation situation in Old Bagan has changed often since the 1990 elections, when the entire village (guesthouses included) was forced to move to a new settlement called Bagan Myothit in 15 days. For several years afterwards, the only places open to foreigners were government-owned hotels in Old Bagan. However, with the continuing privatisation of hotels and guesthouses, there are close to 125 guesthouses and hotels in Old Bagan, Nyaung U, Wetkyi-in, Myinkaba, Bagan Myothit and Tetthe (near the airport). Competition for customers is keen and it's not unusual to meet touts whose job is to persuade tourists to jump from one guesthouse to another.

Bagan Thande Hotel *(☎ 70144, fax 70143; e baganthande@myanmars.net; w www.myanmars.net/baganthande; singles/doubles US$10/15, guesthouse building US$16/20, bungalows US$28/32)* is the best value in Old Bagan. The private hotel has small economy rooms with bathroom and air-con, larger rooms in the two-storey 'guesthouse' building – the upstairs corner rooms are best, as these get cross-ventilation – and eight attractive bungalow units with small verandas. A patio breakfast buffet overlooking the Ayeyarwady is included. According to the manager, the hotel's main building dates from 1922 and its first guest was the visiting Prince of Wales.

Bagan Hotel *(☎ 70146, fax 70313; e baganhotel@myanmars.net; w www.myanmars.net/baganhotel; superior singles/doubles US$55/65, suites from US$80)* is a 108-room hotel and the most attractive of the upmarket hotels in the Bagan area. It actually looks like it belongs to an exotic place like Bagan – something which certainly cannot be said of most Bagan hotels. Brick pathways connect several one-storey buildings on beautifully landscaped grounds with Gawdawpalin Pahto looming to one side and the Ayeyarwady just beyond. A full, lavish breakfast is included, and all rooms have shower and bath, air-con, satellite TV and IDD telephone. There are two very good restaurants on the grounds (one Myanmar, one a la carte) and a large lounge in the lobby decorated with teak furnishings and local artwork. There's also a pool.

Thiripyitsaya Sakura Hotel *(☎ 70289, fax 70286; singles & doubles US$120)*, about 500m south of the Old Bagan city walls and 20-minutes' walk from the centre, is a sprawling, privately owned 60-room, 0.2-hectare hotel. It takes good advantage of its scenic riverside location. There is a wing of well-appointed rooms, but a group of extremely swanky garden bungalows with private verandas is its attraction. All rooms are teak-furnished, with satellite TV, fridge and air-con. Breakfast is not included in the hotel's room price. It also has a stylish swimming pool, comfortable lounge area, and an excellent (if pricey) restaurant featuring both international and Bamar cuisine. An outdoor veranda bar overlooks the river. The hotel also offers the **Thiripyitsaya Spa** *(open 10am-10pm daily)*, a very swish massage and reflexology centre where you can enjoy a full body massage (four hours) for US$50. Bookings can be made through hotel reception.

Golden Express Hotel *(☎ 70101; singles/doubles US$20/30)*, located between Old Bagan and Nyaung U, has 20 spiffy bungalows with air-con, fridge and private bathroom. There's a swimming pool, and bicycle hire is available. Rates include breakfast.

Travellers keen to avoid government-owned hotels should bypass the **Aye Yar Hotel**, north of the city wall, near Bupaya.

Finally, if you want to spend the night in Old Bagan, but not the money, you can usually sleep on a platform at the old Bupaya stupa overlooking the river.

See the Nyaung U & Wetkyi-in, Myinkaba and Bagan Myothit sections later in the chapter for details on other places to stay in the area.

Places to Eat

Of the four hotel restaurants in and around Old Bagan, the food at the **Thiripyitsaya** and the **Bagan** Hotels is particularly good.

Sarabha Restaurant, just outside Tharaba Gateway, is a friendly place serving wonderful, well-seasoned and reasonably priced Bamar, Chinese and Thai food in a simple, quiet, indoor-outdoor setting.

Win Thein Gi Burmese Restaurant *(open 10am-11pm daily)*, inside the city gate and near the Air Mandalay/Yangon Air ticket office, is an excellent-value restaurant serving enormous Burmese buffet meals. For the two-person buffet you'll pay around K1200 and get no less than 13 dishes.

Vegetarian Restaurant & Cold Drinks is a simple and decent place just outside the old wall near Tharaba Gate. It serves a few snacks and curry dishes. It's a nice place to rest from the heat if you're bicycling around. A sign in the small dining room says 'Be kind to animals by not eating them'.

Convenient to the Aye Yar Hotel and next to the boat landing below the hotel is a cluster of local **cafés** and **teashops**. Although they're very rustic, the relaxed atmosphere makes for a pleasant evening.

Shopping

One of the region's best souvenir shops can be found in Old Bagan.

Shwe Wa Thein Handicrafts Shop *(☎ 70032)*, just off the Bagan-Nyaung U Rd, is a treasure trove of trinkets of all shapes and sizes. It's signposted at the main road about 500m from the city gate – take the dirt road from near the MTT tourist information office. Visa cards are accepted.

For other interesting shopping options, spend an afternoon wandering around Nyaung U or Bagan Myothit.

Getting There & Around

Nyaung U and Bagan Myothit are the main transportation centres for the area. See the Getting There & Away and Getting Around sections earlier in this chapter for details.

NYAUNG U & WETKYI-IN

ညောင်ဦး ဝက်ကြီးအင်း

Nyaung U, about 5km northeast of Old Bagan, is the major population centre in the Bagan area; you'll pass through Nyaung U if you arrive in Bagan by road or air, and by river if you take the slow boat from Pyay or Mandalay. It's an interesting little place for a wander – it has lots of shops (look out for the cigar dealers), an excellent and colourful market, and even a Burmese billiard hall. Recently several inexpensive guesthouses have opened their doors to foreigners. Several small restaurants offer Indian, Chinese and Bamar food.

The small village of Wetkyi-in, roughly halfway between Nyaung U and Old Bagan, flanks the mouth of Wetkyi-in Chaung (Wetkyi-in Canal). Along the 2km stretch between Wetkyi-in and Nyaung U are several guesthouses and restaurants for travellers.

Although some of the monuments listed in this section are close to Wetkyi-in and Bagan, or conveniently situated between both, others are located far east of Nyaung U. You'll probably see some of them from the river, or if you fly in or out of Bagan.

For tourist information in and around Nyaung U, drop into **Ever Sky Information**, near the Taungzalat Hotel. This friendly, well-run place offers everything from bus and air tickets to taxi hire, massage and laundry. It's open from between 6.30am and 7.30am to between 9pm and 10pm daily. Bikes can be hired here at K400 per day, and horse carts (and driver) are K3000 per day. There's also a bookshop attached.

Aung Myi Bodhi Dhamma Yeiktha

အောင်မြေဗောဓိဓမ္မရိပ်သာ

Directly opposite Shwezigon Paya near Gubyaukgyi, this *kammahtan kyaung* (meditation monastery) is home to the well-regarded 'Pakistan Sayadaw'. Also known by his Pali name U Ariyawananda, the *sayadaw*

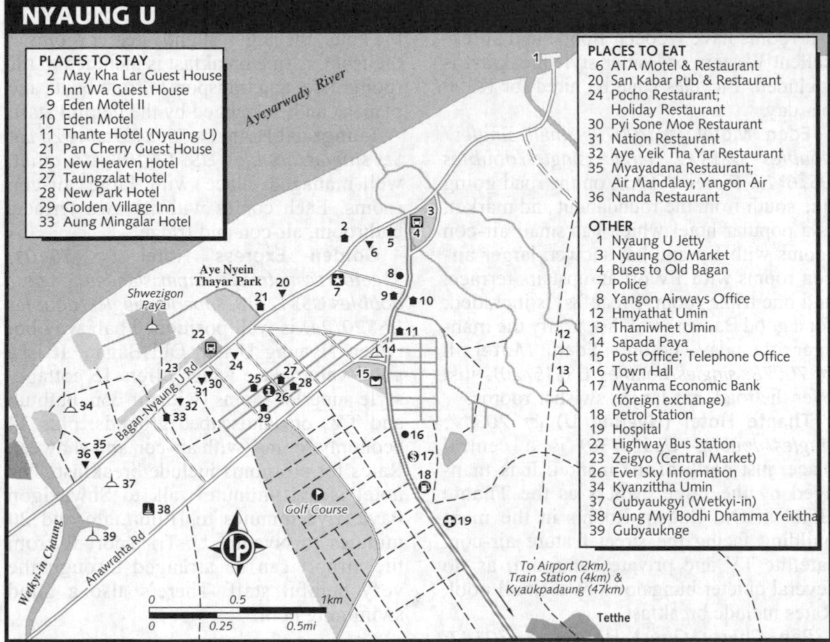

(abbot) teaches a simple technique of breath-and-body awareness that attracts monks and lay practitioners from as far away as Yangon, and even overseas. There's very little to see among the simple collection of huts and buildings – no glittering stupas, just the practice of *dhamma* (Buddhist teachings).

Places to Stay

Places to stay in Nyaung U and Wetkyi-in are increasing in number, turning this side of the Bagan area into a budget accommodation centre. A number of guesthouses and hotels are located near Shwezigon Paya, between Nyaung U and Wetkyi-in. The main advantage to these places is their proximity to the Nyaung U market and Highway bus station. Due to the general activity in the area, these places can be a little noisy during the day, though nights are usually quiet.

Aung Mingalar Hotel (☎ *70406; singles US$10-20, doubles US$15-25)* is a large hotel near the bus station with a wide range of good standard rooms, all with bathroom, air-conditioning and fridge. All rates include breakfast.

Inn Wa Guest House (☎ *70126; economy singles/doubles US$4/8, standard singles/doubles US$5/10)* is a well-managed and friendly place with three storeys, and a rooftop balcony overlooking the street. It has small clean rooms with fan and hot shower, and larger rooms with air-con and a fridge. A great breakfast (Myanmar breakfast on request) is included in the price. Visa card is accepted, with commission.

May Kha Lar Guest House (☎ *70065; economy rooms per person US$4, standard singles/doubles/triples US$8/12/20, luxury singles/doubles US$10/12)*, near Inn Wa Guest House, is friendly and bright with a variety of rooms and prices and is run by the attentive Miss Cho. There are small clean air-con economy rooms with separate bathroom, and larger attractive rooms with private shower, air-con, fan, fridge and TV. All rooms have wooden floors, and an excellent Western or Bamar-style breakfast is included. Bicycles cane be hired for K300 per day.

Eden Motel (☎ *70078; small singles/doubles US$4/5, larger singles/doubles US$6/12, triples US$15)*, on the road going due south from the roundabout and market, is a popular hotel which has small air-con rooms with fan and hot shower, larger air-con rooms with TV off an upstairs terrace, and one triple room. Breakfast is included; for a good Bamar breakfast, notify the manager the day before. **Eden Motel II** (☎ *70078; singles/doubles US$15/20)*, just over the road, has larger, swisher rooms.

Thante Hotel (Nyaung U) (☎ *70317; singles/doubles US$24/30)* is a central place, just north of the market. It is managed by the same owners as the Thante Hotel in Old Bagan. Rooms in the main building facing the street feature air-con, satellite TV and private bathroom, as do several quieter bungalows by a small pool. Rates include breakfast.

Pan Cherry Guest House (☎ *70147; singles or doubles US$3, singles/doubles with air-con US$10/15)*, in Wetkyi-in, is a comfortable guesthouse just northeast of Shwezigon. It has 11 fan-cooled rooms with shared bathroom. The well-constructed, residential-style building stays fairly cool, even in hot weather.

New Heaven Hotel (☎ *70061; Thiripyitsaya – Block 5; singles/doubles US$5/10)* is a small and friendly place a few blocks southeast of Shwezigon Paya in a quiet courtyard setting. Rooms come with fan, air-con, bathroom and breakfast.

Golden Village Inn (☎ *70061; Thiripyitsaya – Block 5; singles/doubles US$4/8)*, in the same residential area as the New Heaven Hotel (and with the same owner) has similar prices and accommodation.

New Park Hotel (☎ *70122;* ⓔ *newparkhotel@myanmars.net; Thiripyitsaya – Block 4; singles US$5-6, doubles US$8-10)* has been recommended by many travellers, and with good reason. It has very good-value, tidy air-con rooms with bathroom. The cheaper, smaller rooms are at the back of the hotel, the larger, slightly dearer rooms at the front. A fine breakfast is included in the room price, and transport to/from boats and planes can be arranged by the helpful staff.

Taungzalat Hotel (☎ *70084; Taung Za Lat St; singles/doubles US$12/15)* is a quiet, well-managed place with large air-con rooms. Each comes with its own terrace, bathroom, air-con and fridge.

Golden Express Hotel (☎ *70101;* ⓔ *getours@mptmail.net.mm; standard singles/doubles US$12/18, superior singles/doubles US$20/24)* is well positioned half way between Nyaung U and Old Bagan. It is a good-value place which offers 15 cottage-style superior rooms (with air-con, bathtub and TV) on landscaped grounds, plus 24 economy rooms (with air-con and shower). Rates for all rooms include breakfast. The hotel is a 10-minute walk to Shwezigon Paya, five minutes to Htilominlo and 20 minutes to Nyaung U. Transport to/from the airport can be arranged through the very helpful staff. There's also a good swimming pool.

Places to Eat

Staying near Shwezigon Paya puts you in the vicinity of several decent places to eat. The **Nation Restaurant** and nearby **Aye Yeik Tha Yar Restaurant** offer the usual fried rice, curries and noodles, and the English-language menus include several brands of beer, yogurt, lassi (yogurt drinks) and fruit juice. The thatched-roof Nation is popular, but service and quality can vary. Nearby is **ATA Motel & Restaurant**, which serves good Pakistani, Indian and Chinese Muslim (halal) food.

Myayadana Restaurant is an excellent place serving a variety of Bamar and Chinese dishes in an indoor-outdoor setting in the village of Wetkyi-in, about 1km toward Old Bagan. Prices are reasonable, and menus are in English and French as well as Burmese; if you're serious about sampling the Bamar food at Myayadana, ask staff in the morning so they can show off their stuff.

Nanda Restaurant is nearby and almost as good as the Myayadana, with a similar menu. Both places put on a low-key marionette show most evenings when enough tourists are in town.

Pyi Sone Moe Restaurant *(dishes K400-500)* is a popular, friendly little restaurant on the main road in Nyaung U, near the bus station, serving a wide range of excellent pork, chicken and vegetarian dishes.

San Kabar Pub & Restaurant, on the main road, serves reasonably priced Italian food until late.

Also worth a look is the **Pocho Restaurant** and **Holiday Restaurant**, both down on Taung Za Lat St.

Shopping

Aside from the all-day central market, several small shops in town sell earthy, utilitarian ceramics, lacquerware and other crafts; what might be called 'folk utensils' elsewhere in Asia are regarded as everyday requisites here.

Getting There & Around

See the Getting There & Away and Getting Around sections earlier in this chapter for transport information to Nyaung U and Wetkyi-in.

MYINKABA

မြင်းကပါ

Only a kilometre or two south of Bagan, Myinkaba has a number of interesting pahto and stupas from the Early Bagan period, including **Gubyaukgyi**, which contains the oldest mural paintings in all of Bagan. Nearby is **Manuha Paya**, built by King Manuha, the 'captive king'. The four Buddhas squeezed within are reputedly representations of the king's own physical discomfort with captivity. Note the north-facing Buddha: north and east positions represent death (with hands flat and feet parallel); south and west represent the relaxed or sleeping position (hands at head, feet crossed).

Excellent lacquerware workshops can be visited in Myinkaba. Some of these accomplish the complete process of producing lacquerware in the one centre, while others specialise in a single phase of the production – such as making the bamboo frames on which the lacquer is coated.

Places to Stay & Eat

Phyo Guest House *(☎ 70086; small singles/doubles US$8/12, large singles/doubles US$10/15)* is a quiet and well-managed place near Gubyaukgyi, at the northern end of the village. All rooms are comfy and well kept, with bathroom, air-con and hot shower. The rates include breakfast. Next door is the excellent Art Gallery of Bagan lacquerware store and workshop.

Down the street, opposite Manuha Paya, are a couple of decent teashops. One of them, the **Aung Mya Thi**, makes very tasty samosas.

Shopping

Art Gallery of Bagan *(☎ 70086, Myin Ka Par Village; open 8am-8pm daily)* is next to the Phyo Guest House and offers some of the country's best lacquerware, made on the premises. Operated by master lacquerware artist Maung Aung Myin, it has everything from chopstick holders to lavishly decorated folding screens – one of which is on display in the British Museum. Tours of the workshop are available on request. Visa cards are accepted.

Getting There & Around

Old Bagan is an approximately 2km walk north of Myinkaba. Bicycles can be rented at Phyo Guest House for touring the ruins. Horse carts are plentiful in Myinkaba. Bagan Myothit is located a few kilometres south – a K40 to K50 horse-cart ride.

BAGAN MYOTHIT (NEW BAGAN)

ပုဂံမြို့သစ်

For the first couple of years after residents of Old Bagan were forced by the government to move to the new town site, Bagan Myothit was a depressing and treeless place with little spirit. Since then, however, the residents have made the best of their unchosen new home, and there are a number of new hotels and guesthouses, restaurants,

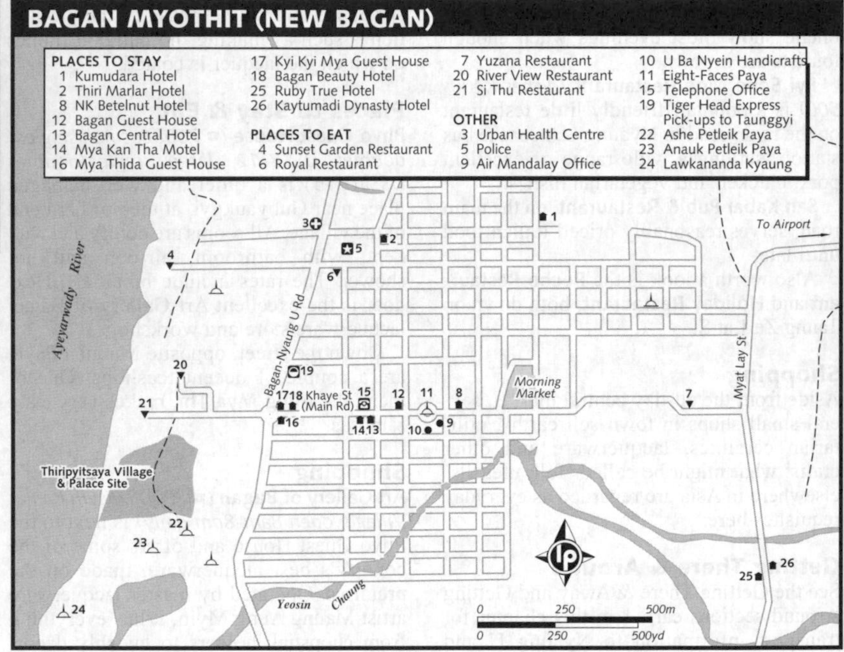

souvenir shops and homes. Nyaung U remains the main population centre in the region, but this growing little town is beginning to show signs of life.

The growth of Bagan Myothit has largely swallowed the small village of Thiripyitsaya that stands at the former site of a Bagan royal palace about 2km south of Myinkaba, and the whole area is now more commonly known as New Bagan. Lots of smaller ruins dot the area, including three very interesting monuments.

A telephone office for making domestic and international calls is on the main road across from Mya Kan Tha Motel.

Places to Stay

Bagan Myothit currently offers a greater choice of mid-range accommodation than any other town or village in the Bagan region.

The main east-west road in town is Khaye St, but most of the businesses there still refer to it as Main Rd, and many new small streets and dirt tracks branch out from it. A string of rather new hotels and guesthouses line both sides of the street.

Bagan Central Hotel *(☎ 70141; singles/doubles US$15/25)*, on the southern side of the main road, is one of the most attractive of the mid-range places to stay. The rooms are large and airy. The hotel lobby opens out to a courtyard of flowers and bungalows, all with air-con, fridge and hot-water bathroom. It's great value.

Bagan Beauty Hotel *(☎ 70238; singles US$5, doubles US$10-15)* is a quiet and friendly place on the main road near the Bagan-Nyaung U road. This thick-walled, two-storey house has three single rooms with shared bathroom and toilet, and nine double rooms with air-con and hot-water bathroom. Breakfast is included, and *mohinga* (noodle, fish and egg dish, pronounced *moun-hinga*) is served on request.

NK Betelnut Hotel *(☎ 70110; singles/doubles US$18/24)*, further east of the Bagan

Beauty Hotel, on the same side of the street, is a new hotel featuring 10 small, but clean and airy, bungalows with air-con, hot water, fan and fridge. Rates include breakfast.

Mya Kan Tha Motel *(☎ 70191; singles/doubles US$15/25)* is a friendly motel opposite the telephone office. Rooms have air-con, hot water, and fridge, and rates include a good complimentary breakfast.

Mya Thida Guest House *(☎ 70036; singles/doubles/triples US$5/8/12)* is a small and clean guesthouse with six air-con, hot-water rooms; rates include breakfast.

Bagan Guest House *(☎ 70021; rooms per person US$5)*, across the road from Mya Thida Guest House, has clean, large rooms with air-con, fridge and hot water. Rates include a simple breakfast.

Kyi Kyi Mya Guest House *(☎ 70037; singles/doubles/triples US$6/10/15)* is one of the cleaner budget places in town. The 10 air-con rooms have fan and hot-water shower.

Thiri Marlar Hotel *(☎ 70134; Thiri Marlar St; singles/doubles US$42/52)* has 21 air-con rooms with bathroom, minibar and good views. Breakfast is included in the rates.

Kumudara Hotel *(☎ 70080; ⓔ kumudara@myanmars.net; cnr 5th & Daw Na Sts; singles/doubles US$40/60)* is a well laid out place with motel-style rooms, many with excellent views, that come with bathroom, air-con, fridge and TV. An attached bar pavilion is open from 9am to 10pm daily.

Ruby True Hotel *(☎ 70262; Myat Lay St; singles/doubles US$42/54)* is typical of Bagan Myothit's upmarket look. It's in the town's southeastern corner. The 30 large air-con rooms have private bathroom, satellite TV, fridge, minibar and telephone, and rates include a full breakfast in the hotel restaurant.

Kaytumadi Dynasty Hotel *(☎ 70123, fax 70124; ⓔ kaytumadi@mptmail.net.mm; Myat Lay St; singles/doubles US$18/25)* has spacious bungalows in a garden setting, each with bathroom, air-con, minibar and TV.

Places to Eat

On the western end of Khaye St, near the Thiripyitsaya Palace site, three restaurants handle most of the upmarket visitor dining trade:

Si Thu Restaurant *(mains around K600-1000)* is near the river and prices on the Bamar/Chinese menu are moderate to high. Check out the large lacquer mural.

The nearby **River View** and **Sunset Garden** restaurants stand on high ground above the river, off the western side of the road. The menu, prices and setting at both are similar to the Si Thu, if a little more expensive. All three restaurants usually feature a marionette show in the evening.

Royal Restaurant, 500m from the River View, is clean and dependable, and the largely Chinese menu is reasonably priced.

Yuzana Restaurant *(Khaye St)* is a decent Chinese/Bamar eatery at the eastern end of Khaye St.

Shopping

U Ba Nyein *(Khaye St)* is one of the largest lacquerware shops in the area, opposite Eight-Faces Paya on the roundabout next to the AM office.

Getting There & Away

Tiger Head Express has its office on the eastern side of the Bagan-Nyaung U road, just north of Kyi Kyi Mya Guest House. See Getting There & Away at the start of this section for details on Tiger Head's pick-ups to Meiktila and Taunggyi.

Getting Around

Pick-ups to/from Nyaung U run roughly four times daily from the market for K20 per person. A horse cart between Old Bagan or the ferry jetty near Old Bagan costs around K150 to K200 each way.

Htun Handicrafts or the Bagan Central Hotel can arrange a car and driver for half-day or full-day use. Expect to pay US$25 to US$30 per day for two or three passengers.

Bicycles are a good way to get around, and they can be rented through any of the hotels or guesthouses for K250 to K350 per day.

MINNANTHU

မင်းနန်သူ

More or less directly south of Nyaung U, Minnanthu's monuments are of a later period than those in the central Bagan area. Temples are off the beaten path, and the track to the village can be very sandy, making bicycle riding difficult. Nevertheless, the temples are well worth the effort to see their faded fresco interiors. Some of the horse cart drivers in Old Bagan make good (if unofficial) guides to Minnanthu and can often find someone to unlock the most frequently locked temples.

PWASAW

ပွားစော

Between Myinkaba and Minnanthu, Pwasaw was the site of the royal palace after it was transferred from Thiripyitsaya, and before it was moved to Bagan in AD 874. There are now two small villages, Anauk (West) Pwasaw and Ashe (East) Pwasaw.

Around Bagan

SALAY

စလေ

During the Late Bagan Era, specifically the late 12th and 13th centuries, Salay (also known as Sale) developed as the expanding spiral of Bagan's influence moved southward along the Ayeyarwady River.

Today, Salay is much more of a religious centre than Bagan, with many more working monasteries than found in Bagan today. Among the Burmese, it's most famous as the historic home of Salay U Ponya, a Bagan Era writer/poet whose works are read by students all over the country.

The British established a presence here, as testified by several old two-storey colonial buildings in town, including one that still bears royal crown reliefs (generally removed in other parts of the country) on the facade. Following independence, the city was virtually abandoned until a Japanese firm built a huge fertiliser plant north of town around 25 years ago. The Japanese eventually turned the plant over to the Burmese, leaving behind the Salay Golf Club – a golf course built to serve the Japanese executives in charge of the project – near the town entrance.

Today the town, with its Bamar majority, is bubbling with activity again. Aside from the atmospheric old colonial buildings and the ruins north of town, the primary attraction is the small museum at Youqson (Yoe San) Kyaung. A trip to Salay is warranted for anyone who develops a passion for Bagan-style architecture. For other visitors less consumed with Bagan, it's simply more of the same, although its laidback atmosphere may be of interest for those who find Bagan and Nyaung U a little too crowded with tourists.

Bagan Era Monuments

Little of Salay's history is known outside a small circle of Burmese archaeologists working with limited funds. Archaeologists from other countries have yet to carry out a thorough study either, so details on the 103 ruins – most of them known only by number rather than name – are sketchy. It is said that most of the monuments in Salay weren't royally sponsored but were built by the lower nobility or commoners. Thus, there are no structures on the grand scale of Bagan's Ananda, Thatbyinnyu or Dhammayangyi.

Salay architects favoured designs similar to those found in the 'outer circle' Bagan monuments of Minnanthu and Pwasaw, particularly mid-sized *gu*-style sanctuaries (small, hollow temples) with prominent *sikhara* (corncob-like temple finials). The latter feature was often inspired by the Bagan namesake copy of the Mahabodhi stupa in Bodhgaya, India.

Among the named sites worth a look is **Payathonzu**, an interconnected complex of three brick shrines with sikhara. All three shrines contain some form of mural painting, but the most extensive painting graces the third one in the series, located to the southwest. This one also has a set of stairs that lead through a very narrow passage to the upper terrace. Legend has it that it was constructed by three sisters, but tripartite pahto exist elsewhere in Salay and Bagan. If Payathonzu is locked, you may have to ask a caretaker for keys, or ask at Youqson Kyaung (see the following entry).

In the same area, near the functioning monastery of **Thadanayaunggyi Kyaung** and the meditation centre of **Mogok Vipassana Yeiktha**, a 19th-century shrine shelters a large lacquer Buddha known as **Nan Paya** (also known as Mann Paya). This image, said to date back to the 13th century, may be the largest lacquer image in Myanmar; the fingertips alone measure about 2m high.

A short walk from Payathonzu stands what the locals call **Hkinkyiza Kyaung**, actually an old brick-and-stucco *pitaka taik* (Buddhist scripture library). Unlike similar libraries in Bagan, this one bears an intact superstructure. There is also some original stucco relief remaining on the lintels and pediments. Of the four entranceways, three are blocked off. The remaining unobstructed passage is bare except for an antique pitaka chest sitting at the back. The interior walls have, unfortunately, been whitewashed, probably covering the murals underneath.

Youqson Kyaung

ရုပ်စုံကျောင်း

On the other side of the main road from Kyaukpadaung is the oldest surviving wooden monastery hall *(museum admission US$3)* in the Bagan area, south of Pakokku. The hall sports a new corrugated metal roof to protect the carved wooden structures below from rain or stray sparks from cooking fires. Despite the metal roof, the interior is surprisingly cool. Only two sides of the 23m-long hall actually bear the original 120-year-old sculptures, which include nearly three dimensional carvings of 19th-century court life, *jataka* (stories of the Buddha's past lives) and *Ramayana* (one of India's best known legends) tales. Some panels are missing and there are some newer woodcarvings mixed in with the old, but those that remain are lovingly cared for by the monks and caretakers, who apply oil regularly to prevent cracking. The monks have also provided detailed English translations identifying the most interesting religious works.

Brick-and-stucco stairs featuring a *naga* (dragon serpent) design lead up to the hall, which is supported by 170 teak pillars 2m off the ground. The structure measures 23m long. Inside the hall is a collection of antique religious objects from the area, including small wooden Buddha figures, heads, old pottery and votive tablets that may date from the 11th to 13th centuries, plus many wooden Konbaung or Mandalay-style images. A wooden Bagan-style naga Buddha is particularly distinctive. A lacquer Konbaung-era Buddha image about 1m high sits in a separate section of the hall, which features a painted, carved-wood ceiling. In the same section is a graceful bronze-and-silver Mandalay-style sitting Buddha in the earth-touching pose; whether by design or not, the head is intriguingly tilted very slightly to the left.

Places to Stay & Eat

Salay has no hotels or guesthouses – for foreigners or Burmese – but determined overnighters might be able to stay in one of the many **monasteries**. The **central market** has the usual noodle and sticky rice vendors, and there are also a few **teashops** around town.

Getting There & Away

Salay is 36km south of Bagan along a new sealed road. You pass through the town of Chauk on the way. From Chauk, another road goes east to Kyaukpadaung.

Nyaung U/Bagan By public transport you can catch an early morning pick-up from Nyaung U to Salay for about K100. If you hire a car and driver in Bagan, expect to pay about US$15 (or kyat equivalent) for a half-day trip. The drive takes about 40 minutes each way.

You could also take a Pyay-bound ferry from Nyaung U, arriving in Salay around noon. The ferry leaves at 5am daily, except Thursday and Sunday, and arrives in Pyay in the late afternoon; the deck-class fare is around K50.

From Pyay The 380km drive between Pyay and Salay takes six to seven hours by private vehicle along a paved road. By public transport you'll have to change buses or pick-ups in Magwe and Kyaukpadaung, making it a very long trip – plan to spend the night in Magwe or Kyaukpadaung and get an early start the next day for onward travel to Salay.

MT POPA

ပုပ္ပါးတောင်

☎ 062

If you look towards the range of hills that rise, shimmering in the heat, behind Bagan, you'll see a solitary peak behind them. Rising to 737m from the flat, surrounding Myingyan Plain, Mt Popa (Popa Daung Kalat in Burmese) is said to be the core of an extinct volcano last active 250,000 years ago. The ground either side of the road is strewn with the remains of a petrified forest.

Volcanic ash makes the surrounding plains fertile and the heights capture the moisture of passing clouds, causing rain to drop on the plateau and produce a profusion of trees, flowering plants and herbs. In fact, the word Popa is derived from the Sanskrit word for flower. One of Mt Popa's presiding nat, Mae Wunna, is considered the patron nat of medicinal and magico-religious herbs, many of which still grow in the area today. At one time, the surrounding forests were home to elephants, rhinos, sambar and tigers; all had disappeared by the time a 1908 mammal survey was undertaken by the British Raj.

GREG HERRIMAN

Once common throughout Southeast Asia, the tiger is now a threatened species.

Mt Popa has been described as the Mt Olympus of Myanmar, and it's considered the abode of Myanmar's most powerful nat. As such, it's the most important nat worship centre. The Mahagiri shrine, at the base of the rock outcropping at the summit, contains a display of mannequin-like figures representing the 37 nat and is a major pilgrimage destination. Burmese superstition says you shouldn't wear red or black on the mountain, nor should you curse, say bad things about other people or bring along any meat (especially pork) – any of these actions could offend the residing nat who might then retaliate with a spate of ill fortune.

Atop the impressive rocky crag clings a picturesque complex of monasteries, stupas and shrines that you can climb to, via a winding, covered walkway, complete with curious monkeys. The 25-minute climb is steep and stiff, but it gets cooler as you get higher. When you reach the top the views are fantastic. You'll meet many other pilgrims along the way, including a class of non-ordained hermit monks called *yeti* (from the Pali-Sanskrit *rishi)* who wear tall peaked hats; part of their meditation involves walking very slowly and mindfully while in the vicinity of Mt Popa.

Special Events

Mt Popa hosts two huge *nat pwe* (spirit festivals) yearly, one beginning on the full moon of Nayon (May/June) and another on the full moon of Nadaw (November/December). Before King Anawrahta's time, thousands of animals were sacrificed to the nat during these festivals, but this practice has been prohibited since the Bagan era. Spirit possession and overall drunken ecstasy are still part of the celebration, however.

[Continued on page 311]

Temples of Bagan

Temples of Bagan

BERNARD NAPTHINE

Title Page: Gawdawpalin Pahto, one of the largest of the Bagan temples, dates to the 13th century. (Photograph by Glenn Beanland)

From Top Left: Facade of the 12th-century Shwegugyi Paya; the unfinished Dhammayangyi temple, built by King Narathu in 1167; the majestic Ananda Pahto with mountain backdrop; Thatbyinnyu Pahto, Old Bagan

ARCHAEOLOGY OF BAGAN

Classification

Classifying the ancient monuments of Bagan by style and age is made difficult by the vast number of archaeological sites. The official count by the end of the 13th century is said to have been 4446. By 1901 surveys found 2157 monuments still standing and identifiable. According to resident Burmese archaeologist U Aung Kyaing, the last count was taken in 1978, when archaeologists found 2230 identifiable sites. However, most contemporary references on the subject quote a figure of 2217. These figures do not include brick mounds, which would give a total of nearly 4000 separate visible sites.

The sheer variety of motifs and measurements to be studied also presents a challenge, though certain unifying factors can be found throughout. For the most part, the proliferation of temples, *stupas* (Buddhist religious monuments) and *kyaung* (monasteries) are constructed of fired brick covered with plaster and decorated with stucco relief, polychromatic murals and glazed tiles. Sculpture materials included bronze, teak, brick and stucco, sandstone and lacquer. The most delicate of these media, the mural paintings, are endangered by the peeling of the plaster behind them, droppings left by bats and soot from cooking fires lit during WWII, when the Burmese sought shelter inside the monuments.

Temple paintings of such figures as Avalokitesvara, Manjusri and Shiva show an unmistakable Mahayana, and possibly Tantric, influence. Much of the mural work at Bagan is thought to be similar to how the interiors of Buddhist temples in Northeastern India may have appeared during the late Pala period, before their destruction at the hands of Muslim invaders.

Looting & Restoration

Looters have made away with many of the sculptures and other religious objects once contained in the monuments. In the 1890s, a German oilman removed glazed plaques from Mingalazedi, Dhammayazika and Somingyi, as well as Vishnu figures from Natlaung Kyaung, all of which ended up at the Berlin Völkerkunde Museum. Around the same time, another German, Th H Thomann, took some of the finest mural paintings known in Bagan from Wetkyi-in's Gubyaukgyi and Theinmazi Pahto. The latter were sold to the Hamburg Ethnographical Museum; the exquisite Wetkyi-in paintings never resurfaced (fortunately Thomann left some murals behind, and they're still visible today).

Another complication comes in deciding what's original and what's been added or reformed since the Bagan period. Restorations of several monuments, for example, were under way when British diplomat

Michael Symes visited Bagan in 1795. Although, for the most part, writings from the colonial era show a great appreciation for Bagan art and architecture, the British did very little to further Bagan archaeology in terms of excavation or exploration.

Surveys

An example of the early carelessness with which research was carried out can be found in the Archaeological Survey of India of the early 1900s. During the survey, a representative from Yangon was accompanied by a local village headman who identified the monuments. When the headman didn't know a monument's name, he simply made one up to please the representative! Many of these names are still in use today.

It wasn't until a couple of decades later that inscriptions were seriously examined to learn Bagan's historical context. The eminent Cambridge scholar GH Luce published a pre-WWII, three-volume study of the Early Bagan period monuments entitled Old Burma-Early Pagan that stands as the classic work. A well-researched art history of Bagan was finally carried out by Scotland's Paul Strachan in 1986 and 1987. Strachan published the results in his book *Pagan: Art and Architecture of Old Burma,* in which he divides everything from artefacts to buildings into three stylistic periods: Early (circa 850–1120), Middle (circa 1100–1170) and Late (circa 1170–1300).

The book has its flaws: for example, the author questions why the reclining Buddha next to Shwesandaw Paya couldn't have been lying on its left side instead of its right – an alternative that would have been a violation of classical Buddhist iconography never dared in Myanmar. Nonetheless, it is a very welcome addition to the literature on Bagan.

Strachan's book notwithstanding, no thorough archaeological study has been published since Myanmar's 1948 independence. Unesco's work focuses on restoration rather than excavation or archaeology; this was perhaps mandated by government fears of any deep historical studies.

Pierre Pichard, an archaeologist from the École Française d'Extrême Orient (EFEO), the same faculty responsible for most of the authoritative work on Angkor and Champa in Indochina, has been working on a new treatise on the archaeology of Bagan for the last 20 years or so. The initial results of his study have appeared in the six-volume *Inventory of Monuments at Bagan,* which provides schematic diagrams of many of the Bagan religious ruins. If and when Pichard takes his work any further, it may very well bring with it a whole new set of intriguing theories about the origins and demise of the kingdom of Bagan.

ARCHITECTURAL STYLES

Though there are a number of distinct architectural styles at Bagan, it is easy even for amateurs to trace the developments of temple design

Principal Bagan-era Monuments

monument	estimated date	location
Ananda Pahto	early 12th C	Old Bagan
Ananda Ok Kyaung	11th C	Old Bagan
Shwegugyi	early 14th C	Old Bagan
Thatbyinnyu Pahto	mid-12th C	Old Bagan
Pitaka Taik	mid-11th C	Old Bagan
Nathlaung Kyaung	10th C	Old Bagan
Gawdawpalin Pahto	late 12th or early 13th C	Old Bagan
Pahtothamya	late 11th or early 12th C	Old Bagan
Bupaya	mid-9th C	Old Bagan
Mahabodhi Paya	early 13th C	Old Bagan
Shwesandaw Paya	late 11th C	Old Bagan
Dhammayangyi Pahto	late 12th C	Old Bagan
Sulamani Pahto	late 12th C	Old Bagan
Mingalazedi	late 13th C	Old Bagan
Mimalaung Kyaung	late 12th C	Old Bagan
Shwezigon Paya	late 11th C	Wetkyi-in
Kyanzittha Umin	mid-11th C	Myinkaba
Somingyi Kyaung	early 13th C	Myinkaba
Lawkananda Kyaung	mid-11th C	Bagan Myothit (New Bagan)
Leimyethna Pahto	early 13th C	Minnanthu
Payathonzu	late 13th C	Minnanthu
Thambula Pahto	mid-13th C	Minnanthu
Nandamannya Pahto	mid-13th C	Minnanthu
Dhammayazika Paya	late 12th C	Pwasaw

over the 240 years of construction. Buildings are primarily either solid *zedi* (stupas) or hollow *pahto* (temples or shrines). The latter large, square buildings, containing arched passageways, are sometimes referred to as temples in their English names. A zedi customarily houses some relic from the Buddha (hair, tooth or bone), while the focal point of a pahto will be a number of Buddha images. The zedi can be seen in an earlier, more bulbous style and in a clearly Sinhalese design before they evolved into the more distinctively Burmese pattern.

Early pahto were heavily influenced by late Pyu architecture, as characterised by the monuments of Bebe and Leimyethna at Thayekhittaya (Sri Ksetra) near Pyay (Prome). These early square temples are characterised by perforated windows and dimly lit interiors. The common Burmese view is that these early Bagan styles are Mon-style buildings, created by Mon architects imported from Thaton after its conquest, although no such architecture exists in the Mon lowlands. The latest theories suggest the Mon influence at Bagan was primarily confined to the religious and literary spheres, rather than the artistic or architectural. Bagan's kings looked instead to the Pyu kingdoms, and to India, for architectural inspiration.

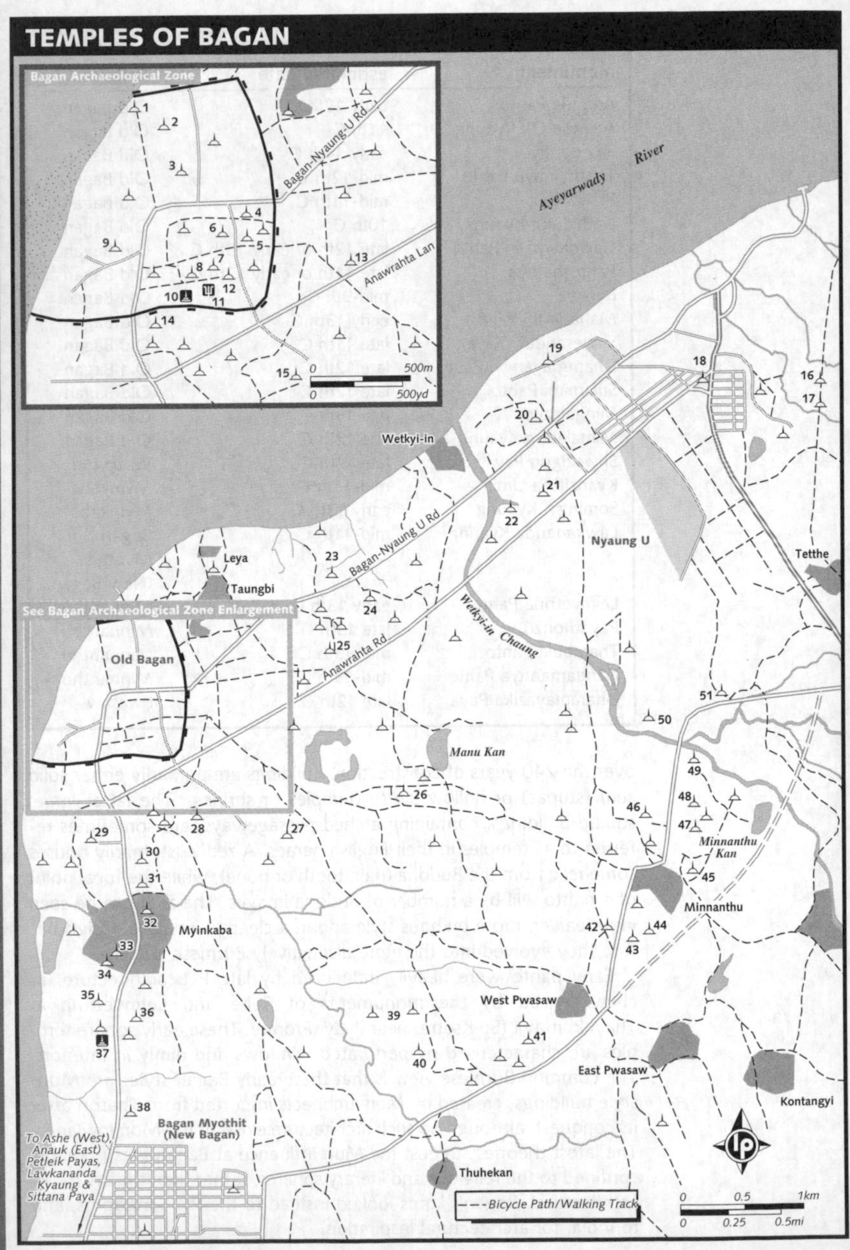
TEMPLES OF BAGAN
Bagan Archaeological Zone
Bagan-Nyaung-U Rd
Anawrahta Lan
500m
500yd
Ayeyarwady River
Wetkyi-in
Nyaung U
Tetthe
Leya
Taungbi
See Bagan Archaeological Zone Enlargement
Old Bagan
Bagan-Nyaung U Rd
Anawrahta Rd
Wetkyi-in Chaung
Manu Kan
Minnanthu Kan
Minnanthu
Myinkaba
West Pwasaw
East Pwasaw
Kontangyi
Thuhekan
Bagan Myothit (New Bagan)
To Ashe (West), Anauk (East) Petleik Payas, Lawkananda Kyaung & Sittana Paya
Bicycle Path/Walking Track
0 0.5 1km
0 0.25 0.5mi

TEMPLES OF BAGAN

1	Bupaya	19	Shwezigon Paya	37	Somingyi Kyaung
2	Pebinkyaung Paya	20	Kyanzittha Umin	38	Seinnyet Nyima Paya & Seinnyet Ama Pahto
3	Mahabodhi Paya	21	Wetkyi-in Gubyaukgyi	39	Thamuti & Kutha
4	Pitaka Taik	22	Gubyauknge	40	Dhammayazika Paya
5	Thandawgya	23	Upali Thein	41	Hsu Taung Pye
6	Shwegugyi	24	Htilominlo Pahto	42	Tawagu
7	Ngakywenadaung Paya	25	Sint Pahto	43	Ashe (West) Zanthi
8	Pahtothamya	26	Sulamani Pahto	44	Anauk (East) Zanthi
9	Gawdawpalin Pahto	27	Dhammayangyi Pahto	45	Leimyethna Pahto
10	Mimalaung Kyaung	28	Shinbinthalyaung	46	Tayok Pye Paya
11	Nathlaung Kyaung	29	Mingalazedi	47	Payathonzu
12	Thatbyinnyu Pahto	30	Gubyauknge	48	Thambula Pahto
13	Ananda Pahto	31	Gubyaukgyi	49	Nandamannya Pahto
14	Nyein Gon Paya	32	Myinkaba Paya	50	Winidho Group
15	Shwesandaw Paya	33	Manuha Paya	51	Izagawna
16	Hmyathat Umin	34	Nanpaya		
17	Thamiwhet Umin	35	Abeyadana Pahto		
18	Sapada Paya	36	Nagayon		

Pahto can be primarily divided into two types: those having one entrance to a vaulted inner area, and few windows, and those having four entrances with images around a central cube. The smaller pahto, characteristic of early Bagan, is often called a *gu* or *ku* (Pali-Burmese for cave temple); these monuments are particularly common around the town of Nyaung U. Seventeen pentagonal monuments – considered the earliest known five-sided buildings in the world – have also been found at Bagan.

Later pahto added Indian design elements to the mix, to produce a truly Burmese design in bright and well-lit pahto like Gawdawpalin, Htilominlo and Thatbyinnyu. Ananda and Dhammayangyi are examples of an earlier transitional phase; indeed, the Ananda is thought by some to have been built by imported Indian labour.

Other unique structures include the *pitaka taik* (Buddhist scripture library), *thein* (ordination hall) and kyaung. These are buildings that would normally have been constructed of wood, and therefore would have disappeared; fortunately, a few were constructed of brick and stone. Monastery buildings served as living quarters and meditation cells for resident monks. At one time, much of the ground space between all the monuments visible today was filled with wooden monastery buildings, said to rival or even exceed the royal palace in design.

Old Bagan

ပုဂံမြို့ဟောင်း

Ananda Pahto One of the finest, largest, best-preserved and most revered of the Bagan temples, Ananda suffered considerable damage in the 1975 earthquake but has been totally restored. Thought to have been built around 1105 by King Kyanzittha, this perfectly proportioned temple heralds the stylistic end of the Early Bagan period and the beginning of the Middle period. In 1990, on the 900th anniversary of the temple's construction, the temple spires were gilded. The remainder of the temple exterior is whitewashed from time to time.

The central square measures 53m along each side, while the superstructure rises in terraces to a decorative *hti* (umbrella-like decorated top) 51m above the ground. The entranceways make the structure a perfect Greek cross; each entrance is crowned with a stupa finial. The base and the terraces are decorated with 554 glazed tiles showing *jataka* (stories of the Buddha's past lives) scenes, thought to be derived from Mon texts. Huge carved teak doors separate interior halls from cross passages on all four sides.

Facing outward from the centre of the cube are four 9.5m standing Buddhas. Only the Bagan-style images facing north and south are original; both display the *dhammachakka mudra* (a hand position symbolising the Buddha teaching his first sermon). The other two images are replacements for figures destroyed by fire. All four have bodies of solid teak, though guides may claim the southern image is made of a bronze alloy. Guides like to point out that if you stand by the donation box in front of the original southern Buddha, his face looks sad, while from a distance he tends to look mirthful. The eastern and western standing Buddha images are done in the later Konbaung, or Mandalay, style.

A small nut-like sphere held between thumb and middle finger of the east-facing image is said to resemble a herbal pill, and may represent the Buddha offering *dhamma* (Buddhist teachings) as a cure for suffering. Both arms hang at the image's sides with hands outstretched, a *mudra* (hand position) unknown to traditional Buddhist sculpture outside this temple. The west-facing Buddha features the *abhaya mudra* (the hands outstretched, in the gesture of no fear).

At the feet of the standing Buddha, in the western sanctum, sit two life-size lacquer statues, said to represent King Kyanzittha and Shin Arahan, the Mon monk who initiated the king into Theravada Buddhism. Inside the western portico are two Buddha footprint symbols on pedestals.

The British built a brick museum next to Ananda Pahto in 1904 in the provincial colonial style. It's now used as a storage facility and is closed to the public. Around the old museum stand a few ordination markers, inscribed stelae and Buddha images.

On the full moon of Pyatho (December/January), a huge *paya pwe* (paya festival) attracts thousands to Ananda. Up to 1000 monks chant day and night during the three days of the festival.

Ananda Ok Kyaung The name of the smaller *vihara* (sanctuary or hall), next door to Ananda Pahto, means Ananda brick monastery. It's one of the few surviving brick monastery buildings from the Early Bagan era. The interior of the building is lined with well-preserved murals, whose colour palette stretches beyond the traditional brown, black and dull red to include a brighter red, plus a little green here and there. The paintings depict everyday scenes from the Bagan period, including Arab traders, market vignettes, bathing and cooking, and musicians playing *hsaing waing* (Burmese drums) and *saung gauq* (Burmese harp).

Although the building is often locked, someone around the temple should have the keys to let you in.

Shwegugyi Built by Alaungsithu in 1311, this smaller but elegant pahto is an example of the Middle period, a transition in architectural style from the dark and cloistered to the airy and light. This brighter design was carried out through the use of more open doorways and windows. The basic profile of the temple, whose name means Great Golden Cave, presages the magnificent Gawdawpalin Pahto with its corncob *sikhara* (temple finial), a scaled-down version of the one at Ananda Pahto, and the move towards verticality.

Shwegugyi is also notable for its fine stucco carvings and for the stone slabs in the inner wall that tell its history, including the fact that its construction took only 7½ months.

Thatbyinnyu Pahto This 'Omniscient' temple, one of the highest in Bagan, rises to 61m and was built by Alaungsithu around the mid-12th century. The structure consists of two huge cubes; the lower one merges into the upper with three diminishing terraces, from which a sikhara rises. Its monumental size and verticality make it a classic example of Bagan's Middle period. Indentations for 539 jataka plaques encircle the terraces; the plaques were never added, leading some scholars to surmise the monument was never consecrated.

In order to better preserve one of Bagan's greatest architectural achievements, since 1994 visitors have been barred from climbing through Thatbyinnyu's amazing inner passages to the top terrace. It was quite a maze climbing to the top – from the main eastern entrance you ascended a stairway flanked by two guardian figures. You then reached a corridor and climbed a narrow, steep flight of steps in the outer wall, and then some external steps to the huge Buddha image on the upper floor. Another claustrophobic stairway within the wall took you to the upper terraces. Of course, military officers and other VIPs are permitted to climb to the top.

In a monastery compound slightly to the southwest of the Thatbyinnyu, you can see the stone supports that once held the temple's huge bronze bell. Northeast of the temple stands a small 'tally zedi', which was built using one brick for every 10,000 bricks used in constructing the main temple.

Ngakywenadaung Paya Close to Thatbyinnyu Pahto, this ruined 9th-century stupa features the bulbous shape favoured by the Pyu. Many of the green glazed tiles that covered it can still be seen.

Left: Cross-section of Thatbyinnyu Pahto, a classic Middle period temple, constructed around 1150.

Pitaka Taik Following the sacking of Thaton, King Anawrahta carted off some 30 elephant-loads of Buddhist scriptures and built this library to house them in 1058. The design follows the basic Early Bagan gu plan, perfect for the preservation of light-sensitive palm-leaf scriptures. It was repaired in 1738. The architecture of the square building is notable for the perforated stone windows, each carved from single stone slabs, and the plaster carvings on the roof which are in imitation of Burmese woodcarvings.

Thandawgya Slightly north of the Thatbyinnyu, this 6m-high stone image of the Buddha was built in 1284, just before the Mongol invasion. It was in poor condition even before the earthquake.

Nathlaung Kyaung Situated slightly to the west of the Thatbyinnyu, this is the only Hindu temple remaining in Bagan. It is said to have been built in 931 by King Taunghthugyi; if true, this was about a century before the southern school of Buddhism came to Bagan, following the conquest of Thaton. In design, it resembles the Pyu Leimyethna, or four-sided shrines of Thayekhittaya.

The temple is dedicated to the Hindu god Vishnu. Gupta-style reliefs of the 10 Avatars, of whom Gautama Buddha was believed by Hindus to be the ninth, were placed around the outside wall; seven of these survive. As a Vaishnava shrine, its main function was to serve as a site for Brahmanic rituals deemed necessary adjuncts for royal ceremonies – an aspect of the Burmese monarchy that continued through the country's last kingship, and one that still survives in neighbouring Thailand.

The central square of brick supports the dome and crumbled sikhara, and once contained free-standing figures of Vishnu, as well as Vishnu reliefs on each of the four sides. The statues were stolen by a German oil engineer in the 1890s, but the badly damaged brick-and-stucco reliefs can still be seen. The temple may have been built by Indian settlers in Bagan, possibly the skilled workers brought to construct other temples. The Bagan scholar Paul Strachan, however, vigorously maintains the work was carried out by indigenous artisans.

This temple's name means Shrine Confining Nat, a reference to a purported time when King Anawrahta tried to banish *nat* (spirit) worship in Bagan. He is said to have confiscated all non-Buddhist religious images – both indigenous Burmese nat and Hindu *devas* (celestial beings) – and placed them in this shrine as part of an effort to establish 'pure' Theravada Buddhism. The king eventually gave in to the cult and standardised the current roster of principal Burmese nat by placing 37 chosen images at Shwezigon Paya. The veracity of this account has never been confirmed, but most Bagan residents – in fact virtually all Burmese – accept it as fact.

Pahtothamya In the same temple-crowded central area, the Pahtothamya (or Thamya Pahto) was probably built during the reign of Kyanzittha (1084–1113), although it is popularly held to be one of five temples built by the nonhistorical king Taunghthugyi (931–64). The interior of this single-storey building is dimly lit, typical of the early type of Pyu-influenced temples, with their small, perforated stone windows. In its vertical superstructure and lotus-bud sikhara, however, the monument is clearly beginning to move forward from the Early period.

Painting remnants along the interior passages may rate as the earliest surviving murals in Bagan.

Gawdawpalin Pahto One of the largest and most imposing of the Bagan temples, Gawdawpalin was begun during the reign of Narapatisithu and finished under Nadaungmya (1211–34) but was very badly damaged in the 1975 earthquake. Reconstruction of the Gawdawpalin probably represents the largest operation undertaken after the earthquake; it was not until the early 1980s that it was completed. The name literally means Platform to which Homage is Paid.

In plan, the temple is somewhat similar to the Thatbyinnyu cube shape, with Buddha images on the four sides of the ground floor, but with several refinements. It features the use of full pediments over the windows, and stairways that ascend through the walls, rather than from within the central cubes. The top of the restored sikhara, which toppled off in the earthquake, reaches 55m in height. Gawdawpalin is considered the crowning achievement of the Late Bagan period.

Although the top terrace was once a popular place to catch the sunset over the Ayeyarwady River, the passageways are now closed to visitors.

Bupaya Right on the bank of the Ayeyarwady, this cylindrical Pyu-style stupa is said to be the oldest in Bagan. Local residents claim it dates to the 3rd century, although there is little proof to support this belief. More likely it was erected about the same time as the city walls, that is around 850, a dating that still distinguishes it as one of Bagan's earliest stupas.

Bupaya was destroyed when it tumbled into the river in the 1975 earthquake, but has since been totally rebuilt. The distinctively shaped bulbous stupa stands above rows of crenellated terraces.

Pebinkyaung Paya If you have been to Sri Lanka, you'll recognise the distinctly Sinhalese character of this small stupa. It was probably built in the 12th century and stands towards the river, near the Bupaya.

Mahabodhi Paya Modelled after the famous Mahabodhi temple in Bodhgaya, India, which commemorates the spot where the Buddha attained enlightenment, this monument was built during the reign of Nantaungmya (1211–34). The pyramidal spire, covered with niches enclosing seated Buddha figures, rises from a square block. Stupas of this nature only appeared during the Late Bagan period; they were most common in the city of Salay, further south.

Bottom: Pahtothamya, a Pyu-style temple with lotus-bud sikhara.

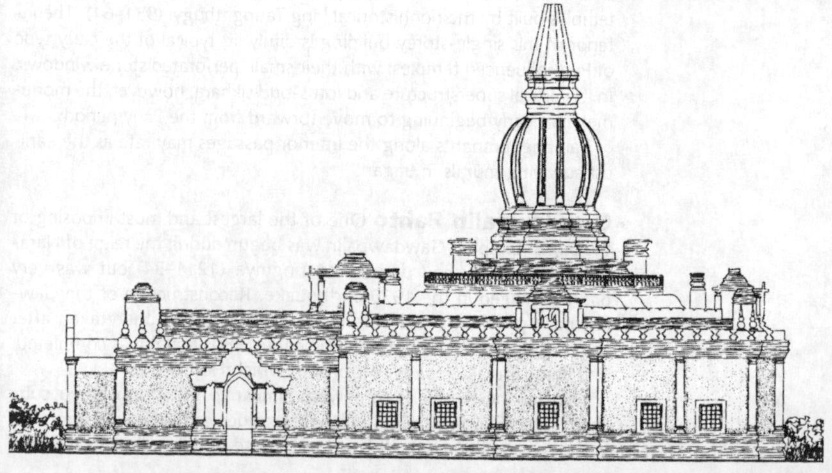

Right: The Late Bagan period Mahabodhi Paya features an unusual pyramidal spire.

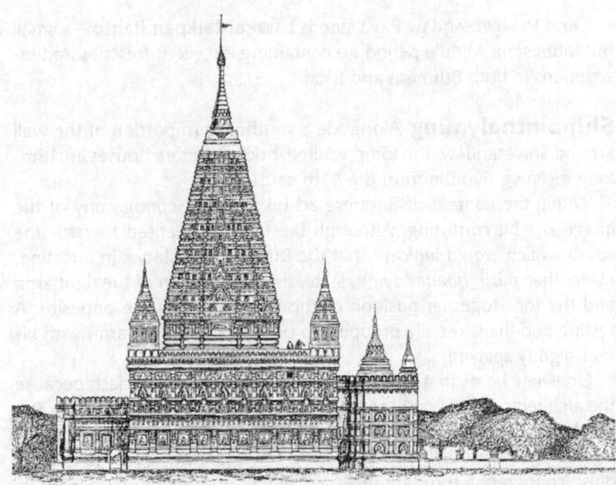

Mimalaung Kyaung A nice set of *chinthe* (half lion/half dragon mythical beasts) guard the stairway leading up this small, square monastery platform, constructed in 1174 by King Narapatisithu. On top of the platform, a tiered-roof shrine contains a large Bagan-style sitting Buddha. Archaeologists discovered a remarkable 6cm dolomite votive tablet here that was so intricately carved it depicted 78 fully sculpted figures.

In front of the monastery stands a brick-and-stucco Tripitaka library next to a large acacia tree. The juxtaposition of venerable tree, library and shrine makes for a special atmosphere, yet few tourists ever visit this easily accessible monument.

Shwesandaw Paya Following his conquest of Thaton in 1057, King Anawrahta built this graceful circular stupa at the centre of his newly empowered kingdom. The five terraces once bore terracotta plaques showing scenes from the jataka, but traces of these, and of other sculptures, were covered by rather heavy-handed renovations. The zedi bell rises from two octagonal bases, which top the five square terraces. This was the first monument at Bagan to feature stairways leading from the square bottom terraces to the round base of the stupa itself. This stupa supposedly enshrines a Buddha hair relic, brought back from Thaton.

The hti, which was toppled by the earthquake, can still be seen lying on the far side of the paya compound. A new one was fitted soon after the quake.

Since the closing of the stairways to the upper terraces of Bagan's tallest monuments, the upper terrace of Shwesandaw Paya has become a very popular sunset-viewing spot. This monument, and Mingalazedi, now offer the highest accessible points within the archaeological zone.

Close to Shwesandaw Paya stands **Lawkahteikpan Pahto** – a small but interesting Middle period gu containing excellent frescoes and inscriptions in both Burmese and Mon.

Shinbinthalyaung Alongside a southeastern portion of the wall around Shwesandaw, this long, vaulted-brick structure houses an 18m-long reclining Buddha from the 11th century.

Within the context of Burmese art history, the iconography of the image is a bit confusing. Although the head is oriented towards the south, which would indicate that the Buddha depicted is in a resting, rather than *parinibbana* (dying) state, the flat position of the right arm, and the toes-together position of the feet, suggests the opposite. A resting Buddha is usually propped up on a crooked right arm, with his feet slightly splayed.

One view holds that the orientation and iconography clash because the architects didn't want the Buddha's back to face Shwesandaw. The builders couldn't simply have placed the figure on its left side, so as to point the head north while still facing Shwesandaw, because in Buddhist iconography throughout Asia reclining Buddha figures always lie on their right side, a preferred sleeping and dying posture with antecedents in Indian yoga (to keep the left nostril clear, thus stimulating the *ida* nerve channel along the spine, to induce a clear, restful state). The historical Buddha was thought to have passed into parinibbana while lying on his right side; even today, Theravada Buddhist monks are often exhorted to sleep on the right side.

Dhammayangyi Pahto Similar in plan to Ananda Pahto, this later temple seems massive in comparison. It is usually ascribed to Narathu (1167–70), who was also known as Kalagya Min (the king killed by Indians – although other sources state that it was the invaders from Sri Lanka who slew him). Other sources believe it was constructed a little earlier, during the reign of Alaungsithu.

As at Ananda, the interior floor plan of the temple includes two ambulatories. Almost all the entire innermost passage, however, was intentionally filled with brick rubble centuries ago. No-one knows for sure why the passage was blocked off; small open places near the top of the passage show intact stucco reliefs and paintings, suggesting that work on the structure had been completed. Local legend says that the work was so demanding – the king mandated the mortarless brickwork fit together so tightly that even a pin couldn't pass between any two bricks – that when the king died, the slave-workers filled the inner ambulatory with rubble in revenge.

Three out of the four Buddha sanctums were also filled with bricks. The remaining western shrine features two original side-by-side images of Gautama and Maitreya, the historical and future Buddhas. Perhaps someday, when Myanmar's archaeological department, or Unesco, or some other party, clears out all the brick rubble, one of the great architectural mysteries of Bagan will be solved.

The interlocking, mortarless brickwork at Dhammayangyi, best appreciated on the upper terraces, is said to rank as the finest in Bagan. Unfortunately, the highest terraces and hidden stairways leading to them are now off-limits to visitors.

Sulamani Pahto Like Htilominlo and Gawdawpalin, this is a prime example of later, more sophisticated temple styles, with better internal lighting. This temple, known as the Crowning Jewel, stands beyond Dhammayangyi Pahto and was constructed circa 1181 by Narapatisithu (1174–1211). Combining the horizontal planes of the Early period with the vertical lines of the Middle, the temple features two storeys standing on broad terraces assembled to create a pyramid effect. The brickwork throughout is considered some of the best in Bagan. The sikhara, badly damaged by the 1975 earthquake, remains unrestored. Stupas stand at the corners of each terrace, and a high wall, fitted with elaborate gateways at each cardinal point, encloses the entire complex. The interior face of the wall was once lined with 100 monastic cells, a feature unique among Bagan's ancient monasteries.

Carved stucco on mouldings, pediments and pilasters represents some of Bagan's finest ornamental work and is in fairly good condition. Glazed plaques around the base and terraces are also still visible.

Buddha images face the four directions from the ground floor; the image at the main eastern entrance sits in a recess built into the wall. The interior passage around the base is painted with fine frescoes from the Konbaung period, and there are traces of earlier frescoes. Stairways lead very close to the top of this temple, from where the views are superb. As at Thatbyinnyu and Gawdawpalin, however, ascents are now prohibited.

A walled enclosure in the north of the compound contains the remains of **Sulamani Kyaung**, a monastery building that housed Sulamani's senior monk and the Tripitaka (Buddhist scriptures); it may also have served as an ordination hall. A water tank in the compound is thought to be the only original Bagan reservoir still in use by local residents.

Mingalazedi Close to the riverbank, a little south of the Thiripyitsaya Sakura Hotel, Mingalazedi (Blessing Stupa) was built in 1277 by Narathihapati. It was the very last of the large Late period monuments to be built before the kingdom's decline, thus representing the final flowering of Bagan's architectural skills.

Mingalazedi is noted for its fine proportions and for the many beautiful glazed jataka tiles around its three square terraces. Although many have been damaged or stolen, there are still a considerable number left. The smaller square building in the zedi grounds is one of the few Tripitaka libraries made of brick; most were constructed of wood, like monasteries, and were destroyed by fire long ago.

Mingalazedi's uppermost terrace is one of the highest points now accessible to visitors. Being the westernmost monument at Bagan, it's a particularly good spot for a panoramic afternoon view of all the monuments lying to the east.

Nyaung U & Wetkyi-in

ညောင်ဦး / ဝက်ကြီးအင်း

Shwezigon Paya Actually standing between the village of Wetkyi-in and Nyaung U, this beautiful zedi was started by Anawrahta but not completed until the reign of Kyanzittha. The latter is thought to have built his palace nearby. Supposedly, the Shwezigon was built to enshrine one of the four replicas of the Buddha tooth in Kandy, Sri Lanka, and to mark the northern edge of the city; the other three tooth replicas went to Lawkananda, a smaller stupa to the south; to Tan Kyi, a stupa on the western bank of the Ayeyarwady; and to Tuyan Taung, a stupa on the summit of a hill 32km to the east.

The stupa's graceful bell shape became a prototype for virtually all later stupas over Myanmar. The gilded zedi sits on three rising terraces. Enamelled plaques in panels around the base of the zedi illustrate scenes from the previous lives of the Buddha. At the cardinal points, facing the terrace stairways, are four shrines, each of which houses a 4m-high bronze standing Buddha. Gupta-inspired and cast in 1102, these figures are Bagan's largest surviving bronze Buddhas. Their left hands exhibit the *vitarka* (exposition) mudra while the right hands are held palms outwards, fingers straight up, portraying the gesture of *abhaya* (no fear).

A 10cm circular indentation in a stone slab, near the eastern side of the stupa, was filled with water to allow former Burmese monarchs to

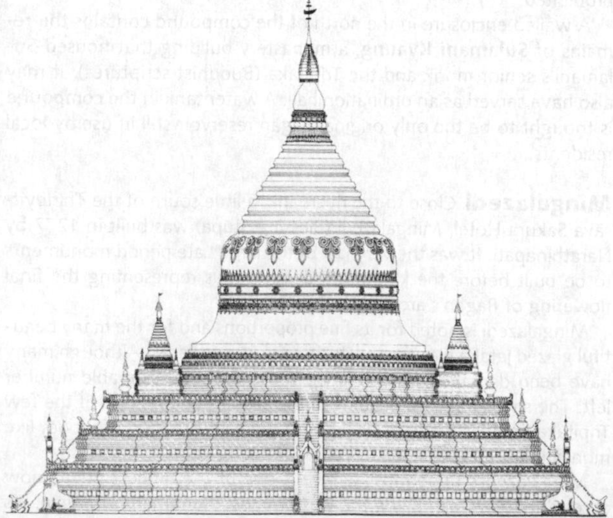

Left: The beautiful bell-shaped Shwezigon Paya – its design became a virtual prototype for all stupas in Myanmar.

look at the reflection of the hti without tipping their heads backwards (which might have caused them to lose their crowns). For a few kyat visitors can view the bejewelled hti through a telescope reserved for that purpose. Surrounding the zedi are clusters of *zayat* (rest houses) and shrines, some of them old, others more modern, though none of them is original.

In addition to ranking as one of the oldest stupas in Bagan, Shwezigon is known as the site where the 37 pre-Buddhist nat were first officially endorsed by the Bamar monarchy. Figures of the 37 nat can be seen in a shed to the southeast of the platform. The 12th-century originals were spirited away by a collector and are now reportedly somewhere in Italy. At the eastern end of the shed stands an original stone figure of Thagyamin, king of the nat and a direct appropriation of the Hindu god Indra. This is the oldest known free-standing Thagyamin figure in Myanmar. Flanked by tigers representing her forest home, another small shrine in the southeastern corner of the grounds is reserved for Mae Wanna, the guardian nat of medicinal roots and herbs.

Caretakers collect a fee from visitors of K10 for the use of still cameras, K25 for videocams.

Kyanzittha Umin Although officially credited to Kyanzittha, this cave temple may actually date back to Anawrahta. Built into a cliff face close to the Shwezigon, the long, dimly lit corridors are decorated with frescoes, some of which are thought to have been painted by Bagan's Tartar invaders during the period of the Mongol occupation after 1287.

Wetkyi-in Gubyaukgyi Close to Wetkyi-in village, this 13th-century 'cave temple' has an Indian-style spire, like the Mahabodhi Paya in Bagan. It is interesting for the fine frescoes of scenes from the jataka, but unfortunately, in 1899 a German collector came by and surreptitiously removed many of the panels on which the frescoes were painted.

This monument is called Wetkyi-in Gubyaukgyi to distinguish it from the temple of the same name in Myinkaba.

Gubyauknge A little southwest of Wetkyi-in Gubyaukgyi, near Wetkyi-in Chaung (Wetkyi-in Canal), this Early-Bagan period temple has some excellent stucco carvings on the outside walls.

Upali Thein Named after Upali, a well-known monk, this ordination hall was built in the mid-13th century and stands across the road from the Htilominlo Pahto. The rectangular building has roof battlements imitative of Burmese wooden architecture, and a small central spire rising from the rooftop. Most buildings of this type were made of wood and have long since disappeared. Inside, there are some brightly painted frescoes on the walls and ceilings from the late-17th or early-18th century. The building is usually kept locked in order to protect them.

Htilominlo Pahto Situated close to the road between Nyaung U and Bagan, this large temple was built by King Nantaungmya in 1218. Nantaungmya erected the temple on this spot because it was here that he was chosen, from among five brothers, to be the crown prince.

Inside the 46m-high temple, which is similar in design to Sulamani Pahto, there are four Buddhas on the lower and upper floors. Traces of old murals are also still visible. Fragments of the original fine plaster carvings and glazed sandstone decorations have survived on the outside. The doorways feature nice carved reliefs.

Hmyathat & Thamiwhet Umin These twin cave temples are about 1km from Nyaung U, towards the airport but off the main road. Dug into hillsides, the caves date from the 13th century.

Sapada Paya Sited close to the road as you approach Nyaung U from Kyauk Padaung or the airport, this Late period zedi from the 12th century was built by Sapada, who originally came from Pathein (Bassein), but became a monk in Sri Lanka. His stupa is Sinhalese in style, with a square relic chamber above the bell.

Other *Monuments* Closer to the river, about 3km east of Nyaung U, you can find the 13th-century **Thetkyamuni** and **Kondawgyi** Pahto. The 11th- and 12th-century **Kyauk Gu Ohnmin** cave temple, further from the river and built into the side of a ravine, is of

Left: Early 13th-century Htilominlo Pahto, similar in design to the earlier Sulamani Pahto.

the same period of Myinkaba's Nanpaya and contains some very impressive sandstone reliefs. It's best visited by boat.

Myinkaba
မြင်းကပါ

Gubyaukgyi Situated just to the left of the road as you enter Myinkaba travelling from Old Bagan, this temple was built in 1113 by Kyanzittha's son Rajakumar, on his father's death. In Indian style, the monument consists of a large shrine room attached to a smaller antechamber. The fine stuccowork on its exterior walls is in particularly good condition.

This Early-period temple is also of particular interest for the well-preserved paintings inside, which are thought to date from the original construction of the temple and to be the oldest remaining in Bagan. The temple is typical of the Pyu, or Early Bagan, style in that the interior is dimly lit by perforated, rather than open, windows; you need a powerful light to see the ceiling paintings clearly. It is generally kept locked – ask in the village for someone to open it. However, in high tourist season (December to February) it's open most of the day.

Right: Gubyaukgyi in Myinkaba, an Early period Pyu-style temple.

Next to the monument stands the gilded **Myazedi** (Emerald Stupa). A four-sided pillar in a cage between the two monuments bears an inscription consecrating Gubyaukgyi and written in four languages – Pyu, Mon, Old Burmese and Pali. Its linguistic and historical significance is great, since it establishes the Pyu as an important cultural influence in early Bagan and relates the chronology of the Bagan kings.

Myinkaba Paya Situated in the village of Myinkaba, this 11th-century paya was built by Anawrahta to expiate the killing of his half-brother, the preceding king, Sokkade, in man-to-man combat. It stands at the Myinkaba stream, into which Sokkade's body and saddle were allegedly disposed. Since it was built before Anawrahta's conquest of Thaton, it is also an interesting example of the religious architecture existing before the influence of the southern school of Buddhism had made itself felt.

Manuha Paya Manuha was named after the Mon king from Thaton, who was held captive in Bagan by Anawrahta. Legend says that Manuha was allowed to build this temple in 1059, and that he constructed it to represent his displeasure at captivity. Stylistically, the dating isn't consistent with the story, though intervening renovations may be responsible for any discrepancies.

The exterior and overall floor plan resemble the more remote Kyauk Gu Ohnmin, a rectangular box topped by a smaller rectangle. Inside, three seated Buddhas face the front of the building, and in the back there's a huge reclining parinibbana Buddha. All seem too large for their enclosures, and their cramped, uncomfortable positions are said to represent the stress and lack of comfort the captive king had to endure. However, these features are not unique in Bagan.

It is said that only the reclining Buddha, in the act of entering parinibbana, has a smile on its face, showing that for Manuha, only death was a release from his suffering. But if you climb to the top of

Left: The mid-11th century Manuha Paya, supposedly built by the captured Manuha.

this paya via the stairs at the entrance to the reclining Buddha chamber at the back of the temple, you can then see the face of the sitting Buddha through a window – from up here you'll realise that the gigantic face, so grim from below, has an equally gigantic smile! In the earthquake, the central roof collapsed, badly damaging the largest, seated Buddha, which has since been repaired.

An outdoor corner of the temple compound is dedicated to Mt Popa's presiding nat, Mae Wanna and her sons Min Lay and Min Gyi. Devotees of Manuha Paya celebrate a large paya pwe on the full moon of Tabaung (February/March).

It is said that, just as King Manuha expressed his dissatisfaction with his captivity by building the paya, nowadays the Burmese people express their dissatisfaction with their 'captivity' by the government by donating freely to the paya.

Nanpaya Close behind the Manuha Paya, this shrine is said to have been used as Manuha's prison, although there is little evidence supporting the legend. In this story the shrine was originally Hindu. Supposedly his captors thought that using it as a prison would be easier than converting it to a Buddhist temple. Recent research now suggests that the temple was constructed by Manuha's grandnephew in the late-11th century.

The masonry work – sandstone block facings integrated over a brick core – is particularly fine. Perforated stone windows are typical of earlier Bagan architecture – in fact it was probably Bagan's first gu-style shrine. It also features interesting arches over the windows.

In the central sanctuary the four stone pillars have finely carved sandstone bas-relief figures of four-faced Brahma. The creator deity is holding lotus flowers, thought to be offerings to a free-standing Buddha image once situated in the shrine's centre, a theory that dispels the idea that this was ever a Hindu shrine. The sides of the pillars feature ogre-like heads with open mouths streaming with flowers. The local Burmese say the face represents a Burmese legend, in which an ogre eats (or, according to others, regurgitates) flowers. In fact the face is a typical representation of the Indian god of time and death, Kala, who devours all in his path.

This temple is generally kept locked but someone at Manuha can usually arrange to have it opened.

Abeyadana Pahto While Kyanzittha sheltered at Nagayon during his flight from Sawlu, his wife Abeyadana waited for him a short distance away. At that site he subsequently constructed this temple, which is quite similar in plan to Nagayon.

The inner shrine contains a large, brick seated Buddha (partly original, partly restored), but the fine frescoes are the main interest here. These paintings are now in the process of being cleaned by Unesco staff. Of the many Buddha niches lining the walls, most are now empty. Some contain Bodhisattvas such as Avalokitesvara and Hindu deities – Brahma, Vishnu, Shiva, Indra – showing a Mahayana influence accredited to the tastes of Kyanzittha's Bengali bride, who was said to have been a Mahayanist.

This temple is usually kept locked, though you can ask around in Myinkaba to find someone to open it.

Nagayon Slightly south of Myinkaba, this elegant and well-preserved temple was built by Kyanzittha. It is generally kept locked to protect its interesting contents. The main Buddha image is twice life-size and shelters under the hood of a huge naga (dragon serpent). This reflects the legend that Kyanzittha built the temple on the spot where he was sheltered while fleeing from his angry brother and predecessor Sawlu – an activity he had to indulge in on more than one occasion.

The outer, dark corridor has many niches with images of the earlier Buddhas. Paintings also decorate the corridor walls. The central shrine has two smaller standing Buddhas as well as the large one. Unfortunately the walls have been whitewashed, obscuring any traces of possible murals.

The small ruined stupa of **Pawdawmu Paya** is nearby.

Somingyi Kyaung Named after the lady who supposedly sponsored its construction, this typical Late Bagan brick monastery is thought to have been built in 1204. A zedi to the north and gu to the south are also ascribed to Somingyi. Many brick monasteries in Bagan were single block structures; Somingyi is unique in that it has monastic cells clustered around a courtyard.

Seinnyet Nyima Paya & Seinnyet Ama Pahto This stupa and shrine stand side by side and are traditionally assigned to Queen Seinnyet in the 11th century, although the architecture clearly points to a period two centuries later. The zedi rests on three terraces and is topped by a beautiful stylised umbrella.

Thiripyitsaya & Bagan Myothit

သီရိပစ္စယာ / ပုဂံမြို့သစ်

Ashe (West) & Anauk (East) Petleik Paya When the lower parts of these twin 11th-century paya were excavated in 1905, it was found that they were built not on a solid base but on vaulted corridors, the walls of which were lined with hundreds of terracotta tiles illustrating scenes from the jataka. New roofs were built over these twin tiers of tiles, many of which are still in excellent condition – particularly in the better-preserved Anauk Petleik Paya. The buildings themselves are unimpressive.

Lawkananda Kyaung At the height of Bagan's power, boats from the Mon region, Rakhaing (Arakan) and even Sri Lanka would anchor by this riverside monastery with its distinctive elongated cylindrical dome. It was built in 1059 by Anawrahta, who is also credited with the Petleik paya. It is still used as an everyday place of worship and is thought to house an important Buddha tooth replica. The views from Lawkananda are good. A couple of vendors on the riverbank provide a selection of snacks and soft drinks.

Sittana Paya This large, bell-shaped stupa is set on four square terraces, each fronted by a standing Buddha image in brick-and-stucco. The stupa was built by Htilominlo and stands slightly south of Thiripyitsaya.

Minnanthu

မင်းနန်သူ

Leimyethna Pahto Built in 1222, this east-facing temple stands on a raised platform and has interior walls decorated with well-preserved frescoes. It is topped by an Indian-style spire like that on Ananda.

Payathonzu This complex of three interconnected shrines (the name literally means Three Stupas) was abandoned shortly before its construction was complete – possibly due to the invasion of Kublai Khan. Dating to the late-13th century, each square cubicle is topped by a fat sikhara; a similar structure appears only at Salay, much farther south along the Ayeyarwady River. The design is remarkably similar to Khmer Buddhist ruins in Thailand.

Two of the shrines contain vaguely Chinese or Tibetan-looking mural paintings that contain Bodhisattva figures. Whether these indicate possible Mahayana or Tantric influence is a hotly debated issue among art historians. Those who say the art is purely indigenous point to the lack of a scriptural context for the paintings; others argue from a purely aesthetic view that the overall iconography suggests Mahayana or Tantric content. The three-shrine design hints at links with the Hindu *trimurti* (triad) of Vishnu, Shiva and Brahma, a triumvirate also associated with Tantric Buddhism. One might just as easily say it represents the Triple Gems of Buddhism (Buddha, dhamma, and sangha), except that such a design is uncommon in Asian Buddhist archaeology, although it does appear in the Hindu shrines of India and Nepal.

The complex is usually locked. It's best to inquire at the museum in Old Bagan to make an appointment for an inspection; in high season, it will probably be open most of the day for group tours.

Thambula Pahto This square temple is decorated with faded jataka frescoes and was built in 1255 by Thambula, the wife of King Uzana. On the eastern wall of the southern transept is an apparently secular painting of a boat race.

Nandamannya Pahto Dating from the mid-13th century, this small, single-chambered temple has very fine frescoes and a ruined, seated Buddha image. The murals' similarity with those at Payathonzu has led some art historians to suggest they were painted by the same hand.

One of the murals represents the 'temptation of Mara' episode in which nubile young females attempt to distract the Buddha from the meditation session that led to his enlightenment. The undressed nature of the depicted females, actually quite tame by all but the most straight-laced standards, shocked French epigraphist Charles Duroiselle, who wrote in 1916 that they were '... so vulgarly erotic and revolting that they can neither be reproduced or described'.

Pwasaw

ပွားစော

Dhammayazika Paya This circular zedi is similar to the Shwezigon or the Mingalazedi, but has an unusual and complex design. Built in 1196 by Narapatisithu, the stupa rises from three five-sided terraces. Five small temples, each containing a Buddha image, encircle the terraces; some of them bear interior murals added during the Konbaung era. An outer wall also has five gateways. Departing from the usual Leimyethna, or four-faced type, the plan adds a fifth aspect in tribute to Mettaya or Maitreya, the Buddha to come. This Buddha plays a major role in historical Mahayana Buddhism. In the context of all the other Mahanayist art seen in Late Bagan temples, one cannot help but wonder if, during the Late period, the kings weren't drifting towards Mahayana Buddhism.

The source of the temple illustrations appearing in this section is *Architectural Drawings of Temples in Pagan* (Department of Higher Education, Ministry of Education, Yangon, 1989).

[Continued from page 288]

There are several other minor festivals, including ones on the full moons of Wagaung (July/August) and Tagu (March/April), which celebrate the departure and return of the famous Taungbyone nat – Min Gyi and Min Lay – each year. The latter nat are brothers who were born to a marriage between Mae Wunna and an Indian Muslim in Anawrahta's employ. The two sons were murdered at Taungbyone, where Anawrahta built a shrine in their honour. Once a year, the Taungbyone nat are believed to travel a spirit circuit that includes Mt Popa, Taungbyone (22km north of Mandalay) and China.

Places to Stay & Eat

On the 1518m mountain (Popa Yoma) to the north of Mt Popa, there's only one, fairly pricey accommodation option.

Popa Mountain Resort *(☎ 70141, fax 70368, reservations: Woodland Travels Yangon office ☎ 01-202071, fax 202074; singles/doubles US$180/200)* was opened in 1999 and commands spectacular views of Mt Popa and the Bagan plain below. There are 24 deluxe chalet-style rooms set in a sandalwood grove, each with all the amenities of an international class resort, including local textiles and teak furnishings. In addition to a pool, terrace restaurant and bar overlooking Mt Popa, the resort offers a number of activities on the mountain, including hiking, bird-watching and horseback riding in the forest. Discounts of 50% are common on published rates.

Most travellers visit Mt Popa as a day trip from Bagan or on their way east of Meiktila or Inle Lake. There's a rather utilitarian **Forestry Guest House** at the base of the mountain that may take visitors; or you could ask at the nearby monastery.

Near the Mahagiri shrine at the bottom of the rock outcropping are several small **cafés** with Bamar food. No beef or pork is served.

Getting There & Away

Mt Popa is about 50km from Bagan or 10km from the railhead at Kyaukpadaung. You can visit Mt Popa by day-tripping from Bagan, or as a stop-off between Bagan and Thazi or Mandalay. Getting there by public transport is time-consuming. One bus leaves Nyaung U daily at 8am for K160. From Kyaukpadaung, pick-ups packed with pilgrims leave frequently for Mt Popa for K60.

With private car charters, more travellers are managing to fit Mt Popa into their itinerary between Bagan and Thazi or Inle. To hire a car and driver for the day to Mt Popa, expect to pay around US$15 to US$20 from Bagan.

A pick-up leaves Nyaung U for Mt Popa at 8.30am, returning around 2pm to 3pm. This should cost K700 to K800 each way.

KYAUKPADAUNG

ကျောက်ပန်းတောင်း

☎ 061

If you're travelling around Myanmar by public bus, you stand a chance of eventually ending up in the junction town of Kyaukpadaung at midnight on your way to Bagan, Salay, Mandalay or Pyay. If so, look for **Pho Pargyi Restaurant** *(☎ 50402)*. In local parlance, it's two furlongs (about 400m) north of the town junction. The owners are experienced in finding either local accommodation (very basic), or a 'saloon' taxi that will take you to Bagan for about US$15 to US$20.

MEIKTILA

မိတ္ထီလာ

☎ 064

Only a short distance west of Thazi, Meiktila is the town where the Bagan-Taunggyi and Yangon-Mandalay roads intersect, just as Thazi is the place where the equivalent train lines intersect. It's an important and prosperous trade centre that also draws revenue from a nearby air force base and training facility. Although there's nothing of particular historical interest here (a bad fire in 1991 almost destroyed the entire town), Meiktila does offer the opportunity to savour the atmosphere of a mid-sized town that until recently has seen very few foreigners.

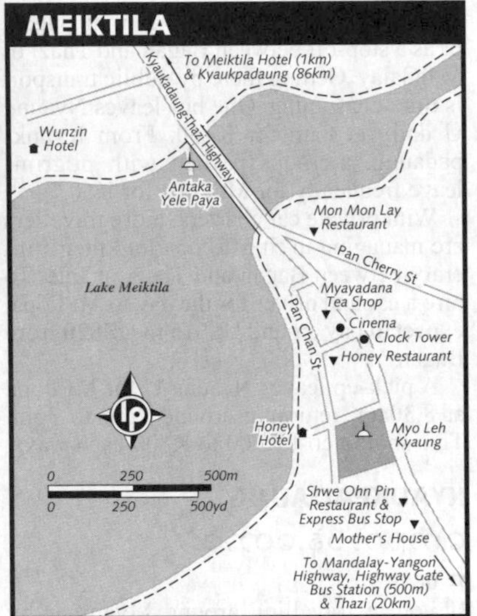

The town sits on the banks of huge Lake Meiktila, bridged by the road from Nyaung U. From one end of this bridge, a wooden pier extends out over the lake to small **Antaka Yele Paya**, a cool spot to rest on warm evenings. The municipality has recently added a promenade around the lake.

Shwebontha Kyaung is a monastery with huge lions out the front – you can't miss this main street landmark while passing through town. Just north of town, by the airfield, there's a WWII Spitfire on display in remarkably good condition.

Places to Stay

Honey Hotel *(☎ 21588; Pan Chan St; singles US$3-5, doubles US$10, singles/doubles with showers US$15/20)* is a friendly place. It is a converted mansion next to the lake, offering large rooms with high ceilings, air-con, private hot showers and good mattresses, or similar rooms with shared bathroom and air-con. An evening breeze often catches the rooms facing the lake. Breakfast is available for US$1, or kyat equivalent.

Wunzin Hotel *(☎ 21848; economy singles US$18, per extra person US$6, standard singles/doubles US$46/42, extra person US$10)*, on the northern edge of the lake, is a friendly place with a variety of rooms in a long two-storey wooden building. Fairly clean standard rooms have concrete floors, mosquito nets, satellite TV, air-con and attached hot-water bathroom. A separate wooden building out the back contains a set of economy rooms with ceiling fans and private large hot-water showers. The best thing about the economy section is that, unlike the main building, it faces the lake and thus catches the cool evening breezes. The **dining room** *(breakfast/lunch & dinner US$1/3)* is quite decent, if rather expensive, by Burmese standards, and the lakeside grounds are pleasant.

Meiktila Hotel *(☎ 21892; singles/doubles US$30/36)* sits near the Yangon-Mandalay highway north of town and offers 24 clean rooms in chalet-style buildings. All rooms have air-con and private toilet and hot-water shower. Rates include breakfast.

Places to Eat

Meiktila has much better food than the typical Burmese town.

Shwe Ohn Pin Restaurant *(Thazi-Kyaukpadaung Hwy)*, on the main road, is the most famous of the local restaurants. A couple of the major express buses between Mandalay and Yangon stop here. One of the house specialities is a delicious curd curry, with big hunks of *hlan no kei* (Indian-style cheese) mixed with cauliflower and okra in a thick and spicy sauce. You can order Chinese dishes from the English-language menu or point at the curry pots for Bamar food. All Bamar meals come with a complimentary dahl stocked with lots of okra and turnips.

Honey Restaurant is a block behind Shwe Ohn Pin, and two blocks northeast of the Honey Hotel (under the same ownership), near the lake. This small, humble wooden restaurant serves decent Chinese food.

Mother's House, next to the Shwe Ohn Pin, is a snack shop with soft drinks, Mars bars and cold beer, along with traveller requisites such as mosquito repellent, shampoo and film. There are a few tables and chairs out the front. The English-speaking father of the owner drops by occasionally to share his English poems with visitors.

Mon Mon Lay Restaurant *(Pan Cherry St)* is at the southeastern end of the lake's bridge, where the road forks. It's a small, reliable Bamar restaurant run by an Indian family.

For tea and snacks, the **Myayadana Tea Shop** near the cinema is a popular spot any time of the day.

Getting There & Away

The public bus stop for Thazi (K30), Mandalay (K180), Pyinmana (K120), Kalaw (K300), Taunggyi (K700) and Yangon (K1000) is located at the Highway Gate bus station. You can also catch buses to Mandalay near the clock tower – this is the stop for buses and pick-ups west to Kyaukpadaung (K100) and Nyaung U (K120).

Sein Kabar (Diamond World) Express and Hnin Thu Wai Express will pick up passengers at the Shwe Ohn Pin on the way to Yangon or Taunggyi.

Getting Around

Horse carts serve the western side of town; many of them park near the southeastern end of the lake's bridge. Trishaws cruise the main streets. A trip from the Honey Restaurant to the Wunzin Hotel costs around K100 by horse cart; from the Honey Hotel to Shwe Ohn Pin by trishaw costs around K40.

PAKOKKU

ပခုက္ကူ

☎ 062

As the region continues to open up, a trickle of travellers are stopping off in Pakokku on the way to Bagan – either by river from Mandalay, or more commonly by private car. A bustling tobacco trading centre, the town itself has little to see, but 20km northeast of Pakokku are the remains of **Pakhangyi**, a 19th-century town with old city walls, an archaeological museum and one of the oldest surviving wooden kyaung in northern Myanmar. The latter is supported by 254 teak pillars. Further west is Myanmar's largest wooden kyaung, a 19th-century structure with 332 teak pillars called **Pakhanngeh Kyaung**.

Besides tobacco, which is cultivated in the surrounding Ayeyarwady floodplain, Pakokku is famous for *jaggery* (palm sugar), *thanakha (Linoria acidissima)* logs, *longyi* (sarongs), and *saun* (checked blankets) made from cotton and wool. Vendors selling these items line up along the pontoon landing whenever a ferry arrives at Pakokku.

One of the town's biggest festivals, Thihoshin, is held from the 8th waxing day to the 8th waning day of Nayon (May/June). The festival is famous for its *pwe* (shows/festivals), both human and marionette.

Places to Stay & Eat

Mya Yatanar Inn *(☎ 21457; rooms per person K500)* is a friendly place that rents very simple rooms; someone from the inn usually meets arriving passengers at the pier. The rough-and-ready facilities don't seem to worry the guests, who have filled a collection of notebooks with effusive praise.

The inn can also arrange meals, or direct you to one of several **rice and noodle restaurants** and **cafés** around town. A trishaw from the pier to the inn costs about K80.

Getting There & Away

The most convenient way to reach Pakokku is by bus or pick-up from Mandalay. These cost around K250 to K300 per person and leave the central/main bus centre at 7am and 11am, a schedule timed with the Chindwin River ferry crossings at 11am and 3pm. Another crossing is to the north at Monywa, which is a scenic route if travelling by car.

You can also travel by bus from Monywa (northwest of Mandalay) to Pakokku. These head off from Monywa three times daily and take about three to four hours. If you catch the early morning bus to Pakokku, you should able to connect with the government-run boat from Pakokku to Nyaung U (Bagan), which departs at 1pm and 2pm daily and takes about 1½ hours. Private boats between Pakokku and Nyaung U can be chartered for around K5000.

Another way to reach Pakokku is via the Mandalay-Bagan ferry – see the Getting There & Away section at the start of this chapter for details.

MYINGYAN

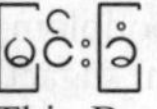

This Bamar-majority township of 260,000 sits on a flat plain along the Ayeyarwady River about midway between Mandalay and Nyaung U. Roads to Mandalay, Nyaung U and Meiktila all intersect here, and long-distance ferries stop here as well. To top it off, a rail line links Myingyan to Mandalay, Thazi and Nyaung U, so the township is a busy transport junction. A modern, two-storey **central market** indicates that trade is an important byproduct of the town's transport function. **Yan Aung Myin Paya**, a standard bulb-tipped, bell-bottomed gilded stupa, is the town's only pride and joy after the market. The townspeople might also boast about the town's tidy green-and-white train station, one of the better-kept stations in northern Myanmar.

In the southern part of town at **Soon Lu Kyaung**, the remains of the well-known Soon Lu Sayadaw are draped in monastic robes and on display in an ornate gilded funerary dais. The sayadaw died 50 years ago; though desiccated, his body is remarkably well preserved.

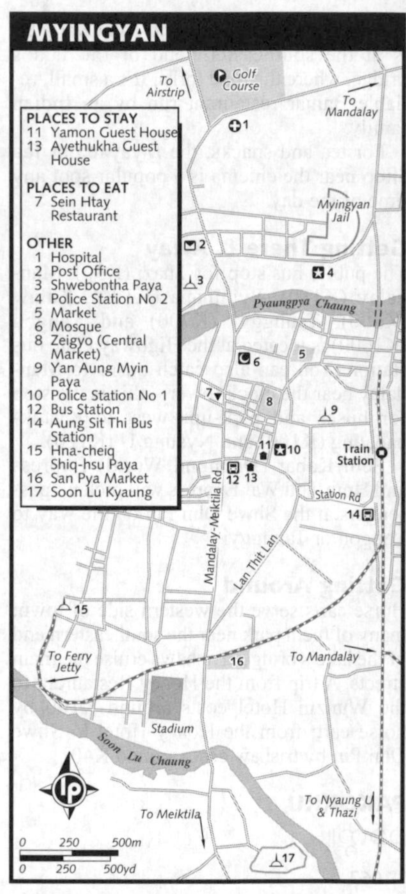

Places to Stay & Eat

The Ministry of Hotels & Tourism's (MHT) licensing division hasn't gotten around to Myingyan yet, but foreigners are occasionally accepted at the **Ayethukha Guest House** or the **Yamon Guest House** opposite one another on Station Rd. Both offer spartan rooms for K500 per person, plus a couple of air-con rooms for around K1000. There are other less palatable places to stay as well.

There are several basic **rice-and-noodle shops** (Burmese signs) opposite the train station and the bus station near the guesthouses.

Sein Htay Restaurant *(Mandalay-Meiktila Rd)* is a few blocks north of the bus station.

Getting There & Away

Around a dozen intercity transport services run buses and pick-ups to Magwe (K400, four hours), Mandalay (K300, three hours), Nyaung U (K300, three hours), Meiktila (K400, four hours) and Yangon (K1000, 15 hours). The main bus station is in the centre of town, near the Ayethukha Guest House.

Myingyan is linked by rail with Thazi, the junction for the Mandalay-Yangon express trains. The train station is on the eastern side of town. One train per day makes the six-hour journey to Thazi. Although the train fare is cheap, buses do the same route (with a change in Meiktila) in around four hours. A newer train line connects Myingyan to Nyaung U and Bagan. The Bagan-Mandalay train stops in Myingyan around noon.

Ferries between Mandalay and points south also stop off in Myingyan. The ferry landing is located west of town.

Getting Around

Trishaws, horse carts and motorised three-wheelers ply the streets of Myingyan. At K40 per kilometre, trishaws are the cheapest option, while motorised three-wheelers and horse carts cost about K80 per kilometre.

MAGWE

မကွေး

Capital of Magwe Division, this mid-size town on the eastern bank of the Ayeyarwady River is 850km north of Yangon and 152km southwest of Nyaung U. The town has an estimated 99% Bamar majority and, like the rest of the area surrounding Bagan, it's very hot and dry from April to May.

There's very little to interest tourists in the town, although the locals will try to send you out to see the famous 1929-vintage **Mya Tha Lun Paya**, a typical Burmese stupa northwest of town on the river. Magwe's main value to the traveller is as a lunch or dinner stopover on long road trips between Pyay and Bagan.

There is considerable boat traffic between Magwe and Minbu, just across the river.

Places to Stay & Eat

Gon Guest House (*rooms K1000*) has good rooms with air-con. To get there it is a K60 trishaw ride from Magwe's Highway bus station in the northeastern part of town.

San Yadana Guest House (*rooms K500*) is a more basic place, near Myoma market, offering drab little box-like rooms.

Padauk Myaing Restaurant, a block east of the police station, serves decent Chinese and Bamar food.

Chitty Htamin Zain is a rice shop near Myoma market which does very inexpensive Indian meals.

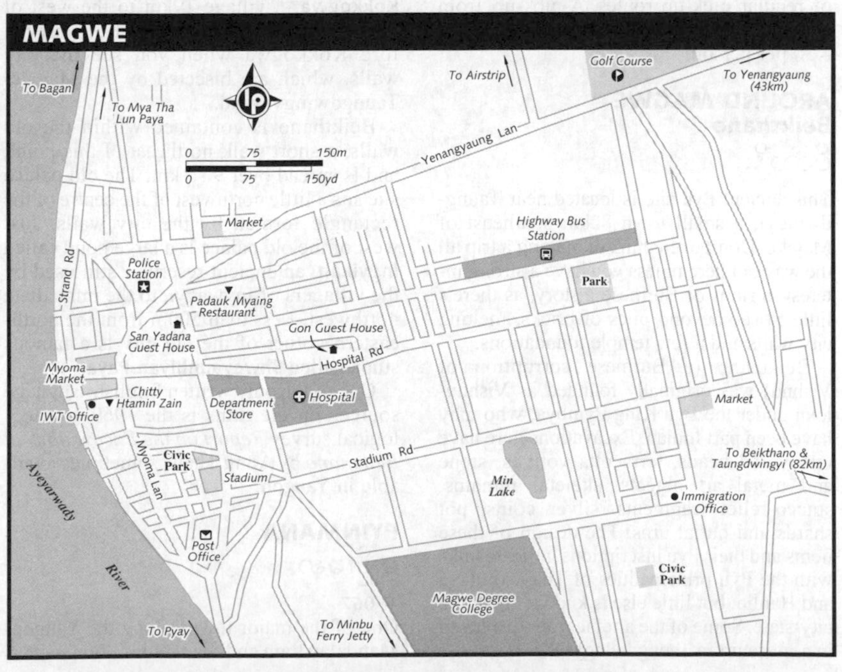

Getting There & Away

Bus & Pick-up The main bus station is in the northeastern part of town; from there you can catch pick-ups and buses to Pyay, Kyaukpadaung and Bagan. There's a bus to Pyay daily at 5am (K700, eight hours). Pick-ups head to Pyay throughout the day (K500, 12 hours).

Boat Ferries from Pyay (deck class K100, upper class K200) arrive on Tuesday, Wednesday and Saturday. However, it makes more sense to travel in the faster downriver direction on the intervening days (Sunday, Monday, Thursday and Friday). From Nyaung U expect to pay about the same as from Pyay. The office of the IWT is near the Myoma market; the ferry landing is south of town.

Getting Around

Trishaws and horse carts are the main forms of local transport, but there are also a couple of regular pick-up routes. A pick-up from Myoma market to the ferry landing costs K30 per person.

AROUND MAGWE

Beikthano

ဗိဿနိုး

This ancient Pyu site is located near Taungdwingyi, a small town 82km southeast of Magwe. Don't even think of making a trip all the way out here unless you have a strong interest in ruins or Burmese history, as there's little to see beyond piles of bricks, melting city walls and a few temple foundations.

Beikthano (a Burmese corruption of Vishnu) was originally founded as Vishnuloka under the Pyu King Pyinbya, who may have been part Indian. Excavations here have uncovered beads, terracotta votives, stone and metal art objects, skeletal remains, stucco-relief fragments, silver coins, pot shards and burial urns. The design of these items and their Pyu inscriptions indicate links with the Pyu principalities of Thayekhittaya and Hanlin, but little else is known about the city-state. Some of the artefacts are displayed in a museum in Taungdwingyi.

With their wheel-and-swastika-shaped bases, the building plans of some of the structures bear a strong resemblance to Buddhist monuments found at Nagarjunakonda in South India. Since *dhammachakka* (dharma wheels) and other Buddhist symbols (but no likenesses of the Buddha himself) were found here, one theory is that the settlement may have been started by Nagarjunakonda missionaries. If true, this would indicate that Beikthano had 3rd-century origins, a period when Buddhists didn't permit the sculpture or worship of Buddha images. Most scholars agree that Beikthano predates Thayekhittaya by about four centuries and that it was destroyed by fire in the 4th to 5th century.

Getting to Beikthano is difficult without wheels. The road to Taungdwingyi is paved, but not in very good condition. During the dry season, there is usually one pick-up per day between Magwe's Myoma market and Taungdwingyi. The ruins lie just north of **Kokkogwa**, a village 19km to the west of Taungdwingyi; you should get off just before Kokkogwa when you see the city walls, which are bisected by the Magwe-Taungdwingyi road.

Beikthano is contained within the old walls, a short walk northeast of this point, and is spread over 9 sq km. The old **palace** site sits a little northwest of the centre of the rectangle formed by the city walls. Just west of the old palace is a large pond called **Ingyikan**, an ancient reservoir still used by the villagers of Inywagyi, to the immediate northwest. Less than 500m from the northeastern corner of the old city is a famous stupa called **Shweyaunhlyan Paya**.

One of the only written English-language sources on the ruins is the 1969 archaeological survey *Report on the Excavations at Beikthano* by Aung Thaw, sometimes available in Yangon.

PYINMANA

ပျဉ်းမနား

☎ 067

One of the major towns along the Yangon-Mandalay train and road routes, Pyinmana is a very leafy place with plenty of trees and many thatched-roof homes at the edge of Shan Lake – a welcome change after visiting the 'dry zone' around Mandalay and Bagan. Overall, it has a more colourful and interesting feel than Taungoo to the south, even though it's of less historic interest. Coconut palms are planted along the Ngalaik River, which passes through town, and you can see the Shan Yoma and Aleh Yoma (mountain ranges) to the east and west. The surrounding valley is carpeted with rice fields, many of which yield two crops a year.

The **Yezin Forest Research Institute**, 15km north of town, is an important facility for the study of Burmese hardwoods. Like Taungoo further south, a fair amount of Myanmar's teak trade is centred here. Korea, Japan, China, Taiwan and Singapore are the major players.

The town's diverse population supports three **mosques** as well as **St Michael's Catholic Church**, a small brick edifice near the river. You may notice more propaganda signs in Pyinmana – they're erected to scare visiting undercover rebels. Insurgent territory begins just 30km east of town: the Kayin (Karen), Kayah and Shan States intersect around 80km southeast of Pyinmana.

Places to Stay

Phoenix (Zar Mani) Motel *(☎ 21646; 183 Bulet Yar St; economy singles/doubles US$7/12, standard singles/doubles US$12/18, superior singles/doubles US$18/24)* is a boxy, four-storey place close to the central market. A group of economy rooms enclose a large central lobby where the TV is on until about midnight. Upstairs are quieter standard rooms with air-con and cold-water shower. The superior rooms are similar but have a TV. A meagre breakfast is included.

Shwe Tharapu Guest House *(Golden Crown Guest House; ☎ 21186; 175 Bo Tar Yar St; rooms per person US$6-7 or kyat equivalent)* is a two-storey house in the central district. The air-con rooms have private cold-water bathrooms. Although the guest house doesn't have a licence to do so, the staff welcome foreigners.

Thukhamyaing Motel *(☎ 21094; rooms K600)* is one other unlicensed place to stay (also known as Pyinmana Co-op Motel), on the main street farther south. It's not particularly clean, but you get a thin mattress, mosquito net and cup of tea in the morning. Bathroom and toilet are separate.

Travellers keen to avoid government-owned accommodation should bypass the **Mingala Kanthaw**.

Places to Eat

There are several very good eateries in Pyinmana.

Yan Naing Restaurant *(1813 Bo Tauk Htain St)* is a popular restaurant on the main street and one of the better places to eat. The menu includes Bamar and Chinese food.

There are several other small, rustic **restaurants** nearby, as this is where most buses stop on their way north or south.

Nearby **Aye Zin Aung Restaurant** *(125 Bogyoke St)* and **Shwe Nadimyit Restaurant** *(2 Bogyoke St)* both serve excellent Chinese and Bamar food.

Getting There & Away

Pyinmana lies close to the southern end of Mandalay Division, just north of the Bago Division border, 303km south of Mandalay and 393km north of Yangon.

From a point near the central market, pick-ups leave frequently for Taungoo; the cost of the trip is K150. Pick-ups depart throughout the day for Meiktila for K150 (K300 front seat).

Two bus companies make the Yangon trip for around K1000. Sein Kabar Express Bus and Mahar Express Bus depart for Yangon at 9.30pm for a 7am arrival at the Highway bus station.

Mandalay-bound buses (K350) cruise the main north-south street for passengers a couple of times each day. The Yangon-Mandalay air-con express buses stop near the Yan Naing Restaurant for meals and to pick up passengers if necessary, but this is not as reliable a stop as Taungoo or Meiktila. Inquire at the Yan Naing for arrival and departure times.

Northeastern Myanmar

Shan State

Nearly a quarter of Myanmar's geographic area is occupied by the Shan State. Before 1989 the area was broken into several administrative divisions collectively known as the Shan States. It's the most mountainous state in the country, divided down the middle by the huge north-south Thanlwin (Salween) River. To the west of the river lies the 1000m-high Shan Plateau, to the east a jumble of north-south mountain ranges and international borders with China, Laos and Thailand.

About half the people living in the Shan State are ethnic Shan, who for the most part live in valleys formed by the Thanlwin River and its tributaries. The traditional Shan ruling system revolves around the *sao pha long* (*sawbwagyi* in Burmese, or Great Sky Lord, a hereditary, feudal leader or prince) installed in each of the original nine Shan states. Under the British, a system of indirect rule created 37 administrative divisions, with a sao pha in charge of the largest ones. After independence, the Shan leadership signed away their hereditary rights in the 1947 Panglong Agreement, which guaranteed a cooperative, semi-autonomous administration of the Shan States. Much of the current conflict in the state dates from this time: Shan commoners were appointed to government positions after the formation of the Union of Burma, much to the dismay of the sao pha, who expected to get the appointments; and from the perspective of most Shan, the degree of expected autonomy never materialised.

In addition to the Shan, the state's major ethnic groups include the Palaung in the mountainous northwestern corner, the Kachin in the far north, the Kaw (Akha) and Lahu (Musoe) in the far east and northeast, the Kokang and Wa in the northeastern mountains, and the Padaung and Taungthu in the southwest. Dozens of smaller groups also inhabit various parts of the state, particularly the mountainous areas.

Because of its elevation, most of the Shan State – even the river valleys – is ill-suited for the cultivation of lowland crops, such as rice. One crop that flourishes even at high elevations is *Papaver somniferum*, the opium poppy, which is the state's main

Highlights

- The serene waters of Inle Lake with its floating gardens and quaint water-borne villages
- Timeless hill-tribe villages in the scenic mountains of the Shan State
- The breathtaking view from the Gokteik Viaduct, a century-old marvel of railway engineering
- A slow boat up the Ayeyarwady to the laid-back and leafy town of Bhamo
- George Orwell's old haunts in Katha, the setting for his classic novel *Burmese Days*
- Colourful markets and ancient monasteries of Kengtung, the capital of the Golden Triangle

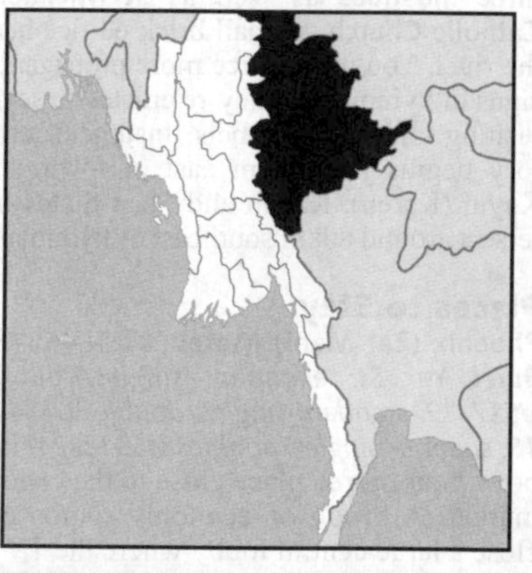

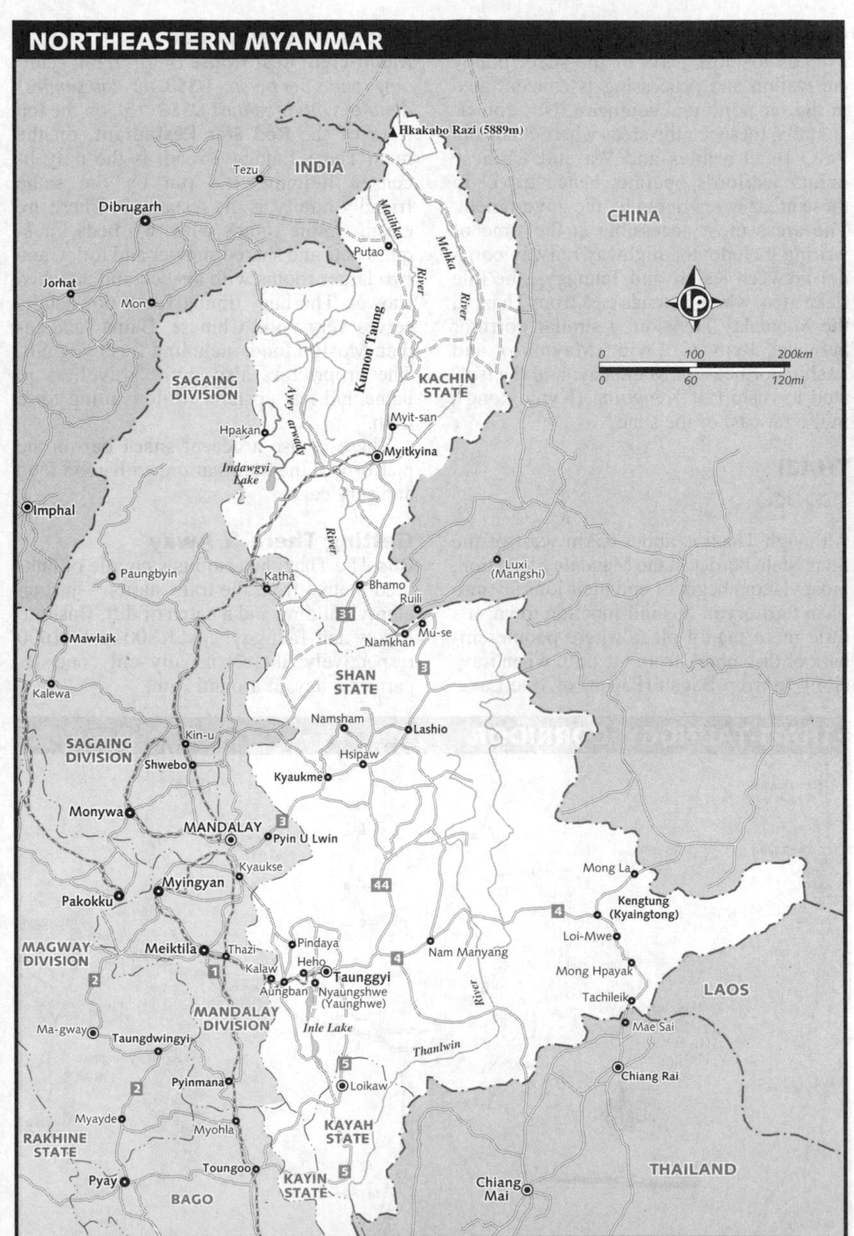
NORTHEASTERN MYANMAR
Hkakabo Razi (5889m)
INDIA
CHINA
Tezu
Dibrugarh
Putao
Malihka River
Mehka River
Kumon Taung
Jorhat
Mon
0 100 200km
0 60 120mi
SAGAING DIVISION
KACHIN STATE
Ayeyarwady
Myit-san
Hpakan
Myitkyina
Indawgyi Lake
Imphal
River
Luxi (Mangshi)
Paungbyin
Katha
Bhamo
Ruili
Mu-se
Namkhan
Mawlaik
Kalewa
SHAN STATE
Namsham
Lashio
Kin-u
SAGAING DIVISION
Shwebo
Hsipaw
Kyaukme
Monywa
MANDALAY
Pyin U Lwin
Kyaukse
Myingyan
Pakokku
Mong La
Kengtung (Kyaingtong)
Loi-Mwe
MAGWAY DIVISION
Meiktila
Thazi
Pindaya
Nam Manyang
Mong Hpayak
Heho
Kalaw
Taunggyi
Aungban
Nyaungshwe (Yaunghwe)
Tachileik
LAOS
MANDALAY DIVISION
Mae Sai
Ma-gway
Taungdwingyi
Inle Lake
Thanlwin
Chiang Rai
Pyinmana
Loikaw
Myayde
Myohla
KAYAH STATE
RAKHINE STATE
Toungoo
THAILAND
Pyay
KAYIN STATE
Chiang Mai
BAGO

source of income. Although the opium trade extends to most parts of the state, poppy cultivation and processing is concentrated in the far north and southeast. Not coincidentally, these are the areas where Shan and Pa-O rebel armies and Wa and Chinese opium warlords operate, hence travel to these areas is restricted by the government. The areas most accessible at the time of writing include: the highway/railway corridor between Kalaw and Taunggyi; the Inle Lake area, which extends east from Thazi in the Mandalay Division; a similar corridor between Pyin U Lwin (Maymyo) and Lashio northeast of Mandalay; and the isolated township of Kengtung (Kyaingtong), in the far east of the state.

THAZI

သာစည်

Although Thazi is about 65km west of the Shan State border in the Mandalay Division, most visitors begin or end their journey into Shan territory in this rail-junction town. It's little more than a place where people embark or disembark from the train when travelling to/from Bagan (Pagan) or Inle Lake.

Places to Stay & Eat

Moon-Light Rest House *(☎ Thazi 56; economy rooms per person US$3, air-con singles/doubles with breakfast US$8/15)*, on the top floor of the **Red Star Restaurant**, on the main Thazi-Taunggyi road, is the only licensed lodging. It's run by the same friendly family as the restaurant. There are clean, simple rooms with two beds, mosquito nets and shared shower and toilet, and two larger rooms with air-con and attached shower. The busy dining room downstairs serves very good Chinese, Bamar and Indian Muslim food, including fresh yoghurt. The proprietors also invite travellers to bathe and rest upstairs while waiting for a train.

There is also a decent **snack bar** on the platform of the train station, with good food and service.

Getting There & Away

Bus The Thazi bus stop is a couple of hundred metres from the train station – just an empty building and a patch of dirt. Buses to Kalaw and Taunggyi cost K800 and K1000 respectively; there's usually only one departure a day, at around 7am.

THAZI-TAUNGGYI CORRIDOR

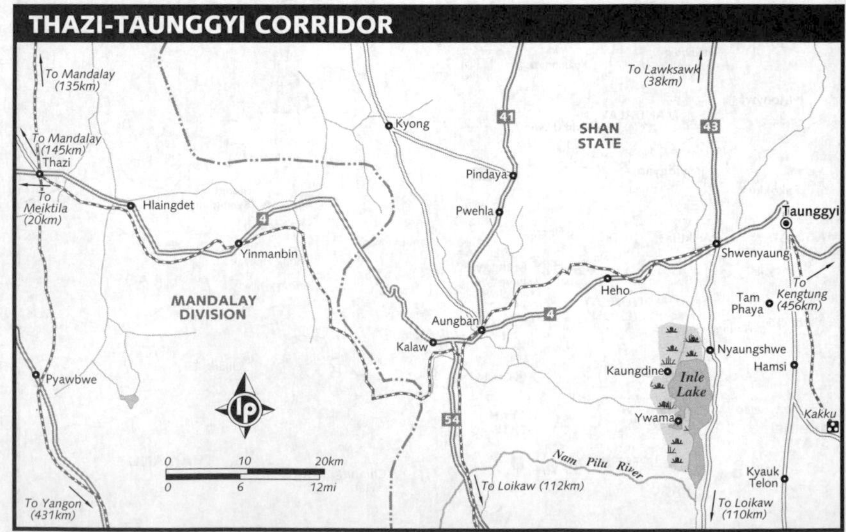

Since a new bypass road was built in 1998, it's now possible to skip Meiktila when travelling between Thazi and Mandalay. Nevertheless, there are more buses going through Meiktila bound for Mandalay. The simple solution is to get to Meiktila by pick-up, then wait for a bus to Mandalay (see the Meiktila section in the Bagan Region chapter for information on buses to Mandalay). The riskier choice is to wait for a Taunggyi-Mandalay bus to come through Thazi and hope you can get on. A passenger pick-up between Meiktila and Thazi costs around K200.

Train See the Getting Around chapter at the start of this book for details on train travel to/from Thazi. Some travellers have managed to get ordinary-class seats from Thazi to Yangon (Rangoon) for US$9, or to Mandalay for US$5. It's more likely, however, that you'll have to buy upper-class tickets.

For information on the train to Shwenyaung, for Inle Lake, see the Inle Lake section later in this chapter.

Car Ask at the Red Star Restaurant about arranging a car tour of northern Myanmar. The going rate is about US$30 (or kyat equivalent) per day, depending on the condition of the vehicle. Though it has become easier to get good rental rates around Mandalay and Bagan, some drivers based in these towns charge a bit more, simply because the steep winding roads of the Shan State require more vehicle upkeep.

KALAW

ကလော

☎ 081

Situated 70km west of Taunggyi, about halfway along the Thazi-Taunggyi road, Kalaw sits high on the western edge of the Shan Plateau. This was a popular hill station in the British days, and it's still a peaceful and quiet place with an atmosphere reminiscent of the colonial era. In fact, if you're looking for colonial architecture, Kalaw y boasts as many, or more, examples than U Lwin, which has lost many colonial structures to modernisation in the past few years. At an altitude of 1320m, Kalaw's pleasantly cool and a good place for hiking amid gnarled pines, bamboo groves and rugged mountain scenery. There is comfortable accommodation, and you can make interesting excursions around Kalaw and treks into the surrounding mountains.

The small population is a mix of Shan, Indian Muslims, Bamar and Nepalis (Gurkhas retired from British military service). As recently as the 1970s, there were American missionaries teaching in the local schools. Because of the British colonial and missionary heritage, many people speak English. About 20,000 people live in and around Kalaw.

Things to See & Do

There are some rather interesting temples to see in town. Perched on the hill overlooking the Thazi-Taunggyi road is the **Thein Taung Paya**. In the town centre is a glittering stupa (Buddhist religious monument), covered in gold-coloured mosaics, called **Aung Chang Tha Zedi**. Just across the street is the dilapidated **Dhamma Yon**, a two-storey temple; it's not particularly interesting in itself, but from upstairs you can get fair views of the town, Dhamma Yanthi Paya and the ruins of **Hsu Taung Pye Paya**, now a field of crumbling stupas behind the Dhamma Yon towards the Kalaw Hotel. Just west of town, **Nee Paya** (also called Hnin Paya) features a gold lacquered bamboo Buddha. It's about 20 minutes away by car.

Less than 1km from the Kalaw Hotel is **Christ the King Church**, a brick Catholic church under the supervision of Burmese Father Paul and, until recently, the late Italian Father Angelo Di Meo, who was based in Myanmar from 1931 until he passed away in 2000. He managed to remain in Myanmar despite Japanese suspicion of his possible British sympathies during WWII, British suspicion after the war, and State Peace & Development Council (SPDC) suspicion up until his death. The Christ figure over the altar came from Italy, and Father Angelo painted the mural background. A stone grotto built behind the church is reputed to

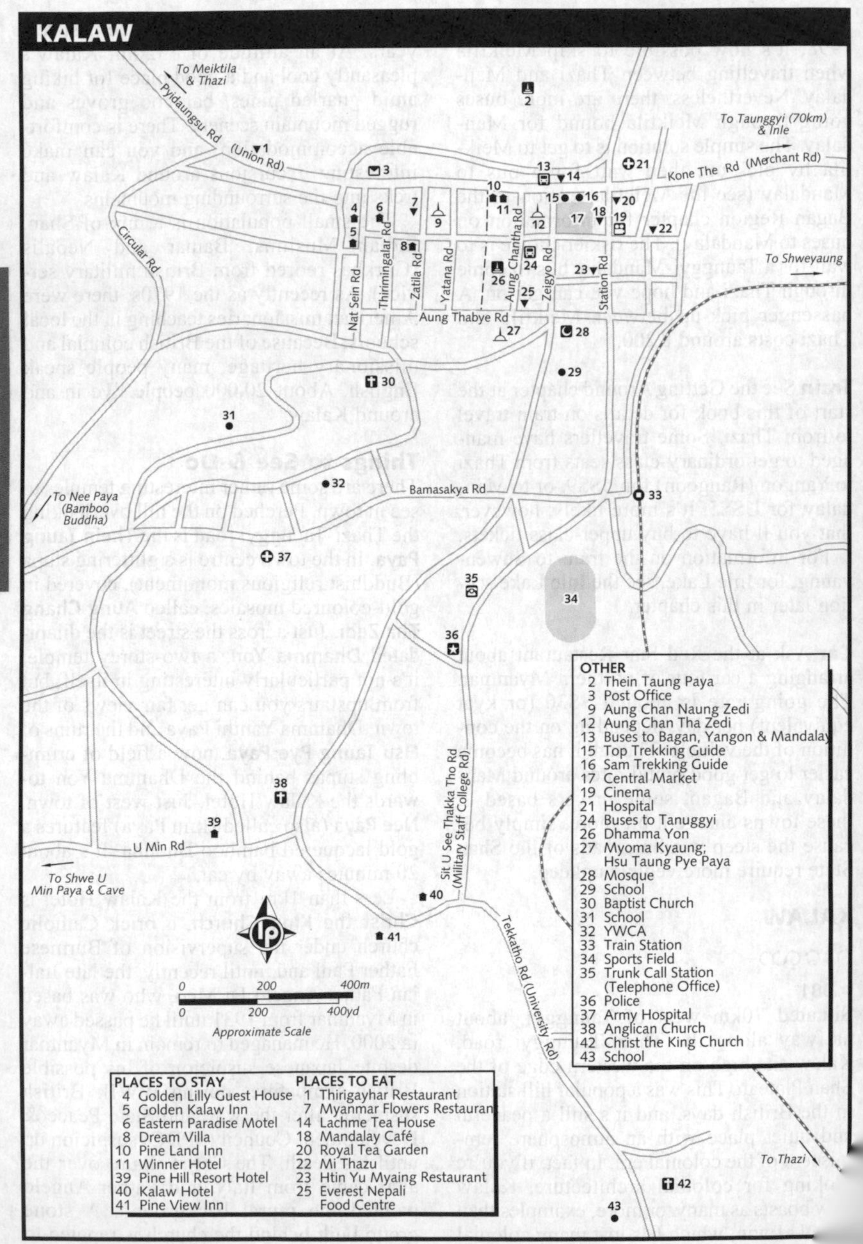
KALAW
To Meiktila & Thazi
Pyidaungsu Rd (Union Rd)
To Taunggyi (70km) & Inle
Kone The Rd (Merchant Rd)
To Shweyaung
Circular Rd
Nat Sein Rd
Thirimingalar Rd
Zatila Rd
Yatana Rd
Aung Chantha Rd
Zeigyo Rd
Station Rd
Aung Thabye Rd
Bamasakya Rd
To Nee Paya (Bamboo Buddha)
Sit U See Thakka Tho Rd (Military Staff College Rd)
U Min Rd
To Shwe U Min Paya & Cave
Tekkatho Rd (University Rd)
To Thazi
0 200 400m
0 200 400yd
Approximate Scale
NORTHEASTERN MYANMAR
OTHER
2 Thein Taung Paya
3 Post Office
9 Aung Chan Naung Zedi
12 Aung Chan Tha Zedi
13 Buses to Bagan, Yangon & Mandalay
15 Top Trekking Guide
16 Sam Trekking Guide
17 Central Market
19 Cinema
21 Hospital
24 Buses to Tanuggyi
26 Dhamma Yon
27 Myoma Kyaung; Hsu Taung Pye Paya
28 Mosque
29 School
30 Baptist Church
31 School
32 YWCA
33 Train Station
34 Sports Field
35 Trunk Call Station (Telephone Office)
36 Police
37 Army Hospital
38 Anglican Church
42 Christ the King Church
43 School
PLACES TO STAY
4 Golden Lilly Guest House
5 Golden Kalaw Inn
6 Eastern Paradise Motel
8 Dream Villa
10 Pine Land Inn
11 Winner Hotel
39 Pine Hill Resort Hotel
40 Kalaw Hotel
41 Pine View Inn
PLACES TO EAT
1 Thirigayhar Restaurant
7 Myanmar Flowers Restauran
14 Lachme Tea House
18 Mandalay Café
20 Royal Tea Garden
22 Mi Thazu
23 Htin Yu Myaing Restaurant
25 Everest Nepali Food Centre

have curative powers. Mass is held daily at 6.30am; and at 8am and 4pm on Sunday.

Places to Stay

In Kalaw there are several places to stay on or close to the main road, and several more on the outskirts of town. The main road goes by several names, including Pyidaungsu Rd (Union Rd) and Thazi-Taunggyi Hwy.

Golden Kalaw Inn (☎ *50311; 66 Nat Sein Rd; rooms per person without/with bathroom US$2/3)* is a friendly hotel offering clean rooms as well as a casual 'lobby' with satellite TV. Eddie, the owner, leads informative treks that are highly recommended. Bus and plane tickets can also be arranged. Breakfast is included.

Golden Lily Guest House (☎ *50108; 5/88 Nat Sein Rd; rooms with private bathroom per person US$3)*, a rambling place with screen doors and a wide veranda, was formerly the Golden Kalaw Inn. Rooms are spartan and a tad rustic. Breakfast is included.

Eastern Paradise Motel (☎ *50087; 5 Thirimingalar Rd; singles/doubles with shared bathroom US$3/6, with private hot-water bathroom US$8/15, with satellite TV & fridge US$10/20)* is a friendly motel on a quiet street, with clean rooms, including some triples. Breakfast is included.

Winner Hotel (☎ *50025; Pyidaungsu Rd; singles with shared bathroom US$3, singles/doubles with satellite TV US$10/12, with satellite TV & fridge US$20/25)*, on the main road, is clean, well managed and good value. As the manager, George, speaks excellent English, this is a good place to ask about local treks. Breakfast is included.

Pine Land Inn (☎ *50026; Pyidaungsu Rd; rooms without/with bathroom per person US$2/3)* is a rambling and shabby two-storey guesthouse, right on the main road through Kalaw. The cheapest place to stay in town, it has very basic two-bed rooms with shared hot-water shower and toilet, and similar rooms with attached bathroom. Spoken English is very basic here. Breakfast is included.

Pine View Inn (☎ *50185; Tekkatho Rd; singles/doubles US$10/20)*, on a quiet street, is good value. It has spacious rooms with desks, plenty of light, and attached hot-water shower. A tasty Bamar or Western breakfast is included, along with a good view. The only drawback is that it's a bit of a walk into town.

Pine Hill Resort Hotel (☎ *50079, fax 50078; 101 U Min Rd; bungalow singles/doubles/triples US$36/42/67, chalet singles/doubles US$60/72)*, though not as historic as the Kalaw Hotel, is the nicest place to stay in Kalaw. Its well-appointed bungalow-style rooms overlooking the surrounding hills have fridge, TV and hot-water bathroom, and breakfast is included in the rates. The hotel restaurant serves very good Bamar and Indian dishes. It's a little far from the town centre.

Kalaw Hotel (☎ *50039; 84 University Rd; new building singles/doubles US$30/36, old building rooms US$48, main building rooms US$60)* consists of three buildings: the oldest, built in 1903, is all wood but the rooms have been recently modernised – only the floorboards are original – and hence have lost much of their charm. The main building, which looks like a cross between a Tudor mansion and a hunting lodge, was built in 1906 and has more character. The new building, built in the past few years, is an eyesore and looks like it's ready to collapse. All rooms have a hot-water shower. The hotel originally served as resort quarters for British officers. The Japanese used it as a hospital during WWII. Set well behind the town, it's a very quiet and peaceful place to stay, and is popular among French package tourists.

Dream Villa (☎ *50144; Zatila Rd; singles/doubles/family suite US$18/24/36)* has decent rooms with hot water, though for the amenities provided it's a bit overpriced. Rates include breakfast. During the low season (May to October), discounts may be available. As with most hotels in cool Kalaw, there is no air-con.

Places to Eat

As in Pyin U Lwin, many Kalaw restaurants have an Indian or Nepali touch.

Everest Nepali Food Centre *(Aung Chantha Rd; open 6.30am-9pm daily)* is clean and modest and one of our favourite places to eat. Two blocks from the main road, it serves tasty and reasonably priced curries, fresh juice and dry chapatis.

Thirigayhar Restaurant *(Seven Sisters; ☎ 50216)* is a popular (though relatively pricey) Shan-Chinese-Indian eatery in a charming cottage on the main road. It often caters to package-tour groups.

Htin Yu Myaing (Pineland) Restaurant, a block south of the central market, serves good Chinese and Bamar fare. **Myanmar Flowers Restaurant**, near Aung Chang Naung Zedi (four blocks west of the market), offers some of the best Bamar dishes in town.

There are quite a few teashops in Kalaw, but they're nothing fancy. The **Royal Tea Garden**, near the cinema, is large and popular.

Mandalay Café *(open 5am-9pm)*, across the street from the Royal Tea Garden, is a tiny Nepali-operated teahouse, which serves very good tea, chapatis and curry, and is open longer than any of the other places.

Lachme Tea House, across the main road from the market, is simple but friendly and stays open later than most; its stereo blaring Burmese rock draws a younger crowd.

Mi Thazu, behind the cinema, is a larger Nepali teashop, where chapatis, tea and *raksi* (Nepali-style homemade liquor) are available.

Getting There & Away

Buses for Kalaw (around K1000) leave Thazi in the morning. Taunggyi-bound buses from either Meiktila or Bagan pass through Kalaw, though you may have to pay the full Taunggyi fare. Travel time is about three hours. From Taunggyi to Kalaw by bus (two to three hours) it's K500. To charter a vehicle to either Thazi or Taunggyi will cost US$20 to US$25. For information on travel to Aungban and Pindaya, see the Pindaya section later in this chapter.

It's possible to take the train from Thazi or Shwenyaung; it takes around 4½ hours from Thazi, about half that time from Shwenyaung. The fare is US$5 in 1st class. Either way, it's a scenic, if slow, trip.

To return to Yangon, it's possible to book a seat through the Winner Hotel, Kalaw Hotel or Top Trekking Guide Service for one of the Taunggyi-Yangon air-con express buses (about K3000). To Mandalay, expect to pay about K2000; to Bagan about K2500. In Yangon, check with Trans-national Express. There's also the usual Mandalay-Yangon train connection via Thazi.

AROUND KALAW

Visiting Nearby Villages

Trekking around Kalaw can vary from a one-day hike to five-day treks into the surrounding hills. The plateau near Kalaw is inhabited by people of the Palaung and Pa-O (Black Karen) tribes. Intha, Shan, Taungthu, Taung-yo, Danu, Kayah, Danaw and Bamar people occupy the mountains to the north and east.

Palaung women wear colourful blue-and-red costumes and families often live in 'long houses'. One of their main sources of income is the cultivation of *thanaq-hpeq* (a large leaf used to wrap Burmese cigars). The Pa-O wear more sombre dark blue or indigo costumes, and are regarded as good businesspeople. Tribespeople come into town on Kalaw's market day, which comes around every five days. On the way home, their woven backpack baskets may be filled with cheroots (Burmese cigars), candles and treats for the children.

When visiting the villages, it's better to contribute cash gifts to the village health fund rather than hand out medicine, toys or food. Pencils, paper notebooks and ball-point pens are also welcome. Your guide should know what's appropriate and what's not. Usually the *sayadaw* (chief abbot) of the village monastery, or the village head-man, handles such donations. Village elders prefer that any gifts intended for children be given to an adult, rather than directly to the children.

Trekking Several nearby villages can b visited in half-day or whole-day hik

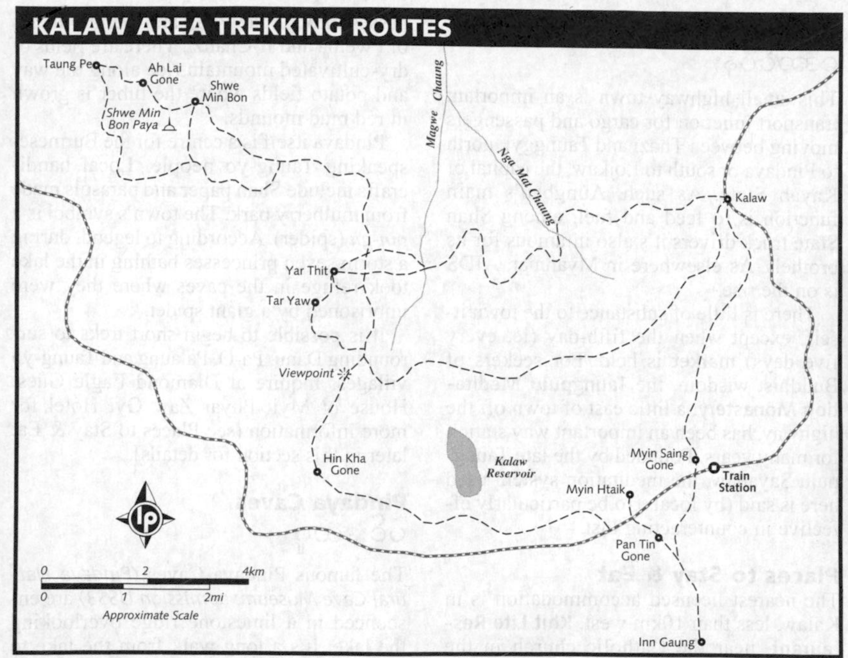

Some guides are beginning to lead multiday trips. Licensed guides in Kalaw generally charge US$4 to US$5 for a day hike, and US$5 to US$7 per day for overnight treks. The cost generally includes food and lodging. Expect to hike for at least six hours a day and cover about 15km.

One advantage of overnight treks is that by evening time people are back home in the village after spending a day tending the fields. Lodging is usually in long houses, occasionally in *kyaung* (monasteries). Be prepared for the lingering smoke of longhouse cooking fires. On the plus side, it keeps mosquitoes at a minimum.

Some of the guide services rate treks as 'hard', 'normal', or 'easy', according to the distance to be covered. All the licensed trekking guides in Kalaw can provide sleeping bags and mosquito nets. Hikers need to e prepared with good shoes and warm thing for the cool evenings. Trekking s on year-round, but during the rainy season (May/June–November) expect muddy conditions.

If you want to trek to nearby villages, there are several sources of information in Kalaw (see that section earlier in this chapter). Many of the hotels (eg, Winner Hotel, Golden Kalaw Inn) and restaurants (eg, Everest Nepali Food Centre) can offer guide assistance. Father Paul at Christ the King Church is also quite helpful.

Several reliable trekking guide services operate from small offices along the main road through Kalaw, just north of the market:

Sam Trekking Guide Service (☎ *50237*) offers one-, two- and three- to four-day treks. Sam's English is quite good, and his daughter speaks reasonable Japanese. Sam takes a maximum of four people on any trek, regardless of its duration.

Top Trekking Guide Service is a few doors down from Sam's and offers similar services, including a three-day trek to a working-elephant camp west of Kalaw.

AUNGBAN
အောင်ပန်း

This small highway town is an important transport junction for cargo and passengers moving between Thazi and Taunggyi, north to Pindaya or south to Loikaw, the capital of Kayah State. As such, Aungban's main function is to feed and fuel; among Shan State truck drivers it's also infamous for its brothels. As elsewhere in Myanmar, AIDS is on the rise.

There is little of substance to the town itself, except when the fifth-day (ie, every five days) **market** is held. For seekers of Buddhist wisdom, the **Taungpulu Meditation Monastery**, a little east of town off the highway, has been an important way station for many years. Founded by the late Taungpulu Sayadaw, the meditation system used here is said (by locals) to be particularly effective in counteracting lust.

Places to Stay & Eat
The nearest licensed accommodation is in Kalaw, less than 10km west. **Khit Lite Restaurant**, near the Catholic church in the centre of town, is a big place serving Chinese food. The café at **Pwint Thit Sa Guest House** offers inexpensive Bamar meals.

Getting There & Away
See Getting There & Away in the Pindaya section later for information on transport from Pindaya and Kalaw to Aungban.

Loikaw is 155km south of Aungban – four to five hours by car or longer by public transport. This road has been closed to foreigners for several years running; there are four military checkpoints between Aungban and Loikaw, so it's virtually impossible to get through undetected.

PINDAYA
ပင်းတယ

☎ 081

About 20km north of Aungban is the town of Pindaya, noted for its extensive limestone caves and picturesque Boutaloke Lake. The scenic Aungban-Pindaya road passes through the Pa-O and Danu villages of Pwehla and Ji-Chanzi. There are fields of dry-cultivated mountain rice along the way and potato fields where the tuber is grown in red mud mounds.

Pindaya itself is a centre for the Burmese-speaking Taung-yo people. Local handicrafts include Shan paper and parasols made from mulberry bark. The town's symbol is a *pin-gu* (spider). According to legend, during a storm seven princesses bathing in the lake took refuge in the caves where they were imprisoned by a giant spider.

It is possible to begin short treks to surrounding Danu, Pa-O, Palaung and Taung-yo villages. Inquire at Diamond Eagle Guest House or Myit Phyar Zaw Gyi Hotel for more information (see Places to Stay & Eat later in this section for details).

Pindaya Caves
ပင်းဒယဂူ

The famous Pindaya Caves *(Pindaya Natural Cave Museum; admission US$3)* are ensconced in a limestone ridge overlooking the lake. It's a long walk from the lake to the foot of the cliff containing the caves; if you've chartered a jeep or car from Kalaw or Taunggyi, make sure that you're driven all the way up to the cliff. Travel from town to the foot of the cliffs costs K1000 by horse cart. A 200-step stairway leads to the cave entrance – or you can take the new lift to the entrance for K100.

Inside the cavern there are more than 8000 **Buddha images** – made from alabaster, teak, marble, brick, lacquer and cement – which have been put there over the centuries and arranged in such a way as to form a labyrinth throughout the various cave chambers. Sadly, somebody recently decided to spruce up the Buddha images by painting them all red and gold. Some of the smaller side-chambers are accessible only on hands and knees, and you may come across people practising meditation.

Among the more unusual features in th cave is a set of **stalagmites** that can struck with large wooden mallets to prod 'gong' tones. In one corner of the cave three 'perspiring Buddhas', sitting images that stay wet because of condensation in the damp cave. Burmese worshippers believe they will gain good fortune and beauty by rubbing the drops of 'sweat' on their faces.

Although many areas within the caves are illuminated by electric lights, power has been known to fail and a torch (flashlight) will help make out the darker corners. Take care on the slippery paths.

From a temple complex built along the front of the ridge you can view the nearby lake and the ruins of **Shwe U Min Paya**, a cluster of low stupas just below the ridge. Beginning on the full moon of Tabaung (February/March), Pindaya hosts a colourful *paya pwe* (pagoda festival) at Shwe U Min.

Padah-Lin Caves

ပဒါးလင်းဂူ

Northwest of Pindaya, near the village of Ye-Ngan, is the most important prehistoric site in Myanmar, the Padah-Lin Caves (also known as Badalin, or Badut Hlaing – Chameleon Cave). The interior of one of the caves is decorated with the remains of very old paintings of animal and human subjects, not unlike Neolithic cave paintings in Europe. Some visitors reckon that these caves are more atmospheric than the heavily touristed Pindaya Caves. To get here you will have to charter a 4WD – this can be added on to a Pindaya trip from either Kalaw or Taunggyi for about an extra K3500 per vehicle. From Ye-Ngan, a rough track leads several kilometres southwest to Yebok village. The two caves are a little over 1km west of Yebok on a footpath.

Places to Stay & Eat

Pindaya is an established tourist destination, and there are several places to stay between Boutaloke Lake and the caves.

Pindaya Hotel *(in Taunggyi ☎ 22409; standard singles/doubles US$12/16, superior rooms US$20/25)* is a clean and comfortable two-storey place about halfway between the town and the caves. The standard rooms have fan and attached shower and toilet. Slightly bigger superior rooms have a fridge and balcony views of the lake. The hotel restaurant serves very decent Chinese and Shan dishes.

Golden Cave Hotel *(in Taunggyi ☎ 23471; singles/doubles US$12/18)* is a friendly place with simple and clean two-bed rooms with attached hot-water shower. Rates include breakfast.

Myin Phyar Zaw Gyi Hotel *(in Taunggyi ☎ 23257; standard singles/doubles US$10/20, superior singles/doubles US$15/25)* has 16 standard rooms with attached hot-water bathroom, and five larger superior rooms with fridge. Rates include breakfast. Its dining room serves mostly Chinese food.

Inle Inn *(Pindaya ☎ 29, in Taunggyi ☎ 21479, fax 21347; singles/doubles US$25/30, larger singles/doubles US$35/40)* is a quiet place set in a bamboo grove. You'll find it by entering Pindaya from the south. All rooms have hot water and a veranda. Rates include breakfast.

Conqueror Hotel *(in Taunggyi ☎ 23257; standard singles/doubles US$37/42, superior singles/doubles US$45/53)* is more expensive and caters largely to tour groups. During the low season (May–October) it often drops its prices by at least 20%. All rooms are duplex bungalows, and come with attached hot-water bathroom, satellite TV, fridge and fireplace.

Diamond Eagle Guest House *(☎ Pindaya 30; rooms per person US$5)* is a friendly, cheap guesthouse next to the lake. Rooms are clean and have a common bathroom, and even offer a view of the lake. Breakfast is not included.

In addition to the standard hotel dining rooms mentioned, good food can be found in the market area in town – the best is at **U Aseik**, where you can get a delicious full Bamar meal for around K60.

Shwe Da Nu Restaurant serves the usual Chinese food but a view of the mouth of the cave sets it apart from the others. **Teik Sein Restaurant** serves delicious Shan food. **Kyanlite Restaurant** has an English menu featuring Chinese fare.

At the cave temple, as well as in the market (between December and March), you can buy delicious local avocadoes (*tawpaq-thi*).

Getting There & Away

From Kalaw it costs K200 to Aungban and another K550 to Pindaya by public transport. It can be difficult to find buses or pick-ups later in the day, especially between Aungban and Pindaya, so leave early in the morning and allow a whole day for the trip. The first pick-up from Pindaya to Aungban leaves from the market area at 6am. There's one bus per day from Taunggyi to Pindaya (K600), at noon; the same bus travels in the opposite direction at 8am the next day.

You can also hire a car and driver in Kalaw to make the day trip to Pindaya for about US$15 or US$20. If you don't want to stay in Pindaya, you can hire a car to take you from Kalaw to Pindaya, have it wait for a couple of hours while you take in the caves and have lunch in town, and then continue on to Nyaungshwe (Yaunghwe) for Inle Lake. This should cost about US$30 or the kyat equivalent for the whole day – it's better to pay in US dollars than kyat. One pick-up can take four or five passengers with baggage. The actual road time is about two hours for the 50km from Kalaw to Pindaya and three hours or more for the 93km from Pindaya to Nyaungshwe. Add waiting time (which can be considerable) in Aungban and Shwenyaung if you go by public transport.

HEHO

ဟဲဟိုး

Another highway town, Heho is about halfway between Aungban and Shwenyaung, which is the junction for the road south to Nyaungshwe and Inle Lake. North of the town is an airstrip that fields Air Mandalay (AM), Yangon Airways (YA) and Myanma Airways (MA) flights from Yangon and Mandalay (see Getting There & Away in the Inle Lake section later for details).

Heho has a dusty **market** area just off the highway that hosts the largest of the five-day markets in the southern area of the Shan State.

The several **guesthouses** in town admit locals only. On the highway near the market area are a couple of decent places to eat, including the **Oasis Café** (tea snacks), **San Restaurant** (Chinese food) and **Island Restaurant** (Chinese and Bamar meals). There is a small **snack bar** at the airport.

SHWENYAUNG

ရွှေညောင်

Few people stop off in Shwenyaung, except to change from a Thazi-Taunggyi pick-up or bus going to Nyaungshwe. Should you find yourself needing overnight accommodation, there is one good choice; in fact it may be good enough to warrant an intentional stopover for those seeking something away from the lake scene.

Remember Inn *(budget singles US$6, standard singles & doubles US$12, superior rooms US$20)* was undergoing renovations when we visited. It's located near the crossroads and has budget singles with shared facilities, standard rooms with air-con, fridge and attached toilet and bathroom, and superior rooms with TV. All rooms are spacious and there's a rooftop terrace with umbrellas and chairs. The proprietors lead treks to local Shan and Pa-O villages.

Getting There & Away

You can get all the way to Shwenyaung by train, but it's time-consuming. From Yangon or Mandalay, the programme would be to take one of the Yangon-Mandalay express trains and disembark at Thazi. See the Getting Around chapter for timetable details.

The train from Thazi to Shwenyaung (US$4/9 ordinary/1st class; eight to nine hours) is rather slow – the average speed must be around 10km/h with occasional sprints of 15km/h – but the route is very picturesque and having the run of a carriage can be more comfortable than sitting in the back of a cramped pick-up on mountain curves. It's a spectacular journey through the Shan mountains and local villages, partially on a zigzagging railway line. Stations en route have masses of fruit, snacks and flowers for sale.

The No 141 Up leaves Thazi at 9am and arrives in Shwenyaung between 5pm and 6pm. The No 142 Down leaves Shwenyaung at 8.30am and arrives in Thazi around 6pm in plenty of time to connect with the Mandalay-Yangon train, which is scheduled to depart from Thazi around 8.30pm but usually doesn't leave till around 9pm.

INLE LAKE

အင်းလေးအိုင်

Inle Lake is 22km long, roughly 11km wide, 875m above sea level and outrageously beautiful – it has very calm waters dotted with patches of floating vegetation and busy fishing canoes. High hills rim the lake on both sides; the lakeshore and lake islands bear 17 villages on stilts, mostly inhabited by the Intha people. Culturally and linguistically separate from their Shan neighbours, the Inthas are thought to have migrated to this area from Dawei (Tavoy) on the Tanintharyi (Tenasserim) peninsula in southern Myanmar. The Intha dialect is related to standard Burmese but also shows similarities with the Mon-influenced Dawei dialect. The Burmese 'th' sound becomes an 's' in Intha, so that the Burmese *beh-thwa-ma-lay?* (Where are you going?) becomes *beh-swa-ma-lay?* among the Intha.

According to one story, two brothers from Dawei came to Nyaungshwe in 1359 to serve a Nyaungshwe sao pha. The latter was so pleased with the hard-working demeanour of the Dawei brothers that he asked them to invite 36 more families from Dawei; purportedly, all the Intha around Inle Lake are descended from these migrant families. Another theory says they migrated from the Mon region in the 18th century to avoid wars between the Thais and Bamar.

Like the Shan, Mon and Bamar, the Intha are Buddhist; there are around 100 Buddhist kyaung around the lake and perhaps 1000 stupas. The Inle style of religious architecture and Buddhist sculpture is strongly Shan-influenced.

The hard-working Intha are famous for propelling their flat-bottomed boats by standing at the stern on one leg and wrapping the other leg around the oar. This trange leg-rowing technique offers relief to e arms – which are also used for rowing – ing the long paddles from one end of the

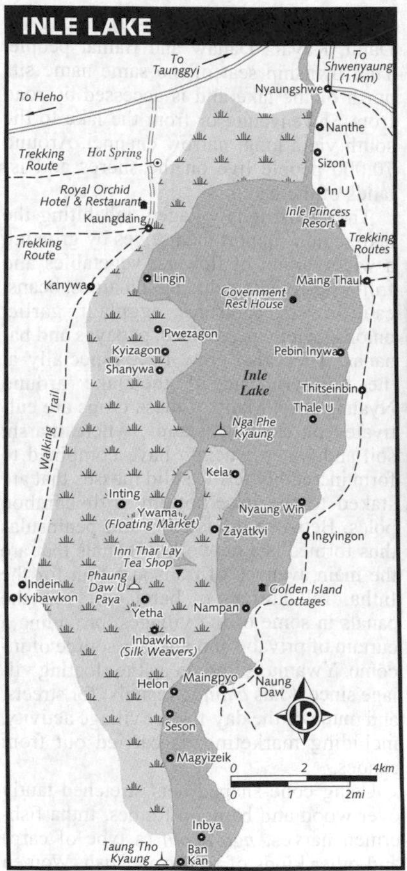

lake to another. It also enables the rower to better see the *kyun myaw* (floating islands) and *beda* (water hyacinth). It's sometimes necessary to stand up to plot a path around the obstacles – and to spot fish. Although diesel motors are used on cross-lake ferries and for carrying tourists to the islands and lakeshore villages, most people still use oars and paddles, thus avoiding fuel shortages, saving money and precluding the hassle of hyacinth-tangled propellers.

The entire lake area is contained in the township of Nyaungshwe and supports a population of 130,000 that consists of

Intha, Shan, Taungthu (Pa-O), Taung-yo, Danu, Kayah, Danaw and Bamar people. The township seat of the same name sits north of the lake and is accessed by road from Shwenyaung or from the lake to the south via a long, narrow channel. Around 70,000 people live on the shores and islands of the lake.

The industrious villagers inhabiting the lake region support themselves by growing a wide variety of flowers, vegetables and fruit year-round, including tomatoes, beans, cauliflowers, cabbages, eggplant, garlic, onions, betel vine, melons, papayas and bananas. They also grow rice, especially at the northern end of the lake around Nyaungshwe. Many of these crops are cultivated on floating islands, where marsh, soil and water hyacinth have combined to form incredibly fertile solid masses that are staked to the lake bottom with bamboo poles. Between the islands and peninsulas thus formed is a network of canals that are the main avenues of transportation for the Intha. Tall lattices of betel vine line the canals in some of the villages, providing a curtain of privacy and another source of income. Ywama is known as the floating village since it has *chaung* (canals) for streets, and much of the day-to-day village activity, including marketing, is carried out from canoes.

Using cone-shaped nets stretched tautly over wood and bamboo frames, Intha fishermen harvest *nga-hpein* (a type of carp) and other kinds of freshwater fish. Women in the villages (especially Ywama and Heya at the southern end of Inle Lake) weave Shan-style shoulder bags and silk *Zinme* (Chiang Mai–style) *longyi* (sarongs) on wooden handlooms. Using raw silk from China, these weavers produce more silk garments than anywhere in the country, after Amarapura.

When they aren't busy with fishing or farming, the men of Inle produce silver and brassware, as well as pottery and lacquerware. The area around Kaungdaing, on the western shore, is famous for its noodles, tofu and other soybean products that end up in kitchens all over Myanmar.

During January and February, the nights and mornings around the lake area are cold, so you should bring socks and a sweater. Hotels and guesthouses have adequate blankets.

Information

To enter the Inle Lake zone, tourists are required to pay a US$3 entry fee at the office of **Myanmar Travels & Tours** *(MTT; Strand Rd)* or, more commonly, at one of the hotels or guesthouses around town. You can arrange a boat tour at your guesthouse, or from a couple of places near the canal leading to the lake.

Special Events

One of the best times of the year to visit Inle Lake is during September and October. The ceremonial Phaung Daw U festival, which lasts for almost three weeks, is closely followed by the Thadingyut festival, when the Inthas and Shan dress in new clothes and fervently celebrate the end of Waso (Buddhist Lent). They are so religious that it's not unusual for families to spend all of their meagre savings during this one annual event.

Exploring the Lake Area

MTT no longer has a monopoly on lake tours and you can hire watercraft from just about anyone who has a boat. The exact price per person or per boat depends on two things: the price of petrol and the distance travelled. An all-day trip around the lake costs less than US$10.

The typical motorboat trip is not bad – you will see the floating gardens, leg-rowers, fishermen, Phaung Daw U Paya and whatever lake commerce is going on. The boat trips usually include stops at souvenir shops near the paya. The selection isn't bad at these shops, but prices are lower at the five-day floating market or at the paya itself. At all these places you'll see Shan shoulder bags, embroidered shirts and longyi, tapestries, pottery, jewellery and all the usual souvenirs.

The lake itself is rich in wildlife, esp cially waterfowl. All avifauna on the l and adjoining wetlands is repor protected by law, as Inle Lake has been an official bird sanctuary since 1985. Egrets fly in formation over the lake every day, about an hour before sunset.

Canoe Trips With all the package tours heading to the southern end of the lake on noisy powerboats nowadays, a quiet canoe paddle through the villages along the lake channel has become an attractive alternative. Unfortunately, following the capsizing of a canoe and drowning of a foreign visitor, non-motorised canoes ferrying foreign passengers are no longer allowed onto the lake itself, but several people in town do shorter canoe trips (K1000 for two or three hours) on the canals branching from the lake and along the Nyaungshwe shore of the lake. Although you won't get to see the more-famous lake sights, life along the canals is itself fascinating and the villagers are friendly. Slow-moving canoes are also better for photography.

One place that can only be visited by canoe is the large **nat shrine** in the middle of a swampy banyan-tree jungle opposite Nanthe village on the main channel. No-one dares cut the trees for fear of angering the *nat* (spirits), so it's a good place to see unfettered nature, including plenty of waterfowl. The house-sized, wooden nat shrine sits on stilts and contains a rustic altar.

Hiking Extended walks to the north or south of Nyaungshwe pass among extensive rice paddies dotted with Shan stupa ruins. Trails into the hills east of town lead to Pa-O villages and panoramic views of the lake area. A good and rugged all-day hike is to the monastery of **Koun Soun Taungbo** and nearby **Ta-Eh Gu** (Cave). You pass through two Pa-O villages on the way. Further away are the ruins of Kakku.

Guided day hikes can be arranged through guesthouses or hotels. Guides typically charge US$5 a day. Multiday trips are not currently allowed. It's a good idea to bring some bottled water on any hike.

Nyaungshwe

ညောင်ရွှေ

☎ 081

Nyaungshwe (Golden Banyan Tree, also called Yaunghwe) is the small town 3.5km from the northern end of the lake. There are a number of places to stay and eat, and boats reach the lake by the wide channel that runs along the western side of town. At first it appears there's not a lot to do around town, but between the lake itself, the nearby villages, countryside walks and historic ruins, there's actually enough to occupy an active visitor for a week or more.

The **Museum of Shan Chiefs** *(Yaunghwe Haw Museum; US$2; open 9.30am-3.30pm Tues-Sun)*, housed in a large teak-and-brick mansion in the northeastern part of town, was the *haw* (palace) of the 33rd and last Shan sao pha, Sao Shwe Thaike. Thaike, who became the first president of Myanmar in 1948, was imprisoned when Ne Win came to power, and died in jail. The museum is the best surviving example of a Shan-style palace since the demolition of the *haw sao pha* (Shan lord's palace) in Kengtung in 1991.

For years, much of the two-storey building, laid out in a double cruciform floor plan, remained in a state of disrepair. Recent renovations have improved things, and many of the rooms contain displays of Shan furniture and royal costumes. Most impressive is the huge teak-floored throne-and-audience hall in the north wing, behind the front building.

Shrines, Monasteries & Stupas The oldest temple in town, **Yadana Man Aung Paya**, is worth visiting for its unique step-spired stupa. Look for the 'you will be old' and 'you will be sick' figures in glass cases in one of the shrine buildings.

There are several good-sized monasteries in the central and southeastern parts of town, including **Kan Gyi Kyaung, Shwe Gu Kyaung** and **Yangon Kyaung**. On the southeastern outskirts of town, the ruin of an old Shan monastery called **Nigyon Taungyon Kyaung** – originally built by the Nyaungshwe sao

pha – features a set of slender whitewashed Shan stupas and some very old plinths with surviving stucco relief. Under the supervision of an old monk, the complex is being transformed into a *kammahtan kyaung* (meditation monastery). A new shrine hall on the grounds contains five alabaster sitting Buddhas in the Mandalay style, and there are a few thatched huts for meditators.

Less than 1km north of the town entrance, an old 18th- or 19th-century monastery called **Shwe Yaunghwe Kyaung** features a venerable wooden *thein* (consecration hall) with unique oval windows. A long, low, rectangular brick-and-stucco *pahto* (shrine) on the premises bears slender Shan *zedi* (bell-shaped stupas) on top and Buddha images of various ages inside.

A short walk south of town along the eastern side of the main channel leads to the small but atmospheric ruins of **Kyaukhpyugyi Paya** next to the Intha village of Nanthe. Surrounded by brick-and-stucco *deva* (celestial beings), chinthe (half-lion, half-dragon guardian deities) and stupas is a huge sitting Buddha, said to be 700 years old. The cloister around the image is lined with intact stucco reliefs, while the stupas behind the main shrine are topped with surrealistically bent and twisted metal *hti* (decorative umbrellas).

Mingala Market The main municipal *zei* (market), near the town's northern entrance, is busiest in the morning, when vendors congregate to sell their wares. In addition to mountains of fresh produce, Shan noodles and other local products, there are a few stalls selling pottery and textiles.

Kaungdaing
ခေါင်တိုင်

Also spelt Kaungdine, this Intha village or the northwestern shore of the lake is know for its soybean cakes and noodles. It's easy

NYAUNGSHWE (NYAUNGSHWE)

PLACES TO STAY
2 Paradise Hotel & Restaurant
4 Remember Inn
10 Hu Pin Hotel
13 Joy Hotel
21 Evergreen Hotel
24 Inle Inn
27 Nandawunn Hotel
28 May Guest House
32 Teakwood Guest House
38 Gypsy Inn
41 Nawng Khan (Little Inn)
46 Mingalar Hotel
54 Pyi Guest House
56 Four Sisters Inn
58 Primrose Hotel

PLACES TO EAT
5 Eden Teashop
7 Shwe Inlay Bakery
8 Hu Pin Restaurant
11 Chow Su Ma Restaurant
12 Shanland Restaurant
16 Thukha Café
23 Golden Kite Restaurant
33 Daw Nyunt Yee Restaurant
34 Big Drum Restaurant
47 Shwe Pye Soe Restaurant

OTHER
1 Monument
3 Museum of Shan Chiefs
6 Bank
9 Bus/Pickup Stop
14 Boat Landing
15 Comet Travel
17 Longyi Shop
18 AM & YA Ticketing
19 Stupa
20 Sri Jagdish Hindu Temple
22 Puppet Theatre
25 Township Office
26 Police
29 Hlaing Gu Kyaung
30 Yangon Kyaung
31 Monastery
35 Boat Landing
36 Moe Ma Kha Boat Hire
37 MTT Office
39 Handicrafts
40 Independence Monument
42 Post Office
43 Shwe Zali Paya
44 Stupas
45 Yadana Man Aung Paya
48 Telephone Office
49 Stupas
50 Shwe Gu Kyaung
51 Kan Gyi Kyaung
52 Monastery
53 Nigyon Taungyon Kyaung
55 Moe Moe Boat & Bicycle
57 Hospital

observe the methods used, as just about every other household is involved in this cottage industry. Pottery and weaving can also be seen. Just outside the village are some interesting Shan temple ruins featuring brick-and-stucco zedi, pahto and *chinthe* (half-lion/half-dragon guardians); the villagers use some of the pahto for storing straw or hay.

A little north of Kaungdaing is a **hot spring** *(open 7am-5pm daily)*. You can bathe in communal baths for a few kyat, but be sure to bring a longyi to wear in the bath. Private rooms are also available (US$2). The water is very hot and is said to be cleanest between May and August. Kaungdaing and the hot springs are a 1½-hour drive from Nyaungshwe around the top of the lake via Shwenyaung on the Heho road, or about 30 minutes across the lake by boat. A boat charter costs K800 (each way) to Kaungdaing. There are a couple of hotels near Kaungdaing.

Inleh Bo Teh

အင်းလယ် ဗိုလ်တဲ

The lake is very shallow and clear – a swim looks inviting and Inleh Bo Teh is a good place to have one; *inleh* means 'middle of', *bo* is 'officer' or 'official', and *teh* is 'house', so Inleh Bo Teh is literally 'an official's house in the middle of a lake'. It's no longer used as such, but makes a good place to stop for a mid-lake picnic or swim.

Maing Thauk

မောင်းသောက်

On the eastern side of the lake, bicycling distance from Nyaungshwe along the dusty track running along the foot of the hills that rise up from the lake, the village of Maing Thauk is divided into 'land' and 'floating' halves. The half-kilometre-long wooden bridge running out to the floating village from the lake's shore was paid for by Lonely Planet and built with the voluntary labour of the villagers in 2001. Just below the boys orphanage on the hillside above the village, a few crumbling **gravestones** are all that remain of the colonial-era Fort Steadman. Further up the hill is the Maing Thauk **forest monastery**.

Ywama

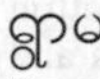

Regular boats run from Nyaungshwe to the village of Ywama – to see the famed floating market, you must calculate the day according to the local five-day market scheme. Unfortunately, you must also take into account what has happened to this once-interesting local event. On market day, Ywama floating market is a traffic jam of tourist boats and souvenir hawkers, with a few local farmers trying to sell their vegetables to a few local buyers. On nonmarket days, it's almost worse because there are only souvenir and tourist boats (at a ratio of about five to one!); of course, the smart vegetable farmers are already at another five-day market. Arriving early won't help; the action is in full swing by 8.30am, and it's downhill from there.

Don't despair, you can enjoy a floating market without fighting the crowds and without adding to the already crazy atmosphere of Ywama. Simply choose a market from the five-day market schedule around Inle. Any guesthouse or hotel in Nyaungshwe will have the current schedule. A secondary five-day circuit rotates among the lake villages of Kaungdaing, Maing Thauk, Nampan, Indein and Thandaung.

The approach to Ywama is quite beautiful despite the market scene, and after the morning rush hour (and before the late-afternoon one) it's a lovely place to see. You pass through floating fields where the Intha people grow everything from vegetables to flowers – an unusual and picturesque sight.

Phaung Daw U Paya The main landing at Ywama stands in front of Phaung Daw U Paya, the holiest religious site in the southern area of the Shan State. Five images, four of which are ferried around the lake during the important Phaung Daw U festival (late September/early October), are enshrined in the centre of the building. Beside the channel are the boathouses sheltering the ornate vessels that carry the images on their annual voyage.

Stalls on the ground floor of the shrine and nearby sell brightly coloured cotton Shan shoulder bags, other local crafts and 'antiques'. Silk and cotton fabrics are a local speciality; there are over 200 handlooms in

Phaung Daw U Festival

The biggest event in the southern area of Shan State takes place at Phaung Daw U Kyaung, one of the state's holiest sites, from the first day of the waxing moon to the third day after the full moon of Thadingyut (September/October). The focus of the large two-storey sanctuary is five gold leaf-covered statues, of which three are said to be Buddha images, while the remaining two are reportedly Arahats (historical disciples of the Buddha). The gold leaf on the figures has become so thick that it's hard to tell what the figures represent; they look a bit like short, squat bowling pins or lopsided dumbbells.

The statues were reportedly fashioned during the reign of King Alaungsithu (AD 1113–67). The gold lumps are so holy that pilgrims rub red strips of cloth against them, then tie the cloth strips to their bikes, cars and trucks to create protective spiritual force fields around themselves and their vehicles.

During the 20 days of the festival, a ceremonial barge carries four of the five Phaung Daw U images around the lake, from village to village, to bless the village monasteries. The smallest of the five figures stays at Phaung Daw U to act as 'guardian' of the temple, following an incident that happened many years ago when the procession used to carry all five images around the lake. About 8km from Phaung Daw U, in the middle of the lake, you can see a pillar mounted by a *shwe hintha* (golden swan figure – actually a *hamsa*, a swan-like creature from Indian mythology). This monument marks the spot where the ceremonial barge once capsized. Only four of the five figures were immediately recovered, but when the stunned crew returned to Phaung Daw U they found the fifth sitting on its pedestal, covered with lake weeds. Ever since the legendary incident, that image has never left the monastery.

Hundreds of other vessels travel in the entourage in a general celebratory atmosphere. Thousands of people from around the Shan State attend this most holy of Shan celebrations.

Joe Cummings

NORTHEASTERN MYANMAR

Ywama. A shady *khamauk* (conical bamboo hat) is another popular purchase here.

Jumping Cat Monastery Just north of Ywama, Nga Phe Kyaung is a wooden monastery on stilts over the lake, built four years before Mandalay Palace. The monks have trained their much-photographed resident cats to leap through small hoops, but a better reason to visit is the modest collection of Buddha images in Shan, Tibetan, Bagan and Inwa styles. The tall, highly ornate wood-and-mosaic pedestals and cases built for the images are just as impressive as the Buddhas themselves. Such pedestals are a speciality of Shan and northern Thai Buddhist art and those at the monastery are over 100 years old. Many of the original Shan images they once contained have been sold or stolen, so the cases mostly contain newer images. A few 150-year-old Shan images are unceremoniously kept off to the side on a smaller altar; crafted by Intha artisans, the gilded wood images feature crowns and royal attire decorated with mosaics.

Indein

အင်းဒိန်

The quaint village of Indein on the western side of the lake is accessed by a winding river that is too shallow to use late in the dry season. The **Nyaung Ohak** (Group of Banyan Trees, or Under the Shade of Banyan Trees) monastery has a nice, old mouldering complex of shrines and stupas at the bottom of the hill. At the top is **Shwe Inn Thein**, reached by a long stairway with over 400 wooden columns. The impressive collection of weather-beaten stupas has, so far, escaped restoration. From the hillside there are great views across the lake to the hills in the east.

Southern End of the Lake

On the western side of the lake, a long walkway leads to the poorly restored hilltop complex of stupas at **Thaung Tho Kyaung**. On the lakeside there's a popular **market** site.

Right at the southern end of the lake, the whole village of **Kyauk Taung** is so devoted to pottery-making that there are pots everywhere. The floating village of **Kyaing Kan East** specialises in weaving robes using threads drawn from the long stems of lotus plants. The lotus robes are specially made for monks, Buddha statues and visiting tourists. They're quite expensive (US$35 to US$50 for a shawl) because of their rarity – lotus plants can only be gathered for six months of the year.

Places to Stay – Budget

There are around 30 hotels and guesthouses in Nyaungshwe, plus a few upmarket places on and around the lake itself. With the increase in hotels and guesthouses in Nyaungshwe, you can expect low-season discounts of 10% to 20%.

Four Sisters Inn *(singles/doubles US$7/12)* used to be a well-known dining spot. The sisters have expanded it into a quiet guesthouse between the canal and a large rice paddy, about 1km south of the main village. Rooms have fan, hot-water shower and good beds. Like most places in town, it can help arrange boat tours and rent bicycles.

Gypsy Inn *(☎ Nyaungshwe 84; Chaung Rd; rooms without/with bathroom per person US$3/5)*, along the canal, is one of the brighter budget spots. The rooms are spacious, if simple, and have fans. Breakfast is included. Because it's next to the canal, you'll hear the early-morning canal boats going by.

Nawng Khan *(Little Inn; ☎ 21448; Phaundawpyan Rd; singles US$6, doubles US$10-12)*, opposite Shwe Zali Paya, has bright, clean rooms with fan and hot-water shower, and breakfast is included. One of the rooms is reputedly haunted, though it's recently been turned into a storage room and guests are no longer quartered there. There's a nice sitting area with a atmospheric view of the nearby kyaung.

Mingalar Hotel *(rooms per person US$4)*, friendly but spartan, is one of the cheapest places in Nyaungshwe. Rates for the small rooms include breakfast, served on a pleasant rooftop terrace.

Teakwood Guest House *(rooms per person US$3)*, three blocks east of the canal, offers good budget lodgings. The large wooden rooms have attached hot-water shower and fan.

May Guest House *(☎ 21416; Myawady Rd; rooms per person US$5)*, opposite Hlaing Gu Kyaung, is another good friendly, budget place. The clean linoleum-floor rooms have hot-water shower and a small veranda, and a Bamar breakfast is included.

Joy Hotel *(☎ Nyaungshwe 83; budget rooms with shared/private bathroom US$2/3, larger singles/doubles US$6/10, triple US$15)*, on a narrow, quiet canal west of the market, has basic but clean rooms in a two-storey house, plus five newer rooms in an adjacent building. The cheapest rooms are in the old building and have a shared bathroom. A few others have bathroom and fan. There are also larger, newer rooms with shared hot-water shower and toilet. And there's one huge triple with a sitting area, desk, bathtub and closet. Breakfast is included, and there's a small sitting area that overlooks the canal.

Pyi Guest House *(☎ Nyaungshwe 76; rooms with private bathroom US$10-12)*, in the southern part of town, three blocks east of the main canal, consists of two buildings: a big wooden house with pleasingly rustic rooms and a new building made of concrete blocks. Of course, the rooms in the old house have the most character. The proprietors sometimes arrange dinner shows with Shan food, music and dancing. A traditional breakfast is included in the price of the room.

Remember Inn *(☎ Nyaungshwe 44; singles/doubles with hot-water bathroom US$4/8)*, opposite the entrance to the Museum of Shan Chiefs, has small rooms in a rather noisy concrete compound, and larger rooms in a new building. There's a good restaurant and sitting area with satellite TV. Burmese massage is available for US$2 per hour.

The **Evergreen Hotel** *(☎ Nyaungshwe 79; singles/doubles with private bathroom US$5/10)* is a long, two-storey place east of Mingala Market on a canal that runs through town. The shabby concrete building is cold and draughty, and there is no hot water – an unfortunate combination.

Places to Stay – Mid-Range

Primrose Hotel *(in Taunggyi ☎ 22709; 40 Mingala Rd; singles/doubles US$18/24)* is in the southern part of town near the Mong Li canal. It's quiet and the service is good. The clean, attractive rooms have bathroom, fan and fridge, and rates include breakfast.

Inle Inn *(in Taunggyi ☎ 21347, Nyaungshwe 16; singles/doubles/triples US$15/18/25)*, on the eastern side of town, is well run and quiet and one of the oldest privately owned inns in the country. Rooms in the main building and in a new wing to the side come with attached toilet and hot-water shower, and rates include breakfast, with *mohinga* (pronounced moon-**hing**-ga; a dish of noodles, fish and eggs) available upon request. There is a pleasant garden sitting area out the back. Good food is served; a Shan dinner and puppet show is available on request.

Nandawunn Hotel *(in Taunggyi ☎ 22600; Youngyi Rd; bungalow singles/doubles/triples US$15/20/32, singles/doubles with larger bed & bathtub US$20/25)* is a few blocks east of the market in a quiet compound. The attractive duplex bungalows have hot water, fridge and TV.

Places to Stay – Top End

Nyaungshwe The top end in Nyaungshwe isn't luxurious but it is comfortable enough for people who desire softer beds, service foyers and more attractive decor.

Paradise Hotel & Restaurant *(in Taunggyi ☎ 22009; 40 3rd St; standard singles/doubles US$30/36, superior rooms US$36/42, suites US$50)*, east of the main road as you come into town and near the Museum of Shan Chiefs, is the best value of the few places in this category. All rooms have hot-water shower, fridge, TV and air-con, and breakfast is included. The 'suite' has a bathtub. The staff are quite helpful with travel and air ticket arrangements. This place is quite popular with French package tourists.

Hu Pin Hotel *(in Taunggyi ☎ 21374, Nuangshwe ☎ 23; singles/doubles US$30/36, larger rooms US$45/60)*, a Chinese-style hotel a block west of Mingala Market, is owned by the nearby restaurant of the same name. The ordinary rooms have attached hot-water shower, TV and fridge; and there are larger rooms with bathtub, fridge and TV. All rates include breakfast at the rooftop restaurant or around the corner at the Hu Pin Restaurant. Although Hu Pin has its own generator, electric power is still erratic.

Around the Lake There are now a number of more expensive hotels on the lakeside or built, like the floating villages, on stilts over the lake.

Golden Island Cottages *(in Taunggyi ☎ 23136; singles/doubles US$35/40, superior rooms US$45)* is a quiet and relaxing place, but the service is rather indifferent. It's run as a Pa-O collective and located on the lake near Nampan. Individual bamboo and hardwood cottages on stilts, each with a private balcony, seem to float on the lake surface. Reservations are required during the high season (November to February), as it's usually fully booked by package-tour groups. The restaurant specialises in Chinese cuisine; Shan and Pa-O dishes are available upon request.

Inle Princess Resort *(in Taunggyi ☎/fax 21347; rooms/bungalows US$90/150)* is 6km from Nyaungshwe and is the most luxurious place on the lake. The rooms are pleasant but the individual bungalows are beautifully designed and decorated. The spectacular dining room and bar area, with its soaring ceiling, is modelled after a Khün monastery building in Kengtung. The Shan food is expensive but excellent and cultural shows are presented regularly. Note that credit cards are not accepted, so bring plenty of cash.

Royal Orchid Hotel & Restaurant *(in Taunggyi ☎ 23182; singles US$24-40, doubles US$30-48)*, near Kaungdaing on the northwestern part of the lake, is a quiet and relaxing place about 50m from the lake's bank. It offers 20 spacious bungalow rooms with private facilities and serene views. Rates vary depending on room size and view.

Places to Eat

Vegetarians will find Inle Lake a fine place to eat because of the year-round variety of vegetables, fruit and soy products. **Mingala Market** is a good place to shop for local produce; there are also plenty of Shan *hkauq-sweh* (noodle soup) **vendors** at the market every morning. Another local delicacy is *maung jeut* (round, flat rice crisps).

Nyaungshwe There are numerous places to eat in Nyaungshwe but there are now also a handful of places to stop for lunch out on the lake.

Eden Teashop *(open 6am-5pm)*, on the northeastern corner of the market, sells good *nam-bya* (flat bread similar to nan) with bean dip. The teashop's location, near an old wooden bridge over the Mong Li canal, makes it great for watching the parade of people coming to market in the early morning.

Golden Kite Restaurant *(open 8am-10pm)*, diagonally opposite the Nandawunn Hotel, is an unassuming little eatery making what is probably Myanmar's tastiest pasta. There are also omelettes and pancakes available, as well as fruit shakes. A vegetarian version of its delicious tagliatelle is also on offer.

The popular **Thukha Café**, in the centre of town near the market, serves a variety of Burmese teashop snacks.

Shwe Inlay Bakery *(open around 5am-6pm daily)*, on the opposite side of the street to the Thukha Café, further north, bakes tasty Chinese and European-inspired pastries.

Hu Pin Restaurant *(open 11am-9pm)* is said to be Nyaungshwe's best Chinese restaurant and is also the cleanest place in town. The English menu is divided into three sections: chicken, fish and pork.

Two popular restaurants near the Joy Hotel are **Chow Su Ma Restaurant** for good Chinese, and **Shanland Restaurant** for tasty Shan cuisine. Both are reasonably priced. Try the cosy **Shwe Pye Soe Restaurant** near Yadana Man Aung Paya for very good Bamar fare.

Daw Nyunt Yee Restaurant *(Phaungdaw Seiq Rd)*, near the canal on the east-west Phaungdaw Seiq Rd, is a good Chinese/Bamar eatery.

Big Drum Restaurant, a set of thatched A-frame shelters on the western bank of the main canal, is a friendly place. A Shan dinner of fish curry, bean soup, fried peanuts, rice and maung jeut costs K400. Chinese food is also available.

Four Sisters Inn is the place to try excellent Shan home-style cooking. The Intha family that live here serve dinner to guests (see Places to Stay – Budget, earlier in this section) by advance arrangement; there's no set charge for the meal but donations are gladly collected. Some nights the sisters dance and sing as well as cook. One of the four sisters is living in Germany now, but the remaining three, plus their brother, carry on the tradition. They also arrange canoe and motorboat trips.

Chinese restaurants are the only places in town that serve beer (and Mandalay rum), although some smaller shops sell *ayeq hpyu* (white liquor) by the shot, which mixes well with lemon-lime soda.

Ywama There are a number of places to eat in the floating village, near the Phaung Daw U Paya. This area of the larger village is sometimes referred to as Thar Lay.

Inn Thar Lay Tea Shop, on the southern side of the canal, near the paya, is really more of a Chinese restaurant and makes a nice lunch stop.

On the other side of the village canal, which is almost like a street with its shops and houses, **Ngwe Zin Yaw Restaurant** and **Mee Ein Shin Restaurant** both have good food and pleasant balconies where you can enjoy your lunch and watch the passing boats.

Getting There & Away

Apart from flying, all the routes to the Inle Lake area are time-consuming, but there are several options to consider that can save you much time and trouble getting there. First of all, there is no need to go to Taunggyi, the main town in the area and the location of the main MTT office. If you want to simply go to the lake, you'll save a couple of hours by skipping Taunggyi.

Air AM, YA and MA fly to Heho, which is 30km west of Shwenyaung, from where it's a further 11km to Nyaungshwe or 20km to Taunggyi. The airstrip at Heho is only 12.5m wide; according to AM this is the smallest ATR aircraft landing strip in the world. For some reason the terminal is completely fenced off and taxis have to stop down the road, over 100m away, where there are a couple of small restaurants.

Both AM and YA provide comfortable and punctual service, and have daily flights from Yangon to Heho, some via Mandalay. During the high season (November to February), you can count on at least two flights per day from Heho with either of these reliable carriers, but during other times of the year, service is sometimes every other day. The Yangon-Heho fare is US$128 on YA and US$131 on AM. From Mandalay the fare is US$48 on YA and US$51 on AM.

For the foolhardy, MA flies from Yangon to Heho (US$85) on Wednesday and Saturday, and from Mandalay (US$40) twice weekly.

AM and YA fly daily from Heho to Bagan with a stopover in Mandalay. Aboard AM or YA, a ticket for this leg costs US$71 and US$68 respectively.

Taxis from Heho to Nyaungshwe cost K6000. The cheaper option is to hike out to the main road and wait for a pick-up or bus to the Shwenyaung junction (K350); from Shwenyaung, another pick-up or bus will eventually go to Nyaungshwe (about K100). If you're continuing to Taunggyi, it's K200. Keep in mind that doing it the cheap way may take half a day.

Bus, Pick-up & Car By road, most people travel to Inle Lake from Bagan, Thazi or Mandalay. Around January, the trip from the plains over the mountains to Inle Lake can be very cold in an open truck – make sure you have some warm clothes.

You can hire a private taxi from Nyaungshwe to Bagan for around US$40. Inquire at **Comet Travel** *(27 Youngyi Rd)* southwest of the market, or at one of the hotels.

Smokin'

Kipling immortalised the Burmese cheroot with his poem dedicated to a 'Burma girl a-settin'...a-smokin' of a whackin' white cheroot'. Such large cheroots (originally from the Tamil *curuttu*, meaning 'roll', and later the Hindi-Urdu *charut*, meaning 'cigar/cigarette'), wrapped in the paper-thin bark of the betel palm *(kun thi hpeq hse leiq)*, are very rarely seen nowadays, but their smaller green cousins are more commonly smoked than regular cigarettes in Myanmar. This mild *hse baw leiq* – similar to the Indian *bidi* but about twice the size – contains a mixture of Virginia-style tobacco leaves and stems that may have been sweetened with tamarind pulp and jaggery before being dried and shredded, along with a sprinkling of wood chips to mellow the smoke and enhance steady burning. The narrow end of the gently cone-shaped hse baw leiq holds a filter made of corn husks wrapped tightly in newspaper pages (adding new meaning to the *New Light of Myanmar)*.

Tobacco is cultivated in Myanmar's dry central plains, particularly in the sandy soils around Pakokku and Myingyan. Planters sow tobacco seeds in September, and the plants are harvested and sun-dried in March. The outer wrapper of the modern cheroot, a large leaf called *thanaq hpeq* that grows well on the mountain slopes of the Shan State, is one of the main cash crops for the Pa-O and Palaung ethnic groups. In lowland Myanmar, rural women still occasionally wrap market tobacco in a white maize husk that resembles the betel-bark wrapper of a hundred years ago. But for most of the country, the slim thanaq hpeq–wrapped hse baw leiq is the norm.

In Taunggyi, widely regarded as the source of Myanmar's finest smokes, a hse baw leiq factory will employ up to 100 women, each of whom may hand-roll up to 1000 cheroots per day. Elsewhere in the Shan State, women take the raw ingredients – tobacco, wrappers, labels, filters and glue – and roll a few 50-cheroot bundles in their spare time. Although the hse baw leiq remains the predominant nicotine delivery device in Myanmar, the more expensive Western-style cigarette is rapidly becoming a status symbol, particularly for young men. Smoking Marlboro, 555 or Lucky Strike cigarettes at K400 to K600 per packet signifies wealth and an imagined cosmopolitanism. Many urbanites can afford only Chinese or Burmese brands, such as Vegas, London or Duya, which sell for less than K250 per pack. Even at these prices, Burmese smokers typically buy only one cigarette at a time or, if feeling flush, a *hse leiq tabwe* (bowl) of five cigarettes.

Vicky Bowman

Thazi & Meiktila The road between Thazi and Taunggyi has improved considerably over the last few years, but it's still a stiff ride of around six hours by public transport, five hours if you have your own vehicle.

The fare for the better Thazi-Taunggyi trucks is about K800. The less expensive trucks don't leave till there are passengers hanging off every protrusion on the truck; the better trucks have more leg room and fewer passengers. Most trucks depart from either town at 9am and 11am. If you're heading for Inle Lake, get off at the Shwenyaung junction and catch one of the frequent pick-ups (from 6am to 6pm only) to Nyaungshwe (K100), which is 11km south. Taxis do the same trip for K2000.

There are also a couple of trucks per day between Shwenyaung and Meiktila (K800).

The staging area for most public transport to/from Nyaungshwe is the street that runs south of the Hu Pin Hotel, one block west of Mingala Market.

Mandalay Buses between Mandalay and the lake area (seven to eight hours) cost around K1500 to K1800 per person, depending on the company. Two of the more reliable express bus companies, Taung Pawthar Express and Shan Maw Mye, have daily departures for Taunggyi. The former departs Mandalay at 7pm (K1800) and the latter at 5am (K1500). As usual, go to Shwenyaung and catch a public pick-up to Nyaungshwe (K100), or a taxi (K2000).

Most hotels and guesthouses in Nyaungshwe can help make bus reservations, so you can be picked up at the Shwenyaung junction when the bus from Taunggyi comes through. **Comet Travel** *(☎ 23172)*, near Mingala Market, is very good at arranging Shwenyaung junction bus connections, as well as handling flight reservations.

Although it's unlikely to be used by buses, a new and shorter route by car leaves the Mandalay-Meiktila road just south of Kyaukse and crosses the hills through Yengan to meet the Aungban-Pindaya road halfway between the two towns.

Bagan Generally, an overland trip from Bagan entails getting to Meiktila or Thazi, then changing to a Nyaungshwe-, Shwenyaung- or Taunggyi-bound bus or pick-up. See the Bagan chapter for more information.

Nyaung Oo Man Company (Golden Moon Express) operates a bus from Bagan Myothit (New Bagan) to Taunggyi (K2300) that leaves at 4am; as usual, get off at Shwenyaung and continue to Nyaungshwe by public pick-up (K100).

Taunggyi A pick-up to Taunggyi costs K200. See Getting There & Away in the Taunggyi section for more information.

Yangon Several companies run buses between Yangon and Taunggyi; see Getting There & Away in the Taunggyi section later in this chapter for details. Two nightly Yangon-bound buses stop briefly in Shwenyaung at around 12.30am. Two bus companies, Ye Thu Aung and Taung Baw Da, charge K2600 per seat and arrive the next morning at Yangon's Highway bus station.

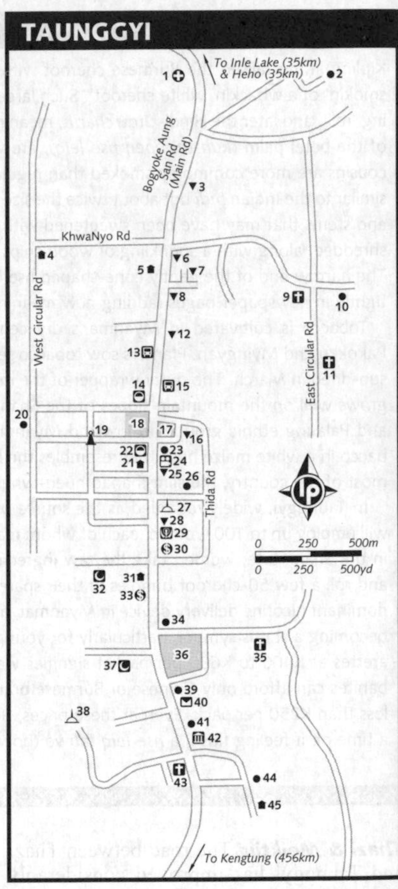

TAUNGGYI

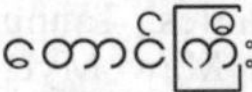

☎ 081

At 1430m, the pine-clad hill station of Taunggyi provides a cool break from the heat of the plains. There are some pleasant walks if you're in the mood, but basically it's a growing trade centre for the southwestern area of Shan State.

Taunggyi is the official end of the line for east-bound foreigners in Myanmar – at least for those travelling by road. Beyond Taunggyi lies a world of black-marketeers, ruby miners, insurgent armies, and opium and methamphetamine warlords. The town was once a place of respite for the perspiring British, although all that remains of the colonial era is an overgrown graveyard, a stone church, a line of cherry trees and a handful of timber cottages, all on the

TAUNGGYI

PLACES TO STAY
4 Paradise Hotel
5 Khemarat Guest House
21 May Khu Guest House
31 Salween Hotel
45 Taunggyi Hotel

PLACES TO EAT
3 Maxim's Restaurant
6 Coca-Cola Restaurant
7 Maw Kan Restaurant
8 Shan Noodle Shop
12 Sein (Diamond) Restaurant
16 Htun Restaurant
25 Lyan Yu Restaurant
28 Brother Hotel Restaurant

OTHER
1 Hospital
2 Gem Market
9 Church
10 Myanma Airways
11 Baptist Church
13 Eastern State Express Bus
14 Taxis, pick-ups to Inle Lake
15 Buses to Yangon, Mandalay, Bagan
17 Old Market
18 New Market
19 Clock Tower
20 GIC Office
22 Taxis & Local Buses, pick-ups
23 Asian Light Supermarket
24 Myoma Cinema
26 Flying Tiger Mashua
27 Myoe Le Dhamma Yon Paya
29 Sikh Temple
30 Myanmar Economic Bank (MEB)
32 Mosque
33 Mayflower Bank (foreign exchange)
34 Yangon Airways
35 Catholic Church
36 Bogyoke Park
37 Mosque
38 Yat Taw Me Paya
39 YMCA
40 Post & Telecom Office
41 Shan State Library
42 Shan State Museum
43 St George Anglican Church
44 Township Offices

fringes of town. The main street is strictly 'socialist realism', with signs done in raised concrete letters, just like China (Myanmar's current benefactor).

Because it functions as a conduit for smuggled goods from Thailand, China and India, and a base for trips to the Maing Shu (Mong Hsu) gem tract to the east, this is one of Myanmar's most prosperous and enterprising towns. Long-haired smugglers in army fatigues saunter down the street alongside turbaned hill-tribe people and sleek-suited Chinese businesspeople. An abundance of black-market consumer goods is displayed in the Taunggyi market, which is located at the edge of a Chinese enclave whose residents include many illegal immigrants. The remainder of the population of 100,000 people includes tribespeople, Shan, Bamar, Sikhs, Punjabis and Nepalis. Along Taunggyi's main streets you'll see various temples, mosques and churches.

There's a fairly ordinary temple on the hill, with views over the plains, Inle Lake and Taunggyi, and the walk itself is pleasant.

Information

Find information on the street and at the **MTT office** (*☎ 21303*) in the Taunggyi Hotel (see Places to Stay later in this section). At the post office near the hotel you can make long-distance calls to Yangon and other parts of Myanmar. International Direct Dial (IDD) phone service is available from the Taunggyi Hotel. The mail is said to be reliable in Taunggyi. Both Myanmar Economic Bank (MEB) and Mayflower Bank on the main street offer foreign exchange.

Special Events

In November, to coincide with the full-moon festival of Tazaungmon (Tazaungdaing), the city hosts a hot-air (or fire-) balloon festival. It is very popular with Burmese tourists, so it may be easier to find accommodation in Nyaungshwe during this three-day event.

Things to See & Do

Taunggyi has an interesting **market** area in the centre of town where you're likely to rub shoulders with hill-tribe people – there's a daily market, plus one that comes to town every five days. That market moves from Taunggyi to Pwehla (on the way to Pindaya), then to Kalaw on the third day, and from there (in turn) to Pindaya, Heho and back to Taunggyi. Basket-making is a popular local handicraft.

There is also a daily **gem market** *(open noon-4pm)* in the northeastern part of town where jade, rubies and sapphires are bought and sold. While it doesn't really compare with the gem markets of Mogok, the well-informed may be able to ferret out a deal or two.

For those interested in the Shan State's cultures, the modest **Shan State Museum** *(admission US$2)* and **Shan State Library**, near the Taunggyi Hotel, are worth a visit. Although only a relatively small number of displays are labelled in English, you can look at items that include local native costume, musical instruments, ceramics and weapons. If nothing else, you may begin sorting out hill tribe names: Kaw for Akha, Tai for Shan, Jin-Phaw (Jinghpaw) for Kachin, Lahta and Yanglai for different Karen groups; and identifying kinds of dress for the 35 different ethnic groups officially recognised in the state. There's also a display of royal Shan regalia and an exhibit of religious art that includes Buddhist sculpture in Shan and Mandalay styles, Shan *jataka* (stories of the Buddha's past lives) paintings, *pitaka* (Buddhist scripture) chests, *kammawa* (Buddhist lacquered scriptures), *parabaik* (folding manuscripts) and ornate votive tablets.

One upstairs room is devoted to the Panglong Agreement of 1947, in which Shan, Kachin and Chin leaders signed a document promising cooperation in the proposed Union of Burma. English-speaking lecturers are available to lead visitors around.

The Pa-O have established a **cultural centre** *(98 Merchant St)* near the market. The small but well laid-out museum contains musical instruments, including a typical Pa-O accordion, as well as banknotes and costumes.

There's a cheroot factory called **Flying Tiger Mashua** on a side street south of the Myoma cinema. The hand-rolling technique is impressive, and cheroot bundlers are able to get cheroots into bundles of 50 without counting – they judge simply by feel.

Places to Stay

May Khu Guest House *(☎ 21431; Bogyoke Aung San Rd; rooms per person US$3)* is an old standby in Taunggyi, a rambling, dark and shabby wooden structure on the main road. Its stark two-bed rooms have a common bathroom.

Khemarat Guest House *(☎ 22464; 48 Bogyoke Aung San Rd; singles/doubles US$8/10, with private bathroom US$15/20)* is newer and cleaner than the May Ghu. Overall, this hotel, owned by Maing Shu gem traders, is the best value in town.

Paradise Hotel *(☎ 22009; 157 Khwanyo Rd; standard singles/doubles US$24/30, with fridge US$36/42)*, a few blocks west from the Khemarat, is a four-storey (no elevator), modern Chinese-style place. The well-appointed but noisy rooms have good mattresses, hot-water showers, polished wood floors and TV. There are also slightly nicer rooms with fridge, and plush sitting rooms at the end of each floor.

Salween Hotel *(☎ 22605; 289 Bogyoke Aung San Rd)* is similar in price and quality to the Paradise.

Taunggyi Hotel *(☎ 21127; rooms US$30-40)*, a privatised and somewhat efficient 56-room place sprawling over landscaped grounds near the southern end of town, has spacious rooms with attached hot-water bathroom. The old Ministry of Hotels & Tourism (MHT)-style bar and restaurant attract a mix of well-heeled businesspeople and military types. Perched on a hillside, the hotel is a short stroll from the town centre and is one of the more comfortable older hotels in Myanmar.

The other places to stay in Taunggyi are all quite central and fairly similar – small and basic.

Places to Eat

A row of small **food stalls** in the market serves decent Chinese and Shan dishes. Very little English is spoken here, however, so brush up on your Burmese and/or point-to-order technique.

Maw Kan Restaurant *(Maokham; open 10am-8pm)* is an unassuming place that serves very good Shan and Chinese fare;

walk east from the main street down the road near the Shwe Innlay Guest House, make an immediate left and it's the unmarked wooden building on the right (Burmese sign).

Maxim's Restaurant, on the way out of town toward Inle, serves decent Chinese and European dishes, though it's on the expensive side.

Coca-Cola Restaurant *(Bogyoke Aung San Rd)*, in the same area as Maxim's, has an all-Chinese menu; it's nothing great, but it's popular.

Lyan Yu Hotel Restaurant prepares good noodle dishes, and also shows them off in a picturesque window display.

Brother Hotel Restaurant, a block south of Lyan Yu Hotel Restaurant, serves decent Chinese meals.

Sein (Diamond) Restaurant (with a Burmese sign) is a Bamar/Shan restaurant worth checking out. It's on the main road north of the market, and a favourite for out-of-town Shan visitors.

Htun Restaurant, equally as popular with the Shan crowd as the Sein Restaurant, is behind the old market in the middle of town and worth a visit.

Just south of the Khemarat Guest House is a very good **Shan noodle shop** (Burmese sign).

Between the Sikh temple and the cinema on the main road are a number of decent **teashops** and **small eateries** that specialise in an extensive variety of pastries and tea snacks, including basic *dan bauk* (biryani).

Getting There & Away

Air There are daily flights from Yangon, Bagan and Mandalay to Heho, 35km west of Taunggyi. A taxi from Heho to Taunggyi costs around US$10 or the kyat equivalent.

Bus & Pick-up Public pick-up trucks to Taunggyi from Inle Lake (K200, 45 minutes) leave frequently from the Nyaungshwe market area between 7am and 5pm. A taxi along the same route costs around US$10 or kyat equivalent.

There's one bus per day from Taunggyi to Pindaya (K300), leaving at 2pm and arriving at 5.30pm. There are frequent pick-ups to Pindaya from the Shwenyaung junction, starting at 6am.

Buses from Mandalay take seven or eight hours to reach Taunggyi (K1500 to K1800). Minibuses from Bagan leave at 7am (K1500) and 2pm (K1900).

Several buses depart for Yangon around noon from a point near the Taunggyi market. Ye Thu Aung and Taung Baw Da both charge K2600, are reliable and fairly comfortable, and arrive in Yangon around 6am the next morning.

KAKKU

ကက္ကူ

Kakku (also spelt Kekku or Ketku) is best described as a vast orchard of stupas, and has only recently been opened to foreign visitors. Some 40km south of Taunggyi in a region populated by the Pa-O people, the site is said to contain over two thousand stupas – most of which are only 3m to 4m high and laid out in neat rows. Constructed in a mixture of Pa-O, Shan and Bamar styles, the stupas are of brick and laterite, and some are covered with ornate stucco motifs. Two larger stupas are also part of the collection; one contains a highly revered Buddha image.

As yet no detailed studies have been conducted to determine the age of this site, but a local legend gives it a (highly doubtful) history dating back to the 3rd century BC, when India's Buddhist emperor, Asoka, is said to have sent missionaries to the region.

In 2000 an all-weather road was built to Kakku, making it easily accessible from Taunggyi. Unfortunately, along with the new road have come concessions to tourists, both foreign and local. The site has been fenced in and paved walkways have been laid around and through the rows of stupas. Work has also begun on the restoration of the stupas themselves. Once again, it's the typical dilemma that has affected Buddhist ruins throughout Southeast Asia. While foreign visitors are drawn to these ancient sites to view them in their 'picturesque', ruined state, local Buddhist pilgrims come specifically to acquire religious merit by contributing money to the restoration of the ruins. Since foreign visitors to Kakku are outnumbered by local pilgrims by about 10 to one, it won't be long before Kakku's crumbling stupas are given new coats of whitewashed stucco and topped with gleaming new golden hti.

Kakku is managed by the same Pa-O collective that owns the Golden Island Cottages at Inle Lake. Before visiting the site, foreign visitors are required to stop at the **Pa-O collective office** *(GIC; ☎ 23136, fax 23970; 65 West Circular Rd)* in Taunggyi and pay a US$3 entrance fee and US$5 guide fee. A Pa-O guide from this office will accompany you to the site, and while their English isn't always up to par, this arrangement will at least enable the Pa-O to earn some of the tourist dollars that they hope their historic site will attract.

Places to Stay & Eat

At the time of writing, foreigners weren't allowed to overnight at Kakku – indeed, so far there aren't any places of accommodation in the immediate vicinity. A huge **restaurant** of the type that caters to busloads of package tourists was recently built overlooking the site, so if the sight of all those stupas gives you the urge to down a few beers, you're in luck.

Getting There & Away

To visit Kakku you must first hire a car. Foreigners aren't allowed to take public transport to the site, even though a new railway line runs from Taunggyi to Kakku. Cars hired through hotels in Taunggyi and Nyaungshwe do the round trip for US$20 and US$30 respectively. This includes waiting time of a couple of hours at the stupas – though some of the Pa-O guides may try to rush your visit.

KENGTUNG (KYAINGTONG)

ကျိုင်းတုံ

☎ 084

Tucked away in the far east of the Shan State, 456km northeast of Taunggyi, 163km north of the border town of Tachileik (opposite Mae Sai, Thailand) and 787m above sea level, Kengtung is the sleepy but historic centre for the state's Khün culture, surrounded by Wa, Shan, Akha and Lahu villages. Built around a small lake, and dotted with ageing Buddhist temples and a few examples of British colonial architecture, Kengtung is probably the most scenic town in the Shan State.

Its opening to foreign visitors in January 1993 came as a complete surprise considering this was – and still is – one of the most remote inhabited mountain valleys in Myanmar. Access is difficult and restricted to YA flights from Myanmar's interior or the rough overland road trip from Tachileik/Mae Sai.

Kengtung is also a strategic Myanmar government stronghold in the middle of the shifting seas of Shan and Wa insurgency and the illicit drug trade. Its position is doubly strategic considering the area is a crossroads with outlets in four different countries – Myanmar, China, Thailand and Laos. As such, it is a critical linchpin in the country's defence. During WWII the town was occupied by Japanese and Thai soldiers, supposedly because it was equidistant from three international borders. In fact, the Thais were keen at the time to take back traditional tributary areas that had been colonised by the British in the 19th century. After the war, Thailand was forced to cede Kengtung back to the British.

Although Kengtung lies about mid-way between the Thanlwin and Mekong River valleys, it is more or less cut off from the former by a series of north-south mountain ranges. Hence, culturally, the area has more of an affinity with the nearby cultures of the Mekong – Laos, Xishuangbanna (southeastern Yunnan Province) and northern Thailand – than for the Shan and Bamar cultures west of the Thanlwin. Indeed, culturally Kengtung feels more like some long forgotten corner of northern Thailand than a part of Myanmar.

The Khün speak a northern Thai language related to Shan and Thai Lü and use a writing script similar to the ancient Lanna script of Chiang Mai in northern Thailand. The original Khün people are said to have been 13th-century migrants from Chiang

Mai, and their rulers claim to be descendants of the Lanna (or Lan Na Thai – Million Thai Rice-Fields) dynasty.

Before the Khün began paying tribute to the Bamar under King Anawrahta, they had their own independent kingdom, variously called Muang Tamilap, Muang Ong Puu, Muang Sanlawachilakam, Muang Khemmaratungkburi (or Khemarattha) and Tungkalasi, before settling on Kengtung, which means 'Walled City of Tung'. 'Tung' is a reference to the kingdom's mythical founder, a hermit named Tungkalasi, who used his magic staff to draw two channels to drain a lake of near-sea proportions, leaving behind the current town lake and the Nam Lap and Nam Khon streams. Remains of the original city walls and gates can still be seen. Today the Thais know the city as Chiang Tung, while in Burmese it is Kyaingtong.

Traditional Khün dress consists of a horizontally striped longyi and Shan-style jacket with a crossover front that ties on the side. Nowadays most Khün dress similarly to their counterparts in neighbouring countries – although older Khün women are still partial to their traditional turbans. About 80% of the township's population of 180,000 people are Khün; roughly 15% are Shan-Chinese and the remainder is a mix of other ethnicities such as Lahu. About half the population is Buddhist, and another 17% is Christian – American missionaries were quite active here, as their imposing churches attest. The rest of the population belong to various spirit cults.

A large percentage of all foreign visitors to Kengtung are Thais seeking a glimpse of ancient Lanna. Few Westerners are seen around town, save for contract employees working for the United Nations Drug Control Project (UNDCP), whose sizeable expenditures lead many of the locals to believe all Western arrivals are similarly rich.

Crossing the Border to Mae Sai

Foreigners are ordinarily permitted to cross the bridge over the Sai River into Tachileik, and to continue by air or road the 163km to Kengtung for two weeks, upon payment of a US$18 fee and the exchange of US$100 for 100 foreign exchange certificates (FECs). You can use the FEC to pay for hotel rooms and plane tickets, but that's about all – or change them for kyat at the going free-market rate (see the Money section in the Facts for the Visitor chapter for more information). Your two-week tourist visa can be extended for up to two months (two weeks at a time) at a cost of US$36 at the immigration office in Kengtung.

In May 1994 Khun Sa's Mong Tai Army (MTA) bombed the Tachileik dike, draining the reservoir that supplied the town with water. The border was closed to foreigners for several weeks, then reopened, but other incidents in April 1995 closed the border. Things were more or less peaceful until fierce fighting between Burmese and Thai troops in February 2001 caused the border crossing to be closed again. At the time of writing the border crossing was open. Although Khun Sa did a deal with the SPDC in 1996, there are still frequent skirmishes between the drug-trafficking United Wa State Army (UWSA) and its Tatmadaw allies, the Shan State Army (SSA) and Thai armed forces.

Hence, if you're contemplating an overland trip to Kengtung from Thailand, you'll simply have to take your chances on finding the border crossing open or closed – more often than not it is open.

Foreigners are not at direct risk from the fighting, although the possibility of getting caught in the crossfire somewhere along the road between Tachileik and Kengtung can't be ruled out. Kengtung itself seems relatively safe; the MTA hasn't attacked the town since the 1980s. See the Tachileik section later in this chapter for more information on border crossings.

Things to See & Do

When the British settled into Kengtung, they centred the town on a large, natural lake. Decaying **colonial-style buildings**, taken over by the Burmese government or by squatters, are reminiscent of British colonial provincial architecture found elsewhere in Myanmar and India. The faded colonial air, along with the pagoda spires of over 30 local temples, the surrounding

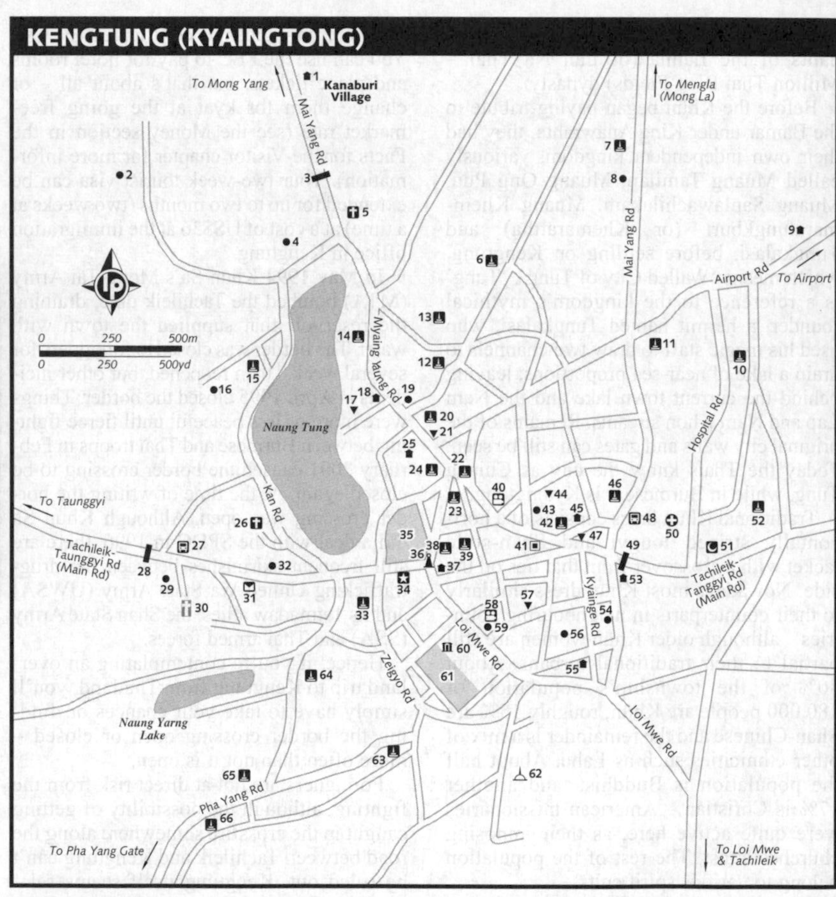

green hills and narrow, winding streets combine to create something of a Burmese counterpart to Luang Prabang in Laos. It's hard to say how long this atmosphere of benign neglect will last, however. Of late, Chinese investors and local drug lords have increased the local cash flow in the town, and old buildings are being knocked down to make way for characterless structures in the modern Thai and Chinese styles.

Kengtung's many well-kept monasteries – called 'wats' rather than 'kyaung' by the Khün – reflect Shan, Siamese, Burmese and Chinese influences.

The most impressive is **Wat Jong Kham (Zom Kham)**, which features a tall gilded zedi topped by a gold hti inlaid with silver, rubies, diamonds, sapphires and jade, and hung with tiny gold bells. The interior walls bear older gold-leaf-on-lacquer jataka, as well as modern painted jataka, sparkling mirrored pillars and a dozen or so Buddha images on an altar draped with gilded cloth. Much intricate tinwork outlines the gables and plinths of the temple. Legend says Wat Jong Kham dates back to a visit by Gautama Buddha and that the zedi contains six strands of his hair. Most likely the site dates

KENGTUNG (KYAINGTONG)

PLACES TO STAY
- 1 Harry's Guest House & Trekking
- 9 Win Guest House
- 18 Noi Yee Hotel
- 25 Kyaing Tong Hotel
- 37 Barami Motel
- 45 Kyi Lin Star Guest House
- 53 Princess Hotel
- 55 Hsam Yawt Guest House

PLACES TO EAT
- 17 Keng House Restaurant
- 21 Millionaire Teashop
- 44 Tai Khun Restaurant
- 47 Golden Banyan Restaurant
- 57 Lauo Tien Lu Restaurant

OTHER
- 2 Chinese School
- 3 Naung Pha Gate
- 4 UNDCP Office
- 5 American Baptist Church
- 6 Wat Kae Min
- 7 Wat Yang Kon
- 8 Pottery Works
- 10 Wat Naung Kham
- 11 Mangala Kyaung (Wat Tamawtaya)
- 12 Wat Jong Kham (Zom Kham)
- 13 Wat In
- 14 Wat Noi Naw
- 15 Wat Chiang Ing (Keng Ing)
- 16 Jail
- 19 Immigration Office
- 20 Wat Chiang Ying (Keng Yun)
- 22 Wat Pha Jao Lung (Maha Myat Muni)
- 23 Wat Ho Kong
- 24 Wat Pha Kaew
- 26 St Mary's Convent
- 27 Buses to Taunggyi
- 28 Yang Kham Gate
- 29 Water Buffalo Market
- 30 Roman Catholic Mission & Immaculate Heart Cathedral
- 31 Fax & Telegram Office
- 32 Myanma Airways
- 33 Wat Asok
- 34 Police
- 35 Sports Field
- 36 Independence Monument
- 38 Maung Ming Kyaung
- 39 Maung Mai Kyaung
- 40 Kengtung Cinema
- 41 Mausoleum of the Khün Princes
- 42 Wat Chiang Jan (Keng San)
- 43 Tai Khun Silverworks
- 46 Wat Ho Kat
- 48 Buses to Tachilek
- 49 Paleng Gate
- 50 Hospital
- 51 Mosque
- 52 Wat Jom Mai
- 54 Chinese Clan House
- 56 Regional Offices
- 58 Khemarat Cinema
- 59 Thai Flying Service
- 60 Town Hall
- 61 Central Market
- 62 Wat Pha That Jom Mon
- 63 Wat Tuya
- 64 Wat Chiang Khom (Keng Khom)
- 65 Wat Si Naw
- 66 Wat Mahabodhi Vipassana (Kamathan Kyaung)

back to the 13th-century Chiang Mai migration. The temple was substantially renovated in 1906 and 1936, when the height of the stupa rose to 38m. The zedi was regilded in 1988 and 1989. Wat Jong Kham is north of the town centre.

Right in the centre of town are a couple of busy and visually striking 19th-century temples, **Wat Pha Jao Lung** (which gets its Burmese name, Maha Myat Muni, from a 1920 replica of the Mandalay Maha Myat Muni image) and **Wat Ho Kong**. Aficionados of rare Buddha images will have a field day at **Wat In**, named after the Hindu god Indra and located on a hill overlooking the lake. Behind the altar of the principal sanctuary is a must-see collection of wooden Buddha images in the Khün style – the robes of which are gracefully carved and inlaid with tiny bits of coloured mirror.

On a hill to the south of town, **Wat Pha That Jom Mon** features an older wood-and-plaster sanctuary with good tinwork. Further up the hill behind the monastery are some very tall dipterocarp trees and two picturesque white stupas. The surrounding hillside provides good views of the town below.

On the road leading west out of town toward Taunggyi, the British-era **Roman Catholic Mission (RCM)** and the 12-year-old **Immaculate Heart Cathedral** are still thriving on a hillside where the original town was founded 1000 years ago. Visitors are welcome. The mission cares for nearly 100 orphaned boys, many from Shan State hill tribes.

One of the great sights in Kengtung was the large **Haw Sao Pha Kengtung**, considered the most outstanding example of Shan-style palace architecture in Myanmar. The stucco-and-teak structure combined Buddhist-temple-style pavilions with Islamic-looking domes, said to have been inspired by the suggestions of a visiting Muslim Indian prince. Despite a protest mounted by a group of monks and Khün residents who appealed to the local army commander to preserve the building, the Burmese government demolished the palace in 1991 to make way for the unsightly

Uneasy Neighbours

Of all Myanmar's neighbours, Thailand seems to have had more than its share of strained relations. The Burmese have repeatedly shelled Thai territory since 1992, while attacking Karen and Shan insurgent armies along the Thai-Myanmar border.

Until the late 1990s, most Thai officials seemed sympathetic to the insurgents' cause – even after one insurgent group took over the Myanmar embassy in Bangkok and held the staff and several innocent bystanders hostage in 1999. The Thai government brokered the hostages' release and the insurgents were given safe passage to the Myanmar border – much to the chagrin of Myanmar officials, who retaliated by temporarily closing the border crossings between the two countries. However, Thai attitudes changed drastically a few months later, when another group of insurgents (some of whom had participated in the Myanmar embassy takeover) crossed the border into Thailand to make political demands while holding hostage the staff of a hospital in Ratchaburi's provincial capital. This time the Thai government sent in elite troops and all of the hostage-takers were killed.

In February 2001, artillery duels across the international boundary between Myanmar's eastern Shan State and Thailand's Chiang Rai Province led to a number of military and civilian deaths on both sides. Thailand claimed that the Burmese military, as well as ethnic-Wa troops, had pursued Shan 'rebels' into Thai territory. The real reason behind the clashes was the lucrative trade in methamphetamine tablets between the two countries (the Thai government estimates that Burmese nationals will smuggle 600 to 700 million methamphetamine pills into Thailand in 2002). Once again, the border crossings were closed, but relations between Myanmar and Thailand improved after the Thai prime minister Thaksin Shinawatra paid a visit to Myanmar in June 2001.

Steven Martin

Kyaing Tong Hotel. All that is left of the old palace are the walls and a sentinel tower on the hotel's perimeter. To get an idea of what the old palace domes looked like, check out the **Mausoleum of the Khün Princes**, opposite Wat Chiang Jan. The compound is walled-in and visitors are not allowed inside, but you can get a good view from the monastery on the other side of the road. The main tomb, belonging to Sao Kon Kyio, is topped with a dome that is identical to the ones that crowned the old palace. To the east of this is another impressive tomb containing the remains of Sao Kong Tai, who was murdered by a relative on the steps of the palace in 1937.

The **central market** draws people from all over the Kengtung district, including a variety of hill-tribe people. Fresh produce and household goods are the market's main emphases, but some handicrafts are also available. Look for Kengtung-style lacquerware, which, like that found in Kyaukka in the Sagaing Division, doesn't employ the polychromatic incising techniques found in Bagan, but rather two-colour lacquer-moulding reliefs. Also interesting are a handful of stalls that specialise in supplying Akha women with the silver coins, buttons and seed beads that they use to decorate their colourful clothing.

The lake in the centre of town, **Naung Tung** (*naung* is the Shan word for 'small lake'), is a popular spot for morning and evening strolls.

Places to Stay

Blackouts are common in Kengtung, so be sure to bring along a torch (flashlight).

Harry's Guest House & Trekking (*☎ 21418; 132 Mai Yang Rd, Kanaburi Village; rooms with bathroom US$5, bungalow US$20)*, 500m north of the Naung Pha Gate at the northern edge of town, has a row of basic rooms and one bungalow. Harry is an English-speaking Kengtung native who spent many years as a trekking guide in Chiang Mai.

NORTHEASTERN MYANMAR

Noi Yee Hotel *(☎ 21298; 5 Myaing Yaung Rd; singles/doubles US$15/20)*, near the Kyaing Tong Hotel, is a former royal residence that has seen better days. The rooms are a tad grubby, but there's some character (high ceilings and antique furniture) as well as attached hot-water bathrooms.

Princess Hotel *(☎ 21319, fax 21159; standard singles/doubles US$24/30, superior singles/doubles US$34/40)*, a newly built, three-storey place just south of the Paleng Gate, is probably the most comfortable in town. All rooms have hot-water bathroom, satellite TV, air-con, fridge and IDD phone. The attached restaurant only serves breakfast, but can do lunch and dinner with advance notice. Of course, like most modern hotels in this part of Myanmar, the amenities come at a price – this place is quite lacking in atmosphere.

Win Guest House *(singles/doubles US$25/30)*, on the road to the airport northeast of town, offers decent rooms, each with private toilet and cold-water shower, in a modern-looking house. Although a bit removed from the town centre, it's quiet.

Hsam Yweat Guest House *(☎ 21235, 21643; 21 Kyainge Rd; singles/doubles US$10/15)* has decent rooms and friendly staff.

Other places in town that may accept foreigners during festival times when everything else is full, include the **Barami Motel** *(☎ 21089; 3 Loimwe Rd)* and **Kyi Lin Star Guest House**, near Paleng Gate. Both plan to ask US$10 to US$15 per person. Travellers who wish to avoid government-owned hotels should bypass the **Kyaing Tong Hotel**.

Places to Eat

When visiting local drinking establishments, particularly the ones along Naung Tung, travellers should be wary of invitations to sit and share a whisky. Although their intentions are genuinely friendly, some local men are fond of lacing their drinks with methamphetamine. Unless you want to be awake all night, offer to buy a round of beers instead.

Two Chinese restaurants a few blocks northeast of the central market get more than their share of regular clientele.

Lauo Tien Lu Restaurant *(also known as Lawt Tin Lu)* is the longest-running and most reliable Chinese restaurant, a branch of one owned by the same family in Thailand's Chiang Khong. It's a simple open-sided restaurant with good southern Chinese food.

Golden Banyan Restaurant *(also known as Shwe Nyaung Bin or Ton Pho Thong)* is the second very popular Chinese restaurant. It's near Wat Chiang Jan (Keng San) and has a view of the Mausoleum of the Khün Princes. The main feature of this restaurant is outdoor tables beneath a huge banyan tree. The food is only fair but the atmosphere makes up for it.

Keng House Restaurant, on the eastern shore of Naung Tung, is a pleasant open-air spot with an extensive Chinese menu; hotpot is a house speciality.

Tai Khun Restaurant, east of Kengtung Cinema, serves authentic Shan/Khün food.

The **Millionaire Teashop**, opposite the Kyaing Tong Hotel, is a good place for morning samosas and *palata* (fried flatbread). It's one of the few places in town where the stereo plays Burmese rock instead of Thai pop.

Getting There & Away

The road between Kengtung and Taunggyi is firmly off-limits to foreigners. At the moment only Burmese citizens are permitted to use this road, and they travel in convoy, as robbery is rife. Fighting between the Yangon government and the Shan and Pa-O insurgents is another factor making the Kengtung-Taunggyi journey potentially hazardous.

Air The airport at Kengtung is subject to the occasional closure, so the information in this section is especially vulnerable. Both YA and AM fly routes linking Kengtung with Tachileik, Mandalay and Yangon . YA currently schedules five flights a week from Tachileik to Kengtung (US$38, 30 minutes, no service on Wednesday and Saturday). AM flies twice a week (US$ 41, Monday and Wednesday). AM flies twice a week from Yangon to Kengtung (US$138, Monday and Wednesday).

NORTHEASTERN MYANMAR

Mae Sai/Tachileik If you're coming to Kengtung from Thailand through Mae Sai, the Myanmar government and local tour agents and drivers have conspired to make it impossible for travellers to ride the Tachileik-Kengtung bus at local prices. Arranging a ride to Kengtung must now be done through an agent. This can be accomplished either at the small tourist office next to the immigration check-point at the border crossing or at the bus station, where a line of agent's offices is located. Either way, you will have to complete a form that includes the name and vehicle registration of the driver of the vehicle in which you intend to ride, and present this to the immigration officials for them to record. A copy of the form must then be given to the driver who will show it on demand at any of the five road-blocks set up between Tachileik and Kengtung.

Foreign passengers are asked to pay in Thai baht or US dollars and are charged US$6 for a seat on the bus, US$14 for a back seat in a Toyota Corolla 'van', or US$17 for the front seat. The trip takes between six and seven hours over a rough dirt road through scenes of some of the worst deforestation in Southeast Asia, as well as numerous Akha, Wa and Shan villages. Along the way the main rest stops are **Talay**, a small town with interesting Shan temples and an army post, and **Mong Hpayak**, the most popular food stop.

Getting Around

Kengtung has a small fleet of motorcycle taxis that charge around K200 for a ride within town, K300 for longer rides, say from Harry's Guest House to the town centre. Look for the cyclists wearing numbered vests to discern which motorcycle is for hire.

AROUND KENGTUNG

Hot Springs

Just south of town on the road to Tachileik is a large public hot-springs spa *(admission K100)* with gender-segregated bathhouses. Shampoo and soap are available for sale, so this is a great spot to clean up if you're staying at one of the cold-water guesthouses in town during the cool season. **Vendors** on the grounds sell noodles and other snacks, so you could easily spend an entire afternoon here. The spa is busiest on weekends.

Hiking

Hiking to nearby Lahu (Musoe), Akha (Kaw), Shan and Wa villages is permitted in the company of a licensed guide, available at the Kyaing Tong Hotel or Harry's Guest House & Trekking for around US$25 a day per person (see Places to Stay in the Kengtung section earlier for details). Overnighting in the villages is not officially permitted.

Yang Kong

ယင်ကောင်

On the northern outskirts of town in the village of Yang Kong, on the road to Mong Ma, you can visit **pottery works** where roof tiles, utilitarian bowls and other ceramic items are made.

Loi-mwe

လွိုင်မွယ်

Although it lies a little outside the permitted radius, no-one seems to care if you visit Loi-mwe, 33km southeast of Kengtung. Located at over 1600m, this 'hill station' features a number of old **colonial buildings** and a century-old Catholic **church**. The main attraction, though, is the scenery on the ascent to Loi-mwe, which passes through forests, terraced rice fields and a lake. You'll have to hire a car or motorcycle, as there doesn't seem to be any regular public transport between Kengtung and Loi-mwe.

Mong La

မိုင်းလား

Eighty-five kilometres north of Kengtung lies the border district of Mong La (or Mengla as it's sometimes spelt). Although Mong La is mainly a Thai Lü district, in a deal worked out with the Myanmar military it's currently controlled by ethnic Wa, who once fought against Yangon troops but now enjoy peaceful relations with the government.

The district receives lots of Chinese tourists, who come to peruse Mong La's well-known wildlife market and to gamble in the district's several casinos. The largest and plushest, the **Myanmar Royal Casino**, is an Australian-Chinese joint venture. Inside are the usual Chinese and Western games of chance with the setup the same as typically seen in Macau, the Genting Highlands (Malaysia) and on cruise ships in the South China Sea. There are also plenty of karaoke, discos (including a thriving gay and transvestite scene) and other staples of modern Chinese entertainment life. The main currency used in town is Chinese yuan.

Many of the paya in Mong La have been built in the past 10 years as part of the SPDC's drive to convert the border areas to Buddhism.

In 1997 a **Drug Eradication Museum** was opened by U Sai Lin, a local Wa/Chinese drug-trafficker turned establishment figure and head of the Eastern Shan State Army (ESSA), who declared, to widespread disbelief, that the area around Mong La was henceforth an 'opium-free zone'. This may be somewhat accurate, as opium has been replaced by methamphetamine as the region's most lucrative illicit drug. As in much of the Shan State, AIDS is a serious problem.

When you pass through the southern gate into Wa territory, a charge of 80 yuan is collected for each four-wheeled vehicle, 10 yuan for a motorcycle, plus 5 yuan per person.

Rooms at the **Mengla Hotel** are available for 270 yuan (about US$32), an astounding figure given the fact the hotel doesn't have running water. You can also stay with the district headman in his Thai Lü–style **house** for around 30 yuan – a much better deal and a more interesting experience.

In order to proceed to Mong La from Kengtung, you must first register at the Kengtung immigration office. The staff at the Noi Yee Hotel or Harry's Guest House & Trekking (see Places to Stay in the Kengtung section earlier) can help you accomplish this.

The obvious question is: Can you cross the border from Mong La into Daluo, China? So far the only third-country nationals that have been able to cross here have done so in 'caravans' – off-road aficionados who pay the Chinese and Myanmar governments large sums for the permission to cross here. Keep in mind also that leaving Myanmar from Tachileik, if you have arrived from Yangon, is expressly forbidden.

Crossing the Border to Laos

About 19km northeast of Tachileik on the Tachileik-Kengtung road, a smaller road branches off from Nam Manyang and heads east-southeast to the Mekong River, the border between Laos and Myanmar. At the small town here, Wan Pasak, you can get a boat across the river to Xieng Kok in Laos. From Xieng Kok there's a road northeast of Muang Sing, which connects with roads to Luang Nam Tha and Udomxai. You *might* be permitted to cross into Laos here if you already possess a valid Lao visa. Then again, you might not! Much depends on the local political situation, obviously, as well as the mood of local officials. It is not a legal international border crossing, yet plenty of Burmese and Lao do use it. Sooner or later, however, this could become an official crossing for all nationalities.

TACHILEIK

တာချီလိတ်

☎ 084

Most travellers coming into Myanmar from Mae Sai in Thailand head straight for Kengtung to the north rather than linger at the border, but it's also possible to arrange a one-day pass to visit Tachileik from Thailand. Besides shopping for Shan handicrafts (about the same price as on the Thai side, and everyone accepts baht) and eating Shan/Bamar food, there's little to do in Tachileik, though. About 3000 to 4000 people cross the bridge to Tachileik daily, most of them Thais who shop for dried mushrooms, herbal medicines, cigarettes and other cheap imports from China.

Border Crossings

A day pass from Thailand to Tachileik costs US$5, paid to Myanmar immigration officials at the border crossing. There is no FEC exchange requirement as there is for longer stays. If you hold a day pass, you're restricted to a radius of 5km. See the Kengtung section earlier for information on longer permits.

The Mae Sai–Tachileik border is usually open from 6am to 6pm weekdays, and until 9pm on weekends and holidays. This early closing time on weekdays can be a problem if you're driving back from Kengtung, given the unpredictability of road conditions between Kengtung and Tachileik.

Should you find yourself stranded in Tachileik after the border has closed you have a few choices, and a couple of them are actually comfortable.

Places to Stay

All hotels here accept both US dollars and Thai baht.

Dream Flower Hotel *(☎ 21318; Padonmar Rd; rooms US$5/200B)* is just south of the main intersection in town. Rooms are clean, if a bit noisy, and have attached bathroom. This place accepts both US dollars and Thai baht for payment.

Golden Triangle Hotel *(☎ 51006; Depar Kyaw St; bungalows/rooms US$15/28, 660/1200B)* is probably the most comfortable place in Tachileik. All 24 rooms have private bathroom, TV and air-con. On a hill overlooking the town, the Golden Triangle has good views and is quiet. There's a Burmese restaurant on the premises and breakfast is included. If you call the hotel, it will send a car to pick you up at the border crossing.

Mya Shwe Ye Hotel *(☎ 51792; 3/52 Mya Shwe Ye St; rooms US$18/600B)* is a newer place with decent rooms, all with attached bathroom, TV and air-con.

Other places you might try are the cheap but spartan **Peacock Hotel** and **Erawan Hotel**, both with rooms in the US$3 to US$10 range. If crossing the border into Thailand is an option, you'll find the accommodation there better in every respect.

PYIN U LWIN TO LASHIO

Gokteik Viaduct

ဂုတ်ထိပ်တံတား

The unusual Gokteik railway viaduct is 55km out of Pyin U Lwin, en route to Lashio. When, on behalf of the British, the Pennsylvania Steel Co built the Gokteik Bridge over the deep Gokteik Gorge over 100 years ago, it was the second-highest railway bridge in the world. A British insurance policy expired years ago, but while it was in effect the Burmese government didn't service the viaduct much; however, it has recently been renovated. Its age shows; trains slow to a crawl when crossing the viaduct, in order to avoid putting undue stress on the structure.

If you go by train, get off at the station before the bridge to get the best view. You're not allowed to go under the bridge, as there's a military camp there. In fact, be careful wandering around the bridge as land mines are reputed to have been planted in some areas – to fend off insurgents who might want to destroy the span. You'll only have a few minutes before you must get back on the train if continuing on to Hsipaw or Lashio. The military supposedly forbids photo-taking from the bridge, but everybody seems to do it.

Getting There & Away From Pyin U Lwin, catch the Mandalay-Lashio train between 7am and 8am for the journey to Gokteik (US$4 1st class, two hours), unless you can wrangle a kyat ticket). Or start at Mandalay aboard the 4.45am train.

You can also go by car or bus to Gokteik via the Mandalay-Lashio road – see Getting There & Away in the Lashio section later in this chapter for details. The road itself, a ribbon of hairpin bends descending into the gorge, is impressive, but the railway viaduct is only visible in the far distance.

Kyaukme

ကျောက်မဲ

The market towns between Gokteik and Lashio are in many ways more interesting and atmospheric than Lashio. Unlike Lashio, which has a large Chinese and Bamar

Gokteik Viaduct

In 1899 Burma Railways solicited bids for the construction of a railway viaduct over the Gokteik gorge, a geographic obstacle that for all intents and purposes cut off northeastern Myanmar from the country's centre. It was an engineering problem of immense proportions for that day and age, and one that drew world attention. Pennsylvania Steel Co vied with several British engineering outfits for the project, coming in with a bid far below those of its competitors in price and scheduling and, according to a 1901 engineering magazine, with a design 'much superior to anything else submitted'.

Work on the bridge began in February 1900. The crew of Americans (including 'a North Carolina negro who spoke Hindustani'), British, Germans and Burmese drove the last rivet in December of the same year. Considered the greatest railway viaduct in the world at the time, Gokteik was the only American-built span in the British Raj.

Joe Cummings

population, Kyaukme and Hsipaw are Shan-majority towns with small numbers of Chinese and Indian traders. Both towns are located on the road and rail routes between Mandalay and Lashio, the main China-Myanmar trade route. Kyaukme is also joined by road with Mogok to the northwest, so it sees a steady stream of gem traders. Several colonial-era buildings are adjacent to the bustling Kyaukme market.

Hsipaw

သီပေါ

☎ 082

Hsipaw (called Thibaw in Burmese) was once the centre of a small Shan state of its own and has become a popular hang-out for travellers, thanks to its cool climate, friendly people and relaxed atmosphere.

Special Events One of the oldest and largest Shan festivals, the **Bawgyo Paya Pwe**, is held here from the 10th waxing day to the first day after the full moon of Tabaung (February/March). Shan festivals traditionally served as important economic and administrative (as well as social) events, since this was when the sawbwa collected taxes and reviewed the accounts of his lieutenants and subjects. The Bawgyo pwe still draws a large encampment of traders and festival-goers who pay tribute, in spirit if not in cash, to the old Shan ways. *Zat pwe* (costumed dance-drama based on jataka stories) is performed nightly. Before dawn on the day of the full moon, hundreds of Palaung pilgrims who come from miles around offer rice to the images. Although the government has officially clamped down on the gambling that used to be the sawbwa's big money-earner, you may be able to find a dice game of 36 animals, which is still secretly played in parts of Shan State.

Things to See & Do A **haw sao pha** *(Shan palace; admission by donation; open after 4pm)* – *sawbwa haw* in Burmese – still stands at the northern end of Hsipaw. Built in 1924, the charming building is European in design – a Shan-style palace that was located nearby didn't survive WWII bombing. The last sao pha was arrested during the military takeover of 1962 and hasn't been heard from since. This story about vanquished royalty is the topic of *Twilight over Burma: My Life as a Shan Princess*, a recent memoir by Austrian-American Inge Sargent who was the popular Mahadevi (sao pha's wife) of Hsipaw from the 1950s until the takeover. The prince's niece and nephew take care of the palace and welcome foreign visitors. The palace is a residence, not a museum, so they ask that you restrict visits to after 4pm and request a donation of at least US$1 per visitor to help with its upkeep. It's a K400 trishaw ride from the clock tower in the centre of town, or about 20 minutes' walk, past the old town jail.

One of the busiest religious sites in Hsipaw is **Mahamyatmuni Paya** at the southern outskirts of town. A shrine in the compound

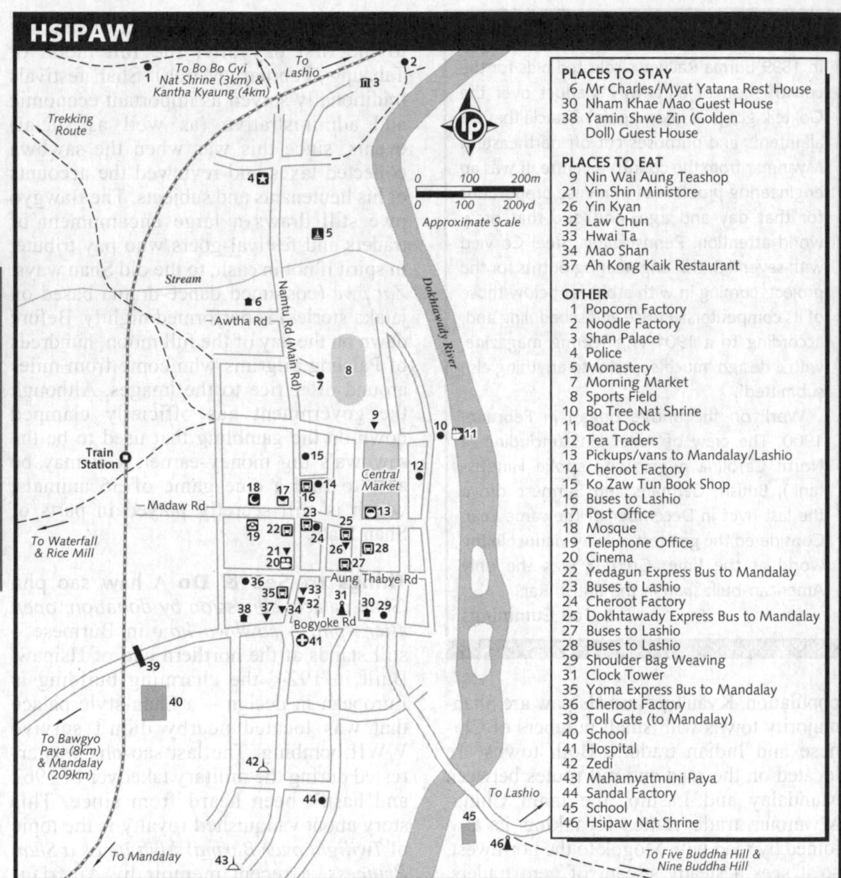

contains a large Buddha image inspired by its Mandalay namesake, Mahamuni Paya.

Eight kilometres southwest of town, off the Mandalay-Lashio road, is the Shan-style **Bawgyo Paya**. This is the most revered paya in northern Shan State – equivalent to Inle Lake's Phaung Daw U Paya in the southern half of the state (see the Inle Lake section earlier in this chapter). It is said that the sagawa tree growing by the paya bends over at the top in deference to the paya. It lost some of its charm following renovations in 1995, during which the building was redecorated to look less Shan and more Bamar – but its situation by the river still gives it some appeal. The paya contains four gold Buddha images.

On a hill to the left, just as you enter the city limits of Hsipaw from Bawgyo, is the overgrown and ruined **mausoleum** of the sawbwa of Hsipaw.

Hsipaw's large **market** is best in the morning when Shan and other tribal people from nearby villages come to trade. The Dokhtawady River (also called the Myitngeh or Namtu), just east of the market, is cool and clear. According to local saying, if you drink the river's water, you will return.

Alternatively, you can do as the locals do and use the river as an impromptu car wash.

To catch a great **sunset** in Hsipaw, walk to either Five Buddha Hill or Nine Buddha Hill. First cross the bridge on the Lashio road, and go about 200m. On your right, look for a path which leads to both small hills.

There are **walking tours** and **boat trips** to nearby villages, a sandal factory that recycles old tires and a cheroot factory near the market. Also worth checking out are looms for weaving shoulder bags and a **'popcorn factory'** that employs an alarmingly explosive technique to make the snack. East of the market are a handful of merchants' shophouses that trade in tea grown in the surrounding mountains. Visit the hospitable and well-informed bookseller Ko Zaw Tun (known as **Mr Book** to many travellers) on the main road for reliable advice on moving around Hsipaw. He also gives out hand-drawn maps to Shan villages that you can hike to from of town. If you visit during the hot season, Mr Book can arrange for you to go tubing down the river.

Places to Stay This small Shan town offers simple and basic accommodation, most with separate bathroom and toilet facilities (mostly squat toilets). Prices are similar at all the guesthouses – about K500 per person. Some of the guesthouses do not provide towels, but you can always buy one at the market, or along the main road, for less than K300.

Nam Khae Mao Guest House (*☎ Hsipaw 88; Bogyoke Rd; rooms with bathroom US$6*), east of the clock tower, has double and triple rooms, plus a large lobby with TV. A few rooms have attached bathroom and Western-style flush toilets. A big drawback is the aforementioned clock tower, which loudly announces the hours throughout the night.

Mr Charles/Myat Yatana Rest House (*☎ 80105; Awtha Rd; rooms without bathroom K2500, singles/doubles with private hot-water bathroom US$6/8*), just off the main road at the northern end of town, has small clean cubicles, and larger rooms with hot-water bathroom and fan. There's a common veranda on the 2nd floor, a great place to enjoy a beer and a good book. Most days at about 8am, Mr Charles leads a three-hour 'morning excursion' to a village or nearby waterfall.

Yamin Shwe Zin (Golden Doll) Guest House (*☎ Hsipaw 66; Bogyoke Rd; cubicles with shared bathroom K500, room with hot-water bathroom K1500*), west of the clock tower, has clean, spartan rooms with screens. Bath and toilet facilities are separate with the exception of one room. The hospitable family owners are a good source of information about the area.

Places to Eat Good Shan-style restaurants and teashops are common in Hsipaw. There are several very good Shan and Chinese restaurants along the main road (Namtu Rd) near the cinema and across the street from the Yoma bus stop. **Hwai Ta** and **Law Chun** are both open in the evening and serve good rice, curry and noodle dishes. Fresh fish is also available at both.

Across the road near the cinema, **Yin Shin Ministore** has plenty of imported Chinese snacks, cookies, soft drinks and beer. **Mao Shan**, a very tasty noodle shop opposite and a few metres south of Law Chun restaurant, is open for breakfast and lunch.

There's good and cheap food to be had in the **market** if you're willing to poke around and look for it. One stall just inside the northern entrance belongs to the very friendly Aung Kyaw, nicknamed 'Mr Bean', and offers a variety of nutritious and tasty bean salads. Try the *lahpeq thouq* (tea-leaf salad) or the *gyin thouq* (pickled ginger salad) which, besides their namesake ingredients, include several kinds of dried beans and peas as well as fried garlic.

Another stall worth seeking out offers Shan sticky noodles with tomato sauce, cilantro (coriander) and pickled mustard greens. This can be eaten as a vegetarian dish or with pork, chicken or dried shrimp on request. This stall is located in the southeastern corner of the market. Both are open until mid-afternoon. Also within the market are a number of stalls where you can have good Shan breakfasts, including *tohu pyaw* (tofu porridge).

Yin Kyan *(sign in Burmese; open lunch only)*, a few doors south of the market and around the corner from the Dokhtawady bus stop, is an excellent small Shan eatery with the best noodles in town. There's no English menu.

Ah Kong Kaik Restaurant, on the road into Hsipaw from Mandalay, serves decent Shan and Chinese fare, and is a favourite of the truck drivers who ply the Mandalay-Lashio road. You can spot the restaurant by the trucks parked along the road.

There are several tea and snack shops in town – look around the northern and southern sides of the market. The rustic **Nin Wai Aung Teashop** (no English sign), just opposite the northern side of the market and next to a big orange-coloured building, opens very early and has a good selection of tea snacks. Teashops on the southern side of the market tend to stay open late – until 11pm or so.

Getting There & Away Yoma Express, Yedagun Express and Dokhtawady Express run between Mandalay and Hsipaw (K1200). Five or six buses depart from Hsipaw daily at about 6am. If you want to get a look at Kyaukme, take the Yoma Express, which stops there for an hour, giving you some time to explore.

The price of a ticket from Hsipaw to Pyin U Lwin is K900. Two buses (5.15am and 6am) to Lashio (K300, two hours), 72km northeast, depart daily from opposite the market and a block down from Dokhtawady Express stop.

Vans to Pyin U Lwin and Lashio are usually parked by the market on Madaw Rd, across from Dokhtawady bus stop. The toll gate to Hsipaw from the Lashio side closes at 6pm – a custom representing both the warlord legacy, and possible threat from Shan rebels to the north and east.

See the Mandalay chapter for information on other public vehicles to Lashio, all of which make stops in Hsipaw.

Train The Mandalay-Lashio (US$4/8 ordinary/1st class) train departs from Mandalay at 4.45am and arrives in Hsipaw at 3pm (with any luck). Tickets must be purchased at least a day before at the Mandalay train station between 6am and 4pm. The same train leaves Hsipaw at about 3.30pm, arriving in Lashio at 7.30pm. The price of a ticket for this leg is US$2/4 for ordinary/upper class. Trains from Lashio to Mandalay arrive in Hsipaw at around 9am and depart at 9.30am.

Getting Around Bicycles are available for rent at most guesthouses. Rates are about K400 for the day. Most places are within easy walking distance. The only public transport around town are trishaws, which cost around K200 for a ride from the market to the Shan Palace.

Namhsan
နမ့်စမ်

A few travellers have made it from Hsipaw as far as Namhsan, although you are likely to be told that this is not allowed. The 80km journey, on a road barely maintained since colonial times, takes at least six hours, and if it is blocked by trucks it can take days.

Namhsan was the capital of the former Shan State of Tawngpeng. It clings to a 1600m-high narrow ridge, surrounded by valleys and mountains which rise to 2000m. The area is stunningly beautiful, and nicknamed the 'Switzerland of Myanmar'. Most of the inhabitants are Shwe (Golden) Palaung and make a living from tea, although opium poppies are never far away. In Namhsan and nearby Payagyi, there are a number of tea factories where tea is roasted, boiled or pickled. The tea harvest runs from April to August, and during the monsoon, overloaded trucks heading for Mandalay are a particular hazard, sometimes blocking the road for hours, sometimes days.

From Hsipaw, the road passes through the lowland Shan villages of Konzaleik, Mo-te and Mali before crossing a bridge over the Dokhtawady and climbing to Panglong (Big Village), a dull market-town on the junction with the road to the mines at Namtu, 43km away. The road then descends to the river again at the small village of Loilu, where there are a few **teashops** and an army checkpoint, before skirting the mountainside through tea plantations that run all the way to Namhsan.

Tawngpeng Palace is unimpressive. It dates from 1931, but was partially rebuilt following bomb damage. Khun Pan Sing, the sao pha, designed it as a long rectangle to fit the narrow ridge and provide a long veranda for pushing prams in rainy weather. His children 'donated' it to the government in 1974, and it is now a hospital. On a nearby hill is a **monastery**, with good views.

A cobbled track leads up behind the town, past typical wooden carved houses that cling to the steep hillside, to a couple of paya, a monastery and the green, shady reservoir that supplies Namhsan with water. It is possible to make **day treks** to Shan and Palaung villages nearby.

If you attempt coming up here in December or January, consider buying a jacket or thick blanket in Hsipaw before you set out. Once the sun goes down the temperature drops like a stone.

Places to Stay & Eat Namhsan has no guesthouses, but **Daw May Saw Nu** and **Daw Saw Mya** have been given permission to put foreigners up for a few hundred kyat a night. They will register you with immigration.

There are several **Chinese restaurants** along the narrow main street. Like the rest of the town, they close early (about 9pm). There are a limited number of **noodle stalls** for breakfast.

Getting There & Away Trucks and buses leave Hsipaw and return from Namhsan when the amount of passengers and cargo warrant a run. Check with Ko Zaw Tun (Mr Book) in Hsipaw to find out where the truck or bus is parked while waiting for passengers. Tickets cost about K800. Breakdowns are common and you may be better off trying to hire a pick-up in Hsipaw. The old road from Namhsan to Kyaukme is not passable by car.

LASHIO

လားရှိုး

☎ 082

This township of mostly Shan-Chinese and Chinese inhabitants is located at the southern end of the infamous Burma Road. Until the early 1990s Lashio was off-limits to foreigners because of its proximity to China – and the hated Chinese communists – as well as ethnic insurgent territory. Since the 1950s, the town has been flanked by the SSA to the west and south, the Kachin Independence Army (KIA) to the north and the Wa fighters of the Burmese Communist Party (BCP) to the east. Fragile truces with most of these groups since 1989, along with the tremendous boost in trade with China, led to an announcement in 1992 that the town of Lashio – and the town only – would be open to foreign visitors.

Shan insurgents are still around, and you're not likely to be allowed beyond the military checkpoints at the northeastern edge of town without special permission from the regional army command. Although the Myanmar government allows foreigners to travel from China to Lashio with permits obtained at the consulate in Kunming, it doesn't sanction travel in the opposite direction (see the Getting There & Away chapter and Mu-se in the Around Lashio section later in this chapter).

Lashio is in a mountain basin at 855m – clouds may form and deliver rain at almost any time of the year. It is divided into two main districts, Lashio Lay (Little Lashio) and Lashio Gyi (Big Lashio), connected by Theinni Rd. Lashio Lay is the newer and bigger of the two districts.

Information

The main post office is opposite the Lashio Motel on Mandalay-Lashio road at the corner of Puta Rd (Station Rd). Telephone and telegraph services are available at the Lashio telephone office on the main road between Lashio Lay and Lashio Gyi. Although direct dialling is only possible within the city (you can direct dial *to* Lashio

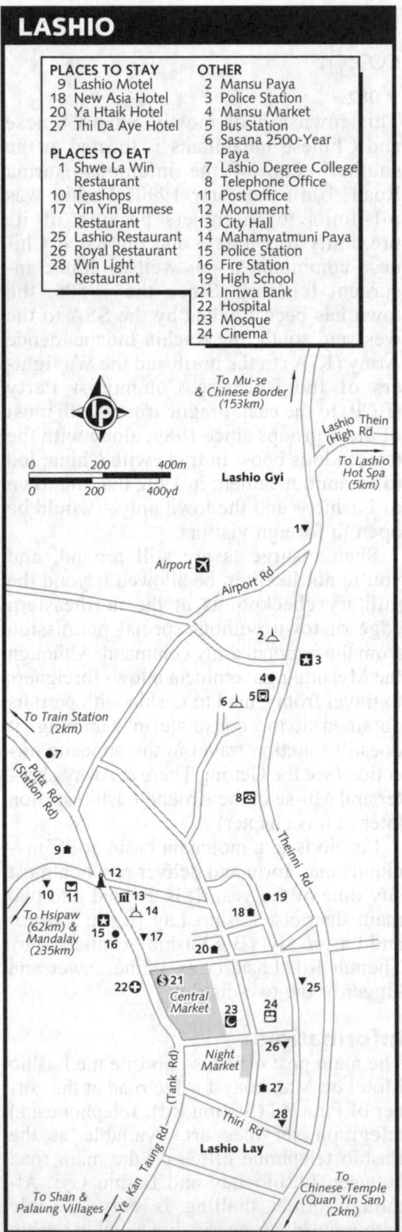

from other places), overseas and trunk calls must be made through the operator, or at the Lashio Motel and Ya Htaik Hotel (see Places to Stay later in this section).

Markets

There's a large **main market** in central Lashio Lay and a smaller one called **Mansu Market** *(Theinni/Hsenwi Rd)* closer to Lashio Gyi. The central market has just about everything, while Mansu Market focuses on fresh produce and foodstuffs. Some visitors to Lashio expect its markets to be very exotic and colourful – if you want to see people from various ethnic groups participating, you're better off in Hsipaw or Kengtung.

Other Attractions

Mansu Paya stands between Lashio Lay and Lashio Gyi on a hill to the western side of Theinni Rd, and is said to be over 250 years old. It is unremarkable, except for the fact that it has no planetary post for Monday; the Monday-born pay homage to the main Buddha image instead. More impressive is the **Sasana 2500-Year (Pyi Lon Chantha) Paya**, reportedly built by the last Shan sao pha in the area, Sao Hon Phan. One of the shrines in the paya complex contains a Bagan-era Buddha image. A second stupa of similar name, **New Pyi Lon Chantha Paya**, sits on Mya Kantha Hill in the northern part of town and offers good views of the city. The latter is also known as Kyaw Hein's Paya because the famous Burmese film actor of the same name paid for its construction. The newly built **Mahamyatmuni Paya**, next to the City Hall, is quite colourful from the street but looks less interesting the closer you get to it.

More interesting than any of the Buddhist shrines in town is the large and busy **Quan Yin San Temple** in Lashio Lay. Built around 40 years ago, it's the main Chinese temple in Lashio and possibly the largest in Myanmar; the steady traffic here bears testimony to Lashio's substantial Chinese population. Nearby is a popular new paya, **Hsu Taung Pye**.

Places to Stay

Once, just about any hotel or guesthouse in Lashio seemed prepared to accept foreign guests. Things are more regulated now, but it's still worth asking. Rates quoted vary between kyat and US dollars, and are sometimes quoted in both.

Ya Htaik Hotel *(☎ 22655; Bogyoke Rd; rooms with shared bathroom US$5, with private bathroom & TV US$15, with fridge US$20)*, a newly built modern Chinese-style place, has spartan but clean budget rooms (some without windows) and larger rooms with the usual amenities.

New Asia Hotel *(☎ 23622; San Khaung Rd; singles/doubles with shared bathroom K1000/1500, with private bathroom K1500/2000)*, northeast of the central market, is a modern four-storey place that has simple rooms with attached bathroom, as well as a few dark rooms with common bathroom.

Lashio Motel *(☎ 21702, 22763; singles & doubles US$15)*, a three-storey motel at the intersection of the Mandalay-Lashio road and Station Rd, has clean, spacious and quiet rooms with a view of the hills. All rooms come with air-con, TV, fridge, toilet and hot-water shower. Prices include breakfast. Favoured by visiting Chinese businesspeople, the motel features an attached karaoke lounge and expensive restaurant.

Thi Da Aye Hotel *(☎ 22165; 218 Thiri Rd; singles & doubles US$15)* has clean and spacious single and double rooms with fan, attached hot-water shower and toilet, plus a nice view of the surrounding hills. Some rooms face a nearby mosque, where the call to prayer begins at 4am.

Places to Eat

Chinese and Shan eateries are abundant in Lashio Lay. The famous **Lashio Restaurant**, a block east of the market, is one of the most reliable for both kinds of cuisine.

Royal Restaurant, on the corner southeast of the cinema, does Chinese food as well as several different types of satay. Cheap draught beer is also available here.

For Yunnanese Muslim (look for the number 786) cuisine, try the **Win Light Restaurant** *(Thiri Rd)*, around the corner from the Thi Da Aye Hotel.

Yin Yin Burmese Restaurant, south of Mahamyatmuni Paya, is the best place for Bamar food – there are also a few Shan and Chinese dishes available.

There are also many **Shan restaurants**, large and small, near the central market on Ye Kan Taung Rd (Tank Rd), and a row of good **teashops** west of the post office. In the evenings a **night market** sets up on the road leading south from the southeastern corner of the market.

There are fewer restaurants in Lashio Gyi, but **Shwe La Win Restaurant** is very good for Chinese and Shan dishes.

Getting There & Away

Air Although Lashio has an airport and MA allegedly flies there once weekly from Mandalay (US$45), it's better to take the train.

Bus From Mandalay there are buses to Lashio (around K3500, eight hours) that operate from the central/main bus centre near the corner of 26th and 82nd Sts. Buses operated by five different companies depart daily between 4am and 6am. Buy tickets at least one day before to get a seat. Buses from Lashio to Mandalay leave at 6am. To break up the trip, it's a good idea to schedule at least a day's stopover in Pyin U Lwin or Hsipaw along the way. The main bus station in Lashio stands on Theinni Rd south of Mansu Paya and near the Mansu Market.

Pick-up Foreigners are not allowed to take pick-ups from Mandalay to Lashio, but it's still possible to travel between Pyin U Lwin and Lashio (K2500) on pick-ups run by the May-Shio company. It takes seven hours going from Pyin U Lwin up to Lashio, an hour less coming down.

Van & Car Small air-con vans (Toyota Super-roofs) travel from Mandalay to Lashio (K6000 rear seats, K8000 at the front); these deliver their passengers door-to-door, but they fill up fast. You can also hire your own car and driver in Mandalay to make the one-way trip for about US$40. A three- or four-day round trip between Mandalay and Lashio costs US$30 to US$40 per day. Inquire at the Nylon Hotel or the Royal Guest House. As usual, rates vary according to the price of petrol.

The road entrances to Lashio from Mandalay and from Mu-se are supposed to close at 6pm. In practice, though, there seems to be plenty of night-time travel in both directions.

Train Since the Mandalay-Lashio road has been upgraded, travelling by bus is much faster (and cheaper) than by train. As usual, though, the train is the better alternative for those who are interested in beautiful scenery and a chance to meet the locals. The No 131 Up leaves Mandalay at 4.45am and arrives in Lashio around 7pm – when it's not delayed by track conditions (late arrivals aren't unusual). The Lashio train departs for Mandalay at 5am, and is very cold in the wee hours of the morning during the cool season.

Along the way you'll crawl across the famous Gokteik Viaduct (see the Pyin U Lwin to Lashio section earlier in this chapter) and wind around four monumental switchbacks. This route was long known among the Burmese as the black-market railway line because of all the contraband goods smuggled on board in both directions. Today, more and more of the trade consists of medicine, TVs and other taxable items from China.

The Mandalay to Lashio fare costs US$6 for ordinary class, US$12 in the only 1st-class (a step down from upper) coach on the train. From Pyin U Lwin the fare drops to US$10. (Officially, ordinary class isn't available to foreigners, but if 1st class is full, it's worth asking. In a pinch, you can just board the train and wait for the ticket collector to come by.)

Tickets for this route can be bought from one to seven days ahead of time, and they sell out very quickly. In Lashio, the train station lies 3km northwest of the centre of Lashio Lay.

Getting Around

The airport is in Lashio Gyi. A taxi pick-up from the airport into town costs around K800.

Pick-ups circulate between the train station, Lashio Lay and Lashio Gyi for K50 per person.

Small vans and taxi pick-ups with black-numbered numberplates park at the Lashio Motel and central market in Lashio Lay, as well as at the train station and airfield.

AROUND LASHIO

If you want to leave town via the northern entrance (toward Mu-se), you must have a permit from the regional military headquarters. Taxi drivers or staff at the New Asia Hotel and Lashio Motel in Lashio can sometimes help to arrange these.

Hot Springs & Caves

Lashio Hot Spa *(admission US$3; open 8am-8pm)* is a hot spring about 5km northeast of Lashio Gyi via Theinni Rd. If you've come from Mandalay or Pyin U Lwin during the cold season, you might want to head there to warm up. The admission fee gives you up to 30 minutes of bath time. There are also outdoor pools. **Vendors** on the premises sell Chinese and Shan snacks.

Although you're not officially allowed to visit them, **Peiqchinmyaing Caves**, 72km northeast of Lashio, feature Buddha-filled caverns up to 793m deep.

Mu-se
မူဆယ်

The Shweli River forms the border between Myanmar's Shan State and China's Yunnan Province at Mu-se. Although it extends all the way to Lashio (and to some degree beyond), the Chinese influence is of course stronger here than elsewhere in the Shan State. You're not likely to be allowed to visit Mu-se from the south. However, package tours entering from China have received permission to enter Myanmar at Mu-se, and travel south to Lashio.

As Mu-se continues to prosper, the situation may open up for foreign independent travellers.

Mu-se's once sleepy frontier-town atmosphere has been swept away by the bustling border trade with China. The town's electricity is supplied by China, so the power cuts common around the country are unheard of here. Chinese tourists flock to Mu-se to shop, keeping the moneychangers busy.

Trucks from Myanmar cross to China with dried fish, rattan, fresh beans and fruit – including tamarind, which is then processed into a soft drink and sold back to Myanmar at a tidy profit. On the return trip from China, the same trucks carry electrical goods and spare parts, cement and other building components. Smuggled goods include teak, cigarettes and alcohol.

The territory surrounding Mu-se is one of the primary pipelines for opium and heroin smuggling from the Shan State to Yunnan Province, and from there to Hong Kong. East of Mu-se, along the border, there are reportedly several major heroin refineries, as well as methamphetamine labs. This area to the east is strictly off-limits to foreigners.

The area around Mu-se is thought to have been the centre of one of the first consolidated Shan kingdoms (called Kawsumpi, or Mong Mao) as early as the 7th century. From this point the Shan dispersed to other river valleys to the west, east and south.

Cut by the Shweli River, the verdant **Namkham Valley**, southwest of Mu-se, is a beautiful patchwork of bamboo and rice paddies. Most of the people living off the land in this area are Shan and other Thai ethnic groups. Namkham itself is renowned as the WWII-era location of Dr Gordon Seagrave's American Medical Center. Doctor Seagrave renounced his associations with the American Baptist Mission in order to offer medical service free of Christian proselytisation; people from all over the northern frontier states emerged from his medical centre trained as doctors and nurses. He and his staff tended to wounded soldiers around the clock during the Allies' siege of Myitkyina in 1944. In 1951 Seagrave was briefly imprisoned by the post-independence Burmese government for his alleged associations with Kachin rebels. After his release he remained in Namkham till his death in 1965.

Places to Stay & Eat The most popular place to stay is **Muse Hotel** *(singles/doubles US$10/15)*. Rooms in this privatised 40-room place have attached hot-water bathroom and air-con, but are noisy and a tad grubby.

There are cheaper places to stay (although not officially licensed to accept foreigners), including the **Yan Yan Guest House**, **Tokyo Motel** and **Lucky Hotel**.

If you are lucky enough to get permission to visit Namkham, you'll find cheap but rustic accommodation at the **Cherry Guest House**, **Yadana Theingi Guest House** and **Friendship Guest House**.

Getting There & Away From Mu-se it's four or five hours by pick-up or car along the famed Burma Road to Lashio, a distance of 176km. With the increased traffic between Mu-se and Mandalay, the road to Lashio has livened up with businesses catering to the truck drivers. Pick-ups (K1000 per person) start at about 6am in either direction – but be forewarned: they're impossibly packed with people and cargo, and very uncomfortable. Air-con shared taxis are available for K2500 per person. Hitching is possible, but any driver who picks you up will want some money for fuel, plus a little extra for stopping.

Since 1992 there has been a bridge over the Shweli River (called Ruili River on the Chinese side), which you'll be permitted to cross from China – if you've brought the proper paperwork from Kunming. There are also one-day border passes available to foreigners for US$10. From Kunming, Ruili can be reached by air (50 minutes) or by bus (24 hours). At time of writing it was not possible to cross the border from Myanmar into China, however.

Kachin State

ကချင်ပြည်နယ်

Myanmar's northernmost state borders India and China to the north and east, the Sagaing Division to the west and the Shan

State to the south. Major rivers flowing north to south – the Malihka, Mehka, Tanainghka and Ayeyarwady (Irrawaddy) – form fertile upland valleys where most of the state's meagre population lives. Above these valleys stand the nation's highest mountain peaks, part of the southern edge of the Himalaya.

Most people living in the Kachin State are of Tibeto-Burman origin, representing four main language groups: Jinghpaw, Maru, Yawyin and Lisu. The Jinghpaw, who are generally known as Kachin, are the majority, and since their language can be written (using a Roman alphabet system devised by 19th-century Christian missionaries), Jinghpaw has become a lingua franca for the state.

Although many Kachin people nowadays are nominally Christian or Buddhist, some of the old beliefs are practised syncretically. Under the British and today, to a much lesser degree, under the SPDC, the Kachin tribes have continued to practice their own form of semidemocratic civil administration, *gumlao-gumsa*. One of the distinctions of this system is that the youngest in the family – rather than the eldest – is the legal heir when a parent dies.

Until the early 1990s, the Kachin Independence Organisation (KIO) and its tactical arm, the KIA, operated throughout the state with near impunity. Following a 1993 truce with the Yangon government, the KIA has ceased active insurgency. The Burmese government, however, still considers the state a sensitive area and the movements of both foreigners and Burmese are strictly curtailed.

The jade trade may also have something to do with travel restrictions in the state. During the Konbaung era, roughly 75% of all Kachin jade ended up in China. China is still the biggest market for Burmese jadeite, which is preferred over China's nephrite, although both minerals can be called jade.

The Manao

မနောပွဲ

Traditionally, the Jinghpaw are animists who recognise a spirit world presided over by Karai Kasang, a supreme deity who requires animal sacrifice. *Duwa* (hereditary chieftains) maintain ceremonial and cultural leadership, especially with regard to the *manao* (also spelt *manau* or *manaw*) – the important festivals held periodically to placate or pay homage to the Jinghpaw nat. There are several types of manao, depending on the region and time of year. One of the most common types, *sup manao*, looks towards the future, ensuring good weather for farming and serving to ward off danger and general ill-fortune; *padang manao*, on the other hand, celebrates a past victory or success.

MARTIN HARRIS

For all their hard work as the traditional tool of the Southeast Asian rice farmer, buffaloes usually meet with a grisly end.

A typical manao involves the sacrifice of 29 cows and/or buffaloes, one for each of the 28 Jinghpaw nat plus one dedicated to all of them. Participants dance to music played on a large doubled-headed drum, brass gong, cymbals and buffalo-horn oboe. These festivities are centred on *manao-taing* (brightly painted totems

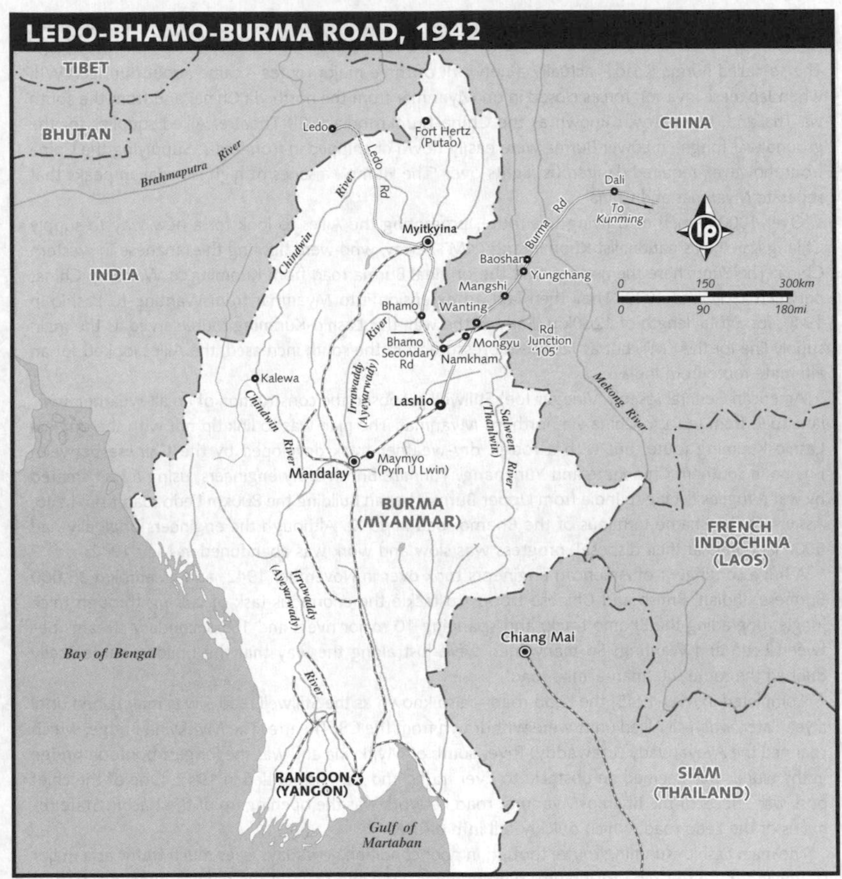

strung with banners of red, black and white) whose colours are considered most attractive to the nat. Dancers often carry fans in imitation of bird feathers; the lead dancer wears a headdress designed to resemble the head and beak of a great hornbill. Other dances mimic the movements of horse-riding, fishing and cattle herding. There is much drinking of local *churu* (rice beer) and feasting on *shat kada* (special meal packets).

On 10 January (Kachin State Day) a major manao in Myitkyina draws Kachin groups from all over the state and beyond.

MYITKYINA

မြစ်ကြီးနား

☎ 074

Set in a flat valley that is extremely hot in the dry season and very rainy during the monsoon, Myitkyina (By The Big River) itself is not very interesting. However, since the 25km-radius travel restriction was lifted, the town now holds possibilities as the starting point for visits to the many Kachin villages in the area. Kachin men living in the lowlands wear dark blue and green longyi, while those from the mountains wear trousers. The

Burma Road

The so-called Burma Road – actually a network of three major routes – came about during WWII, when Japanese invasion forces closed in on Myanmar from the north via China, and from the south via Thailand. In what was known as the China-Burma-India (CBI) Theatre, Allied supplies for the ground war fought in Lower Burma were easily flown or shipped in from India. Supplying the China front, however, required dangerous flights over 'The Hump', a series of high Himalayan peaks that separate Myanmar and China.

Over 1000 airmen died flying this route, prompting the Allies to look for a new way to supply Chiang Kai-shek's nationalist Kuomintang (KMT) army, who were fighting the Japanese in western China. The Yunnanese themselves built the original Burma road from Kunming to Wanting, China, between 1937 and 1939. They then laid an extension into Myanmar from Wanting to Lashio in 1940, for a total length of 1200km. Early in the war, this Lashio-Kunming route served as the main supply line for the KMT, but as Japanese pressure from the south increased, the Allies looked for an alternate route from India.

American General Joseph 'Vinegar Joe' Stillwell proposed the construction of an all-weather, two-lane road from India to China via northern Myanmar. The plan was to link up not with the original Lashio-Kunming route, but with a rough dry-weather track developed by the Chinese between Bhamo in southern Chin State and Yunchang, Yunnan. British army engineers, using a trail created by war refugees fleeing to India from Upper Burma, began building the 800km Ledo road from Ledo, Assam, to the Bhamo terminus of the Bhamo road in 1942. Although the engineers originally had 5000 labourers at their disposal, progress was slow and work was abandoned in May 1942.

A huge contingent of American engineers took over in November 1942, and assembled 35,000 Burmese, Indian, British and Chinese troops to tackle the enormous task of cutting through thick jungle, upgrading the Bhamo track, and spanning 10 major rivers and 155 secondary streams between Ledo and Wanting. So many men were lost along the way that the builders sardonically dubbed the route the 'man-a-mile road'.

Completed in May 1945, the Ledo road – also known as the Stillwell road – was maintained until a year later, when all Allied units were withdrawn from the CBI Theatre. The Myitkyina Bridge, which spanned the Ayeyarwady (Irrawaddy) River south of Myitkyina and was the longest pontoon bridge in the world, was deemed an obstacle to river traffic and was dismantled in 1947. One of the chief post-war effects of the Bhamo-Myanmar road network was the opening up of the Kachin State remains of the Ledo road, which quickly fell into disuse.

The main Lashio-Kunming route, though in poor condition nowadays, sees much traffic as a major smuggling route to China for opium, heroin, gems, jade and teak. In the reverse direction, traders bring finished goods, such as auto parts, pharmaceuticals, processed foods, clothing and homewares. The Yangon government has made such trade – legal and illegal – much easier than in the past by making the border crossing at Mu-se a legal overland port of entry from China.

Joe Cummings

women wear distinctive red and black headdresses, but colourful fashions are reserved for weddings and festivals, events that make any village visit much more compelling.

Hsu Taung Pye Zedidaw is a pretty, gilded, 'wish-fulfilling' stupa on the banks of the Ayeyarwady River. The larger **Andawshin Paya** boasts a silver-plated zedi said to contain tooth relics and a Buddha footprint; there are a couple of adjacent monasteries. Other religious structures of interest include the **Sri Saraswati Gurkha Hindu Temple**, **Ja-me Mosque** and a Taoist-Buddhist **Chinese temple**.

Most of the Kachin people living in and around Myitkyina have been strongly influenced by missionaries and there are now around 15 **churches** in town – mostly Baptist with a few Methodist and Catholic ones sprinkled in. About 14km north is **Praying Mountain**, a sacred site for Kachin and Lisu Baptists and the location of a bible school and seminary. The town is also home to a small Nepali community.

Many older Kachin people speak English as they were educated in mission schools. There are also a few elderly WWII veterans around who like to talk about Merrill's Marauders and the various campaigns fought in the region.

Only a handful of visitors have visited the **Kachin State Cultural Museum** *(Youngyi Rd; admission US$2; open 10am-3pm Tues-Sun)* since it was built in 1994. On display is the usual collection of costumes and Kachin and Shan artefacts, such as pipes, baskets, fishing nets, looms and musical instruments. Upstairs are the conch, chests and a home-made cannon belonging to the former sawbwa of Hkamti Long (Putao). Most labels are in Burmese.

Myit-son

မြစ်ဆုံ

Myit-son, the confluence of the Mehka and Malihka Rivers, 43km north of Myitkyina, forms the beginning of the great Ayeyarwady River. A hotel overlooking the water, to replace the government rest house burned down by Kachin insurgents in the 1960s, has been planned for years. The return-trip taxi fare is about K8000. It's an hour each way.

Another spot formerly off-limits is the jade-mining centre of **Hpakan**, 148km west of Myitkyina. Permission is required and can usually be arranged by any hotel in Myitkyina. The first 80km to Kamaing is via a sealed road; the rest is an unsealed dry-weather road. If you're only interested in buying jade, however, there's plenty in Myitkyina. Southwest of Kamaing is the huge and serene **Indawgyi Lake**.

Places to Stay & Eat

Hotel and restaurant infrastructure in Myitkyina lags behind that found in more-touristed regions of the country, and rates are high.

Popa Hotel *(☎ 21746; singles/doubles US$8/14)* at the train station has simple rooms with a fan and a common bathroom.

YMCA *(beds per person US$5)*, near the Popa Hotel, is friendly, quieter and has a clean, simple dorm room with fan and common bathroom.

Pantsun Hotel *(☎ 22748, fax 22749; singles/doubles US$25)*, a newish, four-storey place behind the YMCA, is the only hotel in town with all the amenities. Comfortable rooms feature air-con, attached hot-water bathroom, satellite TV, IDD phone and fridge.

Sumpra Hotel & Restaurant *(☎ 22298; singles/doubles US$56/69)*. Owned by a cultural minister of the Kachin state, the Sumpra is a collection of modern bungalows on the riverbank. It mainly caters to tour groups. The three-room bungalows have hot-water bath, satellite TV and fridge. For what you get, it's certainly not worth these prices.

Most of the restaurants in town serve Chinese and Kachin food.

Shwe Ainsi (Ein Zay) doesn't look like much but serves quite reasonable food.

Also good is the **Chili Restaurant**, owned by a Ghurkha family.

Getting There & Away

You can reach Myitkyina by air, train or boat – although there are drawbacks to each method of travel, and the town's inaccessibility, combined with the limited number of sights, mean that few visitors bother. Officially, you can't arrive by car.

Air YA flies to Myitkyina from Yangon (US$90, 1¼ hours) with a stopover in Mandalay on Tuesday, Thursday and Sunday. The flight from Mandalay to Myitkyina costs US$70. On Wednesday, MA makes the flight from Yangon to Myitkyina via Bhamo (US$145). The 25-minute flight from Bhamo costs US$35. MA often doesn't fly according to schedule, and tickets are difficult to obtain. There is an MA office in town.

Train The No 55 Up train from Mandalay leaves daily at 1.50pm and is supposed to take 25 hours to reach Myitkyina. In practice it often takes longer – up to 40 hours due to the poor condition of the rail bed. In early 1995 a derailment at the railway bridge near Mohnyin killed over 100 passengers, and a similar accident in 2001 is said to have killed at least that many. The fare is US$33 for an upper-class sleeping berth, and US$27 for a seat. The No 41 Up train from Mandalay departs at 5.45pm and is slightly cheaper: US$26 for a sleeper and US$24 for a seat. Tickets should be purchased at least three days in advance, especially if you want to book a sleeper.

Two private companies run somewhat better trains to Myitkyina on certain days of the week. The problem is that they use the same track, and are therefore subject to the same delays.

Mehka Mandalar Railways departs from Mandalay on Wednesday and Sunday at 4.40pm, arriving in Myitkyina around 24 hours later – usually. A seat costs US$35, or you can get a sleeper for US$40.

Malikha Mandalar Railways charges the same prices as Mehka Mandalar and its trains depart on Monday and Friday at 4.40pm. In the opposite direction, these privately owned trains leave Myitkyina on Tuesday, Thursday and Saturday. Tickets for both companies can be purchased at window Nos 7 and 8 at the Mandalay train station. For the government trains tickets are sold at window Nos 5 and 6. All the signs at the ticket windows are in Burmese (including the numbers) so you might have to ask around to figure things out. Better yet, book the tickets through your hotel or guesthouse and save yourself the frustration.

Road There are no regular public transport services along the road between Mogok and Myitkyina, as road conditions are quite bad between Mogok and Bhamo.

The 188km road between Bhamo and Myitkyina, which runs parallel to the China-Myanmar border, is passable in all weather. Strictly speaking, you're not supposed to arrive in Myitkyina by road. This may change as 'security' improves. Reportedly, the fare for the four- to five-hour trip is K2500 per passenger. We know of a couple of travellers who tried to make the trip from Mandalay by car via Mohnyin, only to be turned back and put on the train less than 160km from Myitkyina.

Boat & Road You could try to catch a ferry north from Mandalay as far as Bhamo, and then continue to Myitkyina by road, though the road was closed to foreigners at time of writing. The ferry trip is fairly straightforward (see the Bhamo and Katha sections later in this chapter for details).

Getting Around

Trishaws and Mazda taxis are easy to hire in Myitkyina, and the YMCA will lend bicycles. Taxis are available from the airport and opposite the market. For trips further afield (eg, to Indawgyi) you will need to arrange an excursion with a registered tour guide and the necessary permission.

BHAMO

ဗန်းမော်

Bhamo (ba-**maw**), 186km south of Myitkyina, is perhaps a bit more leafy and charming than the latter. The **daily market** draws Lisu, Kachin and Shan participants from the surrounding countryside but, as in Myitkyina, there is little to see in the way of traditional costumes. A portion of the old city walls of **Sampanago**, an old Shan kingdom, can be seen around 3km north of town – though the ride out there by horse cart is of more interest than the overgrown pile of rubble. To get there, tell the horse-cart driver to go to Bhamo Myo Haung (Old City of Bhamo). **Theindawgyi Paya**, in the town centre, features an older stupa.

Places to Stay & Eat

Friendship Hotel (*☎ Bhamo 277; rooms with fan & shared bathroom per person K700, windowless basement K600, singles/doubles with private hot-water bathroom, air-con, TV & fridge K3000/4000*) has a monopoly on foreign visitors – it's the only place in town that accepts them. Despite the lack of

NORTHEASTERN MYANMAR

competition, it has decent and clean rooms, though the electricity is not always powerful enough to run the air-conditioning.

Food in Bhamo is limited to a handful of eateries. On the main drag, the Hindu-run **Yamona Tea Shop** has good samosas and a satellite TV tuned in to a Hindi channel. Good Chinese food is available from the **Sein Sein Restaurant**, opposite the cinema.

Getting There & Away

Air During the high season (November to February), YA flies from Yangon to Bhamo via Mandalay (US$140). Between Mandalay and Bhamo the cost is US$47. MA flies to Bhamo from Mandalay (US$55) on Monday and Thursday. This flight originates in Yangon – the fare all the way from Yangon to Bhamo via Mandalay is US$155. It then continues to Myitkyina (US$35 from Bhamo).

Boat Public ferries ply the Ayeyarwady River between Mandalay and Bhamo (US$9/36/54 lower deck/upper deck/cabin) thrice weekly. When the water level is optimum, the upriver journey takes 1½ days, but when the river's low it can take as long as 2½ days. See Getting There & Away in the Katha section later for more details.

The scenery along the upper reaches of the Ayeyarwady is very fine, especially north of Shwegu, where the riverbanks are lush with bamboo and other flora and the boat passes through steep rock gorges.

The Inland Water Transport office (where you can buy ticket for the boat) in Bhamo is located opposite the roundabout near Tat Twin Kyaung (military monastery).

Getting Around

Horse carts to Bhamo Myo Haung can be hired anywhere in town and cost about K400 per person for the round trip. Bhamo is small enough to see on foot.

KATHA

ကသာ

In the Sagaing Division and situated on the Ayeyarwady River roughly halfway up to Myitkyina, Katha is an attractive town with a mixed population of Bamar, Kachin and Chin, plus a small Nepali minority. At first glance it looks quite similar to Myitkyina and Bhamo further to the north, but Katha has a little-known distinction. Eric Blair (known to the world by his pen name George Orwell) was posted here from December 1926 to June 1927 as a colonial police officer, and Katha was the setting for his novel *Burmese Days*. Because of the book's harsh criticisms of the British colonial system, Orwell's London editors rejected it; they later relented after the novel was published in America to rave reviews – but only after Orwell agreed to make certain changes to the story in order to make the setting and characters of the novel difficult to trace. Thus Katha was renamed 'Kyauktada' in the novel.

Although Katha has grown quite a bit since Orwell's time, most of the sites mentioned in the novel are still there, including the police station, the huge walled jail, and the old hospital where Orwell spent some time recuperating from dengue fever and befriended an Indian doctor named Krishnaswami (renamed Dr Veraswami in the novel).

Most interestingly, the old **British Club**, around which much of the novel revolves, is now the headquarters for an agricultural co-op. The club library and billiard table are long gone, but the tennis court is still in use and this is the easiest way to find the former club – ask any local for directions to the tennis court and then follow the path beside it to the wooden building directly behind it. Don't be surprised if the co-op employees seemed bemused by your visit – when we discovered the club during a trip to Katha in 1999, we were amazed to find that the locals had no idea that their humble agricultural co-op was the principal setting for a novel by one of the 20th century's greatest authors.

Places to Stay & Eat

Katha gets few foreign visitors and the rustic accommodation reflects this. The town's three hotels are all located on Kana Rd near the jetty.

NORTHEASTERN MYANMAR

Nedigantha Guest House *(rooms with shared bathroom per person US$5)*, directly opposite the boat landing, is the cheapest and friendliest of Katha's hotels. The wooden rooms are rustic but comfortable and there's a sitting area and small balcony overlooking the jetty – a nice place from which to view the pandemonium that erupts whenever a passenger ferry pulls in. Toilet and shower rooms are downstairs. Very little English is spoken here and the sign reads simply 'Guest House'.

Annawah Guest House *(rooms with shared bathroom per person US$6)*, two doors down from the Nedigantha Guest House, is not particularly good value. Rooms are mere wooden cubicles and the staff are indifferent.

Ayeyarwadi Hotel *(formerly Shwe Naga Hotel; rooms with fan & bathroom US$8-10)*, about 20m to the south of the jetty, was recently renovated and is in a concrete building. It's fairly clean but has little charm.

Katha has a handful of simple Chinese and Bamar restaurants.

Myanmar Restaurant, next door to the Nedigantha Guest House, is a tiny eatery serving Bamar cuisine and Chinese dishes.

A no-name **Bamar restaurant** next to the police station has a selection of Bamar curries. Beside the high school is a good **teashop** that has the usual breakfast tea snacks.

Getting There & Away

Boat The most enjoyable way to reach Katha is by passenger ferry on the Ayeyarwady River from Mandalay or Bhamo. Ferries depart from Mandalay on Monday, Thursday and Saturday at 6am and arrive at Katha around 7am the next day. The ferries are relatively new Chinese-built vessels and have three classes. Lower-deck class is US$7 but there are no chairs provided: you must bring a mat and camp on the lower deck, which is not recommended during the winter months when the temperatures can dip below freezing. Upper-deck class is US$21 and is in a lounge area forward on the second level of the ferry. Mats are also needed but since it's enclosed, blankets aren't as necessary during the cool season. Cabin class costs US$28 and is the most comfortable option. Each cabin has two beds, a sink and a fan. Toilet and bathrooms are located toward the rear, but passengers in cabin class are given keys to their own set of toilet and bathing facilities, which are not shared by the deck-class passengers (a boon if you're squeamish about filthy toilets – the deck-class facilities tend to get fouled rather quickly).

The ferry from Bhamo leaves Monday, Thursday and Saturday at 6am and arrives at Katha around 2pm the same day. Between Bhamo and Katha the fares are US$4 for lower-deck class and US$14 for upper-deck class. The Ayeyarwady scenery between Katha and Bhamo is quite spectacular, especially north of Shwegu when the boat passes through a steep gorge and gibbons can be heard calling from the thick jungle. Pods of rare Irrawaddy dolphins are sometimes spotted north of Katha when the river is low. The Inland Water Transport office in Katha is located opposite the jetty.

Train Katha can be reached by trains from Mandalay or Myitkyina, which make a stop at Naba, approximately 25km west of Katha. A railway spur goes from Naba to Katha, but there is only one train a day and it leaves at 5.30am. Most people opt instead to take a truck between the two towns, which is cheaper and much faster. Trucks wait at the Naba station to take passengers to Katha (K800) whenever a train arrives from Mandalay or Myitkyina.

Government trains from Mandalay to Naba (US$18 upper class) leave daily at 1.50pm and 5.45pm and the trip takes about twelve hours (if you're lucky). Foreigners are not allowed in the lower-class cars but, unless you're some kind of masochist, you wouldn't want to ride them anyway – they're little better than cattle cars. Tickets for the government train can be purchased at window Nos 5 and 6 at the Mandalay

BERNARD NAPTHINE
Yum! Tea snacks at a teashop in Nyaungshwe, Shan State

RYAN FOX
Mystical Mt Popa, Mandalay

RYAN FOX
Shrine on Mt Popa, Mandalay

BERNARD NAPTHINE
Fishing on Inle Lake, Shan State

JERRY ALEXANDER
A lively game of *chinlon*, Inle Lake

BERNARD NAPTHINE
Floating Market on Inle Lake, Shan State

JERRY ALEXANDER

Vendors in Shan State

ANDERS BLOMQVIST

Walkways leading to the Pindaya Caves, Shan State

COREY WISE

Terraced rice paddies cover the hills outside Kengtung, Shan State.

BERNARD NAPTHINE

Sitting Buddha in Nanthe village, Shan State

BERNARD NAPTHINE

Temple detail, Nyaungshwe

railway station, but you might have to bring along a Burmese to help you buy them: signs are in Burmese only – and Arabic numerals are nowhere to be seen! Better yet, purchase your tickets through your hotel in Mandalay – most of them provide this service for their guests.

Two private companies also run trains between Mandalay and Myitkyina that make a stop in Naba. Trains operated by the Mehka Mandalar company depart on Wednesday and Sunday at 4.40pm. Upper-class seats are US$25. The Malikha Mandalar company runs trains on Monday and Friday and the fare and departure time are the same. These tickets can be bought at the Mandalay railway station at window Nos 7 and 8. These trains depart from Myitkyina for Naba on Saturday, Tuesday and Thursday.

Getting Around

So far nobody is renting bicycles in Katha, but it's a smallish town and is easily explored on foot. Trishaws can be hired for short trips. From the jetty to the market should cost about K200.

PUTAO

ပူတာအို

Putao and the surrounding area lie above the tropic of Cancer, in a zone characterised by subtropical conditions, up to 2000m; temperate rainforest from 2000m to 3000m; and subalpine snow forest that becomes alpine scrub, above 3000m. The highlands north of Putao are considered one of the most pristine Himalayan environments in Asia and could become a major ecotourism destination if made accessible to foreigners. The locals often refer to the surrounding peaks as the 'ice mountains'.

Putao itself is small and picturesque, with a population of about 10,000 people. The elevation is 402m above sea level. During the late British colonial era, a military post called Fort Hertz was based in Putao. By the end of WWII most Westerners used this name instead of Putao – it still appears on some older ma[...] the population of around [...] Kachin and Lisu, followed by Bamar, Shan and various other smaller tribal groups.

Things to See & Do

The army has a strong presence here, including its own nine-hole golf course near the military camp. At the **Myoma Market** in town there are bamboo and wooden handicrafts, and medicines made from local plants. On Sunday following morning mass, many in the church congregation go to the market to watch videos. The most interesting feature of the town is found next to the **Mahamuni Paya**, where the chime bell is made from the propeller of a wrecked WWII aircraft.

Hkakabo Razi stands 5889m high and is snow capped year-round. Satellite peaks in adjoining massifs include **Namni-Lka** (4664m) in the Adung Valley and **Diphuk-Ha** (4360m) in the Seingku Valley. A protected 'trans-frontier reserve' has been proposed by neighbouring countries.

Places to Stay & Eat

No 46 Light Infantry Division Rest House is a government-owned resthouse, which we won't review or recommend. Unfortunately, at the time of writing, it was the only accommodation in town that allowed non-Burmese guests.

The town has one Chinese restaurant, **Khamsuko**, near Myoma Market.

The **Yadanapon Tea Shop** serves a few tea snacks, at prices significantly higher than elsewhere in Myanmar.

Getting There & Away

Foreigners are not allowed to travel to Putao by road. Even with permission, the narrow, unsurfaced 356km road is passable only in dry weather.

With permission, you can fly to Putao. At the time of writing, MA was operating flights to Putao on a charter basis only, but this may change in the future. From Yangon it's around a four-hour flight, including stops in Mandalay and Myitkyina.

Kayah State

ကယားပြည်နယ်

This small state is wedged between the Shan State to the north and west, the Karen State to the west and south, and Thailand to the east. Eight ethnic groups reside in this mountainous state, including the Taungthu, Padaung, Yinbaw, Bre, and Kayah, who form the majority.

The culture of the Kayah people, also known as Karenni or Red Karen, appears to the outsider to be a blend of Kayin (Karen) and Shan influences. Hereditary chieftains called *saopya* have obvious similarities with the sao pha of the Shan, while bronze frog drums are used ceremonially as in the Kayin culture. Most of the Kayah are animist, although there are significant numbers of Christians and Buddhists as well. Animists, Buddhists and Christians alike participate in the annual Kuhtobo festival in May, which pays homage to the rain spirits.

The group most known outside Myanmar is the minority Padaung, whose women traditionally stack up to 22kg of brass rings around their necks. The rings depress the collarbone, making it look as if their necks have been unnaturally stretched. No-one knows for sure how the ring custom got started; one theory says it was to make the women's appearance strange enough that men from other tribes wouldn't pursue them. The Padaung also wear thin hoops, made of cane or lacquered cord, in bunches around their knees and calves.

Until the early 1990s, Kayah rebel groups controlled much of the eastern half of the state. The Myanmar government has concentrated on securing the capital, Loikaw, and the very important hydroelectric plant at nearby Lawpita. The recent ceasefire has allowed the government to build a railway between Aungban and Loikaw.

LOIKAW

လွိုင်ကော်

The Kayah State is open by permit only, and permits have yet to be given for the state capital, Loikaw – located near the state's northern tip at an elevation of just over 1200m.

If it ever opens for visitors, Loikaw has a colourful **Thirimingala Market**, frequented by members of several tribal groups, including the Padaung. Naungyar, towards the northern quarter of town, is inhabited by mostly Kayah people; now that a ceasefire with the insurgents is in effect, it's not unusual to see Kayah rebel soldiers in this area. Two small lakes and a stream add visual interest to the town. Visit the **Taungkwe Zedi** on Taungkwe, a twin-peaked mountain on the edge of town, for Loikaw vistas.

Twenty kilometres southeast of Loikaw is a huge hydroelectric facility built by the Japanese as war reparation. A dam impounds the Bilu Chaung (Bilu Canal), which flows from Inle Lake 120km to the north. The facility supplies most of the power in the national grid system and so is highly strategic. Nearby **Lawpita Falls** is said to be beautiful; however, it's in insurgent territory, so you're unlikely to be permitted to visit, despite the ceasefire.

Pinlaung, roughly halfway between Aungban and Loikaw, is the highest point on the road/railway route, at over 1500m. It's inhabited mainly by Pa-O and it can be quite cold in winter.

Places to Stay

Garden Hotel reportedly provides economy singles/doubles for US$10/15, and standard rooms for US$15/20.

Getting There & Away

At the time of writing, travel to Loikaw for foreigners was not permitted.

sometimes misty, light of dawn. Pilgrims chant, light candles and meditate all through the night. Men are permitted to walk along a short causeway and over a bridge spanning a chasm to the boulder and affix gold-leaf squares on the rock's surface. It's also said that if you wedge a short piece of wood or bamboo into the space between the bottom of the boulder and the cliff on which it rests, you can watch it flex as the boulder gently rocks back and forth.

A new terrace allows devotees to view the boulder from below. There are several other stupas and shrines scattered along the ridge at the top of Mt Kyaikto, though none is as impressive as Kyaiktiyo. The interconnecting trails, however, sometimes lead to unexpected views of the valleys below.

Kinpun, about 9km in from the highway and Kyaikto, lies at the base of the mountain. This is the starting point for either beginning the four-hour hike up or catching one of the frequent trucks-with-benches *(lain-ka)* up the winding road. The charge is K350 per person each way. Vehicles are not permitted near the top, so you still have about a 45-minute walk up to the stupa area. Along the way, you pass through an array of village vendors.

Although permits are no longer required, there is now a US$6 entrance fee to the stupa area, payable at the **tourist office** *(open 6am-6pm daily)* opposite the pilgrim truck-loading area. There is a table-and-chair checkpoint near the top, where you can also pay. By the way, your ticket is valid for 30 days, so you may visit again without paying the government another US$6.

Places to Stay

Although Kyaiktiyo can be visited as a d[...] trip from Bago, the advantage of sta[...] near the shrine is that you can catch [...] and sunrise – the most magical t[...] viewing the boulder shrine.

Golden Rock Hotel *(in Ya[...] 532553, fax 527379; eco[...] doubles US$24/30, standard [...] US$36/48)* is better value tha[...]

Hotel (see later in this section), with the exception that it's just up the path from the last truck stop – in other words, a 40-minute walk from the top. The attractive standard rooms have a TV, fridge and phone. The smaller economy rooms also have an attached bathroom.

Mountain View Motel *(in Yangon ☎/fax 01-533846; bungalow singles/doubles US$15/20, superior singles/doubles US$30/40)* is the best value of the upmarket places. It's closer to Kyaikto town than Kinpun at the foot of the hill, although you can usually get a free lift to either location. The very comfortable bungalow-type rooms have a fan and a cold-water shower. Larger 'superior' rooms have a desk and a hot-water shower. Breakfast is included with all rooms, and there is an attractive indoor/outdoor restaurant.

In the town of Kyaikto along the main road from Bago there are several guesthouses; none of them very appealing. Of the lot, the two-story **Nilar Guesthous[e]** *(rooms per person [K]3000)*, on the m[ain] road at the corner [o]f Hospital St, i[s the] most conveniently [lo]cated; Yangon-[bound] buses leave from i[n] front of the h[...] guesthouse has cu[...] rooms [...] and toilets are on the ground [...] nearby **La Min Th[a Gu]estho[use]** *([...] Rd)* is similar.

Closer to the s[...] places to stay are in Ki[npun] [...] of the new [...] gone-tom[...] worth **Thu G[...]** show[...] [...] value i[...] clean an[d] [...] **ar Zar G[...]** [K]600) is f[...] so far.

[...] **Sar Gue[...]** [...] is behi[...]

[Folded-over text from another page:] [...] fan [...]. The [...] Station [...] places to [...] ge. Many [...] the be [...] ere-today- [...] uses but three are [...] el to has separate [...] for. F[...] et facili[...] buse (singles/ [...] /6) is [...] managed place [...] pa vicinity. The [...] House (singles & [...] and the cheapest of [...] (singles & doubles [...] opular Sea Sar Res- [...] ant & Ba[...] s are very basic, with [...] ooden slats [...] squito nets. [...] Travellers [...] to avoid government- [...] owned hot[...] uld stay clear of the

SOUTHEASTERN MYANMAR

Kyaikto Hotel, along the ridge at the top of Mt Kyaikto.

Foreigners aren't permitted to stay in the *zayat* (rest shelters) for pilgrims, nor are they permitted to camp in wooded areas on the mountain.

Places to Eat

Because Kinpun is the starting point for this popular Burmese site, there are a number of good **Chinese and Bamar restaurants** up and down the main street. In addition to the **food stalls** at the Kinpun base camp and along the footpaths, there's a decent **teashop** opposite the front entrance of the Kyaikto Hotel at the summit. In addition to the usual teashop snacks such as flat bread and deep-fried samosas, the tiny kitchen can make fried noodles and fried rice.

If you're coming by road from Bago, **Yadana Oo Restaurant**, just northwest of the town of Waw (3[illegible]km from Bago), serves good Bamar food in clean surroundings.

Getting There & Away

[illegible] individual travel[illegible]rs, Bago makes a bet[illegible] starting point [illegible] road trips to Mt K[illegible]to than Yang[illegible]ince hotel staff there ar[illegible]pt at arra[illegible]ging [illegible]nexpensive alterna-tiv[illegible] guide and[illegible] to Mt Kyaikto can be [illegible]through [illegible] the central Bago hote[illegible] around [illegible]S[illegible]0. The same tour book[illegible] Yangon [illegible] US$80.

Bus & [illegible] from Ya[illegible]p Big[illegible] the High Kya[illegible]n buses straight minibuse[illegible]s sta[illegible]50) leave from malaik bus[illegible] fro[illegible]aller air-con are large b[illegible] for th[illegible]n's Hsim-Bago to Ky[illegible]380) [illegible]ce. There

For travell[illegible]350, [illegible] pick-ups (K[illegible]ting t[illegible]s from Kinpun (12km[illegible] min[illegible] Mt Kyaikto) [illegible]yaikt[illegible]iyo, Kyaikto train [illegible]m a for [illegible]pm. Time of [illegible]betw[illegible] [illegible]mber of passe[illegible] dep[illegible]

[illegible]in A direct trai[illegible] [illegible]$7) leaves daily Bago [illegible]am, arriving three hours later, though many travellers report the trip can take six hours or more. The train from Mottama (Martaban) arrives in Kyaikto around 5pm, sometimes later if the train is delayed.

Car If you're coming to Kyaikto by car, keep in mind that the Sittoung Bridge closes at 6pm.

AROUND KYAIKTO TO MAWLAMYAING

Southeast of Kyaikto is **Bilin**, a dusty town of wooden buildings and a favoured stop for truckers making the Yangon-Mawlamyaing (Moulmein) haul. Among the mechanic shops that line the main road through town are a couple of cheap but quite decent **Bamar restaurants**. A few kilometres southeast of town there's a toll bridge over the Bilin River.

Taunzaung Paya, another large and interesting old *zedi* (stupa), can be found at Zokthok village, slightly south of Bilin. The most famous of the many hillside stupas is **Myathabeiq Paya** (Emerald Alms-Bowl Stupa), which can be reached by road and offers good views of town.

Thaton

သထုံ

Long before the rise of Bagan (Pagan), Thaton was an important centre for a Mon kingdom that stretched from the Ayeyarwady River delta to similar river deltas in Thailand, and possibly as far east as Cambodia. Early on it may have been known as Suvannabhumi, the 'Golden Land' – legend says Asoka, the great Indian Buddhist emperor, sent a mission there in the 3rd century BC – and later as Dvaravati when it reached its dynastic peak between the 6th and 10th centuries AD. The thriving port carried on trade with the south of India and Sri Lanka. Shin Aran, a monk from Thaton, carried Theravada Buddhism north to the Burmese [illegible]ingdom of Bagan, and in 1057 Thaton was [illegible]quered by King Anawrahta of Bagan.

[illegible]day Thaton sits on the main road and [illegible]ne that stretches from Bago to

Mottama. Little of ancient Thaton is visible, as the modern town has been built over the old sites; piles of brick here and there are all that remain of the massive city walls. The town's core is a leafy place, lining each side of the highway with colonial mansions and thatched-roof homes. A few older stupas dot the hillsides surrounding town and a picturesque canal network irrigates rice paddies and fruit orchards.

Shwe Zayan Paya, on the northern side of the road just beyond the clock tower, features a nice set of monastery buildings and a large stupa supposedly built during the early Mon era. A famous 10th-century standing Buddha stele found at this paya was sculpted in the classic Mon style and shows strong similarities with Dvaravati-period Buddhas from central Thailand.

Places to Stay & Eat An overnight rest stop in Thaton might be worthwhile if you're travelling between Yangon and Mawlamyaing without any other stops, although since the road was upgraded most travellers now breeze on through. A large, two-storey, no-name **guesthouse** *(☎ Thaton 186; doubles K1500)*, off the northern side of the main street through town, has clean and comfortable rooms with shared facilities. The friendly staff report that although the guesthouse isn't likely to be officially licensed to accept foreigners, they can arrange permission for overnight stays at the police station on a case-by-case basis.

There are several **teashops** and basic **Bamar-style restaurants** along the busy main street.

Mottama (Martaban)

မုတ္တမ

Double-decker passenger ferries cross the Thanlwin River to Mawlamyaing from the Mottama landing every half hour from 7.15am to 6.45pm. The fare is K15 and the trip takes 20 to 30 minutes, depending on the tides. If you don't feel like waiting, there's a much faster 25-seat outboard across the river for K100, or you can always charter a boat cross the river for about K3000 to K5000.

Less frequent vehicle ferries from Mottama to Mawlamyaing cost K100 per passenger plus K500 per car or van, more for trucks and buses. Departures depend on the tides; the last boat leaves just before sunset and the crossing takes about half an hour.

See the Getting There & Away entry in the following Mawlamyaing section for details on bus and rail transport to Mottama.

MAWLAMYAING (MOULMEIN)

မော်လမြိုင်

☎ 032

Mawlamyaing is an attractive, leafy, tropical town with a ridge of stupa-capped hills on one side and the sea on the other. Although an unsightly row of modern Chinese-style buildings along the waterfront tends to dash the hopes of colonial-architecture buffs, Mawlamyaing does have an impressive collection of ornate and wonderfully decrepit mosques. George Orwell (author of *Burmese Days*) was stationed here for a time in the 1920s during his service with the Indian Imperial Police.

Mawlamyaing served as the capital of British Burma from 1827 to 1852, during which time it developed as a major teak port. Much coastal shipping still goes on, although Pathein (Bassein) and Yangon have superseded it as Myanmar's most important ports. Today it's Myanmar's fourth-largest city with a population of around 300,000 people, composed roughly of 75% Mon or some mixture of Mon, plus Kayin, Bamar, Indian, Chinese and other ethnicities. A look around the old Christian cemetery gives a hint of how cosmopolitan Mawlamyaing was during the 18th and 19th centuries.

Orientation

The city's main north-south thoroughfares begin with North Bogyoke Rd, which runs east-west from the vehicle jetty at the northern end of Mawlamyaing and links wi Htet Lan Magyi (Upper Main Rd) in centre of town. Htet Lan Magyi cont south past several government build the main bus station at the souther town, then connects with the

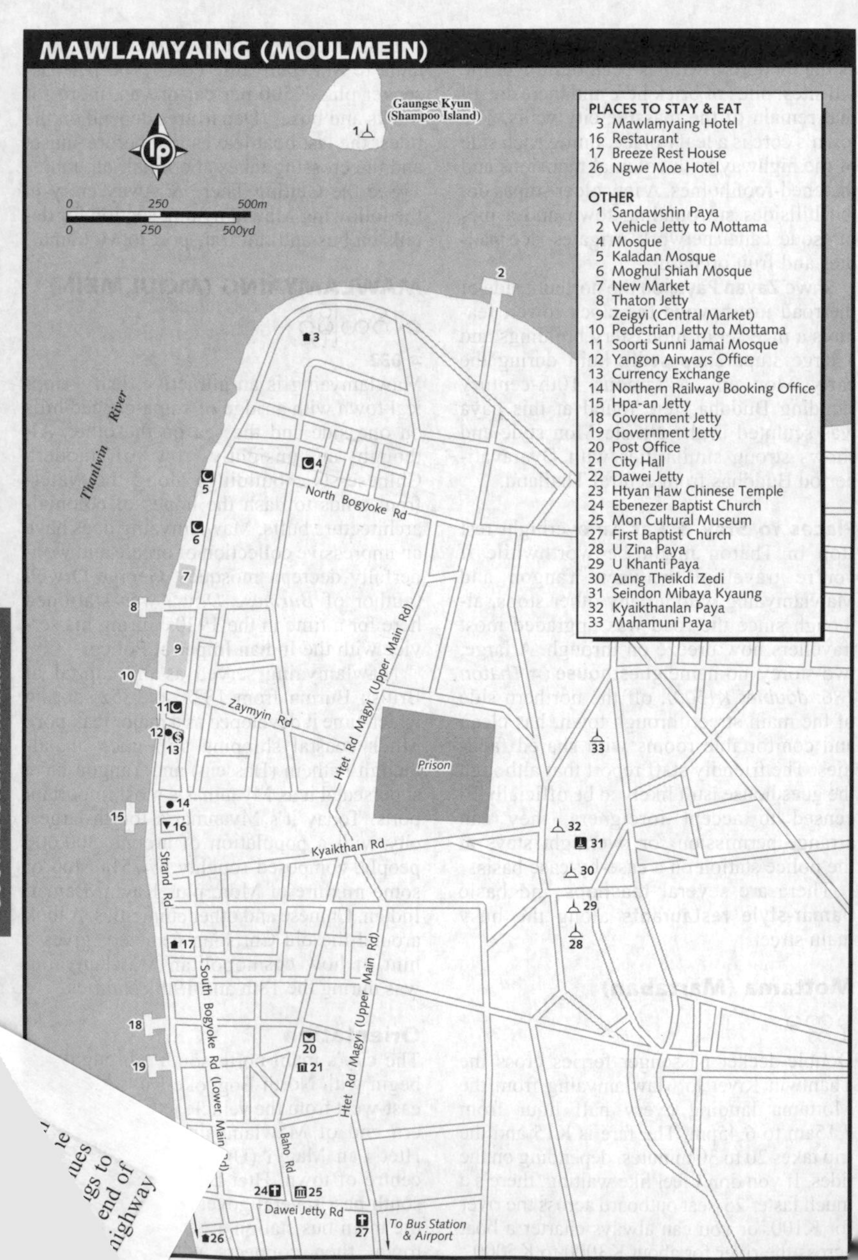
MAWLAMYAING (MOULMEIN)
PLACES TO STAY & EAT
3 Mawlamyaing Hotel
16 Restaurant
17 Breeze Rest House
26 Ngwe Moe Hotel
OTHER
1 Sandawshin Paya
2 Vehicle Jetty to Mottama
4 Mosque
5 Kaladan Mosque
6 Moghul Shiah Mosque
7 New Market
8 Thaton Jetty
9 Zeigyi (Central Market)
10 Pedestrian Jetty to Mottama
11 Soorti Sunni Jamai Mosque
12 Yangon Airways Office
13 Currency Exchange
14 Northern Railway Booking Office
15 Hpa-an Jetty
18 Government Jetty
19 Government Jetty
20 Post Office
21 City Hall
22 Dawei Jetty
23 Htyan Haw Chinese Temple
24 Ebenezer Baptist Church
25 Mon Cultural Museum
27 First Baptist Church
28 U Zina Paya
29 U Khanti Paya
30 Aung Theikdi Zedi
31 Seindon Mibaya Kyaung
32 Kyaikthanlan Paya
33 Mahamuni Paya
Gaungse Kyun (Shampoo Island)
0 250 500m
0 250 500yd
Thanlwin River
North Bogyoke Rd
Zaymyin Rd
Htet Rd Magyi (Upper Main Rd)
Prison
Kyaikthan Rd
Strand Rd
South Bogyoke Rd (Lower Main Rd)
Baho Rd
Dawei Jetty Rd
To Bus Station & Airport

southward to Ye. Along the western side of town, South Bogyoke Rd (Lower Main Rd) connects through the market and commercial districts. Another block west, Strand Rd hugs the waterfront and offers access to various local and long-distance passenger-ferry jetties. From Strand Rd, Kyaikthan Rd runs from west to east and terminates at Kyaikthanlan Paya.

The main west-east avenue is Dawei Jetty Rd, which leads from the Dawei jetty, on the coast across town, to the southern end of the ridge. On the eastern side of the ridge stand several grand colonial-era mansions that have been converted to government offices.

Taungwaing Rd cuts diagonally from near the bus station southeast to the airport and Mawlamyaing University, terminating near Taungwaing Paya.

Mon Cultural Museum

မွန်ယဉ်ကျေးမှုပြတိုက်

This two-storey building *(Baho Rd; admission US$2; open 9.30am-4pm Tues-Sun)* at the northeastern corner of Baho Rd (formerly Dalhousie St) and Dawei Jetty Rd is dedicated to the Mon history of the region. Exhibits are displayed downstairs, while upstairs are reading rooms and toilets.

The museum's modest collection includes: stelae with Mon inscriptions; 100-year-old wooden sculptures depicting old age and sickness (used as *dhamma*-teaching devices in monasteries); ceramics; *thanakha* grinding stones; silver betel boxes; an English-language letter, dated 22 December 1945, from Bogyoke Aung San to Mo Chit Hlaing, a famous Mon leader; lacquer ware; *parabaik* (folding manuscripts); royal funerary urns; Mon musical instruments; and wooden Buddha altars.

In front of the museum is a British cannon dated 1826, plus a huge Burmese gong. Some labels are printed in English though most are in Burmese only.

Religious Monuments

In the city's east, a hilly north-south ridge is topped with five separate monasteries and shrines. At the northern end is **Mahamuni Paya**, the largest temple complex in Mawlamyaing. It's built in the typical Mon style with covered brick walkways linking various square shrine buildings. The main image is a replica of its namesake in Mandalay (see the Mahamuni Paya section in the Mandalay chapter for more information) – without the thick gold leaf. Another difference is that women may enter the main Buddha chamber here. Tile work on the chamber walls includes colourful peacock representations. In the outer cloister several well-executed paintings depict local scenes from the 1920s and 1930s.

Farther south along the ridge stands **Kyaikthanlan Paya**, the city's tallest and most visible stupa. It was probably here that Rudyard Kipling's poetic 'Burma girl' was 'a-settin'…' in the opening lines of *Mandalay*: 'By the old Moulmein Pagoda, lookin' lazy at the sea' (never mind that it's actually the Thanlwin River that's visible from the paya – poetic license).

For K20 you can take a lift to the main platform surrounding the 40m stupa, which offers fine views over the city and harbour. You can also see the plains to the east towards Kyaikmaraw and the coconut tree–shrouded islands in the mouth of the Thanlwin River. The zedi's name comes from the Mon word for stupa, *kyaik*, while *than-lan* is thought to mean Siamese-defeating (than = shan = siam). The defeat refers to the Mon effort in building the highest stupa in the region, rather than a military manoeuvre. A large bell at the shrine's western entry dates to 1855 and weighs 600 *viss* (960kg).

Below Kyaikthanlan is the 100-year-old **Seindon Mibaya Kyaung**, a monastery where King Mindon Min's queen, Seindon, sought refuge after Myanmar's last monarch, King Thibaw Min, took power. On the next rise south stands the isolated silver-and-gold-plated **Aung Theikdi Zedi**.

Farther south, on the western side of the ridge, a view looks out over the city and is a favoured spot for watching sunsets and catching evening sea breezes. Just beyond the viewpoint stands **U Khanti Paya**, built to commemorate the hermit of Mandalay Hill fame; supposedly U Khanti spent some time on this hill as well. It's a rustic, airy sort of place centred around a large Buddha image. Various bells and gongs are suspended by ropes from the steel supports of the sanctuary's ceiling.

U Zina Paya, on the southern spur of the ridge, was named after a former monk who dreamt of finding gems at this spot, then dug them up and used the proceeds to build a temple on the site. One of the shrine buildings contains a very curvy, sensual-looking reclining Buddha topped with the blinking electric halo so popular in Myanmar; a second recliner in the same room has blinking lights all over its body.

In the centre of town towards the waterfront, on South Bogyoke Rd, are three mosques built during the colonial era when many Indians arrived to work for the British. Since the Indian exodus of the 1970s, Muslim congregations have declined substantially but the survival of these grand old buildings makes a walk along Lower Main Rd and its extension South Bogyoke Rd a fleeting exercise in nostalgia.

The most impressive building, **Kaladan Mosque**, is a grey-and-white structure designed by Sunni Muslims in the elaborate 'wedding-cake style' similar to that seen in Penang or Kuala Lumpur. Farther south, on the same side of the street, is the smaller **Moghul Shiah Mosque**, a white Shiite place of worship with austere Moorish arches. A couple of blocks farther, south of the Central Market, the Sunni **Soorti Sunni Jamai Mosque** fills a similar space but presents a more brilliant turquoise-and-white facade.

Just up from Dawei jetty, on the eastern side of Strand Rd, the small but colourful **Htyan Haw** Chinese temple serves the local Chinese community. Of historic interest is the sturdy brick **First Baptist Church**, also known as the Judson Church, on the corner of Htet Lan Magyi and Dawei Jetty Rd. Founded by the American missionary, Adoniram Judson, this was Myanmar's first Baptist church.

Markets

Mawlamyaing's **zeigyi** (central market) is a rambling area on the western side of South Bogyoke Rd, just north of the main pedestrian jetty for Mottama. This market specialises in dry goods, from inexpensive clothes to house wares. Much of the merchandise includes items that have 'fallen off the boat' on the way from Singapore to Yangon, such as untaxed cigarettes and liquor.

Mawlamyaing is renowned for its durian. Don't be put off by the smell – one taste and you might just be hooked!

On the same side of the street a block north is the **New Market**, a large shed built as 'People's Market No 2' during Myanmar's recently ended socialist era. Fresh fruits, vegetables and meats are the attraction here.

A variety of street vendors set up shop along both sides of South Bogyoke Rd in the area of these two markets. Fresh areca nut, pomelo and durian are among the specialities Mawlamyaing is renowned for. The entire district is busiest in the early morning from 7am to 8am; by 9am business is considerably slower.

Gaungse Kyun (Shampoo Island)

ခေါင်းဆေးကျွန်း

This picturesque little isle off Mawlamyaing's northwestern end is so named because during the Ava period the yearly royal hair-washing ceremony customarily used water taken from a spring on the island.

You can hire a boat out to the island for K1000. Other than just walking around and soaking up the island ambience, you can visit **Sandawshin Paya**, a whitewash-and-silver zedi said to contain hair relics, and a nearby Buddhist meditation centre. Among other islands in the river, there is the largest one – **Bilu Kyun** (Ogre Island).

Places to Stay & Eat

Thanlwin Hotel *(☎ 21976; South Bogyoke Rd; singles/doubles US$10/15, with air-con US$15/20)* is a friendly and spacious colonial-era place with wide stairways and open verandas. Air-con rooms feature an attached bathroom, but the economy rooms, which have a separate shower and toilet, are the more atmospheric, with high ceilings and marble floors.

Breeze Rest House *(☎ 21450; 6 Strand Rd; singles/doubles US$6/12, with bathroom & air-con US$10/15)* is the cheapest place in town and it's friendly. Most rooms have two beds, a fan and shared facilities. The English-speaking owner has recently added air-con to a few rooms that have private bathrooms.

Ngwe Moe Hotel *(☎ 24703; Strand Rd; singles/doubles US$27/36)* is the newest accommodation in town. The three-storey place boasts attached bathroom, air-con, IDD phone, fridge and satellite TV in each room. Breakfast is included.

Travellers keen to avoid government-owned hotels should stay clear of the **Mawlamyaing Hotel**, in the northwestern corner of the city.

One **restaurant**, opposite the passenger jetty (to Hpa-an) serves good Chinese food in a clean setting. A few others in the same vicinity serve similar fare, but they're a grubby lot.

The **Thanlwin Hotel** serves lunches and dinners.

Getting There & Away

Bus & Pick-up Several overnight buses costing K1200 to K1500 leave Yangon for Mawlamyaing in the evening, and arrive at Mottama about eight hours later. From there, you take a ferry (K5) or a much faster 25-passenger outboard motorboat (K30) across the river to Mawlamyaing. Bus tickets can be purchased from offices opposite the central train station, and most companies provide free shuttles to the Highway bus station.

Pick-ups leave from west Yangon's Hsimmalaik bus station in the morning for K800.

Recently, permits have been sometimes required to proceed south by road into Tanintharyi Division. However, since travel has been opening up in nearby Mon State and elsewhere, it may be possible to go overland despite vague official restrictions. Mawlamyaing's main station for southbound buses or pick-ups is near the southern end of town off the road to Ye-U, where public vehicles go to Thanbyuzayat, Kyaikkami, Setse, Dawei, or Payathonzu on the Thai border (opposite Three Pagodas Pass).

Train Two express trains run from Yangon to Mottama daily, the No 81 Up at 8am and the No 89 Up at 10pm. Both trains make brief stops in Bago and Thaton. When the trains are running on time the trip takes nine hours – slower than the bus. Still, the scenery from the train is, as usual, much more engaging. Foreigner price for an upper-class seat is US$18. Tickets can be purchased at the train station.

In the reverse direction, the No 82 Down leaves Mottama at 7pm and is scheduled to arrive in Yangon at 4.30am; the No 90 Down leaves at 9am and arrives in Yangon at 6pm. In Mawlamyaing tickets may be purchased one day in advance at the Northern Railway Booking Office, which stands between Strand Rd and South Bogyoke Rd, just north of the Hpa-an jetty.

A separate southern railway line begins at the southern end of the city and terminates at Ye-U. From Ye-U, another local train continues to Dawei. Foreigners have not been allowed to travel on these rail lines for some time, due to a lack of security farther south. With the military presence surrounding a gas pipeline near Dawei, this situation is unlikely to change soon.

Boat See the earlier Mottama section for details on the Thanlwin River ferry crossings to Mawlamyaing. There are two main jetties on the Mawlamyaing side for ferries to/from Mottama: the vehicle jetty at the northern end of town and the pedestrian jetty just south of the central market off Strand Rd. Double-decker passenger ferries depart for Mottama across the Thanlwin River every half hour; the fare is K15 and the trip takes 20 to 30 minutes. Faster 25-seat outboards cross the river for K100 per person.

The next jetty south of the Mottama pedestrian jetty handles boats to Hpa-an in the Kayin (Karen) State. See the Getting There & Away entry in the Hpa-an section later in this chapter for details on once-daily ferries to Hpa-an from Mawlamyaing.

Next south are two jetties reserved for government boats only, followed by the larger Dawei jetty for boats to Dawei and Myeik (Mergui). It can be quite difficult for foreigners to arrange passage on any of these boats. If you want to try your luck, it may pay to inquire in Yangon at the Myanma Five Star Line (MFSL) office.

Getting Around

Motorised *thoun bein* (three wheelers) are the main form of public transport around the city. The highest concentration is on South Bogyoke Rd in front of the zeigyi. The going rate is K200 for a short hop within the centre of town and as much as K500 for a ride up the ridge to Kyaikthanlan. You can also rent bikes from one of the hotels.

AROUND MAWLAMYAING

The authorities often frown upon foreigners travelling south of Mawlamyaing, even though the local tourist brochures are flush with photos of Thanbyuzayat, Kyaikkami and Setse. We have heard from travellers who have gone south without a problem, and from others who were turned back at the bus station. However, **Mudon**, 29km south of the city, is an area of unrestricted travel and there are no checkpoints on the way. Verdant mountains to the east are a source of 'jungle food' – deer, snake and other wild forest species – for restaurants in Mudon. The town is also known for cotton weaving.

Just north of Mudon is a turn-off east to **Azin Dam**, a water-storage and flood-control facility that's also used to irrigate local rubber plantations. A tidy recreation area at **Kandawgyi** – a lake formed by the dam – is a favourite picnic spot; bring your own snacks or rely on the vendors who gather here on weekends and holidays. At the northern end of the lake stands the gilded stupa of **Kandawgyi Paya**.

Just off the road between Mawlamyaing and Mudon are two interesting hill-top shrines at **Kyauktalon Taung** and **Yadana Taung**. The former is a flat-topped limestone crag crowned with stupas. On the opposite side of the road is a similar but smaller outcropping surmounted by a Hindu temple. On Yadana Taung, local Buddhists are constructing a huge reclining Buddha, which when completed (and construction seems to be moving at a snail's pace) will reportedly measure around 160m in length, making it the largest such image in the world. Many other stupas and standing Buddhas dot the countryside around the reclining image.

Most locals will warn against travelling along the roads south of Mudon after 3pm. The government attributes road attacks in this area to Mon or Kayin insurgents, but since the attacks don't discriminate between government and private vehicles, and since the motive always seems to be robbery, it's hard to conceive that the perpetrators are anything other than common highway bandits. One of the methods used is to roll a log across the road to force vehicles to stop, at which time armed men appear and demand money from drivers and passengers.

Incidents between 8am and 2pm are apparently quite rare because that's when most people travel – increased traffic means increased safety. Public transport – buses or pick-ups – are comparatively safer from attack than private vehicles.

Kayah State

ကယားပြည်နယ်

This small state is wedged between the Shan State to the north and west, the Karen State to the west and south, and Thailand to the east. Eight ethnic groups reside in this mountainous state, including the Taungthu, Padaung, Yinbaw, Bre, and Kayah, who form the majority.

The culture of the Kayah people, also known as Karenni or Red Karen, appears to the outsider to be a blend of Kayin (Karen) and Shan influences. Hereditary chieftains called *saopya* have obvious similarities with the sao pha of the Shan, while bronze frog drums are used ceremonially as in the Kayin culture. Most of the Kayah are animist, although there are significant numbers of Christians and Buddhists as well. Animists, Buddhists and Christians alike participate in the annual Kuhtobo festival in May, which pays homage to the rain spirits.

The group most known outside Myanmar is the minority Padaung, whose women traditionally stack up to 22kg of brass rings around their necks. The rings depress the collarbone, making it look as if their necks have been unnaturally stretched. No-one knows for sure how the ring custom got started; one theory says it was to make the women's appearance strange enough that men from other tribes wouldn't pursue them. The Padaung also wear thin hoops, made of cane or lacquered cord, in bunches around their knees and calves.

Until the early 1990s, Kayah rebel groups controlled much of the eastern half of the state. The Myanmar government has concentrated on securing the capital, Loikaw, and the very important hydroelectric plant at nearby Lawpita. The recent ceasefire has allowed the government to build a railway between Aungban and Loikaw.

LOIKAW

လွိုင်ကော်

The Kayah State is open by permit only, and permits have yet to be given for the state capital, Loikaw – located near the state's northern tip at an elevation of just over 1200m.

If it ever opens for visitors, Loikaw has a colourful **Thirimingala Market**, frequented by members of several tribal groups, including the Padaung. Naungyar, towards the northern quarter of town, is inhabited by mostly Kayah people; now that a ceasefire with the insurgents is in effect, it's not unusual to see Kayah rebel soldiers in this area. Two small lakes and a stream add visual interest to the town. Visit the **Taungkwe Zedi** on Taungkwe, a twin-peaked mountain on the edge of town, for Loikaw vistas.

Twenty kilometres southeast of Loikaw is a huge hydroelectric facility built by the Japanese as war reparation. A dam impounds the Bilu Chaung (Bilu Canal), which flows from Inle Lake 120km to the north. The facility supplies most of the power in the national grid system and so is highly strategic. Nearby **Lawpita Falls** is said to be beautiful; however, it's in insurgent territory, so you're unlikely to be permitted to visit, despite the ceasefire.

Pinlaung, roughly halfway between Aungban and Loikaw, is the highest point on the road/railway route, at over 1500m. It's inhabited mainly by Pa-O and it can be quite cold in winter.

Places to Stay

Garden Hotel reportedly provides economy singles/doubles for US$10/15, and standard rooms for US$15/20.

Getting There & Away

At the time of writing, travel to Loikaw for foreigners was not permitted.

railway station, but you might have to bring along a Burmese to help you buy them: signs are in Burmese only – and Arabic numerals are nowhere to be seen! Better yet, purchase your tickets through your hotel in Mandalay – most of them provide this service for their guests.

Two private companies also run trains between Mandalay and Myitkyina that make a stop in Naba. Trains operated by the Mehka Mandalar company depart on Wednesday and Sunday at 4.40pm. Upper-class seats are US$25. The Malikha Mandalar company runs trains on Monday and Friday and the fare and departure time are the same. These tickets can be bought at the Mandalay railway station at window Nos 7 and 8. These trains depart from Myitkyina for Naba on Saturday, Tuesday and Thursday.

Getting Around

So far nobody is renting bicycles in Katha, but it's a smallish town and is easily explored on foot. Trishaws can be hired for short trips. From the jetty to the market should cost about K200.

PUTAO

ပူတာအို

Putao and the surrounding area lie above the tropic of Cancer, in a zone characterised by subtropical conditions, up to 2000m; temperate rainforest from 2000m to 3000m; and subalpine snow forest that becomes alpine scrub, above 3000m. The highlands north of Putao are considered one of the most pristine Himalayan environments in Asia and could become a major ecotourism destination if made accessible to foreigners. The locals often refer to the surrounding peaks as the 'ice mountains'.

Putao itself is small and picturesque, with a population of about 10,000 people. The elevation is 402m above sea level. During the late British colonial era, a military post called Fort Hertz was based in Putao. By the end of WWII most Westerners used this name instead of Putao – it still appears on some older maps. Most of the population of around 10,000 are Kachin and Lisu, followed by Bamar, Shan and various other smaller tribal groups.

Things to See & Do

The army has a strong presence here, including its own nine-hole golf course near the military camp. At the **Myoma Market** in town there are bamboo and wooden handicrafts, and medicines made from local plants. On Sunday following morning mass, many in the church congregation go to the market to watch videos. The most interesting feature of the town is found next to the **Mahamuni Paya**, where the chime bell is made from the propeller of a wrecked WWII aircraft.

Hkakabo Razi stands 5889m high and is snow capped year-round. Satellite peaks in adjoining massifs include **Namni-Lka** (4664m) in the Adung Valley and **Diphuk-Ha** (4360m) in the Seingku Valley. A protected 'trans-frontier reserve' has been proposed by neighbouring countries.

Places to Stay & Eat

No 46 Light Infantry Division Rest House is a government-owned resthouse, which we won't review or recommend. Unfortunately, at the time of writing, it was the only accommodation in town that allowed non-Burmese guests.

The town has one Chinese restaurant, **Khamsuko**, near Myoma Market.

The **Yadanapon Tea Shop** serves a few tea snacks, at prices significantly higher than elsewhere in Myanmar.

Getting There & Away

Foreigners are not allowed to travel to Putao by road. Even with permission, the narrow, unsurfaced 356km road is passable only in dry weather.

With permission, you can fly to Putao. At the time of writing, MA was operating flights to Putao on a charter basis only, but this may change in the future. From Yangon it's around a four-hour flight, including stops in Mandalay and Myitkyina.

sometimes misty, light of dawn. Pilgrims chant, light candles and meditate all through the night. Men are permitted to walk along a short causeway and over a bridge spanning a chasm to the boulder and affix gold-leaf squares on the rock's surface. It's also said that if you wedge a short piece of wood or bamboo into the space between the bottom of the boulder and the cliff on which it rests, you can watch it flex as the boulder gently rocks back and forth.

A new terrace allows devotees to view the boulder from below. There are several other stupas and shrines scattered along the ridge at the top of Mt Kyaikto, though none is as impressive as Kyaiktiyo. The interconnecting trails, however, sometimes lead to unexpected views of the valleys below.

Kinpun, about 9km in from the highway and Kyaikto, lies at the base of the mountain. This is the starting point for either beginning the four-hour hike up or catching one of the frequent trucks-with-benches *(lain-ka)* up the winding road. The charge is K350 per person each way. Vehicles are not permitted near the top, so you still have about a 45-minute walk up to the stupa area. Along the way, you pass through an array of village vendors.

Although permits are no longer required, there is now a US$6 entrance fee to the stupa area, payable at the **tourist office** *(open 6am-6pm daily)* opposite the pilgrim truck-loading area. There is a table-and-chair checkpoint near the top, where you can also pay. By the way, your ticket is valid for 30 days, so you may visit again without paying the government another US$6.

Places to Stay

Although Kyaiktiyo can be visited as a day trip from Bago, the advantage of staying near the shrine is that you can catch sunset and sunrise – the most magical times for viewing the boulder shrine.

Golden Rock Hotel *(in Yangon ☎ 01-532553, fax 527379; economy singles/doubles US$24/30, standard singles/doubles US$36/48)* is better value than the Kyaikto Hotel (see later in this section), with the exception that it's just up the path from the last truck stop – in other words, a 40-minute walk from the top. The attractive standard rooms have a TV, fridge and phone. The smaller economy rooms also have an attached bathroom.

Mountain View Motel *(in Yangon ☎/fax 01-533846; bungalow singles/doubles US$15/20, superior singles/doubles US$30/40)* is the best value of the upmarket places. It's closer to Kyaikto town than Kinpun at the foot of the hill, although you can usually get a free lift to either location. The very comfortable bungalow-type rooms have a fan and a cold-water shower. Larger 'superior' rooms have a desk and a hot-water shower. Breakfast is included with all rooms, and there is an attractive indoor/outdoor restaurant.

In the town of Kyaikto along the main road from Bago there are several guesthouses; none of them very appealing. Of the lot, the two-storey **Nilar Guesthouse** *(rooms per person K3000)*, on the main road at the corner of Hospital St, is the most conveniently located; Yangon-bound buses leave from in front of the hotel. The guesthouse has cubicle rooms with a fan and toilets are on the ground floor. The nearby **La Min Tha Guesthouse** *(Station Rd)* is similar.

Closer to the stupa, the cheapest places to stay are in Kinpun, the base village. Many of the new guesthouses have a here-today-gone-tomorrow feel to them, but three are worth looking for. Each has separate shower and toilet facilities.

Pann Myo Thu Guest House *(singles/doubles US$5/6)* is a well-managed place and the best value in the stupa vicinity. The rooms are clean and light.

Htet Yar Zar Guest House *(singles & doubles K600)* is friendly and the cheapest of the lot so far.

Sea Sar Guesthouse *(singles & doubles US$6)* is behind the popular Sea Sar Restaurant & Bar. Rooms are very basic, with wooden slats and mosquito nets.

Travellers keen to avoid government-owned hotels should stay clear of the

Kyaikto Hotel, along the ridge at the top of Mt Kyaikto.

Foreigners aren't permitted to stay in the *zayat* (rest shelters) for pilgrims, nor are they permitted to camp in wooded areas on the mountain.

Places to Eat

Because Kinpun is the starting point for this popular Burmese site, there are a number of good **Chinese and Bamar restaurants** up and down the main street. In addition to the **food stalls** at the Kinpun base camp and along the footpaths, there's a decent **teashop** opposite the front entrance of the Kyaikto Hotel at the summit. In addition to the usual teashop snacks such as flat bread and deep-fried samosas, the tiny kitchen can make fried noodles and fried rice.

If you're coming by road from Bago, **Yadana Oo Restaurant**, just northwest of the town of Waw (35km from Bago), serves good Bamar food in clean surroundings.

Getting There & Away

For individual travellers, Bago makes a better starting point for road trips to Mt Kyaikto than Yangon, since hotel staff there are adept at arranging inexpensive alternatives. A guide and driver to Mt Kyaikto can be hired through any of the central Bago hotels for around US$40. The same tour booked in Yangon costs US$80.

Bus & Pick-up Big air-con buses straight from Yangon to Kyaikto (K850) leave from the Highway bus station; smaller air-con minibuses leave from Yangon's Hsimmalaik bus station for the same price. There are large buses (K380) and pick-ups from Bago to Kyaikto (K350, three hours).

For travellers wanting to visit Kyaiktiyo, pick-ups (K100, 20 minutes) bound for Kinpun (12km from Kyaikto at the base of Mt Kyaikto) leave from a spot near the Kyaikto train station between 6am and 4pm. Time of departure depends on the number of passengers.

Train A direct train from Bago to Kyaikto (US$7) leaves daily at 4.30am, supposedly arriving three hours later, though many travellers report the trip can take six hours or more. The train from Mottama (Martaban) arrives in Kyaikto around 5pm, sometimes later if the train is delayed.

Car If you're coming to Kyaikto by car, keep in mind that the Sittoung Bridge closes at 6pm.

AROUND KYAIKTO TO MAWLAMYAING

Southeast of Kyaikto is **Bilin**, a dusty town of wooden buildings and a favoured stop for truckers making the Yangon-Mawlamyaing (Moulmein) haul. Among the mechanic shops that line the main road through town are a couple of cheap but quite decent **Bamar restaurants**. A few kilometres southeast of town there's a toll bridge over the Bilin River.

Taunzaung Paya, another large and interesting old *zedi* (stupa), can be found at Zokthok village, slightly south of Bilin. The most famous of the many hillside stupas is **Myathabeiq Paya** (Emerald Alms-Bowl Stupa), which can be reached by road and offers good views of town.

Thaton

သထုံ

Long before the rise of Bagan (Pagan), Thaton was an important centre for a Mon kingdom that stretched from the Ayeyarwady River delta to similar river deltas in Thailand, and possibly as far east as Cambodia. Early on it may have been known as Suvannabhumi, the 'Golden Land' – legend says Asoka, the great Indian Buddhist emperor, sent a mission there in the 3rd century BC – and later as Dvaravati when it reached its dynastic peak between the 6th and 10th centuries AD. The thriving port carried on trade with the south of India and Sri Lanka. Shin Aran, a monk from Thaton, carried Theravada Buddhism north to the Burmese kingdom of Bagan, and in 1057 Thaton was conquered by King Anawrahta of Bagan.

Today Thaton sits on the main road and rail line that stretches from Bago to

Mottama. Little of ancient Thaton is visible, as the modern town has been built over the old sites; piles of brick here and there are all that remain of the massive city walls. The town's core is a leafy place, lining each side of the highway with colonial mansions and thatched-roof homes. A few older stupas dot the hillsides surrounding town and a picturesque canal network irrigates rice paddies and fruit orchards.

Shwe Zayan Paya, on the northern side of the road just beyond the clock tower, features a nice set of monastery buildings and a large stupa supposedly built during the early Mon era. A famous 10th-century standing Buddha stele found at this paya was sculpted in the classic Mon style and shows strong similarities with Dvaravati-period Buddhas from central Thailand.

Places to Stay & Eat An overnight rest stop in Thaton might be worthwhile if you're travelling between Yangon and Mawlamyaing without any other stops, although since the road was upgraded most travellers now breeze on through. A large, two-storey, no-name **guesthouse** *(☎ Thaton 186; doubles K1500)*, off the northern side of the main street through town, has clean and comfortable rooms with shared facilities. The friendly staff report that although the guesthouse isn't likely to be officially licensed to accept foreigners, they can arrange permission for overnight stays at the police station on a case-by-case basis.

There are several **teashops** and basic **Bamar-style restaurants** along the busy main street.

Mottama (Martaban)

မုတ္တမ

Double-decker passenger ferries cross the Thanlwin River to Mawlamyaing from the Mottama landing every half hour from 7.15am to 6.45pm. The fare is K15 and the trip takes 20 to 30 minutes, depending on the tides. If you don't feel like waiting, there's a much faster 25-seat outboard across the river for K100, or you can always charter a boat across the river for about K3000 to K5000.

Less frequent vehicle ferries from Mottama to Mawlamyaing cost K100 per passenger plus K500 per car or van, more for trucks and buses. Departures depend on the tides; the last boat leaves just before sunset and the crossing takes about half an hour.

See the Getting There & Away entry in the following Mawlamyaing section for details on bus and rail transport to Mottama.

MAWLAMYAING (MOULMEIN)

မော်လမြိုင်

☎ 032

Mawlamyaing is an attractive, leafy, tropical town with a ridge of stupa-capped hills on one side and the sea on the other. Although an unsightly row of modern Chinese-style buildings along the waterfront tends to dash the hopes of colonial-architecture buffs, Mawlamyaing does have an impressive collection of ornate and wonderfully decrepit mosques. George Orwell (author of *Burmese Days*) was stationed here for a time in the 1920s during his service with the Indian Imperial Police.

Mawlamyaing served as the capital of British Burma from 1827 to 1852, during which time it developed as a major teak port. Much coastal shipping still goes on, although Pathein (Bassein) and Yangon have superseded it as Myanmar's most important ports. Today it's Myanmar's fourth-largest city with a population of around 300,000 people, composed roughly of 75% Mon or some mixture of Mon, plus Kayin, Bamar, Indian, Chinese and other ethnicities. A look around the old Christian cemetery gives a hint of how cosmopolitan Mawlamyaing was during the 18th and 19th centuries.

Orientation

The city's main north-south thoroughfares begin with North Bogyoke Rd, which runs east-west from the vehicle jetty at the northern end of Mawlamyaing and links with Htet Lan Magyi (Upper Main Rd) in the centre of town. Htet Lan Magyi continues south past several government buildings to the main bus station at the southern end of town, then connects with the highway

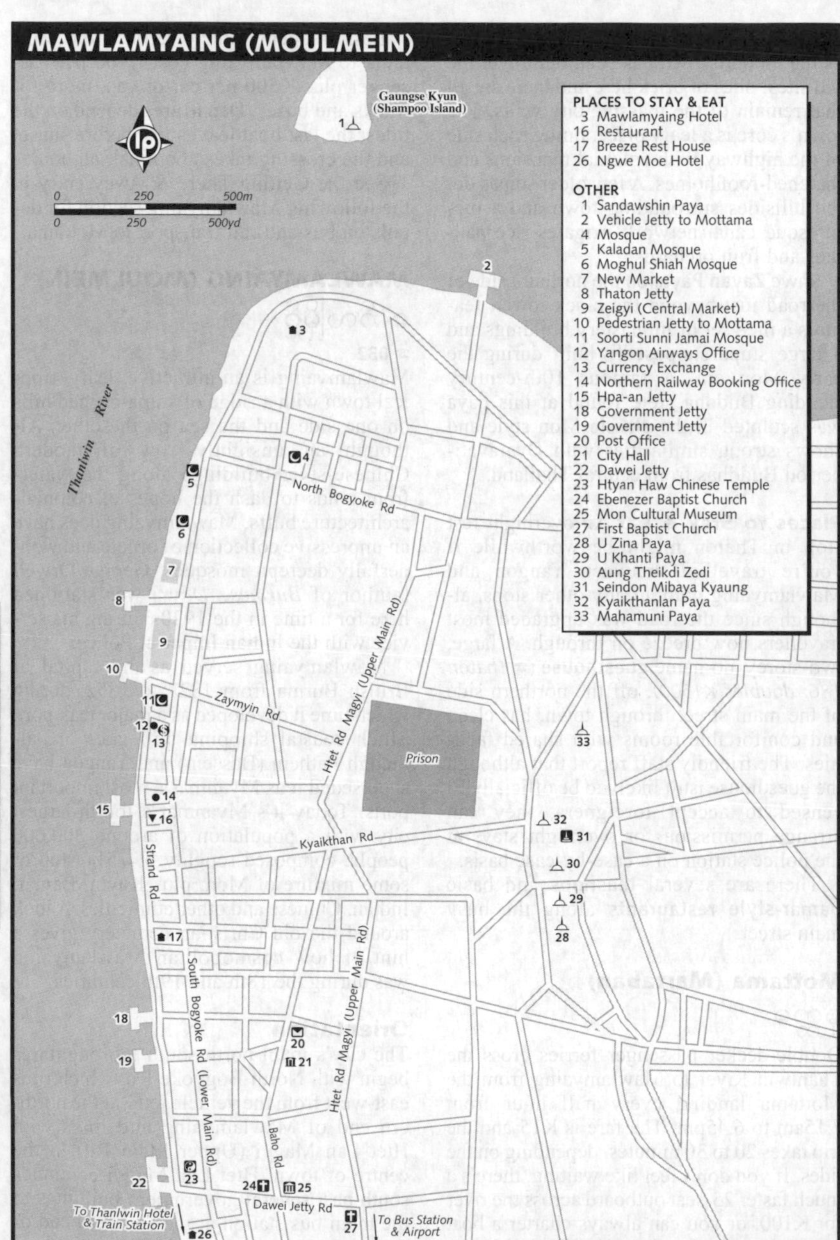
MAWLAMYAING (MOULMEIN)
Gaungse Kyun
(Shampoo Island)
0 250 500m
0 250 500yd
Thanlwin River
North Bogyoke Rd
Zaymyin Rd
Htet Rd Magyi (Upper Main Rd)
Prison
Kyaikthan Rd
Strand Rd
South Bogyoke Rd (Lower Main Rd)
Baho Rd
Dawei Jetty Rd
To Thanlwin Hotel & Train Station
To Bus Station & Airport
PLACES TO STAY & EAT
3 Mawlamyaing Hotel
16 Restaurant
17 Breeze Rest House
26 Ngwe Moe Hotel
OTHER
1 Sandawshin Paya
2 Vehicle Jetty to Mottama
4 Mosque
5 Kaladan Mosque
6 Moghul Shiah Mosque
7 New Market
8 Thaton Jetty
9 Zeigyi (Central Market)
10 Pedestrian Jetty to Mottama
11 Soorti Sunni Jamai Mosque
12 Yangon Airways Office
13 Currency Exchange
14 Northern Railway Booking Office
15 Hpa-an Jetty
18 Government Jetty
19 Government Jetty
20 Post Office
21 City Hall
22 Dawei Jetty
23 Htyan Haw Chinese Temple
24 Ebenezer Baptist Church
25 Mon Cultural Museum
27 First Baptist Church
28 U Zina Paya
29 U Khanti Paya
30 Aung Theikdi Zedi
31 Seindon Mibaya Kyaung
32 Kyaikthanlan Paya
33 Mahamuni Paya

southward to Ye. Along the western side of town, South Bogyoke Rd (Lower Main Rd) connects through the market and commercial districts. Another block west, Strand Rd hugs the waterfront and offers access to various local and long-distance passenger-ferry jetties. From Strand Rd, Kyaikthan Rd runs from west to east and terminates at Kyaikthanlan Paya.

The main west-east avenue is Dawei Jetty Rd, which leads from the Dawei jetty, on the coast across town, to the southern end of the ridge. On the eastern side of the ridge stand several grand colonial-era mansions that have been converted to government offices.

Taungwaing Rd cuts diagonally from near the bus station southeast to the airport and Mawlamyaing University, terminating near Taungwaing Paya.

Mon Cultural Museum

မွန်ယဉ်ကျေးမှုပြတိုက်

This two-storey building *(Baho Rd; admission US$2; open 9.30am-4pm Tues-Sun)* at the northeastern corner of Baho Rd (formerly Dalhousie St) and Dawei Jetty Rd is dedicated to the Mon history of the region. Exhibits are displayed downstairs, while upstairs are reading rooms and toilets.

The museum's modest collection includes: stelae with Mon inscriptions; 100-year-old wooden sculptures depicting old age and sickness (used as *dhamma*-teaching devices in monasteries); ceramics; *thanakha* grinding stones; silver betel boxes; an English-language letter, dated 22 December 1945, from Bogyoke Aung San to Mo Chit Hlaing, a famous Mon leader; lacquer ware; *parabaik* (folding manuscripts); royal funerary urns; Mon musical instruments; and wooden Buddha altars.

In front of the museum is a British cannon dated 1826, plus a huge Burmese gong. Some labels are printed in English though most are in Burmese only.

Religious Monuments

In the city's east, a hilly north-south ridge is topped with five separate monasteries and shrines. At the northern end is **Mahamuni Paya**, the largest temple complex in Mawlamyaing. It's built in the typical Mon style with covered brick walkways linking various square shrine buildings. The main image is a replica of its namesake in Mandalay (see the Mahamuni Paya section in the Mandalay chapter for more information) – without the thick gold leaf. Another difference is that women may enter the main Buddha chamber here. Tile work on the chamber walls includes colourful peacock representations. In the outer cloister several well-executed paintings depict local scenes from the 1920s and 1930s.

Farther south along the ridge stands **Kyaikthanlan Paya**, the city's tallest and most visible stupa. It was probably here that Rudyard Kipling's poetic 'Burma girl' was 'a-settin'…' in the opening lines of *Mandalay*: 'By the old Moulmein Pagoda, lookin' lazy at the sea' (never mind that it's actually the Thanlwin River that's visible from the paya – poetic license).

For K20 you can take a lift to the main platform surrounding the 40m stupa, which offers fine views over the city and harbour. You can also see the plains to the east towards Kyaikmaraw and the coconut tree–shrouded islands in the mouth of the Thanlwin River. The zedi's name comes from the Mon word for stupa, *kyaik*, while *than-lan* is thought to mean Siamese-defeating (than = shan = siam). The defeat refers to the Mon effort in building the highest stupa in the region, rather than a military manoeuvre. A large bell at the shrine's western entry dates to 1855 and weighs 600 *viss* (960kg).

Below Kyaikthanlan is the 100-year-old **Seindon Mibaya Kyaung**, a monastery where King Mindon Min's queen, Seindon, sought refuge after Myanmar's last monarch, King Thibaw Min, took power. On the next rise south stands the isolated silver-and-gold-plated **Aung Theikdi Zedi**.

Farther south, on the western side of the ridge, a view looks out over the city and is a favoured spot for watching sunsets and catching evening sea breezes. Just beyond the viewpoint stands **U Khanti Paya**, built to commemorate the hermit of Mandalay Hill fame; supposedly U Khanti spent some time on this hill as well. It's a rustic, airy sort of place centred around a large Buddha image. Various bells and gongs are suspended by ropes from the steel supports of the sanctuary's ceiling.

U Zina Paya, on the southern spur of the ridge, was named after a former monk who dreamt of finding gems at this spot, then dug them up and used the proceeds to build a temple on the site. One of the shrine buildings contains a very curvy, sensual-looking reclining Buddha topped with the blinking electric halo so popular in Myanmar; a second recliner in the same room has blinking lights all over its body.

In the centre of town towards the waterfront, on South Bogyoke Rd, are three mosques built during the colonial era when many Indians arrived to work for the British. Since the Indian exodus of the 1970s, Muslim congregations have declined substantially but the survival of these grand old buildings makes a walk along Lower Main Rd and its extension South Bogyoke Rd a fleeting exercise in nostalgia.

The most impressive building, **Kaladan Mosque**, is a grey-and-white structure designed by Sunni Muslims in the elaborate 'wedding-cake style' similar to that seen in Penang or Kuala Lumpur. Farther south, on the same side of the street, is the smaller **Moghul Shiah Mosque**, a white Shiite place of worship with austere Moorish arches. A couple of blocks farther, south of the Central Market, the Sunni **Soorti Sunni Jamai Mosque** fills a similar space but presents a more brilliant turquoise-and-white facade.

Just up from Dawei jetty, on the eastern side of Strand Rd, the small but colourful **Htyan Haw** Chinese temple serves the local Chinese community. Of historic interest is the sturdy brick **First Baptist Church**, also known as the Judson Church, on the corner of Htet Lan Magyi and Dawei Jetty Rd. Founded by the American missionary, Adoniram Judson, this was Myanmar's first Baptist church.

Markets

Mawlamyaing's **zeigyi** (central market) is a rambling area on the western side of South Bogyoke Rd, just north of the main pedestrian jetty for Mottama. This market specialises in dry goods, from inexpensive clothes to house wares. Much of the merchandise includes items that have 'fallen off the boat' on the way from Singapore to Yangon, such as untaxed cigarettes and liquor.

LPP

Mawlamyaing is renowned for its durian. Don't be put off by the smell – one taste and you might just be hooked!

On the same side of the street a block north is the **New Market**, a large shed built as 'People's Market No 2' during Myanmar's recently ended socialist era. Fresh fruits, vegetables and meats are the attraction here.

A variety of street vendors set up shop along both sides of South Bogyoke Rd in the area of these two markets. Fresh areca nut, pomelo and durian are among the specialities Mawlamyaing is renowned for. The entire district is busiest in the early morning from 7am to 8am; by 9am business is considerably slower.

Gaungse Kyun (Shampoo Island)

ခေါင်းဆေးကျွန်း

This picturesque little isle off Mawlamyaing's northwestern end is so named because during the Ava period the yearly royal hair-washing ceremony customarily used water taken from a spring on the island.

SOUTHEASTERN MYANMAR

You can hire a boat out to the island for K1000. Other than just walking around and soaking up the island ambience, you can visit **Sandawshin Paya**, a whitewash-and-silver zedi said to contain hair relics, and a nearby Buddhist meditation centre. Among other islands in the river, there is the largest one – **Bilu Kyun** (Ogre Island).

Places to Stay & Eat

Thanlwin Hotel (*☎ 21976; South Bogyoke Rd; singles/doubles US$10/15, with air-con US$15/20)* is a friendly and spacious colonial-era place with wide stairways and open verandas. Air-con rooms feature an attached bathroom, but the economy rooms, which have a separate shower and toilet, are the more atmospheric, with high ceilings and marble floors.

Breeze Rest House (*☎ 21450; 6 Strand Rd; singles/doubles US$6/12, with bathroom & air-con US$10/15)* is the cheapest place in town and it's friendly. Most rooms have two beds, a fan and shared facilities. The English-speaking owner has recently added air-con to a few rooms that have private bathrooms.

Ngwe Moe Hotel (*☎ 24703; Strand Rd; singles/doubles US$27/36)* is the newest accommodation in town. The three-storey place boasts attached bathroom, air-con, IDD phone, fridge and satellite TV in each room. Breakfast is included.

Travellers keen to avoid government-owned hotels should stay clear of the **Mawlamyaing Hotel**, in the northwestern corner of the city.

One **restaurant**, opposite the passenger jetty (to Hpa-an) serves good Chinese food in a clean setting. A few others in the same vicinity serve similar fare, but they're a grubby lot.

The **Thanlwin Hotel** serves lunches and dinners.

Getting There & Away

Bus & Pick-up Several overnight buses costing K1200 to K1500 leave Yangon for Mawlamyaing in the evening, and arrive at Mottama about eight hours later. From there, you take a ferry (K5) or a much faster 25-passenger outboard motorboat (K30) across the river to Mawlamyaing. Bus tickets can be purchased from offices opposite the central train station, and most companies provide free shuttles to the Highway bus station.

Pick-ups leave from west Yangon's Hsimmalaik bus station in the morning for K800.

Recently, permits have been sometimes required to proceed south by road into Tanintharyi Division. However, since travel has been opening up in nearby Mon State and elsewhere, it may be possible to go overland despite vague official restrictions. Mawlamyaing's main station for southbound buses or pick-ups is near the southern end of town off the road to Ye-U, where public vehicles go to Thanbyuzayat, Kyaikkami, Setse, Dawei, or Payathonzu on the Thai border (opposite Three Pagodas Pass).

Train Two express trains run from Yangon to Mottama daily, the No 81 Up at 8am and the No 89 Up at 10pm. Both trains make brief stops in Bago and Thaton. When the trains are running on time the trip takes nine hours – slower than the bus. Still, the scenery from the train is, as usual, much more engaging. Foreigner price for an upper-class seat is US$18. Tickets can be purchased at the train station.

In the reverse direction, the No 82 Down leaves Mottama at 7pm and is scheduled to arrive in Yangon at 4.30am; the No 90 Down leaves at 9am and arrives in Yangon at 6pm. In Mawlamyaing tickets may be purchased one day in advance at the Northern Railway Booking Office, which stands between Strand Rd and South Bogyoke Rd, just north of the Hpa-an jetty.

A separate southern railway line begins at the southern end of the city and terminates at Ye-U. From Ye-U, another local train continues to Dawei. Foreigners have not been allowed to travel on these rail lines for some time, due to a lack of security farther south. With the military presence surrounding a gas pipeline near Dawei, this situation is unlikely to change soon.

Boat See the earlier Mottama section for details on the Thanlwin River ferry crossings to Mawlamyaing. There are two main jetties on the Mawlamyaing side for ferries to/from Mottama: the vehicle jetty at the northern end of town and the pedestrian jetty just south of the central market off Strand Rd. Double-decker passenger ferries depart for Mottama across the Thanlwin River every half hour; the fare is K15 and the trip takes 20 to 30 minutes. Faster 25-seat outboards cross the river for K100 per person.

The next jetty south of the Mottama pedestrian jetty handles boats to Hpa-an in the Kayin (Karen) State. See the Getting There & Away entry in the Hpa-an section later in this chapter for details on once-daily ferries to Hpa-an from Mawlamyaing.

Next south are two jetties reserved for government boats only, followed by the larger Dawei jetty for boats to Dawei and Myeik (Mergui). It can be quite difficult for foreigners to arrange passage on any of these boats. If you want to try your luck, it may pay to inquire in Yangon at the Myanma Five Star Line (MFSL) office.

Getting Around

Motorised *thoun bein* (three wheelers) are the main form of public transport around the city. The highest concentration is on South Bogyoke Rd in front of the zeigyi. The going rate is K200 for a short hop within the centre of town and as much as K500 for a ride up the ridge to Kyaikthanlan. You can also rent bikes from one of the hotels.

AROUND MAWLAMYAING

The authorities often frown upon foreigners travelling south of Mawlamyaing, even though the local tourist brochures are flush with photos of Thanbyuzayat, Kyaikkami and Setse. We have heard from travellers who have gone south without a problem, and from others who were turned back at the bus station. However, **Mudon**, 29km south of the city, is an area of unrestricted travel and there are no checkpoints on the way. Verdant mountains to the east are a source of 'jungle food' – deer, snake and other wild forest species – for restaurants in Mudon. The town is also known for cotton weaving.

Just north of Mudon is a turn-off east to **Azin Dam**, a water-storage and flood-control facility that's also used to irrigate local rubber plantations. A tidy recreation area at **Kandawgyi** – a lake formed by the dam – is a favourite picnic spot; bring your own snacks or rely on the vendors who gather here on weekends and holidays. At the northern end of the lake stands the gilded stupa of **Kandawgyi Paya**.

Just off the road between Mawlamyaing and Mudon are two interesting hill-top shrines at **Kyauktalon Taung** and **Yadana Taung**. The former is a flat-topped limestone crag crowned with stupas. On the opposite side of the road is a similar but smaller outcropping surmounted by a Hindu temple. On Yadana Taung, local Buddhists are constructing a huge reclining Buddha, which when completed (and construction seems to be moving at a snail's pace) will reportedly measure around 160m in length, making it the largest such image in the world. Many other stupas and standing Buddhas dot the countryside around the reclining image.

Most locals will warn against travelling along the roads south of Mudon after 3pm. The government attributes road attacks in this area to Mon or Kayin insurgents, but since the attacks don't discriminate between government and private vehicles, and since the motive always seems to be robbery, it's hard to conceive that the perpetrators are anything other than common highway bandits. One of the methods used is to roll a log across the road to force vehicles to stop, at which time armed men appear and demand money from drivers and passengers.

Incidents between 8am and 2pm are apparently quite rare because that's when most people travel – increased traffic means increased safety. Public transport – buses or pick-ups – are comparatively safer from attack than private vehicles.

Kyaikmaraw

ကျိုက်မရော

This small, charming town 24km southeast of Mawlamyaing is accessible via a sealed road. For the most part, Kyaikmaraw is considered a 'white area' although insurgents or bandits have been known to rob rubber plantations along the road to Mawlamyaing.

Hugging the banks of the Ataran River, a branch of the Thanlwin River, the town consists of mostly wooden homes with thatched-palm or corrugated metal roofs.

Kyaikmaraw Paya The pride of the town is this temple built by Queen Shin Saw Pu in 1455 in the late Mon regional style. Among the temple's many outstanding features are multicoloured glass windows set in the outside walls of the main sanctuary, an inner colonnade decorated in mirrored tiles, and beautiful ceramic tile floors. Painted reliefs appear on the exterior of several auxiliary buildings; one wall of the *thein* (ordination hall) bears a large relief of Myei Sountmatham, the Hindu-Buddhist earth goddess (Ma Dharani in Pali), twisting her wet hair to create a flood to wash away the armies of Mara the tempter.

Covered brick walkways lead to and around the main square sanctuary in typical 15th-century Mon style. The huge main Buddha image sits in a 'European pose', with the legs hanging down as if sitting on a chair rather than in the much more common cross-legged manner. The Burmese call this the 'going to leave' pose, a transition between the canonical sitting and standing/walking postures. A number of smaller cross-legged Buddhas surround the main image, and behind it are two reclining Buddhas, one with eyes open, one with eyes closed. The robes of all the Buddha images in the main sanctuary are gilded; some are encrusted with semiprecious stones. Another impressive feature is the carved and painted wooden ceiling.

A side room to the inner sanctuary contains sculptures depicting the Buddha in various stages of illness and death – other than the traditional *parinibbana* reclining posture, these are unusual motifs for Buddhist temples. Two images show the Buddha lying on his back with hands folded on his abdomen; another depicts an ill Buddha stooping over slightly with one hand clasped to his chest, the other hand against the wall as his disciples reach out to assist him. Another elaborate sculpture display features *devas* (celestial beings) dividing the Buddha's remains to serve as relics while his monastic disciples watch.

Next to the main sanctuary is a small museum with Buddha images, donated by the faithful, on the upper floor; other artefacts from the area are on the lower floor. Some of these objects are more than 500 years old.

Getting There & Away Two kinds of trucks frequently ply the Kyaikmaraw road from Mawlamyaing: bright green Chevy trucks with wooden door panels and wooden passenger compartments (K100, 45 minutes), and smaller white Japanese pickups (K150, 30 minutes). Lined with toddy palms and rubber plantations, the road passes through eight villages before ending at the riverbank in Kyaikmaraw.

Thanbyuzayat

သံဖြူဇရပ်

South of Mudon, little traffic is seen and the hills to the east grow more densely forested. Thanbyuzayat (Tin Shelter), 30km south of Mawlamyaing, was the western terminus of the infamous Burma-Siam Railway, dubbed the 'Death Railway' by the thousands of Allied prisoners of war (POWs) and Asian coolies who were forced by the Japanese military to build it. It was here that the Japanese broke into Myanmar after marching over the rugged mountain range separating Myanmar from Tak in Thailand via Three Pagodas Pass.

The strategic objective of the railway was to secure an alternative supply route for the Japanese conquest of Myanmar and other Asian countries to the west. Construction on the railway began on 16 September 1942 at existing terminals in Thanbyuzayat and

Nong Pladuk, Thailand. At the time, Japanese engineers estimated that it would take five years to link Thailand and Burma by rail, but the Japanese army forced the POWs to complete the 415km, 1m-gauge railway, of which roughly two-thirds ran through Thailand, in 16 months. Much of the railway was built in difficult terrain that required high bridges and deep mountain cuttings. The rails were finally joined 37km south of the town of Payathonzu (Three Pagodas Pass); a Japanese brothel train inaugurated the line. The railway was in use for 20 months before the Allies bombed it in 1945.

An estimated 16,000 POWs died as a result of brutal treatment by their captors, a story chronicled by Pierre Boulle's book *Bridge on the River Kwai* and popularised by a movie based on the book. The notorious bridge itself still stands in Kanchanaburi, Thailand. Only one POW is known to have escaped, a Briton who took refuge among pro-British Kayin guerrillas.

Although the statistics of the number of POWs who died during the Japanese occupation are horrifying, the figures for the labourers, many from Myanmar, Thailand, Malaysia and Indonesia, are even worse. It is thought that 90,000 to 100,000 coolies died in the area.

A clock tower in the centre of Thanbyuzayat stands at a road junction; the road south leads to Ye-U while the road west goes to Kyaikkami and Setse. About 1.5km south of the clock tower, a locomotive and piece of track commemorating the Burma-Siam Railway are on display. A kilometre west of the clock tower in the direction of Kyaikkami, on the southern side of the road, lies the **Htaukkyant War Cemetery**, which contains 3771 graves of Allied POWs who died building the railway. Maintained by the Commonwealth War Graves Commission, the landscaped cemetery is reminiscent of, but much smaller than, the Taukkyan War Cemetery near Yangon. Most of those buried were British, but there are also markers for American, Dutch and Australian soldiers.

Thanbyuzayat is easily reached by public pick-up (K350) from the Mawlamyaing bus station; there are six departures, all before noon. As there is no legal lodging in Thanbyuzayat, start early so you can catch the last pick-up back to Mawlamyaing at around 2pm.

Kyaikkami

ကျိုက္ခမီ

Located 9km northeast of Thanbyuzayat, Kyaikkami was a small coastal resort and missionary centre known as Amherst during the British era. Adoniram Judson (1788–1850), an American missionary and linguist who has practically attained sainthood among Burmese Baptists, was sailing to India with his wife when their ship was blown off course, forcing them to land at Kyaikkami. Judson stayed on and established his first mission here; the original site is now a Catholic school on a small lane off the main road.

Among other accomplishments, Judson developed the first Burmese-English dictionary in 1849 and was the first person to translate the Bible into Burmese. He was imprisoned along with his wife by the Burmese during the first Anglo-Burmese war and served as the official translator to the Burmese court during the negotiations of the treaty that ended the war. Judson died in 1850 and was buried at sea, but the grave of his wife, Anne Judson, who died soon after their release from prison in 1826, can still be seen in Kyaikkami, a couple of hundred metres off the main road near the school.

However, the main focus of Kyaikkami is **Yele Paya**, a metal-roofed Buddhist shrine complex perched over the sea and reached via a long two-level causeway; the lower level is submerged during high tide. Along with 11 Buddha hair relics, the shrine chamber beneath Yele Paya reportedly contains a Buddha image that supposedly floated here on a raft from Sri Lanka in ancient times. According to legend, a gifted Sinhalese sculptor fashioned four different Buddha images using pieces from the original bodhi tree mixed with a cement composite. He then placed them on four wooden rafts and set the rafts adrift on the ocean; the other three landed near Pathein, Kyaikto and Dawei. A display of 21 Mandalay-style Buddha statues sits over the spot where the Sinhalese image is supposedly buried. Some of the seashells for sale on the premises have been fashioned into religious charms.

During the early half of the day there are occasional pick-ups to Kyaikkami from Thanbyuzayat for K130 per person. You can also charter a car for around K4000.

Setse

ဝက်စဲ

This low-key Gulf of Martaban beach lies about half way between Kyaikkami and Thanbyuzayat. It's a very wide, brown-sand beach that tends towards tidal flats when the shallow surf-line recedes at low tide. The beach is lined by waving Casuarina trees and has been a popular spot for outings since colonial times.

A guesthouse on the beach is licensed for foreigners – perhaps an indication that the region will continue to open up. You can stay at the privately owned **A Htou She Guest House** *(rooms with/without bathroom K2500/1500)*. It's on the beach, along with several bungalows for Burmese citizens. **Vendors** sell fresh young coconuts, and a few modest **restaurants** offer fresh seafood. The biggest, **Mya Annawa** (Emerald Sea), serves delicious lobster and prawns.

There is no public transport to Setse as yet; from Thanbyuzayat you can charter a taxi for K5000.

Kayin State

ကရင်ပြည်နယ်

Many districts in Kayin State and Tanintharyi Division (which both share borders with Thailand) are very much off-limits to foreign visitors travelling from Yangon, but things are changing. The Kayin State, homeland to around a million Kayin, has probably received more foreign visitors who have crossed over – unofficially – from Thailand than from any other direction. Many international volunteers have ventured into the frontier area to assist with refugee concerns.

Ever since Myanmar attained independence from the British in 1948, the Kayin have been embroiled in a fight for autonomy. The main insurgent body, the Karen National Union (KNU), controls much of the northern and eastern parts of the state, although recent Yangon military victories have left the KNU and its military component, the Karen National Liberation Army (KNLA), without a permanent headquarters. A split between Christian and Buddhist factions has also weakened the KNU, which had become the de facto centre of the Democratic Alliance of Burma (DAB), an alliance of a dozen rebel groups fighting for regional autonomy. KNU headquarters was also the seat of the National Coalition Government of the Union of Burma (NCGUB), a 'parallel government' established by a group of National League for Democracy (NLD) members who won parliamentary seats in the ill-fated May 1990 national elections, but were denied office by the military. Much of the state remains a potential battleground as sporadic fighting between Burmese troops and the KNLA continues.

HPA-AN

ဘားအံ

You can reach Hpa-an, capital of Kayin State, by road from Yangon across a new bridge over the Thanlwin River, west of the town, or by river ferry from Mawlamyaing – a very scenic trip. Another new bridge across the Gyaing River at Zathabyin, east of Mawlamyaing, links Hpa-an with Mawlamyaing by road. The trip by car takes an hour.

Even though Hpa-an is a small but busy commerce centre, it still has something of a village atmosphere. Away from the jetty, which is crowded with trucks and motorcycles, you can see farmers coming to town in horse carts, or trishaws stacked with baskets or mats to sell in the market. The townspeople are a mixture of Mon, Bamar and Muslim. Burmese is the primary language,

SOUTHEASTERN MYANMAR

but Kayin is spoken by many. The mosque seems to be the town hub, and there are numerous teashops around, along with pick-ups to Thaton and Kyaikto.

Hpa-an is famous among Burmese for the Buddhist village at **Thamanyat Kuang** and the highly respected monk U Winaya, whose solid support of democracy leader Aung San Suu Kyi is well known throughout Myanmar. Thamanyat monastery is about 40km southeast of Hpa-an, and there is a daily flow of small buses to this busy religious site. The fare by bus from Hpa-an is K220.

Places to Stay & Eat

After the leisurely boat ride up from Mawlamyaing, the choice of accommodation in Hpa-an is a disappointment. So far there are only two places to stay.

Royal Guesthouse *(rooms per person US$5)* is about ten minutes' walk from the jetty. The rooms are barely adequate – just cubicles really, with a separate shower and toilet.

Parami Hotel *(rooms per person US$4, with bathroom & TV US$20)*, a few blocks away, is friendly and slightly better value than the Royal. There are rooms with a fan, mosquito net and common bathroom, and a few rooms with a private bathroom and toilet. The roaches rule the roost at this place.

Khit-Thit Restaurant *(New Age Restaurant)* and **Lucky Restaurant** are near the guesthouses; the food is quite ordinary.

Getting There & Away

Bus & Pick-up Shwe Chin The buses (K1000) depart from Yangon's Hsimmalaik bus station at 8pm and arrive at about 7am. Pick-ups from Hpa-an to Kyaikto (K800 front seat) depart from in front of the green mosque. Pick-ups from Thaton cost about K500. Buses depart from near the Parami Hotel at about 6pm for Kyaikto and Bago.

Boat Double-decker ferries leave from the Hpa-an jetty in Mawlamyaing daily at 2.30pm for the four-hour trip up the Thanlwin River to Hpa-an on the river's eastern bank. The fare for foreigners is US$2 for upper-deck class and US$12 for a cabin.

From Hpa-an a rutted, unsurfaced road heads 143km southeast to Myawadi, a town controlled by the Tatmadaw (armed forces) on the western bank of the Thaungyin River (known as Moei River to the Thais) opposite the northern Thai town of Mae Sot. A large number of Kayin refugees fleeing KNLA-Tatmadaw battles are encamped on the Thai side of the border in this area.

PAYATHONZU (THREE PAGODAS)

ဘုရားသုံးဆူတောင်ကြား

The Thai-Myanmar border town of Payathonzu (Three Pagodas Pass), 110km southeast of Thanbyuzayat, can't be visited from the Myanmar side (see Getting There & Away later in this section), and doesn't really have much to recommend it, but it does mark a mountain pass used for many centuries as a route for overland trade as well as military invasion. Three zedi today stand on Thai turf, 12m from the Burmese border crossing. Control of the Burmese side of the border once vacillated between the KNU and the MNLF, as Payathonzu was one of several 'toll gates' along the Thai-Burmese border where insurgent armies collected a 5% tax on all merchandise, including truckloads of logs smuggled into Thailand, passing through.

Kloeng Thaw Falls, 12km from the border, takes a couple of hours by motorcycle to reach from Payathonzu. The road to the falls is only open in the dry season – reportedly the Kayin control the waterfall area during the rainy season. Even in good weather, the two-rut track is very rugged – not recommended for motorcycle novices. Like other sites in the region, this one is subject to closure. Lately, the falls area has been closed more often than it has been open.

Getting There & Away

For the time being, foreigners are only permitted to visit Payathonzu from the Thai side. The nearest Thai town of any size is Sangkhlaburi, 19km from the border crossing, where lodging and food are readily available.

Before crossing the border from Thailand into Myanmar you must stop in Sangkhlaburi to visit the immigration office (around the corner from the Phornphailin Hotel) and apply for a border pass. Be sure to bring two passport-sized photos and copies of the photo- and visa-pages of your passport. At the border, you'll need to pay US$5 on the Myanmar side. The crossing is open from 6am to 6pm, and you must cross back into Thailand before it closes.

Pick-ups to Three Pagodas Pass leave hourly between 6am and 6.40pm from Sangkhlaburi's central market area. The fare is 30B; the last pick-up back to Sangkhlaburi leaves Three Pagodas Pass at around 5pm.

Tanintharyi (Tenasserim) Division

တနင်္သာရီတိုင်း

Known to the outside world as Tenasserim until 1989, Tanintharyi has a long history of trade with India (especially Coromandel) and the Middle East. Because it's joined with Thailand to a relatively slender length of land separating the Andaman Sea/Indian Ocean from the Gulf of Thailand, this trade link included Siam and other nations east of Myanmar's eastern mountain ranges. Routes through Dawei and Myeik were especially important, and for many years, before the arrival of the British in the late 19th century, the Siamese either controlled the state or received annual tributes from its inhabitants.

Most of the people living in the division are of Bamar ethnicity, although splitting hairs one can easily identify Dawei and Myeik subgroups of the Bamar who enjoy their own dialect, cuisine and so on. Large numbers of Mon also live in the division, and in or near the larger towns you'll find Kayin (often Christian) and Indian (often Muslim) residents.

The Tatmadaw have pushed the KNLA and its Mon equivalent, the MNLF, south from their states into rural or forested areas of the Tanintharyi Division. Hence much of the eastern portion towards Thailand – and parts of the southern extent between Myeik and Kawthoung – is considered 'black territory' by Yangon. Road banditry is not uncommon along the main roads in the interior.

Although permits are no longer required for visits to Dawei, Myeik or Kawthoung, none of the towns are accessible by land. To reach them from the north you must fly from Yangon. From the south, it's now possible to travel as far north as Myeik by boat via Kawthoung, which is an official border crossing from Ranong, Thailand. If you are lucky, you may even be able to travel by boat between Dawei, Myeik and Kawthoung, although only a few travellers have managed to do this so far.

DAWEI (TAVOY)

ထားဝယ်

☎ 036

The area near the mouth of the Dawei River has been inhabited for five centuries or more, mostly by Mon and Thai mariners. English trader Ralph Fitch mentions a stop at 'Tavi' during his 1586 sea journey between Bago and Melaka in a written account stating that tin from the area 'serves all India'. The present town dates to 1751 when it was a minor 'back door' port for the Ayuthaya empire in Thailand (then Siam). From this point it bounced back and forth between Bamar and Siamese rule until the British took over in 1826.

Still a port of medium importance, Dawei today is a sleepy, tropical seaside town, only recently connected to the rest of Myanmar by road and rail. Areas to the west and north of town are planted in rice, while to the east lie patches of jungle. Some of the architecture in town is quite impressive, with many old wooden houses in the two-storey vernacular, with hipped rooflines and plenty of temple-like carved wood ornamentation. Mixed in are more modest thatch-roofed bungalows and a few colonial-style brick-and-stucco mansions. Tall, slender sugar palms, coco palms, banana and other fruit trees, along with heliconia and lots of hanging orchids, are interspersed throughout – it's a very green town due to the abundant annual rain that falls on the southern half of Tanintharyi Division. In spite of its remote location – or perhaps because of it – Dawei has become a significant Burmese Buddhist centre.

Dawei's sleepy, laid-back demeanour is threatened by the development of a new Ye-U-Dawei railway, which was largely built using local forced labour. Hundreds of Tanintharyi Division residents fled to Thailand rather than work on the railway. Refugees report conditions that almost rival those described in chronicles of the Japanese army's 'Death Railway'. According to Amnesty International, one of the camps of refugee labourers at the Thai border was attacked by a battalion of Myanmar's 62nd Infantry and some of the refugees were forcefully repatriated.

Dawei is also near the starting point of the massive 700km Yadana gas pipeline, which carries natural gas from fields in the Gulf of Mottama to Ratchaburi Province in Thailand. About 400km of its length runs through the Mon State and Tanintharyi Division, the remainder through Thailand. Reportedly, the Myanmar government relocated villages originally in the pipeline's path with little or no compensation for the villagers. There have also been charges that forced labour was used in building the pipeline.

Because of the pipeline's perceived strategic importance, there is a fairly heavy military presence around Dawei.

A steady trade in marine products (mostly dried fish), rubber, cashews and wolfram (tungsten) has made Dawei a relatively prosperous town for Myanmar, though not as prosperous as Myeik, farther south.

Theinwa Kyaung (Payagyi)

သိမ်ဝကျောင်း (ဘုရားကြီး)

The main Buddhist monastery in town, usually referred to simply as Payagyi (Big Pagoda), contains a complex of sizable Mon-style *vihara* (glittering cubes of reflective mosaics filled with gilded Buddhas). A sculpture of Dharani, the earth goddess, standing in the corner of one of the main thein is a much-venerated object of worship among the people of Dawei, who rub her breasts, thighs and shoulders for good luck.

The best time to visit Theinwa Kyaung is in the early evening, just after sunset, when hordes of local residents come to make offerings and to meditate for an hour or two. To find it, head northwest along Yodaya Rd, past the Royal Guest House on your right, until you come to a large fork in the road. Bear right at the fork, follow the road another 200m and you'll come to the paya on your right.

Shwethalyaung Daw Mu

ရွှေသာလျောင်း တော်မ

Completed in 1931, the largest reclining Buddha in the country – 74m long, 21m high – can be seen at the edge of town (about 5km from the central Strand Rd market). Although not as beautiful an image as the Shwethalyaung in Bago, its sheer scale is indeed impressive.

Shinmokhti Paya

ရှင်မုတ္ထီးဘုရား

About 5km beyond Shwethalyaung Daw Mu on the same road, this paya is the most sacred of local religious monuments. Reportedly constructed in 1438, it's one of four shrines in the country housing a Sinhalese Buddha image supposedly made with a composite of cement and pieces of the original bodhi tree – see the Shwemokhtaw Paya entry in the Pathein section in the Around Yangon chapter, or the Kyaikkami entry in the Around Mawlamyaing section earlier in this chapter for an account of the legend. During religious festivals this is one of the most lively spots in the district.

Municipal Market

The main municipal market is in the centre of town on Strand Rd. Enclosed by brick walls dating to the British colonial era, it's divided into two main sections; there's a spacious open-sided shelter where fresh produce is sold, and an equally voluminous enclosed shed where dry goods, cosmetics, longyi and ready-made clothes are displayed.

American Baptist Sites

The American Baptists had a long and active history in Dawei, beginning in 1828. The **Karen Baptist Church**, founded by an American evangelist in 1957, is still in use in the Shan Malei Swe Quarter. The original hardwood flooring and pews are in good condition; foreign visitors are welcome.

Impressive, thick-walled **Morrow Karen High School** is now Dawei College. The equally impressive former **American Baptist Mission** is now No 3 State High School.

Beaches & Islands

Few foreigners have been permitted to visit coastal areas around Dawei so details are still sketchy. The best local beach, **Maungmagan** (also spelt Maungmakan) is around 18km west of Dawei via a narrow, winding, patched blacktop road over a high ridge and through rubber plantations. A very wide sand beach stretches 8km or 10km along a large, pretty bay. Near the road head a few outdoor vendors offer snacks and beverages in the shade of Casuarina trees and palms. On weekends and holidays this end of the beach draws a crowd, but if you walk 500m or so up the beach you're likely to have it all to yourself, save for the occasional fisherman.

The surf at Maungmagan seems fairly tame, even during the southwest monsoon, and the water is very clean, so it's a good beach for swimming. Just about everyone who comes to this beach swims with their clothes on, or in very modest swimming costumes.

Opposite Maungmagan is a collection of three pretty island groups that were named the Middle Moscos Islands by the British – they are now known as **Maungmagan**, **Heinze** and **Launglon** (or collectively as the Maungmagan Islands). Due to a natural profusion of wild boar, barking deer, sambar and swiftlets (sea swallows), these islands belong to Myanmar's only marine sanctuary – established by the British in 1927 and still officially protected.

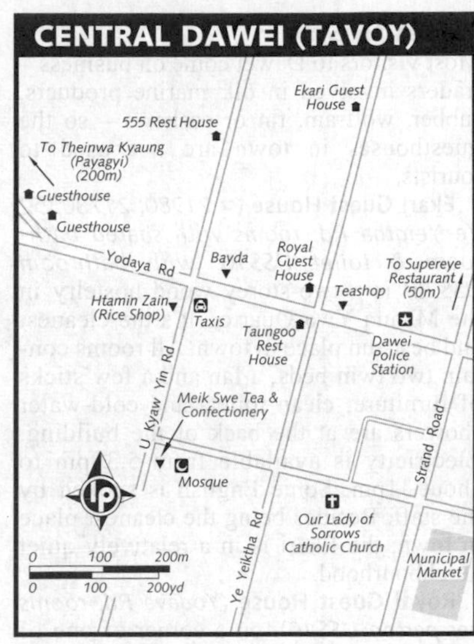

A long peninsula ending in **Dawei A-Ngu** (Dawei Point), about 60km south of Dawei, creates a vast estuarine bay dotted with islands. Because the waters of the lengthy bay are to some degree protected from strong ocean currents, these islands may be more easily accessible by boat than the Maungmagan Islands. **Zalut**, a small town near the tip of Dawei A-Ngu, offers basic services.

Local taxi trucks from the Strand Rd market go to the beach at Maungmagan or to Zalut for about K800 and K1500 per person.

Special Events

During the annual Thingyan festival in April, Dawei's male residents don huge, 4m bamboo-frame effigies and dance down the streets to the beat of the *kalakodaun*, an Indian long drum. The origin of this custom, peculiar to Dawei, seems to be a mystery but it's most likely linked to a similar custom brought by Indian immigrants many decades ago.

Places to Stay

Most visitors to Dawei come on business – traders involved in oil, marine products, rubber, wolfram, tin or cashews – so the guesthouses in town are not used to tourists.

Ekari Guest House *(☎ 21980, 21780; 52 Ye Yeiqtha Rd; rooms with shared bathroom & toilet US$10, with bathroom US$25)* is a two-storey wood hostelry in the Myauq Ywa Quarter. It's the cleanest and best-run place in town. All rooms contain two twin beds, a fan and a few sticks of furniture; clean toilets and cold-water showers are at the back of the building. Electricity is available from 5.30pm to about 11pm. Some English is spoken by the staff. Besides being the cleanest place in town, the Ekari is in a relatively quiet neighbourhood.

Royal Guest House *(Yodaya Rd; rooms per person US$10)*, on a corner of one of the main four-way intersections in the centre of town, occupies a well-restored, two-storey, colonial-era former company office on Yodaya Rd (so called because this road heads east to Thailand, known in Burmese as Yodaya, from Ayuthaya). Rooms are similar to those at the Ekari but not nearly as well kept, and there is some ambient street noise.

Taungoo Rest House *(☎ 21951; rooms US$10)*, right across the street from the Royal, is another big, two-storey colonial building. It's run by an Indian Muslim family, most of whom do not speak English. There is a semi-outdoor café downstairs.

Places to Eat

Neither the Ekari nor the Royal offer food service, but the ground floor *htamin zain* (rice shop) at **Taungoo Rest House** serves good, inexpensive Bamar-Muslim food.

Along Yodaya Rd, one of the main thoroughfares through town, are several small **htamin zain** and **teashops. Supereye** *(Strand Rd)* offers an extensive English-language menu of Chinese and Dawei-style Bamar cuisine, much of it seafood-based. It's relatively clean and the food is good, if a little expensive by Myanmar standards.

Meik Swe Tea & Confectionery *(U Kyaw Yin Rd)* is the best teashop in town. Attached to a mosque on U Kyaw Yin Rd, not far from the Taungoo and Royal guesthouses, it's extremely popular and tends to be half full all day. In addition to good-quality Burmese tea, Meik Swe serves a small but changing menu of Indian-style tea snacks – perhaps *puris* (potato curry) with curry dip one day, *tohsay* (dosa) the next.

About 75m northwest of Royal Guest House is a Chinese-style teashop called **Bayda** (no sign in English) that's also very popular.

Getting There & Away

Air Yangon Airways (YA) fields three direct flights per week from Yangon to Dawei for US$65 per person. The flight time is one hour and 10 minutes. Myanmar Air (MA) also flies this route four days per week, for US$75, but this airline is not recommended (see the Getting Around chapter).

Flights continue to Myeik and Kawthoung before turning around and hitting the same three stops on the way back to Yangon. The YA fare is US$50 between Myeik and Dawei and the ride takes less than an hour. Between Dawei and Kawthoung the fare is US$70.

Bus Various private bus companies now operate buses from Yangon's Highway bus station all the way to Dawei, although foreign travellers aren't usually allowed to take the bus. At the time of writing, flying was the only sure way to get to Dawei from Yangon. If you were allowed to take a bus from Yangon to Dawei, the trip would take about 17 hours. The situation may change so it's always a good idea to ask at the bus station or consult a travel agent in Yangon.

Boat MFSL sails between Yangon, Dawei, Myeik and Kawthoung several times a month, but travel is slow. It takes two days and two nights between Yangon and Dawei, and possibly up to a week in the rainy season.

MYEIK (MERGUI)

မြိတ်

☎ 021

The Tanintharyi coast, in the extreme south of Myanmar where Myanmar and Thailand share the narrow peninsula, is bounded by the beautiful islands of the Myeik Archipelago. Myeik – known to the colonials as Mergui and locally as Beik (Myeik is the written rather than the spoken form) – sits on a peninsula that juts out into the Andaman Sea. Because of the safe harbour offered by the peninsula and facing islands, Myeik became an important port over 500 years ago.

The original Mon inhabitants called their town, at the confluence of the Tanintharyi and Kyaukpaya Rivers, Maw-reik, but the locale was known by several other names as well. A 1545 Portuguese expeditionary chronicle refers to Tanancarim, somewhere along the northwest coast of the Thai-Malay Peninsula, and this Portuguese rendering became Tenasserim in later European records in reference to both Myeik and a town farther upriver now known by that name. The current name for the Tanintharyi Division is the Burmese pronunciation of this name. Myeik, the Burmese mispronunciation of the Mon name Maw-reik, was officially applied to the port by Bamar rulers in 1770.

As Myeik became an important trade entrepot, many European traders and envoys in the employ of the Ayuthaya court settled in the area. The most infamous of these, Samuel White, used his position as harbourmaster of both Mergui (which he called Mergen) and Tenasserim to plunder visiting ships at will and to tax the local population for every shilling he could squeeze out of them.

The British occupied the region following the First Anglo-Burmese War in 1826, so that along with Sittwe, Myeik became one of the first cities in Myanmar to become part of British India. The Japanese invaded in 1941, but by 1945 Myeik was back in British hands, until independence was achieved in 1948.

Until recently Myeik was one of the most picturesque coastal cities in Myanmar, with a wide range of traditional colonial and vernacular architectural styles lining the streets. Increased cash flow due to the exportation of seafood to Thailand caused a mini-boom in building during the 1990s, and many old buildings were replaced by modern ones. Then in 2001, a large portion of the remaining old architecture was razed by fire.

Things to See & Do

The city's most venerated Buddhist temple, **Theindawgyi Paya**, sits on a ridge overlooking the city and harbour. A beautiful, Mon-style ordination hall of wood, brick and stucco contains an impressive painted and carved ceiling, a 'European pose' Buddha towards the front entry, 28 smaller Buddhas (representing different historical Buddhas) along its two sides, a large meditation Buddha in the centre and a sizable reclining Buddha at the back. A mirrored mosaic decorates the lower interior walls and columns. A tall gilded stupa stands on a broad platform with excellent views of the city below and islands in the distance.

Pataw Padet Island, a five-minute boat ride (K100 shared, K800 chartered) from the harbour, is named for two prominent hills at either end of the island. Several religious buildings, stupas and sculptures have been constructed on the island. A large, hollow reclining Buddha, **Atula Shwethalyaung**, lies at the foot of rocky, jungle-covered Padet Hill to the south. At 66m it's the third-longest reclining Buddha in Myanmar – but with a twist: it's a hollow cement form with an interior walkway lined with comic-strip-like *jataka* (stories of the Buddha's past lives) scenes as yet unfinished.

The **harbour front** is worth a stroll to watch stevedores loading and offloading cargo from ships big and small. Towards the southern end of the waterfront, on the eastern side of the street, you may notice what appears to be a large stone-slab box on the footpath. This is the **tomb of Mary Povey White**, the wife of the notorious Siamese-employed harbourmaster Samuel White. Povey died of cholera in 1682 and was entombed on the waterfront. Hardly anyone gives the tomb any notice anymore. The city has grown around it and the uninformed would be excused for thinking it enclosed a fire plug or public well.

Not far from Theindawgyi Paya there's a **Muslim quarter** with two mosques and lots of teashops. The larger of the two, **Lamat Tin Mosque**, is said to be over 50 years old and is quite Arabic-looking. There are seven other mosques in the city.

Near the harbour, **Sibinthaya Zei** *(Municipal Market; open 6am-5pm Mon-Sat; closed Sun & holidays)*, is a very large and colourful collection of enclosed stalls covering a city block.

Myeik Archipelago

မြိတ်ကျွန်းစု

Far beyond the value of any local product – rubber, marine products or swiftlets' nests – is the Myeik Archipelago's huge, almost completely untapped potential in the beach-going and ecotourist market. The Burmese say there are over 4000 islands in the archipelago, though British surveyors recognised only 804. Most are uninhabited, though a few are home to 'sea gypsies', a nomadic seafaring people who sail from island to island, stopping off to repair their boats or fishing nets. Known as Salon to the Burmese, *chao náam* to the Thais, *orang laut* or *orang basin* to the Malays and *Moken* or *Maw Ken* (sea-drowned) among themselves, this may have been the first ethnic group to have lived in what is today Myanmar. With stones tied to their waists as ballast, Moken divers can reportedly descend to a depth of 60m while breathing through an air hose held above the water surface.

Mayanpin Kyun, known to the British as King Island (and locally known both as Kadan Kyun and Kyunsu, the latter the name of the island district's capital), lies a good distance offshore. In spite of its size and geographic variation – at 44,000 hectares it's the largest island in the archipelago – reports say there are no good beaches on the island. A government guesthouse accommodates visitors to a hydroelectric power station – reportedly built with forced labour – on the island. All the power goes to a navy base on the island, while Myeik's civilians rely on part-time diesel generators.

Boats to nearby islands can be chartered for US$60 per day from Myeik's harbour. See the Diving & Snorkelling section under Activities in the Facts for the Visitor chapter for details on dive sites and tour companies that operate overnight archipelago trips.

Places to Stay

Palemon Resort *(☎ 21841; singles/doubles US$20/30)*, opposite the Myeik airport and adjacent to the Myeik Golf Club, has large, plain rooms with comfortable beds, air-con, minifridge, TV and private cold-water shower. It has its own generator, so it has power 24 hours a day. This place was once government owned and is still called the 'government guesthouse'. Some travellers who have recently visited Myeik have reported that the Palemon Resort was the only place in town where foreigners were allowed to stay.

Myeik Golden Pearl (Myeik Shwe Palei) Guest House *(Pyitawtha Rd; rooms US$20)*, near the waterfront, is a modern, two-storey place over a shop house. The musty rooms contain damp carpet, a couple of beds, and an attached shower and toilet. It's very much a second choice. Electric power comes on at night only.

Travellers who wish to avoid Myanmar's government-owned hotels should stay clear of the **Annawa Guest House**, high on a ridge near Theindawgyi Paya.

Places to Eat

When it comes to local cuisine, Myeik can be a real delight. Seafood is abundantly available and inexpensive. One local speciality is *kat gyi kai* (scissor-cut noodles): wheat noodles that have been cut into short strips and stir-fried with seafood and various spices. It's a delicious meal, usually eaten for breakfast or lunch.

Meik Set *(U Myat Lay Rd, Kan Paya Quarter; open 6am-5pm)*, a decade-old wood and thatch teashop/restaurant with a dirt floor

SOUTHEASTERN MYANMAR

and open front, is one of the best places to try kat gyi kai. Other treats available here include *hkauq hnyin kin* (sticky rice steamed with coconut milk in little banana-leaf packets).

Sakura Food & Drinks, on the same street as Meik Set, is a much nicer-looking place with an air-con dining room decorated with wood and thatch, plus an outdoor area with umbrella tables. The chef/owner worked in Singapore for a number of years and has created a unique and very good menu of Southeast Asian seafood dishes, barbecued satay, burgers, omelettes and sandwiches. Considering the high quality of the food and service, it's not expensive, and hence it's very popular with locals.

Pan Myint Zu *(Payakozu Rd, Kan Paya Quarter; open 7am-10pm daily)* is a quiet and semi-rustic, thatched-roof restaurant with good Chinese dishes and seafood.

For traditional Bamar cuisine with local flair, you can do no better than **Shwe Mon Family Restaurant** *(open 7am-8pm daily)*, near the waterfront in the Seik Nge Quarter. Highlights include delicious *bei hin* (egg-and-potato curry), and *balachaung* (chutney-like spices) made with peanuts.

On the same street as Shwe Mon Family Restaurant, closer to the harbour, the **Point Restaurant** is more of a night-time place, with Chinese and seafood dishes, and tables covered with tablecloths. It's not a bad place to down a beer or two and eat appetisers. Later in the evening there's karaoke.

Myeik Restaurant *(Bogyoke Rd)* in the same quarter as Point Restaurant, south of the YA office, occupies a historic building and serves a mixed menu of Chinese, Bamar and seafood.

Between the two mosques in the Muslim quarter, **Pearl World Bakery House** does decent, light pastries.

Behind the Palemon Resort, there's a small **restaurant** serving good Chinese and Bamar food.

Getting There & Away

Air YA flies from Yangon to Myeik three times weekly with a stopover in Dawei for US$90. These flights take a total of two hours and 10 minutes to reach Myeik. Between Myeik and Kawthoung, flights are three times weekly and cost US$70.

MA flies daily from Yangon for US$100, and these flights take one hour and five minutes.

In Myeik, the **YA representative** *(☎ 21160; 115 Bogyoke Rd)* has an office near Sibinthaya Zei (Municipal Market). The MA office is next door to Sakura Food & Drinks on U Myat Lay Rd.

Bus There are daily buses and pick-ups from Dawei, 249km north, but it's highly unlikely foreigners will be permitted to travel by bus to Myeik. The road is so bad – and plagued by bandit attacks – that the trip sometimes requires an overnight stop at Palaw, 73km north of Myeik. Also, there are four ferry crossings, one each at Palauk Chaung (Palauk Canal), Pyicha Chaung, Palaw River and Tomok River.

Boat MFSL sails, on average, twice a month between Yangon, Dawei, Myeik and Kawthoung, but travel is very slow. Regular speedboats also travel between Myeik and Kawthoung (US$25, seven hours), leaving about 6am.

KAWTHOUNG

ကော့သောင်း

This small port at the southernmost tip of Tanintharyi Division – and the southernmost point of mainland Myanmar (800km from Yangon and 2000km from the country's northern tip) – is only separated from Thailand by a broad estuary in the Pagyan River. To the British it was known as Victoria Point and to the Thais it's known as Ko Song (Second Island). The Burmese name, Kawthoung (also spelt Kawthaung), is a mispronunciation of the latter.

The main business here is trade with Thailand, followed by fishing, rubber and cashews. Among Burmese, Kawthoung is most known for producing some of the country's outstanding kickboxers. Most Kawthoung residents are bilingual in Thai and Burmese. Many residents born and raised in Kawthoung, especially Muslims, also speak Pashu, a dialect that mixes the Thai, Malay and Burmese languages.

Kawthoung's bustling **waterfront** is lined with teashops, moneychangers and shops selling Thai construction materials. Touts stroll up and down the pier area, arranging boat charters to Thailand for visitors and traders. A huge **duty-free market** built in pseudo-Bamar style in 1997 sits next to the harbour. Along one side of the harbour lies **Cape Bayinnaung**, named for King Bayinnaung, a Bamar monarch who invaded Thailand several times between 1548 and 1569. A bronze statue of Bayinnaung – outfitted in full battle gear and brandishing a sword pointed at Thailand, not exactly a welcoming sight for visiting Thais – stands at the crest of a hill on the cape.

Five kilometres north of town, the fishing village of **Thirimyaing Lan** is known for its hilltop Third Mile Pagoda, with good sea and island views. Thirimyaing Lan also boasts good local seafood restaurants along its waterfront. Another 11km on is **Paker Beach**, reportedly the best nearby mainland beach.

Islands

The Mergui Archipelago continues south to Kawthoung and many islands lie tantalisingly offshore in this area. Unfortunately, there is no regular transport to any of these islands, except to the closest ones, and boat charters are expensive.

Nearby islands are inhabited by bands of nomadic Moken or sea gypsies. Opposite Kawthoung's harbour the southernmost island in the Myeik Archipelago, **Mwedaw Kyun**, is mounted by two gilded zedi.

Thahtay Kyun Thahtay Kyun (Thahtay – Rich Man – Island; known as Pulau Ru to the Moken), one of the closest isles, sports a large resort known variously as Andaman Club and Andaman Club Resort (see Places to Stay later in this section). There are no beaches to speak of on the island, but the resort offers trips to beaches on Zadetgale Kyun and Zadetgyi Khun, each about 45 minutes away by speedboat.

Farther offshore, **Lampi Kyun**, possibly one of the least disturbed island habitats in Southeast Asia, has been designated as a national park. Extending about 90km long and 8km wide, this rugged landmass features a forested, mountainous interior and two year-round rivers that flow into the sea from the island's western shore. According to *Action Asia* magazine, known wildlife on the island includes white-bellied sea eagles, Brahminy kites, parakeets, hornbills, gibbons, crab-eating macaques, flying lemurs, civets, tigers, leopard cats, boar, barking deer, sea otters, crocodiles and fruit bats. Some naturalists speculate the interior of Lampi might harbour hitherto undiscovered animal species, or species thought to be extinct elsewhere in Southeast Asia, such as the Sumatran rhinoceros or kouprey. A few Phuket-based tour companies operate hiking and river excursions on Lampi – see Diving & Snorkelling under the Activities section in the Facts for the Visitor chapter for a list of outfitters.

Organised Tours

Jansom Travel *(in Ranong, Thailand, ☎ 077 821 576)* offers Kawthoung tours aboard four boats with capacities ranging from 15 to 200 people. A half-day tour costing 750B per person (minimum of 10) sails from Ranong at 8am, visits a couple of pagodas in Kawthoung and returns to Ranong around noon.

Places to Stay

So far there are only two places in Kawthoung approved to accept foreigners. Note that Thai baht are readily accepted in Kawthoung.

Honey Bear Hotel *(in Yangon ☎ 01-229 6190; rooms 700B)*, on the waterfront about 150m from Myoma jetty (the main landing for boats to/from Ranong), this modern and friendly place offers 24-hour power and 39 clean rooms with air-con, satellite TV and cold-water shower.

The mouldy **Kawthoung Motel** *(rooms US$25 or 1000B)*, about 300m beyond the main immigration office and about 500m from the jetty, is the other option. The simple double rooms have private cold-water shower, and rates include breakfast.

Andaman Club Resort *(in Ranong ☎ 077 830 463, in Bangkok ☎ 026 798 389; rooms from US$125-465)*, on nearby 700-hectare Thahtay Kyun, is a huge five-star hotel complex sporting a casino, duty-free shops and a Jack Nicklaus–designed 18-hole golf course. Well-heeled Thai and Singaporean gamblers shack up here. All 191 rooms come with sea views. You can catch a five-minute boat ride out to the island from the Kawthoung jetty for 100B.

Places to Eat

Li Li Flower Restaurant, attached to the Honey Bear Hotel, is an air-con place serving good Thai, Bamar and Chinese food along with well-chilled beer. Around the corner from the hotel is a plain, no-name **Thai restaurant** – look for a glass case out the front filled with pans containing Thai curries.

Smile Restaurant is a Chinese-run place up the hill from the jetty near the Kawthoung Motel. It's one of the few places besides the Li Li Flower offering cold drinks all day. The English-language menu offers several seafood dishes, including a delicious crab curry.

Getting There & Away

It is now legal to travel between Dawei and Kawthoung by plane or ship, or between Yangon and Dawei by plane. Road travel to Kawthoung, however, is forbidden.

Air Flights between Yangon and Kawthoung cost US$130 on YA or US$145 on MA. All flights stop in Myeik and Dawei. See the Getting There & Away entries in the Dawei and Myeik sections earlier in this chapter for details on these individual flight segments.

Bus Buses run between Kawthoung and Myeik, but road conditions are bad and robbery is not uncommon. Hence foreigners are unlikely to be permitted to travel this route.

In 1993 the government began constructing a new Myeik-Kawthoung road that passes through Tanintharyi and Bokpyin. The 486km road passes through some beautiful scenery, including over 300 rivers and streams.

Boat Boats to Kawthoung (50B, 20 minutes) leave the Saphan Pla pier near Ranong regularly from around 7am till 6pm. You can charter a boat for 200B to 400B, depending on the size of the boat and your bargaining skills. After getting your passport stamped by Thai immigration, board one of the boats near the immigration office and you'll be taken to the Burmese immigration office. At this point you must inform immigration authorities whether you're a day visitor – in which case you must pay a fee of US$5 for a day permit. If you have a valid Myanmar visa in your passport, you'll be permitted to stay up to 28 days, but also be required to buy US$200 worth of foreign exchange certificates (FECs). See the Money section in the Facts for the Visitor chapter for more information.

See the Getting There & Away entries in the Dawei and Myeik sections earlier in this chapter for information on ship travel along the coast to/from Yangon.

SOUTHEASTERN MYANMAR

Western Myanmar

The Rakhaing Yoma (Arakan Range) separates the Rakhaing and Chin States from the central Ayeyarwady (Irrawaddy) River plains. Isolated from the Bamar heartland, in many ways the inhabitants of both states have more in common with the peoples of eastern India and Bangladesh.

Highlights

- Impressive and secluded 16th-century temple ruins and murals at Mrauk U
- The historic port town of Sittwe, overlooking the Bay of Bengal
- Indigenous Rakhaing and Chin cultures
- Fishing villages and pristine sandy beaches at Ngapali Beach

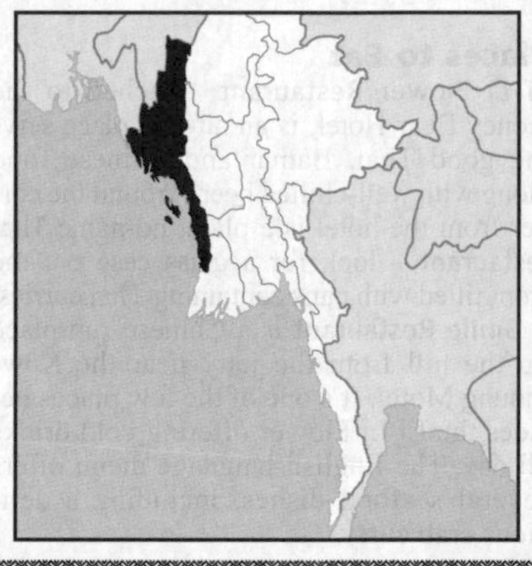

The Peoples of Western Myanmar

The Rakhaing Rakhaing ethnicity is a controversial topic – are the Rakhaing actually Bamar (Burmans) with Indian blood, Indians with Bamar characteristics, or a separate race (as is claimed by the Rohingya insurgents)? Although the first inhabitants of the region were a dark-skinned Negrito tribe known as the Bilu, later migrants from the eastern Indian subcontinent developed the first Hindu-Buddhist kingdoms in Myanmar before the first Christian millennium. These kingdoms flourished before the invasion of the Tibeto-Burmans from the north and east in the 9th and 18th centuries. The current inhabitants of the state may thus be mixed descendants of all three groups: Bilu, Bengali and Bamar.

The Burmese government denies the existence of a Rohingya minority, a group of around three million people who distinguish themselves from the Rakhaing majority by their Islamic faith. Many Rakhaing Muslims – Rohingya as they prefer to be called – have fled to neighbouring Bangladesh and India to escape Bamar persecution.

The Chin The Chin State, to the immediate north of Rakhaing, is hilly and sparsely populated. The people and culture exhibit a mixture of native, Bengali and Indian influences similar to that found among the Rakhaing, with a much lower Burman presence. As in Rakhaing State, there have been clear governmental efforts in recent years to promote Burmese culture at the expense of Chin culture, and many Chin have fled west to Bangladesh and India.

Of Tibeto-Burman ancestry, the Chin call themselves Zo-mi or Lai-mi (both terms mean 'mountain people'), and share a culture, food and language with the Zo of the adjacent state of Mizoram in India. Outsiders name the different subgroups around the state according to the district in which they live, eg, Tidam Chin, Falam Chin, Haka Chin.

Traditionally the Chin practise swidden (slash-and-burn) agriculture. They are also skilled hunters, and animal sacrifice plays a role in important animistic ceremonies. Currently, Chin State has the largest proportion of animists of any state in Myanmar, but the Zo culture is fast disappearing in the face of Christian and Buddhist missionary influences. Some Chin follow the Pau Chin Hau religion, which is based on the worship of a

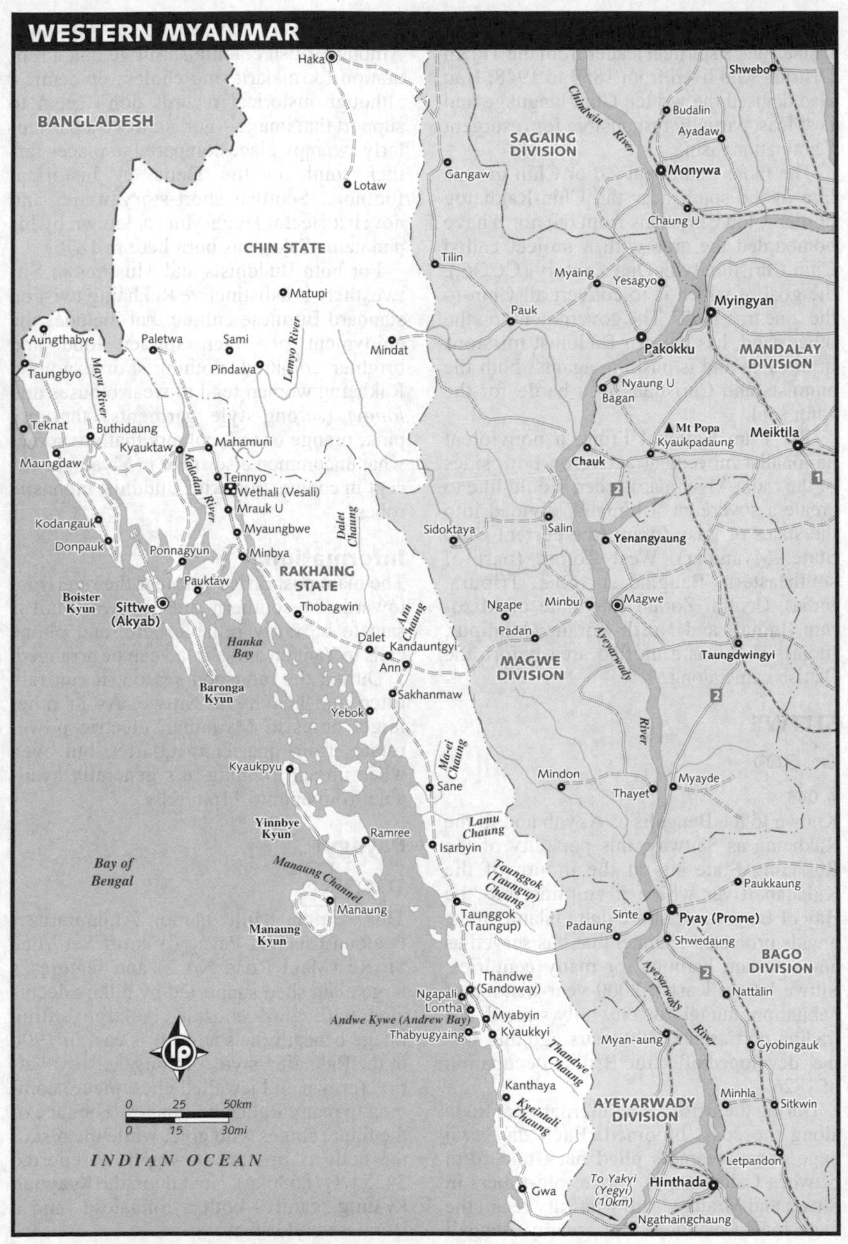
WESTERN MYANMAR
BANGLADESH
CHIN STATE
SAGAING DIVISION
MANDALAY DIVISION
MAGWE DIVISION
RAKHAING STATE
BAGO DIVISION
AYEYARWADY DIVISION
Haka
Lotaw
Gangaw
Tilin
Matupi
Sami
Paletwa
Pindawa
Mindat
Lemyo River
Chindwin River
Shwebo
Budalin
Ayadaw
Monywa
Chaung U
Myaing
Yesagyo
Pauk
Myingyan
Pakokku
Nyaung U
Bagan
Mt Popa
Kyaukpadaung
Meiktila
Chauk
Aungthabye
Taungbyo
Mayu River
Teknat
Buthidaung
Maungdaw
Kyauktaw
Mahamuni
Kaladan River
Teinnyo
Wethali (Vesali)
Mraik U
Myaungbwe
Kodangauk
Donpauk
Ponnagyun
Minbya
Dalet Chaung
Sidoktaya
Salin
Yenangyaung
Pauktaw
Boister Kyun
Sittwe (Akyab)
Thobagwin
Hanka Bay
Dalet
Kandauntgyi
Ann
Ann Chaung
Ngape
Minbu
Magwe
Padan
Ayeyarwady River
Taungdwingyi
Baronga Kyun
Sakhanmaw
Yebok
Kyaukpyu
Ma-ei Chaung
Sane
Mindon
Thayet
Myayde
Yinnbye Kyun
Ramree
Lamu Chaung
Isarbyin
Bay of Bengal
Manaung Channel
Manaung
Manaung Kyun
Taunggok (Taungup) Chaung
Taunggok (Taungup)
Paukkaung
Sinte
Padaung
Pyay (Prome)
Shwedaung
Thandwe (Sandoway)
Ngapali
Lontha
Myabyin
Andwe Kywe (Andrew Bay)
Thabyugyaing
Kyaukkyi
Thandwe Chaung
Nattalin
Myan-aung
Gyobingauk
Kanthaya
Kyeintali Chaung
Minhla
Sitkwin
0 25 50km
0 15 30mi
INDIAN OCEAN
Letpandon
Gwa
To Yakyi (Yegyi) (10km)
Hinthada
Ngathaingchaung
1
2

deity called Pasian and named after Pau China Hau, a spiritual leader from the Tidam District, who lived from 1859 to 1948. Hau also devised the written Chin language and is at least partially responsible for resurgent Chin nationalism.

The more traditional Zo or Chin groups live in the south near the Chin-Rakhaing border. Chin Christians from the north have bombarded the area with a project called Chin Christianity in One Century (CCOC), the goal of which is to convert all Chin to the 'one true faith'. The government, on the other hand, has its own Buddhist missions in the area and is pushing against both the animists and Christians in a battle for the Chin soul.

The Chin National Front, a nonviolent nationalist movement active on both sides of the India-Myanmar border, would like to create a sovereign 'Chinland' divided into the states of East Zoram (the current Chin State, Myanmar), West Zoram (part of southeastern Bangladesh plus Tripura, India), Central Zoram (the state of Mizoram, India), and North Zoram (Manipur, India). This was a unified area before the British came along.

SITTWE

စစ်တွေ

☎ 043

Known to the Bengalis as Akyab and to the Rakhaing as Saitway, this port city of the Rakhaing State sits at the mouth of the Kaladan River where it empties into the Bay of Bengal. Offshore delta islands form a wide protected channel that has served as an important harbour for many centuries. Sittwe has at least a 2000-year history of habitation, though the city only started as a trading port around 200 years ago and further developed after the British occupation of 1826.

During the British era, international trade along the coast bloomed. Each day, two huge cargo steamers plied back and forth between Calcutta and Sittwe; old-timers in Sittwe and Mrauk U still wistfully recall the huge Indian mangoes and creamy Bengali *halvah* (sweet) that arrived on the ships. Among British colonials, Sittwe had a reputation for malaria and cholera epidemics, although historical records don't seem to support that image – nor is Sittwe a particularly swampy place compared to places farther south in the Delta. A historical footnote: Scottish short-story writer and novelist Hector Hugh Munro, known by his pen name Saki, was born here in 1870.

For both Buddhists and Muslims in Sittwe, there is a distinctive Rakhaing twist on standard Burmese culture that includes the enjoyment of much spicier food and brighter coloured clothing. For example, Rakhaing women tend to wear blouses and *longyi* (sarong-style garments) that are pink, orange or red, colours that are somewhat uncommon elsewhere in Myanmar except in conjunction with Buddhist monastic robes.

Information

The main post office sits near the riverfront towards the southern end of town. Mail is said to be fairly reliable here, and phone calls to Yangon and abroad can be arranged.

During the monsoon season, it can rain often and heavily in Sittwe. As in other larger cities in Myanmar, electric power rotates from quarter to quarter, but even when up and running, it's generally available from 6pm to 11pm only.

Payagyi

ဘုရားကြီး

This temple (full name: Atulamarazei Pyeloun Chantha Payagyi) is off Set Yone Su Rd (Main Road No 2) and features a large plain shed supported by pillars decorated with glass mosaic. A large sitting image beneath the shelter was cast in 1900 in the Rakhaing style – minus the 'royal attire' (crown and jewelled chest piece) common to many Rakhaing images. The face of the figure shines with gold, while the rest of the body is bronze. It weighs a reported 5425 *viss* (8680kg). Next door, the **Kyayouq Kyaung** features both a Sinhalese- and a Burmese-style stupa.

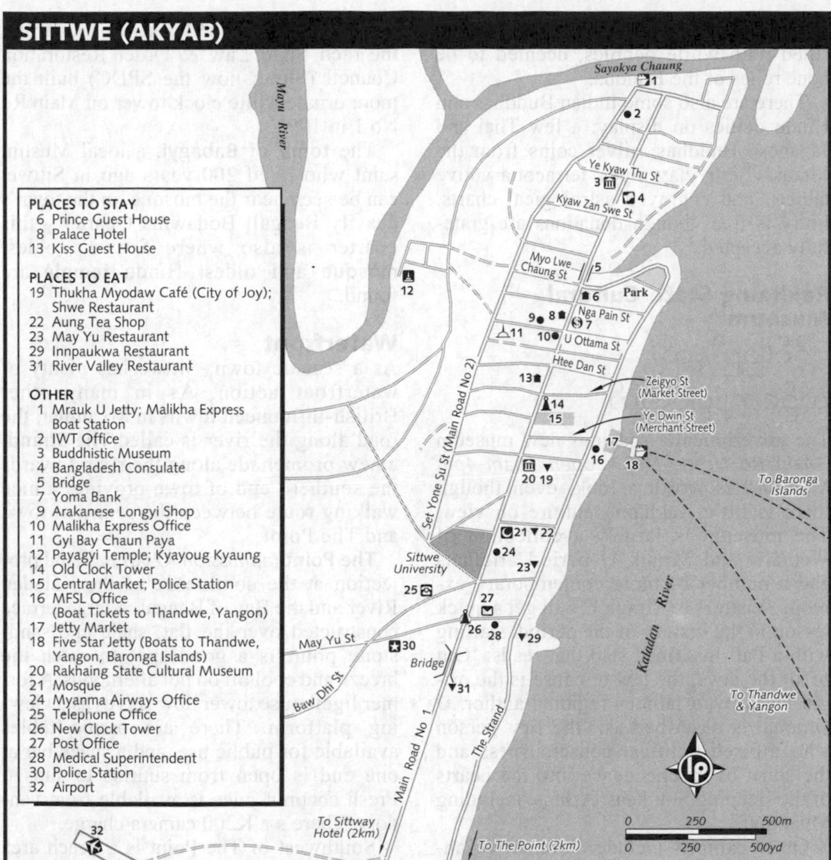

Buddhistic Museum

ဗုဒ္ဓ ပြတိုက်

Housed in a colonial-style building on the grounds of **Mahakuthala Kyaungdawgyi** (Large Monastery of Great Merit), about three blocks south of the *chaung* (canal) that runs behind town, this modest two-storey museum is the best place in Myanmar to view Rakhaing-style Buddha images. Maintained by resident monks, the collection here represents a rare instance of historical preservation in a country where older Buddhas are frequently stolen and sold – partly due to the dire need for foreign exchange, partly because the Burmese generally associate older Buddhas with karmic accumulations that they would rather not contend with.

Most of the images are under a metre in height and feature the royal attire common to Rakhaing Buddhas. The majority date to the Mrauk U period, although a few date as far back as the Wethali era, and are made of bronze, silver, nickel, quartz or alabaster. Unique motifs include Buddhas seated on pedestals, which are in turn supported on the backs of elephants that stand in a circle.

In glass cases are numerous small saucers filled with white pebbles, deemed to be bone relics of the Buddha.

There are also some Indian Buddhas and Hindu deities on display: a few Thai and Japanese Buddhas; silver coins from the Mrauk U era; clay pipes; terracotta votive tablets; and engraved astrological charts. Entry is free, though donations are gratefully accepted.

Rakhaing State Cultural Museum

The government's spacious new museum *(Main Rd No 1; US$2; open 10am-4pm Mon-Sat)* is worth a look, even though there is little Rakhaing culture on view. The museum is largely a collection of Wethali- and Mrauk U–period artefacts and a number of more contemporary exhibits. Visitors to Mrauk U will get a quick lesson in the history of the period, starting with a Pali-inscribed slab that reads: 'Out of all the laws, the law of cause is the origin.' Nearby, a famous regional author, U Ottama, is described as: 'the first person who infused political consciousness and the spirit of independence into the hearts of the sleeping Southeast Asians, including Myanmar.'

Other exhibits include dioramas of ancient cities; replicas of a crocodile xylophone and a coconut-shell violin; local school children's sketches of Mrauk U pictographs; and the famous '64 Kinds of Coiffures of the Mrauk U Period', which adorn a row of mannequin heads in a glass case on the museum's upper floor.

The helpful curator, U Tin Aung Soe, told us that visitors should come to the side door if they find the museum closed for any reason.

Around Town

An old steel **clock tower** topped with a weathervane in the centre of town was erected by the Dutch in the 18th century. As a counter-symbol of Burmese nationalism, the then State Law & Order Restoration Council (Slorc; now the SPDC) built the more ornate white clock tower on Main Rd No 1 in 1991.

The **tomb of Babagyi**, a local Muslim saint who lived 200 years ago in Sittwe, can be seen near the mosque, in the town's heavily Bengali Bodawma Quarter – this quarter is also where Sittwe's oldest **mosque** and oldest Hindu **temple** are found.

Waterfront

As a seaside town, Sittwe has plenty of waterfront action. As in many other British-influenced towns in Myanmar, the road along the river is called **The Strand**; a new promenade along the river towards the southern end of town provides a nice walking route between the centre of town and The Point.

The Point *(admission K250)* is a land projection at the confluence of the Kaladan River and the Bay of Bengal. A large terrace constructed over the flat, shale and sandstone point is a good spot to catch the breeze and cool off on hot afternoons. A former lighthouse tower now serves as a viewing platform. There are picnic tables available for public use, and a snack bar at one end is open from sunrise to sunset. Fresh coconut juice is available from vendors. There's a K200 camera charge.

Southwest of The Point is a beach area with grey-brown sand. Trucks drive onto the beach to collect sand for construction use but overall, it's OK for swimming, especially if you move farther west away from The Point, towards the Sittway Hotel. The main beach hazard is probably hotel guests practising golf.

About halfway up the shore side of town, heading north, is an inlet where fishing boats moor. During low tide, the boats rest on mudflats, and the fishermen retire to a group of huts on shore. Just north of the inlet is the harbour proper, where ocean-going vessels dock including oil tankers, Myanma Five Star Line (MFSL) cargo and passenger ships, and the Malikha Express fast boat.

Places to Stay

At the time of writing, there were only a few places in town licensed to accept foreigners.

Prince Guest House *(☎ 21395; 27 Main Rd; rooms per person US$5, air-con room US$15)* is in the centre of town next door to a small, century-old mosque. The cheery, yellow three-storey wooden building features basic but clean rooms with ceiling fans, and a bathroom down the hall. There is also one huge room with air-conditioning, fridge, private bathroom and beds with decent mattresses and mosquito nets. As it's at the back of the building, this room is quieter than those at the front. There is also a small sitting terrace off the 3rd floor and the family staff are quite helpful.

Palace Hotel *(singles/doubles with cold-water bathrooms US$5/10)*, a three-storey hotel near the Prince Guest House, offers large rooms with ceiling fan that shuts off at 11pm. Even though the rooms have screens, it's a good idea to accept the management's offer of a mosquito net. Breakfast is not included, but the staff will arrange to serve *mohinga* (rice noodles in fish soup) in the lobby if you request it the day before.

Kiss Guest House, on the main road, doesn't yet accept foreigners. If it does in future, we found it to be clean and friendly.

Travellers keen to avoid government-owned hotels should bypass the **Sittway Hotel**, about 1km west of The Point.

Places to Eat

Seafood and spicy Rakhaing curries are what Sittwe kitchens do best. If you can manage to find it, order *kagadit*, a delicious white-fleshed fish caught off the coast of Sittwe, best lightly fried whole and served with a tasty lime-garlic-chilli sauce *(chin ngan za)*.

The attractive **River Valley Restaurant** *(multi-course meals K1000)*, about 200m south of the new clock tower on the main road, is one of the top places in town. The menu is mostly Chinese- and Rakhaing-style seafood. It's best visited by night, when the nearby river isn't so visible.

The all-wood, brightly painted **Innpaukwa Restaurant** *(Strand Rd)*, near the post office on the waterfront, is probably Sittwe's finest. Service can be slow but the food is good. and you can dine indoors or on the terrace, which juts out over the adjacent mangrove swamp.

May Yu Restaurant, just north of Innpaukwa, is one of Sittwe's top three eateries, serving a variety of Chinese and Rakhaing dishes.

Good, hot Rakhaing curries can be obtained from various **street vendors** and **rice shops** *(htamin zain)* around town, especially on the street behind the new culture museum. One of Sittwe's specialities is *moundi*, a Rakhaing version of mohinga. Moundi is usually served dry, but is sometimes served in a light broth, instead of the thicker fish stew native to central Myanmar. It usually comes with grilled onions and garlic, chilli sauce and crumbled dried fish. At night vendors light candles along Main Rd No 1 to sell peanut brittle, and sticky rice and coconut steamed in bamboo joints.

Aung Tea Shop, near the mosque, opens early and by 7am is full of locals savouring the shop's delicious chapati, *nam-bya* (nan), *palata* (fried flatbread) and potato curry.

Thukha Myodaw Café (City of Joy), in the same general vicinity, serves decent *hsi htamin* (turmeric-coloured sticky rice) and *bei palata* (stuffed palata), and what look to be slabs of thick French toast – bread fried in egg batter with banana essence. Just as good, and serving similar fare, is the nearby **Shwe Restaurant.**

Shopping

At the **central market**, or at one of the few **longyi shops** in town, you can purchase the famous Rakhaing-style longyi. These garments feature a supplementary-weft weaving technique that creates dense, geometric patterns with a shimmering patina.

Check out a good selection of fine Rakhaing cloth at **Diamond Longgyi Shop** *(U Ottama St)*.

Getting There & Away

Air Air Mandalay (AM) makes the Yangon to Sittwe flight (US$131, via Thandwe) on Wednesday and Sunday. On Yangon Airways (YA) it's US$128. A government MA flight crashed in January 1998 at Sittwe, killing several passengers. Sittwe's airstrip is only 10 minutes from town.

It costs K800 to charter a pick-up for this short ride, or around K100 per person in a shared pick-up. A small taxi costs K400 and can be arranged from your hotel. Three small shops next to the airport serve fried rice, moundi, tea, coffee, soft drinks and beer. Check-in is chaotic; don't forget to clear immigration and customs, for which there are no English signs.

Boat The Inland Water Transport (IWT) office is near the government Mrauk U jetty, which sits on Sayokya Chaung, a tributary of the Mayu River, which in turn runs northwest off Kaladan River. See the Mrauk U section later in this chapter for details on ferries to Mrauk U.

The fastest (and most expensive) transport option between Taunggok and Sittwe is the Malikha Express, a sleek private passenger craft that sails from Taunggok to Sittwe on Wednesday and Saturday between 7am and 9.30am, and from Sittwe to Taunggok on Monday and Thursday between 7am and 9.30am. The trip takes just over six hours (including a lunch stop in the small port town of Kyaukpyu) and costs US$50 one way. In Taunggok, the Malikha Express boat station is a rambling, unsignposted thatched-roof affair, 200m off the road, on the right, just before the main jetty area. You can buy tickets here, but to be on the safe side, you should first try the Malikha Express office in Taunggok proper, off the main road, not far from the Royal Guest House. In Sittwe, the Malikha Express office is on the main road, diagonally opposite the Yoma Bank.

Malikha Express also whizzes from Sittwe to Mrauk U on Sunday at 7am, and from Mrauk U to Sittwe at 7am on Monday. The trip takes less than two hours, but costs foreigners a hefty US$25. There's no discount for a return trip.

There are also cargo boats that you can ride to Mrauk U. See Getting There & Away under Mrauk U later in this chapter for details.

Road There is a road route of sorts linking Sittwe with Yangon, but it takes 36 to 48 hours, going via Minbu. But the standard of the road is only one hurdle on this route – foreign tourists must also have clearance to travel this way (contact MTT for more details). There is also a road between Sittwe and Mrauk U, but at the time of writing it was not open to foreigners.

Getting Around

Trishaw is the main form of public transport for getting around Sittwe. A ride from Mrauk U jetty to the Prince Guest House costs K100 per person.

A good guide can make all the difference in a region such as Sittwe and Mrauk U. Sittwe hotels such as The Prince can provide guides to pick you up from Sittwe airport or jetty area and take you to Mrauk U (and a Chin State village) and back again as a three-day trip for US$40 (this is the guide fee only).

AROUND SITTWE

Baronga Islands

ဗရွန်းဂါး ကျွန်း

A visit to these three islands (also known as Phaynoka, Bayonga and Bayonka), just offshore, near the mouth of the Kaladan River, makes for an interesting day excursion. Hand-dug, privately owned oil wells are a major source of livelihood on the island of East Baronga. The hereditary owners of the wells, called *twin-zar* (well-eater), typically employ five worker-partners to operate the well, each of whom receives an equal share of the daily production. Simple tripod pumps extract the crude product, which is sold to local agents who refine the petroleum into diesel, kerosene and wax for local distribution. Although the island oil deposits tapped by the twin-zar are generally

MARK WEBSTER

Sea life, Myeik Archipelago, Tanintharyi Division

COREY WISE

Mural at Kyaiktiyo stupa complex, Mon State

RICHARD I'ANSON

An elderly man is carried up the mountain to venerate Kyaiktiyo, Mon State.

JOE CUMMINGS

Theindawgyi Paya, Myeik

MARK WEBSTER

A gaudy sea slug in the Myeik Archipelago, Tanintharyi Division

COREY WISE
The ruins of 16th-century Andaw Paya, Mrauk U, Rakhaing State

COREY WISE
Painted Buddha footprints, Shittaung Paya, Mrauk U

BERNARD NAPTHINE
Serene Buddha face, Mrauk U

COREY WISE
The interior passageway of Kothaung Temple, Mrauk U

too small for industrial purposes, foreign oil companies have recently begun offshore explorations in the area.

Fishermen and coconut farmers live on Middle and West Baronga. The fishing is said to be especially good in the channel between Middle and East Baronga, and there are some decent beaches on the western side of West Baronga and along the southwestern shore of East Baronga. Regular boats to East Baronga leave from the Mrauk U jetty (also called Sayokya jetty) twice a week, but foreigners are supposedly required to gain permission from the regional army command to make this trip. One boat stops at a jetty on the eastern side of the island, while a larger boat operated by Myanma Oil & Gas Enterprises stops on the western side before continuing to Yangon. You can also charter a boat to the islands, costing US$100 to US$200, for the return trip, depending on the boat.

MRAUK U

မြောက်ဦး

Once a centre for one of Myanmar's most powerful kingdoms, Mrauk U (in Burmese, Myauk U) straddles the banks of Aungdat Chaung, a tributary of the Kaladan River, 72km from the coast. The surrounding rice paddies are well watered by the annual monsoon, which brings up to 5m of rain. Also cultivated in the region are coconut, banana, jackfruit, mango, areca nut, citrus, lychee and a variety of vegetables.

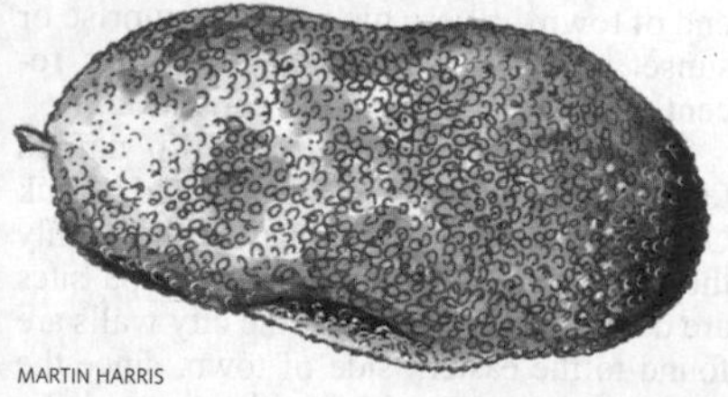

MARTIN HARRIS

Not to be confused with the durian, the jackfruit is bigger, smoother and less challenging to eat!

History

The Rakhaing king, Minzawmun, founded Mrauk U in 1433, although in the common practice of the times, dynastic legends endowed the kingdom with a make-believe 3000-year history. A network of chaung allowed access by large boats, even ocean-going vessels.

In the next century, the city became a free port that traded with the Middle East, Asia, Holland, Portugal and Spain; elephants were one of the main commodities supplied from the Rakhaing region. A Dutchman who visited Mrauk U in the 16th century described it as one of the richest cities in Asia, and compared it with Amsterdam and London in size and prosperity. The remains of a European quarter called Daingri Kan can still be seen southwest of town.

The Mrauk U dynasty, which lasted 352 years, was much feared by the peoples of the Indian subcontinent and central Myanmar, who called the Rakhaing warlords Magh (the origins of this name are lost). Mrauk U kings even hired Japanese samurai as bodyguards against assassination. At Mrauk U's peak, King Minbin (1531–53) created a naval fleet of some 10,000 war boats that dominated the Bay of Bengal and Gulf of Martaban.

Mrauk U was a successor to two earlier kingdoms in the area: Dhanyawady (circa 1st to 6th centuries AD) and Wethali (3rd to 10th centuries AD), the remains of which are still visible to the north. All three kingdoms blended elements of Theravada and Mahayana Buddhism with Hinduism and Islam. In the late 18th century, the Konbaung dynasty asserted its power over the region and Mrauk U was integrated into the Bamar kingdoms centred around Mandalay.

After the First Anglo-Burmese War (1824–26), the British Raj annexed Rakhaing and set up its administrative headquarters in Sittwe, thus turning Mrauk U into a political backwater virtually overnight. The Burmese name gradually changed to Myohaung (Old City), though the Rakhaing continued to call the town Mrauk U.

Today, the original city lies in ruins and a small, poor town with simple buildings of

MRAUK U

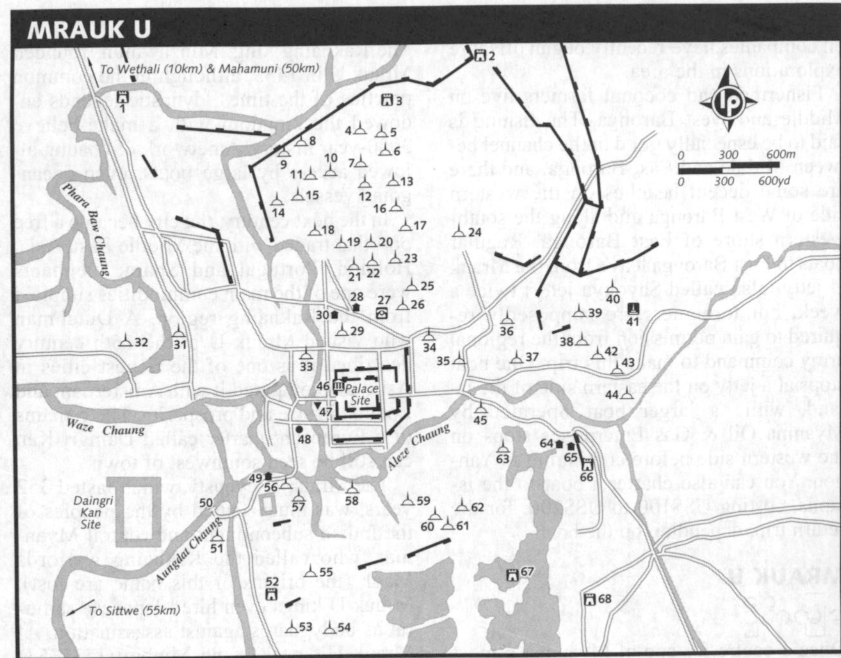

brick, wood and thatch has grown up adjacent to the old city site. It's the kind of town where every man, woman and child seems to chew betel and smoke cheroots. The town is intersected by several chaung, the main source of transport and water. Much daily activity seems to be taken up with water trips to and from the chaung. Instead of the usual clay pots or rectangular oil cans employed in most of the rest of Myanmar, Mrauk U residents carry shiny aluminium water pots (imported from India) on their hips with one arm crooked around the pot's neck.

One of the best times – or worst, depending on your taste – to visit Mrauk U is during the huge *paya pwe* (pagoda festival) held in mid-May. Centred on the large grassy open area to the southern side of Dukkanthein, the festival lasts about a week and features the usual menu of fortune-tellers, craft vendors, seriocomic theatre, music and food.

Temples of Mrauk U

Unlike Bagan (Pagan), where temple ruins are strewn over a vast plain, the ruins of Mrauk U sit on or against bluffs in hilly terrain, interlaced with streams and leafy trees. Overall this lends an intimate, friendly feel to the place. In addition to the major sites 1km or 2km northeast of town, there are lots of stupas next to the town itself, especially on hillocks along the stream at the southern end of town – a very nice area for sunrise or sunset strolls. As at Bagan, there has recently been a great deal of renovation.

Altogether, there are around 70 named temple, stupa or city-wall sites around Mrauk U, plus dozens of other unnamed sites. Only the more significant temple and stupa sites are described here. Most of the city walls are found to the eastern side of town, since the west, north and south provided natural defences in the form of hills and streams. The walls were built to fill in the gaps in these natural barriers, so they appear intermittently.

MRAUK U

PLACES TO STAY & EAT

- 28 Nawarat Hotel
- 30 Mrauk U Hotel
- 47 Pan Thazin Restaurant; Moe Cherry Restaurant
- 49 Royal City Guesthouse
- 64 Prince Hotel; Golden Valley Resort
- 65 Vesali Resort Hotel

OTHER

- 1 Ngwetaung Fortress
- 2 Yenla Fortress
- 3 Ahmyinttaung Fortress
- 4 Pitaka Taik
- 5 Anoma Shwekhyatheing
- 6 Alaisaita
- 7 Htuparyon
- 8 Shantaung
- 9 Tayzayamo
- 10 Thoropavata
- 11 Mokseiktaw
- 12 Laungbanpyauk Paya
- 13 Mahabodhi Shwegu
- 14 Parahla
- 15 Myatanzaung
- 16 Ratanasanraway
- 17 Ratanamhankin
- 18 Laymyetnha
- 19 Dukkanthein
- 20 Ratanabon
- 21 Shittaung
- 22 Andaw Paya
- 23 Ratanathinkha
- 24 Ratanamanaung
- 25 Ngapithema
- 26 U Myawa
- 27 International Telephone Station
- 29 Haritaung
- 31 Lokamanaung
- 32 Parabow
- 33 Yokkhataung
- 34 Shwegutaung
- 35 Htintawmu
- 36 Sakyamanaung
- 37 Wuntnattaung
- 38 Neikbuzar (Middle)
- 39 Neikbuzar (Main)
- 40 Paranyinaung
- 41 Kothaung Temple
- 42 Neikbuzar (Lower)
- 43 Paraoke
- 44 Minkhaung Shwegu
- 45 Myawtawmu
- 46 Museum
- 48 Market
- 50 Jetty
- 51 Naretsa
- 52 Aungminggala Fortress
- 53 Laytanknan
- 54 Kaenawin
- 55 Pagan taung
- 56 Sankartaung
- 57 Pannzeemyaung
- 58 Wuthaie Image
- 59 Tinamanaung
- 60 Sakka Thila
- 61 Minkhamaung
- 62 Kalamya
- 63 Shwetaung
- 66 Ponnomyaung Fortress
- 67 Myataung Fortress
- 68 Laythataung Fortress

Palace Ruins & Museum Walls and gateways of sandstone blocks and earth are all that's left of the royal palace, constructed in 1430 according to some sources; as late as 1553 according to others. A Portuguese monk and envoy to Mrauk U described the palace as it appeared during his visit in the 1630s:

> The royal palaces…have massive wooden columns of such extraordinary length and straightness that one wonders there are trees so tall and so straight. The inside columns are entirely gilt, without any admixture of other materials. In the same palace there is a hall gilt from top to bottom which they call the 'Golden House' because it has a vine of the purest gold which occupies the whole roof of the hall, with a hundred and odd gourds of the same pure gold. There are also in that very rich house seven idols of gold, each of the size and proportions of an average man. These idols are adorned on the forehead, breast, arms and waist with many fine precious stones, rubies, emeralds and sapphires, and also with some brilliant old rock diamonds of more than ordinary size.

Unfortunately, the palace buildings were […]t to fire long ago. A museum *(admission free)* within the old palace walls contains a good collection of religious sculpture and other artefacts unearthed around Mrauk U. In the yard out the front, there are several sandstone figures, including a Hindu yoni, headless Buddhas, Vishnu figures and various stelae.

Inside is a collection of Wethali-, Mrauk U– and Konbaung-period Buddhas and Bodhisattvas; votive tablets; small bronze stupas; Krishna statuettes; Buddha heads; musical instruments; sandstone lintels from 15th-century monuments; some broken pieces of painted frescoes from the Shittaung temple; painted ceramics; a large 4th-century relief from Kyauktaw, depicting the Buddha teaching one of his disciples; *dvarapala* (gate guardians) from the 14th-century Mrauk U palace; and ornate 16th-century Portuguese headstone slabs bearing astrological runes. Among the more historically interesting artefacts are a set of stelae dating between the 8th and 16th centuries and inscribed with several different scripts, including Arabic. Some of the Mrauk U Buddhas on display are exquisite in design.

Opening hours for the museum don't seem to be regular – in fact it's often locked – however it's well worth seeking out the caretaker to get in. Some items are labelled in English, though most appear in Burmese only.

Shittaung The most complex and well preserved of the surviving Mrauk U temples, **Shittaung** (in Burmese, Sittaung) was constructed in 1535 by King Minbin, the most powerful of the Rakhaing kings. Its name means 'Shrine of the 80,000 Images', a reference to the number of holy images found inside. A maze-like floor plan, which vaguely resembles a square-cornered pinwheel, suggests the shrine was originally used for Tantric-like initiation rituals. A walk through each of the interior passages exposed the initiate to different sets of formulaic Buddhist messages carved in sandstone on the walls. With its thick walls, tiny windows and commanding views of the surrounding area, the temple may have also served as a royal fortress during times of attack.

Shittaung sits on a bluff known as Phokhaung Taung and presents a layered quadrangle, studded with straight-sided stupas that curve gently at the top where they are joined to their *sikhara* (finials). Though much fewer in number, the stupas are very reminiscent of Indonesia's Borobudur temple in shape, general absence of ornamentation and in the way they rise from platform to platform. The large central and topmost stupa is flanked by 33 smaller stupas lined up in flaring angles to the northern and southern walls; two significant sandstone stupas sit on the lowest platform – the circular **Nay Win Paya** (Sunset Paya) and octagonal **Nay Htwet Paya** (Sunrise Stupa).

The entire monument features a mortarless assembly of laterite and sandstone blocks, carried to Mrauk U by boat along local rivers and streams. At the northern entrance to the complex stands the **Shittaung Pillar**, a 3m four-sided obelisk brought from Wethali to Mrauk U by King Minbin in 1535. Three sides of the pillar are inscribed in Sanskrit; the earliest inscription, facing east, is for the most part illegible but has been dated to between the 3rd and 6th centuries, in the middle of the Dhanyawady era. The western face dates to the early 8th century and displays a list of Rakhaing kings, while the northern face is ascribed to King Minrazagyi in 1593.

A walking tour of the monument takes you through four separate passages, five if you include the reliefs on the exterior walls. The latter are difficult to see unless you climb out onto the crumbling ledges in front of the reliefs. The reliefs appear to represent figures from Hindu-Buddhist mythologies – considered *nat* (spirits) by the Burmese today – who are both protecting and paying homage to the temple interior. Many of these reliefs have decayed into an unrecognisable state and some are missing altogether.

The first **outer chamber** inside Shittaung features arched passages along the outside wall with pairs of Buddha images sitting back-to-back. The inner wall of the 94m passage features sandstone slabs with high relief cut into six tiers. The lowest tier depicts people in Rakhaing dress engaged in festival-oriented activities (eg, boxing, dancing, drama, wrestling) plus work-related activities using elephants, water buffaloes and oxen. On the middle four tiers, over 1000 separate sculptures chronicle 550 *jataka* (scenes from the Buddha's past lives). Along the top layer of reliefs, male and female figures participate in devotional activities. The teaching impetus of the reliefs perhaps implies that festival-going and making a living are lower sorts of human activities; learning about the history of Buddha represents a step up, and then actually taking an active role in the religion is the highest level. Some of the reliefs bear paint remnants. Small depressions along lower ledges were designed to hold oil for illumination. Nowadays the temple caretakers request a small donation to turn on electric lights in the concentric passageways.

The two **inner galleries** display hundreds of Buddha images in niches, while a Buddha footprint is the terminal point of the innermost passage, taking the visitor from an appreciation for the serenity and wisdom of the Buddha to the knowledge that h actually walked on this spot – or so it is said – during his post-enlightenment travels. The route set by the first three passages moves in the traditional clockwise direction, but when you come to the Buddha footprint you're forced to double back counterclockwise, through the smallest and darkest chamber – a twist perhaps further indicative of Tantric influence. Due to the insulating quality of the surrounding laterite substructure, each passageway feels cooler than the last – a perfect symbol for the psychologically 'cooling' effect of the Buddhist teachings.

The best of the Buddha sculptures are reserved for the **innermost sanctuary** and for the large prayer hall added to the eastern side of the temple, where there was once a courtyard. Throughout the monument, the images represent typical Rakhaing style, though most have been restored and many are badly painted. Several images were gathered from other monuments in the region, including the Wethali and Dhanyawady sites. One Wethali image we couldn't identify looked like it had worms crawling out of its ears.

The **prayer hall** itself features an impressively carved and painted wooden ceiling. A lintel around the large portico into the main chamber has been restored in the original style. A Kala (Hindu god of Time and Death) head over this entry is surrounded by *deva* (celestial beings), and a Brahma sits above Kala – a Hindu schema adopted by the Buddhists to show the devotion practised by Hindu deities in the presence of the Buddha.

It's at this temple that tourists are required to pay a US$5 'archaeological zone fee' for Mrauk U. In the main hall of Shittaung you may also be asked to pay a K500 'donation' to cover lighting in the temple.

Andaw Paya Less than a dozen metres to the northeast of Shittaung stands a smaller, eight-sided monument with a similar linear layout – rectangular prayer hall to the east, multispired sanctuary to the west. Sixteen *zedi* (stupas) are aligned in a square-cornered U-shape around the southern, northern and western platforms. As at Shittaung, small windows admit light and ventilation. In this case there are only two concentric passageways lined with Buddha niches; at the innermost core of the shrine, an eight-sided pillar supports the roof.

The original construction of the shrine is ascribed to King Minhlaraza in 1521. King Minrazagyi then rebuilt Andaw in 1596 to enshrine a piece of the tooth relic supposedly brought from Sri Lanka by King Minbin in the early 16th century. Most likely the roofline sikhara date to his later reconstruction, as their slender, terraced style is very different to that found at Shittaung.

Yadanapon Paya A ring of 24 smaller stupas surround the largest stupa in the area just north of Andaw Paya. According to local chronicles, the mammoth stupa was sponsored by Mrauk U's Queen Shin Htway in 1612. During WWII, it was hit by a bomb but it may have already been damaged by treasure hunters attracted by the name, which means 'pile of jewels' or 'treasure'. It has recently been extensively renovated, although in 2002 the sandstone *chinthe* (half-lion, half-dragon guards) at each of the four corners of the surrounding wall remained semi-intact.

Dukkanthein Said to have been constructed by order of King Minphalaung in 1571, Dukkanthein stands on a bluff 100m opposite and to the northwest of Shittaung. A loose translation of the name is 'ordination hall that spiritually reinforces the town', and it certainly looks like a huge bunker from the outside.

Wide stone stairways lead up the eastern and southern sides of the tall base. Simple dome-shaped stupas, similar to those at Shittaung, stand atop receding terraces over a large, slope-sided sanctuary. Two inner cloisters form a U shape around the central rectangular sanctum, in which a series of steps ascend to an egg-shaped Buddha chamber. The cloisters are lined with 146 Buddha niches, along with sandstone reliefs depicting 64 different types of hairstyles for the wives of Mrauk U nobility. A tall entrance on the east side admits light into this interior chamber.

Laymyetnha Looking like a squashed-up version of the adjacent Dukkanthein, this temple dates from 1430. The name means 'four-faced pagoda' and the squat, square base has four entrance projections, topped by small stupas at the four corners around a stubby central stupa. Inside there's a circular passageway with eight Buddhas facing out in eight directions while 20 niches shelter images facing in wards.

Pitaka Taik This compact, highly ornate building is now surrounded by rice paddies, in a secluded site accessible by a narrow path, around 300m northeast of Dukkanthein. It was built in 1591, under King Minphalaung, as a repository for the Tripitaka (Three Baskets; the Buddhist canon); only a few of the 48-such Mrauk U–period libraries have survived. Originally, it is said to have contained 30 *pitaka* (scripture collection) sets brought from Sri Lanka in the mid-17th century, though at the moment it contains nothing but a pile of brick rubble.

The rectangular structure stands only 2.75m high, with a floor plan that measures 12 sq metres. The monument's most distinguishing features are its five-tiered roofline and beautifully decorated east-facing entrance.

Laungbanpyauk Paya Built in 1525 by order of King Minkhaungraza, this zedi stands roughly midway between Yadanapon Paya and Pitaka Taik. Locally it's known as the Plate Pagoda because a wall in front of the structure is embedded with plate-like tiles in bright yellow, red, white, celadon and blue. Not all the tiles are intact though; many broken pieces lie strewn on the ground.

Stylistically, the octagonal stupa somewhat resembles the sikhara atop Andaw Paya, with a receding terrace effect from the base to halfway up each side, followed by a smoothly rising bell shape, topped by a lotus-bud sikhara that's only half intact. Before the latter toppled, the zedi is reputed to have reached 37m in height; today it measures only 23m. Sixteen Buddha niches surround the base of the zedi; unfortunately, thieves have emptied some entirely and taken the heads off the remaining figures. However, the carved lintels over the niches are still impressive.

Mahabodhi Shwegu This squat little hilltop stupa has a long, narrow passageway leading to a central Buddha image, watched by four Buddhas in niches. Scenes from the jataka line the inner side of the passageway. The stupa is shaped like an eight-sided bell, with decorative stonework at the joins, and dates from 1448.

Sakyamanaung Paya Approximately 1km northeast of the old palace walls, this graceful zedi was erected in 1629 under King Thirithudhammaraza. At this point in the development of Mrauk U architecture, the stupa had been modified into a more vertical and highly ornate form, an obvious absorption of Bamar, especially Shan, styles, by way of Bagan and Ava.

The lower half of the well-preserved, 85m zedi features a multi-tiered octagonal shape as at Laungbanpyauk Paya, but beyond this the bell reverts to a layered circular shape which is mounted by a decorative *hti* (umbrella-like top). The western gate into the surrounding compound is guarded by a pair of half-kneeling, half-squatting *yakka* (giants).

Kothaung Temple A couple of kilometres to the east of the palace site, recent restorations have revealed some of the inner corridors of the fortress-like 'Shrine of 90,000 Images'. The temple dates from 1553, and it's said its creator built it to top the 80,000-image Shittaung built by his father, King Minbin. At one corner of the 77m square base, five tiers of tiny stupas have been restored. In the centre of the enclosure, a stupa shelters four Buddha images but it is the thousands of small Buddha **bas-reliefs** on the walls of the outer passage which make the temple so interesting.

Places to Stay

Royal City Guesthouse *(rooms per person US$5)* is a pleasant budget lodging house near the jetty with simple, tidy upstairs

WESTERN MYANMAR

rooms for foreign guests and a common bathroom overlooking the river. The bathroom also overlooks a timber yard, but it usually quietens down after 5pm.

Pleasant Island Bungalows *(bungalows US$10)*, across the chaung from the Royal City Guesthouse, deserves a rave review simply for being located on its very own tiny island. Accessible by a wooden bridge, this cute little establishment is very handy to the jetty and offers a viewing deck overlooking the river.

The friendly but basic **Prince Hotel** *(rooms with private bathroom per person US$5, bungalows US$10)* is a funkier version of the Prince in Sittwe. The standard rooms are a bit on the shabby side, and you should request a mosquito net. Breakfast is included in the price.

Golden Valley Resort *(rooms per person US$5, bungalow US$10)* is similar in price and facilities to its neighbour, the Prince Hotel, and is an attractive enough budget option.

Vesali Resort Hotel *(Yangon office ☎ 01-525609, fax 526325; ⓔ myathiri@mpt mail.net.mm; bungalow singles/doubles with hot-water bathroom US$30/35)* is a serene, beautifully designed place with teak-floored, high-ceiling bungalows set around a picturesque garden and lily pond. It is the perfect retreat after a hard day's pagoda exploring. The staff are friendly and a great breakfast is included in the price.

Nawarat Hotel *(Yangon office ☎ 01-703885, fax 661159; singles/doubles US$30/35)* is bright and well-equipped. The modern air-con rooms have fridge and satellite TV. Breakfast is included. The restaurant, although a little pricey, has excellent food.

Travellers keen to avoid government-owned hotels should stay clear of the rather grim **Mrauk U Hotel**.

Places to Eat

The Rakhaing menu at **Moe Cherry Restaurant** *(meals & beer K1500; open 7am-11pm)* features several tasty curries and appetizers, and cold beer is served. When we visited, the owners were enjoying a Charlie Chaplin video. Like most establishments in town, the electricity is on from 6.30pm to 11pm. Moe Cherry will also prepare a lunch box for you to take on an excursion around Mrauk U or for the ferry back to Sittwe.

Pan Thazin Restaurant, next door to Moe Cherry, is an excellent place and even better than its popular neighbour for traditional Bamar cuisine. Prices are similar to Moe Cherry, and the service here is also very good, although it lacks the open-air, upstairs ambience of Moe Cherry.

Getting There & Away

With the price of fuel quite high in this area, government ferries have stopped running between Sittwe and Mrauk U. Private ferries often carry at least twice the number of passengers they were designed to. The lower steel deck is chaotic, while the upper deck is also quite crowded, but has a limited number of sling chairs, plus a salon cabin. The standard fare for foreigners is US$9 each way. You can rent a sling chair for K500, but do so immediately upon boarding because they go fast.

The salon cabin has 10 or so wooden chairs and a table. It's the coolest part of the boat since it gets direct breezes through windows, and it has an attached toilet room. The cabin costs US$54 (US$90 return), although it's really not worth that sort of money. Buy your ticket at the jetty; it's quite informal, but allow an extra 20 minutes to fill out a form at a table amid coils of rope, wooden crates and thick stacks of tattered forms wrapped in brown paper.

Ferries leave daily from the Mrauk U jetty on Sayokya Chaung, at the northern end of Sittwe. Departure times depend on the tide, but boats usually depart from Sittwe at 7am on Monday and Thursday, and depart from Mrauk U at 7am on Friday and Tuesday.

There's nearly always a small cargo boat heading from Sittwe to Mrauk U, and back again in the morning around 7am or 8am for US$10. There are no chairs as such, but you can usually lounge under cover quite comfortably on deck. To find a cargo boat, simply ask at the jetty area.

You can also charter boats between Sittwe and Mrauk U. These are usually medium-sized (to seat a large group), timber boats, often with the name of a tour company painted on their sides. They can be found at the jetty area in Sittwe or Mrauk U, or through one of the hotels. A round trip (two nights) will cost K45,000, or US$65, per boat. You can also take the ferry one way, and a private boat the other (starting at either Mrauk U or Sittwe). Most types of boats take anything from five to seven hours, usually slightly longer on the way back to Sittwe. Inquire at the jetty, any Sittwe hotel, or the Moe Cherry restaurant in Mrauk U for charter boat information.

For part of the way, boats move against the current on the Kaladan River, then turn east onto the Theinganadi River and go with the current before turning upriver again on the Henyakaw River. The government boat terminates in Kyauktaw, another four hours north of Mrauk U on the Kaladan River, connected to Mrauk U by the Theinganadi River.

On the way, private boats stop at the town of **Ponnagyun (Brahman Island)** on the 26km-long island of the same name. On a hill opposite, over a suspension bridge, you can see the stupa of **Uritaung Paya** (Buddha's Skull Pagoda), supposedly erected in AD 993 and renovated in 1521, 1641 and 1688. The lower half of the large bell shape is whitewashed, the upper half gilded. The village of Ponnagyun has a lively market and plenty of good little food stalls.

Getting Around

A US$5 'zone fee' is collected at the main pagoda of Shittaung. A guide should cost about US$10 per day.

Mrauk U is small enough to explore on foot, but a delightful alternative is to hire a horse and cart, which is easily done through most of the main hotels. A horse, cart and driver will chauffeur you in style around Mrauk U's sites for around K3000 per day.

Sturdy five-seat Willys Jeeps with driver are available for hire through the main hotels for around K8000 per day, while six-seat vans can be hired for around K10,000 per day.

AROUND MRAUK U

Wethali

ဝေသာလီ

Almost 10km north of Mrauk U are the remains of the Wethali, or Vesali (Waithali in the local parlance), kingdom. According to Rakhaing chronicles, Wethali was founded in AD 327 by King Mahataing Chandra. Archaeologists believe that this kingdom lasted until the 8th century. Of the oval-shaped city boundaries that remain, only parts of the moat and walls are still visible amid the rice paddies. Many of the hillocks around this area are actually overgrown stupas. A central palace site, its walls relatively well-preserved, measures about 500m by 300m. The palace prayer hall is now used as an irrigation tank during the rainy season.

Other than these meagre, unexcavated ruins, there is only one other sight worth seeing in Wethali. The **Great Image of Hsu Taung Pre** *(Pye)* sits in the base of a large *pahto* (temple) that is missing all of its superstructure. Now covered with a corrugated metal roof, the 5m Rakhaing-style sitting Buddha and its pedestal are said to be carved from a single piece of solid stone and date to AD 327. The highly revered image is swathed in embroidered red holy cloth and attended by monks and nuns; an umbrella painted with runes stands over the figure. Pilgrims are starting to gild the image from the top down by handing gold-leaf squares to an attendant, who climbs a bamboo scaffold to affix them to the head of the image.

Regular public transport to Wethali from Mrauk U is scarce, but you can arrange to charter a jeep or pick-up through the Moe Cherry Restaurant for around US$15 for a return trip. The once- or twice-daily pick-up north to Mahamuni and Kyauktaw passes Wethali.

Mahamuni Paya

မဟာမုနိဘုရား

The Mahamuni Paya, 40km north of Mrauk U and about 10km east of the farm town of Kyauktaw, sits at the northeastern corner of the old Dhanyawady city site. This was the original site for Mandalay's famous Mahamuni Buddha, a huge and very old bronze image which Rakhaing kings believed provided supernatural protection for their successive kingdoms. When the Bamar, under King Bodawpaya, invaded Rakhaing in 1784, they dismantled the image into three pieces and hauled it over the Rakhaing Yoma to Amarapura to further legitimise the Konbaung dynasty.

Some Rakhaing say the Bamar unknowingly took a counterfeit figure and that the true Mahamuni image lies hidden somewhere in the jungle. Nowadays, three smaller stone images sit on the pedestal where the Mahamuni image once sat. A famous sandstone stele found there depicts a Gupta-style Buddha dating from AD 400 to AD 500.

The current Konbaung-style shrine buildings date to the 18th or 19th centuries, as the earlier ones were destroyed by fire. One of the infamous *yadaya* bells used by Rakhaing rulers to keep invaders at bay was displayed here but has disappeared in recent years.

You can reach the town of Mahamuni by taking a boat to Kyauktaw (four hours from Mrauk U) and from there catching a pick-up east to Mahamuni. It's quicker to go to Kyauktaw by road from Mrauk U (50km, about three hours) but this involves a vehicle charter.

Chin State

For information on visiting the Chin State from neighbouring Mrauk U, see the Excursions into Southern Chin State section, at the end of this chapter.

NGAPALI BEACH

ငပလီ

Of the beach resorts most accessible to Myanmar visitors, Ngapali is easily the prettiest. The origin of the name is something of a mystery, though the most popular story says a homesick Italian who lived here for a while told everyone the beach reminded him of beaches near Naples. The Burmese name does have a meaning of its own – roughly, 'cajoling fish' It's the kind of name that should come with a story, but no-one in the area seems to know it, so perhaps the meaning has been grafted to the Burmese pronunciation.

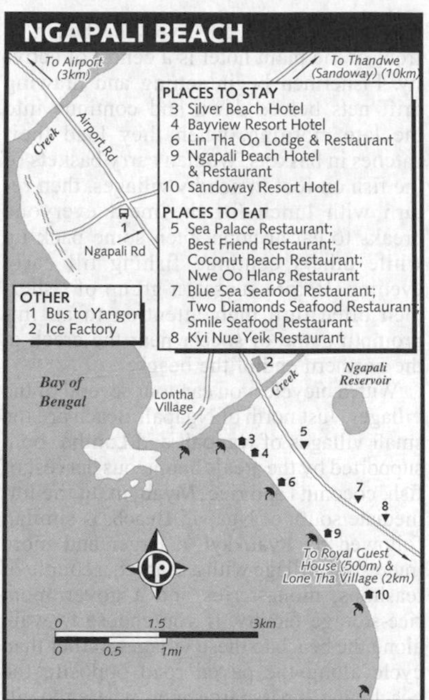

Backed by swaying palms and casuarinas, the Ngapali area is a good place to relax and take a break from the rigours of Myanmar road travel. The very broad, pristine stretch of sand known as Ngapali Beach stretches over 3km, and is separated from several other beaches by small, easily negotiated rocky headlands. Surfing is possible during the monsoon season (mid-May through to mid-September). With the opening of several new hotels and guesthouses, it is now possible to find a room at Ngapali year-round. In the past, the few beach hotels tended to close down because of the heavy rains. Malaria precautions should be taken.

There's more to do around Ngapali than just sit on the white sand and splash around in the sea, though for many people that's reason enough to go. Even the beach in front of the main hotel is a centre of activity. Fishermen begin setting and drawing drift nets before dawn and continue into the late morning, when they load their catches in baskets. Women carry baskets of the fish on foot to nearby villages, then return with lunch for the men; everyone breaks to eat at noon, then some pack up while others continue fishing till early evening. Before sunset, a group of fishermen often turn their attention to an impromptu game of soccer near the creek at the northern end of the beach.

With a bicycle, you can tour several of the villages. Just north of Ngapali Beach are the small villages of **Ngapali** and **Lontha**, both supported by the area's bounteous harvest of fish, coconuts and rice. **Myabyin**, to the immediate south of Ngapali Beach, is similar, followed by **Kyaukkyi**, a larger and more interesting village with a market, a couple of teashops, monasteries and a government rice-storage facility. If you choose to walk along the beach to these villages, rather than cycle along the paved road opposite the beach, you'll pass large areas where the villagers sun-dry fish, shrimp and coconut on cane mats spread over the sand. Just offshore, near these villages, are several small, rocky islets reachable during low tide, and a bit farther south there's a mangrove swamp. Farther offshore are the larger islands of **Balet** and **Kayi**; a two-hour boat trip to these islands can be arranged at any of the hotels or guesthouses for around K5000.

Even farther south is the village of **Lontha** and an inlet of the same name backed by a sweeping curve of mangrove and sand. It's prettiest at high tide; during low tide the bay becomes muddy and rocky. There's a pier here, and the inlet is used heavily by smaller fishing boats, since it's the most protected harbour in this area. The inlet is connected to a larger bay called **Andwe Kywe** on recent government maps, Andrew Bay on older colonial maps (the latter is still the term used by most Burmese). All of these villages are connected by a sealed, two-lane road that ends at the Lontha jetty.

On the other side of the bay (accessible only by boat from this point, or by taking another road farther inland) is the village of **Thabyugyaing**. This village has an MFSL jetty used by big fishing trawlers, MFSL ships and a large seafood processing plant nearby.

Places to Stay

Since AM started a weekly service to nearby Thandwe, the beach area has continued to sprout new accommodation.

Bayview Resort Hotel *(singles/doubles US$40/60)*, at the northern end of the beach, is a joint Burmese-German venture with large air-con rooms, shaded verandas and hot-water showers. The Bayview also features The Catch Restaurant, specialising in seafood and pizzas.

Silver Beach Hotel *(☎ Ngapali 25, in Yangon ☎ 01-294587; singles/doubles with cold-water bathroom US$30/36)* sits in a shaded compound along the beach. The two-bed bungalows have a small veranda, and standard toast-and-eggs breakfast is included in the rates. Prices may be lower outside the popular November-March season. Each room has a fan (electricity from 6pm to 11pm only). There are two large screened windows for a breeze. The management like to come by around sunset to blast each room with bug spray. If this isn't your idea of enjoying sunset on the veranda, you may request that they skip your room.

At the other end of the beach to the Bayview Resort, **Sandoway Resort Hotel** is another joint venture (Burmese-Italian) with similar facilities to the Bayview, though the rates are a good notch up from those at the Bayview.

Linn Thar Oo Lodge *(☎ Ngapali 10, 9, in Yangon ☎ 01-229928; Yangon office 788/L Bogyoke Aung San St; budget bungalows per person US$5, standard singles/doubles US$15/20, larger singles/doubles US$20/25)* has the widest range of room prices and standards, with several four-room wooden bungalows with common bathroom and several standard rooms with cold-water shower and small veranda. There are also two larger and brighter rooms with a large private veranda. Prices include breakfast. The attached restaurant is very good (see Places to Eat).

Royal Guest House *(singles/doubles with shared bathroom US$8/10, triples with bathroom US$20, annexe singles/doubles with bathroom US$20/25)* is a budget option at the far southern end of the beach, beyond the Sandoway Resort Hotel; it's nicely secluded and good value.

Travellers who wish to avoid government-owned hotels should stay clear of **Ngapali Beach Hotel & Restaurant**.

Places to Eat

Lin Thar Oo Lodge Restaurant *(mains from K400)* is right on the beach and nestled into the resort of the same name. This open-air delight has a huge menu of Chinese, Bamar and European specialities and the service is particularly good.

Nwe Oo Hlang Restaurant is a small, friendly, family-run place with fresh seafood plus Bamar and Chinese dishes – and an English-language menu.

Several other family-run restaurants that specialise in fresh seafood are across the road, just north of the Ngapali Beach Hotel. Very little separates these eateries in terms of quality of food, they all deserve more customers than they usually get. These include **Blue Sea Seafood Restaurant**, **Two Diamonds Seafood Restaurant**, **Smile Seafood Restaurant** and **Kyi Nue Yeik Restaurant**.

Similarly, there's a good bunch of local eateries, all prettily lit up at night, near the Bayview. These all offer generous seafood dishes in Bamar and Chinese style, at good prices. They include **Sea Palace**, **Best Friend**, **Coconut Beach** and **Nwe Oo Hlang Restaurant**.

Getting There & Away

See Getting There & Away in the Thandwe section for details on air and road travel to Thandwe, the transport hub for the region.

Getting Around

A pick-up from Thandwe to Ngapali Beach costs about K200 per person. But if you've just touched down at Thandwe airport, there will be a row of buses from most of the Ngapali Beach resorts ready to whisk you away free of charge, whether you have a reservation or not. Thandwe, Kyaukkyi, Myabyin and Lontha are all linked by narrow sealed roads and can be visited by bicycle. At night, a torch is handy for strolling around Ngapali. It's probably easiest to walk along the beach at night, as most lodgings or restaurants front the bay.

Bicycles can be rented from most of the hotels or guesthouses at around K100 per hour.

THANDWE (SANDOWAY)

သံတွဲ

Located 10km northeast of Ngapali Beach, Thandwe (also spelt Thantwe) is the seat of a township by the same name with a population of approximately 80,000. Around 25% of the population is Muslim, most of whom live in the small township and attend the five mosques there. For the most part, the surrounding villages are Buddhist.

Thandwe has been a key Rakhaing centre for many centuries and may originally have been an independent principality with the Sanskrit name of Dvaravati (which roughly translates as 'gated kingdom', a name borrowed from India's epic poem *Ramayana*). Thandwe (Iron-Fastened) may in fact be a Burmese variation of this name. When the British stationed a garrison here around the turn of the century, they twisted the name into Sandoway.

The town boasts a network of sealed and unsealed roads lined with two-storey buildings that range from 50 to 100 years of age, and are constructed of masonry on the ground floors and wood on the upper floors. Away from the centre of town, virtually all houses are made of thatch. A former British jail in the centre of town is now used as a market where vendors sell medicinal herbs, clothes, textiles, hardware and free-market consumer goods. Among the many small shops surrounding the market are a number of gold shops, which suggests that the area is marked by some wealth.

Along the road between Thandwe and Ngapali you'll see a number of rubber plantations, including terraced ones – a deviation from the usual flat groves seen in most parts of the world. Rice and coconuts are also heavily farmed in the area. A battalion from the Burmese 55th Regiment has replaced the old British garrison outside town – so it's not unusual to see trucks overflowing with men in green on the roads.

Three stupas perched on hillsides at the edge of town are of mild interest. **Sandaw Paya**, reportedly built in AD 784 by the Rakhaing king Minyokin to house a Buddha hair relic and rebuilt by the Burmese in 1876, is a fairly ordinary stupa that affords good views of the town, river and surrounding hill. **Nandaw Paya**, on a higher hill opposite, was supposedly erected in 761 by King Minbra to enshrine a rib or piece of a rib of the Buddha. **Andaw Paya**, on a lower hill, claims a molar relic and a dating of 763. Outside one of the shrine buildings at Nandaw stands an old sculpture of a Rakhaing king that reportedly dates to the 6th century. A stone niche, inscribed in the Pali language using Rakhaing script, says the king reigned AD 525–75.

Places to Stay & Eat

San Yeik Nyein Guest House *(rooms per person K500)* is a set of bare but adequate wooden rooms with shared facilities, set over a 'video house' a block south of the market. It wasn't accepting foreigners when we checked.

Thandwe has little in the way of restaurants despite its apparent relative prosperity. **The Point** is a very good teashop, next to the market and opposite a large mosque, and offers whitewashed chairs instead of the usual tiny stools. Sticky rice and palata are available here, as well as nam-bya, which is cooked in an outdoor oval oven painted like a soccer ball. The quality of the tea is very good here, but if you want it less sweet, remember not to stir it. You can also use the ever-present Chinese tea to thin it.

There are several other **tea and cold drink shops** in this area, and in the market itself there are a few rather questionable-looking **noodle vendors**. On the next street south, a few blocks west of the San Yeik Nyein Guest House, **Jupiter Food & Drink** serves a mix of Chinese and Indian pastries, including *paug-si* (steamed buns), *ei-kya-kwe* (long fried pastries), and samosas.

Getting There & Away

Air AM flies from Yangon to Thandwe and back on Wednesday, Friday and Saturday. The flight takes 50 minutes and costs US$111. YA does it for US$108.

MA also flies between Thandwe and Yangon on Tuesday and Friday. For this route MA usually employs an F-27. The fare from Yangon is US$55. On the same days, and with the same aircraft, MA flies from Sittwe via Kyaukpyu for US$50. The flight segment from Thandwe to Kyaukpyu costs US$30.

MA doesn't usually fly to Thandwe during the rainy season (mid-May through to mid-September). AM usually cuts back flights outside the November to April high season, but with new hotels recently opening in nearby Ngapali Beach, expect regular if limited service year-round.

MA maintains a ticket office in the centre of Thandwe. AM has no office in Thandwe as yet; eventually it may establish a local office, most likely at one of the hotels. Until then, the only time you can speak with a representative is when there's an AM plane on the runway at Thandwe airport – the rep accompanies each flight from Yangon, spends about an hour taking care of business at the airport, then boards the return flight to Yangon. If you want to buy or confirm a ticket out of Thandwe, be sure to turn up at the airport around 5pm on days when the AM flights are scheduled to arrive.

An MA flight crashed at Thandwe in 1998.

Bus A variety of buses, pick-ups and taxis operate regionally out of Thandwe. A private bus, Mihara Express, operates between Thandwe and Yangon's Highway bus terminal and costs about K2500. Departure is at 3pm, and the trip takes a rather hellish 16 or 17 hours one way, with breaks at Taunggok and Pyay. From Thandwe to Taunggok it's a three-hour trip. The more mountainous leg between Taunggok and Pyay takes nine to 10 hours – the Taunggok Pass in the Rakhaing Yoma was only breached in 1960. But the road between Pyay and Yangon is one of Myanmar's best, and makes for a smooth four- to five-hour run. Thandwe's bus station sits at the side of the road that leads to Andaw Paya on the edge of town, but if you make a reservation, the bus will pick you up at any Ngapali Beach hotel or guesthouse. There is a Mihara ticket counter in the Emerald Tea Shop at the airport junction, midway between Ngapali Beach and the airport.

Taunggok MTK and Yoma Express buses leave Pyay daily for Taunggok at around 1pm and 7pm, taking about 10 hours. A one-way ticket is K1500, or US$7.

In Taunggok, the **Royal Guesthouse** *(K500 per person)* is on the main street near the bus station. It doesn't have a licence for foreigners, but that doesn't seem to matter in out-of-the-way Taunggok. The **Royal Restaurant** *(meals K700)* opposite the guesthouse dishes up fine, spicy Bamar food. If you're heading for Taunggok's jetty area from downtown Taunggok, a trishaw should cost around K300 and take about 30 minutes, as it's a rough old road.

A longer and more scenic bus route to Thandwe starts in the delta region at Pathein and takes you up the coast. Many of the roads are unsealed and subject to flooding. A bus runs from Pathein northwest to Ngathaingchaung (K150, four or five hours). Buses continue along a decent road from Ngathaingchaung to Gwa (K300, six hours or more, mornings only), on the coast. From Gwa, one bus per day heads straight north to Thandwe (K200, nine hours) on a dusty, unsealed road. Much of the trade on this route is cargo rather than passengers.

There's also a bus route between Thandwe and Pathein that takes you via the small town of Yakyi. It takes about 18 hours, not counting the several hours you may spend waiting in Yakyi for a connecting bus. The leg between Pathein and Yakyi costs K600, and between Thandwe and Yakyi it's around K2500.

Car You can travel the routes described above by private vehicle, depending on the time of year and possible flooding along many coastal roads. Cars can be hired at a cost of about US$40 in Pyay to make the trip to Thandwe.

Boat MFSL sails passenger boats from Yangon to Thabyugyaing jetty, south of Thandwe, once or twice a week, on their way to Sittwe. There's an MFSL office in Thandwe around the corner from the MA office. Dates for voyages to Yangon are posted on a chalkboard. At least one of the government vessels is an express ship, making the trip between Taunggok and Sittwe in a day and a half, with an overnight stay in a village along the way. The fare is US$9 for the boat, and another K150 to stay in the village.

By far the fastest (and most expensive) transport option between Taunggok and Sittwe is the Malikha Express, a sleek private passenger craft that sails from Taunggok to Sittwe (US$50, six hours) on Wednesday and Saturday between 7am and 9.30am, and from Sittwe to Taunggok on Monday and Thursday between 7am and 9.30am. The trip includes a lunch stop in the small port town of Kyaukpyu.

In Taunggok, the Malikha Express boat station is a rambling, unsignposted thatched-roof affair 200m off the road, on the right, just before the main jetty area. You can buy tickets here, but to be on the safe side, you should first try the Malikha Express office in Taunggok proper, off the main road, not far from the Royal Guest House. In Sittwe, the Malikha Express office is on the main road, diagonally opposite the Yoma Bank.

Chartered boats go from the Thabyugyaing jetty to the Lontha jetty for K1200. From Lontha, regular buses to Thandwe cost K20.

It may be difficult to find a cargo boat in Yangon, but not in Taunggok. There is usually some kind of boat going north or south every day. In Taunggok, you need to go to the jetty and ask about departure times. For example, a cargo boat to Sittwe may cost anything from US$9 to US$25 for a two-night/three-day trip. You sleep on the deck with potato and onion sacks, but the crew does cook for you.

Getting Around

Most of Thandwe is easily seen on foot. Trishaws for short trips around town cost about K100.

Local minibuses, as well as pick-ups, cruise several times a day from Thandwe to Lontha for K20; you can get off at Ngapali Beach along the way.

Sometimes you can ride for free to Thandwe from Ngapali with one of the hotel drivers on their way to the morning market to buy food for the hotel restaurant.

KANTHAYA

ကမ်းသာယာ

The Rakhaing coast's latest beach resort is 26km north of Gwa, a small town on the coast just north of the Ayeyarwady Division border, and 130km south of Thandwe. Kanthaya extends a sandy 5km, but few people know about the place yet, partly because access is very limited and partly because Chaungtha Beach to the south and Ngapali Beach to the north are drawing more and more visitors.

It's about six to seven hours by car from Yangon via Ngathaingchaung, about four to five hours from Pathein, or five hours from Ngapali. See the Getting There & Away section under Thandwe for details on public transport to Gwa from Ngathaingchaung and Thandwe.

An old airfield outside Gwa may eventually be renovated for use by AM/MA flights.

EXCURSIONS INTO SOUTHERN CHIN STATE

Although it's possible to visit the northern part of the Chin State by road from Kalewa in the Sagaing Division, the true heart of traditional Chin culture is found in the south. **Paletwa**, just over the state line from the Rakhaing State, can be reached via boat along the Kaladan River from Sittwe or Kyauktaw. There is a road between Mahamuni and Paletwa allowing vehicles to travel direct from Mrauk U, but at the time of writing this road was not open to foreign tourists.

In the Chin Hills some women still have traditionally tattooed faces, though it's a custom that's fading fast. At higher elevations they wear thick, striped cotton blankets draped over the body, and copper and bronze ornaments. Among the Khamui, a subtribe that inhabits the lower elevations of southern Chin State, unmarried women wear short skirts and little else. Chin men tend to wear simple Western-style dress.

The easiest way to reach a Chin village is by organising a day trip up river through one of the hotels in Mrauk U. Permission fees cost US$30 per person, a guide US$20, a charter boat K22,000, and a horse and cart K3,000. The horse and cart will meet you at the jetty, and the boat price includes stops at villages along the way, and a packed lunch on board. You should provide at least half a day's notice to allow guides to organise one of these very worthwhile day trips for you.

Language

PRONUNCIATION

Mastering Burmese pronunciation is a dizzying proposition for the average traveller. While there are elements that don't exist in English, with a little practice it's not as daunting as it at first seems.

Vowels

Burmese vowel sounds occur in open, nasalised and stopped forms. Nasalisation of vowels is like that in French; speakers of English or other languages can approximate this by putting a weak 'n' at the end of such a syllable. In this guide the nasalisation is indicated by **n** after the vowel, eg, *ein* (house).

non-nasalised

i	as the 'e' in 'be'
e	as the 'a' in 'bay'
eh	as the first 'e' in 'elephant'
a	as in 'father'
aw	as the British pronounce 'law'
o	as in 'go'
u	as the 'oo' in 'too'

nasalised		stopped	
in	as in 'sin'	**iq**	as in 'sit'
ein	as in 'lane'	**eiq**	as in 'late'
		eq	as in 'bet'
an	as in 'fun'	**aq**	as in 'mat'
oun	as in 'bone'	**ouq**	as in 'boat'
un	as in German *Bund*	**uq**	as in 'foot'
ain	as in German *mein*	**aiq**	as in the English 'might'
aun	as in 'brown'	**auq**	as in 'out'

Consonants

Consonants only occur at the beginning of a syllable; there are no consonants that occur after the vowel. The consonants **b**, **d**, **j**, **g**, **m**, **n**, **ng**, **s**, **sh**, **h**, **z**, **w**, **l** and **y** are pronounced as in English; the 'w' sound can occur on its own, or in combination with other consonants. Another difficulty is in saying the **ng** at the beginning of a syllable; try saying 'hang on', then leave off the 'ha' to get an idea of the sound. The following consonants and combinations may cause confusion:

th – as in 'thin'
dh – as in 'the' or 'their'
ny – similar to the consonants at the beginning of the British 'new'
hm, hn, hny, hng, hl – made with a puff of air just before the nasal or **l** sound
ng – as the 'ng' in 'hang'; try saying this word without the 'ha' and imagine starting a word with the 'ng' sound

Aspirated Consonants

The aspirated sounds are made with an audible puff of air after the consonant; in English, the letters 'p', 't' and 'k' are aspirated when they occur at the beginning of a word. Unaspirated examples of these sounds occur in words such as 'spin', 'stir' and 'skin'.

The unaspirated **c** and aspirated **c'** are similar to the 'ch' in 'church'. Remember that **sh** as in 'ship', **s** as in 'sip' and the aspirated **s'** are three different sounds.

Tones

Burmese tones seem very tricky, but are essentially a matter of relative stress between adjoining syllables. There are three tones, plus two other possibilities.

Creaky High Tone

This is made with the voice tense, producing a high-pitched and relatively short, creaky sound. It's indicated by an acute accent above the vowel, eg, *ká* (dance).

Plain High Tone

The pitch of the voice starts quite high, then falls for a fairly long time, similar to the pronunciation of words like 'squeal', 'car' and 'way'. It's indicated by a grave accent above the vowel, for example *kà* which, conveniently, is also the Burmese word for 'car'.

Low Tone

The voice is relaxed, stays at a low pitch for a fairly long time and does not rise or fall in pitch. If a vowel is unaccented, it indicates a low tone, eg, *ka* (shield).

Stopped Syllable

This is a very short and high-pitched syllable, cut off at the end by a sharp catch in the voice (a glottal stop); it's similar to the 'non' sound in the middle of the exclamation, 'oh-oh', or the Cockney pronunciation of 't' in a word like 'bottle'. It's indicated by a 'q' after the vowel, eg, *kaq* (join). However, the 'q' is not pronounced.

Reduced (Weak) Syllable

This is a shortened syllable, usually the first of a two-syllable word, which is said without stress, like the 'a' in 'ago' in English. Only the vowel 'a' (sometimes preceded by a consonant) occurs in a reduced syllable; this is indicated by a small 'v'-like symbol above the vowel, eg, *ălouq* (work). Any syllable except the last in a word can be reduced.

Transliteration

The system used in this language guide is just one of many ways that Burmese script can be represented using the Roman alphabet – the process known as 'transliteration'. In Burmese writing, the sounds **c**, **c'**, **j** are represented by the letters for **k**, **k'**, **g** plus **y** or **r**; so anglicised forms of Burmese often represent them as **ky**, **gy** and so on. One example of this is the unit of currency, *caq*, which is usually written 'kyat' in the Roman alphabet. Aspirated consonants (**k'**, **s'**, **t'** and **p'**) may be transliterated with an 'h' either before or after the consonant. A creaky tone may be indicated by a final **t**, eg, Hpakant (a town in Kachin State).

Various combinations of letters may be used to represent the same vowel sound: **e** and **eh** are both often transliterated as 'ay'; **ain** may be represented as 'aing', **auq** as 'auk' and so on.

There is no 'r' in Burmese but the sound appears in some foreign words such as *re-di-yo* (radio). Sometimes it's substituted with a **y**. Similarly there is no 'f' or 'v' in Burmese; loan words containing these consonants often use **p'** and **b** respectively.

In this guide, hyphens have been used to separate syllables (with the exception of the reduced syllable **ă**) to make it easier to determine the divisions between syllables. However, you'll notice that native speakers don't speak with such clear division between words or syllables.

Greetings & Civilities

Hello. (lit. It's a blessing)
min-găla-ba
မင်္ဂလာပါ။

How are you/Are you well?
k'ămyà (m)/*shin* (f) *ne-kaùn-yéh-là?*
ခင်ဗျား/ရှင် နေကောင်းရဲ့လား။

(I) am well.
ne-kaùn-ba-deh
နေကောင်းပါတယ်။

Have you eaten?
t'ămin sà-pì-bi-là?
ထမင်းစားပြီးပြီလား။

(I) have eaten.
sà-pì-ba-bi
စားပြီးပါပြီ။

Where are you going?
beh thwà-măló-lèh?
ဘယ်သွားမလို့လဲ။

To this, a general, non-specific reply is *di-nà-lè-bèh,* (lit: Just around here). However, you could say:

I'm going back to my hotel.
ho-teh-go pyan-táw-meh
ဟိုတယ်ကို ပြန်တော့မယ်။

I'm leaving now. (Goodbye)
thwà-ba-oùn-meh
သွားပါဦးမယ်။

While in Myanmar, a smile is often enough, it's always appreciated if you say 'thank you' in Burmese.

Thanks.
cè-zù-bèh
ကျေးဇူးပဲ။

Thank you.
cè-zù tin-ba-deh
ကျေးဇူးတင်ပါတယ်။

It's nothing (You're welcome).
keiq-sá măshí-ba-bù
ကိစ္စ မရှိပါဘူး။

Language Difficulties

Do you understand?
nà-leh-dhălà? နားလည်သလား။

I understand.
nà-leh-ba-deh နားလည်ပါတယ်။

(I) don't understand.
nà-măleh-ba-bù နားမလည်ပါဘူး။

Please say it again.
pyan-pyàw-ba-oùn ပြန်ပြောပါအုံး။

I can't speak Burmese.
băma-zăgà lo măpyàw-daq-bù
ဗမာ စကား မပြောတတ်ဘူး။

I speak English.
ìn-găleiq-zăgà lo pyàw-daq-teh
အင်္ဂလိပ်စကား ပြောတတ်တယ်။

Can you speak English?
k'ămyà (m)/*shin* (f) *ìn-găleiq-zăgà lo pyàw-daq-thălà?*
ခင်ဗျား/ရှင် အင်္ဂလိပ်စကား ပြောတတ်သလား။

What do you call this in Burmese?
da băma-lo beh-lo k'aw-dhălèh?
ဒါ ဗမာလို ဘယ်လိုခေါ်သလဲ။

Small Talk

What's your name?
k'ămyá (m)/shín (f) *na-meh beh-lo k'aw-dhălèh?*
ခင်ဗျား/ရှင့် နာမည် ဘယ်လို ခေါ်သလဲ။

My name is ...
cănáw (m)/*cămá* (f) ... *ló k'aw-ba-deh*
ကျွန်တော့်/ကျွန်မ ... လို့ ခေါ်ပါတယ်။

I'm glad to meet you.
k'ămyà (m)/*shin* (f) *-néh twé-yá-da wùn-tha-ba-deh*
ခင်ဗျား/ရှင်နဲ့ တွေ့ရတာ ဝမ်းသာပါတယ်။

Yes.
houq-kéh ဟုတ်ကဲ့။

No. (for questions containing nouns)
măhouq-pa'bù မဟုတ်ပါဘူး။

Getting Around

Where is the ...?
... *beh-hma-lèh?* ... ဘယ်မှာလဲ။

airport
le-zeiq လေဆိပ်

railway carriage
mì-yăt'à-dwèh မီးရထားတွဲ

railway station
bu-da-youn ဘူတာရုံ

bus station
baq-săkà-geiq ဘတ်စကားဂိတ်

riverboat jetty
thìn-bàw-zeiq သင်္ဘောဆိပ်

When will the ... leave?
... *beh-ăc'ein t'weq-mălèh?*
... ဘယ်အချိန်ထွက်မလဲ။

plane
le-yin-byan လေယာဉ်ပျံ

train
mì-yăt'à မီးရထား
bus
baq-săkà ဘတ်စကား
riverboat
thìn-bàw သင်္ဘော
jeep
jiq-kà ဂျစ်ကား
taxi
ăhngà-kà အငှါးကား
bicycle
seq-bein စက်ဘီး
motorcycle
mo-ta s'ain-keh မော်တော်ဆိုင်ကယ်
rickshaw/side-car
s'aiq-kà ဆိုက်ကား
express train
ămyan-yăt'à အမြန်ရထား
local train
law-keh-yăt'à လော်ကယ်ရထား

Where does this bus go?
di baq-săkà beh-go thwà-dhălèh?
ဒီဘတ်စကား ဘယ်ကိုသွားသလဲ။
Where should I get off?
beh-hma s'ìn-yá-mălèh?
ဘယ်မှာဆင်းရမလဲ။

I'd like ...
cănaw (m)/*cămá* (f) ... *lo-jin-ba-deh*
ကျွန်တော်/ကျွန်မ ... လိုချင်ပါတယ်။
one ticket
leq-hmaq-dăzaun
လက်မှတ်တစ်စောင်
two tickets
leq-hmaq hnăsaun
လက်မှတ်နှစ်စောင်

What time does the boat leave?
thìn-bàw beh-ăc'ein t'weq-mălèh?
သင်္ဘော ဘယ်အချိန်ထွက်မလဲ။

Signs

အဝင်	**Entrance**
အထွက်	**Exit**
ဝင်ခွင့်မရှိ	**No Entry**
တယ်လီဖုန်း	**Telephone**
ဆေးလိပ် မသောက်ရ	**No Smoking**
အမျိုးသမီးများ မဝင်ရ	**Women Forbidden**
ဓါတ်ပုံ မရိုက်ရ	**No Photographs**
တားမြစ်နယ်မြေ	**Prohibited Area**
အိမ်သာ/ရေအိမ်	**Toilets**
မ	**Women**
ကျား	**Men**

Can I get on board now?
ăk'ú teq-ló yá-dhălà?
အခု တက်လို့ရသလား။
Can I get there by ...?
... néh thwà-ló yá-mălà?
... နဲ့ သွားလို့ရမလား။
Please go slowly.
pyè-pyè thwà-ba
ဖြည်းဖြည်းသွားပါ။
Please wait for me.
cănaw (m)/*cămá* (f) *-go saún-ne-ba*
ကျွန်တော်/ကျွန်မကိုစောင့်နေပါ။ .

Stop here.
di-hma yaq-pa
ဒီမှာ ရပ်ပါ။

Directions
Is this the way to ...?
di-làn ... thwà-déh-làn-là?
ဒီလမ်း ... သွားတဲ့လမ်းလား။

What ... is this?
da ba ... lèh?
ဒါ ဘာ ... လဲ။

town *myó* မြို့
street *làn* လမ်း
bus *baq-săkà* ဘတ်စကား

How do I get to ...?
... ko beh-lo thwà-yá- dhălèh?
... ကို ဘယ်လိုသွားရသလဲ။

Can I walk there?
làn-shauq-yin yá-mălà?
လမ်းလျှောက်ရင် ရမလား။

Is it nearby?
di-nà-hma-là?
ဒီနားမှာလား။

Is it far?
wè-dhălà? ဝေးသလား။

left
beh-beq ဘယ်ဘက်

right
nya-beq ညာဘက်

straight (ahead)
téh-déh တည့်တည့်

very far away
theiq wè-deh သိပ်ဝေးတယ်။

not so far away
theiq măwè-bù သိပ်မဝေးဘူး။

north
myauq-p'eq မြောက်ဘက်

south
taun-beq တောင်ဘက်

east
ăshé-beq အရှေ့ဘက်

west
ănauq-p'eq အနောက်ဘက်

Around Town

Where is the ...?
... beh-hma-lèh?
... ဘယ်မှာလဲ။

bank *ban-daiq* ဘဏ်တိုက်
market *zè* ဈေး
museum *pyá-daiq* ပြတိုက်
post office *sa-daiq* စာတိုက်

I'd like to make a call.
p'oùn-s'eq-c'in-deh
ဖုံးဆက်ချင်တယ်။

Can I send a fax?
fax pó-ló yá-dhălà?
ဖက်စ်ပို့လို့ ရသလား။

I want to change ...
... lèh-jin-ba-deh
... လဲချင်ပါတယ်။

dollars
daw-la ဒေါ်လာ

pounds
paun ပေါင်

foreign currency
nain-ngan-gyà ngwe နိုင်ငံခြားငွေ

money
paiq-s'an ပိုက်ဆံ

travellers cheques
k'ăyì-c'eq-leq-hmaq ခရီးချက်လက်မှတ်

How many kyat to a dollar?
tădawla beh-hnăcaq-lèh?
တစ်ဒေါ်လာ ဘယ်နှစ်ကျပ်လဲ။

Please give me smaller change.
ăkywe lèh-pè-ba
အကြွေ လဲပေးပါ

Accommodation

Is there a ... near here?

... di-nà-hma shí-dhălà?

... ဒီနားမှာရှိသလား။

hotel *ho-teh* ဟော်တယ်

guesthouse *tèh-k'o-gàn* တည်းခိုခန်း

Can foreigners stay here?

nain-ngan-gyà-thà di-hma tèh-ló yá-dhălà?

နိုင်ငံခြားသား ဒီမှာတည်းလို့ရသလား။

May I see the room?

ăk'àn cí-bayá-ze?

အခန်း ကြည့်ပါရစေ

Is breakfast included in the price?

ăk'àn-k'á-dèh-hma măneq-sa pa-dhălà?

အခန်းခထဲမှာ မနက်စာ ပါသလား။

Can I pay in kyats?

caq-néh pè-ló yá-là?

ကျပ်နဲ့ပေးလို့ရလား။

I will stay for two nights.

hnăyeq tèh-meh

နှစ်ရက်တည်းမယ်။

How much is ...?

... beh-lauq-lèh?

... ဘယ်လောက်လဲ။

one night

tăyeq တစ်ရက်

two nights

hnăyeq နှစ်ရက်

a single room

tăyauq-k'an တစ်ယောက်ခန်း

a double room

hnăyauq-k'an နှစ်ယောက်ခန်း

This room is good.

di ăk'àn kaùn-deh

ဒီအခန်း ကောင်းတယ်။

clean

thán-deh သန့်တယ်

dirty

nyiq-paq-deh ညစ်ပတ်တယ်

fan (electric)

pan-ka ပန်ကာ

noisy

s'u-nyan-deh ဆူညံတယ်

pillow

gaùn-oùn ခေါင်းအုံး

Shopping

Where is the ..?

... beh-hma-lèh?

... ဘယ်မှာလဲ။

bookshop *sa-ouq-s'ain* စာအုပ်ဆိုင်

chemist/pharmacy *s'è-zain* ဆေးဆိုင်

market *zè* ဈေး

shop *s'ain* ဆိုင်

Where can I buy ...?

... beh-hma weh-yá-mălèh?

... ဘယ်မှာဝယ်ရမလဲ။

Do you have ... ?

... shí-là

... ရှိလား။

How much is ...?

... beh-lauq-lèh?

... ဘယ်လောက်လဲ။

matches

mì-jiq မီးခြစ်

shampoo

gaùn-shaw-ye ခေါင်းလျှော်ရည်

soap
s'aq-pya ဆပ်ပြာ
toothbrush
dhăbuq-tan သွားပွတ်တံ
toothpaste
thwà-taiq-s'è သွားတိုက်ဆေး
toilet paper
ein-dha-thoùn-seq-ku အိမ်သာသုံးစက္ကူ

Do you have a cheaper one?
da-t'eq zè po-pàw-da shí-dhălà?
ဒါထက် ဈေးပိုပေါတာ ရှိသလား။

OK (lit. 'good')
kàun-ba-bi ကောင်းပါပြီ။
expensive
zè-cì-deh ဈေးကြီးတယ်
cheap
zè-pàw-deh ဈေးပေါတယ်

In the Country

beach	*kàn-gye*	ကမ်းခြေ
countryside	*tàw*	တော
field (irrigated)	*leh-gwìn*	လယ်ကွင်း
hill	*taun/koùn*	တောင်/ကုန်း
island	*cùn*	ကျွန်း
lake	*ain*	အိုင်
lake (small/ artificial)	*kan*	ကန်
map	*mye-boun*	မြေပုံ
river	*myiq*	မြစ်
sea	*pin-leh*	ပင်လယ်
town	*myó*	မြို့
track/trail	*làn-jaùn*	လမ်းကြောင်း
village	*ywa*	ရွာ
waterfall	*ye-dăgun*	ရေတံခွန်

Time & Date

What time is it?
beh-ăc'ein shí-bi-lèh?
ဘယ်အချိန်ရှိပြီလဲ။

At what time?
beh-ăc'ein-hma-lèh?
ဘယ်အချိန်မှာလဲ။

7am
măneq k'ú-hnăna-yi
မနက် ခုနှစ်နာရီ

1pm
né-leh tăna-yi
နေ့လည် တစ်နာရီ

4.30pm
nyá-ne lè-na-yi-gwèh
ညနေ လေးနာရီခွဲ

10.15pm
nyá s'eh-na-yi s'éh-ngà-măniq
ည ဆယ်နာရီဆယ့်ငါးမိနစ်

hour
na-yi နာရီ
minute
măniq မိနစ်
morning (6am to noon)
măneq မနက်
midday (noon to 3pm)
né-leh နေ့လည်
afternoon/evening (3pm to 7pm)
nyá-ne ညနေ
night (7pm to 6am)
nyá ည
today
di-né ဒီနေ့
tomorrow
măneq-p'yan မနက်ဖြန်

day after tomorrow
dhăbeq-k'a သဘက်ခါ

next week
nauq ăpaq နောက် အပတ်

yesterday
măné-gá မနေ့က

Sunday
tănìn-gănwe-né တနင်္ဂနွေနေ့

Monday
tănìn-la-né တနင်္လာနေ့

Tuesday
in-ga-né အင်္ဂါနေ့

Wednesday
bouq-dăhù-né ဗုဒ္ဓဟူးနေ့

Thursday
ca-dhăbădè-né ကြာသပတေးနေ့

Friday
thauq-ca-né သောကြာနေ့

Saturday
săne-né စနေနေ့

Numbers

1	၁	*tiq/tă*	တစ်/တ
2	၂	*hniq/hnă*	နှစ်/နှ
3	၃	*thòun*	သုံး
4	၄	*lè*	လေး
5	၅	*ngà*	ငါး
6	၆	*c'auq*	ခြောက်
7	၇	*k'ú-hniq/ k'ú-hnă*	ခုနှစ်/ ခုနှ
8	၈	*shiq*	ရှစ်
9	၉	*kò*	ကိုး
10	၁၀	*(tă)s'eh*	တစ်ဆယ်
11	၁၁	*s'éh-tiq*	ဆယ့်တစ်
12	၁၂	*s'éh-hniq*	ဆယ့်နှစ်
20	၂၀	*hnăs'eh*	နှစ်ဆယ်
35	၃၅	*thòun-zéh-ngà*	သုံးဆယ့်ငါး
100	၁၀၀	*tăya*	တစ်ရာ
1000	၁၀၀၀	*(tă)t'aun*	တစ်ထောင်
10,000	၁၀၀၀၀	*(tă)thaun*	တစ်သောင်း
100,000	၁၀၀၀၀၀	*(tă)thèin*	တစ်သိန်း
one million	၁၀၀၀၀၀၀	*(tă)thàn*	တစ်သန်း

(One hundred thousand is often called one *lakh*.)

Health

Where is the ...?
... beh-hma-lèh?
... ဘယ်မှာလဲ။

chemist/pharmacy
s'è-zain ဆေးဆိုင်

doctor
s'ăya-wun ဆရာဝန်

hospital
s'è-youn ဆေးရုံ

Please call a doctor.
s'ăya-wun kaw-pè-ba
ဆရာဝန် ခေါ်ပေးပါ။

I'm allergic to penicillin.
cănaw (m)/*cămá* (f) *pănăsălin-néh mătéh-bù*
ကျွန်တော်/ကျွန်မ ပင်နီစလင်နဲ့ မတည့်ဘူး။

I'm pregnant.
baiq cì-ne-deh/ko-wun shí-deh
ဗိုက်ကြီးနေတယ်/ကိုယ်ဝန်ရှိတယ်။

Emergencies

Help!
keh-ba ကယ်ပါ။

Go away!
thwà-zàn သွားစမ်း။

Thief!
thăk'ò သူခိုး။

Call a doctor!
s'ăya-wun-go k'aw-pè-ba!
ဆရာဝန်ကို ခေါ်ပေးပါ။

Call an ambulance!
lu-na-din-gà k'aw-pè-ba!
လူနာတင်ကားခေါ်ပေးပါ။

I'm ill.
ne-măkàun-bù
နေမကောင်းဘူး။

I'm lost.
làn pyauq-ne-deh
လမ်းပျောက်နေတယ်။

I've been raped.
mú-dèin cín-k'an-yá-deh
မုဒိမ်းကျင့်ခံရတယ်။

I've been robbed.
ăk'ò-k'an-yá-deh
အခိုးခံရတယ်။

It hurts here.
di-hma na-deh
ဒီမှာ နာတယ်။

I vomit often.
k'ăná-k'ăná an-deh
ခဏခဏ အန်တယ်။

I feel faint.
mù-lèh-deh
မူးလဲတယ်။

asthma
(pàn-na-)yin-caq ပန်းနာရင်ကျပ်

have diarrhoea
wùn-shàw-deh/ ဝမ်းလျှောတယ်/
wùn-thwà-ne-deh ဝမ်းသွားနေတယ်

have a fever
p'yà-deh ဖျားတယ်

have a headache
gàun kaiq-ne-deh ခေါင်းကိုက်နေတယ်

have a stomachache
baiq na-deh ဗိုက်နာတယ်

aspirin
eq-săpărin အက်စပရင်

bandage (for sprain)
paq-tì ပတ်တီး

FOOD

Is there a ... near here?
... di-nà-hma shí-dhălà?
... ဒီနားမှာရှိသလား။

Shan noodle stall
shàn-k'auk-swèh-zain ရှမ်းခေါက်ဆွဲဆိုင်

Chinese restaurant
tăyouq-s'ain တရုတ်ဆိုင်

food stall
sà-thauq-s'ain စားသောက်ဆိုင်

restaurant
sà-daw-s'eq စားတော်ဆက်

breakfast
măneq-sa မနက်စာ

lunch
né-leh-za နေ့လည်စာ

dinner
nyá-za ညစာ

snack/small meal
móun/thăye-za မုန့်/သရေစာ

food ('edibles')
sà-zăya စားစရာ

At the Restaurant

Please bring (a) ...
... yu-pè-ba
... ယူပေးပါ။

chopsticks	*tu*	တူ
fork	*k'ăyìn*	ခက်ရင်း
spoon	*zùn*	ဇွန်း
knife	*dà*	ဓား
glass	*p'an-gweq*	ဖန်ခွက်
plate	*băgan-byà*	ပန်းကန်ပြား
bowl	*băgan-loùn*	ပန်းကန်လုံး
cup	*k'weq*	ခွက်

I can't eat meat.
ăthà măsà-nain-bù
အသား မစားနိုင်ဘူး။

Do you have any drinking water?
thauq-ye shí-dhălà?
သောက်ရေရှိသလား။

What's the best dish to eat today?
di-né ba-hìn ăkaùn-zoùn-lèh?
ဒီနေ့ဘာဟင်းအကောင်းဆုံးလဲ။

I didn't order this.
da măhma-bù
ဒါ မမှာဘူး။

Typical Burmese Dishes

clear soup
hìn-jo ဟင်းချို

sizzling rice soup
s'an-hlaw-hìn-jo ဆန်လှော်ဟင်းချို

'12-taste' soup
s'eh-hnămyò-hìn-jo ဆယ့်နှစ်မျိုးဟင်းချို

mohinga (rice vermicelli in fish sauce)
móun-hìn-gà မုန့်ဟင်းခါး

Mandalay moun-ti (noodles & chicken/fish)
móun-di မုန့်တီ

coconut noodles with chicken and egg
oùn-nó-k'auk-swèh အုန်းနို့ခေါက်ဆွဲ

coconut rice
oùn-t'ămìn အုန်းထမင်း

fried rice
t'ămìn-gyaw ထမင်းကြော်

beef curry
ămèh-dhà-hìn အမဲသားဟင်း

beef in gravy
ămèh-hnaq အမဲနှပ်

chicken curry
ceq-thà-hìn ကြက်သားဟင်း

fried chicken
ceq-thà-jaw ကြက်သားကြော်

fried spicy chicken
ceq-thà-ăsaq-ceq ကြက်သားအစပ်ချက်

grilled chicken (satay)
ceq-thà-gin ကြက်သားကင်

pork curry
weq-thà-hìn ဝက်သားဟင်း

pork curry in thick sauce
weq-thà s'i-byan ဝက်သားဆီပြန်

red pork
weq-thà-ni ဝက်သားနီ

sweet chicken
ceq-thà-ăc'o-jeq ကြက်သားအချိုချက်

fish salad
ngà-dhouq ငါးသုပ်

prawn/shrimp curry
băzun-hìn ပုဇွန်ဟင်း

steamed fish in banana leaves
ngà-baùn-douq ငါးပေါင်းထုပ်

vegetable curry
hìn-dhì-hìn-yweq-hìn/thì-zoun-hìn
ဟင်းသီးဟင်းရွက်ဟင်း/သီးစုံဟင်း

steamed sticky rice
kauk-hnyìn-baùn
ကောက်ညှင်းပေါင်း

packet of sticky rice
kauk-hnyin-douq
ကောက်ညှင်းထုပ်

bamboo section of sticky rice
kauk-hnyìn-ci-dauq
ကောက်ညှင်း ကျည်တောက်

purple sticky rice
kauk-hnyìn-ngajeiq
ကောက်ညှင်း ငချိပ်

sticky rice cake with jaggery
móun-zàn
မုန့်ဆန်း

sago/tapioca in syrup
tha-gu-móun သာဂူမုန့်

sweet fried rice pancakes
móun-s'i-jaw မုန့်ဆီကြော်

toddy palm sugar cake
t'àn-thì-móun ထန်းသီးမုန့်

Meat

beef
ămèh-dhà အမဲသား

chicken
ceq-thà ကြက်သား

pork
weq-thà ဝက်သား

Seafood

catfish
ngăk'u ငါးခူ

eel
ngăshín ငါးရှဉ့်

fish
ngà ငါး

seafood
pin-leh-za/ ပင်လယ်စာ/
ye-thaq-tăwa ရေသတ္တဝါ

shellfish
k'ăyú ခရု

squid
pyi-jì-ngà ပြည်ကြီးငါး

steamed carp
ngà-thălauq-paùn ငါးသလောက်ပေါင်း

steamed fish
ngà-baùn ငါးပေါင်း

Vegetables

banana flower
hngăpyàw-bù ငှက်ပျောဖူး

beans
pèh-dhì ပဲသီး

cabbage
gaw-bi-douq ဂေါ်ဖီထုပ်

carrot
moun-la-ú-wa မုန်လာဥဝါ

cauliflower
pàn-gaw-p'i ပန်းဂေါ်ဖီ

chick peas
kălăbèh ကုလားပဲ

corn (cob)
pyaùn-bù ပြောင်းဖူး

cucumber
thăk'wà-dhì သခွါးသီး

eggplant/aubergine
k'ăyàn-dhì ခရမ်းသီး

mushrooms
hmo မှို

onion
ceq-thun-ni ကြက်သွန်နီ

pumpkin
p'ăyoun-dhì ဖရုံသီး

tomato
k'ăyàn-jin-dhì ခရမ်းချဉ်သီး

vegetables
hìn-dhì-hìn-yweq ဟင်းသီးဟင်းရွက်

white radish
moun-la-ú-p'yu မုန်လာဥဖြူ

zucchini/gourd
bù-dhì ဘူးသီး

Fruit

fruit
thiq-thì/a-thì သစ်သီး/အသီး
apple ('flower-fruit')
pàn-dhì ပန်းသီး
avocado ('butter-fruit')
t'àw-baq-thì ထောပတ်သီး
banana
ngăpyàw-dhì ငှက်ပျောသီး
breadfruit
paun-móun-dhì ပေါင်မုန့်သီး
coconut
oùn-dhì အုန်းသီး
custard apple ('influence-fruit')
àw-za-thì ဩဇာသီး
durian
dù-yìn-dhì ဒူးရင်းသီး
lemon
shauq-thì ရှောက်သီး
lime
than-băya-dhì သံပရာသီး
lychee
lain-c'ì-dhì လိုင်ချီးသီး
mango
thăyeq-dhì သရက်သီး
orange
lein-maw-dhì လိမ္မော်သီး
papaya ('boat-shaped fruit')
thìn-bàw-dhì သင်္ဘောသီး
peach
meq-mun-dhì မက်မွန်သီး
pear
thiq-taw-dhì သစ်တော်သီး
pineapple
na-naq-thì နာနတ်သီး
plum (damson)
meq-màn-dhì မက်မန်းသီး
jujube plum
zì dhì ဆီးသီး
pomelo
cwèh-gàw-dhì ကျွဲကောသီး
rambutan ('cockscomb fruit')
ceq-mauq-thì ကြက်မောက်သီး
tamarind
măjì-dhì မန်ကျည်းသီး
watermelon
p'ăyèh-dhì ဖရဲသီး

Spices & Condiments

betel quid
kùn-ya ကွမ်းယာ
butter
t'àw-baq ထောပတ်
cardamon
p'a-la-zé ဖါလာစေ့
cashews
thi-ho-zí သီဟိုစေ့
chilli sauce
ngăyouq-ye ငရုတ်ရည်
chilli
ngăyouq-thì ငရုတ်သီး
coriander
nan-nan-bin နံနံပင်
coconut cream
oùn-nó အုန်းနို့
fish sauce
ngan-pya-ye ငံပြာရည်
galangal (white ginger-like root)
meiq-thălin မိတ်သလင်
garlic
ceq-thun-byu ကြက်သွန်ဖြူ
ghee
kalà t'àw-baq ကုလားထောပတ်
ginger
gyìn ဂျင်း
honey
pyà-ye ပျားရည်
lemongrass
zăbălin စပါးလင်
lime (for betel)
t'oùn ထုံး

peanuts
mye-bèh မြေပဲ
fried peanuts
mye-bèh-jaw မြေပဲကြော်
raisins
zăbyiq-thì-jauq စပျစ်သီးခြောက်
rose syrup
hnìn-ye နှင်းရည်
sago/tapioca
tha-gu သာဂူ
salt
s'à ဆား
sesame
hnàn နှမ်း
soy sauce
pèh-ngan-pya-ye ပဲငံပြာရည်
sugar
thăjà သကြား
tofu (beancurd)
tó-hù/tó-p'ù တို့ဟူး/တို့ဖူး
turmeric
s'ănwìn ဆနွင်း
vinegar
sha-lăka-ye ရှာလကာရည်

DRINKS

Cold Drinks

alcohol
ăyeq အရက်
beer
bi-ya ဘီယာ
coconut juice
oùn-ye အုန်းရည်
lime juice
than-băya-ye သံပရာရည်
milk
nwà-nó နွားနို့
orange juice
lein-maw-ye လိမ္မော်ရည်
soft drink
bí-laq-ye/ ဘိလပ်ရည်/
p'yaw-ye ဖျော်ရည်
sugarcane juice
can-ye ကြံရည်
toddy
t'àn-ye ထန်းရည်
water
ye ရေ
boiled cold water
ye-jeq-è ရေကျက်အေး
hot water
ye-nwè ရေနွေး
cold water
ye-è ရေအေး
bottled water ('clean water')
thán-ye သန့်ရေ
soda water
s'o-da ဆိုဒါ
wine
wain ဝိုင်

Hot Drinks

plain green tea
lăp'eq-ye-jàn/ye-nwè-jàn
လက်ဖက်ရည်ကြမ်း/ရေနွေးကြမ်း
coffee
kaw-fi ကော်ဖီ
Indian tea
leq-p'eq-ye လက်ဖက်ရည်
with milk
nwà-nó-néh နွားနို့နဲ့
with condensed milk
nó-s'ì-néh နို့ဆီနဲ့
with lime
than-băya-dhì-néh သံပရာသီးနဲ့
with sugar
dhăjà-néh သကြားနဲ့

Glossary

acheiq longyi – *longyi* woven with intricate patterns and worn on ceremonial occasions
a-le – opium weights
a-nyeint pwe – traditional variety *pwe*
ayeq hpyu – 'white liquor', a strong alcoholic beverage distilled from rice or palm sap

bama hsan-jin – Burmese-ness; also *myanma hsan-jin*
Bamar – Burman ethnic group
bedin-saya – astrologer
bei moq – Burmese cake made with poppy seeds
betel – the nut of the areca palm, which is chewed as a mild intoxicant throughout Asia
Bodhi tree – the sacred banyan tree under which the Buddha gained enlightenment; also 'bo tree'
Brahman – pertaining to Brahma or to early Hindu religion (not to be confused with 'brahmin', a Hindu caste)
Buddha footprints – large, flat, stylised sculptures that represent the Buddha's feet, distinguished by 108 identifying marks; footprint shrines mark places where the Buddha himself is reputed to have walked

cantonment – the part of a colonial town occupied by the military, a carry-over from the British days
chaung – *(gyaung)* stream or canal; often only seasonal
cheroots – Burmese cigars; ranging from slim to massive, but very mild as they contain only a small amount of tobacco mixed with other leaves, roots and herbs
Chindits – the 'behind enemy lines' Allied forces who harried the Japanese during WWII
chinlon – an extremely popular Burmese sport in which a circle of up to six players attempts to keep a rattan ball in the air with any part of the body except the arms and hands
chinthe – half-lion/half-dragon guardian deity

dah – long-bladed knife, part of the traditional dress of the Shan and several hill tribes
dan-bauk – biryani
deva – Pali-Sanskrit word for celestial beings
dhamma – Pali word for the Buddhist teachings; called *dharma* in Sanskrit
dobat – rural musical instrument; a small, two-faced drum worn around the neck

ei-kya-kwe – deep-fried pastries
eingyi – traditional long-sleeved shirt worn by Burmese men

flat – covered pontoon used to carry cargo on the river, often up to 30m long
furlong – obsolete British unit of distance still used in Myanmar; one-eighth of a mile

gaiq – yard (measurement)
gaung baung – formal turban-like hat made of silk over a wicker framework, for men
gyo-daing – 'planetary post', a small shrine near the base of a zedi containing a Buddha image to which worshippers make offerings according to the day of the week they were born; there are usually eight posts, one for each day of the Burmese week (Wednesday is divided into two days)

haw – Shan word for 'palace', a reference to the large mansions used by the hereditary Shan *sao pha*
hgnet – a swallow-tailed boat
hin – curry dishes
hin jo – light soup
hintha – mythical, swan-like bird; *hamsa* in Pali-Sanskrit
hka – stream or river in Kachin State
hkauq sweh – noodles
hneh – a wind instrument like an oboe; part of the Burmese orchestra
hpongyi – Buddhist monk
hpongyi-byan – cremation ceremony for an important monk
hpongyikyaung – monastery; see also *kyaung*
hsaing – traditional musical ensemble

hsaing waing – circle of drums used in a Burmese orchestra
hsinbyudaw – royal white elephant
hsingaung – head elephant man, above an *u-zi*
htamin – rice
htamin zain – rice shop
htan – *(tan)* sugar palm
htan ye – palm toddy, a slightly alcoholic drink made from the sap of the sugar palm
hti – umbrella-like decorated pinnacle of a stupa
htwa – half a *taung*

in – lake; eg, Inle means little lake

Jataka – stories of the Buddha's past lives, a common theme for temple paintings and reliefs

kalaga – embroidered tapestries
kamma – Pali word for the law of cause and effect; called *karma* in Sanskrit
kammahtan – meditation; *kammahtan kyaung* is a meditation monastery
kammawa – lacquered scriptures
kan – *(gan)* beach; can also mean a tank or reservoir
karaweik – (Pali: *karavika*) a mythical bird with a beautiful song; also the royal barge on Inle Lake
kat gyi kai – scissor-cut noodles; wheat noodles cut into short strips and stir-fried with seafood and various spices
keinnayi – (Pali: *kinnari*) a mythical creature that is human from the waist up, bird from the waist down; the female is called *keinnaya* (Pali: *kinnara*)
kon – *(gon)* hill
kunya – betel-nut chew
kutho – merit, what you acquire through doing good; from the Pali *kusala*
kyaik – Mon word for paya
kyauk – rock
kyaung – *(gyaung)* Burmese Buddhist monastery; pronounced chown
kye waing – circle of gongs used in a Burmese orchestra
kyi – *(gyi)* big; eg, Taunggyi means big mountain
kyun – *(gyun)* island

lan – road or street
lapheq – pickled tea
lei-myet-hna – four-sided Buddha sculpture
lin gwin – cymbals in a Burmese orchestra
Lokanat – Avalokitesvara, a Mahayana Bodhisattva (Buddha-to-be) and guardian spirit of the world
longyi – the Burmese unisex sarong-style lower garment, sensible wear in a tropical climate; unlike men in most other Southeast Asian countries, few Burmese men have taken to Western trousers

Mahayana – literally, Great Vehicle; the school of Buddhism which thrived in north Asian countries like Japan and China, and also enjoyed popularity for a time in ancient Southeast Asian countries; also called the Northern School of Buddhism.
makara – mythical sea serpent
Manuthiha – a half-lion/half-human mythical creature; visible around Shwedagon Paya
mara – the tempter, the Buddhist equivalent of Satan
maya ngeh – 'lesser wife', a man's second wife
mi-gyaung – crocodile lute
mohinga – traditional and very popular dish found at many street stalls (pronounced moun-hinga); it consists of rice noodles, fish and eggs
mudra – hand position, used to describe the various hand positions used by Buddha images, eg, *abhaya mudra* (the gesture of fearlessness)
Myanma let-hwei – Burmese kickboxing
myit – river
myo – town; hence Maymyo (after Colonel May), Allanmyo (Major Allen) or even Bernardmyo
myothit – 'new town', usually a planned new suburb built since the 1960s

naga – multiheaded dragon-serpent from mythology, often seen sheltering or protecting the Buddha
nam-bya – flat-bread cooked in a clay oven, similar to *nan* bread in India
nat – spirit being with the power to either protect or harm humans

nat-gadaw – spirit medium (literally 'spirit bride'), embraces a wide variety of nat
nat pwe – dance performance designed to entice a nat to possess a spirit medium or *nat-gadaw*
ngapi – fermented fish or shrimp paste, an all-purpose Burmese flavouring
ngwe – silver
nibbana – enlightenment, the cessation of suffering, the end of rebirth; the ultimate goal of Buddhist practice

o-zi – a long-bodied, goblet-shaped, one-faced drum used for accompanying folk music in the country

pagoda – generic English term for zedi or stupas as well as temples; see also *paya*
pahso – *longyi* for men
pahto – Burmese word for temple, shrine or other religious structure with a hollow interior
palata – fried flatbread
Pali – language in which original Buddhist texts were recorded; the 'Latin' of Theravada Buddhism
pa-lwe – bamboo flute
paq-ma – Burmese bass drum
parabaik – folding Buddhist palm-leaf manuscripts
parinibbana – literally, final nibbana, the Buddha's passing away
pattala – bamboo xylophone used in the Burmese orchestra
paya – a generic Burmese term meaning holy one; often applied to Buddha figures, zedi and other religious monuments
pe-sa – palm-leaf manuscripts
pin – *(bin)* banyan tree
pi ze – traditional tattooing, believed to make the wearer invulnerable to sword or gun
pwe – generic Burmese word for festival, feast, celebration or ceremony; also refers to public performances of Burmese song and dance, often all-night (and all-day) affairs
pyatthat – wooden, multiroofed pavilion, usually turret-like on palace walls, as at Mandalay Palace
Pyithu Hluttaw – Peoples' Congress or parliament, now defunct

ro-ro – 'roll on, roll off', a ferryboat that carries vehicles; see also *zed craft*

Sanskrit – ancient Indian language and source of many words in the Burmese vocabulary, particularly those having to do with religion, art and government
sao pha – 'sky lord', the hereditary chieftains of the Shan people
saung gauq – 13-stringed harp
sawbwa – Burmese corruption of the Shan word *sao pha* or 'sky lord', the hereditary chieftains of the Shan people
saya – a teacher or shaman
sayadaw – 'master teacher', usually the chief abbot of a Buddhist monastery
shinpyu – ceremonies conducted when young boys from seven to 20 years old enter a monastery for a short period of time, required of every young Buddhist male; girls have their ears pierced in a similar ceremony
shwe – golden
shwe leinmaw – orange brandy distilled in the Shan State
sikhara – Indian-style, corncob-like temple finial, found on many temples in the Bagan area
sima – see *thein*
soon – alms food offered to monks
stupa – see *zedi*

Tatmadaw – Myanmar's armed forces
taung, daung – mountain, eg Taunggyi means 'big mountain'; it can also mean a half yard (measurement)
taw – *(daw)* a common suffix, meaning sacred, holy or royal; it can also mean forest or plantation
tazaung – shrine building, usually found around *zedi*
tea snacks – snacks, such as Chinese steamed buns or Indian samosa, served in tea shops
thabeiq – monk's food bowl; also a traditional element of stupa architecture
thanakha – yellow sandalwood-like paste, worn by many Burmese women on their faces as a combination of skin conditioner, sun block and make-up
thein – ordination hall; called *sima* in Pali

The Thirty – the '30 comrades' of Bogyoke Aung San who joined the Japanese during WWII and eventually led Burma (Myanmar) to independence
Theravada – literally, the Word of the Elders; the school of Buddhism that has thrived in Sri Lanka and Southeast Asian countries such as Myanmar and Thailand. Also called Southern Buddhism and Hinayana.
thilashin – nun
thoun bein – motorised three-wheeled passenger vehicles
thouq – light, spicy salads; also, *lethouq*
Tripitaka – the 'three baskets'; the classic Buddhist scriptures consisting of the Vinaya (monastic discipline), the Sutta (discourses of the Buddha) and Abhidhamma (Buddhist philosophy)
twin – *(dwin)* well, hole, mine
twin-zar – (literally, well-eater) owners and workers of small oil wells in the Barong Islands, near Sittwe

u-min – *(ohn-min)* cave, usually artificial and part of a temple
u-zi – elephant handler or *mahout*

vihara – Pali-Sanskrit word for sanctuary or chapel for Buddha images
viss – Burmese unit of weight, equal to 1.6kg
votive tablet – inscribed offering tablet, usually with images of the Buddha

wa – mouth or river or lake; Inwa means 'mouth of the lake'
wa leq-hkouq – bamboo clapper, part of the Burmese orchestra

yagwin – small cymbals
Yama pwe – Burmese classical dancing based on the Indian epic *Ramayana*
ye – water, liquid
yediya – the superstitious belief that fate can be averted by carrying out certain, sometimes contradictory, activities
yodaya zat – Ayuthaya theatre, the style of theatre brought into Myanmar with Thai captives after the fall of Ayuthaya in 1767
yoma – mountain range
youq-the pwe – Burmese marionette theatre
ywa – village; a common suffix in place names such as Monywa

zat pwe – Burmese classical dance-drama based on *Jataka* stories
zawgyi – an alchemist who has successfully achieved immortality through the ingestion of special compounds made from base metals
zayat – an open-sided shelter or resthouse associated with a *zedi*
zed craft – large vehicle ferry
zedi – stupa, a traditional Buddhist religious monument consisting of a solid hemispherical or gently tapering cylindrical cone, and topped with a variety of metal and jewel finials; zedi are often said to contain Buddha relics
zei – *(zay)* market
zeigyo – central market

ABBREVIATIONS

AM – Air Mandalay
BCP – Burmese Communist Party
FEC – Foreign Exchange Certificate
IWT – Inland Water Transport
KIA – Kachin Independence Army
KNLA – Karen National Liberation Army
KNU – Karen National Union
MA – Myanma Airways
MAI – Myanmar Airways International
MFSL – Myanma Five Star Line
MHT – Ministry of Hotels & Tourism
MNLF – Mon National Liberation Front
MTT – Myanmar Travels & Tours
NLD – National League for Democracy
NMSP – New Mon State Party
Slorc – State Law & Order Restoration Council
SPDC – State Peace & Development Council
SSA – Shan State Army
UWSA – United Wa State Army
YA – Yangon Airways

Thanks

Many thanks to the travellers who used the last edition and wrote to us with helpful hints, useful advice and interesting anecdotes.

Ruth Abraham, Dan Adams, Airell Hodgkinson, Masud Akhtar Zaman, John-Paul Alexandrowicz, Chrissy Allott, Kim Ames, Kimberley Ames, Dave Atlee, Zmrouthe Aubozian, Olivier Aumont, Dan Bachmann, Chris Bain, Robert Banbury, Robert Barnes, Assaf Barnes, David Barnett, John Barnett, Maria Bartolini, Brad Bay, Janny Beare, Robert W Beckman, Geoff Becque, Val Becque, Nina Bert, Riccardo Bertoncelli, Marnix Beugel, Gary Bezer, Marta Billarelli, Lene Bille, Graham Bird, Marc Biver, Dennis Blackmore, Shannon Blackmore, Rodolphe Blary, Cedar Blomberg, Dr Eginhard Blunk, Michael Boller, Thomas Bon, Chris Boorman, Laura Bowers, David Boyall, David Boyd, Felicity Boyd, Sandy Brayshaw, Edwin Briels, Jan-Henk Bruijn, Richard Buckley, Joy Budd, Linda Burgin, Meritxell Busqueta, Ronald Carlson, Matt Carr, Emmanuel Chabas, Ross Chalmers, Charles Chew, Davide Chiapasco, Chirs C Chin, Uwe Christner, Daniel Clarke, Samantha Colclough, Prof Cook, A Corcoran, Caroline & Iago Cornelius-Jones, Steve Craig, Alain Cuzin, Robin Daus, Les davenport, Soren Davidsen, Maike de Bot, Terry Deane, Christian Debenath, Albert G Dempster, Peter & Verena Demuth, J Despature, Beatrice Dettmann, Fredrik Divall, Denis Doolan, Ellen M Dragotto, M L Drayer, Kari Dukeshire, Nicky Dunnington-Jeffeson, Helmut Eberhary, Darren Eddy, Jane Edwards, Richard Embray, Angie Eng, Cati Esteva, Karen & David Eubank, Sheila Eustace, Denis Fargier, Ruthcarol Feldman, Ignacio Fernandez, Hanne Finholt, Eric Fisher, Ralph Flores, Ted Foon, Jennifer Foster, Simon Fox, Blaise Fracheboud, John Steven Friedman, Kevin Furuta, Markus Gabathuler, Ruth Gerson, Silvio Giroud, Mrs Giulj, Mrs & Mr Giulj, Sascha Grabow, Carmen Grau, Peter Gregory, Matthew Gubb, Frank Hammette, Paul Hannon, Camerom Hansen, Ray Hegarty, Zutta Hell, Rob & Val Helliwell, Barry Henshaw, Scott Herbstman, Shachar Hershman, Jo Heyvaert, David Hogarth, Carol Holley, Lee Chee Hoong, Tony Hughes, Connie Van Der Hulst, Geoff Hutcheison, Pancho Ilamas, Christine Ingemorsen, Simone Jakobs, Paul Jansen, Juliette Jeffries, Phillip & De Jeffries, Mary Jenkins, Stewart Johnston, Ronaele Jones, Rosanne Jones, Roger Joyner, S Karn, Tej Kaur, John Keep, Ulli Keil, Mary Rose Kent, Miranda Kerklaan, Noa Kfir, Bernard Kilchoer, C Kim, Dave King, Jane King, Andreas Klett, L Knight, Benjamin Knor, Ko Ku, David Kulka, Roger Lapalme, Kfir Lapid, R & D Le Viet, Alida Lehnort, Mikelson Leong, Yael Levy, Leslie & Robert Lewinter-Suskind, Cas Liber, Keith Liker, Joan Longley, Marilyn Longmuir, Joris Loos, Lieuwke Loth, Ng Man Fei, Delyan Manchev, Carl Mandabach, Aaron W Maness, Lorraine & Robert Mann, Rebecca Martin, Jose Angel Martinez, Nuno Martins, Alexander Matskevich, Janet Mccarraher, Walsh McGuire, Henry Meester, Brett Melzer, Ken Merk, John J Merrick, Patrik Mertens, Don Miller, Thomas Ming, Bernard Mire, Michael & Cristina Moffett, J Morris, Dominique Muet, George Mulder, Liz Mulqueen, Chan Mya Tun, Taro Naotsuka, Carol & Peter Nelson, Gloria Neumeier, Jonathan Newton, Marjol Nijnens, Yoav Noam, Cheryl Noble, Ian & Delia Norris, Martin Novak, Andrzej Nowak, Damia Obrado, John O'Donnell, Arron Ofner, Mick Olsen, Mohammad Iqbal Bin Omar, Anja Oosterwijk, Ken Opprann, Sachiko Osada, Len Outram, Patrice Palmer, Mario & Silvia Paloschi, Nurit Paltiel, Amanda Parfitta, Julie Parker, David Patel, Sebastian Pearson, Giorgio Perversi, Michael Pfeiffer, Bruce Pickering, Kalai Pillay, Clifford Raisbeck, Sarah Ramsden, Thomas Rau, Claudia Rees, Frederico Riberio, John Richards, Francis Riezouw, Thane Roberts, Judith Robertson, Paul Roer, Low Puay Hwa Roger, Andrea Rogge, Yvette Rogier, Jay Ruchamkin, Andrea Michele Sacripanti, L & M Samson, Stuart Sangster, Gabriele Santambrogio, Chong Sau Long, Dr Julia Saurazas, Claudia Schlup, Martin Schmidt, Esther Schuhmacher, Martin Schulte-Middelmann, Claus Schumann, Werner Schwab, Nadia Sebati, Andrew Selth, Runn & Sharon Shabtai, Matthew Sheader, Samira Shehadeh, Daniel Sher, Noa Sher, Yum Shoen Liang, Lee Silver, Stans Slaats, Les Smith, Lorraine Smith, Sara Stahl, Paul A H Steele, Brian Stewart, John Stonham, Joanne Sugiono, Chris Sullivan, Evelyn Tan, Jeff Tan, Corine Tap, Samir Thapa, Nolan Thompson, E Thornes, Roslyn Thurn, Ross Tinley, Jennifer Tradewell, Katrina Tudor, Charles Tyler, Ute Ultsch, Peter Van, Edith van berkel, Hendrik van Dam, Paulien van der Linden, J W J Van Dorp, R van Klaveren, Kris van Kooten, Remko van Yperen, Carlijn Vandehn, Margaret Vannan, Peter van't Westeinde, Elwin Verheggen, Ron Vermeulen, Frank Villante, Christel Visser, Cor Visser, Jan von Doetinchem, R C Wadkar, Clive Walker, Hugh Waters, Gavin & Emma Watson, Rich Westlake, Bien Weytens, J Wheaton, Jorgen Wide, John Winward, Corey Wise, Rowena Wong, W C Wong, Dr Frank Woten, Nyunt Wynn, Malou Xavier, Hoe Kah Yang, C-h Yee, W-b Yee, Bob Young, Amy Zimmer, Maarten Zonjee.

LONELY PLANET

You already know that Lonely Planet produces more than this one guidebook, but you might not be aware of the other products we have on this region. Here is a selection of titles that you may want to check out as well:

South-East Asia on a shoestring
ISBN 1 86450 158 8
US$21.99 • UK£12.99

South-East Asia phrasebook
ISBN 0 86442 435 3
US$6.95 • UK£3.99

Read This First: Asia & India
ISBN 1 86450 049 2
US$14.95 • UK£8.99

Healthy Travel Asia & India
ISBN 1 86450 051 4
US$5.95 • UK£3.99

Travel Photography
ISBN 1 86450 207 X
US$16.99 • UK£9.99

Burmese phrasebook
ISBN 1 74059 048 1
US$7.99 • UK£4.50

Hill Tribes phrasebook
ISBN 0 86442 635 6
US$5.95 • UK£3.99

Buddhist Stupas in Asia
ISBN 1 86450 120 0
US$34.99 • UK£24.99

Lonely Planet Unpacked
ISBN 1 86450 062 X
US$12.95 • UK£6.99

Available wherever books are sold

ON THE ROAD

Travel Guides explore cities, regions and countries, and supply information on transport, restaurants and accommodation, covering all budgets. They come with reliable, easy-to-use maps, practical advice, cultural and historical facts and a rundown on attractions both on and off the beaten track. There are over 200 titles in this classic series, covering nearly every country in the world.

Lonely Planet Upgrades extend the shelf life of existing travel guides by detailing any changes that may affect travel in a region since a book has been published. Upgrades can be downloaded for free from **www.lonelyplanet.com/upgrades**

For travellers with more time than money, **Shoestring** guides offer dependable, first-hand information with hundreds of detailed maps, plus insider tips for stretching money as far as possible. Covering entire continents in most cases, the six-volume shoestring guides are known around the world as 'backpackers bibles'.

For the discerning short-term visitor, **Condensed** guides highlight the best a destination has to offer in a full-colour, pocket-sized format designed for quick access. They include everything from top sights and walking tours to opinionated reviews of where to eat, stay, shop and have fun.

CitySync lets travellers use their Palm™ or Visor™ hand-held computers to guide them through a city with handy tips on transport, history, cultural life, major sights, and shopping and entertainment options. It can also quickly search and sort hundreds of reviews of hotels, restaurants and attractions, and pinpoint their location on scrollable street maps. CitySync can be downloaded from **www.citysync.com**

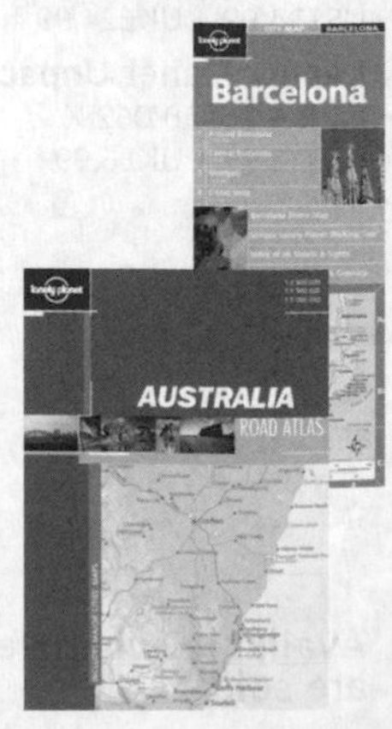

MAPS & ATLASES

Lonely Planet's **City Maps** feature downtown and metropolitan maps, as well as transit routes and walking tours. The maps come complete with an index of streets, a listing of sights and a plastic coat for extra durability.

Road Atlases are an essential navigation tool for serious travellers. Cross-referenced with the guidebooks, they also feature distance and climate charts and a complete site index.

LONELY PLANET

ESSENTIALS

Read This First books help new travellers to hit the road with confidence. These invaluable predeparture guides give step-by-step advice on preparing for a trip, budgeting, arranging a visa, planning an itinerary and staying safe while still getting off the beaten track.

Healthy Travel pocket guides offer a regional rundown on disease hot spots and practical advice on predeparture health measures, staying well on the road and what to do in emergencies. The guides come with a user-friendly design and helpful diagrams and tables.

Lonely Planet's **Phrasebooks** cover the essential words and phrases travellers need when they're strangers in a strange land. They come in a pocket-sized format with colour tabs for quick reference, extensive vocabulary lists, easy-to-follow pronunciation keys and two-way dictionaries.

Miffed by blurry photos of the Taj Mahal? Tired of the classic 'top of the head cut off' shot? **Travel Photography: A Guide to Taking Better Pictures** will help you turn ordinary holiday snaps into striking images and give you the know-how to capture every scene, from frenetic festivals to peaceful beach sunrises.

Lonely Planet's **Travel Journal** is a lightweight but sturdy travel diary for jotting down all those on-the-road observations and significant travel moments. It comes with a handy time-zone wheel, a world map and useful travel information.

Lonely Planet's eKno is an all-in-one communication service developed especially for travellers. It offers low-cost international calls and free email and voicemail so that you can keep in touch while on the road. Check it out on **www.ekno.lonelyplanet.com**

FOOD & RESTAURANT GUIDES

Lonely Planet's **Out to Eat** guides recommend the brightest and best places to eat and drink in top international cities. These gourmet companions are arranged by neighbourhood, packed with dependable maps, garnished with scene-setting photos and served with quirky features.

For people who live to eat, drink and travel, **World Food** guides explore the culinary culture of each country. Entertaining and adventurous, each guide is packed with detail on staples and specialities, regional cuisine and local markets, as well as sumptuous recipes, comprehensive culinary dictionaries and lavish photos good enough to eat.

LONELY PLANET

OUTDOOR GUIDES

For those who believe the best way to see the world is on foot, Lonely Planet's **Walking Guides** detail everything from family strolls to difficult treks, with 'when to go and how to do it' advice supplemented by reliable maps and essential travel information.

Cycling Guides map a destination's best bike tours, long and short, in day-by-day detail. They contain all the information a cyclist needs, including advice on bike maintenance, places to eat and stay, innovative maps with detailed cues to the rides, and elevation charts.

The **Watching Wildlife** series is perfect for travellers who want authoritative information but don't want to tote a heavy field guide. Packed with advice on where, when and how to view a region's wildlife, each title features photos of over 300 species and contains engaging comments on the local flora and fauna.

With underwater colour photos throughout, **Pisces Books** explore the world's best diving and snorkelling areas. Each book contains listings of diving services and dive resorts, detailed information on depth, visibility and difficulty of dives, and a roundup of the marine life you're likely to see through your mask.

LONELY PLANET

OFF THE ROAD

Journeys, the travel literature series written by renowned travel authors, capture the spirit of a place or illuminate a culture with a journalist's attention to detail and a novelist's flair for words. These are tales to soak up while you're actually on the road or dip into as an at-home armchair indulgence.

The range of lavishly illustrated **Pictorial** books is just the ticket for both travellers and dreamers. Off-beat tales and vivid photographs bring the adventure of travel to your doorstep long before the journey begins and long after it is over.

Lonely Planet **Videos** encourage the same independent, tough-minded approach as the guidebooks. Currently airing throughout the world, this award-winning series features innovative footage and an original soundtrack.

Yes, we know, work is tough, so do a little bit of deskside dreaming with the spiral-bound Lonely Planet **Diary** or a Lonely Planet **Wall Calendar**, filled with great photos from around the world.

TRAVELLERS NETWORK

Lonely Planet Online. Lonely Planet's award-winning Web site has insider information on hundreds of destinations, from Amsterdam to Zimbabwe, complete with interactive maps and relevant links. The site also offers the latest travel news, recent reports from travellers on the road, guidebook upgrades, a travel links site, an online book-buying option and a lively travellers bulletin board. It can be viewed at **www.lonelyplanet.com** or AOL keyword: lp.

Planet Talk is a quarterly print newsletter, full of gossip, advice, anecdotes and author articles. It provides an antidote to the being-at-home blues and lets you plan and dream for the next trip. Contact the nearest Lonely Planet office for your free copy.

Comet, the free Lonely Planet newsletter, comes via email once a month. It's loaded with travel news, advice, dispatches from authors, travel competitions and letters from readers. To subscribe, click on the Comet subscription link on the front page of the Web site.

Lonely Planet Guides by Region

Lonely Planet is known worldwide for publishing practical, reliable and no-nonsense travel information in our guides and on our Web site. The Lonely Planet list covers just about every accessible part of the world. Currently there are 16 series: Travel guides, Shoestring guides, Condensed guides, Phrasebooks, Read This First, Healthy Travel, Walking guides, Cycling guides, Watching Wildlife guides, Pisces Diving & Snorkeling guides, City Maps, Road Atlases, Out to Eat, World Food, Journeys travel literature and Pictorials.

AFRICA Africa on a shoestring • Botswana • Cairo • Cairo City Map • Cape Town • Cape Town City Map • East Africa • Egypt • Egyptian Arabic phrasebook • Ethiopia, Eritrea & Djibouti • Ethiopian Amharic phrasebook • The Gambia & Senegal • Healthy Travel Africa • Kenya • Malawi • Morocco • Moroccan Arabic phrasebook • Mozambique • Namibia • Read This First: Africa • South Africa, Lesotho & Swaziland • Southern Africa • Southern Africa Road Atlas • Swahili phrasebook • Tanzania, Zanzibar & Pemba • Trekking in East Africa • Tunisia • Watching Wildlife East Africa • Watching Wildlife Southern Africa • West Africa • World Food Morocco • Zambia • Zimbabwe, Botswana & Namibia
Travel Literature: Mali Blues: Traveling to an African Beat • The Rainbird: A Central African Journey • Songs to an African Sunset: A Zimbabwean Story

AUSTRALIA & THE PACIFIC Aboriginal Australia & the Torres Strait Islands •Auckland • Australia • Australian phrasebook • Australia Road Atlas • Cycling Australia • Cycling New Zealand • Fiji • Fijian phrasebook • Healthy Travel Australia, NZ & the Pacific • Islands of Australia's Great Barrier Reef • Melbourne • Melbourne City Map • Micronesia • New Caledonia • New South Wales • New Zealand • Northern Territory • Outback Australia • Out to Eat – Melbourne • Out to Eat – Sydney • Papua New Guinea • Pidgin phrasebook • Queensland • Rarotonga & the Cook Islands • Samoa • Solomon Islands • South Australia • South Pacific • South Pacific phrasebook • Sydney • Sydney City Map • Sydney Condensed • Tahiti & French Polynesia • Tasmania • Tonga • Tramping in New Zealand • Vanuatu • Victoria • Walking in Australia • Watching Wildlife Australia • Western Australia
Travel Literature: Islands in the Clouds: Travels in the Highlands of New Guinea • Kiwi Tracks: A New Zealand Journey • Sean & David's Long Drive

CENTRAL AMERICA & THE CARIBBEAN Bahamas, Turks & Caicos • Baja California • Belize, Guatemala & Yucatán • Bermuda • Central America on a shoestring • Costa Rica • Costa Rica Spanish phrasebook • Cuba • Cycling Cuba • Dominican Republic & Haiti • Eastern Caribbean • Guatemala • Havana • Healthy Travel Central & South America • Jamaica • Mexico • Mexico City • Panama • Puerto Rico • Read This First: Central & South America • Virgin Islands • World Food Caribbean • World Food Mexico • Yucatán
Travel Literature: Green Dreams: Travels in Central America

EUROPE Amsterdam • Amsterdam City Map • Amsterdam Condensed • Andalucía • Athens • Austria • Baltic States phrasebook • Barcelona • Barcelona City Map • Belgium & Luxembourg • Berlin • Berlin City Map • Britain • British phrasebook • Brussels, Bruges & Antwerp • Brussels City Map • Budapest • Budapest City Map • Canary Islands • Catalunya & the Costa Brava • Central Europe • Central Europe phrasebook • Copenhagen • Corfu & the Ionians • Corsica • Crete • Crete Condensed • Croatia • Cycling Britain • Cycling France • Cyprus • Czech & Slovak Republics • Czech phrasebook • Denmark • Dublin • Dublin City Map • Dublin Condensed • Eastern Europe • Eastern Europe phrasebook • Edinburgh • Edinburgh City Map • England • Estonia, Latvia & Lithuania • Europe on a shoestring • Europe phrasebook • Finland • Florence • Florence City Map • France • Frankfurt City Map • Frankfurt Condensed • French phrasebook • Georgia, Armenia & Azerbaijan • Germany • German phrasebook • Greece • Greek Islands • Greek phrasebook • Hungary • Iceland, Greenland & the Faroe Islands • Ireland • Italian phrasebook • Italy • Kraków • Lisbon • The Loire • London • London City Map • London Condensed • Madrid • Madrid City Map • Malta • Mediterranean Europe • Milan, Turin & Genoa • Moscow • Munich • Netherlands • Normandy • Norway • Out to Eat – London • Out to Eat – Paris • Paris • Paris City Map • Paris Condensed • Poland • Polish phrasebook • Portugal • Portuguese phrasebook • Prague • Prague City Map • Provence & the Côte d'Azur • Read This First: Europe • Rhodes & the Dodecanese • Romania & Moldova • Rome • Rome City Map • Rome Condensed • Russia, Ukraine & Belarus • Russian phrasebook • Scandinavian & Baltic Europe • Scandinavian phrasebook • Scotland • Sicily • Slovenia • South-West France • Spain • Spanish phrasebook • Stockholm • St Petersburg • St Petersburg City Map • Sweden • Switzerland • Tuscany • Ukrainian phrasebook • Venice • Vienna • Wales • Walking in Britain • Walking in France • Walking in Ireland • Walking in Italy • Walking in Scotland • Walking in Spain • Walking in Switzerland • Western Europe • World Food France • World Food Greece • World Food Ireland • World Food Italy • World Food Spain **Travel Literature:** After Yugoslavia • Love and War in the Apennines • The Olive Grove: Travels in Greece • On the Shores of the Mediterranean • Round Ireland in Low Gear • A Small Place in Italy

Lonely Planet Mail Order

Lonely Planet products are distributed worldwide. They are also available by mail order from Lonely Planet, so if you have difficulty finding a title please write to us. North and South American residents should write to 150 Linden St, Oakland, CA 94607, USA; European and African residents should write to 10a Spring Place, London NW5 3BH, UK; and residents of other countries to Locked Bag 1, Footscray, Victoria 3011, Australia.

INDIAN SUBCONTINENT & THE INDIAN OCEAN Bangladesh • Bengali phrasebook • Bhutan • Delhi • Goa • Healthy Travel Asia & India • Hindi & Urdu phrasebook • India • India & Bangladesh City Map • Indian Himalaya • Karakoram Highway • Kathmandu City Map • Kerala • Madagascar • Maldives • Mauritius, Réunion & Seychelles • Mumbai (Bombay) • Nepal • Nepali phrasebook • North India • Pakistan • Rajasthan • Read This First: Asia & India • South India • Sri Lanka • Sri Lanka phrasebook • Tibet • Tibetan phrasebook • Trekking in the Indian Himalaya • Trekking in the Karakoram & Hindukush • Trekking in the Nepal Himalaya • World Food India **Travel Literature:** The Age of Kali: Indian Travels and Encounters • Hello Goodnight: A Life of Goa • In Rajasthan • Maverick in Madagascar • A Season in Heaven: True Tales from the Road to Kathmandu • Shopping for Buddhas • A Short Walk in the Hindu Kush • Slowly Down the Ganges

MIDDLE EAST & CENTRAL ASIA Bahrain, Kuwait & Qatar • Central Asia • Central Asia phrasebook • Dubai • Farsi (Persian) phrasebook • Hebrew phrasebook • Iran • Israel & the Palestinian Territories • Istanbul • Istanbul City Map • Istanbul to Cairo • Istanbul to Kathmandu • Jerusalem • Jerusalem City Map • Jordan • Lebanon • Middle East • Oman & the United Arab Emirates • Syria • Turkey • Turkish phrasebook • World Food Turkey • Yemen **Travel Literature:** Black on Black: Iran Revisited • Breaking Ranks: Turbulent Travels in the Promised Land • The Gates of Damascus • Kingdom of the Film Stars: Journey into Jordan

NORTH AMERICA Alaska • Boston • Boston City Map • Boston Condensed • British Columbia • California & Nevada • California Condensed • Canada • Chicago • Chicago City Map • Chicago Condensed • Florida • Georgia & the Carolinas • Great Lakes • Hawaii • Hiking in Alaska • Hiking in the USA • Honolulu & Oahu City Map • Las Vegas • Los Angeles • Los Angeles City Map • Louisiana & the Deep South • Miami • Miami City Map • Montreal • New England • New Orleans • New Orleans City Map • New York City • New York City City Map • New York City Condensed • New York, New Jersey & Pennsylvania • Oahu • Out to Eat – San Francisco • Pacific Northwest • Rocky Mountains • San Diego & Tijuana • San Francisco • San Francisco City Map • Seattle • Seattle City Map • Southwest • Texas • Toronto • USA • USA phrasebook • Vancouver • Vancouver City Map • Virginia & the Capital Region • Washington, DC • Washington, DC City Map • World Food New Orleans **Travel Literature**: Caught Inside: A Surfer's Year on the California Coast • Drive Thru America

NORTH-EAST ASIA Beijing • Beijing City Map • Cantonese phrasebook • China • Hiking in Japan • Hong Kong & Macau • Hong Kong City Map • Hong Kong Condensed • Japan • Japanese phrasebook • Korea • Korean phrasebook • Kyoto • Mandarin phrasebook • Mongolia • Mongolian phrasebook • Seoul • Shanghai • South-West China • Taiwan • Tokyo • Tokyo Condensed • World Food Hong Kong • World Food Japan **Travel Literature**: In Xanadu: A Quest • Lost Japan

SOUTH AMERICA Argentina, Uruguay & Paraguay • Bolivia • Brazil • Brazilian phrasebook • Buenos Aires • Buenos Aires City Map • Chile & Easter Island • Colombia • Ecuador & the Galapagos Islands • Healthy Travel Central & South America • Latin American Spanish phrasebook • Peru • Quechua phrasebook • Read This First: Central & South America • Rio de Janeiro • Rio de Janeiro City Map • Santiago de Chile • South America on a shoestring • Trekking in the Patagonian Andes • Venezuela **Travel Literature**: Full Circle: A South American Journey

SOUTH-EAST ASIA Bali & Lombok • Bangkok • Bangkok City Map • Burmese phrasebook • Cambodia • Cycling Vietnam, Laos & Cambodia • East Timor phrasebook • Hanoi • Healthy Travel Asia & India • Hill Tribes phrasebook • Ho Chi Minh City (Saigon) • Indonesia • Indonesian phrasebook • Indonesia's Eastern Islands • Java • Lao phrasebook • Laos • Malay phrasebook • Malaysia, Singapore & Brunei • Myanmar (Burma) • Philippines • Pilipino (Tagalog) phrasebook • Read This First: Asia & India • Singapore • Singapore City Map • South-East Asia on a shoestring • South-East Asia phrasebook • Thailand • Thailand's Islands & Beaches • Thailand, Vietnam, Laos & Cambodia Road Atlas • Thai phrasebook • Vietnam • Vietnamese phrasebook • World Food Indonesia • World Food Thailand • World Food Vietnam

ALSO AVAILABLE: Antarctica • The Arctic • The Blue Man: Tales of Travel, Love and Coffee • Brief Encounters: Stories of Love, Sex & Travel • Buddhist Stupas in Asia: The Shape of Perfection • Chasing Rickshaws • The Last Grain Race • Lonely Planet ... On the Edge: Adventurous Escapades from Around the World • Lonely Planet Unpacked • Lonely Planet Unpacked Again • Not the Only Planet: Science Fiction Travel Stories • Ports of Call: A Journey by Sea • Sacred India • Travel Photography: A Guide to Taking Better Pictures • Travel with Children • Tuvalu: Portrait of an Island Nation

Index

Text

Bold indicates maps.

N

O

P

Bold indicates maps.

Boxed Text

MAP LEGEND

CITY ROUTES

Freeway — Freeway
Highway — Primary Road
Road — Secondary Road
Street — Street
Lane — Lane
On/Off Ramp
Unsealed Road
One-Way Street
Pedestrian Street
Stepped Street
Tunnel
Footbridge

HYDROGRAPHY

River; Creek
Canal
Lake
Dry Lake; Salt Lake
Spring; Rapids
Waterfalls

REGIONAL ROUTES

Tollway; Freeway
Primary Road
Secondary Road
Minor Road

BOUNDARIES

International
State
Disputed
Fortified Wall

TRANSPORT ROUTES & STATIONS

Train
Underground Train
Metro
Tramway
Cable Car; Chairlift
Ferry/Jetty
Walking Trail
Walking Tour
Path
Pier or Jetty

AREA FEATURES

Building
Park; Gardens
Market
Sports Ground
Beach
Cemetery
Campus
Plaza

POPULATION SYMBOLS

CAPITAL — National Capital
CAPITAL — State Capital
CITY — City
Town — Town
Village — Village
Urban Area

MAP SYMBOLS

Place to Stay
Place to Eat
Point of Interest

Airport
Bank
Bus Stop/Terminal
Cathedral/Church
Cinema/Theatre
Embassy/Consulate
Fortress/Mountain
Golf Course
Hospital
Internet Cafe
Monument/Museum
Mosque
Paya
Petrol Station
Police Station
Post Office
Pub or Bar
Ruins/Tomb
Stately Home
Swimming Pool
Taxis/Telephone
Temple/Monastery
Temple (Chinese)
Temple (Hindu)
Temple (Sikh)
Tourist Information
Transport (Pick-ups)
Zoo

Note: not all symbols displayed above appear in this book

LONELY PLANET OFFICES

Australia
Locked Bag 1, Footscray, Victoria 3011
☎ 03 8379 8000 fax 03 8379 8111
email: talk2us@lonelyplanet.com.au

SA
0 Linden St, Oakland, CA 94607
0 893 8555 TOLL FREE: 800 275 8555
10 893 8572
info@lonelyplanet.com

UK
10a Spring Place, London NW5 3BH
☎ 020 7428 4800 fax 020 7428 4828
email: go@lonelyplanet.co.uk

France
1 rue du Dahomey, 75011 Paris
☎ 01 55 25 33 00 fax 01 55 25 33 01
email: bip@lonelyplanet.fr
www.lonelyplanet.fr

World Wide Web: www.lonelyplanet.com *or* AOL keyword: lp
Lonely Planet Images: www.lonelyplanetimages.com